AQA GCSE

Religious Studies

SPECIFICATION A

Christianity, Islam, Judaism and the Religious, Philosophical and Ethical themes

UPDATED EDITION

Lesley Parry
Jan Hayes
Sheila Butler

Approval message from AQA

This textbook has been approved by AQA for use with our qualification. This means that we have checked that it broadly covers the specification and we are satisfied with the overall quality. Full details of our approval process can be found on our website.

We approve textbooks because we know how important it is for teachers and students to have the right resources to support their teaching and learning. However, the publisher is ultimately responsible for the editorial control and quality of this book.

Please note that when teaching the ***AQA GCSE Religious Studies Specification A*** course, you must refer to AQA's specification as your definitive source of information. While this book has been written to match the specification, it cannot provide complete coverage of every aspect of the course.

A wide range of other useful resources can be found on the relevant subject pages of our website: www.aqa.org.uk.

hachette LEARNING

The Publishers would like to thank the following for permission to reproduce copyright material.

Photo credits

Cover © Sunshine Pictures/Alamy Stock Photo; **p.1** © Marc Rasmus/ImageBROKER/Alamy Stock Photo; **p.4** © Duncan Noakes/123RF; **p.5** © PanjarongU/iStock/Thinkstock; **p.12** Sheila Butler; **p.16** © Marc Rasmus/ImageBROKER/ Alamy Stock Photo; **p.17** *t* © Pakhnyushchyy/Fotolia, *c* © Kesu/Fotolia.com; **p.19** © Tim Graham/Alamy Stock Photo; **p.20** © Chronicle/Alamy Stock Photo; **p.25** © Cretzu/iStock/Thinkstock; **p.39** © Renata Sedmakova/stock.adobe.com; **p.42** © The Picture Art Collection/Alamy Stock Photo; **p.43** © Hugo Martin/Alamy Stock Photo; **p.45** *cl* © ChiccoDodiFC/iStock/Thinkstock, *cr* © Lynne Sutherland/Alamy Stock Photo; **p.46** © Ruth Hofshi/Alamy Stock Photo; **p.47** © GRANGER – Historical Picture Archive/Alamy Stock Photo; **p.48** *tr* © Pawelosi/iStock/Thinkstock, *cr* © Michael Nolan/Robertharding/Alamy Stock Photo; **p.49** © Bahnmueller/ImageBROKER/Alamy Stock Photo; **p.53** © Godong/Alamy Stock Photo; **p.54** © L'Osservatore Romano/Pool Photo/Associated Press/Alamy Stock Photo; **p.57** © Maciej Dakowicz/Alamy Stock Photo; **p.58** © Jeff Morgan 13/Alamy Stock Photo; **p.59** © Logo used by kind permission of Serving In Mission; **p.60** © by_Djenka/iStock/Thinkstock; **p.62** © Suburbanium/Shutterstock.com; **p.63** © Arthur Edwards/The Sun/PA Images/Alamy Stock Photo; **p.64** © Helmuth Lohmann/Associated Press/Alamy Stock Photo; **p.68** © Libby Welch/Alamy Stock Photo; **p.69** © armvector/iStock/ Thinkstock; **p.77** © Aidar Ayazbayev /123 RF; **p.85** *tr* © Mr. Bundit Chailaipanich/123 RF, *cr* © jerbarber/iStock/Thinkstock; **p.92** © Hikrcn/123 RF; **p.94** © ZUMA Press, Inc./Alamy Stock Photo; **p.95** © Art Directors & TRIP/Alamy Stock Photo; **p.97** © JD Dallet/ArabianEye FZ LLC/Alamy Stock Photo; **p.100** © Fred de Noyelle/Stone/Getty Images; **p.103** *tr* © Sonia Halliday Photo Library/Alamy Stock Photo, *cr* © CM Dixon/Print Collector/Getty Images; **p.103** © British Library/Robana/REX/Shutterstock; **p.106** © The British Library archive/Bridgeman Images; **p.109** *tl* © Fine Art Images/Heritage Images/Alamy Stock Photo, *tr* © Granger,NYC/TopFoto; **p.125** *tl* © Aidar Ayazbayev /123 RF, *c* © Mohamed LOUNES/Gamma-Rapho/Getty Images; **p.125** *cl* © Cem Oksuz/Anadolu Agency/Getty Images, *bl* © Mawardi Bahar/Alamy Stock Photo; **p.126** tl © Mawardi Bahar/Alamy Stock Photo, *c* © Abid Katib/Getty Images News/ Getty Images, *cl* © epa european pressphoto agency b.v./Alamy Stock Photo, *bl* © Cem Oksuz/Anadolu Agency/Getty Images; **p.127** © Lesley Parry; **p.128** *tl* © kirill4mula/ iStock/Thinkstock, *cl* © Vincent_St_Thomas/iStock/Thinkstock, *c*, *cr* & *tr* © Lesley Parry; **p.129** *tr* © Mark/stock.adobe.com, *cr* © Godong/Stockbyte/Getty Images, *l* & *br* © Lesley Parry; **p.135** © Pictures From History/CPA Media Pte Ltd/Alamy Stock Photo; **p.141** *cl* © Giuseppe Ciccia/Pacific Press/Alamy Stock Photo, c © ADEK BERRY/AFP/GettyImages, *c* © PaulCowan/iStock/ Thinkstock, *cr* © NIKLAS HALLE'N/AFP/Getty Image; **p.142** © Lesley Parry; **p.151** © Board of Deputies; **p.153** *l* © Alex Segre/Alamy Stock Photo, *r* © Board of Deputies; **p.164** © World History Archive/Alamy Stock Photo; **p.169** © Mike FANOUS/Gamma-Rapho/ Getty Images, *br* © World Jewish Relief; **p.187** © Lebrecht Music and Arts Photo Library/Alamy Stock Photo; **p.192** © Michael Bracey/Alamy Stock Photo, *br* © Board of Deputies; **p.193** *tl* & *bl* © Lesley Parry; **p.194** tl, *cr* & bl © Board of Deputies; **p.195** © Board of Deputies; **p.196** *cr*, *c* & *cl* © Lesley Parry; **p.198** *tr* © MENAHEM KAHANA/AFP/Getty Images, *cl* & *bl* © Board of Deputies; **p.199** © Board of Deputies; **p.200** © Board of Deputies; **p.202** © Lesley Parry; **p.203** *tr* & *br* © Lesley Parry; **p.206** *bl* © Ungvar/Shutterstock, *r* © Board of Deputies; **p.210** © Lesley Parry; **p.211** © Ira Berger/Alamy Stock Photo; **p.217** *r*, *c* & *l* © Lesley Parry, *br* © Keith Larby/Alamy Stock Photo; **p.218** © Carl D. Walsh/Portland Press Herald/Getty Images; **p.219** © Lesley Parry; p.222 © Ilan Rosen/Alamy Stock Photo; **p.223** *t* © Board of Deputies, *c*, *bl* & *br* © Lesley Parry; **p.231** © Sunshine Pictures/Alamy Stock Photo; **p.259** © Lesley Parry; **p.261** *tr* © Justin Hobson/Royal Geographical Society/Alamy Stock Photo, *br* © Classic Image/Alamy Stock Photo; **p.267** *tr* © Stockbyte/ Photolibrary Group Ltd/Environmental Issues DV 48, *tc* © Lesley Parry; **p.268** *bl* © Janniwet wangkiri/123 RF, *br* © Olaf Krüger/imageBROKER/ Alamy Stock Photo; **p.269** © Elly Godfroy/Alamy Stock Photo; **p.270** © Lesley Parry; **p.271** © Jack Star/Photodisc/Getty Images/Environmental Concerns 31; **p.272** © Stockbyte/ Photolibrary Group Ltd/Environmental Issues DV 48; **p.274** cr, *br* & *c* © Lesley Parry; **p.275** © Dmitry Korotayev/Epsilon/Getty Images; **p.278** *tl* © Christian Darkin/Science Photo Library, *cl* © Dr G. Moscoso/Science Photo Library, *tr* © Edelmann/Science Photo Library, *c* © Prof Stuart Campbell/Shutterstock, *cr* © Blend Images/Alamy Stock Photo; **p.295** © Alex Segre/Alamy Stock Photo; **p.297** *tl* © Louise Batalla Duran/Alamy Stock Photo, *tc* © lamart1971/ iStock/Thinkstock, *tr* © KoBoZaa/iStock/Thinkstock; **p.303** *tr* © imagez/iStock/ Thinkstock, *cl* © Purestock/Thinkstock, *cr* ©David *t* Gomez/iStockphoto.com; **p.307** *tl* © TeessideLive, *tr* © REUTERS/Ali Jarekji, *cl* © STR/Association Images/Alamy Stock Photo, *cr* © MUFTY MUNIR/AFP/Getty Images; **p.314** © Lesley Parry; **p.315** *tl* © CHROMORANGE/marco campagna/Alamy Stock Photo, *tc* © Masatoshi Okauchi/Shutterstock; **p.325** *cl* © Lesley Parry, *cr* © Photoshot/TopFoto; **p.328** *tr* © Gokhan Sahin/Getty Images News/Getty Images, *cr* © Shutterstock, *br* © Yanice Idir/Alamy Stock Photo; **p.330** *tl* © STR/AFP/Getty Images, *tc* © Alain Le Garsmeur "The Troubles" Archive/Alamy Stock Photo; **p.341** © World History Archive/Alamy Stock Photo; **p.342** © Masatoshi Okauchi/REX/Shutterstock; **p.361** © Stuart Miles/123 RF; **p.366** © Richard Gardner/Shutterstock; **p.368** *br* © Associated Press/Alamy Stock Photo; **p.370** *tl* Candle logo © Amnesty International, *tr* © Brooks Kraft LLC/Sygma/Getty Images; **p.385** *tl* © Klaus-Werner Friedrich/imageBROKER.com/Alamy Stock Photo, *cr* © Sally and Richard Greenhill/Alamy Stock Photo, *tc* © D Johnson/Alamy Stock Photo, *cr* © George Sweeney/Alamy Stock Photo; **p.389** © Shutterstock; **p.391** *tl* © Huntstock/Thinkstock, *tc* © K-King Photography Media Co. Ltd/Photodisc/ Thinkstock, *br* © Hektor Pustina/Associated Press/Alamy Stock Photo; **p.392** © Fawcett Society; **p.393** © Chris Dorney/123 RF; **p.397** © Cliff Hide News/Alamy Stock Photo; **p.401** © The Salvation Army's red shield logo.

Acknowledgements

The Publishers would like to thank the following for permission to reproduce copyright material.

Bible quotes are from THE HOLY BIBLE, NEW INTERNATIONAL VERSION®, NIV® Copyright © 1973, 1978, 1984, 2011 by Biblica, Inc.®

Used by permission. All rights reserved worldwide.

Qur'an quotations are from The Holy Qur'an translated by Abdullah Yusuf Ali.

The Publishers would like to thank representatives from the Hindu Forum of Britain Mrs t Patel, Mrs H Shukla MBE and Dr R Pattni for reviewing the content on pages 235–406 of this publication.

To order, please visit www.HachetteLearning.com or contact Customer Service at education@hachette.co.uk / +44 (0)1235 827827.

ISBN: 978 1 0360 1960 0

First published in 2016

This edition published in 2025 by Hachette Learning
(a trading division of Hodder & Stoughton Limited),
An Hachette UK Company
Carmelite House
50 Victoria Embankment
London EC4Y 0DZ

www.HachetteLearning.com

The authorised representative in the EEA is Hachette Ireland, 8 Castlecourt Centre, Dublin 15, D15 XTP3, Ireland (email: info@hbgi.ie)

Impression number 10 9 8 7 6 5 4 3 2 1

Year 2029 2028 2027 2026 2025

Cover photo © Sunshine Photos / Alamy Stock Photo
Illustrations by Tony Jones, Oxford Designers & Illustrators
Typeset by Aptara Inc.
Printed in the UK by Bell & Bain Ltd.

A catalogue record for this title is available from the British Library.

Contents

The study of religions

Religious, philosophical and ethical studies

The study of religions

1 CHRISTIANITY

An introduction to Christianity

Beliefs and teachings

Over 2000 years of existence, Christianity has seen many changes. Many different groups (denominations) belong to it, with different names, but all calling themselves 'Christians'.

It began as the Catholic (universal) church; everyone who was a Christian was a Catholic. However, time has seen disagreements about beliefs, leadership, organisation and practices, so new groups have been formed.

Each group is known as a **denomination**. The **Orthodox Church** was the first to break away from the Catholics in 1054CE, which was known as the Great Schism. The main factors causing this were an attempt by Rome to force all Christians to use Latin as their religious language, mistreatment of Orthodox Christians by Western Crusader knights and differences in interpretation of creeds. This created the Eastern Orthodox and the now **Roman Catholic** Church, representing the Church in the East and the West, respectively. In Europe, until the sixteenth century, the vast majority of people were Roman Catholics. However, a new movement grew up and '*protested*' against Rome, becoming known as the **Protestant** movement. European countries set up churches of their own. Therefore, in Britain the Church of England was born, with Henry VIII as its head. As time progressed, many disagreements occurred and people protested against the State form of the Church and began to form new groups with separate leadership. These were known as Non-Conformists as they refused to conform to the rules of the State. The table below shows you this:

Roman Catholic	Found worldwide – the largest Christian group
Orthodox Church	Example of groups – Russian Orthodox, Greek Orthodox, Ethiopian Orthodox
Protestant Church	Examples of groups – **Church of England** Non-Conformist – **Methodist**, Baptist, Elim Pentecostal, United Reformed Church, Congregational Church

The **Trinity** is a key belief for all Christians. They believe in one God, who has three Persons (aspects); God the Father in heaven, God the Son incarnate in Jesus and now in heaven and God the Holy Spirit, which is the power of God remaining at work in the world today. (See pages 9–10 for further explanation.)

The **Bible** is the holy book. It is a single collection of 66 books. Now available in most languages of the world, it can be found in old, modern and even children's versions. It is divided into two sections: the Old Testament and New Testament.

The Old Testament begins with the book of Genesis. With 39 books in total, it contains the history of the Jewish people – so we hear about the lives of Adam, Noah, Abraham, Isaac, Jacob, Moses and David, and this history leads up to the life of Jesus (who was Jewish by birth).

With 27 books in total, the New Testament starts with the **Gospels** – four of them (Matthew, Mark, Luke and John) all relating the life of Jesus. Gospel means good news. Then there are the books and letters that record the spread of early Christianity. The Bible can be interpreted in many different ways.

Many Christian Churches have **statements of faith** (creeds), which were put together by Christian Councils in the early centuries of the Christian Church, for example the **Nicene Creed** (381CE) and the **Apostles' Creed** (c. sixth to seventh century CE). They sum up the basic beliefs of the Christian faith.

Practices

Each Church has its own **leader**, with leadership levels below them to support this individual. The leader of the Roman Catholic Church is the Pope, who is chosen from leaders worldwide and lives in the Vatican City in Rome. The leader of the Orthodox Church is the Patriarch, known as the Patriarch of Constantinople. The Church of England has the King as its head as a ceremonial leader, but the Archbishop of Canterbury leads in reality.

Church buildings are all different too. From the outside, traditional churches are easily recognisable; it is the more modern ones that you might miss. However, on the inside these buildings often share some common key features, such as the altar, the pulpit, the lectern, stained glass windows and, of course, the symbol of the cross. On most occasions it would be very clear that the building you were inside was a church, but it is not always called a church. You might hear the term **cathedral** (a church which is presided over by a bishop, often very big and ornate) or **chapel**. Different names, different styles – but all for the purpose of worshipping God. The church leaders have different names too (priests, ministers and pastors, for example) but essentially their roles are the same; to look after the people in the community and to lead church services. Most services, though not all, have a combination of hymns, prayers, Bible readings, teachings and sermon, and most churches have some kind of celebration of the meal eaten by Jesus at his Last Supper, which included bread and wine.

The **Christian calendar** follows a predictable pattern every year. Some events, like Christmas, are celebrated on a fixed date and others, like Easter, can vary. *Advent* consists of the four Sundays leading up to *Christmas* (birth of Jesus); *Epiphany* (when the wise men visited Jesus) on the 6th January; *Ash Wednesday* (the first day of the 40 days of Lent) remembering the temptations of Jesus; *Holy Week* (including Good Friday) and Easter mark the death and **resurrection** of Jesus; **Ascension** Day commemorates Jesus being taken up to heaven and *Pentecost* which celebrates the gift of the Holy Spirit and the birth of the Church. There are others and indeed each Church has variations on how they celebrate each of them.

Some Churches, such as the Roman Catholic Church, the Orthodox Churches and some Anglican Churches, have seven of these special occasions. They are seen as rites; events of special significance. Many Protestant Churches have two, **Baptism** (of a child or adult) and Holy Communion, as these are required of Christians in the Gospels. You will learn about these two later.

Key Christian teachings

- A creed is a statement that a person believes in. The **Apostles' Creed** (below) is a short statement of Christian faith, summarising core beliefs about God, Jesus and the Holy Spirit, and in fact provides a good outline of everything you need to know for this part of the course.

I believe in God, the Father almighty,
creator of heaven and earth.

I believe in Jesus Christ, His only Son,
our Lord,
who was conceived by the Holy Spirit,
born of the Virgin Mary,
suffered under Pontius Pilate,
was crucified, died, and was buried;
he descended to the dead.
On the third day he rose again;
he ascended into heaven,
he is seated at the right hand of the Father,
and he will come to judge the living and the dead.

I believe in the Holy Spirit,
the holy catholic Church,
the communion of saints,
the forgiveness of sins,
the resurrection of the body,
and the life everlasting.
Amen.

Some things the book refers to, which you might not know:

'The Gospels' are the first four books of the New Testament – Matthew, Mark, Luke and John. They are called *gospel* which means *good news*, as they tell the story of the life of Jesus.

'The Catechism of the Catholic Church' is a collection of the key teachings which Catholics should believe and follow.

1.1 Beliefs and teachings

The nature of God

Christians believe that God is totally different from anything in the universe and ultimately beyond human understanding. However, they believe that He has revealed something of Himself through nature, the insights of the Bible and personal experience. From this, Christians believe that God has many attributes (qualities) and can describe these.

God as omnipotent

'Omnipotence' means 'all-powerful'. This is sometimes misunderstood as meaning that God can do absolutely anything, such as making a square, a circle or doing something that is morally wrong. However, by omnipotence most Christians mean that God can do anything that it makes sense for God to do. The idea of a square circle is just nonsense and doing something morally wrong would be contradictory for a God who is all good. Christians do mean that God's power is immense – immeasurable even.

For Christians, God's omnipotence can be seen in many ways, for example:

- the creation of the universe itself
- the wonders of the universe, which owes its existence to His creative and sustaining power
- the **miracles** performed by Jesus and the miracles which are claimed to sometimes occur in the modern world.

Above all, Christians believe that however bad things may seem in the world, nothing can ultimately defeat God's power.

A storm at sea

What the Bible says about God's omnipotence

There are many stories about God's omnipotence. The Creation, the Flood and the Ten Plagues are just three of them.

In St Mark's Gospel there is the story of Jesus and his disciples out on Lake Galilee in a boat. Sudden storms are common on this lake and can be very dangerous, though they end as suddenly as they begin. On this occasion, while Jesus was sleeping, a violent storm blew up and the disciples feared the boat would sink. They woke Jesus, saying, 'Teacher, do you not care if we drown?' Jesus got up and spoke to the wind and waves. 'Quiet! Be still!' Immediately the storm ended and the disciples were amazed at his power.

Some Christians think that:

- this story happened exactly as Mark told it, or
- the story can be explained as coincidence, or
- Jesus was speaking to the disciples and it was their panic, not the storm which was causing the problem, or
- it was a story created by the Church to show Jesus' divine power.

Many Christians claim this story illustrates God's power at work, as they believe that Jesus is the Son of God (see page 2, on the Trinity).

The Basics

1. What is meant by omnipotence?
2. How might Christians claim God has shown his omnipotence?
3. What is meant by all-loving and agape?
4. Explain how God is all-loving.

God as loving

Christians believe that God is all-loving. When referring to God's love, the New Testament writers used the word **agape**, which refers to a self-giving, self-sacrificial love. Christians see Jesus' death on the cross as the supreme example of that love: 'for God so loved the world that He gave His only Son' (John 3:16). They believe this showed love because the sacrifice of Jesus then allowed human beings the chance to enter heaven in the afterlife (see page 14). Many people find it hard to believe that there is an all-loving God when they see so much suffering in the world. When they experience it themselves, some lose any belief that they had in God, as the God they believed in would have helped them. Suffering actually leads some Christians to feel closer to God; they feel that God is sharing their pain and giving them strength to cope.

How God's all-loving nature is shown in the Bible

Much of Jesus' teaching is about the love of God, which is universal and unconditional. Universal means for everyone everywhere, unconditional means without conditions (regardless of what they have done). This is why Christians believe that even those who do the most evil things are still loved by God and can still come back to God and be forgiven.

Jesus told the Parable of the Prodigal Son, illustrating this love (Luke 15:11–32). A man has two sons, one claims his inheritance and leaves to waste it all. He returns to ask for a job on his father's farm, and is welcomed home. His father has forgiven him. This does not mean he gets another inheritance – everything now belongs to the elder son – but he does get a fresh start because of his father's love.

The parable of the prodigal son shows God's all-loving nature.

In the teaching known as the Sermon on the Mount, Jesus said:

> 'You have heard that it was said, "Love your neighbour and hate your enemy." But I tell you, love your enemies and pray for those who persecute you, that you may be sons of your Father in heaven. He causes his sun to rise on the evil and the good, and sends rain on the righteous and the unrighteous … Be perfect, therefore, as your heavenly Father is perfect.' *(Matthew 5:43–45, 48)*

The Basics

1 Think about events that happen in the world. Make a side-by-side list of those that might show God as loving and those that might suggest God is not loving. Make a second list to show God's power, or non-power. As an extension, for each one, explain each of your decisions.
2 **All suffering can be used to show God's love.** Do you agree with that statement? Explain your view.

God as just

To be 'just' means to be fair, to operate in a way which gives everyone equal value and equal rights, rather than being discriminatory. Christians believe that God is just.

However, it does not always seem that God is just. Many Christians think that the idea of suffering as a test of faith does not fit with believing in a loving and just God. The fact that terrible things happen in the world where there is supposed to be an all-loving God is called 'the problem of evil'. It is made worse by the fact that suffering often seems excessive and pointless. Some people argue that God is not fair or just since He allows it. (He is omnipotent, remember.) The only answer to the problem of suffering, in the view of Christian philosophers like John Hick, is that ultimately, it cannot be explained. Those who experience the love of God in other ways simply have to be prepared to accept what they cannot understand and to believe that God is indeed a God of justice.

Why it is important for Christians to believe God is just

The news often makes us think there is no justice, only terrible situations in which people suffer, and wicked people get away with their behaviour. Believing in Judgement Day or the afterlife and that God is just, means that you believe these things will be addressed and made fair.

The Bible portrays God as just and says that He expects believers to behave justly. This means not only treating their fellow human beings fairly, but also doing what it takes to relieve suffering and injustice. Many Christians work for justice in society because of this. The Bible contains rules for life, such as the Ten Commandments, which believers are expected to obey. The prophet Amos told his audience to 'let justice roll on like a river'. Jesus taught that God would judge all people according to how they had cared, or not cared, for those in need and that whatever they did for others, they did for him. He said, 'In everything, do to others what you would have them do to you' (Matthew 7:12).

The Ten Commandments (Exodus 20:1–17) – which ones might promote justice?

The Basics

1 What do Christians mean when they say God is just?
2 How might Christians reflect this belief in justice in their lives?
3 Explain, giving two reasons for each, why some people think that God is not loving and not just.
4 Explain how Christians might argue against these views.

The problem of evil and suffering

You have just learned some of the characteristics which Christians believe God is:

- All-loving: God loves each and every person as a unique individual.
- All-knowing: God knows everything it is possible to know, much more than human beings can know. This is omniscience.
- All-powerful: God has unimaginable power. Nothing is beyond God.
- Just: God is completely fair and just, so that all will be judged fairly without discrimination.

Christians are also very aware of the evil and suffering going on in the world.

Moral evil is a term given to suffering inflicted by people on each other, for example, murder. Suffering is the pain (physical or emotional) which a person goes through for any reason. Nature is responsible for a lot of the suffering in the world, for example, through natural disasters like a tsunami.

I believe in God. My God is all-loving, all-powerful and all-knowing. My God is also fair. I know there are terrible things happening in the world all the time. Some are because of people's greed, hatred and selfishness. Some I can't explain except to say the person was just evil. I have tried to understand where evil comes from, and why God allows the suffering. It is difficult, maybe even impossible. But I still believe.

The problem Christians have is how to reconcile their idea of God with the reality of suffering and evil. They have to be able to make sense of God allowing this evil and suffering to continue to happen.

Check the news for the next five days to create a short record of all the bad news events that are reported on.

How do Christians try to solve the problem of evil and suffering?

The problem of evil and suffering is why God (who is all-loving, all-knowing, all-powerful and just) allows evil and suffering.

Evil is easier to explain than the suffering caused by nature. Many Christians believe in the existence of an evil force, which they call the Devil or Satan. This being tries to tempt human beings into behaving badly and disobeying God. So, evil perpetrated by them is a result of the Devil's work.

Not all Christians believe in the Devil. Many believe that as human beings have free will, they have the ability to choose their actions. This free will was given to Adam and Eve in the Garden of Eden, and they abused it by disobeying God (they ate the fruit from the tree of knowledge). So, for many Christians, freedom of choice when mixed with greed, selfishness or hatred lead to evil doings. Humans, not God, are responsible for this kind of evil.

Suffering caused by nature is more difficult to understand. After all, God created the world, so why does it seem so flawed in its design? God must be allowing the suffering to continue as God is all-loving, all-powerful and all-knowing. In other words, He knows about the evil and suffering, loves us enough to want us not to suffer, and has the power to deal with anything. So why is there still suffering?

Is nature a flawed design?

The solution to this dilemma has been sought for many centuries by Christians, and it is not resolved. Here are some suggested explanations as to why God allows suffering.

- Suffering is a **punishment** for wrongdoing. Everyone does things wrong and so everyone might deserve to be punished.
- Suffering is a **test of faith** in God. Human beings should view suffering as a test which they must try to get through. If they do, the reward from God will be great.
- Suffering is a form of **education** for our souls. By suffering, we grow spiritually and also we learn to take responsibility and help others.
- Suffering is needed as a **balance** – to appreciate good, we have to be able to recognise evil/bad. It is impossible to have one without the other.

Is suffering fair?

These look like valid solutions – but they become problematic when examined. There will always be an example of suffering which simply cannot be explained satisfactorily. Think about a newborn baby, born with a painful and serious disability, could any of the solutions above explain that? Or a person who had always followed God's rules, worshipped Him and was genuinely good. Would any of the solutions explain their suffering a terrible and painful death?

Whatever suffering is, it is a fact of life.

The final attempt to explain why God allows suffering is to say that human beings simply must accept it. John Hick and many other Christians would claim that they experience God's love in other areas of their lives. So when they experience suffering that seems excessive or pointless, they are prepared to accept what they cannot understand. They are prepared to trust in God's goodness and love for them. Humans cannot possibly understand God and His purposes, and so suffering must just be accepted.

The response is more important than the cause.

For Christians, the point is not to question why God allows suffering, but rather to look at how they can respond positively to suffering, whether it be their own or that of others. Suffering becomes a trigger for action, for showing the love of Jesus to their fellow humans.

The Basics

1 What is the problem of evil?
2 How do Christians explain the existence of evil and suffering?
3 **It is impossible for God to be all-loving and allow evil and suffering.** Do you agree? Explain your arguments.

The Oneness of God and the Trinity

Christianity is a monotheistic faith, in other words, Christians believe in one God. Most Christians believe that God's nature has been revealed to the world in distinct ways:

- as the loving creator and sustainer of the universe (God the Father)
- as the saviour who became incarnate (born in human flesh) and lived, died and rose again (God the Son)
- as the source of strength which Christians find at work in their hearts (God the Holy Spirit).

The Trinity concept is an attempt to explain what the Bible says about the nature of the relationship between the Father, the Son and the Holy Spirit. Christians believe that the One God is a Trinity of these Three Persons. The word 'Person' in relation to the Trinity is used in a very different way from its meaning in modern everyday life. It does not mean that God consists of three individuals or that God has three properties. God can be known in three ways and each way has its own characteristics, but they are three forms of the same single entity. The Trinity is also often called the Godhead.

However, believing something to be both three and one at the same time can be a confusing idea. Christians accept this to be the case, but say that:

- God cannot be known. The nature of God is totally beyond human understanding. So it should not be possible to make full sense of it.
- Belief in God as Trinity makes the best sense of what they read in the Bible and experience in their lives. In the Bible it says that when Jesus was baptised, the Holy Spirit descended like a dove and a voice said, 'You are my Son …' At his final meeting on earth with his disciples, Jesus said to them, 'Go therefore and make disciples of all nations, baptizing them in the name of the Father and of the Son and of the Holy Spirit.' (Matthew 28:19)

Symbols of the Trinity

Christians often use symbols that show the concept of the Trinity, showing the idea of 'three in one'. Perhaps the earliest and simplest symbol is an equilateral triangle, with each of its sides representing one of the Persons of the Trinity.

1 One of the most famous is the shamrock, which St Patrick is said to have used when teaching the Christian faith in Ireland.

2 Another symbol, taken from mathematics is that of the Borromean rings. Taken together they are inseparable, but if one is removed the other two fall apart. They are seen as a symbol of strength in unity. The circle is a symbol of the unending and eternal nature of God.

3 The ancient Celtic spiral triskelion shape is also used by Christians.

Shamrock

Borromean rings

Triskelion

Task

Using research, find and draw the following symbols of the Trinity: triquetra, trefoil, fleur-de-lis, shield of the faith (*scutum fidei*). Underneath each of your drawings, explain how each relates to the idea of God as Trinity.

How belief in the Trinity influences Christians

In baptism ceremonies, which are a symbol of welcome into the Christian Church, we mention the Trinity throughout. In the Church of England, for instance, I will say, '(Name), I baptise you in the name of the ***Father and of the Son and of the Holy Spirit****. Amen.' Before the baptism can take place, the person being baptised (if old enough) or the parents and godparents declare their faith in* ***God as Three-in-One****. I ask if they believe in* ***God the Father, God the Son and God the Holy Spirit*** *and finally everyone present says, 'This is our faith.* ***We believe and trust in one God, Father, Son and Holy Spirit****.'*

So … where else is this idea used?

Vicar

*You may have heard the prayer '****The grace of Our Lord Jesus Christ, and the love of God, and the fellowship of the Holy Spirit****, be with us all evermore. Amen'. This is said at the end of most services. Many hymns mention the Trinity, and at the end of saying or singing a psalm, there are the words: 'Glory be to the* ***Father and to the Son and to the Holy Spirit****.'*

Parishioner

And … what does it all mean?

The Trinity has been explained as being like a relationship based on love and equality … hence the equilateral triangle. Human beings are said to be created in the image of God, so they should show that same unity of love and equality in their relationships with others. This should make a big difference to a Christian lifestyle – Christians must try to show their fellow human beings the same love and respect that flows between the three Persons of the Trinity.

Challenging the idea of the Trinity

Some Jewish people, Muslims and others suggest that Christians believe in tritheism. This means belief in three separate gods who are linked in some way. In other words, they claim that Christians believe in three separate gods.

Secular critics, such as Richard Dawkins, state that belief in the Trinity makes no logical sense whatsoever. They say it confirms their view that religion is just superstitious nonsense based on old-fashioned and out-dated thinking.

Task

Research Christian hymns or poems which refer to the Trinity. For example, 'Lead us, Heavenly Father' (James Edmeston) or 'The Trinity – A poem' (Neil Booth). Make notes on what they say about the Trinity and how they explain it.

The Basics

1. Explain the Christian belief in the Trinity.
2. Explain how believing in the Trinity might influence a Christian's life.
3. **Christians believe in three gods, not one.** Do you agree? Explain your reasons.

Christian beliefs about creation

God is transcendent (beyond space and time, controlled by neither). Christians believe God created the world (if you do not know the story read page 155), as both Christians and Jewish people have the same teaching.

One of the most fundamental beliefs of Christianity which separates it from other religions, is that of the Trinity (see pages 9–10, to remind yourself about the Trinity concept).

If God is the Trinity, then the Trinity must have existed before the creation – because God did. So for Christians, the Trinity is the way in which the world was created.

Creeds are statements of belief. The Nicene Creed begins with: 'We believe in one God, the Father, the almighty, maker of heaven and earth.' '**Father**' is a metaphor that expresses the life-giving, creative nature of God. This statement reflects the opening verse of the Old Testament: 'In the beginning, God created the heavens and the earth' (Genesis 1:1).

St John's Gospel also opens with the phrase 'in the beginning': 'In the beginning was the Word, and the Word was with God, and the Word was God. He was with God in the beginning. Through him all things were made; without him nothing was made that has been made.' This picks up the idea of God creating through His Word, for example, 'And God said, "Let there be light," and there was light.' However, there is more to the term 'Word' than this. The author of St John's Gospel linked the Word with Jesus (the **Son**) in the statement: 'The Word became flesh and lived for a while among us. We have seen his glory, the glory of the one and only [Son] …' (John 1:14). Christians understand this as referring to the Second Person of the Trinity, who might be referred to both as the Word and the Son of God. So God and Jesus are 'one'.

The Genesis account of creation also states: 'Now the earth was formless and empty, darkness was over the face of the deep, and the **Spirit of God** was hovering over the face of the waters' (Genesis 1:2). Christians see this as a reference to the Third Person of the Trinity, the Holy Spirit. The Spirit shows God in action, transforming chaos into order, as seen in the rest of Genesis 1. Commentary on Genesis 1 compares this to the hovering of a dove.

In the beginning God created the heaven and the earth. And the earth was without form, and void; and darkness was upon the face of the deep. And the Spirit of God moved upon the face of the waters. 'And God said, "Let there be light," and there was light.' *Genesis 1:1–3*

'In the beginning was the Word, and the Word was with God, and the Word was God. He was with God in the beginning. Through Him all things were made; without Him nothing was made that has been made.' *John 1:1–3*

The Basics

1. Why is God called the Father? What is the role of the Father?
2. Explain how the three Persons of the Trinity were all part of the creation (hint – you will need to refer to each of the three parts).
3. **The Trinity is the most important belief in Christianity.** Explain arguments to agree and disagree with this.

Genesis 1:1–31

This describes God's creation of the universe over a period of six days, starting with the day and night and ending with the creation of human beings (see page 155), with a seventh day of rest. Some Christians believe the story literally: that is, that it tells us exactly how creation happened. They believe that the authors of the writings in the Bible were directly inspired by God, so that what they wrote contains no mistakes.

However, many Christians think that the story is a myth: that is, a fictional story with a profound message, delivered through symbolism. It is the message or symbolism that is important rather than how and when it all happened. In this case, it is trying to teach religious truths about the nature of God and His relationship with His creation.

The message is:

- God is the sole and omnipotent Creator.
- God is the source of everything in the universe and sustains it.
- God created a universe that was ordered not chaotic.
- Every aspect of God's creation was good: that is, it fulfilled His purposes for it.
- Human beings are created in God's image, so they reflect God's capacity for creativity and relationship.
- Human beings are given authority over the rest of the created world.

> 'God saw all that He had made, and it was very good.' *(Genesis 1:31)*

The importance of beliefs about Genesis 1 for Christians

Christians believe that the message within Genesis 1 is true and that they live in an ordered world, created and sustained by God. The universe does not exist by chance and human lives have meaning and purpose. This belief encourages Christians to adopt a positive approach to life. Even when things go wrong, they retain this positivity, and they do not ignore issues but rather they think things through and then act on their beliefs.

The statement that human beings are made in the image of God is highly significant for Christians. To be human is to have potential and this can be seen in the tremendous achievements made in the arts, science, medicine, sport, and so on. Being in the image of God applies to all human beings, which means that all human lives are of value, regardless of their physical, mental or intellectual capacity.

Christians therefore believe they have a responsibility to treat everyone equally and to show love and respect to all created beings, both human and non-human. The power that human beings have been given over the rest of creation entails responsibility, not privilege and most Christians interpret it in terms of stewardship, not domination leading to exploitation.

Created in the image of God

The Basics

1. Read Genesis 1:1–31 and use it to create a comic strip cartoon, showing the stages of creation.
2. **It does not matter if the Creation story is not true.** Do you agree with this statement? Explain your reasoning.

Interpretations of the Genesis 1 creation story

Christians interpret the creation story in different ways. Here are three different ways of understanding the creation story in Genesis 1.

If I interpret a creation story in this way, I believe it is literally true. Every word in it is the word of God, who is always correct, and tells only the truth. God dictated the holy book, including the creation story. Whatever I read in the story must be absolutely correct. It isn't difficult to believe this, as I also believe that God is all-powerful (omnipotent) and all-knowing (omniscient), so God is more than capable of creating the world. For a fundamentalist, the Genesis creation story is word-for-word true – God did create the world in just seven days, as described. Where questions are raised about fossil evidence, this is seen as a test from God.

Does this interpretation seem reasonable to you? Explain your views.

My view is slightly different. I believe the account in Genesis 1 contains the truth. The Bible, and so the creation story, do tell us what really happened. However, God did not dictate the story, God inspired it. This means that there is room for error in the way it is told. One way to look at Genesis 1 is to see it as a general description. For example, in Genesis, we are told the creation took seven days. The word for 'day' in the original language can mean period of time, so maybe that's actually what it meant. Maybe it is saying that God raised the level of the development of the world at regular intervals over a long period of time, the most crucial example being when God created humans.

Does this interpretation seem reasonable to you? Explain your views.

I have a different view of the creation stories in Genesis. I don't believe God told what is in the Bible directly to humankind. I believe whoever wrote them was inspired by the world around them and a sense of God. This means that I shouldn't try to read them as versions of what happened. Instead they are answering questions like 'Why did the world come to be?' and 'Have I got a purpose on earth?' In the case of Genesis, the writer is trying to show that we each have a place in the world, and that the world is a good place. So it doesn't matter whether science can prove the story wrong, because the story isn't trying to state facts anyway. What is crucially important is the message – there is a loving God, who created each of us as special beings, and gave us a world to live in, live from and to look after.

Does this interpretation seem reasonable to you? Explain your views.

Task

Consider each of those interpretations. What influence might belief in each have on the life and behaviour of a believer?

Beliefs about the afterlife

If people are asked to describe what happens after we die, many would say something along the lines of: 'You die, your soul leaves your body, goes to be judged and then goes to heaven or hell, depending on whether you have been good or bad.' This is a popular idea which we see reflected in films and books, so it is part of our culture. It is, in very simple terms, what Christians believe about life after death.

Christianity teaches that death is not the end. It separates life on earth (temporary and subject to the limitations of time and space) from life with God (eternal and beyond time and space). Death is not something to be feared. Many believe that they will be reunited with loved ones who have already died, which helps them with the awful pain of bereavement.

The Christian hope about the afterlife is expressed as follows in Revelation: 'He [God] will wipe every tear from their eyes. There will be no more death or mourning or crying or pain, for the old order of things has passed away' (Revelation 21:4).

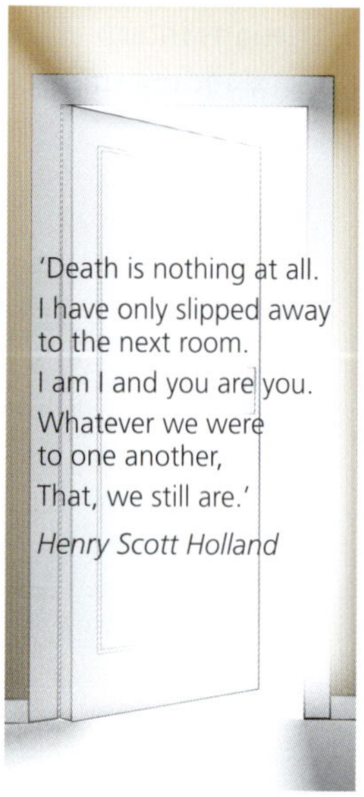

The importance of belief in the resurrection for Christians

Most Christians believe in resurrection – that the dead will be restored to life. This belief is based on the teaching of Jesus and that he overcame death through resurrection. **St Paul** said that belief in Jesus' resurrection was central to Christian faith: 'And if Christ has not been raised, your faith is futile ... If only for this life we have hope in Christ, we are to be pitied more than all men' (1 Corinthians 15:17, 19). If death was really the end for Jesus, then Christianity is in effect nothing more than the worship of a martyr whose life ended in failure with a shameful death. Christians believe that Jesus lives and, after death, so will they in a state of unimaginable joy.

Belief in resurrection treats the physical body as an integral and valuable part of what it means to be human. The body is 'a temple of the Holy Spirit' and should be treated with respect. Some believe it will be restored to life; for them the concept of resurrection is of a physical resurrection. Others believe that the resurrection body will be spiritual, not physical.

The Basics

1 What do people mean when they talk about the afterlife?
2 Look at the poem on the door. What do you think it means?
3 Explain why many people believe in an afterlife.

What Christians mean by resurrection

I believe in ... the resurrection of the body, and the life everlasting. Amen *(Apostles' Creed, final part)*

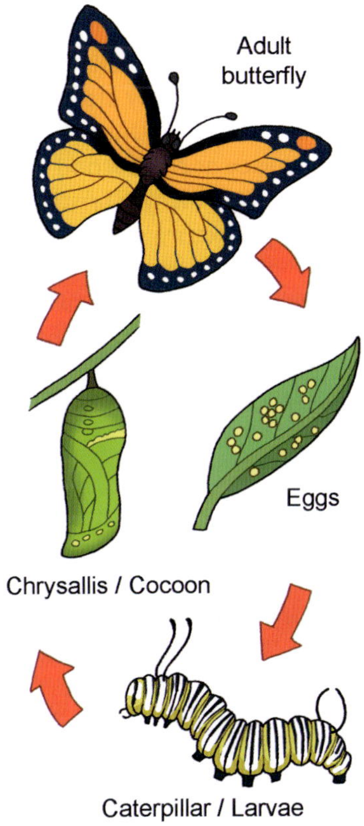

A creed is a statement of belief but Christians know that after death the physical body decomposes. So what do Christians mean by resurrection of the body? Clearly it cannot be the reassembling of the bodies that people have now! Even so, some Christians reject the idea of cremation because of their belief in that physical resurrection – they believe God will raise them back to life before Judgement Day.

When Jesus was questioned about the idea of resurrection, he said, 'When the dead rise, they will neither marry nor be given in marriage' (Mark 12:25). The new mode of existence would be different from the earthly one. St Paul tried to explain this – 'The body that is sown is perishable, it is raised imperishable ... it is sown a natural body, it is raised a spiritual body' (1 Corinthians 15:42, 44). Sometimes the lifecycle of the butterfly is used to illustrate Christianity's teaching that there is a continuity of identity between the person's earthly life and the resurrection life. The caterpillar and butterfly have a totally different appearance, but there is a continuity of identity throughout.

Roman Catholics believe in purgatory. This is believed to be an intermediate state of existence between death and the afterlife. After the death of the body, the soul goes to purgatory if it is destined for heaven. Purgatory is a place of purification for the soul, so that it can become pure and holy enough to enter heaven. It is not a physical place.

Different views about the afterlife

There has always been debate about what resurrection really means. If we are all physically resurrected, where is the place we will go to? How will we all recognise each other? Will we be resurrected in the body which died, which may be very damaged? These are some of the problems raised. Many Christians say that God has the answers, and human beings must trust in that as we cannot understand.

There is no scientific proof of resurrection, nor evidence beyond the Biblical stories of, and early historical writings about Jesus. Many believe our souls are what live, not the physical body; the soul is eternal and it will be in heaven after the Judgement. This fits with what Jesus and St Paul said, whilst a physical resurrection does not.

Increasing numbers of people ask to have humanist funerals when they die. Humanist funerals are non-religious ceremonies that can be held in a variety of locations and focus on celebrating the life of the deceased. Humanists do not believe in the afterlife, whereas a Christian funeral has references to the afterlife and the resurrection.

The Basics

1. What is a creed? Name two Christian creeds.
2. Explain what Christians mean by 'resurrection'.
3. Evaluate the claim that **belief in life after death makes no sense.** Try to give reasons for and against this statement.

Judgement

Aside from whether a person is Christian or not, Christian beliefs about an afterlife and Judgement Day have had a very big impact on our culture.

How does belief in Judgement Day influence people now in their lives? Does it only influence people who claim to be Christian?

Jesus taught that God's love and mercy are unconditional, though many of his parables speak about God's judgement after death. Christianity teaches that there will be a Judgement Day at the end of time and all will be judged by Jesus according to how they behaved.

The Nicene Creed states that Jesus 'will come again in glory to judge the living and the dead.' This is showing Jesus will make and deliver the judgement.

The Catechism of the Catholic Church (a summary of Roman Catholic teaching) states that there are two judgements: the particular and the general judgements. The particular judgement occurs immediately after each individual's death. The general/final judgement takes place at the Second Coming, which is when many Christians believe that Jesus will return in glory to earth, bringing the age of time and space to an end. He will judge those still alive and those who are dead, as a result of which they will be assigned to either heaven or hell.

Many Christians believe absolutely that after they die, their souls will wait for Judgement Day. From there, they will be rewarded with heaven or punished with hell. The problem is that words cannot describe the afterlife adequately, not least because no one has the experience to speak from. Some Christians reject the idea of the Second Coming and final judgement. They think Jesus was trying to express something human beings cannot fully understand, but in a way that they could make some sense of. They also believe the creeds should be understood in the same way. They do not deny that humans will be called to account for their lives, but they disagree about the context and the way in which it is to be interpreted.

Judgement in Jesus' teaching

A number of Jesus' parables relate to judgement. The parable of the rich man and Lazarus (Luke 16:19–31) warns that ignoring the needs of others may have eternal consequences.

Another parable is that of the sheep and the goats (Matthew 25:31–46). The message is that on Judgement Day, some will be rewarded with heaven for helping others, whilst others are sent to hell because they did not.

The Basics

1 Explain the Christian belief about judgement.
2 **It makes sense for everyone to live as if they believe in a Judgement Day.** How far do you agree with this statement? Explain reasons for and against it.

Heaven and hell

Heaven

If people are asked to describe what they think heaven will be like, their answers might well relate to what they see as most desirable in their present lives. So for those living in a land frequently suffering from drought, heaven might be a well-watered garden with an abundance of trees and flowers. Those who have to face extreme heat might think of somewhere with cooling breezes. Children might imagine heaven as a party with lots of ice cream and chocolate. Christians themselves use earthly images to explain their understanding of heaven, but Christianity teaches that heaven is a state of being, not a physical place. It is being with God outside time and space. In a newspaper interview Desmond Tutu said of heaven: 'It is difficult for us to conceive of an existence that is timeless, where you look at absolute beauty and goodness and you have no words. It is enough just to be there. You know how it is when you are sitting with someone you love and hours can go by in what seem like moments? Well, in heaven, eternity itself will pass in a flash … heaven is a community.'

Hell

The Bible depicts hell as a place of unquenchable fire. Again, this is metaphor but it led to the most horrific paintings in the Middle Ages. As a way of frightening people into obeying the rules of the Church, some artists painted nightmarish scenes of devils tearing people apart and eating them. Many Christians have rejected those literal views of hell. They teach that hell is eternal separation from God. This separation results from the deliberate rejection of any relationship with Him. So hell is not what God decides for people. It is not what God wants. It is down to human free choice. Many Christians who believe in hell would agree with this statement: 'God predestines no one to go to hell; for this, a wilful turning away from God … is necessary and persistence in it until the end' (Catechism of the Catholic Church).

Different beliefs about heaven and hell

Some Christians reject any idea of hell because they think its existence would mean that God's love would not triumph over evil. They think that ultimately everyone will respond to God's love and that whatever evil things people may have done, they will repent and be forgiven. This belief is called universalism.

The Basics

1. Describe Christian ideas of heaven and hell.
2. Explain why a person might find themselves in heaven or in hell after death.
3. **The existence of hell does not fit with a belief in an all-loving God.** Argue for and against this statement.

The incarnation – Jesus the Son

The incarnation is a central Christian belief. The word literally means 'embodiment', and the term refers to the belief that God took on human form as Jesus. This belief is stated in John 1:14: 'The Word became flesh and lived for a while among us. We have seen His glory, the glory of the one and only [Son], who came from the Father, full of grace and truth.'

Christians believe that Jesus was both fully divine (the pre-existent Word of God) and fully human (conceived by and born of Mary). As the Catechism of the Catholic Church states: '... Jesus is inseparably true God and true man. He is truly the Son of God who, without ceasing to be God and Lord, became a man and our brother.'

As with the idea of the Trinity, this teaching about the incarnation is impossible to fully understand, but it refers to how his disciples and the early Christians experienced Jesus. Those who wrote the books in the New Testament struggled to express their belief that Jesus was both divine and human, but were convinced that this was the case and that it was essential to the Christian faith: 'If anyone acknowledges that Jesus is the Son of God, God lives in him and he in God. And so we know and rely on the love God has for us' (1 John 4:15–16).

The New Testament: Jesus as the Son of God

Throughout the New Testament it states that Jesus is the Son of God. Stories relating to Jesus' birth are found in St. Matthew's and St Luke's Gospels and the title 'Son of God' is used to refer to Jesus again and again. Both Gospels state that Mary was a virgin; according to Luke 1:35, Mary was told that she would conceive through the power of the Holy Spirit. This is taken up in the Nicene Creed's statement that Jesus was 'conceived by the Holy Spirit, born of the Virgin Mary'. Christians hold different views on the idea of the virgin birth. Some accept it as what actually happened and that this was the most appropriate way in which Jesus could be conceived. However, others think it is a myth, believing that a metaphor was being used to show that Jesus was not simply a human being but was in a unique sense the Son of God – he was fully divine and fully human. At Christmas, carols are sung telling the story of the birth of Jesus from the Gospels and often including beliefs about the person of Jesus.

Christmas carols often tell the story of Jesus' birth

The Basics

1. What does incarnation mean?
2. Look at the John 1:14 quote in the first paragraph. What does it mean?
3. What does the Bible tell us about the birth of Jesus?
4. **It is easy to believe the story of the Virgin Birth.** Do you think this statement is true? Explain your reasons to agree and disagree. Include what Christians might say.

What about Jesus' knowledge?

One problem that Christians have with believing in Jesus as both fully God and fully human is how to understand the knowledge of Jesus. There are many occasions recorded in the Gospels when it appears that Jesus' knowledge was limited. For instance, Mark writes about a time when the people of Jesus' home town rejected him, which meant he was unable to perform any miracles there. When speaking about the end of the world, he said to his disciples that no one, not even he, knew when that would happen. If Jesus was really divine, how could he not do or know these things?

One possible answer to this can be found in Paul's letter to the Christians at Philippi, a Christian community in Macedonia. There he quotes from what many Christians think was a very early Christian hymn. It says that at the incarnation, Jesus willingly became fully human. Paul describes Jesus as coming in 'the nature of a servant', which might point to Jesus being born into a poor family, shown because they could give only the 'poor man's offering' when they went to the Temple after Jesus' birth. Christian writers say that God could only be properly human by giving up most of His divine knowledge. Jesus was still fully God in his relationship with and understanding of God, but he made this act of supreme self-giving.

'Who, being in very nature God, did not consider equality with God, something to be used to his own advantage; rather, he made himself nothing by taking the very nature of a servant, being made in human likeness. And being found in appearance as a man, he humbled himself by becoming obedient to death—even death on a cross!' *(Philippians 2:5–11)*

The importance of belief in the incarnation for Christian lifestyle

Belief in the incarnation is central to how Christianity understands the extent of God's love for humanity, but it also has great significance for how Christians believe they should live. The author of 1 John wrote: 'This is love: not that we loved God, but that He loved us and sent His Son as an atoning sacrifice for our sins. Dear friends, since God so loved us, we also ought to love one another' (1 John 4:10–11).

This humility and selfless love for others can be seen in the lives of some Christians. For example, Mother Teresa left the relative comfort of her convent to live among the most disadvantaged people in India as one of them, and Father Kolbe offered his own life in order to save another's in Auschwitz.

Mother Teresa

Task

It is always good to have examples you can refer to in your answers. Find out about one of the following Christians: Colin Parry (father of Tim who died in an IRA bombing), Corrie ten Boom (who helped many Jewish people escape from the Nazis during the Second World War), Thomas Barnardo (founder of homes for poor children), Óscar Romero (South American priest). Explain how the person you have chosen fulfilled the command given in I John to show selfless love for others.

The crucifixion

Jesus' ministry of teaching and healing lasted for about three years and ended with his death by crucifixion. The Jewish religious authorities arrested, tried and convicted him of blasphemy – a crime which was punishable by death in Jewish law. However, they were not allowed to carry out the death sentence under Roman rule so they handed him over to the Roman governor, Pilate, on a charge of treason. He was found guilty and sentenced to death. Crucifixion was the method of execution for those who were not Roman citizens. It was a humiliating and inhumane method that led to a slow and agonising death. All four Gospels contain accounts of Jesus' crucifixion and it was also referred to by Tacitus, a first-century Roman historian.

The crucifixion of Jesus

Mark 15:21–39

According to Mark, a man named Simon was made to carry the crossbeam to the place of execution, perhaps because the whipping prior to crucifixion meant that Jesus was unable to carry it himself. The crucifixion took place at Golgotha. Jesus was stripped of his clothes, nailed through the wrists to the beam, hoisted up and nailed through the ankle and heel to the vertical post. He was offered wine mixed with myrrh but refused it. A sign stating his charge (claiming to be king of the Jews) was attached to the cross. Two criminals were crucified on either side of him. As he hung there, those who had come to watch or who were passing by shouted insults. It took six hours for Jesus to die, and Mark recorded that for the final three hours the whole land was dark. Some Christians think that Mark invented this as a symbol of the judgement falling on Israel for its rejection of the **Messiah**. Shortly before his death, Jesus shouted, 'My God, my God, why have you forsaken me?' The crowd misunderstood, thinking he was calling on the prophet Elijah to come to his aid and they tried to prolong his life by offering him some wine. Jesus, however, gave a loud cry and died. According to Mark, the Temple curtain that separated the most sacred part of that building from the rest was torn in two. Again, many Christians think this was intended to symbolise that Jesus' death destroyed the barrier of sin that had separated humanity from God, making it possible for everyone, Jew and non-Jew, to have access to God. This may explain the last point in the Biblical story, when the Roman officer on duty, hearing Jesus' cry and seeing how he died, commented, 'Surely this man was the Son of God.'

The Basics

1 Describe the events leading up to Jesus' death.
2 Describe the events of Jesus' crucifixion.
3 Why is the crucifixion important to Christians?
4 Why do you think Jesus felt 'forsaken'?
5 **If Jesus died to help us, it is the greatest sacrifice ever made.** How might you agree with this statement?

Why did the Son of God have to die?

There are three key reasons why Jesus had to die. Two of them are about the time he lived in.

Jesus was born in Palestine at the time when the Romans controlled Palestine as part of their Empire. The Romans allowed the Jewish religious leaders to have a level of control, stopping short of allowing them the ability to sentence people to death. Practice of the religion was allowed to continue. The Jewish religious leaders made up the **Sanhedrin** – the ruling council – who had a lot of power. Jesus, with his new interpretation of the religious law of the Torah, came into conflict with them. For example, he helped people on the Sabbath which was a breach of laws forbidding work on the Sabbath. Some of the things he said and did, they considered blasphemy. The reception people gave him was a threat to their own authority.

At the time of Jesus, various groups, for example, the Zealots, were agitating against the Roman occupation of their country. Pilate, the Roman Governor, needed to solve the problem. He put down rebellions with brutality, always making it more likely that they would recur rather than be solved. His superiors in Rome, from which the Empire was controlled, were not impressed with his actions in Palestine and ended his tenure soon after Jesus' death. According to St John's Gospel, Pilate said he intended to release Jesus, but the crowd warned him that if he did so, he was no friend of Caesar (ruler of the Roman Empire). It is possible that fear of reprisal from Rome for setting free a Jewish rebel forced Pilate to sentence Jesus to death.

Finally, one theological understanding is that Jesus had to die to fulfil God's commands for him. Without Jesus' death, human beings could not be reunited with God and could not enter heaven. Human beings had strayed from God's ways, separating themselves from Him; Jesus' sacrificial death would atone (make up for) that separation. We will see this in more detail later (see pages 22–23).

The Basics

1. Explain why the Sanhedrin wanted Jesus dead.
2. Explain how and why Pilate was responsible for Jesus' death.
3. **No one was to blame for the death of Jesus.** What do you think? Explain your reasoning.

Christian beliefs about the role of Christ in salvation

John 3:16 sums up what Christians believe: 'For God so loved the world that He gave His one and only Son, that whoever believes in Him shall not perish but have eternal life.' They believe that the death of Jesus was central to God's plan of salvation (see pages 26–27).

For Christians, the crucifixion was no unfortunate accident. In the Garden of Gethsemane, Jesus pleaded with God as he did not want to die, yet at the same time he said, 'Your will, not mine, be done.' The belief that he was carrying out God's will was what enabled him to get through the arrest, the trials, the flogging and the crucifixion.

Christians often see Jesus' death as an atonement. The New Testament authors express the idea in various ways, the main approaches which link to each other, being:

- On the Cross Jesus bore the consequences and penalty of human sin.
- This was God taking the initiative in reconciling humanity to God.
- It inspires human beings to take the moral lead in reconciliation in the world today.

The Cross is an example and inspiration.

And he said, Abba, Father, all things are possible unto thee; take away this cup from me: nevertheless not what I will, but what thou wilt. *(Mark 14:36)*

Jesus' death – paying the debt caused by human sin

This view starts from the point that human nature is sinful. Human beings have deliberately turned away from God, refusing to obey His will. Being just, God must judge and punish human beings for this wilful disobedience. However, God is also loving and merciful, so He made it possible to be forgiven through the incarnation and Jesus taking on himself the punishment for sin. Christians adopting this approach speak of Jesus' death as a ransom for human sin.

Many Christians struggle with this understanding of Jesus' death, where God is a judge whose justice needs to be satisfied through retribution, and where Jesus bears a penalty which is not his own.

Is this what God is like?

Task

Read again what pages 5–6 say about Christian views on God being all-loving and just. Then in small groups discuss whether you think that what is written there fits in with the view that Jesus died to pay the debt caused by sin. Tell the rest of the class what you think and give reasons for your view.

How Jesus' death was an act of atonement and reconciliation

Atonement means making up for, or making amends. Literally it can be seen as 'at one ment'; the idea that two people who were estranged are now at one with each other, differences put aside. The traditional and still common view of atonement is that because human beings often create a barrier between themselves and God by thinking only of themselves, Jesus' death was a necessary atonement, because human beings could not deal with this problem of selfishness themselves.

Reconciliation is the restoration of friendships or relationships. Christians believe that the relationship between God and human beings was so damaged that drastic action was needed.

Christians believe that human beings needed to be reconciled with God so that they could be reunited with Him in heaven. Human beings could not make that happen, it was up to God through a drastic event; this was God's self-sacrifice in the form of Jesus. They believe Jesus went willingly into this because he knew it was the only way for reconciliation to happen.

Christians believe that by his death, Jesus triumphed over evil

How Christians can take the initiative in reconciliation

Some twenty-first century Christians see that they may have to follow Jesus even to death. Just as Jesus surrendered himself to God's will, so Christians should offer themselves to the service of God, trying to carry out His wishes to the best of their ability. As Jesus said to his disciples, 'Greater love has no one than this; that one lay down his life for his friends. You are my friends if you do what I command' (John 15:12–14). Fortunately for most, death is not required, they can show their beliefs by other actions. For example, a Christian might work as a volunteer with the homeless to bring social justice, or train and take a job as a nurse to be able to help others, or give time to do pastoral work with older members of the congregation. In all these things, they are following Jesus' example and showing love for others. They are taking the initiative and trying to repair the world, not leaving it to someone else.

The Basics

1 What is meant by reconciliation and atonement?
2 Explain how Christians believe human beings had separated themselves from God and how God addressed that problem.
3 **Christians should be prepared to follow Jesus even to death.** Explore and analyse this statement, showing you have thought about more than one point of view.

Tasks

Research Maximilian Kolbe to find out about an example of someone following Jesus' example to the extreme. Research the work of Mother Teresa to find out about how a Christian followed Jesus' example in a different way.

The resurrection

According to the New Testament, a man named Joseph was given permission by Pilate to have Jesus' body taken down from the cross and handed over to him for burial. Jesus was buried in a rock tomb, but the women who accompanied Joseph could not take care of the body because the Sabbath was about to start, meaning no work could be done. A huge boulder was rolled across the entrance to stop animals from getting in. The women returned as soon as it was light on the Sunday to do this work, only to discover that the stone was rolled to one side. The Gospel accounts vary slightly in what followed, but all agree that the body was no longer there and the women were told that Jesus had risen. According to Mark, a young man in white told them this and said that they were to return to Galilee, where they would meet the risen Jesus. The women were terrified and fled, telling no one at first about what they had experienced. According to John, this person revealed himself to Mary Magdalene as Jesus come back to life. John says she returned to the disciples and told them she had seen him.

Matthew, Luke and John's Gospels give accounts of Jesus appearing during the next 40 days to his disciples and to other believers. These are called 'resurrection appearances', (Jesus appearing after he had resurrected from the dead). In most of them, Jesus was not immediately recognised, either there was something different in his appearance, or nobody expected to see him. The stories all stress the physical nature of Jesus' appearance, as if to show it was not a ghost.

The ascension – the fortieth day after the resurrection

St Luke's Gospel ends with what Christians call the ascension of Jesus. Another, longer account of the ascension, in Acts 1:3–11 (New Testament) describes Jesus taking his disciples to a place called Bethany and blessing them. Then he is 'taken up to heaven', which in pictures is usually shown to be him rising up into the sky. In Acts, it says a cloud 'received him out of their sight'. Most Christians think this story was not intended to be taken literally as if Jesus was lifted up and taken to heaven by God's power. Rather, the writer uses imagery to stress the finality of this appearance, the successful completion of Jesus's work on earth and also his divine kingship. Some **fundamentalist** Christians do take the event literally in terms of Jesus being hidden by a cloud and disappearing into another dimension.

The Basics

1 What happened after Jesus had been crucified?
2 Read Luke 24:13–35. Either write an account of the story, as if you were Cleopas, or draw a comic strip cartoon with the title: The journey to Emmaus.
3 Describe the ascension.
4 **The ascension is just a made up story to show Jesus was special.** Explain reasons for and against this statement, including what Christians might say.

Why Jesus' resurrection is important to Christians

For most Christians, belief in Jesus' resurrection is a central element to their faith. If death was the end for him, then Jesus' life ended in failure. At best he was a martyr, dying for his beliefs. At worst, he was just someone whose delusions got him into trouble with the authorities. Christians interpret his resurrection from the dead as the ultimate proof that he is the Son of God, showing God's triumph over evil and death. A Christian symbol of the resurrection shows a Passover lamb (representing Jesus' sacrificial death) carrying a banner of victory (over death).

Did Jesus rise from the dead?

No, he did not	Replies to the points
The women went to the wrong tomb and when the young man said 'He is not here. See the place where they laid him', he was redirecting them.	The women knew where he was buried as they had accompanied Joseph when taking the body to the tomb.
Jesus was not actually dead when taken off the cross. He came round in the tomb and either got himself out or someone came and got him out.	He would not have been capable of getting himself out. If someone got him out, surely someone would have seen him. He could not have been hidden forever.
The disciples were deluded; the appearances of Jesus were just wishful thinking.	Jesus' resurrection was the last thing that the disciples expected. They were in hiding for fear of being arrested themselves.
The story was made up by the disciples to gain prestige.	The disciples gained anything but prestige. They were persecuted from the start when they began to talk about Jesus and most became martyrs; they were killed for their beliefs.

What decides the debate for many Christians is the transformation of the disciples, especially Peter. When Jesus was arrested, Peter ran away in terror. He did go to the high priest's palace to find out what was happening to Jesus, but was recognised and challenged. Three times he denied all knowledge of Jesus. From then on he was in hiding. Yet, just a few weeks later, he was proclaiming to anyone who would listen that Jesus was sent by God and was risen from the dead. Even when threatened by the high priest he refused to stop, saying 'Do we obey God or you?' He was eventually martyred in Rome. Christians think that Peter would not have done this for something he knew to be a lie or as a result of a delusion. Only something that actually happened could explain the transformation.

Just before his death, Jesus said to Peter, 'Today – yes tonight – before the cock crows twice you will deny me three times.'

The Basics

1 Why is the resurrection important for Christians?
2 How might believing in the resurrection affect the way people live their lives?
3 Using the information in the table above, evaluate the claim that **'Jesus' resurrection is a lie.'**

Sin

The story of original sin (the Fall) is found in Genesis 3. In the story Adam and Eve disobey God's command not to eat fruit from the tree of good and evil. The serpent tempted them to think that God's command arose out of His concern for Himself and not from what was best for them. He said that they would become like God Himself, and they gave in and ate the fruit. This was the first (original) sin. As a result, God gave certain punishments and Adam and Eve were thrown out of Eden.

For many centuries most Christians took the story literally. They thought that humans were all descended from Adam and Eve and that their act of disobedience led to all their descendants being tainted with what they called original sin; an inbuilt tendency to disobey God. This meant they were separated from God and in danger of receiving eternal punishment. It also meant they would continue to sin and do wrong, hurting others. Their sinfulness meant that they could not themselves put this right; only God was able to deal with the barrier caused by sin. God did this through the incarnation and then the sacrificial death of Jesus (see pages 22–23). God in Christ offered salvation: that is, the cancelling out of original sin and the promise of eternal life. Most Christians today do not take Genesis 3 literally, but many think that it conveys a religious truth, that humans seem to have a natural inclination to do what they are told not to. This extends to disobeying God, which damages their relationship with God.

Adam and Eve brought original sin.

God removed it through the sacrifice of Jesus.

Salvation through law

Salvation means being accepted by God and so being assured of eternal life. In Jesus' time, his fellow Jewish people thought that in order to be accepted by God they had to obey the law. This meant following all the commandments as laid down in the scriptures and as interpreted by their religious leaders. Before becoming a Christian, St Paul agreed with them.

Some Christians have adopted a similar approach. It is known as 'salvation through works'. In other words, a right relationship with God has to be earned. Throughout the centuries there have been Christian groups that claimed salvation depended on keeping to all the rules that they put in place. However, most Christians reject the idea that salvation can be earned through obedience to the law. Jesus in his teachings taught about what pleases his Father, saying that the thoughts in our minds and the love in our hearts for God and for others is far more important. Putting those thoughts into Christian actions towards and for one another is of primary importance for most Christians today.

The Basics

1. Explain what is meant by the terms *original sin* and *salvation.*
2. Some people think that God set Adam up to fail. What do you think they mean by this?
3. Explain how different Christians have believed that humans can earn a good relationship with God.

Salvation: grace and the Spirit

Amazing Grace

How sweet the sound

That saved a wretch like me

I once was lost but now am found,

Was blind but now I see

What do you think 'Amazing Grace' is about? What do you think 'grace' means? How does the way it is written make it personal?

The word 'grace' occurs many times in the New Testament. It refers to the unconditional love that God shows to everyone, even when it seems undeserved. In other words, God loves humans despite what we do or do not do. In Jesus' parable of the Prodigal Son (see page 5) the son certainly did not deserve the 'welcome with open arms' that he received, but that is how, according to Jesus, God treats humanity. Paul experienced this when he became a Christian: 'For I … do not even deserve to be called an apostle, because I persecuted the church of God. But by the grace of God I am what I am …' (1 Corinthians 15:9–10). Christians believe that this love of God was shown in His offer of salvation as a free gift to all who believe that Jesus is the Son of God. They refer to this as 'salvation through grace and Spirit' and claim that this was made possible through the atoning death of Jesus. Jesus' actions made forgiveness for the sins of the world and reconciliation possible.

Christians believe that they continue to receive God's grace through the presence in their hearts of the Holy Spirit which enables them to try and show love as Jesus did.

The story of 'Amazing Grace'

This well-known hymn was written in the eighteenth century by John Newton. He had been an enslaver, running his own ship, and he was known for his heavy drinking and foul language. He was not religious. On 10 May 1748 he was trying to steer his ship through a terrible storm and thought he would die. In panic he said 'Lord have mercy on us'. The ship and crew survived, which he saw as an act of God's grace. He continued trading in enslaved people for several more years, but treated those on his ship humanely. Then he left to become a Church of England priest. He wrote the hymn 'Amazing Grace', which expressed his belief that God had saved him. So many people came to his parish that the church had to be extended. When he went to work in a church in London, he encouraged the crowds who came to hear him preach to campaign for the abolition of the trade in enslaved people. One of those he influenced was William Wilberforce, who played a key role in ending the trade in enslaved people in Britain.

The Basics

1. What is meant by *grace?*
2. What is meant by *salvation through grace?*
3. Read the full lyrics to the hymn 'Amazing Grace'. Look at each verse. What is the message in them?
4. How did John Newton feel that the grace of God helped him in his life?

Testing your knowledge

One-mark Questions

Multiple-choice question

For the one-mark multiple-choice question, you must choose the correct answer from the four you are offered.

Focusing on the first section of Christianity, on beliefs that you have now studied, try the following:

1 What is meant by omnipotence?

A all-creative B all-knowing
C all-loving D all-powerful

2 Where was Jesus born?

A Bethlehem B Corinth
C Jerusalem D Rome

3 Which of the following is not one of the Three Persons of the Trinity?

A God the Creator B God the Father
C God the Holy Spirit D God the Son

4 What is meant by atonement?

A to forgive B to make amends for sin
C to put to death D to say sorry

5 What is meant by salvation?

A the third person of the Trinity B to do wrong to God
C to save the soul D to substitute

Make up four answers to each of the following and test your partner. Do not forget: only ONE can be correct!

1 Which of these is not one of the Gospels?
2 In which book would we find the Christian creation story?
3 Which of these is the word for God's love?
4 Which of these is not part of the Trinity?
5 What is meant by resurrection?

Short response question

The one-mark short response question is asking you to write a brief response.

You will have to name or give an example of a belief, practice, key term or religious concept.

You may also be asked for a brief definition.

Do not waste time writing too much, but make sure you write enough to answer the question. Don't leave the examiner guessing at what you mean, or how what you have written does answer the question. Don't be vague!

1 Name one characteristic of God.

2 What does the term 'atonement' mean?

3 Give one reason why Jesus had to die.

4 Name one type of salvation.

5 Give one Christian belief about judgement.

Make up three one-mark short response questions to test your partner.

Influence Questions

Four-mark questions

These questions are where you show your understanding of the religion you have studied, and how a person's beliefs have an influence on their lives. It is clear that when people believe things, their thoughts, words and actions become shaped by their beliefs; these questions want you to show that. They might look a bit scary at first, but if you get used to them, they become quite straightforward.

You will have to answer one of these questions in each of the beliefs sections of your chosen two religions. They are always worth four marks, and always ask you to explain two ways.

The wording will always begin: 'Explain two ways in which ...'

Followed by one of these, or something similar:

- 'belief in/about ...'
- 'learning about ...'

Finishing off with: 'influences Christians today'.

Here are some examples for you to see how that works (and to try):

1 Explain two ways in which belief in the resurrection of Jesus influences Christians today.

2 Explain two ways in which beliefs about the creation of the world might influence Christians today.

3 Explain two ways in which belief in the crucifixion might influence Christians today.

4 Explain two ways in which believing that God is all-loving might influence Christians today.

5 Explain two ways in which believing that God is just might influence Christians today.

Go back through your answers to those five questions. Using AQA's mark scheme, how could you improve them?

Look at the following answers. Which do you think is better, and why? Think about how clear the answer is, how detailed it is and whether you can clearly see the influence or effect on the believer.

Explain two ways in which believing that God is just influences Christians today.

Answer 1

One way that believing God is just influences Christians today is that they think he will judge them fairly on Judgement Day. Another way is that they think they should show the same type of fairness and justice to other people.

Answer 2

They believe he will treat them justly on Judgement Day. This means they will not be punished unfairly, and especially not if they are truly sorry for what they did wrong. It also means that they will be fairly rewarded for the good they have done. God will balance these two to make a just decision about whether they go to heaven of hell.

Answer 1: This gives two good ways, however, it doesn't explain either way. You could improve this for them by explaining their ideas.

Answer 2: This gives one way only, but does it in a lot of detail. You could improve this answer by adding a second way which you explain

Explaining Beliefs and Teachings

Six-mark questions

These questions ask you to explain two beliefs and/or teachings from the religion.

The wording will always begin: 'Explain two Christian teachings ...'

Finishing off with: 'Refer to sacred writings or another source of Christian belief and teaching in your answer.'

They will be marked against AQA's mark scheme which can be found on the AQA website.

From the question wording and mark scheme, we can work out how to answer the question effectively. Each question is different, but in this case you would:

- choose your two teachings and then explain each one
- develop your explanations fully
- use a relevant quotation/teaching, show how it links to the question and include its source of authority. This is who or where a quote/teaching comes from, for example a holy book (Bible) or religious leader.

Remember this is just one example to help you practice. In the exam, you will need to think carefully and respond to the actual question you are given.

What does 'fully develop' mean?

When students in RS explain something, it is quite often the case that they just write a sentence in explanation. Whilst correct, that is a 'simple explanation'. For these questions, you have to 'fully develop' your explanation, which means giving more detail about each point you make. Below is an example. The explanation and further development are highlighted so that you can see them clearly.

Explain two Christian teachings about judgement. Refer to sacred writings or another source of Christian belief and teaching in your answer.

Sample answer

In the Apostles Creed[1], it says that Jesus 'will come to judge the living and the dead'[2]. This means that there will be a Judgement Day when everyone is raised from the dead to be judged[3]. The Judgement will be done by Christ, based on how people have behaved in this life[4].

Looking at the sample answer:

[1] it opens by saying where the belief comes from, i.e. the source of authority, here The Apostles Creed;

[2] this is what the Apostles Creed says about judgement;

[3] this explains that belief by mentioning Judgement Day and what it involves – it clearly applies to the quote that was used;

[4] it further explains by saying who will do it.

Of course, the answer needs a second teaching about judgement, written in the same way.

Practise the following questions for yourself:

1. Explain two Christian teachings about the creation. Refer to sacred writings or another source of Christian belief and teaching in your answer.
2. Explain two Christian teachings about God. Refer to sacred writings or another source of Christian belief and teaching in your answer.
3. Explain two Christian teachings about salvation. Refer to sacred writings or another source of Christian belief and teaching in your answer.

Analyse and Evaluate

For GCSE RS you have to be able to show you can react to a given statement. This means you consider what the statement says, present arguments to agree and disagree and come to a conclusion of what you think of the statement. You also have to demonstrate what a Christian would say and what arguments they might use. In the religious section of the paper it will be impossible not to include religious ideas, so do not worry too much about this. However, you must use Christian arguments. This type of question takes the most thinking, so needs the most time.

It is always a good idea to work to a formula when you answer this type of question. This structures your answer which makes it clear and also makes sure you meet all the necessary criteria to do well. Here is one formula you might consider using:

DREARER × 3 = C

D = Disagree
R = Reason to disagree
E = in-depth Explanation of that reason
A = Agree
R = Reason to agree
E = in-depth Explanation of that reason

It is good to try to include at least three reasons on each side.

R = Make sure you have used a number of Religious arguments, not just secular ones.

C = Conclusion – This is where you evaluate the strengths and weaknesses of the different points of view.

1 **For a Christian, believing that God is all-powerful is not important.**

Evaluate this statement. You should:
- refer to Christian teaching
- give reasoned arguments to support this statement
- give reasoned arguments to support a different point of view
- reach a justified conclusion.

2 **Christians should focus on living life here and now rather than focusing on an afterlife.**

Evaluate this statement. In your answer you should:
- refer to Christian teaching
- give reasoned arguments to support this statement
- give reasoned arguments to support a different point of view
- reach a justified conclusion.

3 **It is more important to follow Jesus' example than to spend time in worship.**

Evaluate this statement. You should:
- refer to Christian teaching
- give reasoned arguments to support this statement
- give reasoned arguments to support a different point of view
- reach a justified conclusion.

4 **If God were all-powerful there would be no suffering.**

Evaluate this statement. You should:
- refer to Christian teaching
- give reasoned arguments to support this statement
- give reasoned arguments to support a different point of view
- reach a justified conclusion.

You need to learn to think on your feet and state not only what you think but also other opinions as well. The point of these questions is to challenge your application of knowledge and to make you show your skills in analysis and evaluation. In your conclusion, try not to repeat the same ideas you gave in your for and against sections as you will have already been credited for these.

Want more practice? Go back through the section and redo the evaluation questions using these ideas.

1.2 Practices

Forms of worship

You need to study four forms of worship:

- liturgical worship
- non-liturgical worship
- informal worship
- private worship.

Task

At home, watch religious programmes on TV ('Songs of Praise') or on the internet. It will help you be able to describe different types of worship and understand why people prefer each.

Liturgical worship

This type of worship is found in services in the Roman Catholic, Orthodox and Church of England (**Anglican**) churches. Some acts of worship require a liturgy (a set order/pattern), for example, a Roman Catholic **Mass**. Features of liturgical worship are: a set structure to the service, the use of set prayers and readings. The service follows the text of a prayer book and is not improvised at all. Some Christians see it as 'old fashioned' or 'very traditional'.

Liturgical worship often takes place in a church, but not always, for example, a papal open-air Mass or an Anglican Eucharist in the home of a sick person. Some Christians prefer liturgical worship: the familiarity of the service makes them feel secure and they can join in with ease. They know exactly what to expect even in a church where they have never been before. They like the dignity that is typical of liturgical worship and think there is variety and choice within the set structure.

Non-liturgical worship

Other Christians prefer a more informal style of worship. They think that liturgical acts of worship stifle genuine worship.

Non-liturgical worship is typical of some nonconformist churches and tends to be Bible-based. It often follows a structure (for example, hymn, prayer, reading, hymn, sermon, prayer, hymn) but the service leader has free choice within that structure. They may choose a relevant theme for events in the world or community.

The minister or person leading worship will choose Bible readings that will be based on the theme of the sermon. Prayer is usually in the person's own words and personal style, known as *extemporary prayer*.

Informal worship

Charismatic worship

Charismatic worship is a form of informal worship. The service has the characteristics of other forms of worship (hymns, sermon, prayer, readings), but is very free-flowing.

In charismatic (spirit-inspired) worship, the worshippers often speak in tongues (outbursts of praise in words that are not intelligible, but which express the person's devotion to God). This is seen as a gift of the Holy Spirit. Singing, often accompanied by music, is lively. This has a much more relaxed feel to it. Some Christians believe it comes more from the heart.

Evangelical churches are often charismatic in style. These have become more popular in recent church history in Britain.

Charismatic worship

The Bible

Regardless of the type of worship, it will always have a focus on the Bible. Many Christians believe the Bible to be inspired by God and for some it is the word of God. So it has a central place and importance in any act of worship.

Use of the Bible in worship

- The Bible may be processed
- Many hymns are based on the Bible, for example, 'The Lord's My Shepherd' (Psalm 25)
- Portions of the Bible are read aloud
- Sermons are often based on a Bible passage

Quaker meetings

Quakers (The Society of Friends) have a very distinctive form of informal worship. There is no leader and no set structure at all. Those present usually sit in chairs forming a circle around a table on which there are a Bible and the book of Quaker writings. The worshippers sit in silence, until someone feels called to share thoughts with others.

The Basics

1 Describe the key features of each of these types of worship.
2 Explain the differences between these types of worship. Write your answer as a comparison using words like: however, whereas, but, and so on.
3 **It does not matter how worship is done**. How might a Christian respond to this statement? Explain reasons to agree and disagree.

Private worship

Christians believe that private worship (worshipping on their own) is just as important as public worship. It can take place anywhere. It may be liturgical in structure, for example, an Anglican saying Morning and Evening Prayer every day, or a Roman Catholic saying the **Rosary**. Some Roman Catholics say three times daily the Angelus, which is a structured series of short meditations on the incarnation. It may be non-liturgical, perhaps starting with reading a passage from the Bible or meditating. Christians might go into a church while they are out shopping, so that they can spend a short time worshipping God, shutting out the pressures and concerns of daily life. Those travelling, for example by train, might use the time for silent worship. Worshipping alone allows worship to be exactly how the person wants it and for them to feel close to God as they are alone with God and their thoughts.

The Rosary

The Rosary is a string of beads with a crucifix attached. Saying the Rosary involves running one's hands through the set of beads and saying certain set prayers (the Lord's Prayer, the Hail Mary and the 'Glory be to the Father …') while touching each bead.

Do some research to find out more about the Rosary and its symbolism.

Meditation

Meditation is thoughtfulness, focused on a religious truth. Christians often use a stimulus, for example, they might sit in front of a lighted candle, focusing on 'Christ the Light of the world'. They might meditate on a picture, which may be specifically religious (perhaps an icon of Jesus) or show a beautiful scene from nature. Other Christians might read a passage from the Bible and think about its message. In a church, a Christian might stand before and meditate on each of the Stations of the Cross (visual portrayals of the suffering of Jesus).

Why worship is important for Christians (the form is irrelevant)

- In worship Christians *praise* God as the eternal Being and source of everything that exists – 'Alleluia' (or 'Hallelujah') means 'Praise the Lord'.
- It brings a sense of togetherness as a community.
- It makes them feel closer to God.
- It is an external expression of their faith.
- It is peaceful – allowing for prayer and meditation.

There are many other reasons. Can you think of any?

The Basics

1 Why is it important for many Christians to be able to worship privately?
2 What is meditation? Why do people meditate?
3 What is the Rosary and how is it used?
4 **Private worship is more important than group worship.** Explain arguments to agree and disagree, including religious arguments.

Prayer

Prayer is not just about asking God for things and expecting to get them. For Christians it is about listening, being open to the guidance of the Holy Spirit and doing what God wants them to do.

'I believe; help my unbelief.' *(Mark 9:24)*

A prayer that might be said by many Christians who struggle with doubt

There are several types of prayer. A way of remembering them is to think in terms of 'the hand of prayer'. Praise is the basis of all prayer. It has been said that the whole of life should be an act of thanksgiving. The forefinger is used to point in accusation – so it represents the opposite in prayer. Christians believe that balanced prayer includes many or all of these aspects.

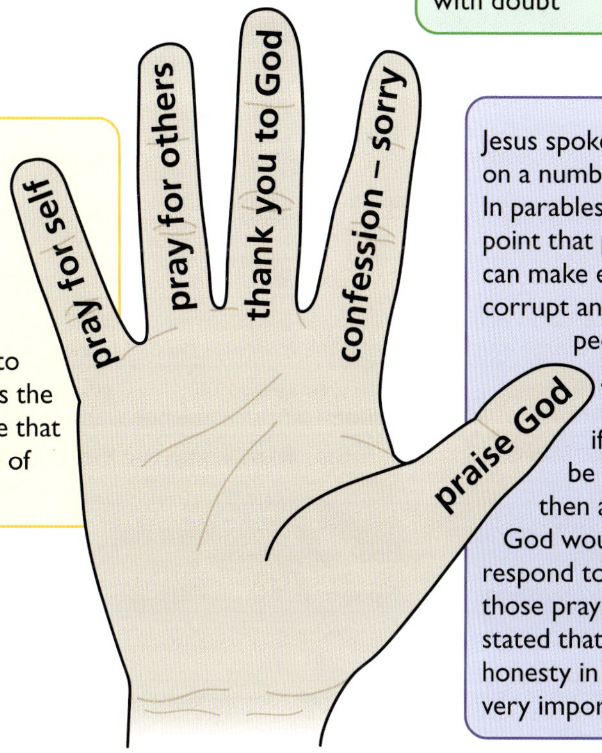

Hand of prayer

Jesus spoke about prayer on a number of occasions. In parables, he made the point that persistence can make even the most corrupt and self-centred people sometimes give in. Jesus' point was that if humans could be persuaded, then an all-loving God would definitely respond to the needs of those praying. Jesus also stated that humility and honesty in prayer were very important.

Set prayers

Set prayers form a key part of liturgical worship, but many Christians also use them for private prayer. Many were written by great thinkers, literary figures and above all, deeply religious men and women. Some come from the Bible, such as the prayer starting with 'The grace of Our Lord Jesus Christ …' that is often said in both public and private worship and is taken from 2 Corinthians 13:14.

Perhaps the simplest of all set prayers is the Jesus Prayer which says 'Lord Jesus Christ, Son of God, have mercy on me, a sinner'. It is an Eastern Orthodox prayer which dates back to the fourth century, but it has become popular with Christians in other denominations as it is so simple, yet so profound. It is meant to be said and repeated many times, like chanting. Whilst repeating it, a person meditates. Some also use rhythmic breathing as they say the prayer. The first part is said while inhaling and the second part while exhaling.

The Basics

1 Complete this chart of Jesus' teaching on prayer.

Text	Summary of Jesus' teaching
Matthew 6:5–8	
Matthew 7:7–11	
Luke 11:5–8	
Luke 18:1–8	
Luke 18:9–14	

2 Why do you think Christians believe prayer is important?
3 **God already knows our needs, so prayer is not necessary**. Give an opinion on this statement trying to show different viewpoints.

The Lord's Prayer

This prayer is especially important for Christians, as it was the prayer that Jesus himself taught his disciples when they asked him how they should pray. It contains some of the key aspects of prayer: praise, confession, prayer for others and for oneself.

The Lord's Prayer	Its meaning
Our Father in heaven	The term 'Father' reminds Christians that the God who created the universe loves and cares for each individual. The 'our' is a reminder that God's love knows no boundaries and that Christians are part of a community. 'In heaven' is a reminder that God is not a human father. It stresses His eternity and transcendence.
Hallowed be your name	May God be treated with honour and respect.
Your kingdom come	May God's kingship and authority be recognised and accepted by all.
Your will be done, on earth as it is in heaven	May God's purposes be carried out as fully in the created world as they are within the eternal sphere of heaven.
Give us today our daily bread	Christians ask God to give them (and everyone) all they need for the day. This includes spiritual and emotional as well as physical needs.
Forgive us our sins	Christians acknowledge that they fail to live up to their calling and are in need of God's forgiveness.
As we forgive those who sin against us	A reminder that if they are unforgiving, they make themselves unable to receive God's forgiveness.
And lead us not into temptation	A prayer not to be tested beyond their powers to resist.
But deliver us from evil	Acknowledgement of their need of God in the struggle against all that is evil in the world.
For the kingdom, the power and the glory are yours now and forever	All the previous petitions are possible because God is the omnipotent and majestic ruler of all.
Amen	A Hebrew word that means 'so be it'. Christians end their prayers with this word to show they mean and assent to what they say.

Tasks

1 Read the parable of the unmerciful servant (Matthew 18:21–35). Create a comic strip cartoon illustrating the parable and underneath write a sentence explaining its meaning.
2 Evaluate the claim that human beings cannot be expected to forgive everyone in the same way that God does.

Informal prayer

In public worship, this takes the form of extemporary prayer. Most Christians use their own words at least some of the time in their private prayers. Many prefer informal prayer to set prayers as they seem to come more directly from the heart, meeting their particular concerns. One type of informal prayer is known as the arrow prayer. These are very short prayers addressed to God spontaneously at a time of urgent need or in response to a particular situation. In a time of personal crisis a Christian might pray 'Help me God' or respond to getting through the crisis with 'Thank you God'.

Explain how a Christian might respond to the statement that God never answers prayer.

The sacraments

The term 'sacrament' has been defined as 'the external and visible sign of an inward and spiritual grace'. In other words, a sacrament is something people can experience with their senses (see, taste, smell, hear, touch), but there is a deeper reality to it which cannot be experienced through the senses.

The Protestant traditions generally acknowledge only the two sacraments of baptism and the Eucharist (see figure opposite). They are known as Gospel sacraments because they were authorised by Jesus and there are many references to their use in the books of the New Testament.

Roman Catholics, Orthodox Christians and some Anglicans recognise seven sacraments. They believe that they are all are implied by the ministry of Jesus as recorded in the Gospels and the practice of the Early Church described in the rest of the New Testament. These seven sacraments are: baptism, confirmation (chrismation in the Orthodox Church), the Eucharist, reconciliation (sometimes referred to as confession), healing, marriage and **ordination** (becoming a priest).

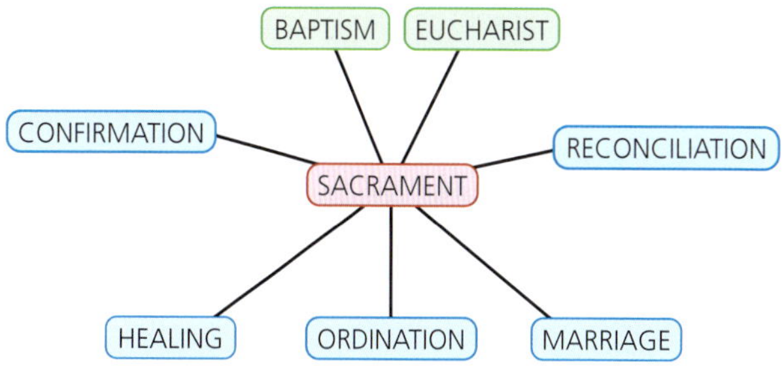

These Christians believe that through the sacraments God imparts particular gifts and powers. For many Christians, they are of central importance to the practice of their religion. Some of the seven sacraments are intended for all Christians, notably baptism, confirmation, the Eucharist, healing and reconciliation. Roman Catholics refer to the sacraments of baptism, confirmation and the Eucharist as the three *rites of initiation*. Marriage is for those who get married. Ordination is for those who believe that God has called them to the priesthood.

Sacrament	Outward and visible sign	Inward and spiritual grace
Baptism	Water and Trinitarian formula	Receiving the Holy Spirit The removal of original sin Entry into the kingdom of God/the Church
Confirmation	The laying on of hands by the bishop	Strengthening/sealing the gifts of the Holy Spirit in the person Becoming an 'adult' member of the Church
Eucharist	Bread and wine	Spiritual 'feeding' with the body and blood of Christ
Reconciliation	Words of absolution (forgiveness)	The forgiveness of sins
Healing	Anointing and the laying on of hands	Spiritual and sometimes physical healing Preparation for death
Marriage	Ring(s)	The endless love between the couple
Ordination	The laying on of hands by the bishop	The special gifts of the Holy Spirit needed by a deacon or priest

The symbolism of the seven sacraments

The Basics

1. What is a sacrament? Name all seven.
2. How does belief in the sacraments differ within Christianity?
3. Research to find out what happens in the sacraments of confirmation and Eucharist.
4. **The most important sacrament is that of baptism.** How far might a Christian agree with this statement? Explain your arguments.

The importance of sacraments for Catholic Christians

For many, the sacraments are God's gifts of grace offered to them at appropriate points in their Christian lives. Some can be seen as rites of passage, as they move from one stage of life into another. Baptism marks the start of the Christian life, giving the strength needed for the journey ahead. Confirmation reinforces baptism, as now those being confirmed make the commitment for themselves. The Eucharist is unique in that it is the only sacrament intended to be received frequently. Christians believe that it unites them with the risen Christ. Reconciliation enables Christians to think about how they have fallen short of God's will for them. They show their **penitence** through confessing their sins and performing a special task set for them by the priest and they are assured of forgiveness through the priest's words of absolution. The sacrament of marriage is believed to unite the couple with each other and with God in what is to be a lifelong loving relationship. Healing is given at times of serious or prolonged illness, not necessarily just when a person is dying. It is believed to give strength and peace of mind. However, when given to those who are dying it is intended to prepare them for death by enabling them to accept peacefully and trustingly what will come. The Eucharist which is given at this point is known as the viaticum, that is, the food for the journey. Ordination sets apart those who believe God has called them to the priesthood, giving them the gifts needed to carry out their ministry. For some Christians, the seven sacraments are the means by which they can grow closer in love to God and are as essential to their spiritual lives as oxygen is to physical life.

Why some Christians do not believe in the sacraments

Quakers and members of the Salvation Army reject all sacraments. They claim that there is no reference to most of the seven in the Bible. They also think that Jesus did not intend either baptism or his words and actions over the bread and wine at the Last Supper to become rituals for his followers to follow. Above all, they believe that God speaks directly to the believer's heart and that there is no need of any form of 'go-between'. Symbols and ritual are a distraction from true religion.

The Basics

1. Explain why each of the sacraments is considered to be important.
2. How might a believer's life be influenced through keeping the sacraments?
3. Why do some Christians not believe in the sacraments?
4. What do you think is most important for a Christian: believing the right things, receiving the sacraments, or praying regularly? Is there anything that should be more important for a Christian than any of these?

Baptism

Baptism in the Bible

Baptism was a ritual that the Jewish people of Jesus' day practised when being cleansed from ritual defilement (impurity) or as part of the process of a non-Jewish person becoming a Jewish person. However, when John the Baptist baptised people, it was as a symbol of forgiveness of sins. This was in preparation for the new way of life that would start with the coming of the Messiah (Jesus).

Jesus was baptised by John, who was his cousin. By being baptised, he was identifying with what John was doing. At first, John refused to baptise Jesus, as he believed Jesus should be the one doing the baptising (as the Messiah). However, he did do as asked and during the baptism, Jesus experienced the Holy Spirit entering his life and heard God's assurance that he was the Son of God. The Gospels say the Holy Spirit came in the form of a dove, so some Christians believe this literally happened.

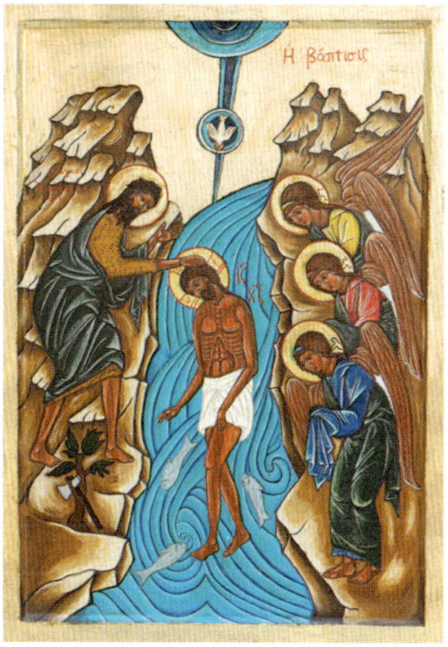

John baptised Jesus in the River Jordan

Just before his ascension, Jesus told his disciples to: 'Go and make disciples of all nations, baptising them in the name of the Father and of the Son and of the Holy Spirit.' Baptism was the rite of initiation into the Christian community right from the start and there are many references to baptism throughout the New Testament.

The gifts of the Holy Spirit

Baptism is a Gospel sacrament practised by almost all Christian Churches (although in different forms), so it could be considered the most important of all sacraments. The structure of the baptism service varies in the different denominations, but all use water and the Trinitarian formula: 'I baptise you in the name of the Father and of the Son and of the Holy Spirit. Amen.' Baptism is important to Christians for many reasons:

- It is the rite of initiation into the Christian community, making it possible to receive the other sacraments later.
- The person is cleansed from original sin.
- The person dies from their old way of life and is reborn into eternal life.
- The person is united with Christ as a child of God (all those baptised are of equal importance and value). Paul wrote: 'You are all sons of God through faith in Christ Jesus. There is neither Jew nor Greek, slave nor free, male nor female, for you are all one in Christ Jesus' (Galatians 3:26–27).
- The person receives the gifts of the Holy Spirit.

Romans 6:3–4

'Or don't you know that all of us who were baptized into Christ Jesus were baptized into his death? We were therefore buried with him through baptism into death in order that, just as Christ was raised from the dead through the glory of the Father, we too may live a new life.'

The Basics

1 Describe Jesus' baptism.
2 Why did Jesus' disciples carry out baptisms?
3 Explain why Christians believe baptism is important.

Infant baptism

Many Christian denominations practise infant baptism (the baptising of a baby). The actual service differs from denomination to denomination and even within denominations (depending on the priest/minister). However, central to all is the use of (blessed) water combined with the use of the Trinitarian formula. Roman Catholic and Anglican churches use a font, pouring water three times over the baby's head. In the Orthodox church the naked baby is immersed totally in the font. This use of water symbolises washing away original sin and spiritual rebirth. Other features found in many baptism services are:

1 Bible reading and prayers
2 anointing with two different oils at different points in the service as a sign of receiving strength to fight evil and of salvation
3 making the sign of the cross on the child's forehead to show that the child is called to fight against all that is wrong and to remain faithful to Christ
4 promises by parents and godparents on behalf of the child to reject evil, repent of sins and submit to Christ, and acceptance of the Church's faith as set out in the **Apostles' Creed**
5 clothing the newly baptised child in a white robe
6 the lighting of a candle, often from the Church's Paschal (Easter) candle, and giving it to the child as a sign that they have received the light of Christ and is to shine as a light in the world
7 the reminder to the parents and godparents that they now have the duty to bring up the child in the Christian faith both in the home and as part of the Christian community, leading at the appropriate stage to the child receiving the sacraments of Eucharist and confirmation in the Eastern Orthodox, Catholic and Anglican traditions.

Why many Christians support infant baptism

Here are some of the reasons given:

- It is in line with baptism of whole households in the early church, for example, Acts 16:14–15, 31–33, and is part of the Christian tradition.
- It is natural for Christian parents to want to bring up their child as a practising Christian right from the start.
- The child receives the seven gifts of the Holy Spirit (see page 39), which are as essential to spiritual growth as food is to physical growth. These are qualities such as wisdom and patience.
- It enables the child to receive the other sacraments as soon as it is appropriate.
- If a newborn baby is unlikely to survive, it comforts the parents to know that he or she has become part of the Christian family before dying.

Infant baptism is practised across most denominations. For Catholics, Anglicans and the Orthodox, it welcomes the child, confirming them as a Christian and member of the church, and absolving of sin. In other churches, a Service of Thanksgiving can be held simply to name and welcome the child.

The Basics

1 What is infant baptism?
2 Describe the features of an infant baptism.
3 Explain why infant baptism is important in Christianity.
4 Why do you think different denominations have different ways of carrying out this ritual? Do you think it matters that they do different things?

Believers' baptism

The Baptist and Pentecostal Churches practise only believers' baptism, which is for teenagers and adults. As with infant baptism, the central ritual is the use of water together with the Trinitarian formula. The baptism does not take place in a font as it involves total immersion. Many churches have a baptistery built in the church. There is a large tank that can be filled with water that comes up to the thighs. They often have a set of steps down into it and up out of it, so the person enters at one end and exits at the other. Sometimes baptism takes place in a river, lake or even in a swimming pool.

Key elements in the baptism service are:

- White clothes are often worn as a sign of the new life that is about to begin.
- The testimony, which is a statement by the person (candidate) about to be baptised, explaining how they came to believe and their reasons for seeking baptism.
- Declaration of penitence, of being truly sorry for sin, of faith in Christ as their personal Saviour and of the intention to show lifelong dedication to the service of Christ.
- The candidate goes down one set of steps into the water, symbolising the end of the old life of sin and separation from God. At least one person, often but not necessarily a church minister, is in the water and tips the person back, right under the water, stating 'I baptise you in the name of the Father, and of the Son and of the Holy Spirit. Amen.' This baptism is a powerful symbol of death and resurrection. The newly baptised person then comes out of the water by another set of steps, symbolising the start of their new life as a Christian. The candidate may go off to get dried.
- They may be given 'the right-hand of fellowship' by the minister on behalf of the whole Christian community. This is a handshake done to welcome them into the community on behalf of the whole community.

Why many Christians support believers' baptism

- Only those old enough to really know what they are doing and be fully committed to the decision should be baptised. This means they have to be (young) adults and it means that baptism will mean much more to them.
- Jesus himself was baptised as an adult, as were most people in the Early Church.
- When they are older, children might resent promises made on their behalf when they were babies.
- The idea of cleansing sin does not make sense for a baby.
- For many people, infant baptism is just a meaningless practice that just names a child.
- Many of those who have been baptised do not go to church again, except if they decide to marry in a church.

The Basics

1. What is meant by believers' baptism?
2. Describe the key features of a believers' baptism.
3. Explain why some Christians think baptism should only happen to young people and adults.
4. **All Christians should be baptised.** Do you agree with this statement? Explain arguments for and against it, including religious arguments.

The Eucharist

The Last Supper

Jesus' last meal was with his disciples on the night before he died. It was probably the Passover meal, which commemorated the Israelites' escape from enslavement in Egypt. What Jesus said and did gave this meal a new significance. Paul, in a letter to the Christians in Corinth, described how in the course of the Last Supper Jesus 'took bread, and when he had given thanks, he broke it and said, "This is my body, which is given for you; do this in remembrance of me." In the same way, after supper he took the cup, saying, "This cup is the new covenant in my blood; do this, whenever you drink it, in remembrance of me."'

Jesus linked the bread and wine to his imminent death, and it was a sign of the new covenant (relationship) established by his death between God and all believers. Ever since the start of the Church, in obeying Jesus' command most Christians have celebrated the Eucharist wherever they are and sometimes in secret. During the Second World War prisoners in Japanese POW camps did not have bread, so the Eucharist was celebrated instead with rice.

The Eucharist is celebrated by almost all Christian denominations (though not by Quakers and the Salvation Army). It has many names, such as the Lord's Supper, the Breaking of Bread, the Liturgy, Holy Communion, Mass. The central features are the same: the connection with the Last Supper, the giving of thanks for the bread and wine (consecration) and using Jesus' words at the Last Supper. The consecrated bread and wine are then shared among the congregation. However, the structure of the service and the interpretation of its meaning differ considerably between the Christian denominations. So, for example, Roman Catholics believe the bread and wine become the actual body and blood of Christ (**transubstantiation**), whereas Protestants do not believe this. Many Protestants see the ceremony as an expression of faith and obedience, whereas the Catholic, Orthodox and Anglican traditions see it as a way to receive God's grace. Not all denominations use wine, many of the Non-Conformist churches use a non-alcoholic substitute.

Task

Find out about services held for the sacrament of the Eucharist in two denominations. What happens and what symbolism is involved?

The Basics

1. Outline the story of the Last Supper.
2. What do you think Jesus' disciples might have thought at the time?
3. What are the central features of most Eucharist celebrations?
4. **The Eucharist is the most important part of Christian living.** What do you think about this statement? Argue for and against it, including using religious arguments.

Orthodox Divine Liturgy

In the Orthodox Church, the Eucharist is known as the Divine Liturgy. A typical service would include:

- The wine and home-made bread are prepared on the altar of preparation, behind the iconostasis (a screen separating the holiest part of the church from the rest). The iconostasis is a wall of painted religious icons with doors in the middle called Royal Doors.
- In preparation, the bread is divided into four. The Eucharistic Prayer is said over three parts of the bread consecrating them, through which the Orthodox believe they come to 'coexist' with the actual body and blood of Christ.
- The service includes Bible readings, a sermon and prayers, before the procession of the Gospel/Bible through the Royal Doors.
- The *cherubic hymn* is sung, to bring everyone present into the presence of the angels around the throne of God. Then the bread and wine are carried through the Royal Doors, which are then closed.
- The Royal Doors are opened and the priest invites all baptised members of the Orthodox Church to receive the consecrated bread and wine, administered from a silver chalice (cup) on a spoon. The bread is in the cup with the wine.
- At the end of the service, all those present may take home to share with others the fourth unconsecrated piece of the loaf, known as the antidoron.

Roman Catholic Mass

- Introductory and penitentiary rites – worshippers confess their sins to God, and forgiveness is given.
- Bible readings, a sermon and prayers; the Nicene Creed is recited.
- After the bread and wine are brought to the altar, the Eucharistic prayer is said (whilst the bread and wine are consecrated).
- The Lord's Prayer and other prayers are said; the congregation stand before the priest to receive consecrated bread which is placed on their tongue or in their hands.
- There is a post-Eucharist prayer, followed by a blessing and dismissal.

Eucharist in Protestant Christianity – the Lord's Supper

The services in most Protestant and Non-Conformist forms of Christianity are very much simpler than in the Orthodox, Catholic and Anglican forms of the religion. Sometimes the service is additional and outside a normal Sunday service. Whereas in the other denominations, a person should have been baptised, here they may only need to be a Church member, or there may be no such requirement. It can also be a monthly service rather than offered daily or weekly as in the other denominations.

The format can be very simple:

- Those wishing to participate gather at the front of the church.
- A minister will read the Gospel story of the Last Supper, or St Paul's version from Corinthians.
- The bread and wine (often a non-alcoholic drink) are shared with those who want to join in. Others are simply blessed. The 'wine' is given in individual glasses, not a single chalice.
- Depending on the church, hymns may be sung. A prayer will certainly be said in addition to the Lord's Prayer which is said by all.

Task

Research the details of Eucharist services in two denominations of Christianity. Find pictures to illustrate each part of these services. Present your findings in the form of flow charts. State the similarities and the differences between each and try to account for the differences.

The Eucharist	The word means 'thanksgiving' and the Eucharist is a thanksgiving for all that God is believed by Christians to have done for the world, and especially for the sacrificial death of Jesus.
Holy Communion	The word 'holy' is a reminder that the service is sacred/special. The word 'communion' means 'fellowship' and reminds Christians that they are joined in fellowship with Christ and with one another.
The Mass	This comes from the Latin words used at the end of the service: *ite, missa est* (Go, you are sent out). It is a reminder of the congregation's Christian mission to the world.
The Divine Liturgy	'Divine' reminds Christians of the sacred mystery of the service. The word 'liturgy' means 'work of the people', in their praising of God.
The Breaking of Bread	This is a reminder of what Jesus did at the Last Supper and of what is still done at the Eucharist today. It is also a reminder of Jesus' body broken on the cross.
The Lord's Supper	A reminder of Jesus' Last Supper with his disciples.

The significance of the different names used for this service

The significance of the Eucharist for Christians

The Christian denominations that celebrate the Eucharist attach great significance to it. Some celebrate it daily or weekly, believing it to be so important that frequent celebration is necessary. Others celebrate it monthly or less because they think it is so important that they want to avoid the danger of losing its significance by overuse.

Christians interpret it in different ways. The Orthodox Church resists any attempts at precise definition of what happens at the consecration/blessing of the bread and wine (because it is essentially a mystery that humans cannot explain), but believes that Christ is mystically and truly present.

Roman Catholics believe in transubstantiation; that the bread and wine are invisibly transformed 'in their substance' into the actual body and blood of Christ.

Anglicans hold a range of beliefs, some identifying with Roman Catholic thinking and others believing that the bread and wine hold the spiritual presence of the body and blood of Christ rather than becoming it.

Others, like Methodists, believe the Eucharist is just a memorial; the bread and wine being purely symbolic of Jesus' death, which brought salvation. Many Christians believe this alongside other views.

The Eucharist is for Christians a taste of heaven. The worshipper is united in love with Christ and also with all other Christians. This is shown when those present shake hands with one another in the part of the service known as the Peace. Christians believe it is food for the soul that gives them strength to live their everyday lives to God's glory.

The Basics

1. Giving examples, explain the different beliefs about the bread and wine.
2. Why is it important for many Christians to participate in this service?
3. Explain how participating in the ritual of Eucharist might have an impact on a believer's daily life.

Pilgrimage

A pilgrimage entails a visit to a place regarded as holy for the believer. Often, the journey is also special. Pilgrimage has always played an important role in the history of Christianity, though it is not a compulsory duty and many today see no need to go on pilgrimage. Places of pilgrimage have special meaning, often making people feel a sense of spirituality and that they are closer to God. They are usually linked to Jesus or a saint, to event/s of religious significance or to healings that are seen as miraculous (inexplicable by science).

Christianity has many places of pilgrimage. Some are very ancient, for example, Jerusalem, the place of Jesus' crucifixion and resurrection. Pilgrimage tours of the **Holy Land** can be undertaken.

Others have become places of pilgrimage for Christians within a specific country, for example Canterbury in England and Iona in Scotland. They link to a key person in the history of Christianity in that place. English Christians often include the journey from London to Canterbury in their pilgrimage.

Others are very recent, for example, Medjugorje in Bosnia and Herzegovina, which became a pilgrimage site in the 1980s when some children claimed to have had visions of and received messages from Mary, the mother of Jesus.

This book will cover two places of pilgrimage, Lourdes in France and Iona in Scotland.

Lourdes

Iona

St Bernadette at Lourdes

Bernadette was born in 1844, in Lourdes, France. Her early childhood was very happy. She found learning difficult and was illiterate. In 1854 her father suffered an accident, plunging the family into poverty. They had to move into a tiny dark room that had formerly been a prison. Bernadette struggled with asthma and cholera.

On 11 February 1858, while she and a friend were at a cave on the banks of the River Gave, she received the first of eighteen visions. The last one was 16 July. In one vision, she was told to dig away the growth clogging the spring and drink the water, which was at first muddy and then clear. Soon after that, a friend put her dislocated arm into the water and it was healed. The authorities at first doubted Bernadette's claims. However, the priest was convinced. Bernadette had claimed the woman she saw said she was the 'Immaculate Conception'. There was no way that she could have known this phrase, let alone its link to the Virgin Mary. Crowds accompanied Bernadette on her visits to the grotto.

From 1858 to 1862 the bishop of that area carried out an enquiry, interviewing Bernadette and others several times. He concluded that the visions were genuine and that a number of inexplicable healings had occurred to some of those who drank or bathed in the grotto's waters. Over time, pilgrim numbers increased. Bernadette herself entered a convent there, dying in 1879.

The Basics

1. What is pilgrimage?
2. Give the names of two Christian places of pilgrimage.
3. Explain why Lourdes is a place of pilgrimage for some Christians.

Pilgrimage to Lourdes

Pilgrims come in their tens of thousands throughout the year from all over the world to visit the churches at Lourdes, take part in the processions with candles and services (saying the Rosary and Mass), to touch the walls of the grotto, light candles and drink and/or bathe in the spring's water. Many pilgrims take home with them Lourdes water, and many shops in Lourdes sell religious artefacts, for example, statues of Mary. Some go to Lourdes on holiday as well as on a pilgrimage; there are many activities provided in the surrounding area.

In the UK, Roman Catholic churches organise pilgrimages for sick or disabled people, their families and volunteer helpers. Special provision is made for the needs of sick people in purpose-built accommodation that has full medical facilities. The volunteers who accompany the sick pilgrims look after their rooms and push hand-drawn carts enabling them to take part in the processions.

Every Easter there is a pilgrimage for 1,000 children, who are sick or have special needs. The participants are accompanied by volunteer helpers, doctors and nurses.

Healings at Lourdes

The official Lourdes website claims that, since the first cure in 1858, 70 cures have officially been recognised as miraculous by the Catholic Church (they are inexplicable by current medical and scientific knowledge). All claims of healing undergo a rigorous and lengthy assessment by a large panel of medical experts. Any case termed as an 'unexpected cure', that is, a lasting cure where no medical explanation can be found, is referred to the bishop of the area where the person lives. It is he who will declare whether or not the cure is a miracle. Danila Castelli had many operations for the removal of growths and was found to have a tumour which caused others. Medical treatment was not effective, but in 1989 she bathed at Lourdes and claimed to have been cured. It was not until 2010 that the Lourdes Office of Medical Observations certified the cure. In 2011 the Lourdes International Medical Committee concluded that her cure 'remains unexplained according to current scientific knowledge' and all the information was then sent to Danila's bishop. In 2013 he recognised her healing as miraculous.

Healings at Lourdes – miracles or mind over matter?

Most of those who go to Lourdes do not experience such healing, but almost all come away feeling that they have been healed spiritually. They are enabled to come to terms with their illness or disability and have peace of mind. Those with terminal illness often feel able to face their imminent death more positively.

The Basics

1. Why do you think people go to Lourdes? Try to give four reasons.
2. What do people do when they go to Lourdes?
3. On the Lourdes website there are claims that people have been cured. What is your opinion of these claims? Give reasons for your answer.
4. Why might other people claim the opposite view to your own?

Iona, an ancient centre of pilgrimage

Iona, the 'cradle of Christianity in Scotland', is a small island off the west coast of Scotland. In 563CE Columba, an Irish monk, settled there. He had left Ireland because of his part in a family feud that killed 3,000 people. The Gaelic rulers gave Iona to Columba so that he could build a monastery. The monks went out from Iona in small groups, living amongst the pagan people they came across, caring for them and preaching the Gospel as far away as north-eastern Scotland.

Columba had a close relationship with the king as an advisor and a diplomat and he travelled to neighbouring countries on the king's behalf. The ruler's sons were educated in his monastery. In return for this, the monastery was given land and protection.

Columba died in 597CE, but the monastery's influence continued, leading to the foundation of new monasteries in Ireland and at Lindisfarne (an island off the north-east coast of Northumberland). Many came on pilgrimage and a system of Celtic crosses and processional roads were built for the pilgrims. Rulers of several lands were buried there. The Book of Kells, an illuminated manuscript of the Gospels, was produced there. Repeated Viking invasions, beginning in 794CE, ended Iona's influence. Columba's remains were removed in 849CE and divided as religious relics across a number of churches in Scotland and Ireland.

In the early Middle Ages, Iona again became a centre of pilgrimage when Benedictine monks built a monastery with a beautiful abbey church on the island. Pilgrims did a circuit of all the sites, culminating in arriving at St Columba's shrine, and from there they went into a crypt beneath the abbey church to see relics of the saint.

The Book of Kells produced on Iona

Iona, a modern centre of pilgrimage

In 1938, George MacLeod, a minister in Glasgow, brought to Iona a group of unemployed skilled craftsmen and men training to become ministers. His plan was that they should rebuild the actual monastic buildings which had fallen into ruin and disrepair. At the same time, they would rebuild the community life which Columba had first set up by living together and sharing everything. That led to the foundation of the ecumenical Iona Community. **Ecumenical** means one which includes all Christian denominations. This group of men and women are committed to a way of life that reflects the Gospel and is relevant to the modern world. It has a global membership who are committed to a Rule that requires daily prayer and Bible reading, stewardship of time and money, regular meeting with other members and an active concern for justice, peace and the environment.

The Basics

1 How did Iona become a place of pilgrimage?
2 How has Iona's status as a place of pilgrimage changed over time?
3 Describe the Iona community set up by George Macleod.
4 **All Christians should make a pilgrimage to a holy place.** Analyse and evaluate this statement. Give arguments to agree and disagree, including religious arguments.

Pilgrimage to Iona

Iona has a longer history than Lourdes. Its rich history has newly made it a centre of pilgrimage. Individuals and family groups go. Others come as part of larger groups from churches or schools. Guests and staff share the practical tasks, for example, the washing up. Special programmes are organised for those staying within one of the Community's two centres, as well as 'Open Weeks' that have a range of activities and workshops. As well as meeting together for worship, visitors hold discussions, often on issues relating to justice, peace and conservation of the environment. They spend one day in pilgrimage around Iona, visiting the many sacred sites. There is also time for reading, reflection, boat trips, entertainment and craft sessions. People go to Iona to reflect and to live in a specific type of community – not for miracles, which is the reason why many go to Lourdes.

Different views on pilgrimage

People hold very different views on the importance and value of pilgrimage.

For some Christians it is a very important part of their faith. These are some of the reasons why:

- It enables time to be taken out from the often very pressured and secular everyday lives they lead. They return from pilgrimage refreshed, renewed and with a new vitality to cope with the demands of life.
- It offers an opportunity for spiritual growth. They have the time to pray and to meditate.
- Visiting places associated with Jesus or the great holy men and women of the past gives inspiration and encouragement to them to lead lives that more closely reflect the values of the Gospel.
- They may have a particular purpose in going to a holy place, for example, a sick person going to Lourdes for healing.
- They meet Christians from very different backgrounds and cultures. This deepens their faith as they gain new insights.

Evaluate the claim that going on pilgrimage is just an excuse for having a holiday.

Others, both Christian and non-Christian, do not think pilgrimage has any value. Here are some of the reasons for their view:

- It is often costly and shows poor stewardship, as the money could be put to better use.
- It is not necessary, as spiritual development, can be gained through regular attendance at church and through daily Bible reading and prayer.
- Reading about Jesus and about the great Christians of the past gives the same insights as pilgrimage.
- Any spiritual 'high' may well be temporary and the effects may soon wear off when everyday life kicks in again.

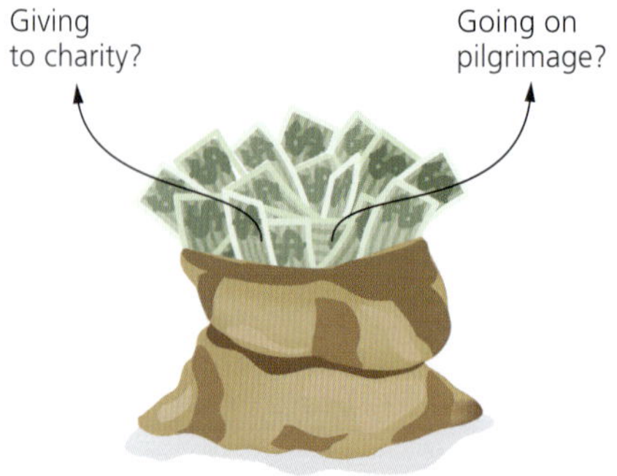

Christmas

Christmas is when Christians celebrate the birth of Jesus. For most Christians it is 25 December, but for the Eastern Orthodox section of Christianity it is 6 January. Neither was the date when Jesus was born. Indeed, if Luke's birth stories are historically accurate, the details relating to the shepherds imply that Jesus' birth might have occurred in spring. For the first two centuries of Christianity, it would seem that unlike Easter, Christmas was not celebrated and there was considerable disagreement about what date it should be celebrated on. Eventually the Western Church chose 25 December and the Eastern Church 6 January.

There are two possible reasons for the choice of 25 December:

- 25 December was the date for Saturnalia (a pagan celebration), and in 250CE the Emperor chose that date to celebrate the *Sol Invictus* (the Unconquered Sun). In fixing Christmas Day on this date, Christians might have been encouraging the replacement of paganism with Christianity.
- There was a tradition that Jesus' conception and death occurred on the same date. Based on Passover dating, some Christians fixed the crucifixion on 25 March. This became the date commemorating the annunciation (the day Mary was told she was with child) and so Jesus' birth occurred nine months later.

The Christmas story

There are two accounts of the birth of Jesus. The one in St Luke's Gospel is perhaps the better known and many of the forms of celebration are based on it.

According to Luke, Joseph and Mary had to leave Nazareth, where they lived, to be registered in the census that had been ordered by the Emperor. All had to register in their ancestral town. Joseph, whose descent was from David, had to go to Bethlehem. On their arrival they found that there was no space in the inn for them, so they had to go where the animals were stabled. It was there that Mary gave birth to Jesus. As was the custom, she swaddled the baby and laid him for warmth and safety in the manger. They were visited by shepherds who had been told by angels of the Messiah's birth while tending to their flocks.

Tradition says that this was the birthplace of Jesus

Many Christians believe that Luke's account of Jesus' birth is what actually happened. Others think it was a story that developed in the early years of the Church, based on Old Testament prophecies that the Messiah would be of Davidic descent and that Bethlehem would be his birthplace. However, all Christians agree that it stresses the humility of the incarnation. He was born into a poor peasant family and was visited by men whose work made them outcasts in the eyes of many. Traditional Nativity plays also include the three wise men, who appear in Matthew's Gospel, and who give gifts to Jesus, but this does not detract from the poverty of Jesus' birth.

Task

Read the accounts of Jesus' birth in Luke 2:1–20 and Matthew 2:1–12. List the similarities and the differences. Choose one and either write an account of it or draw a comic strip with captions.

Christmas celebrations in Britain today

What is Christmas all about for you? Decorations, gifts, cards, parties, food? For Christians, although all this is still part of their celebration, it is also a time of simplicity, family and friendship with their church at the centre of celebration and remembrance.

The most important celebration for many Christians in Britain is in church on Christmas Eve (often at midnight) or on Christmas Day. At midnight Mass, as it is known by many Christians, the Eucharist begins in near darkness, the church being lit only by candles. When the Gospel reading takes place the lights come on, symbolic of the birth of Christ the Light of the World. Special hymns known as carols are sung, churches are beautifully decorated with flowers and Christmas trees. Often in the church there is a Christmas crib showing Mary, Joseph and Jesus together with the shepherds and animals, which will be blessed at the start of the service. The three wise men are not added until the feast of the Epiphany, which is on 6 January.

Many churches also celebrate Christmas with a Christingle service, which came originally from Eastern Europe. Children are given Christingles. The service consists of Christmas carols, readings and prayers, and a collection is taken, often for a children's charity.

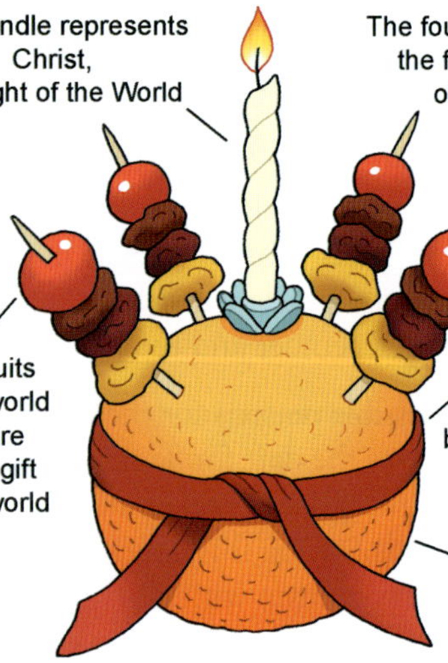

A Christingle

Most Christians send Christmas cards, often with religious themes, though some donate the cost of cards to charity instead. They may have a Nativity scene as part of their decorations.

For children, the central part of Christmas is the exchange of presents on Christmas Day, symbolising the gifts Jesus received from the three wise men. There is also the traditional family Christmas dinner and some families invite someone who is alone. Some Christians serve meals to unhoused people, or visit those without family.

The importance of Christmas to Christians in Britain today

Christmas is important for many reasons:

- Christians thank God for, and celebrate with joy, the incarnation.
- It is a time for both giving to and receiving from loved ones, so is a symbol of love shared.
- It is a time to remember those who, like Jesus and his family, live in difficult circumstances. Christians should give generously to charities that support those in need.
- It highlights Christmas and its meaning to non-Christians.

The Basics

1. What does Christmas celebrate?
2. Given that 25 December is unlikely to have been the real date of Jesus' birth, explain why that date was chosen.
3. Evaluate the following statements. In your answers you should give developed arguments for and against the statement, including Christian teachings, and reach a justified conclusion.
   Statement 1 – **Christmas is only important because it shows Jesus to have been special.**
   Statement 2 – **Christmas is too commercialised.**

Easter

Easter follows Holy Week. The most solemn feelings (remembering the suffering of Jesus) of Holy Week turn to joy at Easter with the story of Jesus' resurrection to overcome death. In order to understand why Christians see Easter as their most important festival, we need to go back briefly to Holy Week.

The origins of Holy Week and Easter

	What happened	**Brief explanation of event and significance**
Palm Sunday	Jesus rides into Jerusalem on a donkey	It was normal for Jewish people to make their way to Jerusalem at Passover time, so Jesus and his disciples did the same. Rumours about Jesus had by this time spread and so when he arrived in the city he was welcomed by Jewish people. They thought he was the Messiah, the figure they had been waiting for ... the person to lead them to victory over the oppressive Roman regime and re-establish Israel. Jesus rode in on a donkey ... humbly ... not on a horse as a warrior king who would lead an uprising.
Monday	Jesus turns the traders' tables over in the Temple	Trading in this part of the Temple complex was normal, but Jesus was angry when he saw traders and money changers cheating people in the Temple itself. He tipped over the tables saying that they had turned his Father's house into a den of thieves.
Tuesday	Jesus gave further teaching in the Temple	Jesus was challenged by priests about his authority and where it came from. He taught the parable of the wedding banquet and about paying taxes.
Wednesday	Jesus spent the day with Martha and Mary in Bethany Judas agreed to betray Jesus	These were two sisters whose brother Jesus brought back from the dead when he saw the weeping and distress of the two women. They lived just outside Jerusalem and it was good for Jesus to get away from the chaos of Monday's events. Many have suggested that Judas was a revolutionary – part of the Jewish underground movement trying to organise an uprising against the occupying Romans. He may have been disappointed because he thought Jesus was the man to lead this.
Maundy Thursday	Last Supper, arrest and trials begin	Jesus shares the meal that included bread and wine ... preparing his friends for his death (though they did not see this at the time). Jesus is later arrested after being betrayed by Judas, and put through trials with the Sanhedrin (the ruling council of the Jewish people) and King Herod.
Good Friday	Trial with Pontius Pilate who sentences Jesus to death Jesus is whipped, nailed to the cross and left to die	Jesus had to die as atonement for the sins of human beings. At his death he commended his soul to God. He said that the criminals beside him would be with him in Paradise – showing it was now open to humans. The temple shroud – separating the Holy of Holies from the rest of the temple – was ripped apart showing all had access to God. Given Sabbath was about to start, so no work done, the body could only be laid in the tomb.
Saturday	Shabbat – Jesus' body lay in the tomb	Jesus' body was laid in the tomb, and the disciples hid, fearing they would be arrested. Losing Jesus had challenged their faith.
Easter Sunday	In the morning, the women went to the tomb to anoint the body – it was gone A young man told them Christ was risen.	The tomb was empty because Jesus had resurrected from the dead. Christians see this as a victory over death.

These events are varyingly listed and described in the Gospels.
For more detail research the story in each Gospel.

How do Christians in Britain remember and celebrate the key events of Holy Week?

Palm Sunday

The first Sunday of Holy Week is called Palm Sunday, which commemorates Jesus' triumphant entry into Jerusalem where he rode a donkey, and the crowd greeted him with palm branches, symbolising victory and royalty. Christians are given palm crosses at church to take home to keep until the start of Lent the following year. On Ash Wednesday (the first day of Lent) the old palm crosses are symbolically burned and then replaced on the next Palm Sunday.

Easter is important to me because it is a new start for all. The principles of love and forgiveness are central, and key in our world today.

Maundy Thursday

Christians go to church on this evening to celebrate the Last Supper. They remember with sadness the predictions that Jesus made about two of his closest friends: that Judas would betray him and that Peter would deny even knowing him in his hour of need. The King in Britain, as the Head of the Church of England, gives out Maundy money (silver coins) to selected older people. For many it reminds them of the 30 pieces of silver that Judas betrayed Jesus for to the Jewish religious leaders. Jesus prayed that same night too, for God his Father to take away the suffering that was to come. Nevertheless he does what he knows God wants him to.

I love the sense of remembrance, reflection and community that Easter brings to my church.

Good Friday

For Christians this is the most solemn day of the year. Many churches have been cleared of all colourful and celebratory items. The altar and lectern cloths are removed. Candles remain unlit. The vicar will just wear black robes. Everything is very plain and simple. Jesus died one of the most terrible deaths possible; eventually dying from suffocation as his body became too weak to support itself and his lungs collapsed. It was not a quick death either. Christians believe that to go through this suffering God is really showing how much He loves humankind.

Good Friday is a real reminder what Jesus did for us – his suffering must have been terrible, and it was done out of love for us. Nothing is more important, or humbling.

In many towns, groups of Christians will walk through the streets following someone carrying a heavy wooden cross just as Jesus was forced to do. They then erect it in the town square as a reminder to everyone of what this festival is all about. Contrastingly, in the Philippines, it is common to see someone nailed to a cross as part of the procession, such is their devotion to their faith. To be chosen for this role is a great honour (of course, they do not die).

Christians often eat fish on this day rather than red meat (which would reflect the blood that Jesus shed). Traditionally, red meat was not even sold on Good Friday. It is called '*Good*' Friday which might seem a strange word to use given what Jesus went through on that day because Christians believe Jesus died for the good of all humankind.

The Basics

1 Describe the events of Holy Week.
2 How do Christians show the importance of Good Friday?
3 **Jesus' sacrifice was the greatest sacrifice ever.** Do you agree with this statement? Explain your opinion.

Easter Day and its celebrations

Easter Day comes at the end of the long period of Lent and Holy Week. Many Christians will have fasted during this time, remembering the 40 days and nights Jesus spent in the wilderness being tempted by the Devil. It is important to different Christians for many reasons, for example:

- His resurrection from the dead proved Jesus to be the Son of God.
- Jesus' predictions of his death and resurrection came true, so it means the rest of his teaching can be trusted.
- There is no need to fear death as Jesus' victory over death has opened up the possibility of eternal life for humanity.
- The message of Easter is one of the victory of light over darkness, good over evil, hope over despair and life over death. However hard life might be, there is the assurance that God's love will triumph.

The Easter Vigil – the start of the celebrations

In Roman Catholic and many Anglican churches, the Easter Vigil is held on Easter Eve (the evening or night before Easter Day or in the early hours of Easter Day itself). This ceremony goes back to the very early days of the Church, when converts were baptised and admitted to the Eucharist. The details vary, but there are four key parts to the ceremony and the word 'alleluia' occurs often in the spoken ritual and the Easter hymns. *Liturgy*, remember, is the special word for ritual.

Service of Light	The church itself is dark and this first ceremony takes place outside the church. A new fire is lit and blessed. The Paschal candle (symbol of Christ the Light of the world) is prepared by the priest and is then lit from the fire. It is then carried in procession through the church, with the deacon or priest saying three times 'The Light of Christ' and the congregation replying, 'Thanks be to God'. Everyone has a candle which is lit from the Paschal candle. Then the Easter hymn (the Exsultet) is sung or recited. It recalls and celebrates the history of salvation, linking the story of the Exodus from Egypt to the sacrificial death of Christ and his victory over death.
Liturgy of the Word	This is the part where scripture is read. It follows the same pattern that would be seen in a usual Sunday Eucharist, but with extra Old Testament readings. One of them is the account of the Exodus from Egypt (Exodus 14).
Liturgy of Initiation	This is a time when some people will be baptised. Sometimes confirmation may occur. All those present renew their baptismal promises.
Liturgy of the Eucharist	The Eucharist then continues, ending with many repetitions of 'alleluia'.

The Basics

1 What is the Easter Vigil and what happens?
2 Explain why Easter is important for Christians.
3 **Easter should be the happiest time of the year for Christians.** How far do you agree with this statement? Explain arguments to agree and disagree.

Other Easter celebrations by Christians

For most Christians, Easter Sunday is a day to attend church. Often, churches will hold congregational meals either before or after the church service, to emphasise the joy of the community. The service itself will focus on the belief that Christ was resurrected. This shows that human beings can also be resurrected and be accepted into heaven with God. Hymns, prayers and Bible readings all follow this theme, as does the sermon.

In Rome on Easter Day, the Pope celebrates Mass in St Peter's Square. Thousands of Roman Catholic pilgrims come from all over the world to celebrate Easter in the very heart of their Church. For those unable to attend, this service is screened live on the internet or television.

Many Christians send Easter cards that, unlike secular Easter cards, have a picture or symbol associated with Jesus' resurrection and/or an appropriate quotation from the New Testament.

The best-known form of Easter celebration is the giving of Easter eggs to children. In the UK these are usually made of chocolate, but some families follow the tradition common in Europe of hard-boiling eggs in water containing a harmless dye and then eating them for breakfast. It is very easy to forget the religious significance of Easter when eating chocolate eggs or painting hard-boiled ones. However, eggs are important because of their symbolism. They were used in the early church to represent the resurrection of Christ and spiritual regeneration (rebirth of Christians). Today they are a sign of new life, and when they are broken open, they can be seen to represent the opening of Jesus' tomb and opening up for humanity the possibility of eternal life.

St Peter's Square

In the Orthodox Church a high point of the Easter Liturgy is when the priest shouts '*Christos anesti*' ('Christ is risen') and the congregation replies '*Alithos anesti*' ('He is risen indeed'). Throughout the day, Orthodox Christians greet one another with this call and response. Orthodox Christians dye eggs red as they hard-boil them. This is a symbol of the blood of Jesus shed on the cross. It is also a custom to have an egg-cracking competition and as they crack their eggs against someone else's egg, they use the greeting and reply. Towards the end of the Divine Liturgy, fireworks are set off.

The Basics

1. Describe some of the ways that Christians celebrate on Easter Sunday.
2. Do you think it is important to celebrate religious festivals in a way which engages children? Explain why.

Explain why some might say that going to church only at Christmas and Easter is not enough for a person to call themselves Christian. What do you think? Explain the reasons for your own point of view.

The role of the church in the local community

The different Christian churches in the UK work both individually and together to try to make their local communities better places for everyone to live in. The Church has always been involved in caring for others. For example, in the Middle Ages the monasteries provided education, hospitality for travellers and treatment for sick people. In the mid-twentieth century it was a London church that set up the first Samaritans phone service for those feeling suicidal. With all the social and economic problems in the UK today, Christians of all denominations feel called to respond where they see need. There is a wide range of involvement by local churches. Here are some examples:

> Can you work out all the different categories of help that Christians are giving to the community? Make sure you have not missed any by comparing your list with other members in the class.

Reasons why Christians are involved

In his parable of the sheep and the goats, Jesus told his disciples that whatever they did or failed to do for someone, however insignificant the deed or the person, they did/failed to do it for him (Jesus). This encourages a sense of helping others. The author of 1 John wrote: 'If anyone has material possessions and sees his brother in need but has no pity on him, how can the love of God be in him? Dear children, let's not love with words or thoughts but with actions and in truth' (1 John 3:17–18). Jesus himself always had time for people. When he and his disciples crossed Lake Galilee for some peace and quiet, they discovered a crowd there already waiting for him, but instead of sending them away or going somewhere else, he went on to teach and to feed them. This is interpreted to mean that Christians should not turn their backs. Jesus deliberately sought out those whom society rejected, notably tax-collectors and sex workers, and the religious leaders criticised him for welcoming sinners and eating with them. This encourages Christians, who believe that they are called to reflect Jesus' teaching and examples in their lives, to work with modern-day 'sinners and outcasts'.

Helping those in need

Food banks: the Trussell Trust

Food banks, where people volunteer to help collect, sort and distribute food to those in need, are increasingly common in many areas of Britain today. Some people argue that there should not be a need for such groups, but there is. Many people help because of their religious background, some because they simply want to help others and some as a form of service.

In 1997, Paddy Henderson and his wife, Carol, started the Trussell Trust to help disadvantaged people in Bulgaria. During a fund-raising initiative in the UK, Paddy received a phone call from a mother in Salisbury who was struggling to feed her family. This led to Paddy and Carol starting a food bank in their garage and garden shed, delivering three days of supplies to those in need. In 2004, they launched the first (and now biggest) UK-wide food-bank network, teaching churches and communities how to set up food banks in their areas. Its vision is to end poverty and hunger in the UK through giving compassionate, practical help and campaigning for justice.

Professionals such as the police, doctors and social service workers identify those in need of help and issue vouchers. The food bank then exchanges vouchers for three days' worth of nutritionally balanced and healthy food. The food has been donated by the public, with supermarkets playing a prominent role (you may have seen food-bank boxes seeking donations from shoppers), and volunteers sorting out the food.

Showing faith in action is more important than praying and worshipping in Church. How true do you think this is? Explain your answer using examples.

'For I was hungry and you gave me something to eat, I was thirsty and you gave me something to drink, I was a stranger and you invited me in, I needed clothes and you clothed me, I was sick and you looked after me, I was in prison and you came to visit me.' *(Matthew 25:35–36)*

The Salvation Army

The Salvation Army is a Christian denomination founded in the nineteenth century by William and Catherine Booth. Its members were shocked by the deprivation they saw around them and also by the apparent indifference of many churches.

Salvation Army members work with those in poverty and disadvantaged in many ways. Their work includes:

- setting up soup kitchens and hostels for the homeless
- toy distribution at Christmas
- advice that helps people to get rid of and stay out of debt
- giving employment guidance and information
- giving emergency assistance, for example, food, meals, clothes, baby supplies, showers
- providing community vegetable gardens where people can grow their own food
- collecting and redistributing unwanted furniture
- raising awareness of the issue of human trafficking.

The Basics

1 Explain why Christian groups try to help their communities.
2 Explain how Christians might respond to vulnerable people in their local communities.
3 Explain how a belief in Jesus as a role model might make a Christian do more for the 'sinners and outcasts' of our society.
4 **Christians should focus on their religion and their family, not interfere in other people's lives.** What do you think of this statement? Present arguments that both agree and disagree with the statement, showing you have thought about more than one point of view.

Street Pastors

Street Pastors is a network of Christian charities, whose members go out onto the streets of many towns and cities (usually on Friday and Saturday nights from about 10 pm until 4 am) to care for the physical and spiritual needs of young people who might be clubbing, drinking heavily, getting into fights, and so on. They are there to care for, listen to and help all they come across, regardless of their views and their behaviour.

They undergo several months of training locally or regionally before being given the role (commission). They have a special service to seek God's blessing on this particular and very challenging kind of ministry within the local community. Before going out, they will gather for prayer.

Street Pastors was founded in 2003 in Brixton, South London as a response to the rise in gang violence and knife crime, but it has since spread across the UK and globally. Each project is set up by The Ascension Trust, which is their governing body, and the work is carried out in partnership with the police, the local council and other official bodies. In the UK there are over 20,000 street pastors. In Sheffield, for instance, the group began after a spate of gun crime. The street pastors went out to talk to people in pubs, shops and on the streets.

St Vincent de Paul Society

The St Vincent de Paul Society (SVP) is a Roman Catholic society that has been given a Big Society award from then prime minister David Cameron in recognition of its work in improving the lives of people with different needs in the UK. It was founded in the nineteenth century by a French professor, Frederic Ozanam, who said: 'In my life I want to become better and do a little good.' Its mission is to help those in poverty, and address the root causes of poverty. Help is given to anyone who needs it, irrespective of race, culture and religion. There are many SVP groups attached to churches, schools and universities and their members are of all ages.

The society is involved in all kinds of work, for example:

- repairing and restoring donated furniture to give to those who need it
- support centres giving debt advice, counselling and providing training in literacy, numeracy and ICT
- providing support for asylum seekers
- running community shops and food banks in areas where there is great poverty
- providing holidays for disadvantaged children and families
- running hostels for newly released prisoners, unhoused people and those with mental illness
- a range of activities for people with disabilities
- soup kitchens.

The Basics

1. Explain why there are street pastors.
2. Describe the work of street pastors.
3. Explain the work of the Society of St Vincent de Paul.
4. Explain why organisations as those you have been reading about on pages 55–56 are important in society and to religion.

Task

Find out more about:

- the work of street pastors, particularly in the town or city nearest to where you live on **www.streetpastors.org**
- the work of the St Vincent de Paul Society on **www.svp.org.uk**

Church growth – Christian mission and evangelism in the UK

Mission and evangelism go together. Mission literally means 'a sending' and in Christian terms it is about the belief that you have been 'sent' to do something. Evangelism is the term used for spreading the Word, by way of preaching the gospel. Christianity has always been a missionary faith and over the centuries it has spread throughout the world. In the twenty-first century, the Church continues to grow in many parts of the world, for example, Africa. However, in Europe it has suffered decline. Many people have become alienated from traditional forms of worship that seem tied to the past rather than looking to the future. Therefore, in recent years, there has been a renewed focus on Europe, preaching the gospel in ways that are relevant to the modern world and encouraging new forms of worship. Many churches are trying to combine these fresh approaches with what they believe to be the timeless values from the past and without compromising key beliefs. Some churches support individuals who act as missionaries to the local communities.

Vidas and Rita Rimkai live in Gloucester. They have received training from the European Christian Mission (ECM) and work as missionaries alongside local churches. They welcome people into their homes, turning general conversation into worship. They organise meals and a free shop at their local Baptist church for refugees and asylum seekers.

Many Christians believe that they too can be missionaries in their daily lives, simply by showing love of God and neighbour.

One activity offered by the Church Army for young people who have difficult home lives

The Church Army

The **Church Army** is a lay (not ordained) Anglican organisation committed to evangelism. Its evangelists are trained over four years and are licensed by the Church of England and Ireland to work throughout the UK. They are committed to enabling people to find faith, showing the love of God as revealed in Christ. In particular, they bring the gospel of salvation to the vulnerable and marginalised in society, and encourage the Church as a whole and locally to live up to its calling.

The Church Army is involved in:

- running clubs for children, and working with families
- projects for young people. For example: the Church Army bus that is somewhere for teenagers to chat with each other over a coffee; an adventure project for troubled and vulnerable teenagers
- working with drug addicts
- acting as chaplains, for example, in hospitals or prisons
- visiting older people and providing luncheon clubs for them
- providing alternative forms of Church.

Christian mission can even take the form of coffee mornings

The Basics

1. What is meant by the terms *mission* and *evangelism*?
2. Why have Christian denominations begun to do missionary work in Europe?
3. **Religion is not relevant in the modern world.** What do you think? Explain your opinion on this statement.
4. Research the Church Army's projects. You will find information and videos on **www.churcharmy.org.uk.** How are they showing Christian mission?
5. Describe the work of the Church Army. Do you think its work is important? Explain your answer.

Christian mission and evangelism in the world

Serving In Mission (SIM)

Serving In Mission
United Kingdom & Ireland

Whilst a lot of missionary work now occurs in Europe, there is still a need further afield. Serving In Mission (SIM) is an international evangelical and interdenominational organisation with a base in the UK. They send mission workers to more than 70 countries across the world. For instance, the support of their church in Hampstead has enabled the Curry family to work with SIM in West Africa. Andrew teaches English to university students, and to those who wish to hear it he proclaims the gospel. Sue works in a medical clinic with a special focus on people living with diabetes and children suffering from malnutrition. Both see their work as carrying out the commission given by Jesus to his disciples.

In Nigeria, the Boko Haram terrorist group has shown very high levels of violence towards Christians. The Nigerian branch of SIM has a project in an area where Boko Haram destroyed all the churches. The people there have suffered terribly, and SIM is enabling twelve pastors to return to their work there. SIM Nigeria is also sending four specially trained pastors to run trauma healing workshops and to organise the building of temporary structures for worship. These people are working with victims in several ways. It is not just about preaching the Gospel, because they realised these people also need specialised mental health treatment if they are to recover.

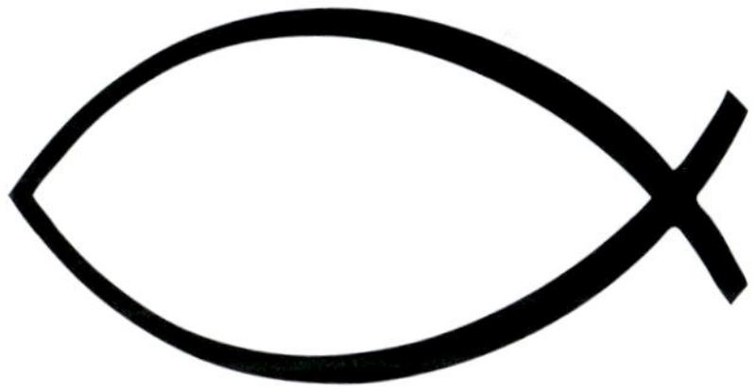

The ichthus symbol represents the phrase 'Jesus Christ, God's Son and Saviour'

The Ichthus Christian Fellowship

Although attendance in many traditional churches is declining in the UK, there is growth in other denominations, particularly in the evangelical and Pentecostal Churches. The Ichthus Fellowship takes its name from the ancient Christian symbol of a fish which was used by Christians to represent Jesus Christ, God's Son and Saviour. This fellowship started with the intention of evangelising by planting churches throughout London and Kent. 'Planting churches' means establishing new churches in communities, so that, like plants, the Christian community thrives and grows. This movement has now spread and there are many *link* churches throughout the UK and abroad, such as the King's Church, which operates in many cities. These are *linked* to a central church, but are not physical churches in their own right. Ichthus' central aim is a simple one: to worship Jesus. Members do this through worship, Bible studies, shared meals, serving those in need, and so on. Services in these churches attract hundreds of people of all ages. The structure of the organisation is threefold and shows how Ichthus differs from traditional denominations:

- *celebrations* where people from a number of churches come together
- *congregations* where local churches meet for worship and service to the community
- *cells* where smaller meetings for prayer, discussion and support in the faith occur in homes.

The Basics

1. Explain the work of SIM.
2. Explain why the Ichthus Fellowship is important in the UK Christian movement.
3. **Helping those in need abroad is the most important part of Christian mission.** Do you agree with this statement? Give reasons for your opinion.

'Fresh Expressions of Church'

The Church of England came up with this term, which is also used by the Methodist Church. It describes new churches that are different in approach from the churches that planted them because they are intended for a different group of people from those already attending the original church. It is not a 'one size fits all' approach. The form of the new church is one that suits the location and the context of its planting; it is often not a traditional church building. So, for instance, there is a church for surfers and another for young people in a skate park. Other 'fresh expressions' of church can be found in pubs, cafes and schools. These churches are intended for those who have never been to church or who have been and do not want to go back. The aim is to attract new 'disciples for Christ'. When Jesus called his first disciples, he said: 'Follow me and I will make you fishers of men.' This is what those who plant new churches see themselves as doing.

In Margate, the Salvation Army has planted a church for the large Roma community which came there from Eastern Europe. In this new church, the Roma people have been enabled to develop a form of worship that suits their culture. Those members of the Salvation Army who founded it are now helping individuals from the Roma community to become evangelists themselves.

Fresh Expressions reaches out to everyone

In Bradford, as part of the Sorted Project the Church Army has planted a church for young people run by young people. It attracts about 150 young adults, teenagers and children each week, and many as a result have been baptised and confirmed.

Mission and evangelism at Spring Harvest

Spring Harvest is a Christian organisation that holds events for people of all ages at Butlin's holiday camps in Skegness and Minehead. It is open to individuals or families and also groups from schools or churches. Different age groups have different meetings, but all follow a common theme. There are two priorities: to deliver excellent Bible teaching and to seek God's presence in worship inspired by the Holy Spirit. A wide range of age-appropriate activities are run for children and teenagers and special provision is made for those with special needs. There are also discussion groups, prayer sessions, craft activities and time for games and fun. There are two intentions: to help some have a first personal experience of God, and to deepen the commitment of others.

The Basics

1. What is Fresh Expressions of Church?
2. Explain, using examples, what it means to be 'planting churches'.
3. What is Spring Harvest? What are its priorities?
4. Explain why it is important for the Church of England to have developed Fresh Expressions. Use examples to explain your ideas.
5. **Christians in the UK must focus on the UK if they want their religion to continue.** How far might a believer agree with this statement? Give reasons for your answer. How far would you agree with the statement? Give reasons for your answer.

New Testament responses to persecution

Persecution is hostility and ill-treatment, usually because of prejudice. The early Christian community faced extreme persecution, including being hunted and executed.

It is likely that Jesus and his disciples met hostility during his life. By 70CE Jesus' followers had been shunned within Judaism, and were soon to be cut off altogether. Jesus had said to his disciples: 'Blessed are you when people insult you, persecute you … Rejoice and be glad, because great is your reward in heaven' (Matthew 5:11–12). This shows they must have faced persecution even when with him. He taught them to love their enemies and pray for their persecutors, not respond with violence.

In the New Testament, the First Letter of Peter was written to Christians who were suffering persecution for their faith. They were told to see persecution as a form of purification so their sufferings would make them more fit for eternal life with God. Also, that they were sharing in the sufferings of Christ and should trust God to help them in their time of trial.

This teaching has inspired Christians throughout the centuries to respond to persecution with forgiveness and love rather than with vengeance and hate. It has also encouraged Churches which are not suffering persecution to support those who are. This concern extends to those of all/no faiths who suffer persecution. So it is common to see Christians getting involved in protests and arguments about persecuted groups, in order to try to help them and to change law and society.

> 'I have decided to stick with love. Hate is too great a burden to bear.'
>
> Martin Luther King's response to persecution

Brother Andrew

'Brother' Andrew was born in Holland in 1928. He left school early and at the age of 18 he joined the Dutch army, but was shot in the ankle. He was impressed by the faith of the nuns who nursed him and began to read the Bible, and became a Christian. In 1952, he went to a Bible college in Glasgow then travelled to Warsaw in Poland (then under Communist rule). He saw how difficult life was for Christians who were persecuted for their faith. So he travelled throughout Eastern Europe, smuggling in Bibles and other Christian literature, despite the risk of arrest, assault and imprisonment. Once Communist rule came to an end in Eastern Europe, Christians were free to practise their faith and so he started to help persecuted Christian communities in other areas of the world. It is estimated that he helped Christians in 125 countries before his death in 2022.

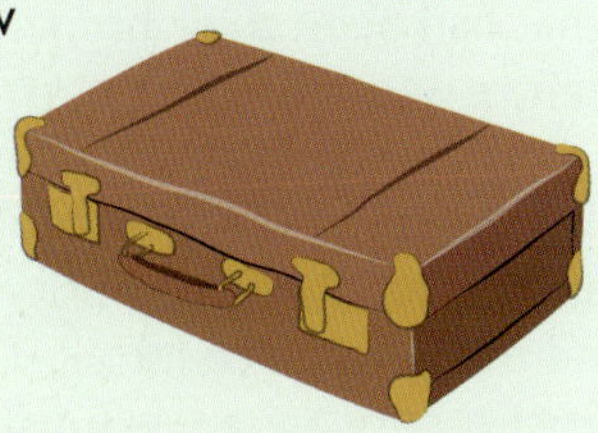

The Basics

1 What does persecution mean?
2 What evidence do we have that the early Christian community was persecuted?
3 Explain what Christians' response to persecution should be.
4 Describe how the work of Brother Andrew might have helped Christians.
5 **True faith is shown through helping the persecuted.** Think about this statement. Give two reasons for and against it.

The work of Open Doors

Open Doors is an organisation that is committed to support persecuted Christians wherever they are. This support is given in many ways:

Open Doors support

- Different forms of training are given. Trainees receive theological training to become pastors and teachers, and learn how to help people traumatised by persecution. Open Doors offers trauma counselling to enable healing and a spirit of reconciliation. Literacy and vocational training programmes are delivered for women and girls, enabling them to gain confidence and find employment.
- Practical support is given to those who have fled from violence. For instance, 3 million Nigerians fled the territory invaded by Boko Haram. Open Doors helped them rebuild their lives, providing food and helping them to find work. Food, medical kits, literacy classes and vocational training are given for refugees and women whose husbands have been killed are given the means to help them support their families. For instance, one woman was enabled to start a firewood business and then to run a farm for breeding chickens. Christian children forced to flee to other countries are given safe homes, education and healing through counselling.
- It fights for justice and religious freedom in the UK and internationally through meeting with politicians and public campaigning.
- Awareness is raised in churches in the UK, which through prayer, fund-raising and volunteering support Open Doors programmes. Open Doors runs special campaigns of prayer for persecuted Christians in specified countries.
- It delivers Bibles for distribution to Christians who often have to practise their faith and meet in secret. In 2014, 3.1 million books were sent and radio broadcasts were increased for Christians in North Korea.

James and Stephen Smith

James and Stephen Smith and their mother, all practising Christians, were shocked when they visited Yad Vashem, the Jewish Holocaust memorial centre in Jerusalem. Returning to England they turned what had been their home, in Laxton, into the National Holocaust Centre and Museum (**www.nationalholocaustcentre.net**) as a permanent memorial to the Jewish people who suffered in the Holocaust. Educational programmes encourage people of all ages to take personal responsibility for challenging all types of discrimination and to seek justice for all. The brothers then founded the Aegis Trust (**www.aegistrust.org**) which works in a similar way in other countries where persecution has occurred. In 2004, they opened the Kigali Memorial Centre in Rwanda. Medical, counselling, financial and educational support is given to the many women and children widowed and orphaned by the 1994 **genocide**.

Open Doors helps those fleeing from persecution

Tasks

Imagine that you are trying to encourage a church to support the work of Open Doors or of the Aegis Trust. Create a presentation and give it to the rest of the class.

Working for reconciliation

Reconciliation, not revenge!

The word 'reconciliation' means 'bringing people together to be friendly again'. Christians believe that Jesus' death was an act of reconciliation. In St Mark's Gospel, the tearing of the Temple curtain at the point of Jesus' death is a symbol of reconciliation (see page 20). In a letter to the Christians of Corinth St Paul wrote that in Christ, God reconciled the world to himself and that God gave to believers the ministry of reconciliation. He had founded the Christian community there and felt responsible for its well-being, but they often challenged his authority and his guidance because there was conflict within the church. He worked to reconcile these differences. Working for reconciliation is necessary for all Christians, although it is often a very painful process. The twenty-first century is full of conflict within and between families, religions, racial/ethnic groups and nations.

Christians believe they are called to use what influence they have in these areas of life to create a family, a community, a nation and a world in which all feel valued and secure and in which all can flourish.

Corrymeela

This is both a centre and a movement. The movement began in Belfast in the 1960s with the concerns of the Dean at Queen's University and some of the students about the growing sectarian tensions. Sectarian tensions are discrimination and hatred between groups within society, in this case, the Nationalists and Unionists of Northern Ireland. The movement wanted to establish 'an open village where all people of good will' could learn to live together. In October 1965, their dream came true and the site known as **Corrymeela** was officially opened. Its work continued right through the Troubles (the conflict which ran between 1968 and 1998 in Northern Ireland) and it continues still. There are now 40 full-time staff, 20 volunteers who work there on year-long terms and hundreds of other short-term volunteers. Throughout the year it runs various programmes:

- working with families needing help to work through difficult times or needing respite support
- helping those aged 18–25 to deal with issues of concern to young adults
- working with schools to help children to encourage positive and active citizenship
- it is currently working with the City of London University's Olive Tree programme involving Israeli and Palestinian students, helping them to understand their own situation through learning about and from the Troubles.

Every day starts with prayer in a space of worship called 'The Croi'.

Tasks

1 Research Corrymeela, including how it came to exist. Create a 'Key details' card covering its origins, its work and its successes. This is something you can do for each organisation you study, keeping the cards as revision tools.

2 Corrymeela can be interpreted as 'hill of harmony' or 'lumpy road'. In pairs discuss what that might mean and which of these is the better interpretation. Give reasons for your opinion to the rest of the class.

King Charles and Queen Camilla arrive at Corrymeela Centre

Community of the Cross of Nails

On 14 November 1940, Coventry Cathedral was bombed by the German air force and reduced to a ruin. The next day, the Provost (head) of the cathedral chalked on the wall of the ruined chancel the words 'Father Forgive', words now properly inscribed on that wall. In a broadcast on Christmas Day 1940, the Provost stated his commitment to forgiveness and working for reconciliation, once the war was ended, with Britain's former enemies. In the ruins, there were two charred beams which had fallen in the shape of a cross. These were bound to retain that shape and set on an altar of rubble. Three nails from the original building were made into a cross and this *Cross of Nails* became a powerful symbol of friendship and hope once the war was over. After the war, Coventry created links with three German cities and gave a Cross of Nails to Berlin. A new cathedral was built alongside the ruins of the old one, with the ruins remaining as a witness to the need for reconciliation. In 2011, they became a memorial to all civilians who have been killed or injured (physically or emotionally) by conflict world-wide. Every weekday at noon, the Coventry Litany of Reconciliation is prayed.

Coventry Cathedral became a world Centre for Reconciliation and the Community of the Cross of Nails was born. There is now an international network of over 260 churches, all committed to praying for peace, justice and reconciliation. The network includes churches, schools and prisons.

Archbishop Desmond Tutu

Desmond Tutu was a retired Archbishop from South Africa. For much of his life, he was subject to South African apartheid, a political system that enforced total separation of black people from white people in every aspect of life. Apartheid ensured the mistreatment and reduced life chances of black people and people from other minority ethnic groups. From childhood, Desmond was aware of the many injustices and humiliations faced by non-white South Africans. Initially a teacher, he later became an Anglican priest. He eventually became Archbishop of Cape Town, using his position to speak out against apartheid and to campaign for social justice, but rejecting any violent methods. When apartheid ended and Nelson Mandela became President of South Africa, Archbishop Tutu chaired the Truth and Reconciliation Commission where the perpetrators of the most horrific acts of violence and their victims came face-to-face. The perpetrators asked for, and victims granted, forgiveness. After that he was involved in the search for reconciliation between Israel and the Palestinians, before his death in 2021.

The Basics

1. How does the Cross of Nails demonstrate reconciliation?
2. How does the life of Desmond Tutu show a belief in reconciliation?
3. **The world would be a far better place if everyone was prepared to reconcile.** What do you think of this statement? Explain your opinion.

Task

On **www.coventrycathedral.org.uk** click on the tab Resources and read out the Coventry Litany of Reconciliation. What does it tell us about reconciliation?

Poverty in less economically developed countries

Less economically developed countries (LEDCs) are the poorest countries of the world. Many are found in Asia and Africa. Religious voluntary aid agencies such as Cafod, Christian Aid and Tearfund help people in LEDCs because of the extreme poverty in which so many people live.

Why do these agencies choose to help these countries?

They are the poorest countries in the world, so need the most help. Since they are poor, things like healthcare and education are often quite limited, so the people struggle to make more of their lives or to even survive. In addition many nations have corrupt leaders or there is corruption within those with power in their communities; this means a selfish attitude limits the opportunities and life chances of the poorest.

Religious voluntary aid agencies also help because they are able to do so. Many Christians live in privileged situations, especially compared to those in LEDCs. They are able to thank God for this by helping others. The agencies are putting this attitude into practice. It is perhaps true to say that they can make the most difference in the poorest countries, where the need is so glaringly obvious.

Helping LEDCs

Generally speaking, the agencies you will study in the next few pages help in similar ways. They provide several different types of aid, as follows:

Emergency aid is an immediate response, generally to a disaster. Food and bottled water are essential to prevent hunger, dehydration and water-borne diseases. Medical kits are often requested to deal with injuries and with outbreaks of life-threatening diseases such as cholera. There may be an urgent need for tents and blankets or temporary shelters. Teams of specialists like doctors and engineers may be needed.

Short-term aid then takes over as the emergency teams start to leave and the process of rebuilding begins. Families need uniting, homes need to be rebuilt and children need to be back at school, especially if they are orphans. They will not have the means to recover easily from the situation.

Long-term aid (development) is a vital part of support for LEDCs. This is about tackling the root cause of the problem and enabling communities to become self-sufficient (so they can look after themselves) instead of becoming aid-dependent, as has sometimes happened in the past. Examples of long-term development are educational programmes, well-digging and the training of medical and health workers.

Tasks

Think about how aid agencies might help LEDCs through the different types of aid they provide. Keep these ideas in mind when you learn about the work of the religious agencies.

The Christian response to poverty

Christianity has a very long history of trying to help those in need and you have already read that this is a core part of following Jesus' example. For this course, you need to know about the work of one of the following organisations: Cafod, Tearfund or Christian Aid. The next few pages give you lots of information about each, but you should supplement this with your own research.

Aid agencies often already have their own links to countries in need, and are therefore not reliant on media coverage. They may even learn about problems sooner than the media, as corrupt governments may try to cover up a disaster. They set to work wherever they can.

Cafod, Christian Aid and Tearfund are all part of the Disasters Emergency Committee (DEC) which responds to crises such as a natural disaster or the mass displacement of people in a civil war that creates refugees. DEC's appeals on radio and television are free, saving vital money that can be used to respond. The humanitarian agencies involved all work together to raise money from the public. All three of these aid agencies work through partner organisations in the affected country who can be relied on to know what is most needed and where.

Work in the UK

Aid given abroad is made possible by work done in the UK. There are three main ways in which Cafod, Christian Aid and Tearfund work:

- **Campaigning.** Putting pressure on those in positions of power, particularly the government, for example by lobbying, sending petitions or peaceful protest. This can lead to more determination from government to secure justice for LEDCs.
- **Increasing public awareness.** Often achieved through persuading sympathetic celebrities to speak out in the media. Educational resources are produced for schoolchildren of all ages who are the ones in the future who will bring change and justice.
- **Fund-raising.** The three charities all have their own particular ways of raising money, but all three spend most on their emergency and long-term development work. A small amount is used for costs associated with fundraising and administration.

This work then enables a constant flow of money to resource their work in LEDCs.

All three charities encourage their supporters to support the Fairtrade movement. Farmers and producers are paid fair prices for their goods. This means better wages, so they can look after their families better. Some Fairtrade producers provide housing and a school so that children are educated whilst parents work. Tea plantations in Sri Lanka are an example of where this happens.

The Basics

1. Why are some countries affected by poverty?
2. Explain the three forms of aid, giving examples of each.
3. How do the religious organisations operate in the UK so that they can do their work abroad?
4. Is the Fairtrade movement important? Research Fairtrade to be able to give good detail in your answer.

Catholic Agency for Overseas Development

In 1960, the Catholic Women's League in the UK organised their first ever Fast Day to raise money for mothers in the Caribbean islands. This action spread and so much support was given that, in 1962, the English bishops realised that the fund-raising should be co-ordinated so as to make it more effective. They founded the Catholic Agency for Overseas Development (Cafod), which now gives support to over 500 partners in LEDCs. Cafod is a member of the international network of Catholic Aid agencies known as *Caritas Internationalis*. When emergency aid is needed because of a natural disaster, Cafod not only gives emergency assistance but also puts in place disaster risk-reduction strategies. For instance, in earthquake-prone areas, as well as providing temporary shelters for victims, Cafod will advise and train local people in constructing homes less vulnerable to earthquakes. Once the emergency is over, Cafod often remains to put in place long-term sustainable development. Programmes for long-term projects are planned and delivered in conjunction with local partner organisations as they are the people who have knowledge from the inside of how to tackle problems in their areas. A central principle in the long-term work they do is that communities must themselves see the need and be part of the project. When a community asks for specific help, and – after their request has been vetted and often modified a little – they have helped to carry out that project, they gain confidence. This breeds self-belief and often becomes the seed for much greater change. Most of Cafod's money comes from Catholic communities, both churches and schools. Above all, it is important to remember that Cafod's help is given to those in extreme poverty, regardless of race, religion, gender or political belief.

'I am sometimes asked why, as a Catholic organisation, we deliver aid to people of other faiths ... My answer is that we help people not because they are Catholics, but because we are Catholics.'

Sally-Anne Knight (Director General of Caritas Internationalis)

Cafod project in southern Zambia

There is terrible poverty in Zambia with many people living on less than 60p per day. Life expectancy is 52 years. In the village of Kalisowe, a drought meant that people had to walk 15 km to a water supply and additionally had to dig to reach the water. Cafod has provided the village with two solar-powered water pumps which supply water for 300 homes, the school and for watering plants. This water is clean, which prevents water-borne diseases, and the villagers no longer have to use the same water as their animals. Families have more varied diets because they can grow (more) fruit and vegetables. A school has been set up, whereas previously there was none, giving children of the village much better prospects for their future. The school garden provides food and training in agricultural skills. From solar-powered wells, to educating and feeding a community which drives up aspirations and changes life for all. This is a good example of Cafod's work.

The Basics

1 How did Cafod begin?
2 Describe the work of Cafod, both in the UK and in its development work.

Task

Find out from the GCSE area of the Cafod site **www.cafod.org.uk** more about the Kalisowe project or another project.

Christian Aid

You may have heard of this charity even if you do not know exactly what is does. The envelope on the right is put through all letterboxes in the UK during Christian Aid Week (usually May). Volunteers then come to collect them.

Christian Aid (originally called Christian Reconstruction in Europe) was set up at the end of the Second World War in response to the terrible refugee crisis in Europe. Its work was then extended beyond Europe to helping newly independent countries and responding to natural disasters. In the 1960s it became Christian Aid. Since then, it has continued to give emergency aid but has been increasingly involved in long-term sustainable development and in campaigning for justice. In promoting long-term aid, Christian Aid uses the proverb: 'Give a person a fish and you feed them for a day; teach a person to fish and you feed them for a lifetime.' From 2012, it has focused on ending poverty and generating global justice by empowering those who are currently exploited and disadvantaged.

Christian Aid works through partner organisations, responding to a wide range of needs. Those in poverty are supported, whatever their race, religion, and so on. Money is raised from various sources. Most comes from governments and institutions, but individuals also donate, either during Christian Aid Week, volunteers drop red envelopes through letterboxes which ask for donations and then collect them.

To ensure global justice, Christian Aid is focusing on five areas:

- giving ordinary people political power
- ensuring essential services, such as water and sanitation, for everyone
- seeking a fair and sustainable share of the world's resources for all
- eliminating discrimination of any form and ensuring equality of treatment for all
- tackling violence and building reconciliation and peace.

Christian Aid project in Myanmar (Burma)

Myanmar is vulnerable to a wide range of natural disasters due to its geographical position, a situation made worse by the government that was in power until 2016. Malaria is a huge problem, killing 7 per cent of children under the age of five. Through its partners in that country, Christian Aid is training healthcare workers to detect the early signs of malaria using a diagnostic kit, so that its victims start treatment sooner. They distribute insecticide-treated mosquito nets, train villagers in basic healthcare and hygiene and encourage them to seek medical help when they are unwell. It will be some time before vaccination against malaria can be implemented, so Christian Aid's work is invaluable in saving lives and improving health.

The Basics

1. How did Christian Aid originate?
2. What are the principles which Christian Aid uses to underpin its work? Can you think of examples of projects which might fit with each of those principles?
3. **All Christians should donate money to Christian Aid.** What do you think about this statement? Give reasons to agree and disagree with it.

Task

Research at least one other Christian Aid project in an LEDC. You will find the information you need by going onto **www.christianaid.org.uk**

Tearfund

In 1960, Christians concerned about the terrible suffering of 40 million refugees created by war in the world sent money to the Evangelical Alliance. This money was put into a special fund and then shared among evangelical agencies who were caring for the refugees. Money continued to come in, so in 1968 Tearfund was born.

Prayer is at the heart of the movement and the principle of 'following Jesus to where the need is greatest' is a strong factor in its motivation and work. Several celebrities, themselves evangelical Christians, have given their support, which has helped raise awareness among the general public.

Much of its money is raised through fund-raising by evangelical churches and individuals. It encourages young Christians in the UK to become involved through becoming part of its projects through gap years or mission trips.

Like Cafod and Christian Aid, Tearfund provides both emergency aid and sustainable long-term development. However, its work is not just about the physical needs, it is also concerned with the spiritual needs of those it serves. Work includes preaching the Gospel and Tearfund claims that over a period of five years 15 million people's lives have been changed and 67,000 churches have been created or helped. Projects work through Christians and local churches in the areas served. A particular area of concern for the past fifteen years has been human trafficking.

Prayer is central to Tearfund's work

A Tearfund project in Ethiopia

Tearfund supports the creation of self-help groups which help communities to lift themselves out of poverty. Senait lives in the town of Nazret and before joining the self-help group, like most of her neighbours she could not afford education for her children. With a Tearfund loan and support, she was able to establish a kindergarten that charges low fees and gives free education to the very poorest people. Children learn to read and write and receive three meals a day. This enables mothers to work and earn money for their families. Senait gives counselling to poor families, encouraging them to save.

The Basics

1. How did Tearfund begin?
2. What makes Tearfund different to Cafod or Christian Aid?
3. Why do you think Tearfund supports self-help projects? Give examples.
4. **Helping one person out of poverty makes no difference.** How might different people respond to this statement? Analyse and evaluate it, giving explanations for your arguments.

Task

Find out more about Tearfund's fight against human trafficking at **www.projectact.org**.

Why Cafod, Christian Aid and Tearfund respond to need

While these organisations were formed in response to different issues, they all share the same motivation: to respond to need. We have already come across many relevant reasons why Christians want to help others while studying other aspects of Christianity.

Can you think of the reasons why Christians would want to help others and why they would set up organisations for this purpose?

Here are some other reasons from the Bible. How does each act as a reason to help?

- The eighth-century BCE prophet Amos said that what God required above all was justice and fairness: 'Let justice roll on like a river, and righteousness like a never-failing stream' (Amos 5:24).
- Old Testament laws encouraged generosity to those in poverty. For instance, when harvesting, farmers were not to cut the corn right to the very edges of their fields and if they dropped any, they should leave it lying there. This was so that they could come and gather what was left.
- The first Christians in Jerusalem practised a form of communism. Those with money to spare gave it to the apostles, who then shared it out among those in poverty. Barnabas had land in Cyprus (his homeland). He sold it and gave the proceeds to the apostles (Acts 4:32–37).
- When there was a famine in Jerusalem, which meant prices would have rocketed, the Christians living in Antioch in Syria made a collection and sent the money to Jerusalem so that the people there could afford to buy food.

'Clothe yourselves with compassion, kindness …' *(Colossians 3:12)*

Different views on supporting LEDCs

There are different views on whether people in the UK should give aid to LEDCs. Pick out the reasons from the statements below which agree with helping, and those which do not.

In the past, money given for health and education has been spent on weapons or on rulers' palaces.

Developed countries are responsible for much of the poverty in LEDCs, so they have a duty to put things right.

We should treat others as we would want to be treated.

Where corruption is a problem, the LEDCs must themselves put that right.

We are all God's children, with responsibilities for one another.

The UK has enough problems of its own, so our own needs should come first.

Christians should see helping others as helping Jesus.

Giving aid makes countries aid-dependent – they need to become self-reliant.

Tasks

Evaluate these statements. In your answer you should:

- refer to Christian teaching
- give developed arguments to support this statement
- give developed arguments to support a different point of view
- reach a justified conclusion.

a The UK should leave LEDCs to sort out their problems themselves.
b The world will never solve the problem of poverty.
c Only religious believers have a duty to help the poor of the world.

Testing your knowledge

One-mark Questions

Multiple-choice question

For the one-mark multiple-choice question, you must choose the correct answer from the four you are offered.

Focusing on the second section of Christianity, on practices that you have now studied, try the following:

1 What is meant by liturgical worship?

A free worship B prayers and hymns
C set pattern D worship in private

2 What is the prayer called that Jesus taught his disciples?

A Christian prayer B Lord's Prayer
C Jesus Prayer D Our Father

3 Which one of these is not a sacrament?

A baptism B confirmation
C funeral D marriage

4 What is meant by pilgrimage?

A a holiday B a sacrament
C a special journey D an act of giving to charity

5 Which event in the life of Jesus do Christians celebrate at Christmas?

A baptism of Jesus B birth of Jesus
C death of Jesus D resurrection of Jesus

Make up four answers to each of the following and test your partner. Do not forget: only ONE can be correct!

1 Which of these is a place of Christian pilgrimage?
2 What is the symbol of the sacrament of marriage?
3 Which of these is not a Christian organisation working to reduce the impact of poverty?
4 What is meant by evangelism?
5 What does reconciliation mean?

Short response question

The one-mark short response question is asking you to write a brief response.

You will have to name or give an example of a belief, practice, key term or religious concept.

You may also be asked for a brief definition.

Don't waste time writing too much, but make sure to write enough to answer the question.

1 What is meant by the term 'street pastor'?

2 Give one alternative name for the Eucharist.

3 Give one reason why someone might have a believer's baptism.

4 Give one reason why Holy Week is important to Christians.

5 Give one reason why charities work in LEDCs.

Make up three one-mark short response questions to test your partner.

Differences Questions

Four-mark questions

These questions are where you show your understanding of the diversity within the religion you have studied – that not everyone in the same religion does or believes exactly the same things. This is why there are different denominations within Christianity, and they have different ways of practising their faith.

You will have to answer one of these in each of the practices sections of your chosen two religions. They are always worth four marks, and always ask you to contrast two practices.

The wording will always begin: 'Explain two different (Christian) ...'

Followed by one of these, or something similar:

- 'views on/about ...'
- 'ways in which ...'
- 'rituals associated with ...'

Here are some examples for you to see how that works (and to try):

1 Explain two different Christian views about the importance of pilgrimage.

2 Explain two different ways in which Christians celebrate the Eucharist.

3 Explain two different ways Christians play a role in the local community.

Go back through your answers to these three questions. Using AQA's mark scheme, how could you improve them?

Look at the following answers. Which do you think is better, and why? Think about how clear the answer is, how detailed it is and whether you can clearly see the influence or effect on the believer.

Explain two different ways Christians play a role in the local community.

Answer 1

They go round and tell people about their religion and how it helps them to feel better in their lives. This is called evangelising. They also help out in areas where there are unhoused people, giving them food and warm clothes and trying to help them get off the streets.

Answer 2

Some Christians will go to train to be a street pastor. They will then go into towns late at night and help people who are drunk, or in difficulty. They are showing God's love by helping them, and might also minister to them about their work. This must help these people, as often they are in no state to help themselves, so they get a better impression of the religion. Other Christians might set up a new church in their community based at a youth club, so it is for young people.

Answer 1: This gives two good ways, but the response is simple, because it gives no detail and no examples. You could improve this for them by being more detailed about the two ways.

Answer 2: This gives two ways, but only the first has enough detail. You could improve this answer by adding more detail to the second way.

Explaining Practices

Six-mark questions

These questions ask you to explain two ways in which Christians put their beliefs into practice, or two ways they believe practices to be important.

> The wording will always begin:
>
> 'Explain two ways in which …'
>
> Finishing off with: 'Refer to sacred writings or another source of Christian belief and teaching in your answer.'

They will be marked against AQA's mark scheme which can be found on the AQA website.

From the question wording and the mark scheme you can work out how to answer the question effectively. Each question is different, but in this case you would:

- choose your two ways and then explain each one
- develop your explanations fully
- use a relevant quotation/teaching, show how it links to the question and include its source of authority. This is where the quote/teaching comes from for example a holy book (Bible) or a religious leader.

Remember this is just one example to help you practice. In the exam, you will need to think carefully and respond to the actual question you are given.

What does 'way' mean?

The question wants you to explain the reasons why something is important. Don't get caught out in the pressure of an exam – practise a lot of questions beforehand.

Here is an example:

Explain two ways in which Christians think worship is important. Refer to sacred writings or another source of Christian belief and teaching in your answer.

Sample answer

In Matthew's Gospel[1], Jesus warned people about being boastful in their prayer so that everyone could see and hear them[2]. For this reason, many Christians think that they should worship privately[3]. They believe that worship is important if it is done from the heart to God, not for others to see[4]. This means it is more honest as nothing can be hidden from God and it is only being done for God[5].

Looking at the sample answer:

1 it opens by saying where the belief comes from, i.e. the source of authority – here Matthew's Gospel, which is in the Bible;

2 this is what Matthew's Gospel says about how Christians should worship;

3 this links the teaching to the question;

4 this explains what the teaching means;

5 the final sentence extends the explanation, and links back to what Matthew said.

Of course, the answer needs a second teaching about the importance of worship, written in the same way to ensure the best response.

Practise the following questions for yourself:

1. Explain two ways in which Christians celebrate Easter. Refer to sacred writings or another source of Christian belief and teaching in your answer.
2. Explain two ways in which pilgrimage is important to Christians. Refer to sacred writings or another source of Christian belief and teaching in your answer.
3. Explain two ways in which Christians respond to world poverty. Refer to sacred writings or another source of Christian belief and teaching in your answer.

Analyse and Evaluate

For GCSE RS you have to be able to show you can react to a given statement. This means you consider what the statement says, present arguments to agree and disagree and come to a conclusion of what you yourself think of the statement. You must also demonstrate what a Christian would say and what arguments they would use. This type of question takes the most thinking, so needs the most time.

The focus of your answer must be the statement. Be careful not to just write about the topic itself.

It is always a good idea to work to a formula when you answer this type of question. This structures your answer, making it clear and ensuring you meet all the necessary criteria to do well. Here is one formula you might consider using:

Reason to agree	Explanation of that reason	Further explanation	Example to demonstrate
Reason to disagree	Explanation of that reason	Further explanation	Example to demonstrate

Building bricks

Imagine you are building a wall of reasoning to answer the statement. In the formula above you have to develop your arguments from left to right: you give a reason, and explain it. Your explanation is given in-depth and includes an example to demonstrate, so it is a strong argument in its own right. Follow this process two to three times in agreeing and two to three times in disagreeing.

After each argument, or at the end of your answer, you should make evaluative statements. This means explaining which side of the argument is stronger, and why that is so. It might include personal opinions as well.

Have a go at using this formula to answer the following questions:

1 **No child should be baptised.**

Evaluate this statement. You should:
- refer to Christian teaching
- give reasoned arguments to support this statement
- give reasoned arguments to support a different point of view
- reach a justified conclusion.

2 **Charities should focus more on helping the poor in Britain.**

Evaluate this statement. You should:
- refer to Christian teaching
- give reasoned arguments to support this statement
- give reasoned arguments to support a different point of view
- reach a justified conclusion.

3 **It is more important to help the poor than to worship in church.**

Evaluate this statement. You should:
- refer to Christian teaching
- give reasoned arguments to support this statement
- give reasoned arguments to support a different point of view
- reach a justified conclusion.

4 **Pilgrimages are a waste of money.**

Evaluate this statement. You should:
- refer to Christian teaching
- give reasoned arguments to support this statement
- give reasoned arguments to support a different point of view
- reach a justified conclusion.

The more practice you get at this type of question, the better. You could go back and use this formula to redo earlier evaluation questions.

Christianity Glossary

Agape Christian love

Anglican a worldwide denomination that includes the Church of England

Apostles' Creed a statement of Christian belief from the Early Church

Ascension Jesus being taken up to heaven on the fortieth day after Easter

Atonement the action of making amends for wrongdoing. The idea of being at one with God

Baptism a ceremony to welcome a person into the Christian religion

Believers' baptism a ceremony to welcome a young person or adult into the Christian religion using full immersion

Cafod a charity: Catholic Agency for Overseas Development

Catechism of the Catholic Church a summary of Roman Catholic teaching

Christian Aid a charity working in the developing world, providing emergency and long-term aid

Church Army an evangelistic organisation founded within the Church of England

Church of England the Protestant Church set up by Henry VIII to be the church of state in England, and rejecting Papal authority

Confirmation an initiation ceremony carried out by a bishop bestowing the gift of the Holy Spirit

Corrymeela a Christian community based in Northern Ireland promoting peace and tolerance

Crucifixion capital punishment used by the Romans which nails a person to a cross to kill them

Denomination the name for the different branches of the Christian Church

Ecumenical relating to the worldwide Christian Church

Eucharist the Christian service/ceremony to recall the Last Supper, in which bread and wine are consecrated and consumed

Evangelism preaching of the faith in order to convert people to that religion

Food banks charity groups collecting donated food to distribute to the poor in Britain

Fundamentalist Christians who take the Bible literally, i.e. word for word true

Genocide the deliberate and indiscriminate killing of a group of people belonging to a particular ethnic group or nationality

Gospel the first four books in the New Testament about Jesus' life and teachings: Matthew, Mark, Luke and John

Grace unconditional love that God shows to people who do not deserve it

Holy Communion another name for the Eucharist

Holy Land the land of Israel

Incarnation means God in human form

Infant baptism ceremony to welcome a child into the Christian religion

Iona an island in Scotland with a fourth-century monastery used by Christians today as a religious retreat as it is a place of tranquillity and peace

Liturgical worship a church service with a set structure of worship

Lourdes a town in France where the Virgin Mary was said to have appeared; now a place of pilgrimage

Lord's Prayer the prayer Jesus taught his disciples to show them how to pray

Mass another name for the Eucharist

Messiah the anointed one who is seen as the saviour by Christians

Methodist a Protestant Christian group founded by John Wesley in the eighteenth century

Miracles events that have no scientific explanation for them happening; these were performed by Jesus and described in the Gospels

Mission an organised effort to spread the Christian message

Nicene Creed a statement of belief used in Christian services

Non-liturgical worship informal structure of worship found in some church services

Omnipotent the idea that God is all-powerful

Oneness of God the idea that God is 'One'

Ordination the process by which someone becomes a priest

Orthodox Church a branch of the Christian Church

Penitence to feel regret for one's sins

Protestant a branch of the Christian Church that broke away from the Roman Catholic Church

Quakers the Society of Friends Christian group

Reconciliation the process of making people in conflict friendly again

Resurrection the physical return of Jesus on the third day after he died

Roman Catholic the largest Christian group, based in Rome with the Pope as its leader

Rosary a set of beads used to count prayers especially in the Roman Catholic Church

Sacrament the outward and visible sign of an inward and spiritual grace

Salvation the saving of the soul from sin

Sanhedrin the ruling council of the Jewish people in ancient Israel

Secular relating to worldly as opposed to religious things

St Paul a man who taught the teachings of Jesus – originally Saul of Tarsus before his conversion

Street Pastors a Christian organisation of people working on the city streets at night caring for people who need help or are involved in anti-social behaviour

Tearfund a Christian charity working to relieve poverty in developing countries

Transubstantiation the change in the bread and wine to become the actual body and blood of Christ

Trinity the belief in God the Father, God the Son and God the Holy Spirit

The study of religions

2 ISLAM

An introduction to Islam

Beliefs and teachings

Islam is not an easy religion to understand, so you will have to get used to words from the Arabic language to explain key terms. Islam, like Judaism and Christianity, is not one united religion; it has many groups within it. For this GCSE Specification it is the **Sunni** and **Shi'a** branches you will focus on. They both have beliefs that underpin their lives:

Sunni – One God, angels, holy texts, prophets, Day of Judgement, supremacy of Allah's will.

Shi'a – One God, prophethood, resurrection, imams and **justice** of Allah.

You can see the similarities, but there are differences and this is where diversity questions can come from to explain the differences in beliefs.

Allah – The Arabic name for God. Muslims have 99 names for Allah, but they are more like qualities to help them try and partially understand His nature. Words like oneness, **immanence** (involved in the world), **transcendence** (beyond time and space), **omnipotence** (all-powerful), **merciful**, kind and forgiving, fair and just are used to describe Allah for **all** Muslims.

Muhammad ﷺ – All Muslims believe in Muhammad ﷺ, the last chosen prophet of Allah. It was he who received the Qur'an (Allah's ultimate message) and he who started the early Muslim community and set up **Makkah** as the House of Allah for worship. It was after his death that everything changed. There was a power struggle. Arguments broke out as to the leadership; should it be passed down Muhammad's ﷺ family line or elected? This created a divide between two groups of Muslims (Sunni and Shi'a), that remains to this day.

Qur'an – The ultimate book of guidance dictated to Muhammad ﷺ through Angel Jibril. It has never been changed and supersedes other early books. You will hear '**Surah**' as well – this is the word for chapter, and each chapter has a name and number, for example, Surah al-Fatihah. The **Hadith** are simply the teachings of Muhammad ﷺ and the **Sunnah** is the way of life of the prophet. Muslims use all of these to live their lives as Muslims.

Akhirah – All Muslims believe in life after death; this life is the test for the next one. They believe their actions will determine a place in paradise. There are differences of opinion as to how the next life will come about, but essentially this life earns a place in an existence where Allah rules and is perfect. However, getting there is not easy.

Practices

Much of Islamic practice is focused on the **mosque**, which is the Islamic place of worship. Festivals are celebrated there, fast is broken there, disputes are resolved there. It is the centre of the community. Whilst many Muslims try to attend mosque for as many of the prayers as they can each day, the main Muslim act of worship is led by an **imam** on Friday each week. Mosques in the UK are very well-attended for this prayer, which also includes religious teachings.

Sunni have **Five Pillars** – five compulsory acts they have to do to be a Muslim and a duty of **jihad** (to struggle for the success of their faith in the world).

Shi'as have **Ten Obligatory Acts** – Five Pillars plus jihad plus four other key concepts.

So, Sunnis and Shi'as have practices in common and Shi'as have extra compulsory acts.

These compulsory acts are called **Pillars** as they hold up the religion. The first Pillar is **Shahadah**, the statement of faith (like a creed). The other four Pillars are actions: prayer, charity, fasting and visiting Makkah. Within these you will find lots of key Arabic terms. It is fine to use the English, but it is more impressive if you use Arabic.

In Islam, these actions are done from the heart and considered essential for a true Muslim. All are equally important and following them serves as part of the test for this life. In fact, according to Islam, this life is a test in preparation for the next life.

The concept of **jihad** is often misunderstood, so make sure you fully understand its meaning. There are two main aspects for some Muslims: greater and lesser jihad (see page 137). Greater jihad is the personal, inner struggle to follow the Islamic religion to the best of one's ability.

Festivals

There are a number of festivals, only some of which you need to study.

Eid ul-Fitr (or Id-ul-Fitr which is a different spelling but refers to the same festival) ends the fasting month of **Ramadan**. It is a festival of celebration and should set Muslims up for their life in the coming year. It reminds them of what is important in life and Allah should be at the forefront of that.

Eid-ul-Adha (or Id-ul-Adha which is a different spelling but refers to the same festival) ends the period of **hajj** and is celebrated both on hajj and at home. It is well celebrated, but also has more of a spiritual meaning, as it makes Muslims think about the tests that Allah puts in front of them.

Ashura is important to all Muslims, but both its meaning and celebrations are very different for the Sunni and Shi'a. This sacred day commemorates significant historical events, and also serves as a reminder of why Islam split into two main sects.

2.1 Beliefs and teachings

Diversity of believers within the religion

Before you start to study Islam, it is important you know why Islam has two main sects. You will need to study the topics to be able to demonstrate your knowledge of the differences in beliefs and practices that exist between the Sunni and Shi'a, especially if you are aiming for the higher grades.

> 'Muhammad ﷺ is not the father of one of your men, but the messenger of Allah and the **Seal of the Prophets**.' *(Qur'an 33.40, Surah al Ahzab)*

Division of Islam into Sunni and Shi'a

Sunni

Sunni form the majority of the Muslim community. Four successors, called **caliphs**, were appointed to lead the Muslim community after the death of Muhammad ﷺ in 632CE: Abu Bakr, Umar, Uthman and Ali. These men were chosen in turn, and, known as the 'four rightly guided caliphs', led the community for the next 24 years.

Sunni Muslims believe in the authority of the Qur'an and Hadiths, interpreted by leading Muslim scholars.

Sunni comes from the word Sunnah, which means 'custom' or 'way'. Sunni believe they are the true followers of the way of the Prophet Muhammad ﷺ. They believe that as Prophet Muhammad ﷺ did not choose his successor, election is the right way. About 90 per cent of all Muslims are Sunni.

Shi'a

Shi'a is the second largest branch of Islam. Shi'a refer to their chosen leader as the imam and they believe that each imam must be chosen by the previous imam. All Shi'a believe that Prophet Muhammad ﷺ appointed Ali as his successor. They claim the first three caliphs ignored the Prophet's choice, so they are only seen as companions. Shi'a believe the imams have authority from Allah and can interpret the Qur'an and the Laws of Islam. They believe the last imam disappeared or went to the sky without dying. This hidden imam, Mehdi, is present in the world, yet is unseen. He helps those in need and tries to convert all humankind to Islam. They believe he will appear again at the end of the world and establish Allah's kingdom.

After Ali's death, Shi'as believed his son, Hasan, should be the next leader, but there was disagreement. Ali himself had been opposed by Muawiya (Uthman's cousin) and Hasan agreed that his family would lead the caliphate only after Muawiya died. Unfortunately, Hasan died and Muawiya made his son, Yazid, the leader. Hasan's brother, Husayn, refused to accept Yazid and war broke out.

Although there are many Shi'a subsects, modern Shi'a Islam has been divided into three main groupings with Twelver Shi'a being the largest and most influential group, and the one this course focuses on.

These differences caused a split amongst the Muslim community, which we still see today. There are some within each Muslim sect who believe no government can be accepted if it is not based on the Laws of Islam and the rule of Allah alone.

The six articles of faith

'The Oneness of Allah' is the concept of tawhid meaning 'oneness, absolute, alone'. Surah 112:1–4 says:

> 'He is Allah, the One, Allah is Eternal and Absolute. None is born of Him, He is unborn. There is none like unto Him.'

This means that Allah is the creator and sustainer of life. He is beyond any human limitations like age and death because He was not born and cannot die. He has no partners or children and nothing is like Him.

Angels do the work of Allah. They deliver revelations via the prophets so that Muslims know what Allah wants them to do. They record the words and actions of each individual person, so that they have a book to account for their lives. They receive souls at death. Angels do not have free will like humans and they obey Allah's commands.

Muslims believe in several revealed scriptures: the Torah of Moses, the Psalms of David, the Gospels, the Scrolls of Abraham, and the Qur'an. According to Muslims, the first four scriptures have been altered or lost in their original form. The Qur'an is the only revealed scripture still preserved in its original form and serves as the ultimate source of authority in Islam, alongside the authentic Hadith of the Prophet Muhammad. It is the direct Word of Allah as revealed through Angel Jibril.

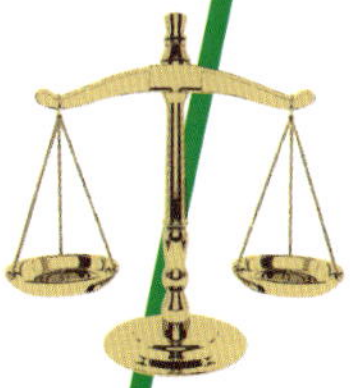

Muslims believe in the supremacy of Allah's will. Sunni believe that Allah knows everything. Qadr means everything is ordered by Allah; nothing is random or by chance. Humans do have free will though, but as Allah knows the past, present and future their choices are already known to Him, but not to them.

Muslims believe that there will be a day (the Day of Judgement) when all Muslims and others stand alone in front of Allah, who decides whether they go to heaven or hell based on their deeds. Everyone must answer for themselves and must accept the consequences of their thoughts and actions on earth. Human life acts as a test for the eternal life to come.

Prophets and messengers are chosen by Allah to deliver His message to humankind. Muslims believe that Allah has revealed messages throughout time to guide humanity and that Prophet Muhammad ﷺ was the last (Seal) of the prophets; he was given the ultimate guidance in the Qur'an. As a result of this, there is no need for any more prophets.

> 'Muhammad ﷺ is not the father of any of your men, but the messenger of Allah and the Seal of the Prophets.' *(Qur'an 33:40).*

Why are the six articles important?

These six articles underpin religious life for Muslims. They influence all aspects of life. If Muslims believe in the absolute power of Allah, then they will live their lives according to His will. The angels are writing up all thoughts and actions, and people will have to justify them, so this makes Muslims think about how they approach life and the people around them. This shows that life here is a test for the afterlife and few have a guaranteed place in paradise because it has to be earned.

To know what is the right thing to do, Muslims have the teachings of the prophets, along with the examples of the lives of the prophets, such as Muhammad ﷺ and Ibrahim, and the ultimate guide in the Qur'an. If they are to live according to how Allah wants, then paradise is on offer to them. Muslims know that they can easily follow the wrong path and that they have to make the right choices with the free will they have been given. Allah knows our actions before we even think about what we do.

Think about how believing in these articles of faith affects how Muslims live their lives today. *How might belief impact on what Muslims say and do? Do you think these beliefs are equally important?*

Complete the questions below. You will see that there are different question types. You need to learn how to structure your answers. The more practice you get the better your answers will be.

The Basics

1 Name one of the articles of faith.
2 Explain briefly what is meant by the 'Oneness of Allah'.
3 Explain the three ways Allah communicates with humankind.
4 Explain ways in which belief in these six articles of faith influences Muslims in their lives today.
5 **Belief in the Oneness of Allah is all a Muslim needs to have.** What do you think about this statement? Give arguments for and against the statement and explain your answer.

The five roots of Usul ad-Din in Shi'a Islam

Usul ad-Din means 'the foundations of the faith'. These are the principles underpinning Shi'a belief, and from them come the Ten Obligatory Acts (see page 134). The **Twelver Shi'a** (the largest group within Shi'a Islam) follow Usul ad-Din and are encouraged to be able to explain them – what they mean and why they are the five key roots to belief – and to understand how they link to their own religious practice in all its elements. Of the five roots, tawhid, prophethood and resurrection are key to all Muslim belief. To be a Muslim means to accept them completely and without question. If a Muslim rejects the other two (imamate and justice), then they are still Muslim, just not Shi'a Muslim.

Tawhid – 'Oneness'

This means the same as in Sunni beliefs, that Allah is One. Allah is the Almighty and unique in His Oneness. Shi'a use Qur'an Surah 112 to explain why they believe Allah is One. Allah cannot be associated with anything as 'none is like Him'; to do so is to commit the greatest sin, namely 'shirk'. This means 'association' in Arabic and therefore nothing and no one can be compared to Allah. Allah is the creator of all, pre-existent, beyond time and space and beyond all human understanding.

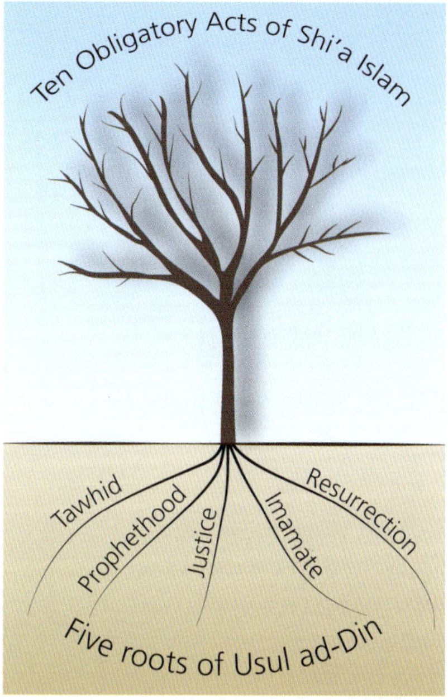

Al-Ma'ad – resurrection

The Shi'a believe that there will be a Day of Judgement (Yawm al-Qiyyamah). Every Muslim and non-Muslim will be judged by Allah. Humans will be physically resurrected to stand to be judged and they will be asked to account for the words and actions of their lives on earth. The events of this day are described in both the Qur'an and Hadith.

Adalat – justice of Allah

Allah is 'The Just' and 'The Wise' which means He does no wrong. Shi'a believe they need to be aware there is good and evil in everything, but that Allah commands them to do good. Surah 16:90 says: 'Indeed Allah commands you towards Justice.' Humans will be held responsible for all their actions, good and bad. Allah acts with a purpose which humans cannot understand. Sometimes justice can be hard to see but the Shi'a should try to understand as much as they can.

Nubuwwah – prophethood

Shi'as believe that Allah sent messengers to guide people to the right path and that Prophet Muhammad ﷺ was the last of them. The 'right path' means a peaceful way of life, lived in total submission to Allah. Prophets deliver the messages to spread the religion. The imam protects the messages so that people do not forget and leave the faith in the absence of prophets.

Imamate – leadership

Some believe that Prophet Muhammad ﷺ said that twelve imams from his own tribe (the Quraysh) would succeed him as leaders. Shi'as believe that the first eleven led the community, and some were killed, but that the twelfth disappeared after his father's death. This imam will appear again when Allah decides at the end of time. Currently he is alive and in hiding. All imams are seen as infallible (can do no wrong) and must be obeyed. They are protectors of the faith, ensuring the teachings do not become corrupted or spoiled.

'I'm a Shi'a Muslim living in Britain today'

My total belief in Allah as One God governs my life. He is my creator, with ultimate power. To know Allah is there as 'One' there is no confusion, to follow His path means I'm doing the right thing. The world is run by one power and I need to run with that power.

I know on the Day of Judgement I will have to answer for my thoughts and actions. I cannot hide from Allah, so I need to do the best I can in terms of intentions. This life is short in comparison to the next and I need to pass the tests that Allah puts in my way.

Prophethood means I am not alone in life. The guidance is there in history and in the present in the Qur'an. I can clearly see what I need to do to please Allah.

'How the five roots influence my life'

Belief in justice is not easy to understand. I know Allah always has a purpose and His actions are based on wisdom, but I cannot always see that purpose even though I search for understanding. I just accept Allah is true and knows best.

The imamate is important to me as without prophets we need leaders who we trust to protect the religion and guide us in the right way. It's easy to go off track when living in a modern world.

Getting prepared

How religious beliefs influence a person's choices and behaviour is a key part of this course at GCSE level. You need to be able to write about how beliefs affect or influence the lives of Muslims today. Read over the last four pages and make your own notes to show how these core beliefs affect both Sunni and Shi'a Muslims.

What if you were asked: Explain how belief in Usul ad-Din influences Shi'as today. (6 marks) Could you answer that?

The Basics

1. What are the five roots of Usul ad-Din?
2. Explain each of the five roots clearly. You might use this template:
   One of the roots is ____________.
   This means _________________.
3. Explain how each of the five roots influences the lives of Shi'a Muslims today.

Nature of Allah – Oneness and omnipotence

Have you ever wondered about Allah? What the nature of Allah is? What qualities we assume Allah to have? Are any qualities more important than others, and if so, why?

Oneness (tawhid)

Muslims believe that Allah is One God, indivisible and absolute; nothing comes close to Him as the ultimate source of power and creation. He is totally supreme. There is nothing that can be likened to Him. He is beyond human understanding. Everything belongs to Allah; everything humans have is on loan from Allah. Humans only exist because Allah wills them to. Muslims are what Allah makes them. They believe any talents come from Allah, so it is wrong to be arrogant. Nothing happens without Allah allowing it. Allah has absolute compassion, so even suffering is Allah's will and for a reason. Muslims should not question this and should never forget His power. Humans cannot obstruct Allah or indeed try to fool Allah as He knows their every thought and intention. Anything that goes against these beliefs breaks tawhid.

If Muslims liken themselves to Allah or to His qualities, then they commit the sin of shirk. For example, Muslims believe that Jesus could not have been the Son of God, as he could not have had God's qualities (which also means there is no Holy Trinity). The Christian belief in the Trinity divides Christianity and Islam in the modern world.

Many positives can come from belief in tawhid. Having total *faith*, *humility* and *modesty* should mean a Muslim cannot be jealous of what does not belong to them. They can *trust* in Allah and know everything happens for a reason. If they dedicate themselves to Him, they will be *courageous* and *determined* in their lives to please Him.

He is Allah, One,

Allah the eternal refuge.

He neither begets nor is born,

Nor is there to him any equivalent.

(Qur'an 112:1–4)

Omnipotent

Allah is Al-Qadeer – (all-powerful). The idea that 'He is able to do all things' ensures a Muslim's submission to Him. Humankind will always need Him and there is a reason for everything that happens. Muslims can be secure in knowing that Allah knows what is happening in the world. He sees their every action and knows their innermost thoughts and desires and He *hears* when they *call* Him. There are hidden blessings to everything that happens.

'... He who is the All-knowing, the All Powerful, able to do anything' *(Surah 30:54)*

As a Muslim I believe that the omnipotence of Allah affects my life because He is always there for me. To me, the impossible is never impossible. I know I can trust Allah, and that trust brings me peace. I am weak; Allah strengthens me. It is all part of His design and weakness is for my own good, so that I always come back to Allah even if I stray. I cannot be content without Allah.

Nature of Allah – immanence and transcendence

We do not only have questions about what Allah is. Have you ever thought about where Allah is? Look at the following comments: *Discuss with a partner the ideas within them.*

'Allah is everywhere'. Where is everywhere, though?

'How does Allah connect with us if He isn't in this world?'

'Allah must be very close to us all, all of the time, if He knows *everything* we say and do!'

'Is Allah with us here in this world?' But He is not physical … is He?'

'Allah is not here … He transcends everything … but then how is He with us?'

'If Allah is not born and eternal He has to be transcendent … doesn't He?

Is it possible to be immanent and transcendent … after all He is omnipotent?'

Immanence

'We are closer to human than his jugular vein.' *(50:16)*

'And He is with you wherever you may be.' *(57:4)*

These quotes from the Qur'an show Allah is vital to human existence. If the jugular vein is cut, humans die so trying to live without Allah is worse than death.

Allah knows humans so well that, for example, He knows what someone will say even before they say it.

Muslims believe Allah must be in this world to help and guide, to give people the purpose and ability to live this life. This is what immanence means; that Allah is very active in the world.

Transcendence

'No vision can grasp Him … He is above all comprehension.' *(6:103)*

'Nothing there is like Him.' *(42:11)*

He is outside this world, outside everything that He created.

Allah is outside time, whereas humans are subject to time.

Allah has no beginning or end, so He cannot be part of time.

Allah is beyond human understanding, limitless and therefore He is not part of this world.

Transcendence is being separate to the world, beyond it, which allows Allah to control and act in the world, but not be affected by it.

The Basics

1. Explain how belief in the Oneness of God influences the life of a Muslim. (Remember this could be positively, negatively or both.)
2. Explain why Muslims believe Allah is omnipotent and what this means.
3. **Allah is immanent not transcendent.** Give and explain reasons to agree and disagree with this statement. Refer to Islam in your answer.

Nature of Allah – beneficence and mercy

Have you ever thought about all the suffering in the world? Wondered why it happens? Some suffering happens because of natural events, whilst some is caused by the actions of others, often called moral evil. We have just looked at Allah being 'All Powerful' and 'All Knowing' and it is often puzzling to us when we see all that happens around us.

Look at the following news clips below. Discuss whether they are natural suffering or moral evil. Also can you think why these things happen? How could Allah allow these to happen? Could/should He stop them?

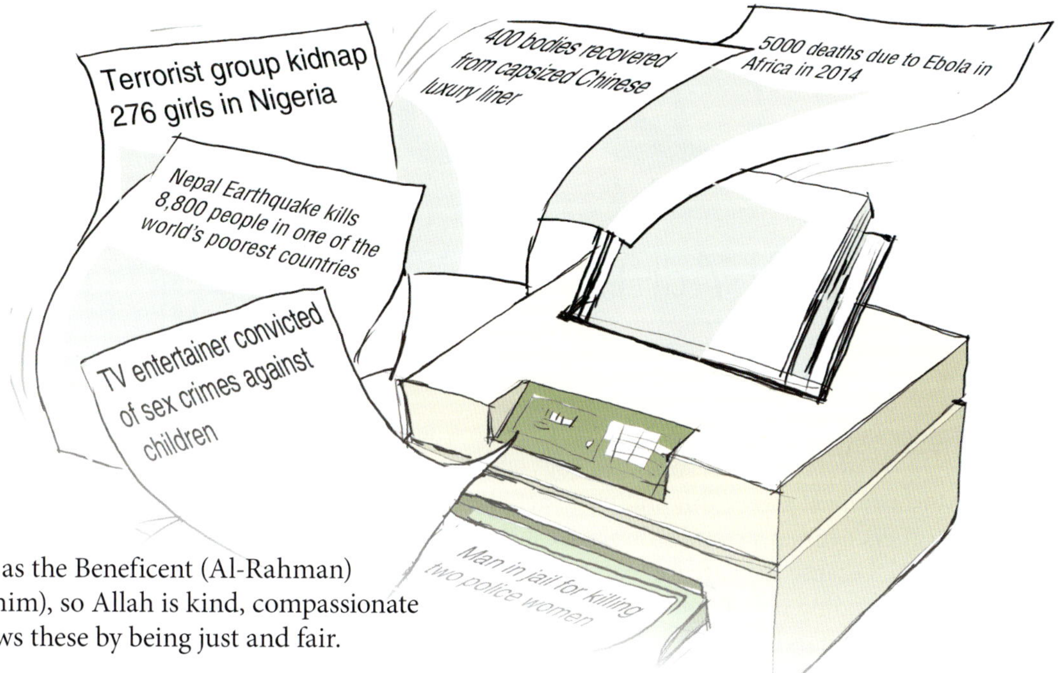

In Islam Allah is known as the Beneficent (Al-Rahman) and the Merciful (Al-Rahim), so Allah is kind, compassionate and forgiving. Allah shows these by being just and fair.

In the Qur'an, Allah is referred to 57 times as the Beneficent and over 160 times as the Merciful. In daily prayer the names are recited seventeen times. So how is Allah beneficent and merciful in a world of suffering and evil?

1 He sent prophets as guides to the right path … so He is compassionate and humans have free will to follow His path.
2 The mercy of Allah is reflected in the rules within the Qur'an.
3 Making mistakes is part of being human, but Allah always forgives those who repent. Out of mercy Allah forgives and even repeated sin is forgiven. Muslims have the chance to make up for bad deeds.
4 Allah's mercy allows humans to exist, to live, to love and to care. Muslims are never alone. Allah's compassion surrounds them and mercy helps them deal with being human.
5 Suffering clearly exists, but it is a test of faith to see how humans respond even where it seems beyond comprehension.
6 Humans should focus on the good (charity, loving kindness, family togetherness, selflessness) of which there is much. They should not think only of the bad, for example, war, crime, poverty, disease.

The Basics

1 What is meant by mercy and beneficence? Give the Arabic terms.
2 Explain how Allah shows mercy and beneficence.
3 Explain why some people might doubt Allah's mercy and beneficence in the world we live in.
4 **It is enough to trust in Allah in our world today.** How far do you agree with this statement? Explain your reasons. Explain what a Muslim might say.

Nature of Allah – fairness and justice

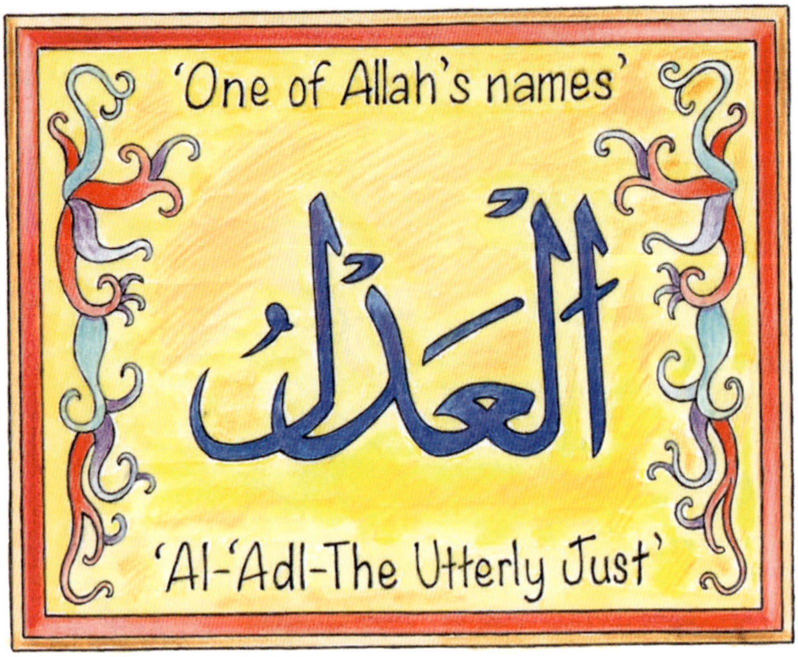

Justice (**adalat**) means fairness, that is, to do what is right. Allah is absolute, so always does what is right. Muslims must accept this and try to act in a fair way to others. Humans cannot always see justice being served, because they are incapable of fully understanding how Allah acts. Allah is just in His creation, in His laws and in all His actions. Allah created all things perfectly through His true wisdom. Allah rewards a good act with a good act and an evil act with consequences. Allah's divine justice rules the universe.

Humans are commanded to be just and fair in their actions: 'Be steadfast witnesses for Allah in equity and let not hatred of any people seduce you that you deal not justly' (Surah 5:8) and also 'We have made you a moderate nation' (Surah 2:143). The Five Pillars exist to help Muslims in life.

This belief should influence Muslims in their lives to never be extreme, to deal with people in the right way, to be fair to others and to do good deeds. So a Muslim must never be too angry or too calm, too courageous or too weak, too clever or too foolish. All Muslims should strive to live their lives in a balanced way. Extreme actions cannot be justified.

Shi'a Muslims believe that the justice of Allah is absolute. Everything belongs to Allah, so humans can never lose anything. Humans only have things by the grace of Allah. Allah punishes humans for any *bad* deed. Any situation which seems negative is actually for our own good as Allah would never be cruel or carry out injustice. At least 40 verses of the Qur'an discuss the justice of Allah and on the Day of Judgement each individual will face justice for their own actions.

Task

Look at the news for the week. How would believing in a just God help Muslims to make sense of the stories?

Think about recent problems or issues in your life. Would you have dealt better with them if your focus had been justice and fairness? Give some examples.

The Basics

1 What is meant by adalat?
2 How does this apply to Allah?
3 How might humans show fairness and justice in their lives?
4 **It is impossible for humans to be truly just.** Argue for and against this view.

How does the nature of Allah influence Muslims today?

Read the three accounts below:

Hi ... My name is Tariq. I'm a mature student in my first year at uni. I'm studying Maths which I'm finding hard! I try to be as good a Muslim as I can, but that is hard too! I believe that my talents were given to me by Allah in His beneficence. It's up to me to make the most of my chances. I know He is always with me (immanent) but I also know I can never succeed on my own. The maths must be hard for a reason, because this is Allah's design. Although why I have to struggle I don't know … It may be a test of my determination. If I fail there will be a lesson for me to learn. I know Allah only acts in a way that is best for me … it's just hard not knowing His plan … but that's a problem for us all, isn't it?

I'm Amina, 35, and I'm an aid worker for UNICEF. I'm in Turkey working at a refugee camp for Syrian people who have left their country due to the civil war. It is a tough job right now – families split up, old people not knowing if their sons are living or dead, people whose homes are just rubble, children who are missing out on their childhood through school and playing in the streets with their friends. When I see this I struggle with my faith. Why does my loving God let this happen? He has the power to stop it doesn't He? Where is His omnipotence, His beneficence, His fairness and justice? So much suffering. It's easy to let these things go through my head but there is good to see too … I'm here for a start helping others, each refugee tries to help the other, there is always someone who has greater suffering than them … it brings out the good in us all for those who want to see it. Evil people will suffer the consequences in the hereafter that's for sure. So I guess that even in the worst of conditions Allah's light is shining through … all we have to do is see it.

Hi I'm Imran. I'm a Shi'a Muslim and the teaching of Allah the Just (adalat) is not to be extreme but to treat people fairly, in a fair way – with justice and equality. I spend some of my time working with young British Muslims to help them see this way, so that they can make a positive contribution to their communities. This is one way to make the world a better place, as we accept others and live in peace with them – regardless of their differences. I have taught my children not to be prejudiced and to try to understand those with different attitudes and beliefs – this is all part of Allah's magnificent design.

Task

Having read the three accounts, discuss how belief in the nature of Allah influences the lives of each of these Muslims. In your written answer include which qualities of Allah have influenced their lives and how.

Authority – the concept of risalah

What is risalah?

Muslims believe Allah is the ultimate creator of the world. But why did He create this world? The Qur'an tells us that Allah told the angels that He was going to put humans on earth. The angels questioned this, as they believed that humans would simply cause chaos. Allah told them that He knew best and asked the angels to bow down before Adam. All the angels obeyed except Azazil believing he was better than Adam. Allah then sent Azazil, now named Iblis, to earth to test humanity. What was he testing though? Human action? How can humans be tested without knowing the rules? Allah had a duty to give people a code to live by. If it is a duty to love, serve and submit to Allah, then humans have to know how to achieve this to be reunited with Allah at death. Allah is just, so it must be the case that He has revealed what He wants from humans.

Adam was the first prophet appointed by Allah. Prophets are guided in the truth and understand it. Their love of Allah prevents them sinning. They deliver the messages Allah sends as guidance. Muslims believe that there were 124,000 prophets who developed the religion over time. Some prophets are also messengers 'rasul' (given divine revelation to deliver everywhere), whilst others are 'nabi', who have been given revelation or news (of an important nature, immediately concerning themselves or their communities).

Muhammad ﷺ, last of the prophets, known as 'the Seal'. Muslims believe that over time previous messages had become lost or changed. Judaism and Christianity contain some truths, but they are not the original messages. Allah then decided to call Muhammad ﷺ and gave him revelations which became the Qur'an. Being written down they could not be changed so no more prophets would be needed. The Qur'an is the direct Word of Allah, containing everything humankind needs to do to pass the test for the next life.

Angels have no physical form. They are messengers of Allah. They are known as bodies of light, which are in constant contact with the world. They are there when we pray. Angels have been seen by specifically chosen individuals in human form, for example, Angel Jibril to Muhammad ﷺ, but they are not human. Muslims believe that we all have two guardian angels who record our actions, which is why they turn to the left and right at the end of daily prayer as if to greet the angels on both shoulders.

Throughout time there have been books to guide Muslims in the right way. Holy Books include the Suhuf of Ibrahim, Tawrat of Musa, Zabur of David (Dawud) and Injil or the Gospels of Jesus. Muslims believe that these books contain some true guidance but have been altered and are incomplete. The Qur'an is the directly dictated Word of Allah in its original form; it is absolute.

Risalah flows through the whole of life. Humans are born, go through the stages of life listening to Allah's guidance from the prophets and reading the holy books and finally die to be resurrected in the afterlife to paradise.

Task

Create a mind map with the word 'risalah' in the middle. On the first ring, name the forms of risalah; the second – key points about what they are; the third – how they provide guidance for humans. Keep them simple with only pointers to remind you. If there are any you find difficult to remember, jot a few notes on the back of the card. Then test yourself. Take two minutes to look at the mind map, visualise the information in each section of the card – total focus. Then see how much of the card you can reproduce. This is a useful revision tool in all subjects.

Prophet Adam

> 'Indeed I am going to set a vicegerent (earthly representative of Allah) on the earth.' *(Qur'an 2:30)*

> '... I am going to create a human out of clay ... so when I have made him, and breathed life into him ...' *(Qur'an 38:71–72)*

The angels collected soil, red, white, brown and black, smooth and gritty, soft and hard. It came from mountains and valleys, from dry deserts and green fertile lands.

Allah honoured Adam. He blew life into his soul. He ordered his angels to bow down before Adam as a sign of respect and honour. His descendants were to be as diverse as the clay he was created from.

So what do we know about Adam?

Everything was created for Adam and his descendants so to be able to worship and know Allah. Adam was to be the caretaker of the earth. Adam was taught everything by Allah, and granted the ability to identify and give names, to communicate and use language. Allah gave him a thirst for learning, and the ability to reason, evaluate and make choices.

To prevent loneliness, Adam was given Hawwa (Eve) as a companion. Allah told Adam and Hawwa to enjoy all the things made for them, but not to eat from one tree. Iblis (a jinn, or supernatural creature) managed to tempt Adam and Hawwa to taste the fruit, hence disobeying Allah. They also became aware of their nakedness and covered themselves. As punishment, Allah banished them to earth, but He forgave them because they asked for mercy. They became ordinary people living on earth instead of in the Garden of Bliss (Eden). On earth, Allah sent guidance to Adam, so he could teach people about Allah.

Adam and Hawwa had many children, the most famous being Qabeel (Cain) and Habeel (Abel). Allah instructed Adam to have his sons offer a sacrifice. Habeel offered a better sacrifice to God than his brother Qabeel. This made Qabeel jealous and he killed Habeel, fulfilling a prophecy in the Qur'an. When Adam died, he named his son Seth as successor but over time his descendants split up and moved apart.

Why is Adam important in Islam?

1. He is the father of all humankind.
2. He was a prophet until his death.
3. He taught the revelations to his sons.
4. He taught about the work of Iblis and how to protect themselves from jinn.
5. He taught that life on earth was temporary, eternal life is in the next life.
6. He built the Ka'aba as the first place of worship, with the help of the angels after he was sent to Earth.

What can Muslims learn from Adam?

Iblis and Adam disobeyed Allah. However, Adam repented his sins straight away and regretted it all his life, so finding salvation. He openly criticised himself for falling into Iblis' trap but he hoped he could make amends and receive Allah's mercy. Iblis did not show repentance or regret. He lost all hope and was forever tormented.

Task

In groups, carry out a silent debate (communication is only through writing) using a large piece of paper and different coloured pens. Respond to the statement: **Prophet Adam can teach Muslims all they need to know.**

Prophet Ibrahim

Overview of his life

Ibrahim lived in Ur in Mesopotamia about 1900BCE. He sold small statues (idol gods) for his father, Azar, who was a sculptor. One day, he decided to test the power of the idols. He threw them into the river to show they did not have any power to save themselves – they sank, proving his point. He realised there was no power in these statues. He began to search for the truth, and looking at the sun, moon and stars became convinced there was just one true power; a single One God. Allah called him to be a prophet and Ibrahim submitted to Him. 'For me, I have set my face towards the One who created the skies and the earth. I will never make partners with Allah' (Qur'an 6:79). He then tried to convert his father and save him, but his father threatened to kill him and sent him away.

Ibrahim preached in public but people did not listen. They ridiculed him. He went into their temples and destroyed all the idols except one. The people were angry and questioned his motives. Ibrahim told them to ask the remaining idol for answers, which of course did not answer. Ibrahim asked them why they worshipped useless idols. Furious, the people shouted for him to be burned. A fire was built and Ibrahim was chained up then catapulted into it. An angel spoke to him in the fire asking what he wanted most, but Ibrahim said he wanted only to please Allah. As a result, Allah commanded the fire to be cool. People were amazed: the chains were burned, but Ibrahim was untouched. Ibrahim continued to receive revelations and wrote them on scrolls called the Suhuf. People including his nephew, Lut, began to follow him. After a disagreement with Nimrud, the King of Ur, Ibrahim realised that he would have to leave. With his family, he set off to the Promised Land (Qur'an 21:71). On the journey quarrels led the group to split. Lut went to the plains east of the Dead Sea and Ibrahim carried on to the Promised Land.

Ibrahim married Sarah and later took on Hajar as a second wife because Sarah was unable to have children. Hajar had a son, Ismail, whom Ibrahim loved greatly. He dreamt he was told to sacrifice Ismail, and when he told Ismail of the dream both agreed to do what Allah commanded. As both were willing, the test was passed and a ram was sacrificed instead. Clearly, Ibrahim was willing to give up everything for Allah. Allah then granted Sarah with a son, Ishaq. It has been said that Hajar and Sarah were jealous of each other, so Hajar and Ismail left to live elsewhere. They were on their own, but they never gave up hope and when they ran out of water, Allah gave them a well, which Hajar named Zamzam. In thanks to Allah for the lives of his families, Ibrahim built (or rebuilt) the Ka'aba with Ismail.

Later, Ismail took his father's place as a prophet and led the first community in the valley of Makkah.

The Basics

1 What are the qualities of Ibrahim which Muslims could try to copy? Do you think that would be difficult?
2 Explain how Ibrahim was responsible for the development of Islam at this time in history.
3 How does the life of Ibrahim influence Muslims in their lives today?
4 **Ibrahim is the perfect role model for modern Muslims.** Write some reasons to agree and disagree with this statement and explain them. What is your overall opinion?

The life of Prophet Muhammad ﷺ

Why Muhammad ﷺ was chosen to be the Prophet of Allah

You have probably studied the life of Prophet Muhammad ﷺ already in previous lessons and so already know the key events in his life, such as his early childhood, his meeting with Angel Jibril, his work in Makkah, the **Hijrah**, his migration to **Madinah**, the battles to retake the city of Makkah and his death. Makkah and Madinah are cities in modern-day Saudi Arabia. If you are not aware of any of these key events, use the internet to research them. Jot down what you do not know.

What you need to do as part of this course, is to look at the importance of Prophet Muhammad ﷺ for Islam at the time and for Islam today.

In 610CE, at the age of 40, Muhammad ﷺ was called to serve Allah. Why Muhammad ﷺ though, and why at this point? Muhammad ﷺ had a tough life, he never knew his father because he had died before Muhammad ﷺ was born. He became an orphan at age six when his mother died, and he had to grow up very quickly, earning his keep by looking after his grandfather's sheep and then working as a merchant for his uncle Abu Talib. Many boys might have struggled with this. For Muhammad ﷺ it made him stronger, developing characteristics of responsibility, determination, patience, courage, honesty, trustworthiness and self-discipline. By age 40 he was married to Khadijah, had children, had his own successful business and was highly respected in the community.

This was all part of Allah's plan; Muhammad's ﷺ role would now be as Prophet to deliver a message that was never going to be changed or corrupted. Prophet Muhammad ﷺ had the task of converting the people of Makkah and beyond to the ways of One God and laying down the basic structures for a religion.

What did Muhammad ﷺ do as a prophet?

The conversion of Makkah was not straightforward, and Muhammad ﷺ had to escape to Madinah (the Hijrah) after his religious message was rejected and his life came under threat. In Madinah, he became the ruler of the city both spiritually and politically. This was the first Islamic community to be set up. He later did fulfil his task of converting the people of Makkah to Islam.

Task

Without Prophet Muhammad ﷺ, Islam would never have developed as a religion. Do you agree? Show that you have thought about more than one point of view by presenting explained arguments to agree and disagree.

The call of Muhammad ﷺ to prophethood

Muslim pilgrims visit the cave where the Angel Jibril first appeared to Muhammad ﷺ

Given we are thinking about the prophethood of Muhammad ﷺ, we need to go back to when he was living in Makkah. He was a wealthy merchant, but was disillusioned with life in Makkah; people behaved in an immoral way, cheated people out of money, gambled, prostitution was rife and idol worship the norm. He began to spend time alone outside the city, meditating in a cave to find peace of mind and the right path to follow. Most scholars agree on the account that on Allah's command Angel Jibril appeared beside Muhammad ﷺ, commanding him to 'Recite!' Muhammad ﷺ said he could not read. The angel squeezed him tight three times before he said the words. When the angel left, Muhammad ﷺ left the cave, trembling from what had happened. He returned to Khadijah to tell her the story. (In the Shi'a tradition they believe that Muhammad ﷺ was not terrified and that he was in fact expecting it.) After reassurances from Khadijah and her Christian cousin, three years passed with Muhammad ﷺ spending more time in meditation and spiritual contemplation. The revelations continued. Allah commanded him to preach to close family friends and then the people of Makkah about Islam and One God.

Why was it important for Muhammad's ﷺ prophethood to happen at that point?

1 It was all part of Allah's plan for it to happen then.

2 People were becoming more distanced from the ways of Allah, earlier revelations were being ignored; Makkah was becoming a centre for idol worship as it grew as a trade centre.

3 Previous holy books had been lost or changed.

4 The religion now needed structure in its organisation in the same way that Judaism and Christianity had.

5 Muhammad ﷺ was a role model that people could follow and trust in. It is said he stood for the truth when truth was lost, was gracious to those who persecuted him, always compassionate and respectful, was concerned with the welfare of others (human or animal), loved children, taught equality, lived humbly and was the model husband, father and friend.

The Basics

Use pages 93 and 94 to answer the following:

1 Where was Muhammad ﷺ called to be a prophet?
A Mt Thaw B Mt Hira C Makkah D Madinah

2 Explain briefly what is meant by the term 'prophet'.

3 Explain what Muslims believe happened when Muhammad ﷺ was called by Allah.

4 Explain ways in which the life of Muhammad ﷺ has influenced Muslims today.

5 **Muslims can never lead their lives as well as Muhammad ﷺ did.** Explore arguments for and against this statement in detail. Refer to Islam in your answer.

Muhammad's ﷺ Sunnah and Hadith

The Qur'an has supreme authority for Muslims, but the second most important source of authority is the Sunnah. The Sunnah are the practices, customs and traditions of Prophet Muhammad ﷺ. These give the perfect example for Muslims to follow. They are found in the Hadith (sayings of the prophet) and other texts. Different groups of Muslims accept different collections of Hadith as reliable sources of authority. Reading the Hadiths helps Muslims learn how Muhammad ﷺ explained the teachings from the Qur'an. The language and style of the Qur'an do not lend themselves to easy interpretation, so Hadiths are helpful. The Shi'a, in addition to using the Hadith narrated by Muhammad ﷺ, also refer to the teachings of the 'Imams'. Sunni Muslims believe that the Hadith are important because the Qur'an says:

> 'A similar (favour you have already received) in that We have sent among you a Messenger of your own … and instructing you in Scripture and Wisdom, and in new knowledge' *(2:151)*.

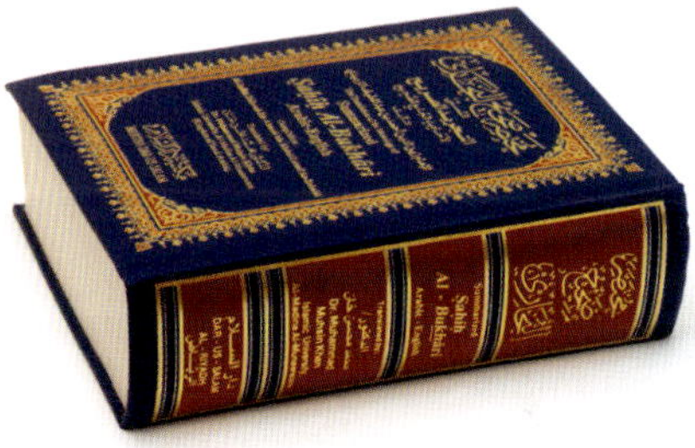

Also

> 'You have in the Messenger of Allah a beautiful pattern for any one whose hope is in Allah and the Final Day' *(33:21)*.

The role of Muhammad ﷺ was to teach and live by the Qur'an so that humankind could understand it and live by it. Muhammad ﷺ should never be worshipped (as Jesus is by Christians, for example).

What does the Sunnah tell Muslims?

The Sunnah covers many areas of life including:

Sunnah for marriage.

Sunnah for rituals for birth of children.

Sunnah towards animals.

Sunnah to have good sense of humour.

Sunnah for helping those in need.

Sunnah to always remember Allah.

The Sunnah is the guideline for Muslim life and there is a Sunnah for everything.

Task

Research 'The Sunnah of Muhammad ﷺ'. Choose **three** areas from the above list and find out what rules apply in your chosen areas.
Give an evaluation of these Sunnah. Are they easy or difficult to implement? Why/why not?

What impact does Prophet Muhammad ﷺ have on Muslims today?

Muhammad ﷺ the individual

Muslims believe he is the perfect example of a man serving Allah without question. Firstly, that he was a man without godlike qualities, meaning there is no reason why they themselves cannot aim to live as good a life as Muhammad ﷺ did. He did not have it easy; he had to be determined to succeed all his life. He had to have patience in his prophethood before it brought results. He rejected the immorality he saw around him. He always focused on Allah. He was humble, modest, caring, prayed and knew Allah would help when difficulties arose. He is the best example to follow for all those reasons. He was a better human being because of his sense of morality, of duty and his belief in the importance of his community. Regardless of a person's position in society, Muslims believe everyone could learn from him, then and now.

Muhammad ﷺ the leader

Muslims claim that Muhammad ﷺ was the greatest political and religious leader of all time, managing to combine the two roles perfectly. He set up a community where individuals were respected. He allowed religious freedom, gave women rights, looked after older people and sick people, welcomed strangers and created rules which allowed the best possible outcomes for everyone. He had charisma as a leader so that people followed him in religion, in ordinary life and militarily. Ten thousand men went into battle for him in Makkah. The Islamic Empire spread from southern Europe to northern Africa and across Asia, in his name and the name of Islam. Today, thirteen centuries later, 1.3 billion Muslim followers repeat his name daily and many people study his life worldwide.

Muhammad ﷺ the family man

Muslims consider Muhammad ﷺ to have been an exemplary family man. In the Qur'an there is a theme of family men: Adam, Noah, Lut, Jacob, Ibrahim and then Muhammad ﷺ. Islam sees the family as the basic unit for the well-being of society. If family works well, society works well. Muhammad ﷺ said 'The best of you is he who is best to his family' (Hadith). Muhammad ﷺ led a strong family unit. He loved his first wife, Khadijah, and cared for her extended family after she died. He also cared for his other wives and dealt with any issues justly. He had four daughters whom he educated (not the tradition at the time), marrying them to decent men, and he was a good grandfather. He also suffered the loss of his own sons and needed his faith in Allah to help him through this. As a loving father, he never forgot his sons.

Muhammad ﷺ the teacher

He was the greatest teacher, because of what he said. He lived every aspect of Islamic life, so others could learn and follow. He spoke with authority, but made it easy for others to learn. He spoke clearly and precisely, making learning easier. He spent thirteen years in Makkah teaching people the Word of Allah. Many initially rejected his teachings and though he faced hatred and violence, he carried on. Muhammad ﷺ realised that everyone can learn with the right method and the patience to succeed. His determination to teach Allah's way meant he had the patience he needed.

Task

One new aspect of this course is to look at how people, teachings and practices influence the lives of Muslims today. Give a variety of ideas in your answer.

- **a** Briefly outline the key events in the life of Muhammad ﷺ.
- **b** Explain how Muslims can try to live up to Prophet Muhammad's ﷺ example in their lives in Britain today.

The Qur'an – its revelation and compilation

Revelation of the Qur'an

The Qur'an has 114 chapters (Surah) which contain 6,237 ayahs (verses). During his thirteen years in Makkah, 86 Surahs were revealed to Prophet Muhammad ﷺ, the remaining 28 were revealed in his ten years in Madinah. The original first revelation happened on The Night of Power (see page 94). It is believed that the first revealed message was 'Recite! In the name of your Lord, Who created all that exists.' It was the direct message from Allah through Angel Jibril with no change or alteration. In Surah 10:15 it states that whilst Muhammad ﷺ received the revelations, he had no authority to change them. What was revealed was the will of Allah – Allah Himself was not seen. Muhammad ﷺ was said to have described the receiving of revelations like the ringing of a bell, but also that some were painful, as if his soul was being ripped from him. Once received, he recited them in public, instructing one of his scribes to write them down. He appointed Zayd ibn Thabit as his lead scribe to record, organise and keep the messages.

Each Surah begins 'In the Name of Allah, the Most Merciful, The Most Compassionate'. Zayd and 48 other scholars recorded the Qur'an in written form, though it was only later that this was compiled as one book. Sunni and Shi'a Muslims believe the revelations were complete by the time Muhammad ﷺ died.

The Basics

1. For each of revelation and compilation, list key words, one idea under the other to remind you of the order of events. Your list will help you with the following questions and is a good revision tool.
2. Explain what Muslims believe about how the Qur'an was revealed.
3. Explain the different views of how the Qur'an was compiled.
4. **It does not matter how it was revealed or compiled, it is the fact Muslims have the Qur'an that is important.** Explore this statement to find reasons to agree and disagree.

Compilation of the Qur'an

Some Hadith say that Muhammad ﷺ left behind two examples: the Qur'an and the Sunnah. The word used is Al Kitab meaning a compiled book. As Muhammad ﷺ put so much importance to the Qur'an he would have had it written down in full. Others disagree; they believe the Qur'an was collected and ordered as the Prophet had recited, but not in one book. Shi'a Muslims believe that Imam Ali had all the Surahs in the right order six months after Muhammad's ﷺ death, but not as a complete book. Other Muslims claim Ali's version had non-authentic verses in it, so rejected this copy.

The majority of Sunni Muslims believe that Umar insisted Abu Bakr (the first caliph) have one copy completed. Certainly, the need for one single volume was urgent, because many scholars and many **hafiz** (those who memorised the Qur'an word for word) had died in the battle of Yamama; including Salim a teacher of the Qur'an. The Qur'an was compiled, passed onto Umar who became the second Caliph. He then handed it over to Hafsa, his daughter and wife of Muhammad ﷺ. The next Caliph, Othman, made sure that as Islam spread, copies of Hafsa's version were sent out, so that everyone was reading the same book.

Since the seventh century CE there have been many forms of the Qur'an from different scholars using different calligraphy and bindings, but the teachings remained the same. The first mass-printed version did not appear until the 1920s, produced in Cairo, Egypt. This version very quickly became accepted by Sunni and Shi'a alike as the 'official' Qur'an.

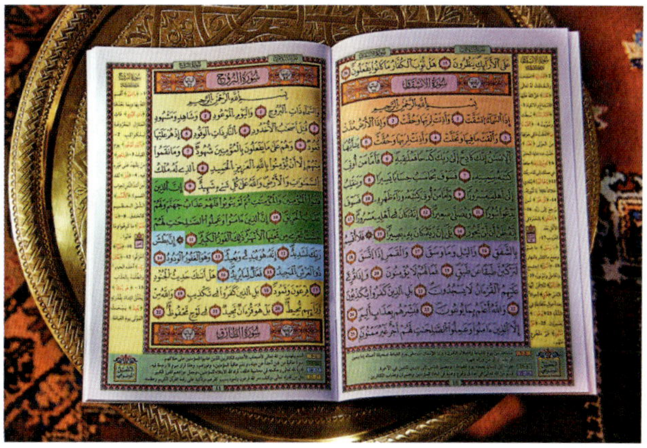

The Qur'an and its authority

Why is this book so important to Muslims? Is it because of where it comes from and why? Or is it about what is contains? The answer to both these questions is 'partly'.

Belief and origins

The Qur'an is the direct Word of Allah and therefore has His authority.

It is infallible (without error) and remains in its original form:

> 'Falsehood shall never come to it' *(Qur'an 41:42).*

It supersedes other books like the Torah and Injil.

The Qur'an was revealed to the Seal of the Prophet (Muhammad ﷺ) and because no man would be capable of writing such a book, it made him even more important.

> 'If all men and jinn should combine to bring about the likes of the Qur'an, they could not bring the like of it, even if they helped one another.' *(Surah 17:88)*

Muhammad ﷺ was illiterate, making the Qur'an the first great miracle.

A written book (the Qur'an) was needed to formalise the religion.

What the Qur'an contains

The Qur'an has authority because it covers every aspect of life: past, present and future.

It influences a person throughout their lives: birth, ceremony, marriage, death and in daily prayers.

It contains the basics of worship which Muhammad ﷺ developed.

It contains the legal (**Shari'ah Law**) and social systems.

It explains the creation and other ultimate questions like why we are here and what happens when we die.

It has been suggested by some that science and the Qur'an go together; they are compatible and the Qur'an reveals ideas that scientists did not even know at the time.

It provides personal and spiritual guidance for all life's situations and challenges.

If Muslims combine all these ideas there is no reason to not believe that the Qur'an has supreme authority. It is a timeless book. Equally though, other religions also believe that their holy books are as important to them and have as much authority. Christians, for example, may say that where the Bible comes from is a secondary issue, what is far more important is how it speaks to people when they read it. In other words, God speaks to them individually in their hearts when the Bible is read. Other books have been translated, but in general the meaning still exists. What is more important is that people can read it in their own language and it is available to all. The Qur'an is only infallible in its original language (Arabic), and translation is exactly that: a translation and not the Word of Allah.

Task

Now that you have the ideas about why the Qur'an has supreme authority for Muslims, research one other religion and see why they believe their holy book has authority for them.

Getting prepared

If you're studying at the higher level, make sure you understand religious diversity and can compare different religious views.

The Qur'an as the basis for Shari'ah

'It is not for a believing man or a believing woman, when Allah and His messenger have decided a matter, that they should (thereafter) have any choice about their affair. And whoever disobeys Allah and His messenger have certainly strayed into a clear error.' *(Surah 33:36)*

What makes up the Shari'ah?

Shari'ah (Islamic law) means 'a path to life-giving water' and goes back to Ibrahim. Shari'ah considers:

1 the Qur'an – containing direct guidance from Allah
2 the Sunnah – many of the prophet's teachings and actions putting the Qur'an into practice.

Leading scholars use these to make decisions (ijma', which means consensus). Muslims believe that any devout Muslim has the right to make judgements in keeping with the Qur'an and Sunnah where there is no guidance. The opinions of the Prophet's companions, such as Abu Bakr and Qatadah, are like laws, later ijma' are only seen as guidelines. There is the belief that these can be changed as time moves on.

Why is there a need for Shari'ah?

Allah's laws are always superior to human-made laws, because He knows and understands the world humans live in far better than they ever could. Also, Allah is without prejudice or favour, so is absolutely objective, whereas humans are biased. Laws are needed for society to function properly and fairly. Shari'ah Law covers five main areas: behaviour and manners; ritual worship; beliefs; transactions and punishments. If the laws in a country are not based on absolute justice, then Shari'ah Law is more important to follow. Muslims are taught to obey the laws of the country they live in, but some Muslims do want Shari'ah to be used alongside government law in dealing with matters of religion. This subject has been debated in Britain as radical Muslims called for Shari'ah Law to be the law of the UK. However, Shari'ah is not meant to be imposed on people, it must be part of the consensus. Some parts of Shari'ah are used in Britain, for example, in relation to marriage.

Sunni and Shi'a diversity

For Sunni Muslims there are four schools of thought within Islamic Shari'ah Law (each known as a **madh'hab**): the Hanafi, Maliki, Shafi'i and Hanbali schools. Some Sunni also accept the Shi'a Ja'fari school of thought. Shi'a Muslims only accept the Ja'fari school, which is made up of learned individuals called mujtahids (living religious scholars or ayatollahs representing the twelve imams). Their opinions must still be based on the Qur'an and Sunnah.

Categories of behaviour

1 Fard or **Wajib**: compulsory actions, for example, prayers.
2 **Mustahab** and Mandoob: things that are recommended for Muslims, for example, nafil prayer.
3 **Mubah**: things that are allowed, but neither recommended nor forbidden.
4 **Makruh**: allowed actions which are disliked or disapproved of, for example, divorce.
5 **Haram**: forbidden actions, for example, adultery.

Task

In groups of five give each person one of the boxes on this page to research. Each person should then feed back to the group so that notes can be made.

How does Shari'ah fit in a modern world?

Shari'ah Law comes from 1,400 years ago. How can they apply today? Are our lives too complex today? Should religion really govern our actions, for example, telling me whether I can drink alcohol? Muslims see all the rules as Allah looking after us, helping us stick to the right path, rather than them being seen as restricting us. They are all there to help.

The Torah (Tawrat) and the Scrolls of Ibrahim

The Tawrat

The Tawrat is the Arabic word for the Torah, which are the revelations given to Musa (Moses) by Allah on Mount Sinai. Some Muslim scholars say that the Tawrat is the first five books of the Bible (the Pentateuch). Other Muslim scholars say the Tawrat is equal to all of the Old Testament. The Qur'an states that it confirms what was before, that is, the Torah and the Gospels, although those texts have themselves become corrupted. Some scholars believe these earlier books to be 'lost' and no longer existing in any form.

The Tawrat does not exist in its original language or its original text. It was put together by the followers of Moses a long time after his death. The compilers changed the text, so some is the Word of Allah and some is human addition.

That being said, some believe that Allah preserves the books, so they have not been lost or added to. This view is supported by these teachings:

1 Allah is all-powerful and His Word cannot be changed. 'None can change His words for He is the one who hears and knows all.' (Surah 6:115)

2 A proverb given to Prophet Sulayman says: 'Do not add to His words or He will rebuke you.'

3 Deuteronomy 4:2 says: 'Do not add to what I command and do not subtract from it …'

4 The fact that Muhammad ﷺ was told if he was ever unsure to search out meaning from those who had received scripture, suggests that the original scriptures were still believed to be reliable at the time the Qur'an was written.

Whatever the case, the Qur'an refers to the Tawrat as 'guidance and light', revealed by Allah and clearly very important. On retiring to bed at night, Muhammad's ﷺ prayer put his life into Allah's hands (the creator and lord of everything, the source of the Tawrat, the Gospels and the Qur'an) and asked for protection from Shaytan (the Devil). The Qur'an also seems to suggest that the Torah was not only taught by Musa, but by all prophets and priests.

The Scrolls of Ibrahim

> 'Or has he not been informed of what is in the scriptures of Musa and Ibrahim.' *Surah 53:36*

> 'Verily, this is the earliest scripture, the scripture of Ibrahim and Musa.' *Surah 87:18*

Very little is actually known about these scrolls (often called Suhuf). The revelations were said to have been received by Ibrahim on the first day of Ramadan and contained parable-like stories about worship, reflection and building a livelihood. Ibrahim is termed 'the upright one', always faithful to Allah. The scrolls were written on parchment but perished over time. It is generally agreed that they were not a 'book' rather individual revelations.

The Basics

1 Explain briefly what is meant by the Tawrat.
2 Explain the different ideas held about the Tawrat, what it is and what it means.
3 Describe what the 'scrolls of Ibrahim' are.
4 **The scrolls of Ibrahim are of no use today.** Try to argue for and against this statement, explaining your ideas.

The Psalms (Zabur) and the Gospels (Injil)

The Psalms – Zabur

One of the other two holy scriptures of Islam, the Zabur (Psalms) of Dawud are a collection of prayers to Allah (some refer to them as poems). Dawud was a great king, whose people were God-fearing and righteous. In Surah 4:163 it says '*we gave Dawud the Zabur*.' They contain lessons of guidance for the people and he recited them in song version.
A fragment of an Arabic translation of Psalm 78 from the second century CE was found in Damascus, Syria.

One important message in the Zabur is the idea of the Masih (Messiah). The Masih was to be a symbol of hope for the future in a world where many had failed to obey Allah's commands. Isa (Jesus) also referred to what had been said about the Masih in the Gospel of Luke, 'Everything must be fulfilled that is written about me in the Law of Moses, the Prophets and the Psalms (Zabur).' He taught in a way which allowed people to understand the scriptures. For Muslims, Jesus was the Messiah and will return.

The Gospels – Injil

This is the good news about Isa (Jesus) written by his disciples. Muslims highly respect Isa because there are revelations in the Qur'an about him. Muslims believe:

- He was born of a virgin mother.
- He was the Masih.
- He was not the son of Allah (as Allah can have no partners).
- He followed Allah.
- He was not crucified (but did not die; rather he ascended to heaven).
- He did not die to save sins (Allah is **all-compassionate**, so He will forgive sins, so this sacrifice would have been unnecessary).
- The gospels in their current form contain mistakes because they were written by disciples many years after the death of Isa, having had only weak understanding of his teachings in the first place.

So … what about the authority of these four books?

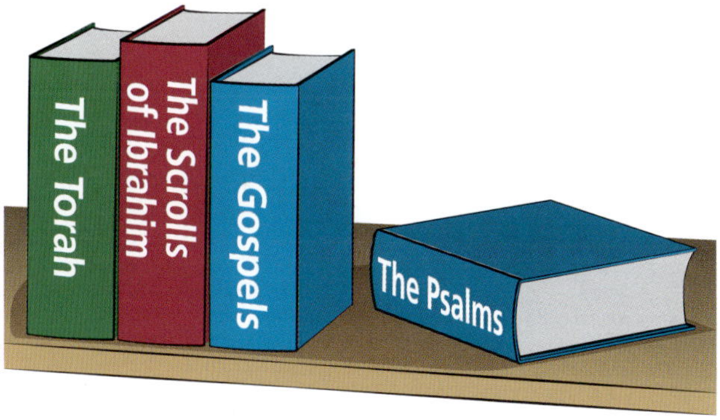

All four books are referred to in the Qur'an, so they are important.

Muhammad ﷺ referred to them to affirm the continuity of divine revelation, highlighting the Qur'an as the final and unaltered culmination of God's message.

They were associated with key prophets and their revelations which gives them importance.

However ...

Some are lost and no one knows what they said.

It is alleged they have been changed, so do they still have *some* authority?

Why were they not preserved like the Qur'an if they were that important?

Having been so changed, Muslims cannot use them, so they have no impact/authority today.

All about angels

What are angels actually?

As stated on page 81, believing in angels is one of the six articles of faith. The Qur'an tells us that humans are made from clay; jinn are made from smokeless fire; angels are made of elements of light. Angels are said to have wings and can move at the speed of light. They can appear in human form, but dazzle so are not like humans. They have no gender and are part of the unseen world. What they do we cannot see and they always complete what Allah asks. Their purpose is to obey Allah as they have no free will. Surah 19:64 says:

'We don't descend except for the command of our Lord.'

What do angels do?

Angels watch over humans, bringing peace to believers and instilling fear in unbelievers. They record every thought and action to report on Judgement Day. One angel delivers all Allah's messages to humans and has appeared to all the prophets. Angels can cause natural disasters when Allah commands them to. There is the Angel of Death who takes the soul at death (it is taken gently or with extreme pain depending upon a person's life). There are angels who question each soul, either punishing or soothing it as it waits for Judgement Day. Angels greet those who enter paradise, two stand at each gate to wish peace upon those entering. In hell there are angels who throw people into the pits of hell and do not let people escape. On Judgement Day one angel will blow the horn at Allah's command to signify the end of the world.

'They do not precede Him in speech and (only) according to His commandment do they act.' *(Surah 21: 73)*

Some famous named angels in the Qur'an

Nakir and Munkir

Malik

Israfil

Kiraman and Katibeen

Task

Research each of the four angels or pairs of angels named. Jot down some notes about what each does and why each of them is important for Muslims in their lives today. Look at the images as the pictures will give you clues as well.

Jibril – the 'Angel of Holiness'

Jibril is the most famous angel, and in Islam, the most important. You might be familiar with him as Gabriel (the angel who visited Mary to tell her she would give birth to Jesus). The Qur'an also records his visits to Maryam the mother of Prophet Isa (Jesus). 'Jibril' is said to mean 'God is my strength'. So what do we know about him? Does the Qur'an give us any ideas?

Jibril is known as the 'spirit of holiness' as he always brings good news. In the Hadith, Muhammad ﷺ was said to have described Jibril as having 600 wings. Each wing filled the horizon as far as the eye could see in all directions. Jibril was the first thing to be given life by Allah and he was sent to look at paradise. On seeing it, he claimed that no one would ever stray away from it for its beauty and wonder. He was sent a second time to look at it when it was surrounded by a barrier of difficulties and hardship. His reaction then was that no one would ever reach it. He was then sent to look at hell; he said that no one would want to go there. So Allah surrounded hell with desires and lusts, at which Jibril said that no one would ever be able to avoid it. *What do you think is the message here?*

Jibril spoke with many prophets who received revelations from Allah. He is mentioned five times in the Qur'an but also in the Hadith. These include:

1 He helped **Ibrahim** when he was thrown into the fire.

2 He opened up the Zamzam well so that **Hajar** could give her dying son water.

3 When **Yusuf (Joseph)** was thrown into a well by his brothers, Jibril caught him and was his protector.

4 He told **Zakariyya (Zechariah)** about a son he was to have in his old age, Yahya (John).

5 Jibril told **Maryam** she would have a son, Isa (Jesus).

6 Jibril spoke to **Muhammad** ﷺ in Cave Hira, over 23 years dictated the Qur'an directly from Allah, and taught him the Sunnah and the Five Pillars, teaching him that faith meant believing in Allah, angels, books and messengers.

Task

Belief in angels has no impact on the life of Muslims today. Evaluate this statement. In your answer you should:
- apply religious arguments
- give developed arguments to support this statement
- give developed arguments to support a different point of view
- reach a justified conclusion.

The Angel Mika'il

Most of what is known about Mika'il is from Islamic tradition rather than the Qur'an. He is mentioned as one of the most important angels. Angel Mika'il not only assisted Muhammad ﷺ with his spiritual mission, but still does that for people today. He is often known as the giver of rain and sustenance. He was one of the first to bow to Adam and he was put in charge of the plants and rain. Muslim teachers think this is symbolic to mean that Mika'il provides spiritual help to the soul and material help to the body. Mika'il had to prepare Muhammad ﷺ by providing the water that Jibril used to purify him, before Jibril took Muhammad ﷺ to the seven heavens and the throne of Allah.

Some Islamic tradition says that Mika'il lives in heaven, has wings of a dark green colour and hairs of saffron. Each hair has a million faces and mouths that can communicate in all languages, all asking for Allah's mercy for humankind. He is mentioned as helping Muhammad ﷺ at the Battle of Badr, which was fought for Makkah.

On Judgement Day both Jibril and Mika'il will help with the weighing of a person's actions. Mika'il has seen hell and how easy it is to get there, as opposed to how hard it is to get to paradise, so it is believed that he does not smile. He is the friend of humankind as he knows what awaits; the path to paradise being thinner than a human hair.

Angels of the seven heavens

Islam believes in other angels, who have specific jobs, and some of whom are named:

Hafaza is the guardian angel, whilst Jundullah (the army of Allah) helped Muhammad ﷺ in battle. There are angels whose job it is to maintain order, angels who protect people from death until the given time, angels who carry Allah's throne, angels who bestow blessings from Allah, angels who ensoul each foetus and angels who travel the earth finding those who worship Allah.

The Basics

1. Explain briefly who Jibril was.
2. Describe what we know about what he did.
3. Explain why Jibril is important for Muslims.
4. Who was Mika'il? What does Mika'il do?
5. **Mika'il is more important than Jibril.** Do you agree? Show that you have thought about more than one point of view. Refer to Islam in your answer.
6. Explain how belief in angels might influence the lives of Muslims today.

Akhirah – belief in life after death

What happens after we die is one of life's biggest mysteries. Philosophers call it an 'ultimate question', which is one that has no answer that can be empirically tested or even agreed upon. What happens when we die is something some people fear as it is a move into the unknown. There are many possibilities given as 'answers' (resurrection, reincarnation, heaven, hell) whilst others think that death is the end and that is it.

What do you think? Discuss in small groups in a silent debate the phrase **Death is simply death!** Present the ideas and further discussion as a class.

How does Islam explain life after death for its followers?

- Akhirah definitely exists. The Qur'an says it does and as the Word of Allah, is right.
- Life after death makes sense of our short existence on earth – why we are here at all.
- On earth, Muslims' lives are tested by Allah and the end result is akhirah in one form or another.
- Most of the prophets state that Muslims were created deliberately, and people will be accountable for their actions in order to complete the journey back to Allah.

People face different tests in their lives, not always equal tests either. Some suffer; others live very well. Both are a test, even if it is hard to understand or might seem very unfair, even to the point of questioning if Allah is fair or not. Muslims believe that no one will face a test beyond what they are able to face. It is how a person faces up to what happens in life that is important.

What is actually being tested, though? Everything: a person's whole way of life, how they treat others, the qualities they show, their reactions to what happens to them and how they face up to difficulties or use good fortune.

There are two angels who keep a record of everything. This idea can be quite scary because it is very easy to be selfish and negatively affect others, whilst being good can seem far harder. Every action taken can either help or harm in relation to the afterlife, which is determined only by a person's actions. A good record in this life will earn a place in paradise. Muslims believe a bad one is not even worth contemplating!

The 'Angel of Death' – the grave and Barzakh

When a person dies, their soul is taken by the Angel of Death, Azra'il. The soul hovers around the corpse, seeing everything but unable to communicate. It watches the burial, as it is no longer part of the body. Two angels visit to ask three questions:
1. Who is your Lord? 2. What was your life like? 3. Who is your prophet? If these are answered correctly it is believed that the soul is made comfortable to sleep until the Day of Judgement. If not, it is tormented by angels. This is known as the punishment of the grave. After this stage, waiting for the Day of Judgement is called Barzakh. Barzakh means 'barrier'. This is not governed by time and there is no return to life even to warn or help others.

Akhirah – the end of the world

Surahs 81 and 82 describe what will happen when this time comes. The Angel Israfil will sound the trumpet, there will be blinding light and the sky will be cut. The earth will be destroyed, with mountains becoming dust and oceans boiling over with fire. The earth will be transformed and the dead raised up. The living will die instantly

The Mahdi (guided one; Messiah) will come to earth and Isa will return to help the Mahdi to fight against false prophets. It is believed that the Qur'an will be taken up to paradise and not even hafiz (those who know the Qur'an by heart) will remember its words. New heaven will also replace the old. Forty days after the trumpet, there will be smoke covering the world. A second trumpet will then sound when the dead will rise to await judgement.

While you need to know what the afterlife is, it is important to understand how belief in the afterlife affects Muslims in their lives. Let's take a closer look at this issue.

Muslims believe that death and judgement are certainties in their lives that they must face up to. Everything in their lives leads to these, so the afterlife gives a purpose to the here and now. Things happen for a reason and actions have consequences. Often people ask the question: Why are we here? For Muslims, the answer is 'to secure afterlife in paradise'. Believing as fact that angels are recording thoughts and actions encourages Muslims to think about their actions, do the right thing, regret doing when they do a wrong thing, and seek forgiveness. The Qur'an describes paradise as far more beautiful than humans could ever imagine and so how could any Muslim not want to work to get there. Human life is short, whereas the afterlife is eternal. At the same time hell sounds horrible. Muslims have the two places on offer to them and it is up to them which they work for.

As the dead will be raised, Muslims believe they need their physical body, so are never cremated. This belief affects some Muslim attitudes to transplant surgery and organ donation, as they feel they need to be whole (though this can be over-ridden by the need to help others). Many will try to resist post mortems on relatives for the same reasons.

'Whoever remembers the hereafter more, their sins decrease.'

Imam Ali

The Basics

1. Explain briefly the term akhirah.
2. Describe why Muslims believe in an afterlife.
3. Explain the role of Azra'il.
4. **Religious believers have no proof that an afterlife exists.** What do you think of this statement? Argue for and against it, explaining your points.
5. Explain how belief in an afterlife could influence the life of a Muslim today. Include some examples in your answer.

Al-Qadr and human freedom

> Say, 'Never will we be struck except by what Allah has decreed for us; He is our protector.' And upon Allah let the believers rely.' *(Surah 9:51)*

Al-Qadr means that everything happens as a result of Allah's *will* and nothing is ever random or without reason. It means predestination of the will of Allah; that Allah is *in charge* of everything in life and has a purpose for everything as part of His plan.

What is the point in life then for humans? Why does Allah design humans to be able to do things wrong? Why punish humans? Why not prevent misbehaviour to avoid punishment? Are humans like puppets with Allah pulling the strings? In which case, are humans really independent? If Allah already knows who is going to paradise or hell then what is the point?

Think again

Actually, according to Islam, it is not really like this at all. Humans control themselves, for example, thoughts, feelings, emotions, responses, choices, decisions, which can all be good and bad. Some things are not controllable, for example, the weather, how people treat you, who helps you, which family a person is born into or where they are born and people certainly do not choose the sufferings they go through. Though not able to always control what happens, humans can control their reaction. This is human free will. However, Allah already knows a person's choices. Whilst Allah controls the boundaries of a person's life, each person has control over the part they play. Undoubtedly humans control their own lives, as they have free will, but they do not know what their destiny is, only Allah knows that.

Responsibility and accountability

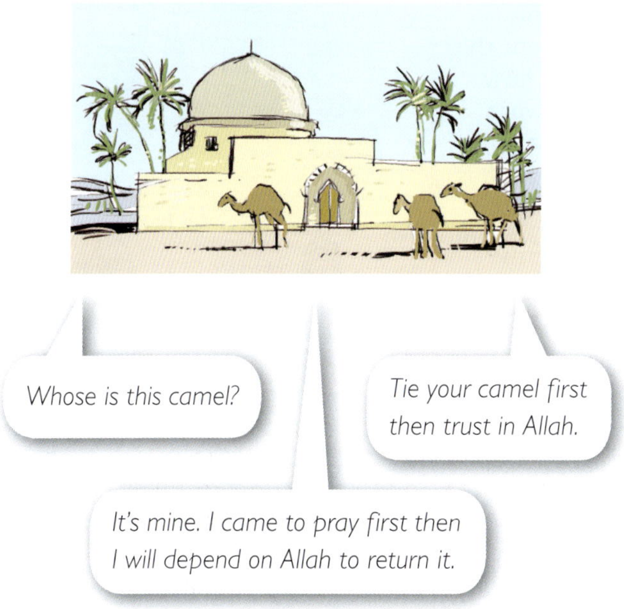

Often Muslims use the words 'Insha'Allah' (if Allah wills). However, everything cannot just be left to Allah, humans have to take responsibility for as much as they can and then put their trust in Allah.

Being responsible also means being accountable for actions. Surah 16:93 states '… and most certainly you will be questioned as to what you did.' This will lead to paradise or hell.

What does this story mean? What does it say about Muslim responsibility?

Task

Think about the last week in your life. What have you done that you would not want to be held accountable for? How could you put these things right? How easy would it be? If you had this time again would you do things differently and why?

Day of Judgement

Task

Look at the images on this page. Research The Islamic Day of Judgement. Write your own account of what will happen. The images give you the outline, but you need to fill in more detail. Think back to when you looked at Mika'il and his reaction to what Allah showed him. At the end of your description, write a simple paragraph explaining how important this day is for Muslims and how they might feel about what they are told will happen. Surah 9:51 states that *'Allah is our protector'*. How does this fit with the Day of Judgement for Muslims?

Paradise and hell – (Jannah and Jahannam)

'No soul knows what delights of the eye are kept hidden from them of joy, as a reward for what they did.' *Surah 32:17*

Jannah

What kind of place is Jannah (paradise)?

- It is magical and mystical, where all wishes/desires are fulfilled.
- No growing ill, old or dying and no pain or worries.
- It is a reward and a gift from Allah.

What is done to get there?

- It cannot be reached by any known means.
- A person must have lived religiously and asked for Allah's forgiveness.
- Good beliefs and actions provide the entrance ticket.

The entry itself:

- People will be invited in, 'Enter among my servants! Enter My Paradise!' (Qur'an 89:29–30)
- People will arrive over the As-Sirat Bridge, joy overwhelming.
- There are eight gates. People are called to a gate (each represents a good action) and the gate that calls you will represent the good action you did the best.
- Two angels welcome people, saying 'Peace be upon you', 'Enter here and live within.'
- People will say 'Praise be to Allah who has fulfilled his promise to us.'

The Qur'an and Muhammad ﷺ gave detailed descriptions of Jannah, but it is beyond human imagination. There are seven levels of Jannah; those with the most reward will gain the higher levels. People will be asked to read from the Qur'an; the more they can read, the higher they go. That layer is their paradise. Families will be reunited, no one will be alone. There will be: rivers, gardens, beautiful weather, creatures to look after everyone, as much food as wished for and wine that does not get you drunk. Clothes will look splendid and radiant. Surah 35 implies people will never grow tired of the pleasures and delights.

Jahannam

'Oh humanity – your sins are against your soul. It is an enjoyment of the life of the present … we will show you the truth of what you did.' *Surah 10:23*

What kind of place is Jahannam (hell)?

- It is a fire seventy times hotter than any flame on earth.
- People will wail in misery.
- Boiling water will be poured over their heads, they will experience pain everywhere, be dragged in chains, have black smoke in their eyes.
- Anyone trying to climb out is pushed back in.

What is done to get there?

- Live a wicked life full of evil.
- Reject the teachings of the Qur'an.
- Make excuses and not take responsibility; try to blame others for your own sins.

What is the fire pit like?

For the worst, fire will burn off their skin but it will be replaced to repeatedly suffer in this way. For the least of the sinners, their boots will be filled with fire but it feels like their brains are boiling. There are seven levels of Jahannam. Some will be left there for a set time, others forever. There will be different punishments for each kind of sin, for example, those who did not pray will have their heads smashed against boulders, people who gossiped will have their lips cut off, arrogant people will be reduced to the size of an ant.

Task

Explain how belief in paradise and hell could influence the life of a Muslim.

Testing your knowledge

One-mark Questions

Multiple-choice question

For the one-mark multiple-choice question, you must choose the correct answer from the four you are offered.

Focusing on the first section of Islam, on beliefs that you have now studied, try the following:

1 What is meant by 'tawhid'?

A Declaration of Faith B life after death
C Oneness of Allah D prophethood

2 What is Shari'ah?

A a chapter of the Qur'an B a prophet
C Islamic law D prayer

3 Who were the Zabur (Psalms) written by?

A David B Ibrahim
C Jesus D Moses

4 What are angels made of?

A clay B elements of light
C fire D gold

5 Who was asked by Allah to sacrifice his son?

A Adam B Ibrahim
C Moses D Noah

Make up four answers to each of the following and test your partner. Do not forget: only ONE can be correct!

1 Which of these is not one of the six articles of faith?
2 What is the name of the place where Muhammad ﷺ received the Qur'an?
3 Name the angel who will blow the trumpet at the end of the world.
4 What is meant by al-Qadr?
5 What is the imamate?

Short response question

The one-mark short response question is asking you to write a brief response.

You will have to name or give an example of a belief, practice, key term or religious concept.

You may also be asked for a brief definition.

Don't waste time writing too much but make sure to write enough to fully answer the question. Don't leave the examiner guessing at what you mean, or how what you have written does answer the question. Don't be vague!

1 Give one Muslim belief about 'akhirah'.

2 Name one of the prophets of Islam.

3 Give one reason why the Qur'an is important to Muslims.

4 Name one of the books of authority for Islam.

5 Give one of the roles of angels in Islam.

Make up three one-mark short response questions to test your partner.

Influence Questions

Short response question

These questions are where you show your understanding of the religion you have studied, and how a person's beliefs have an influence on their lives. It is clear that when people believe things, their thoughts, words and actions become shaped by their beliefs – these questions want you to show that. They might look a bit scary at first, but if you get used to them, they become quite straightforward.

You will have to answer one of these questions in each of the beliefs sections of your chosen two religions. They are always worth four marks, and always ask you to explain two ways.

The wording will always begin: 'Explain two ways in which ...'

Followed by one of these, or something similar:

- 'belief in/about ...'
- 'learning about ...'

Finishing off with: 'influences Muslims today'.

Here are some examples for you to see how that works (and to try):

1 Explain two ways in which belief in the afterlife influences Muslims today.

2 Explain two ways in which beliefs about Allah being just (adalat) might influence Muslims today.

3 Explain two ways in which believing in risalah (prophethood) influences Muslims today.

Go back through your answers to these three questions. Using AQA's mark scheme, how could you improve them?

Look at the following answers. Which do you think is better, and why? Think about how clear the answer is, how detailed it is and whether you can clearly see the influence or effect on the believer.

Explain two ways in which believing in risalah (prophethood) influences Muslims today.

Answer 1

One way that believing in risalah influences Muslims today is that they think they should follow the teachings of the prophets, especially Prophet Muhammad ﷺ. Another way is that they think they should read their books, like the Sunnah, and do as they did.

Answer 2

Muslims believe that risalah is Allah's way to communicate His message (what He wants them to do) to human beings. By following the teachings in the holy books, and by following the examples of the prophets, they can do as Allah wants them to. This means they will please Allah, and be rewarded in heaven.

Answer 1: This gives two good ways, however, it doesn't explain either way. You could improve this for them by explaining their ideas.

Answer 2: This gives one way only, but does it in a lot of detail. You could improve this answer by adding a second way which you explain.

Explaining Beliefs and Teachings

Six-mark questions

These questions ask you to explain two beliefs and/or teachings from the religion.

The wording will always begin: 'Explain two Muslim teachings about ...'

Finishing off with: 'Refer to sacred writings or another source of Muslim belief and teaching in your answer.

They will be marked against AQA's mark scheme which can be found on the AQA website.

From the question wording and the mark scheme you can work out how to answer the question effectively. Each question is different, but in this case you would:

- choose your two teachings and then explain each one
- develop your explanations fully
- use a relevant quotation/teaching, show how it links to the question and include its source of authority. This is who or where the quote/teaching comes from, for example holy book (Qur'an), Prophet Muhammad ﷺ etc.

Remember this is just one example to help you practice. In the exam, you will need to think carefully and respond to the actual question you are given.

What does 'fully develop' mean?

When students in RS explain something, it is quite often the case that they just write a sentence in explanation. While correct, that is a 'simple explanation'. For these questions, you have to 'fully develop' your explanation, i.e. give more detail about each point you make. Below is an example. The explanation and further development are highlighted so that you can see them clearly.

Explain two Muslim teachings about paradise. Refer to sacred writings or another source of Muslim belief and teaching in your answer.

Sample answer

In the Qur'an[1], it says that Muslims will go to paradise – 'Enter among my servants! Enter My Paradise' (89:27)[2]. This means that those people who become Muslims, and follow the teachings of Allah will go to paradise[3]. They will have to have lived as a good Muslim, for example, following Muhammad's ﷺ example closely to be able to go to paradise[4].

Looking at the sample answer:

1 it opens by saying where the belief comes from, i.e. the source of authority, here the Qur'an;

2 it gives a quote about who can enter paradise;

3 it explains the relevance of the quote by saying that a person who follows the teachings of Allah counts as a Muslim;

4 it extends the point by saying that Prophet Muhammad ﷺ is a good example to copy.

Of course, the answer needs a second teaching about paradise, written in the same way to ensure the best response.

Practise the following questions for yourself:

1 Explain two Muslim teachings about the creation. Refer to sacred writings or another source of Muslim belief and teaching in your answer.

2 Explain two Muslim teachings about the imamate in Shi'a Islam. Refer to sacred writings or another source of Muslim belief and teaching in your answer.

3 Explain two Muslim teachings about the Qur'an. Refer to sacred writings or another source of Muslim belief and teaching in your answer.

Analyse and Evaluate

For GCSE RS you have to be able to show you can react to a given statement. This means that you consider what the statement says, present arguments to agree and disagree and come to a conclusion of what you yourself think of the statement. You also have to demonstrate what a Muslim would say and what arguments they would use. In the religious section of the paper it will be impossible not to include religious ideas so do not worry too much about this. This type of question takes the most thinking. In fact, together these questions will be worth 50 per cent of your exam, so it is essential you practise them.

It is always a good idea to work to a formula when you answer this type of question. This structures your answer which makes it clear and also makes sure you meet all the necessary criteria to give a full answer. Here is one formula you might consider using:

DREARER × 3 = C

D = Disagree
R = Reason to disagree
E = in-depth Explanation of that reason
A = Agree
R = Reason to agree
E = in-depth Explanation of that reason

It is good to try to include at least three reasons on each side.

R = Make sure you have used a number of Religious arguments, not just secular ones.

C = Conclusion – This is where you evaluate the strengths and weaknesses of the different points of view.

1 **For a Muslim, believing that Allah is all-powerful is not important.**

Evaluate this statement. You should:

- refer to Muslim teaching
- give reasoned arguments to support this statement
- give reasoned arguments to support a different point of view
- reach a justified conclusion.

2 **Muslims should be more concerned with this life than the next.**

Evaluate this statement. You should:

- refer to Muslim teaching
- give reasoned arguments to support this statement
- give reasoned arguments to support a different point of view
- reach a justified conclusion.

3 **The Sunnah is more important than the Qur'an as a guide to life for Muslims today.**

Evaluate this statement. You should:

- refer to Muslim teaching
- give reasoned arguments to support this statement
- give reasoned arguments to support a different point of view
- reach a justified conclusion.

4 **The Muslim idea of paradise is just wishful thinking.**

Evaluate this statement. You should:

- refer to Muslim teaching
- give reasoned arguments to support this statement
- give reasoned arguments to support a different point of view
- reach a justified conclusion.

The more practice you get at this type of question the better, as you need to be able to give different points of view. The point of these questions is to challenge your application of knowledge, and to make you show your skills in analysis and evaluation. Your conclusion is only valuable if it gives a different viewpoint to what you have already written.

For more practice, go back and redo evaluation questions using this formula.

2.2 Practices

The Five Pillars of Islam

As you can see from the diagram, there are five key practices or duties for Muslims: Shahadah, salah, zakah, sawm and hajj. Both Sunni and Shi'a keep these, though Shi'a have them as part of the Ten Obligations (see page 134). We will look at each in turn.

Shahadah

Shahadah is the Muslim declaration of faith:

> I declare that there is no God but Allah
>
> And Muhammad ﷺ is His messenger
>
> I bear witness that Ali is the beloved of Allah and the rightful trustee
>
> Of the Prophet, and his immediate successor.

The third and fourth statements above are added by only the Shi'as. They sum up the basic beliefs of Islam. The first statement is the declaration that Muslims reject anything but Allah as their focus of belief. They totally surrender to the will of Allah as found in the Qur'an. The second statement recognises the role of Muhammad ﷺ and that his life was to be an example of all to follow. By following the Sunnah they also believe in risalah (prophethood) and akhirah (life after death).

Every Muslim knows the words of the Shahadah in Arabic, but not all can translate a meaning. The words are whispered into the ears of a newborn baby; they are a section of the **Adhan** (call to prayer), heard five times every day; they are repeated each night before sleep and Muhammad ﷺ suggested they should be the last words a person utters before death. They are words from the heart. Many people can pray or fast, for example, but still fail as Muslims because these words do not come from their heart.

As the first of the Pillars or the central one, many think Shahadah must be the most important.

All the Pillars have to be equal or the roof would not fit. At the same time without this belief, the other Pillars would not happen, so Shahadah has to be first or central Pillar. However, it is important to treat all five as important or else the metaphorical building would collapse. With this belief as a start point, the practices then flow, as does a Muslim way of life. Setting a good example encourages others to become Muslims. Muslims must live in a way so as to be able to return to Allah and Shahadah is key to this aim. People who fully follow the Shahadah are called 'Ibad Allah' (servants of Allah).

Task

Think about something you believe in. How does this affect your everyday life? Discuss your belief with a partner. How might belief in Shahadah affect a Muslim? Compare answers to each of these. List the similarities/differences.

Salah – the preparation for salah (prayer)

The call to prayer – the Adhan.

Allah is the Greatest (×4)

I declare that there is no God but Allah (×2)

I declare that Muhammad ﷺ is the Messenger of Allah (×2)

(I testify that Ali is the wali (close friend) of God – said by some Shi'a groups at this point)

Come to prayer (×2)

Come to success (×2)

(Come to the best of actions – said twice by Shi'a Muslims)

Allah is the Greatest (×2)

There is no God but Allah (said twice by Shi'a Muslims)

These words are spoken by the **mu'adhin** (caller to prayer) by loudspeakers so that people will not miss prayer. *Can you see the reasons why prayer is good for Muslims?*

Once these words are heard men will make their way to the mosque. Some women do as well, but they pray separately from the men. Most women will pray at home. *What do you think about this? Is it fair? Is this discrimination? What good reasons are there for this?*

Salah is a prescribed duty that has to be performed at the given time by the Qur'an (4:103)

The Basics

Use pages 115–116 to answer these questions.

1 Explain how Muslims get ready for prayer.

2 Explain why they do each of these things, showing their importance.

It is tradition in most Eastern countries that shoes are taken off before entering a house. As the mosque is the House of Allah shoes are removed; symbolising respect, but also practically, to keep the place clean.

Wuzu is the washing process designed to purify the mind and body for prayer. Muhammad ﷺ said the key to salah is cleanliness. Sins are said to be forgiven also. The niyyah (intention) is made clearing the mind, then the wash begins: right hand/left hand three times each; the mouth then nose three times each; water over the face; right and left arm up to elbow three times; wet hands are run over the head to the back of the neck; the ears follow; and finally both feet washed up to the ankle. There are many clips on the internet to show you this process but for now: *Why do you think these parts of the body are cleansed?*

Salah – the preparation for salah (prayer)

The body must be covered to retain modesty. All must cover their heads; men with a **topi** or prayer hat, women with a **hijab** or scarf. This shows that Allah only looks at the concerns of the heart, not appearance.

Men make their way to the prayer hall (or women to the women's area) and stand shoulder to shoulder facing the Ka'aba, the House of God, in Makkah. Everyone is equal, no special place is reserved. All Muslims throughout the world do the same so it unites them in brotherhood (**ummah**).

The Iqamah (second call to prayer) signals the intention to start to pray. Muslims should have now blocked worldly issues out, are purified physically and have total focus on Allah.

Task

Think about each stage of salah – what do you think goes through a Muslim's mind at each point? How do you think this process affects their daily lives?

The Basics

1. Describe how Muslims carry out prayer.
2. Explain the differences between Sunni and Shi'a prayer, and why they may have occurred.
3. **Preparation for prayer is as important as the prayer itself.** What do you think?

All Muslims say five prayers a day. Each time of prayer involves a set sequence of movements and words known as rak'ah (see page 117). Each sequence has key actions that must be done.

Sunni	Sunni Rak'ahs	Shi'a	Shi'a Rak'ahs
Fajr – dawn	2	Fajr	2
Zuhr – afternoon	4	Zuhr and Asr together	4 + 4 = 8
Asr – late afternoon	4		
Maghrib – dusk	3	Maghrib and Isha together	3 + 4 = 7
Isha – night	4		
Sunni Muslims pray five prayers, each at different times	17 sequences of prayer throughout the day	Shi'a Muslims pray five prayers, but at three different times	17 sequences of prayer throughout the day

Salah – rak'ah and recitations

1

Takbir –
Muslims raise their hands to their ears and say: 'Allahu Akbar' (God is supreme)

2

Qiyam – Standing, Muslims recite Surah Al-Fatiha (the first Surah):

'In the name of Allah, the compassionate ...' *(Surah 1:1–7)*

then they choose a Surah, such as **Surah Al-Ikhlas**:

'He is God, the One; He is eternal Absolute, none is born of Him,

And neither is He born. There is none like unto Him.'

3

After repeating Allahu Akbar again, Muslims bow to the waist saying:

'Glory be to my Great Lord, and praise be to Him.'

4

After declaring Allahu Akbar again, Muslims sink to their knees (sujud) saying:

'Glory be to my Lord, the Most Supreme. Allah is Greater than all else.' They kneel again and then sujud is repeated saying: 'All praise be to my Lord the Most High.'

5

Finally 'Allahu Akbar' is said and Muslims then stand. The next rak'ah begins. At the end of the second rak'ah, after sujud, Muslims sit in a kneeling position and say the first part of the Tashahhud prayer 'All purity; prayer and goodness belong to Allah. Peace be upon you Prophet Muhammad ﷺ, and Allah's mercy and blessings. Peace be upon all righteous servants of Allah.' If the prayer is longer than two rak'ahs, after the sujud the second part is said: 'I declare that there is nothing more worthy of my allegiance than Allah. He is the One with no partners, and I declare that Muhammad ﷺ is His Messenger.' Muslims then turn heads to the right and left to acknowledge other worshippers and their guardian angels.

There are some differences. Shi'a Muslims do not cross their hands whilst standing in qiyam, but have them by their side; they touch their forehead to a wooden block or clay tablet from Karbala (a holy city for Shi'a) rather than the floor when prostrating (sujud); and they position their feet differently during salah (Shi'a Muslims fold both their feet behind them in the sitting position, Sunni often bend the right foot and rest it on their toes).

Why is it important for Muslims to pray?

Some people might think that having to pray five times a day and offer du'a (private) prayers as well seems a little excessive. Some may say it is repetitive. Some might think it would lose its meaning. Some would say surely there are better things to be doing to show faith, like helping others? Some might ask 'Does Allah need all these prayers?' Work with a partner to try to find answers to these questions from a Muslim perspective. What could you say to agree or disagree with any of these ideas?

Why pray?

Surah 96:19 says to *'Prostrate and draw near to Allah.'* Muslims believe a person is closest to Allah when praying. Five prayers were instructed by Allah, so whoever does them will be admitted into paradise. It is believed that prayer brings knowledge, because by praying sincerely a person's heart is opened to Allah and helps them become more aware of Allah, and so more faithful. Muhammad ﷺ considered anyone not praying five times a day to not be a good Muslim or counted as an unbeliever. People who pray properly will benefit on Judgement Day.

Why pray so often?

Prayer is spread throughout the day so that Allah is the focus of a Muslim's mind all the time. From waking to the evening, a Muslim is either going to prayer or returning from it. They should have said sorry for their actions, and be mindful of Allah, and their dependency on Him. Muslims are taught that this life is very hard, almost impossible without Allah and so their prayer gives them support. If they did not pray throughout the day their sins would build up, they could be tempted by Shaytan (the Devil) and be overcome by bad emotions such as arrogance, immodesty and pride. If prayers are accepted, then all other actions will be too. Prayer at the mosque is congregational (with others), and Muslims believe the rewards are far (27 times) greater than from praying alone, so Muslims try to attend mosque as often as possible.

What actual benefits do Muslims gain from prayer?

Prayer with others in the atmosphere of the mosque is a reminder of the greatness of Allah (and the insignificance of humans). It also reminds Muslims that everything comes from and belongs to Allah. It encourages positive and respectful behaviour, as it reminds Muslims of good qualities such as modesty, humility, kindness and peace. The process to prepare for prayer reminds Muslims of cleanliness, purity and determination. Standing with others reminds Muslims of the need to work with others as a community and the equality of all. So the benefits are to the character of a person, and eventually to their judgement in the afterlife.

The Basics

1. Discuss the questions at the beginning of the page. How do you respond now?
2. What do you think are the three most important reasons for prayer? Explain why.
3. Explain fully how prayer might affect the lives of Muslims in a positive way.
4. **Prayer is not important.** Give reasoned arguments for and against this statement.

Jumu'ah prayer (Friday prayer)

Salat al-Jumu'ah are the congregational prayers at the mosque on a Friday. They are the most important prayer in the week and last the longest. They take place just after noon when the first adhan is said. Men are expected to go to the mosque. To miss four Fridays would make a person like an unbeliever. Muslims should first perform wuzu for purity. Many offer du'a and/or read the Qur'an as they wait for the **khatib** to deliver the sermon (**khutbah**). A second adhan is then spoken to bring silence when the khatib is seated in the **minbar** (raised platform). This is the only day that a sermon is delivered, so is the only day the congregation are being given direct spiritual guidance in the mosque. The khatib then stands and gives the khutbah in two parts. Firstly, he speaks in the language of the community, perhaps about local world issues, giving the congregation guidance and Islamic teachings. He is trying to show how Muslims should respond to these issues in a way true to the faith. There is then a brief pause before the second sermon starts, which is done in Arabic and is a set speech. Following this the Iqamah is read and then the imam (the khatib) leads the two rak'ahs of compulsory prayer. Many Muslims do Sunnah salah (these are extra prayers that Muhammad ﷺ did), four rak'ahs by themselves before the two Fardh (compulsory behind the imam) and two after. This prayer is the best attended of the week, and in Muslim countries it is common to see Muslims praying outside the mosque which is actually full.

Prayer at home

Women mostly do their prayers at home. They carry them out in the same way as men, using a prayer mat and facing Makkah. Women are required to pray just as much as men and get just as much reward for doing so. Prayers are also said before mealtimes to thank Allah for the blessings of food, as a family to break fasts on each day of Ramadan and on special occasions like Eid. Personal prayers (du'as) are done at home to talk to Allah on a more personal level, maybe to ask for mercy or help for others. As these are not set they do not require rak'ahs.

Prophet Muhammad ﷺ also prayed at night. Prayers called Tahajjud are performed by some showing real discipline. These are not a one-off, they are done regularly.

The Basics

1 Explain what happens at Friday prayer.
2 Explain why it is important to have Friday prayer.
3 Describe prayer in the home for Muslims. Do you think it is important?
4 **Jumu'ah prayer is no more important than prayers on other days.** What do you think about this statement? Explain differing opinions on this.

Sawm – fasting during Ramadan

> 'Oh believers! Fasting is prescribed for you as it was for those before you that you may learn self-restraint.' *(Qur'an 2:183)*

> 'Ramadan is the month in which the Qur'an was sent down as a guide to humanity; and to provide clear guidance and judgement. So everyone who is present during that month should spend it fasting.' *(Qur'an 2:185)*

Ramadan is the ninth month of the Muslim calendar. It was in this month that the Night of Power took place. *(Read Surah 96:1–5 to check what happened).* The Call of Muhammad ﷺ (page 94) also gives you the account of what happened. During the month of Ramadan, Muslims do not consume any food or drink between sunrise and sunset.

Fasting links to the spiritual side of religion throughout history, as it symbolises that craving and desires have to be overcome. There is no bigger craving than food. Prophets before Muhammad ﷺ told their people to fast. Successful fasting is about mind over matter; the spiritual over the material. It is made more difficult because as soon as we say we are not going to have something, the craving gets worse and we often want it more!

A month is a significant period of time and fasting for a month is a way of retraining minds and bodies to focus on the important things in life. In today's world, proper practice of religion is often fitted in around busy lifestyles, whereas Islam believes that religion should be at the forefront.

Ramadan gives Muslims a chance to redress their lives, be better Muslims in all aspects of life and then hopefully continue this for the rest of the year. However, humans are vulnerable and it is easy to slip off the correct path, so Muslims are reminded every year in Ramadan. It is as if sawm is designed to keep putting people back on the right path. Muslims must also remember that some people in the world will never have any of the things they can give up, so they should appreciate what Allah has given them. Ramadan is hard for Muslims especially in hot weather and long daylight hours. It falls eleven days earlier each year, as the Muslim calendar is based on a lunar system. In summer a Muslim needs to be very determined so that they do not give in. Allah sees all and knows our intentions. Fasting is important for all Muslims because of the self-discipline they can gain, and it is said to be a shield against the fires of hell, which is another good reason if you believe in Islam.

Tasks

Research Ramadan to prepare for the next lesson. What exactly does fasting require? Why is it done? Do you think it is a good idea?

Thinking questions

1. **If Muslims lived their lives according to Allah's will, there would be no need for Ramadan.** Why might someone believe this to be true? Explain your ideas. Can you think of any arguments against it? Explain them.
2. **Fasting during Ramadan makes people kinder to those living in poverty.** Why might someone believe this to be true? Explain your ideas. Can you think of any arguments against it? Explain them.

Sawm – what are the duties of fasting?

Fasting for most people is simply about not eating; in Islam the idea is much more than that. Yes, they give up eating and drinking from dawn to dusk so that they never forget that some of the ummah in the world live like this all the time. However, they should also refrain from sexual relations during these hours. They should consider their behaviour towards others, making it always friendly and helpful. They should spend time in the mosque praying and it is recommended that they read the whole of the Qur'an. Time should not be wasted on the material things in life; it should be purposely used. Watching TV, playing video games and idle chat can all be considered wasted time as they serve no real purpose in life and are often done thoughtlessly.

Days are lived as normal, so Ramadan should not be used as an excuse to avoid things that Muslims know they should do but do not really want to. This would in fact break the fast because the intention is incorrect. Muslims get up early and eat before the Fajr prayer and then at dusk they eat iftar, which is usually something sweet like dates, before going to maghrib prayer. After this Muslims will eat dinner before spending the evening reading the Qur'an or praying du'as. Often there are later prayers in the mosque called tarawih prayers with twenty rak'ahs behind the imam. On one of the last ten nights of Ramadan, Lailat-ul-Qadr happens. Muslims stay all night in the mosques to remember the first revelation of the Qur'an. Surah 97 indicates that keeping this night is greater than one thousand months of worship.

Who is exempt from fasting and why?

- The young (under 12) and older people do not fast, as they need additional nourishment.
- People who are sick and pregnant women do not fast, as both need food and possible medications for health reasons.
- Travellers and women who are menstruating do not fast, but they can make up for missed days later.

Benefits of fasting

- It brings Muslims closer to Allah.
- They rediscover religion as the focus of their lives.
- It is the month of forgiveness. Muhammad ﷺ said all sins are forgiven for those who fast.
- It serves as a reminder of the plight of the poor; zakah (welfare tax) is given in Ramadan.
- It builds personal qualities like self-determination, piety, humility and courage.

Tasks

1 Design an information leaflet for Ramadan, which would help a younger student understand what it is, how it is done and why it is important.

2 Discuss in groups: **Ramadan makes Muslims better people.** Think about reasons to agree and disagree. Find ways to explain these reasons.

Zakah

What is zakah?

It is the giving of alms in order to cleanse or make pure.

> 'Be steadfast in prayer and giving.' *(2:110)*

This is a directive from the Qur'an to pay zakah and for those who do not it says:

> 'And those who hoard gold and silver and spend it not in the way of Allah – give them tidings of a painful punishment. The Day when it will be heated in the fire of Hell and seared therewith will be their foreheads, their flanks, and their backs, [it will be said], this is what you hoarded for yourselves, so taste what you used to hoard' *(9:34–35)*.

Muslims are expected to be kind, compassionate and help others. After all, their wealth is on loan from Allah. Muslims are encouraged to give to charity as the need arises. This is called sadaqah. Whilst sadaqah is voluntary giving, zakah as one of the Five Pillars is compulsory giving. It is a payment given once a year of 2.5 per cent paid on income and savings. It is given by any adult Muslim who has paid all debts and expenses, and has over a certain amount left over (it differs depending on what valuables and cash are being considered). The actual percentage varies depending on what a person owns; their wealth may be in animals, properties, businesses, and so on. It is not a tax, as it is only paid by those who can afford it. You could do some research to find out about the nisab.

Dangers with zakah

Some people give reluctantly or give as little as they can; it is seen as ungrateful to not want to pay as you have the benefit of these blessings. However, since no one records what is given, and the giving is secret, only Allah knows what a person gives, and only Allah can deal with that. Read the quotes at the top of the page. What do they tell us about non-payment?

How is it given?

In Muslim majority countries, zakah is paid to the government, which then distributes it to those who need it. In non-Muslim countries it is either collected by the mosques during Ramadan, or given directly to specific organisations or individuals. The first use should be locally to benefit the Islamic community. It is given anonymously so that the money remains pure and so there is no pride or arrogance or smugness in the amount given. Below are some of the causes it can be used for.

Those who receive zakah should not be made to feel embarrassed. No one actually owns anything, so in fact people are receiving a blessing from what is Allah's anyway. If a person is poor, that is the test that Allah has given them and so to receive from the rich is the will of Allah. Everyone has a different test. The rich have a duty to help, and someone who accepts zakah is helping others fulfil their duty of giving. Zakah should be paid with good grace, not grudgingly. To help one another is to help Allah.

Zakah – the benefits of giving

The purpose of giving zakah is to cleanse or to purify; giving zakah makes a person's remaining money clean and unsullied. By paying it Muslims share their blessings from Allah with others and at the same time reduce chances of their own greed. Money is for the welfare of the people of the ummah (community of Muslims); giver and receiver. The Qur'an says that Muslims will be given back 'a hundred fold' rewards in the afterlife and they do not need to fear Judgement Day. Zakah is a test, but the benefits are great. Muslims say that anyone who gives will feel love in their heart for others, get the satisfaction which comes with helping others, and know that by helping others they have strengthened the ummah.

For those individuals who receive zakah it can practically improve their lives, for example, by providing decent food for a period of time. Imam Ali said that if all people paid their zakah then there would be no more poor people. On a community level zakah can support the community in its religious practice, but can also be used to spread it further.

All Muslims are expected to pay zakah, but from the Shi'a perspective the kinds of things that it is payable on are outdated, for example: wheat, barley, dates, raisins, camels and sheep, none of which fits modern life in the developed world. They recognise that lifestyles have changed and money is made differently, so use the idea of khums. This is tax set at 20 per cent of any yearly surplus (money after all expenses and bills paid). Check forward to page 136, it is worth noting Imam Ali's words. He said that if sadaqah, zakah and khums were all paid in full, people's lives would be more equitable. This is probably true of the wider community across all religions; if we all gave what we could, poverty and inequality could be solved.

To cleanse and purify

Shares Allah's blessings

Money for welfare

Brings love to the heart

Improves lives

Tasks

1 Think about these statements:
'The rich should help the poor.'
'People who give to others are richer than those who do not.'
'The poor can become too reliant on the money of the rich.'
'The poor should help themselves.'
'Zakah should be used to help the needy, not to develop the religion.'
'The benefits for the giver are greater than for the receiver.'
In groups discuss your responses and feedback as a class.

2 **For a Muslim the greatest act is to give zakah.** Explore this statement from different points of view, explaining any points you make. Refer to Islam in your answer.

Hajj – pilgrimage to Makkah

Hajj is pilgrimage to Makkah. It takes place in the last month of the Muslim calendar (Dhu al-Hijjah). All Muslims should go at least once in their lifetime, or every time they can afford it.

1 **Ihram** – Muslims dress in two pieces of white cloth (ihram), one around the waist, the other over the shoulder. Women also wear white (though this is optional). All Muslims stand equal before Allah and dressing so simply shows that. Muslims bathe, put on ihram clothing, pray two rak'ahs and recite the Talbiyah Du'a: 'Here I am O God, here I am …'

2 Muslims then go to the Great Mosque in Makkah to perform 'Tawaf' (seven times circling of the Ka'aba anticlockwise). The Ka'aba is covered with a black cloth (**Al-Kiswah**). They say: 'At your command Lord, at your command.' Muslims raise their hands towards the black stone. If close enough they touch it.

3 Muslims then drink water from the Zamzam well, take some home and dip their garments in it to be used at their burial.

4 Al-Safa and Al-Marwa – two small hills joined by a walkway. Muslims walk between them seven times, an activity called 'sa'y'. There is a section in the walkway for older people and people with disabilities.

5 Mount Arafat is the Mount of Mercy. Muslims perform 'Wuquf' here. They stand from noon to sunset meditating, praying and asking for forgiveness. In the evening they listen to a sermon from the top of Arafat and spend the night in the open thankful for forgiveness from Allah.

6 Muslims move to Muzdalifah (to camp with two million other Muslims). They collect pebbles here for the next day; seven are needed to hit each of the three jamarat (stone pillars).

7 At Mina, Muslims throw pebbles at the three jamarat which represent Shaytan. A sacrifice is also made here called **Qurbani**. Men also shave their heads and women cut a lock of hair.

8 Eid ul Adha is celebrated here. It is a serious rather than celebratory festival. Sheep and goats are sacrificed as Ibrahim did, the meat being distributed to the poor.

9 Some Muslims take the option to travel to Madinah at this point to visit the Prophet's Mosque and burial place.

10 The journey is completed by returning to Makkah, carrying out Tawaf and sa'y again. After every Tawaf they perform two rak'ahs. There is then a farewell Tawaf before leaving.

For many Muslims this is a once in a lifetime journey. When they are in the House of Allah they believe they are as close to Allah as they can be whilst still on earth. It is a very emotional time. Today, many more Muslims can afford to travel to Makkah, and some stay in nearby hotels for the duration of the hajj.

The Basics

1 Describe the key events of the hajj.
2 Research to find out why each activity within the hajj is carried out.
3 What might prevent a Muslim going on hajj?

What is the significance of the places visited on the hajj journey?

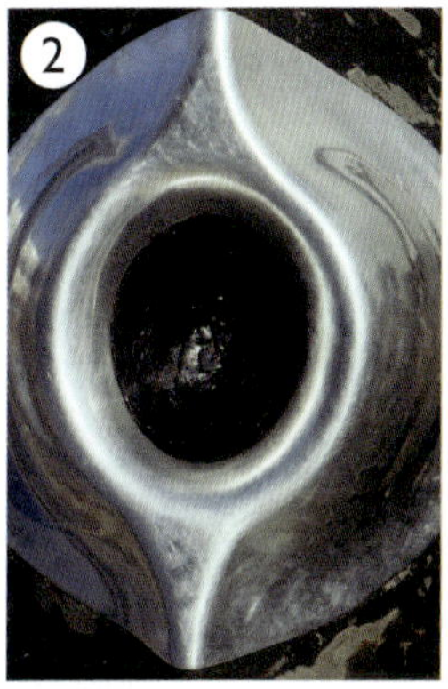

The *Ka'aba* (1) is known as the Baitullah (the House of Allah). For Muslims it is the oldest shrine to Allah on earth. It was built by Prophet Adam, rebuilt by Nuh (Noah to Christians) after the flood, and then again by Ibrahim and his son Ismail. Each year this cube-shaped building is covered by a new black cloth, embroidered in gold. It gives the direction and focus for salah for Muslims all over the world every day.

When Muhammad ﷺ captured Makkah he smashed the idols, setting it up as a place for the worship of the One God – Allah. Muslims re-enact Muhammad ﷺ circling the Ka'aba. Many Muslims are overwhelmed when they experience the Ka'aba; they know it is a once in a lifetime experience. The circling shows a Muslim's devotion to Allah.

The *black stone* (2) existed before Muhammad ﷺ, being referenced by the writer Maximus in the second century BCE. Tradition varyingly suggests it was brought to Adam from paradise by Jibril, or that it was given to Nuh after the flood, or that is was dug out of the earth by Ismail on the instructions of Jibril. Whatever the source, Muslims believe it came from heaven to earth as a gift from Allah.

Zamzam (3) – Ibrahim escorted his second wife from Jerusalem to Arabia, so she could settle there. After a while Hajar and their son Ismail ran out of water. She ran frantically searching for water for her dying son. A spring came up out of the sand where Ismail lay. Muslims believe this water has life-giving qualities. Muhammad ﷺ said it was a cure for whatever it was taken for. For Muslims today it demonstrates that humans are dependent upon Allah. That water is vital for actual life, so Allah is vital to spiritual life. Allah provides for all needs.

Al-Safa and Al-Marwa (4) – this is associated with the same story. As Ismail lay dying, Hajar's solution was not just to give up on her son; she searched and searched for water. As a reward Allah produced the Zamzam well. In life today Muslims are presented with many difficulties, it is their test. By re-enacting Hajar's search with the run between the two hills Muslims are saying that they will not give up when their lives are difficult.

If Muslims complete just these stages it is known as umrah (the lesser pilgrimage). For those completing hajj, there is a short break at this point.

The Basics

1 Explain the significance for Muslims today of each of the four places they visit on this part of hajj.
2 **As long as a Muslim visits Makkah, they have shown enough devotion to their faith.** What do you think about this statement? Do you agree or disagree? Explain your points.

The significance of the other places visited to complete hajj

Mount Arafat (5) – the Mount of Mercy is believed to be the place where Adam and Hawwa were reunited after being sent to earth from paradise. Muhammad ﷺ also gave his final sermon there. Muslims spend time here praying for mercy, as it is here where their own sins can be forgiven, and they believe that with sincere requests, Allah will forgive. They offer prayers and are often moved to tears when they realise the amount of sin they have to admit to. They walk away feeling they have been given a second chance and many change their lives completely.

Muzdalifah (6) is where Muslims collect pebbles for the next day. How many does vary. Seven pebbles are needed to hit one Jamarat the next day. For the next two days they hit each of the three pillars with seven pebbles again (totalling 49). Some Shi'a texts say 70 are needed. They also need to prepare their minds for their own battle with Shaytan. Muslims often gather together here to read the Qur'an, and pray together with Muslims from all different places, which helps them to appreciate the unity of Islam.

The three pillars (Jamarat) (7) at Mina represent three places where Shaytan tried to persuade Ibrahim not to sacrifice his son. At all three Jamarat, Jibril told Ibrahim to 'Pelt him', so Ibrahim threw seven pebbles and Shaytan left. The three Jamarat represent Ibrahim rejecting Shaytan and also Hajar refusing to stop searching for water, and Ismail volunteering to be sacrificed (thus also rejecting Shaytan). Muslims reflect on their own lives, hoping that whatever Allah asks of them they will be able to do. They pray the test will never be as hard as Ibrahim's.

Madinah (8) is the sacred city that was the first to welcome Muhammad ﷺ. It had the first mosque and the first structured Islamic community. Muhammad ﷺ loved Madinah and returned there to die after conquering Makkah. The Prophet's Mosque is there today over his original burial site along with the burial sites of the first two caliphs, Abu Bakr and Umar. In its south-east corner is incorporated the original house of Aisha, Prophet Muhammad's ﷺ wife. In the mosque there is an area which stretches from his burial tomb to his minbar called the 'Gardens of Paradise'. Muslims believe that no prayer said there will ever be rejected. There is also a grave for Isa (Jesus) with the idea that he will come again to earth and be buried here.

The Basics

1. Explain the significance for Muslims today of each of the places they visit to complete hajj.
2. **Standing on Mount Arafat is the most important part of hajj.** What do you think about this statement? Do you agree or disagree? Explain your points.

How does the hajj journey influence the lives of Muslims today?

On the journey

In Makkah I felt like a member of something really special. The whole unity and equality thing was humbling. We didn't connect with people for who they were or what they wore; they were just fellow Muslims from all over the world, all doing the same thing from their hearts. You can never feel this in normal society. To see the Ka'aba was more beautiful than I had imagined, very emotional actually. Praying seemed more real as I didn't have to imagine the Ka'aba … I could see it, felt so close to Allah and the words meant more. Imagining history, Muhammad ﷺ showing his love of Allah and I was doing the same as I did Tawaf. I realised that from now on prayer would be far more of a highlight in my daily life. Doing the sa'y taught me that I should only really be running around for the essentials in life and that essential was Allah. Material stuff had no real significance. On the stand at Mount Arafat, I thought about many things: how many things I did wrong, people I had hurt, not intentionally but I had; how my thoughts and actions weren't right. It was quite sobering to get my head around it all. I felt a weight off my shoulders and was determined not to put it all back on!! Allah had forgiven me so I need to make the most of it. Temptation … well we all fall into it as Shaytan is around us … but I have made a conscious decision to not always take the easy path as that is usually the wrong one! Hajj changed me for the better, but I need to keep that in mind and not slip back to old ways.

On returning home

I am from a village just outside Cairo. My village saved up for me to go on hajj. No one else will go for a long time as we are poor farmers. On returning my house had been painted outside with the Ka'aba and I was treated with total respect. I was looked upon as someone to advise others – I had kind of become a village religious elder. I had had the religious experience of hajj and therefore people saw me as more spiritual and expected me to understand more about religion. It was a big responsibility, but it also made me try to keep the promises I had made myself on the journey itself. It is easy to be Allah-centred on hajj – just not so easy back in the real world. I felt I had to now though, with the way people were treating me.

Decorations on the house of someone who has been on hajj

The Basics

1. Why might someone go on hajj?
2. How might a person be changed by their experience of hajj?
3. **Going on hajj is always a life-changing experience.** Do you agree? Give explained reasons to agree and disagree with this statement.

The mosque – outside design

The mosque is not on the course specification, however, it is important that you know about it as it underpins many of the other topics. Islam is a religion based around the authority of the Qur'an and the sayings of Muhammad ﷺ, and the Hadith. Community leadership and spiritual leadership come from the mosque; which is the centre of the community. You will already recall that, for example, Muslims must pray five times a day – this happens at the mosque. Of course, even though you will not be asked direct questions about the mosque; you will be able to use the mosque in your answers to other questions.

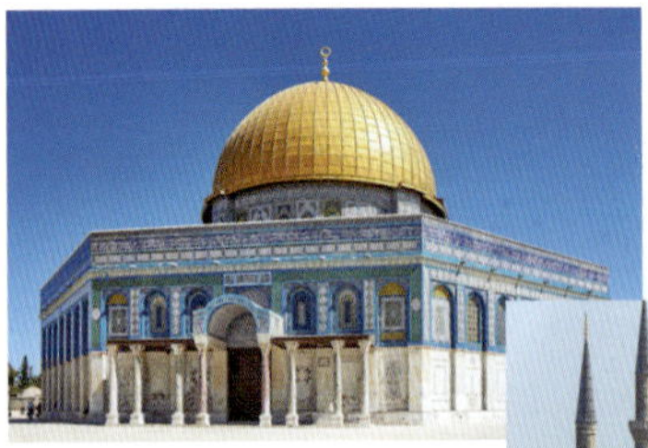

'Whoever builds a masjid (mosque) in which the Name of Allah is mentioned, Allah will build a house for him in Paradise.' *(Hadith 735 Al-Bukhari)*

The word mosque means a 'place of prostration', that is, somewhere to bow down. The first mosques were deliberately very simple in design, so as not to cause distraction. A mosque is usually a physical building, but it does not have to be:

Muhammad ﷺ said: *'Wherever the hour of prayer overtakes you, perform it. That place is a mosque.'*

Many mosques are magnificent in many areas of the world. Being the House of Allah, some Muslims believe that they should reflect his beauty and splendour. The architectural design, with tiled patterns and ornate calligraphy, reflect the nature of Allah. It shows how important the religion is to them, to the wider world. However, many mosques are kept very simple, maybe like a house mosque.

A dome is a semi-circular shape structure on the roof of the mosque. Some have more than one. It can represent the worldwide community of Islam, but also it allows air circulation inside and the voice of the imam to not echo, so he can be heard more clearly.

A **minaret** is a tall tower. Some mosques have several. Their purpose is for the call to prayer to be made. Many today are fixed with loudspeakers so the call can be heard over the city or village. Traditionally the mua'dhin used to climb to the top and call out each prayer time.

The star and crescent is the symbol of Islam usually found on top of the dome. Some say it was the position of the Moon and star when Muhammad ﷺ was first spoken to, whilst others say the Moon is the symbol of the lunar month of the hijrah (Muhammad's ﷺ flight to Makkah). Some say the star is symbolic of a Muslim's belief in Allah as the light in their lives.

Many mosques are open courtyards with great pillars holding up the roof. They are cool, light and airy in hot countries.

The mosque – inside design

Washrooms – Muslims must perform wuzu, so a source of water is required. In modern mosques it can be a tiled washroom, but in others it could be a fountain. Water allows purity of body before standing before Allah. There is a separate wash area for women to use. Washing is crucial as part of getting ready for salah; a Muslim must come before Allah pure, which the washing represents.

Mihrab – This is the semi-circular indented archway in the **Qiblah** Wall in the prayer hall. It shows the direction of the Ka'aba in Makkah. It is symbolic of Allah's presence in the heart of the worshipper. Many are shell-shaped, like a scallop shell, which comes to the surface at night, open, to take in fresh water, symbolising that the heart should be open to receive the Word of Allah in prayer. It is often ornately decorated with texts from the Qur'an or the 99 names of Allah. It reminds the worshipper of the qualities of Allah.

Minbar – This is the only piece of furniture in the prayer hall. It is a set of steps like a pulpit used by the imam for the Friday khutbah. Its size is dependent upon the size of the mosque. Its practical use is so the worshippers can clearly see and hear the speaker. Symbolically it shows the Word of Allah comes down from on high to them and is far greater than they are.

Prayer hall – This is a large open space with the floor separated into rectangles, either in the tiles or the carpet. This denotes a space for each worshipper, in lines with enough room to carry out the prayers. There is no special place for anyone, confirming the equality of all worshipping. There is usually a set of six clocks, five for the times of prayer (remember, these will change as the dawn and dusk times change) and the sixth for Friday Jumu'ah prayers. The mosque has no pictures as, for example, a church might have. This is to avoid distraction and idol worship, but they are still beautiful buildings. Texts from the Qur'an are hand painted in calligraphy text, intricate stonemasonry and coloured tiled mosaics are often used. There is also a women's section either in a divided part of the prayer hall or perhaps upstairs. Qur'ans are available for du'a prayer and study.

Task

Draw a small square in the middle of the page. Make a bigger one around it and three around that. Each section needs to be bigger than the last as there is more to write in each section.
In the middle one write the words describing inside features of a mosque.
Around the next layer write the names of the inside features.
In the next, describe what the feature looks like.
In the next, explain how it is used.
In the next, explain its symbolism or significance to the Five Pillars.

The mosque – what is the building used for?

Worship

Muhammad ﷺ saw the mosque as the centre for all aspects of Muslim life. He saw religion as part of everyday life and therefore used the courtyard mosque as a place for study and teaching, for business, prayer, shelter and a place for the poor to rest, as well as for congregational prayer. For Muslims, it should be central to their spiritual life and development.

The mosque is primarily a house for salah (prayer), five times every day. Men and women gather separately to bow in prostration to Allah. *Can you think of ideas why it should ONLY be used for prayer? Discuss in small groups, and then as a class.*

Muslims have to exist in a modern world and therefore need to be educated both about their religion and about how, as a Muslim, they should react to modern issues that affect them. The sermon (khutbah) is for this purpose. *Why might this be important in British mosques?*

The mosque is used as a madrassah, which is a school for Muslim children to learn Arabic and to study the Qur'an. This teaching usually happens for two hours each night. We must remember that Arabic is not the first language for most of the world's Muslims. People who learn the whole Qur'an off by heart are known as 'hafiz'. There is an increasing need in the modern world for mosques to teach people an understanding of the Qur'an as well as just the recitation of it. *Why do mosques need to educate Muslim children?*

The Basics

1. Think back to all you have studied so far. How does the mosque link to the different things you have studied?
2. Explain what you think is the most important use of the mosque.
3. Explain why a holy building should be used for community and social uses.
4. **The mosque is more important than the home in the Muslim community.** Explore this statement, explaining reasons to agree and disagree with it.

Social and community uses for the mosque

The mosque is often decorated with bright lights for the Eid ul-Fitr festival. Morning Eid prayers are held before the celebrations of the day. Muslims thank Allah for the strength he gave them to succeed in the month of Ramadan. Many Muslims break their fast each night at the mosque.

Why do you think many Muslims break their fast at the mosque and not at home?

Eid ul-Fitr is a day for every Muslim to attend mosque – what does that tell you about the importance of the ummah?

The mosque can be used as a law court. Some parts of Shari'ah Law are applicable in Britain today. Divorces are often settled at the mosque if couples were only married 'Islamically'. Financial disputes can be resolved here.

Do you think it is right that there are law courts within religions?

What happens when religious laws and secular laws do not agree – which should a citizen follow?

Social and community uses for the mosque

Family events are often associated with the mosque; for example, funeral rites are performed there, like the washing of the body. It can be used for large functions celebrating the birth of a child or a marriage.

How does this use strengthen the ummah?

What does it tell you about the closeness of religious and secular life in a Muslim community?

Where Muslims live in non-Muslim countries, the mosque acts as a social centre for young people to gather, to play games and chat with each other, rather like a community centre.

Do you think it is important for young people to have places to go and spend recreation time?

Can you think of what British society offers its young people, and whether that is enough?

Think about it

How might it be said that the mosque influences every aspect of a Muslim's life?

Where in the world …

A map of Sunni and Shi'a Muslims in the world today

Some facts …

Approximately 23 per cent of the world's population is Muslim, around 1.57 billion in number.

10–15 per cent of that number are Shi'a.

Islam is the main religion in over 50 countries. Indonesia has the largest Muslim population.

Iran is the main Shi'a country and leads Shi'a Islam in the world.

Shi'a Islam is the majority religion in the following countries: Iran (90 per cent), Azerbaijan (75 per cent), Bahrain (70 per cent), Lebanon (65 per cent), Iraq (66 per cent) and Yemen (45 per cent). (Percentages are approximate.)

Other countries with a high proportion of Shi'a Muslims are Kuwait (35 per cent), Albania (25 per cent), India (23 per cent), Pakistan (20 per cent), Turkey (20 per cent), Saudi Arabia (18 per cent), UAE (16 per cent), Afghanistan (15 per cent), Qatar (15 per cent), Syria (15 per cent).

How many of these countries have you heard of? Do you know where they are? Do you know why you have heard of them?

Sunni Muslims also live in most of these countries, generally without problems. Unfortunately there is much trouble between Sunni and Shi'a worldwide as well as some Muslim nations and some non-Muslim nations – as you may have spotted in the news.

As we have already learned, the two religious groups are similar in very many ways, but there are some differences in religious practices and also the interpretation of historical events. What divides these groups is far less than what brings them together, yet it is often the divisions that are emphasised. In the next few pages we will be focusing on the Shi'a group and their beliefs. As we go through think about the similarities and differences between Sunni and Shi'a.

Life as a Shi'a Muslim …

In Britain

I am 15 years old and a Shi'a Muslim. I live with my family in the north of England. There is a large Muslim community here, but it is a Sunni community. My parents wanted a good education and for me to fit in, so along with my sisters I attend a Church of England school. My dad has a small bakery and mum helps him make the bread and naans. They didn't want me to attend a Muslim school as the local schools are all Sunni. It can be a little weird with school assemblies and of course I cannot pray my early afternoon prayers as I'm in lessons. My eldest sister is due to be married but it's been really difficult for my parents to find a marriage partner as only one in seven Muslims here are Shi'a. The mosque we attend is 25 miles from where I live … it's the nearest so I don't go to madrassah. I only get to my mosque with my dad at weekends, but I want to go everyday … so we pray at home together. I do have Sunni friends outside school, but sometimes I feel it a bit funny because some of them think I'm not a proper Muslim. It's only really at this point I feel different as most non-Muslims just see me as a Muslim and don't know there are different groups. My school teaches about Eid festivals but not about Ashura and how important the month of Muharram is for Shi'a Muslims … Shi'a history is not something that is taught regularly.

In Iran

I am 15 years old too and my family live in Tehran, the capital city. I attend an all-boys school – there are no mixed schools. I am lucky as Iran is a majority Shi'a country, so things work around my religion. There are loads of mosques and many Shi'a shrines that I am able to visit. I am able to pray as school stops for prayer times. Festivals are celebrated as the whole country stops for days. Last year on Ashura my dad took us to Karbala in Iraq as it's the neighbouring country. We saw the shrines and it was awesome! All my friends are Shi'a and so for us Shi'a Islam is the norm. There are Sunni in Iran but it's our sect that is seen as the major group. I know many Shi'as find it difficult where they live because they are the minority, so I feel very lucky in my life.

Task

Pick out the similarities and differences between the lives of these two boys as Shi'a Muslims. Why do you think there are differences in their lives?

Ten Obligatory Acts of Shi'a Islam

There are Ten Obligations for a Muslim according to the Shi'a branch of Islam. According to Shi'a, study and defining of law comes from Muhammad ﷺ and the twelve imams. Today there are clerics who are seen as the guardians of Islamic law. They base their decisions on the Qur'an and Hadith in order to have responses to modern-day issues. This is known as ijtihad. Clerics like the Ayatollahs (religious leaders in Iran) make these decisions. The Obligatory Acts are what Shi'as should follow:

1. prayer (salah)
2. fasting (sawm)
3. almsgiving (zakah)
4. pilgrimage (hajj)
5. struggle (jihad)
6. one fifth – 20 per cent tax on yearly earnings after deduction of household expenses (khums)
7. directing others towards good/commanding what is just (**Amr-bil-Maroof**)
8. forbidding evil (**Nahi Anil Munkar**)
9. expressing love towards good – those in Allah's path (**Tawalla**)
10. expressing hatred/disassociation with those who oppose Allah (**Tabarra**)

The first four are the same as the Pillars of Islam looked at earlier in the book. Jihad also applies to all Muslims. It is the final five in the list that are not part of the Sunni tradition. Shi'a Muslims believe khums should be paid on business profits as an extra to zakah. The Qur'an says:

> 'And there should be a group amongst you who invite towards good, order for acknowledged virtues, forbid from sin and these it is that are the successful ones' *(3:104)*

This is the source for Obligations 7 and 8. Tradition has it, according to Imam Ja'far as-Sadiq, that Muhammad ﷺ said 'the best and strongest channel of intercession is to have friendship for the sake of Allah and to harbour enmity (opposition) for the pleasure of Allah. Loving the friends of Allah and expressing dislike for the enemies of Allah' (al-Kafi Volume 2 page 125). This is the source for Obligations 9 and 10.

I am a Shi'a Muslim, so I try to keep the Ten Obligatory Acts. Sunni friends all keep the first four – can you remember them? I know we do these things a little differently though. The other six are what make me as a Shi'a different. They aren't easy, but life is a test from Allah. I work hard hoping I pass it.

Task

Research the last five actions on the list. Find out a little more about them in preparation for a more in-depth study. It is always useful to attend lessons with some already acquired knowledge. This lets you get more involved in the lesson and contribute more to discussion, rather than just soaking up information.

Salah and sawm – a Shi'a perspective

Salah

Earlier in the book, we looked at some differences that exist between the practice of salah in the Sunni and Shi'a traditions. Look back to pages 115–118 as a recap. Here we are going to consider specifically Shi'a attitudes and elements.

The Twelve Imams

Regarding wuzu – the fifth imam, Imam Baqir, said 'the wuzu is a divine order (hadd) from among the divine orders of Allah so that he may know who obeys and who disobeys Him.' Imam al Ridha, the eighth imam, built on this by saying 'so that the servant is pure ... purified of filths and impurities and also because it does away with laziness and repels drowsiness and purifies the heart before standing before Allah.' This means that wuzu takes on even greater importance for Shi'a, and can never just be a ritual they go through. They have to see it as an integral part of prayer, not the preparation for it.

Regarding the actual prayer – Imam Sadiq says that 'people should know that Allah sees each person in prayer even if they do not see Him', and Imam Baqir says 'prayer reinforces sincerity and eliminates pride'. For Shi'a Muslims prayer has specific purposes which were summed up by Imam al Ridha: to cancel out all sins, to affirm the Almighty Allah whilst also affirming the insignificance of humans, and to restate a person's obedience to Allah in submission five times every day. It is the level of humility and discipline which is a strong focus for Shi'a, and without being in this mindset, prayer is not valid for them.

Sawm

Imam Ali, the first imam said of sawm 'Bring to mind by your hunger and thirst in Ramadan, the hunger and thirst of Judgement Day' and the eleventh imam, Imam Askari says that the purpose of Ramadan is to experience the pain and hunger of the poor, in order to become generous with gifts to the poor. For Shi'a Muslims therefore, there are two purposes to fasting: to give generous practical help to the poor having realised something of what their lives are like, and as a reminder of what awaits on Judgement Day. It is also expected that each Muslim undertaking the fast will benefit and grow spiritually themselves, so as to live a better life in the year to come. It will help them to be stronger at rejecting evil (munkar) and at doing what is good (ma'roof) and beneficial to all.

The Basics

1 Explain what the purpose of prayer is for Shi'a Muslims.
2 Explain why Shi'a Muslims carry out sawm.
3 Compare and contrast different Muslim beliefs about sawm.
4 How might sawm help Muslims to 'reject evil and do what is good'?

Zakah, khums and hajj

Zakah

Imam Ali says that the purpose of zakah is to test the rich and provide for the poor, and that if all people paid their zakah, no one would be poor any longer. *What do you think Imam Ali is trying to say here?* For Shi'a Muslims zakah is an obligatory tax specifically on silver and gold coins, cows, sheep, goats and camels and on wheat, barley, dates and raisins. Imam Sadiq was asked about other items like rice, but the imam insisted that it could not be obligatory because the law did not name it. He was being absolutely precise to the letter of the law. Zakah is a complicated issue in terms of what it has to be paid on and how much. This is possibly why it is not always paid in full, and that fact makes it difficult to see how it can solve poverty as Imam Ali said it should.

Khums

This is unique to Shi'a. Most pay khums, as a 20 per cent tax upon annual surplus income. Khums should be split six ways: Allah, Muhammad ﷺ, relatives of Muhammad ﷺ, orphans, the needy, anyone who is away from home and has no money to return.

A Muslim cannot pay khums directly to Allah, so originally this portion went to Muhammad ﷺ to be spent for the good of Allah. After Muhammad ﷺ died, and at the time of the first 11 imams, the first three portions used to go to the imam of Muhammad's ﷺ family to be spent in the same way. Now it can be paid to religious teachers. However, as khums is a particular Shi'a act (and only 10–15 per cent of Muslims are Shi'a) the poor do not receive as much as they would if all Muslims paid it.

Hajj

For Shi'a Muslims hajj has the same significance as for all other Muslims. It has an effect on the individual, the family and the community as a whole. Imam Sadiq says that for a believing man in a village who stays in Arafat, Allah will forgive the sins of all in the village, and for a single man of a believing family Allah will forgive the sins of all that family. Many of the eleven Shi'a imams have spoken of the importance of personally seeing the Ka'aba, the black stone, Arafat, Mina and the animal sacrifice.

The fourth imam, Imam Abedin said 'Perform the hajj and the umrah so that your bodies become healthy, your sustenance is expanded and your faith improves.' These words really show the value of this journey.

The Basics

1. Explain the purpose of zakah for Shi'a Muslims.
2. Explain briefly what is meant by khums.
3. What is the significance of hajj for Shi'a Muslims?
4. How are Sunni and Shi'a beliefs and practices for zakah and hajj similar, and how are they different? Do you think this can cause any problems?
5. **If everyone gave money to charity, the problem of poverty would be solved.** Explore this statement from more than one point of view. Give reasons to agree and disagree, and explain those reasons. Refer to Islam in your answer.

Jihad

This is one of the Obligatory Acts of Shi'a Islam. It is important to all Muslims, especially in its sense as trying to follow Allah's teachings in the world. Actually every religious person might say they have a similar duty in their own faith; to keep to their laws and beliefs in the best way possible.

Prophet Muhammad ﷺ said:

> 'The person who struggles so that Allah's Word is supreme is the one serving Allah's cause.'

The word jihad means to struggle or to strive. It comes from the word 'juhd' which means to 'make effort'. Muslims today use jihad in two contexts. First, jihad is a Muslim's internal struggle to serve Allah as best they can. It is the spiritual struggle a person needs to make to conquer their own selfishness, lust or greed to stay on the right path. Secondly, jihad can refer to the attempt to uphold justice and protect the faith. For some situations, this includes self-defence. The first idea is commonly known as greater jihad, the second, the lesser jihad.

Jihad is the internal struggle for Allah

The idea of jihad is often misunderstood. Most Muslim scholars believe that the internal struggle is the greater jihad, based on what the Prophet Muhammad ﷺ said. Others believe that these Hadith are not reliable and that holy war is the better interpretation. There are many references in Islamic writings to jihad meaning a military struggle, often having a meaning similar to 'crusade'. This is referred to as lesser jihad. In the modern world where war is prevalent, claims that the war is for the will of Allah often means that non-Muslims interpret jihad simply as holy war. So we will explore these two terms and what they mean.

Jihad is to defend Islam

Jihad is in everyday life – giving to the poor, following the Pillars, forgiving others

The greater jihad

Firstly, many Muslims do not accept this term at all. Those that do, claim that it applies to the everyday life of a Muslim. It is simply following a moral and virtuous life. A person engaged in jihad is called a mujahid. Examples of jihad are:

- following the Pillars; striving to do them properly
- those who are hafiz, as they have made the effort to learn the Qur'an
- forgiving someone who had insulted you
- giving up things for the poor or working for social justice.

Jihad is striving for peace

According to public opinion polls taken in Muslim countries such as Lebanon, Kuwait, Jordan and Morocco, most people referred to jihad as a 'duty to God' or 'worship of God' or 'striving for peace and cooperation' with no reference to war. So whatever scholars think, many modern-day Muslims indicate that jihad for them is a struggle to live rightly, worship Allah and have total faith in Him.

There are those who also believe there is a third kind of jihad: namely, striving to create a better community. Majid Khadduri, an Iraqi academic, said there were four jihads: by having jihad of the heart, jihad of the tongue, jihad of the hand and jihad of the sword. All these point to believing, thinking, saying and doing the right things.

The lesser jihad

The following two teachings from the Sunnah are attributed to Muhammad ﷺ:

> 'The best jihad is the word of justice in front of an oppressive ruler.'
>
> 'The best jihad is the one in which your horse is slain and your blood spilled.'

It is the existence of such quotations that causes some Muslims in the modern world to take up arms against any enemy of Islam as they see it. Holy books can often be interpreted in many ways and now, 1400 years after Muhammad ﷺ, there are believers who focus on such teachings and use them to justify lesser jihad (defending Islam from threat).

However, even if these quotes are adhered to, there are rules that should apply to lesser jihad concerning when and how it is carried out. For example, it should not be used to force people to accept Islam. It should only be used to defend the faith, rather than to gain territory or wealth. It should also not target innocent civilians or the leaders (or buildings) of other faiths. This is why the majority of Muslims today believe teachings about lesser jihad can never justify terrorism, and that the actions of extreme groups like ISIS, Al Qaeda and Boko Haram are wrong.

'The hope is to have a community for worship for all people.'

Rules for lesser jihad

The following rules apply to lesser jihad:

- to defend Allah and not be used for conquest
- to gain freedom from tyranny and restore peace
- fought until the enemy lays down their weapons
- women and children should not be harmed nor crops damaged; mosques should be protected absolutely
- mercy should be applied to enemy captives, injured soldiers treated, women left unharmed not abused or raped and the enemy should never be executed

Border disputes, wars for personal power, and wars to exploit others are not jihad.

> 'Repel evil with what is seen as better, then your enemy will become your friend.' *Surah 41:34*

Defence of Allah

No harm done

Restore peace

Freedom

Mercy

Respect and protection

The Basics

1. Explain the differences between greater and lesser jihad.
2. Discuss in groups why in the modern world these terms are often confused or misunderstood. Write down some of the reasons you come up with.
3. **It is never right to fight in holy war.** Do you agree with this statement? Explain your arguments.

Amr bil-Ma'roof and Nahi 'Anil-Munkar

Amr bil-Ma'roof: Directing others towards good/justice.

Nahi 'Anil-Munkar: Commanding what is just and forbidding evil.

Ma'roof means anything that is approved by Shari'ah or that is generally recognised as a beneficial/just action. Munkar means that which is not approved by Shari'ah, or what is detestable or disagreeable.

So the title phrase means 'to bring together what is good and approved and not allow that which is evil and disapproved of'. In simple terms the seventh and eighth Obligatory Acts do include the more well-known terms of halal (allowed practices) and haram (forbidden practices). However, they go further than that simplistic meaning. The Qur'an states:

> '... and whatever the Messenger has given you – take; and what he has forbidden you – refrain from' *(59:7)*

How do these beliefs affect the lives of Muslims?

- Promoting what is good is a key characteristic of a Muslim believer – a compulsory responsibility.
- Success in this world and the afterlife depends on meeting this Obligation.
- Men and women are equally obligated – 'the believing men and women are allies of each other'.
- Hypocrites promote wrong and forbid what is right – Allah forgets those who have forgotten him.
- Muhammad ﷺ believed that some people act as role models, whilst the rest just follow their lead – this can be true for good or bad.
- Anyone who does not promote halal and disapprove of haram, their du'as (private prayer) will be unheard.

In the Hadith Muhammad ﷺ gave these instructions:

- If you are capable, use your power and influence to physically stop wrong – it is a necessary action (Fard) for those in power.
- If you are incapable, at least speak out against it.
- If neither is possible – disapprove of it in your heart.
- Anyone who commits evil affects themselves and the community. Hence they should be stopped because it could destroy the whole of society.

The Basics

1 What is meant by ma'roof and munkar?
2 Explain how believing in these obligations affect the lives of Shi'a Muslims today.
3 Explain, using examples, how some Muslims in the world today are not promoting ma'roof and munkar.
4 **It is impossible to always do ma'roof (right things).** Consider this statement. Using explained reasons, argue to agree and disagree with the statement. Use examples in your answer to support your arguments.

Tawalla and Tabarra – the 9th and 10th Obligations

Tawalla: 'Expressing love towards Good – those in Allah's path'.

Tabarra: 'Expressing hatred/disassociation with those who oppose Allah'.

It is obligatory to love those in Allah's path and to not be associated with those who oppose Allah, including the enemies of Muhammad ﷺ and his family. However, the enemy of the Prophet and his family is not defined anywhere, so it is down to the individual to decide who that is. For example, some Shi'a Muslims believe the first three caliphs to be enemies, as they believe Ali was the rightful caliph. Mu'uwiyah and Yazid, because of their actions to Muhammad's ﷺ grandson, are also enemies. Shi'as will ask Allah to withdraw His mercy from such people.

Sunni Muslims do not have this belief and there are scholars today who say that Tawalla and Tabarra should be rejected as they cause division in the religion, so rejecting them would help bring Muslim unity. Muslim history makes unity impossible, without rejecting the Obligations. Shi'a Muslims believe they have been persecuted since the death of Muhammad ﷺ. For example, in the seventh and eighth century CE, Mu'ayiyah, Yazid and Ziyad all killed or tortured anyone who was a Shi'a or spoke in support of the teachings of Ali. Many Sunni cannot accept the Tawalla (Shi'a love of Ali as the good). They believe that visiting imams' shrines is blasphemy as they are 'worshipping' there, and it is also seen as blasphemous to seek advice of imams over the Qur'an. But this can be seen as a misrepresentation of Shi'a belief and practice.

It is true that Shi'a Muslims visit shrines and from doing so they gain great spirituality, but in no way does this overtake their love of Allah. They do believe that the imams are there to offer advice in a modern world, but always in the light of the Qur'an, Hadith and Shari'ah – or else how do Muslims react to modern-day issues?

Sometimes beliefs can be misrepresented and whether divisions can be related to Tawalla and Tabarra is debateable. However, Shi'a Muslims stick with their Obligations as key principles of their faith.

Task

Discuss how these key Shi'a beliefs have caused problems between Sunni and Shi'a groups. Research the issue for yourselves. Should what happened in history have happened? Should religion be able to overcome such differences?

Islamic festivals – Eid ul-Fitr

Imam Ali said:

> 'Verily it is only a festival for he whose fast Allah has accepted and whose prayers he has acknowledged …'

The Eid festival is celebrated at the end of Ramadan. It is the start of the new month, Shawwal, brought in by the sighting of the new moon. As Ramadan has focused on spirituality and the aim to renew faith, it has also been a challenge. In contrast, Eid is welcomed by all Muslims. Look at the photographs below to give you ideas of how the festival is celebrated.

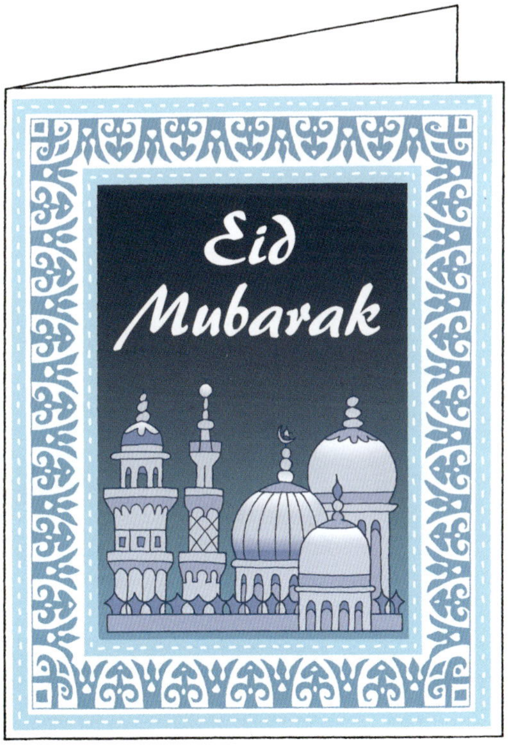

1 Preparations are made for the day; cards are sent, houses decorated, food bought, gifts and sweets for children organised.

2 Mosques in Britain wait for the sighting of the new Moon in places like Saudi Arabia, Syria and Pakistan, so this accounts for the variances in when it is announced and celebrated.

3 Joyous greetings of Eid Mubarak are made though the fast is broken by the simple eating of dates.

4 On the moning of Eid, men attend Eid prayers at the mosque including two sermons explaining the rules for paying zakah.

5 The day is a family day, visiting friends and relatives, visiting cemeteries to remember the dead, exchanging gifts for the children, new clothes and a special meal in the evening.

6 Muslims in Britain are allowed the day off work and school and in Muslim countries it is a public holiday.

The Basics

1 Describe how Eid ul-Fitr is celebrated by Muslims in Britain today.
2 Research the celebration of Eid ul-Fitr in Saudi Arabia and either Turkey, Egypt or an African country. Do you notice any differences because of national traditions or cultures?
3 **Eid is just an excuse for a big party**. How far do you agree with this statement? Explain the reasons for your arguments.

Islamic festivals – Eid ul-Adha

We have already seen this festival mentioned in the section on hajj (see page 124).

Eid ul-Adha takes place on the 10th day of the month of Dhu al-Hijjah each year. This day is within the period for hajj, and anyone on hajj will celebrate the festival as part of that Pillar. Eid ul-Adha is the Festival of the Sacrifice, so is also called Bakr-Eid (Sacrifice Feast).

Why is this festival celebrated?

It dates back to the time of Prophet Ibrahim, who dreamt he was told by Allah to sacrifice his own son, Ishmael. Ibrahim spoke to Ishmael about the dream, and they both agreed that they had to do as Allah commanded. Ibrahim showed his faithfulness to Allah by being prepared to carry out this terrible command. Even when Shaytan (the devil) tried to persuade Ibrahim to protect not sacrifice his son, Ibrahim kept to his orders. Ibrahim threw stones at Shaytan to make him leave (which is why pilgrims throw pebbles during hajj). Muslims believe that Ibrahim did attempt to cut his son's throat, in the manner of ritual slaughter. However, when he looked down at what he had done, it was a ram which had been slaughtered, and his son was safe. He had passed the test.

How is the festival celebrated?

The central element of the festival is the sacrifice of a lamb, called adhiya or qurbani. The meat from the lamb is split three ways – one third for the family who have paid for the sacrifice, one third to relatives, friends and neighbours, and the remaining third to the poor. Many families pay charity money in place of having a lamb sacrificed.

The Sunnah of Eid

The Sunnah are the practices of Muhammad ﷺ, which Muslims are encouraged to follow as he is the perfect example. Muslims are encouraged to prepare themselves for Eid by completing the pre-sunrise prayer (Fajr), and dressing up in new clothes. Eid prayers have to be offered at the mosque with other Muslims – congregational prayer is important. There will always be a sermon at the mosque for this festival, and the theme will be focused around Ibrahim, commitment, the poor and a Muslim's responsibilities. After the service is completed, people exchange greetings and gifts. Many Muslims will visit relatives, and have special meals.

The Basics

1 Why do Muslims celebrate Eid ul-Adha?
2 Explain why many Muslims are away from home when they celebrate Eid ul-Adha.
3 How do Muslims celebrate Eid ul-Adha?
4 **Eid ul-Adha is only about remembering Ibrahim's sacrifice.** How far do you agree with that? Explain your reasons.

The importance of Eid ul-Fitr

The importance of the Eid festival is the same for Sunni and Shi'a Muslims, but the Eid prayers vary slightly. In the Sunni tradition there are two rak'ahs – the prayer starts with niyyah or intention to pray, followed by 'Allahu Akbar'. The next is to recite 'Takbir Al- Ihram' and 'Allahu Akbar' seven times, with the raising of hands to the ears each time. The Shi'a have five raising of the hands in Takbir with a small du'a being recited. Then the imam reads the Surah Al-Fatiha and Surah Al-'A'lá and the congregation performs ruku and sujud. For Sunni, in the next rak'ah five Takbirs are said, whereas the Shi'a just repeat what they did in the first rak'ah. In both traditions the prayer ends with a sermon.

Muslims have gone without food for the fast and glimpsed how hard life is for fellow Muslims who regularly go hungry. Therefore their zakah has to be given by the day of Eid. In some mosques, a board displaying the names of families is placed in public. Names are crossed off the list once families have given their zakah. This provides transparency and encourages participation within the community.

The importance of this festival is both in reflecting on what has gone before and looking into the future for the next year. Reflecting on Ramadan, Muslims have had many reminders about the role of religion in their lives:

1. Allah needs to be the focus of everything.
2. Time should not be wasted on the material things in life – the Qur'an and prayer should dominate time.
3. Behaviour should be modest, polite, peaceful, kind and generous to others.
4. Their wealth is not their own and it should be used as Allah would want – to benefit the community.

In 2015, some Muslim fundamental groups called for Ramadan to be used as a time to promote Islam by violent means. Bombing and killings took place on one of the Fridays of Ramadan in Tunisia, Kuwait and France. These calls for violence totally contradict Islamic teachings. In Iraq in the city of Mosul, ISIS banned Eid prayers, claiming that the prayers were more a social gathering than a religious activity, and that there was no foundation in the Qur'an for them, so they were not appropriate. However, the social aspect as well as the personal striving is integral to the purpose of Ramadan, so this ban of prayers was criticised by Muslims worldwide.

In terms of looking ahead, the actions of Ramadan have bettered those who have fasted, the harder part is to maintain that state throughout the next year. Muslims believe Allah knows that people wander from His path, hence Ramadan is annual as a reminder. Eid celebrates achievement and betterment, so these ideas should continue so as to make the community a better ummah and improve each Muslim's prospects for a good afterlife.

Eid is very important to me. As a British Muslim, it is the day my religion is fully recognised – I have a day off school, my dad gets the day from work. We celebrate as a family but with the community.

Halima

I know that Muslims everywhere are celebrating this festival. We all celebrate at the same time – one huge community.

Ammad

The Basics

Eid celebrates the end of the Holy Month of Ramadan. Explain why this festival is important for Muslims personally and communally.

Islamic festivals – Ashura

Both Sunni and Shi'a observe this festival on the tenth day of the Muslim month of Muharram. However, their reason for and way of celebrating is very different. Ashura just means 'tenth'.

Sunni

Tradition states that when Muhammad ﷺ was in Madinah he saw the Jewish people fasting on the tenth of the month of Muharram. He asked them what they were doing and they explained that it was a day to remember when the Israelites were saved from the Pharaoh. They said that Musa fasted on this day. He replied 'we are closer to Musa than you.' So he fasted on the day and told the people to fast. There are no Hadith to support this, but many Muslims accept its authenticity. Ramadan was established later in Madinah replacing the fast in Muhurram.

Many Muslims remember Ashura as a Day of Atonement, that is, a day sins are forgiven if repented. Many fast, often on the eighth, ninth and tenth of Muharram. However, it is not compulsory in Sunni Islam to do so.

Sunni Muslims do not accept the whipping of their bodies because according to teaching the body should not be harmed. However, this used to be a common practice for Shi'a Muslims.

Shi'a

For Shi'a Muslims this is a really significant festival based in sorrow. For Shi'a, it remembers the martyrdom of Hussein, the grandson of Muhammad ﷺ who was killed in the battle of Karbala on 10 Muharram, 680CE along with 72 members of his family. He was killed by Yazid, a ruler who had demanded Hussein give him his allegiance. He refused because of the corruption, use of enslavement and injustices first of Mu'awiyah, then of his son, Yazid, whom he saw as illegitimate leaders. Hussein had taken his family to Makkah, hoping he would be safe in the holy city. On his way to Kufa in Iraq, he and his family were intercepted and driven into Karbala by 30,000 soldiers. They were held without water. Hussein realised it was him they wanted and told the others to leave, but they refused and were soon attacked. Hussein was beheaded, the camp set on fire and everyone murdered. Bodies were mutilated and left unburied. Later, they were buried respectfully in Damascus.

How the Shi'a observe Ashura

1 It is a festival of sincere sadness.
2 Many wear black as a sign of grief.
3 Mosques are covered in black cloths.
4 After the afternoon prayers, poems about the tragedy are read and people often cry.
5 Some gather to beat themselves with whips and chains in sorrow, especially in Karbala, but this practice is becoming less common.

For Shi'a Muslims there is a great deal to learn from this festival. Hussein should never be forgotten, nor the actions of the imams. Muslims must stand up for justice to better society. A Shi'a's love for Allah is shown through their love of the imams.

The Basics

1 What does the festival of Ashura recall?
2 Explain the difference between the Sunni and Shi'a observance of Ashura.
3 **It is wrong to call Ashura a celebration.** Explore this statement, explaining arguments for and against it.

Testing your knowledge

One-mark Questions

Multiple-choice question

For the one-mark multiple-choice question, you must to choose the correct answer from the four you are offered.

Focusing on the second section of Islam, on practices that you have now studied, try the following:

1 What is meant by the term 'Shahadah'?

A chapter of the Qur'an
B Declaration of Faith
C Islamic law
D prayer

2 What is the adhan?

A call to prayer
B leader of the mosque
C prayer time
D washing process

3 Which of these is not a Muslim festival?

A Ashura
B Easter
C Eid ul-Adha
D Eid-ul Fitr

4 What is meant by the term 'khums'?

A eating halal food
B to be kind to others
C to reject evil
D 20 per cent annual tax

5 What is meant by the term 'Tawalla'?

A approved actions
B express hatred
C express love towards Allah
D just actions

Make up four answers to each of the following and test your partner. Do not forget: only ONE can be correct!

1 What is the name for the washing process in Islam?
2 Which is **not** a place included in hajj?
3 When would a Muslim perform rak'ahs?
4 What is meant by jihad?
5 Which of these is a Muslim festival?

Short response question

The one-mark short response question is asking you to write a brief response.

You will have to name or give an example of a belief, practice, key term or religious concept.

You may also be asked for a brief definition.

Do not waste time writing too much but make sure to write enough to fully answer the question. Don't leave the examiner guessing at what you mean, or how what you have written does answer the question. Don't be vague!

1 Give one reason why Shahadah is the first Pillar.
2 Name one of the Five Pillars of Islam.
3 Give one way that Muslims can demonstrate jihad.
4 Name one of the Ten Obligations for Shi'a Muslims.
5 Give one way in which khums can be given.

Make up three one-mark short response questions to test your partner.

Differences Questions

Four-mark questions

These questions are where you show your understanding of the diversity – that not everyone in the same religion does or believes exactly the same things.

You will have to answer one of these in each of the practices sections of your chosen two religions. They are always worth four marks, and always ask you to contrast two practices.

The wording will always begin: 'Explain two different (Muslim) …'

Followed by one of these, or something similar:

- 'views on/about …'
- 'ways in which …'
- 'rituals associated with …'

Here are some examples for you to see how that works (and to try):

1 Explain two different Muslim views about the importance of sawm.

2 Explain two different ways in which Muslims celebrate Eid ul-Adha.

3 Explain two different ways in which Muslims celebrate the festival of Ashura.

Go back through your answers to these three questions and use AQA's mark scheme to see how you could improve them.

Look at the following answers. Which do you think is better, and why?

Explain two different ways Muslims celebrate the festival of Ashura.

Answer 1

Shi'a Muslims see it as a sad day, because they remember Hussain's death. He was the grandson of Prophet Muhammad ﷺ, and he was murdered. Sunni Muslims see it as a day to think about their wrongdoing, so they fast.

Answer 2

Some Sunni Muslims celebrate Ashura by fasting, that is, they don't eat all day. They do this because Muhammad ﷺ had seen Jewish people doing it to remember the day the Pharaoh freed the Israelites from slavery. Prophet Musa had fasted on this day, so Prophet Muhammad ﷺ said the Muslims should copy his example. Many Muslims will also spend the day thinking about what they have done wrong, and being sorry for that.

Answer 1: This gives two good ways, but the response is simple, because it gives no detail and no examples. It also focuses more on why they do things (murder of Hussain, and seeking forgiveness) than how they are celebrated. You could improve this for them by being more focused on how they celebrate, and giving more detail.

Answer 2: This gives two ways, but only the first has enough detail. You could improve your answer by adding more detail to the second way. This answer only describes what Sunni Muslims do, but it does give two different ways to celebrate, so it is valid.

Explaining Practices

Six-mark questions

These questions ask you to explain two ways in which Muslims put their beliefs into practice, or two ways in which Muslims believe practices to be important.

> The wording will always begin: 'Explain two ways in which ...'
>
> Finishing off with: 'Refer to sacred writings or another source of Muslim belief and teaching in your answer.'

They will be marked against AQA's mark scheme which can be found on the AQA website.

From the question wording and the mark scheme you can work out how to answer the question effectively. Each question is different, but in this case you would:

- choose your two ways and then explain each one
- develop your explanations fully
- use a relevant quotation/teaching, show how it links to the question and include its source of authority, i.e. who or where the quote/teaching comes from.

Remember this is just one example to help you practice. In the exam, you will need to think carefully and respond to the actual question you are given.

What does 'way' mean?

The question wants you to explain the reasons why something is important. Don't get caught out in the pressure of an exam – practise a lot of questions beforehand.

Here is an example:

Explain two ways in which Muslims think zakah is important. Refer to sacred writings or another source of Muslim belief and teaching in your answer.

> ### Sample answer
>
> In the Hadith al-Bukhari[1], it says a Muslim must not withhold their zakah from Allah[2]. For this reason, many Muslims believe zakah is very important to give because Allah has decreed they must give it, so by giving it they follow his commands[3].
>
> By following the commands of Allah, they will be rewarded in the afterlife[4].

Looking at the sample answer:

1. it opens by saying where the belief comes from, i.e. it names the source of authority, here the Hadith;
2. this is what that source says about zakah, an answer that infers importance;
3. this explains the importance because it is a decree of Allah;
4. this further explains that importance by saying what happens if Muslims give zakah.

Of course, the answer needs a second teaching about the importance of zakah, written in the same way.

Practise the following questions for yourself:

1. Explain two ways in which Muslims celebrate Eid ul-Fitr. Refer to sacred writings or another source of Muslim belief and teaching in your answer.
2. Explain two ways in which Muslims view the Salah (prayer) as important. Refer to sacred writings or another source of Muslim belief and teaching in your answer.

Analyse and Evaluate

For GCSE RS you have to be able to show that you can react to a given statement. This means that you consider what the statement says, present arguments to agree and disagree and come to a conclusion of what you yourself think of the statement. You have to demonstrate what a Muslim would say and what arguments they would use. This type of question takes the most thinking, so needs the most time.

It is always a good idea to work to a formula when you answer this type of question. This structures your answer which makes it clear and also makes sure you meet all the necessary criteria to give a good answer. Here is one formula you might consider using:

SOCs

S = Some people might say ...

O = Other people might say ...

C = In Conclusion, I think the strongest answer is ... because ...

s = make sure you have several points in each of the above

Some other tips

- Focus on the statement inself, not the topic the statement sits within, for example, 'Hajj is the most important Pillar' isn't asking you to write all about hajj, rather its status.
- 'Some' and 'other' must be differing (opposing) views.
- Aim to give in-depth explanations of each argument.
- Examples are a good way to further develop your arguments and demonstrate good understanding.

Have a go at using the formula and tips to answer the following questions:

1 **Prayer is more beneficial than going on hajj.**

Evaluate this statement. You should:
- refer to Muslim teaching
- give reasoned arguments to support this statement
- give reasoned arguments to support a different point of view
- reach a justified conclusion.

2 **Shahadah is the most important of the Five Pillars.**

Evaluate this statement. You should:
- refer to Muslim teaching
- give reasoned arguments to support this statement
- give reasoned arguments to support a different point of view
- reach a justified conclusion.

3 **Ashura should be the main festival for all Muslims.**

Evaluate this statement. You should:
- refer to Muslim teaching
- give reasoned arguments to support this statement
- give reasoned arguments to support a different point of view
- reach a justified conclusion.

4 **The expectations of Ramadan should be the everyday expectations for a Muslim.**

Evaluate this statement. You should:
- refer to Muslim teaching
- give reasoned arguments to support this statement
- give reasoned arguments to support a different point of view
- reach a justified conclusion.

The more practice you get at this type of question the better. You need to learn to think on your feet and state not only what you think but also other opinions as well. The point of these questions is to challenge your application of knowledge.

Islam Glossary

Adalat justice in Shi'a Islam

Adhan the call to prayer five times a day

Akhirah belief in life after death/the afterlife

Al-Kiswah the black cloth that covers the Ka'aba in Makkah

All-compassionate all-loving, benevolent, ever forgiving and not vindictive

Al-Qadr predestination of the will of Allah; the belief that Allah has decreed everything that is to happen in the universe

Amr-bil-Maroof commanding what is just

Beneficence an act of charity or kindness in an effort to do good for others

Caliph a successor of Muhammad ﷺ as the spiritual leader of Islam

Hadith the teachings of Muhammad ﷺ

Hafiz a person who has memorised the Qur'an by heart

Hajj pilgrimage to Makkah and the Fifth Pillar of Islam

Haram forbidden for Muslims (includes food, actions, etc.)

Hijab head scarf worn by some Muslim women

Hijrah Muhammad's ﷺ escape journey from Makkah to Madinah

Ihram the white clothing worn by pilgrims on hajj in Makkah

Imamate leadership

Immanence the belief that Allah is closer to us than our heartbeat and is involved in the world

Jihad the greater or lesser striving for the way of Allah

Jumu'ah (Jummah) Friday prayers where the khutbah is read

Justice fairness in society or the right thing to do

Khatib the person who delivers the sermon on Fridays – usually the imam

Khums tax in Shi'a Islam

Khutbah the name for the sermon on Friday in mosques

Madinah holy city in Saudi Arabia as the place where Muhammad ﷺ set up the first Muslim community and the place where Muhammad ﷺ is buried

Makkah holy city of Islam in Saudi Arabia with the Great Mosque housing the Ka'aba

Makruh a detestable act

Merciful to show forgiveness and compassion to those who do wrong

Mihrab indented archway in the mosque showing the direction of the Ka'aba

Minaret tower on the outside of the mosque used for the call to prayer (adhan)

Minbar the raised platform used by the imam to deliver the Friday sermon

Mu'addhin the caller to prayer

Mubah an action which is neither forbidden nor recommended

Mustahab favoured or recommended actions

Nahi Anil Munkar forbidding what is evil

Night of Power the night Muhammad ﷺ received the first revelations of the Qur'an

Omnipotence the belief that Allah is all-powerful

Predestination the idea that everything that happens has been decided already by Allah

Psalms the books written by David (Zabur)

Qiblah the direction of Makkah

Qurbani the sacrifice of animals during Eid-ul-Adha

Rak'ah a sequence of prayer containing actions and recitations

Ramadan the holy month of fasting for 29/30 days

Risalah communication between humans and Allah in the form of books, angels and prophets

Salah compulsory prayer five times a day and the Second Pillar of Islam

Sawm Pillar of fasting

Seal of the Prophets Muhammad ﷺ the last prophet chosen by Allah and given the Qur'an

Shahadah Declaration of Faith – to believe in One God and Muhammad ﷺ as the Prophet of Allah

Shari'ah Law a legal system which comes from the religious rules of Islam

Shi'a a Muslim who adheres to the Shi'a branch of Islam; Shi'a Islam is followed by about one-tenth of all Muslims

Sunnah the way of life of Muhammad ﷺ as an example to follow

Sunni Muslims who follow the Sunnah, the Way of the Prophet

Surah the name for chapters in the Qur'an

Tabarra expressing hatred towards evil

Tawalla expressing love towards good

Tawhid the belief in the Oneness of Allah and the unity of His being

Topi prayer hat worn by Muslim men

Torah the revelations given to Musa (Tawrat)

Transcendence Allah is outside the world, beyond everything and outside time

Twelver Shi'a part of the Shi'a sect of Islam who believe in the Twelve Imams as leaders

Ummah the brotherhood/community of Islam

Usul ad-Din the foundations of faith in Shi'a Islam

Wajib something that is an obligatory duty for a Muslim

Wuzu the symbolic washing and purification of the mind and body before salah

Zakah almsgiving to the poor which benefits the Muslim community

The study of religions

3 JUDAISM

An introduction to Judaism

Beliefs and teachings

Judaism began some 4000 years ago, pre-dating Christianity and Islam. The Jewish people were originally known as Israelites, a tribal people in the Middle East. They were a people held in enslavement by the Egyptian Pharaoh and almost wiped out of existence. They travelled back to the land of Israel, for some Jewish people a historical homeland and for others a religious/spiritual homeland. Judaism has spread to many parts of the world today.

Over time, Judaism in the UK has developed to have two main groups: Orthodox Judaism and Progressive Judaism (including Reform and Liberal Judaism).

In terms of background, most of your study will be based on early Judaism, where you will focus on the relationship between the Jewish people and **G-d**. That is where you will hear the term '**Covenant**'. G-d makes agreements with Noah, Moses and Abraham; all of which bind the Jewish people to G-d and have directed their history.

Jews follow the Ten Commandments, along with another 603 rules (known as **mitzvot**) found in the Torah. There is also the Jewish **oral law**, which helps to explain how to fulfil the 613 mitzvot. Covering almost every aspect of Jewish life, these rules govern their relationship between G-d, humankind and each other.

Jewish people believe that G-d is the one, ultimate creator and Law-Giver. He is just and judges everyone. G-d has a presence in the world known as **Shechinah** and Jewish people believe that He involves Himself in this world.

In terms of **Holy Books** there isn't just one, so it will help you to know the following.

TORAH	The five books of Moses.
TENAKH	The five books of Moses plus the Nevi'im (Prophets) and Ketuvim (Writings) – total of 24 books.
TALMUD	A commentary on the **Torah** originating in the second century CE. Its purpose is to teach and is made up of the **Mishnah** and **Gemara**.
MISHNAH	The original written version of the oral law.
GEMARA	The scholarly record of the discussions following the writing of the Mishnah.
HALAKAH	The collection of Jewish laws based on the written and oral Torah. It includes the 613 mitzvot, Talmudic law, scholarly law and the customs and traditions in the Shulchan Aruch.

The **Messiah** and the **Messianic Age** are important terms in Judaism, though are very difficult to define. They look to the future, to a time when the world is perfect and peaceful. Rather than focus on the unknown afterlife, though, Jewish people are far more concerned about life here and now.

Practice

Historically, Jewish practice was centered around the **Temple** in **Jerusalem**. Currently, only the **Western Wall** remains standing. Today, Jewish people worship in **synagogues** which were created after the destruction of the Temple. There are differences in design between Orthodox and Reform synagogues and these often reflect the differences of belief between the two.

Shabbat is the Jewish Holy Day celebrated both in the home and the synagogue. Judaism in the home is seen as more important than in the synagogue; Judaism is a way of life and a Jewish person is at home far more than in the synagogue.

Jewish people have many **rituals** and **festivals.** The birth of a Jewish boy is marked with the **Brit Milah** ceremony. At the age of twelve or thirteen, boys and girls are welcomed as an adult into the religion with a **Bar Mitzvah** (for boys) and a **Bat Mitzvah** (for girls). Marriage is very important in Judaism for the future of the religion, so an outline of the ceremony will need to be studied. Jewish festivals are a key to not forget the past and serve as a reminder of the struggles Jewish people have had. They form an essential part of the Jewish year both in remembrance and celebration – New Year, the Day of Atonement and Passover are part of your study.

Kosher are dietary laws and affect the preparation of food and food types and combinations that can and cannot be eaten. Kosher is part of the mitzvot so there is a link here between teachings and everyday practices.

Judaism

Who are the Jewish people?

Judaism is one religion, but has different groups within it, so it is important to have some understanding of who these groups are, before looking at their beliefs and lifestyle. There are four main branches of the religion, which are highlighted below, but within each group there are sub-groups. In 2023, there were approximately 15.7 million Jewish people in the world, with most of them living in Israel or the USA. Sizeable Jewish communities are also found in most European countries, as well as in Russia, Canada, Argentina, Australia and Brazil. Small Jewish populations are also found across Asia and Iran. In other words, the Jewish people are racially diverse and spread across the world.

Judaism is a way of life based upon beliefs. It began 4000 years ago with Abraham, who is seen as the Father of the Nation. The Jewish people believe they can have a special relationship with G-d as His Chosen People if they fulfil specific responsibilities.

Orthodox Judaism

Orthodox Jewish people believe that the 'written law' of the Torah is the word of G-d, given by G-d to Moses, and therefore has total authority for modern-day life. Also they believe in the 'oral law' of the Talmud, which was given alongside and so has equal authority to the Torah. They have traditional beliefs about daily worship, kosher, separation of men and women in the synagogues, prayers and ceremonies and the importance of the study of the Torah. They keep strict observance of the Sabbath. In Britain in Orthodox Judaism, there are different levels of strict application; some keep themselves separated from general society, whilst others choose to observe Judaism but within secular British society, and some are Orthodox because of family tradition, but do not observe the mitzvot fully. In 2023, 19 per cent of Jewish people in Britain identified as Orthodox or Haredi (strictly Orthodox).

Reform (part of Progressive Judaism)

This group began in 19th century Germany to try to bring historical Jewish beliefs into modern-day life without the need to follow strict Jewish law to the letter. These Jewish people believe in G-d, the Torah and Israel. They believe that humans are created in the image of G-d and the Torah is revealed continuously allowing Judaism to move with the times. For example, they strive to bring peace and harmony to the world, and they ordain female **rabbis** and **cantors**.

Masorti Judaism

This group sits between Orthodox Judaism and Reform Judaism. It has been described as 'traditional Judaism but practised in a spirit of open-minded enquiry and tolerance, that is, open to the modern world.' Masorti Jewish people support the modern state of Israel, and the Hebrew language as key aspects of the people of the faith. They stress the importance of (studying) the Torah and religious law to govern life.

Liberal (part of Progressive Judaism)

Liberal Judaism is slightly more radical than the British Reform Judaism. It wants change to happen quicker, to see Judaism flourish in a modern world. It believes that religious laws should be reassessed to see if they are suitable for a modern world, and (like Reform Judaism) that people should make their own decisions within the Jewish framework. In Britain there are about 30 Liberal synagogues all governing themselves. Since Liberal Jewish people believe that the Torah was human-written, they believe it to have been affected by the context of the day and to contain outdated ideas and rules. It is G-d-inspired rather than G-d-written, so they see it as a valuable source of wisdom and guidance, but also believe that it must be interpreted in the light of issues today. Liberal Jewish people also have different views on the coming of the Messiah, resurrection and the concept of the afterlife.

'In general Jewish people can be viewed as two groups: as religious Jewish people (who adhere to the practices and beliefs of Judaism) and secular Jewish people (who view Judaism as their heritage and ethnicity rather than their religion). When we talk about Jewish people in this book, we are mainly referring to religious Jewish people.'

More about the Orthodox

In Europe, most Orthodox Jewish people are members of two main geographic groups: Ashkenazic or Sephardic. Some Jewish people are known as Mizrachi (as their families travelled through and lived in Northern Africa and the Middle East).

Ashkenazic

- Ashkenaz is the Hebrew word for 'Germany' as this group descended from Germany, France and Eastern Europe.
- They developed a rich cultural tradition.
- In tenth and eleventh-century Europe, they developed trades as merchants, businessmen and money lenders – in most countries this was because of laws on what trades they were allowed to do.
- Yiddish was developed as a language.
- Due to persecution, the Jewish communities moved around and settled in tight-knit groups, often separated from the rest of society, all over Europe.
- They may carry out some mitzvot a bit differently to Sephardic Jews.

Sephardic

- Sepharad is the Hebrew word for 'Spain' as Sephardic Jewish people travelled through and lived in Spain and Portugal.
- In 1442CE, they were expelled from Spain by the Catholic king. Some escaped, many were persecuted and killed, some adopted Roman Catholicism, often as a disguise to save their own lives.
- Most Sephardic Jews are Orthodox.
- They may carry out some mitzvot a bit differently to Ashkenazi Jews.

Task

Create two circles, one each for Orthodox and Progressive Judaism. Around them highlight the distinctive features. Research Ashkenazi and Sephardic Jewish people, making some simple notes for each.

3.1 Beliefs and teachings

The nature of G-d

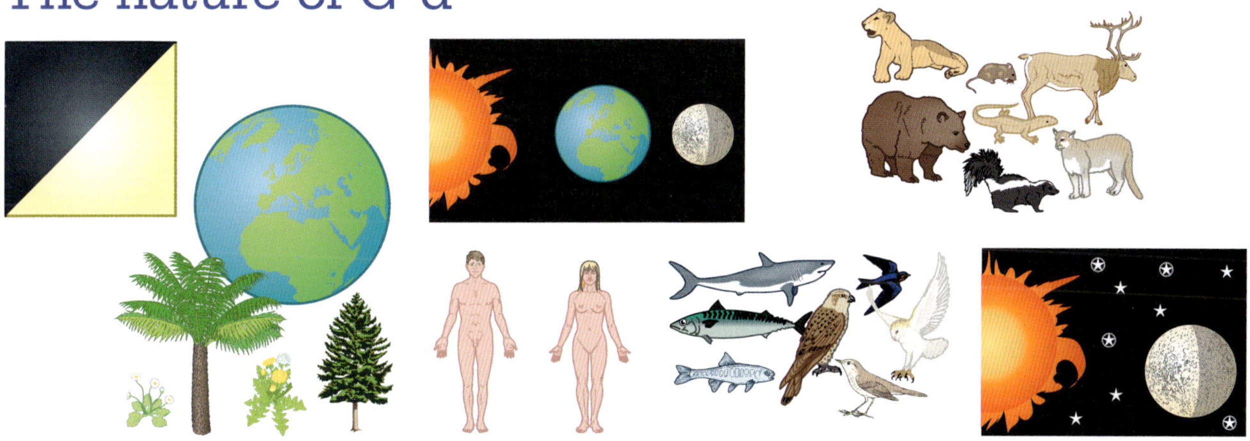

Bereshit 3:1–2:1   Genesis 1:1–2:3

Day one

In the beginning was nothing but darkness, the earth was without form and the wind blew over the restless waters. Then G-d said 'let there be light' and there was light. G-d said it was good and he called the darkness, night, and the light, day.

Day two

G-d then separated the firmament from the waters. He called the firmament 'Heaven'. The heavens were above the earth with a space in between.

Day three

G-d said 'let the waters under the heavens be gathered together and let the dry land appear.' G-d called the dry land earth and the waters seas. G-d said it was good. He then created vegetation on the land, grass, herbs, and fruits of all kinds from the trees.

Day four

G-d said 'Let there be lights in the firmament to divide the day from the night, the seasons and for the days and years.' G-d made the moon and the stars for the night and the sun for the day.

Day five

G-d created fish for the waters, whales and small fish and birds to fill the air. G-d blessed each of them saying 'Be fruitful and multiply, fill the waters and the skies.'

Day six

G-d said 'Let the earth be filled with living creatures, creeping things, cattle, beasts of every kind. Let us also make humans in our image and give humans dominion (power) over the seas, the skies and the earth.' He created male and female alike. G-d then blessed them and told them to be fruitful and multiply. G-d had given humankind everything he had made and it was all good.

Day seven

On the seventh day G-d ended his work and he rested from His work. G-d blessed the seventh day and made it holy.

G-d as One and as the Creator

Jewish people believe there is One G-d. The **Shema** is the Jewish statement of belief and it begins:

> 'Hear O Israel, the Lord is our G-d, the Lord is One.' *(Deuteronomy 6:4)*

This monotheistic belief separated the Israelites (later Jewish people) from other peoples who believed in different gods. Believing in One G-d means having to believe that everything is created by that One G-d; also that G-d is indivisible and complete. G-d cannot be divided into parts. G-d is the only one Jewish people should pray to and praise.

The creation story on page 155 shows how Jewish people believed G-d made the world. He made it '*ex-nihilo*' (from nothing). This also means that He made it exactly how He wanted to, without relying on the materials from somewhere else. He is the ultimate creator. Jewish people believe that G-d revealed Himself through His works of creation; however, He remains incomprehensible to the human mind.

For Jewish people, the world exists because G-d wills it to exist – which is how He could make it out of nothing. G-d's creative powers make things exist. G-d is pre-existent and eternal, so G-d continues to create (in fact, some Jewish people pray daily that His creation continues). The world continues to exist because of G-d's will.

Isaiah 45:6–7

> ... so that from the rising of the sun to the place of its setting,
>
> people may know there is none besides me. I am the Lord, and there is no other.
>
> I form the light and create darkness, I bring prosperity and create disaster;
>
> I, the Lord, do all these things.

This statement from the Prophet Isaiah shows the belief that G-d created everything. He has ultimate power (omnipotence), is all-knowing (omniscient) and exists everywhere (omnipresent). G-d is the beginning and the end, the light and the dark, and the good and the bad. In other words, nothing happens without G-d letting it happen. However, humans do have free will with G-d trying to help us make the right choices.

Reminder

The Genesis **creation** story is the story for both Jewish people and Christians of how the world was created by G-d. The Jewish scriptures are considered later in Topic 3.2 of Judaism. Those people studying Christianity meet the Tenakh as well (Christians call it the Old Testament).

The Basics

1. Explain the Jewish idea of G-d as the Creator.
2. Describe the Genesis creation story.
3. Explain why Jewish people believe 'G-d is One'.
4. Explain how belief that G-d created the world might influence how Jewish people live their lives.
5. **Jewish people should spend all their time trying to understand G-d.** What is your opinion of this statement? Try to give arguments both for and against it.

The nature of G-d – Law-Giver and Judge

The basic Jewish belief is that G-d, having created humankind, wants them to live a certain way. If people follow this way, they will be serving G-d. The first rule was given to Adam and Eve in the Garden of Eden, at the beginning of human life, when G-d told them they could not eat the fruit of the Tree of Knowledge. Jewish people believe G-d is the Ultimate Law-Giver, and has given many sets of laws.

Genesis 9 describes how G-d sent a flood to punish evil people and he only saved Noah and his family. After the flood he gave seven laws to Noah. These laws are for everyone and if followed would make the world an ideal place. They are a spiritual and ethical code of practice.

The Torah describes three separate Covenants (agreements) made with Noah, Abraham and Moses. Covenants are designed to allow both parties to benefit. Jewish people believe that their relationship with G-d is like an agreement, with the Jewish people doing what G-d asks of them.

Deuteronomy 10:12–13 says:*'Now, Israel, what does the Lord your G-d require of you? ... to keep the Lord's commandments and His statutes which I am commanding today for your good.'*

The Hebrew word for 'commandment' is 'mitzvah' (the plural is mitzvot) and these are the rules that come from G-d; those who follow the rules will be rewarded spiritually. There are 613 Laws that the Torah asks Jewish people to keep, although it is impossible to keep them all as some apply to men, some to women, some during Temple times; they are represented on the Jewish Tallit (prayer shawl) in the form of knotted tassels. Some Jewish men (in Orthodox communities) and women (in Progressive communities) wear these all the time (in the smaller version – tallit katan) to show how close G-d's laws are in daily life. The 613 laws include the seven laws of Noah and the **Ten Commandments** given to Moses. They cover all aspects of life; they build the individual's character, provide guidance for a disciplined life and they are a test of faith. The law-giving nature of G-d is present in all life's aspects.

The Tenakh is the canon of holy Jewish texts. It is in three sections, the first being the Torah. In the Tenakh are recorded examples of where G-d has punished people when they fail to follow his way. Adam was punished after eating the fruit in Eden, people of Noah's time were punished by the flood, the people of Sodom were punished for immoral behaviour by fire. In today's world Jewish people believe G-d will judge each individual, which will lead to their punishment. So G-d in Judaism is the Ultimate Judge as well.

Laws given to Noah

- Idolatry is forbidden
- Blasphemy is forbidden
- No murder
- No theft
- No sexual misconduct
- No cruelty to animals
- Justice for all

Task

Find out more about the 613 mitzvot. What do you think about the laws?
How would they affect a person's life?
Discuss if they have any value in the world today. Are some more important than others? Which mitzvah might be difficult to follow in the twenty-first century?

Shechinah – The Divine Presence

The word Shechinah was used to express how G-d is involved in the world. Humans cannot *see* G-d, but people have said that they have felt the *presence* of G-d. Commenting on the Jewish scriptures, **Maimonides** (a Jewish scholar) described this as a light created to act as a connection between G-d and the world. This idea developed into a physical presence, like being surrounded by clouds or fire. Shechinah is not a word found specifically in the Tenakh, but the scriptures do refer to 'the Glory of G-d' surrounding people or 'dwelling' in a certain place. Shechinah is referred to by rabbis in the Talmud, though.

Let's look at some of the Tenakh references to this presence of G-d, so that you can refer to them in answers:

1 Ezekiel 43:2 states that 'the earth shone with His glory.' Many Jewish people believe the world's design reveals the presence of G-d in the world.

2 Exodus chapters 1–18 tell the story of the escape from slavery in Egypt. In Exodus 13:20 it says 'The Lord went before them in a pillar of cloud by day to guide them and in a pillar of fire by night.' Exodus 14:24 says that 'the Lord looked down upon the Egyptian army from a pillar of fire and cloud and threw them into panic …', thus allowing the crossing of the Red Sea. Later, Exodus 24:15 tells the reader that Moses went up Mount Sinai, which was covered by cloud; the presence of G-d, on the Seventh Day, was seen as fire on the top of the mountain.

3 Exodus 40:33–34 describes when Moses finished building the Tabernacle, the cloud covered the Tent of Meeting and G-d's presence filled it.

4 When the Israelites entered the Promised Land, I Kings 6:11–13 says that the presence of the Lord would 'dwell' in the Temple of Solomon. II Chronicles 5 says that the presence would transfer from the Tabernacle to the Temple. So it is believed by the Jewish people to have been in the Temple which was first built in 957BCE by King Solomon. Later this Temple was destroyed, and since the people were wicked, the presence left the Temple. It returned only when the second Temple was built, after the Jewish people had been captive in Babylon. There it remained until 70CE, when Jerusalem was under siege and the Temple again destroyed. The presence left and returned to heaven. It is believed by many Jewish people it will return with G-d's rebuilding of the Temple for his chosen people in the future.

Task

1 What is the Shechinah?
2 Describe how the Jewish people believe that the presence of G-d was shown in the world.
3 Why do you think things like fire, cloud and bright lights are often used to describe G-d's presence?

The Jewish relationship with G-d

The Chosen People of G-d

> 'For you are a holy people to the Lord your G-d. Out of all the peoples on the face of the earth, the Lord has chosen you to be His treasured possession.' *(Deuteronomy 14:2)*

The Jewish people believe that this idea of being chosen is a responsibility on them. It does not give them privileges, rather it gives them the job of serving G-d through observance of the mitzvot (religious laws). This responsibility is exclusive to them in how it must be done, but they also believe that others can also have a responsibility to G-d, but just a different one.

Jewish people also believe that this status of being chosen will never change.

> 'I will establish my covenant between me and you and your descendants after you in their generations, for an everlasting covenant, to be G-d to you and your descendants after you.' *(Genesis 17:7)*

> '... because the Lord loved you, He would keep the oath which He had sworn to your ancestors.' *(Deuteronomy 7:8)*

If you look at Deuteronomy 33:2 and Habbakuk 3:3, these suggest the offer to be G-d's chosen people was made to every other nation, but it was the Jewish people who accepted the offer.

Can you think of the implications arising from being a member of the chosen people?

The Covenants

> 'You are standing this day all of you before the Lord your G-d that you may enter into the Covenant of the Lord your G-d ... that He may set you this day for Himself and that He may be to you a G-d.' *(Deuteronomy 29:10-13)*

A Covenant (brit) is an agreement between G-d and humankind. They are a permanent link between the past, present and future and can never be dissolved. There are three covenants. The idea of the Covenants is that G-d needed a people who He could 'dwell' within, who would serve Him and prepare the world for a future time when all humans would know G-d. If the Jewish people did this, then G-d would never abandon them. Each Covenant consists of a promise made by G-d to His people, a promise made by humankind to G-d and a physical sign to seal each agreement.

Abraham – G-d promised to look after the descendants of Abraham, give them the Promised Land and help them: humankind would only worship One G-d and be obedient to Him and the sign was the circumcision of all Jewish males.

Moses – G-d promised to free the Jewish people from slavery, make them a nation of holy priests and make them His chosen people (thus carrying out His agreement to help them): humankind would obey the rules of G-d and the sign was/is the Sabbath Day and keeping it special.

How hard are these agreements to keep for humankind? Explain why it is or it is not hard.

Abraham

Moses

The Covenant with Abraham – the first of the Patriarchs

Abraham was called Abram when he was born in Ur (modern-day Iraq) about 1800BCE, the son of Terach an idol merchant. One story about Abraham is that as he grew he questioned his father's belief in many gods. Abram believed the world was created by one god and tried to persuade his father of this. One day Abram smashed all the idols and told his father the largest idol had done it, to which his father replied: 'How can they, these idols have no power or life.' Abram replied: 'Why do you worship them then?' Abram began to teach his own belief in one god.

The Covenant between Abraham and G-d

G-d promised Abraham three things: land, descendants and a blessing and redemption. Abraham did not have to make any promises, though he did only worship the One G-d. The sign of Abraham's acceptance of the covenant was circumcision. This is found in Genesis 12:1–3.

The impact of the Covenant with Abraham

For the Jewish people this Covenant means that there are rights and responsibilities on each side. The Covenant was very important before the Torah was written because it was their connection with G-d. Abraham had his faith in the One G-d tested ten times, the first being leaving home. However, the tenth was his greatest test; G-d commanded him to offer his son Isaac as a sacrifice. It was also a test of Isaac's faith because Jewish people believe he knew he was to be sacrificed and did not resist, rather Isaac helped his father build the altar that would be used. At the last moment, G-d stopped Abraham; he had passed the test, and G-d provided a ram instead. Interestingly, child sacrifices were not uncommon at this time in history, but Judaism has always strongly opposed them. After this event G-d knew Isaac had faith strong enough to continue his father's work.

Look up the story in Genesis 25 to see what happened.

Abraham's connection with Jewish people today:

1 Abraham is as the Father of the Jewish nation (the founding father).

2 The Covenant he made binds the Jewish people to G-d.

3 The circumcision of all males unites all the children of Israel.

4 For G-d's part this is the beginning of the idea of the Promised Land, which most Jewish people hold so dear to their hearts. A nation needs a homeland, and this is where it can develop fully and be a 'light to the nations'. No longer a wandering nomadic people, being forced to move from country to country due to persecution as their ancestors had to, Jewish people today believe their homeland is G-d-given land. This is why many Jewish people are encouraged to return and settle with their families in Israel. Unfortunately many Jewish people believe, due to anti-Semitism throughout history, that it is the only place they will be safe.

The Basics

1 Describe the events which led to the Covenant with Abraham.
2 How difficult do you think the things G-d asked of Abraham were? What might Jewish people learn for their own lives from this?
3 Explain why Abraham is important to many Jewish people today.
4 Give a brief outline of the life of Moses. Which part of his life do you think was the most important? Explain why.
5 Explain the Covenant given to Moses.
6 How might each of these Covenants affect the lives of Jewish people today?
7 **Abraham is a role model for all.** Explore this statement, giving explained arguments to agree and disagree, including Jewish arguments.
8 **Abraham's Covenant was more important than the one given to Moses.** Do you agree with this statement? Explain your reasons.

The Covenant with Moses

Moses is probably one of the most famous characters in the Torah. Most people have heard or seen the story of Moses in childhood books, cartoons or films. Look at the images below. *Can you work out an outline of his life? Write it down in pairs.*

Moses was an Israelite. Egyptians saw the Israelites as a threat and forced them into enslavement. To reduce the number of Israelites in Egypt, the Pharaoh ordered the killing of Israelite babies. To save him, Moses' mother placed him in a reed basket and put it into the River Nile, where he was found by an Egyptian princess. Moses was then brought up as an Egyptian, but when he killed an Egyptian guard who was attacking an enslaved person, he had to flee Egypt. G-d spoke to him, telling him to go and see the Pharaoh to demand release of the enslaved Israelites. It took a while and ten plagues, but eventually they were released, and Moses led them in the wilderness. He was given the Ten Commandments and the Torah by G-d, and though he himself was not allowed to go into the Promised Land, when he died he was within sight of it.

The Sinai Covenant

What happened on Mount Sinai was very important to the Israelites at the time and for Jewish people today. Moses was given the Ten Commandments along with an explanation of the laws and how they were to be interpreted, known as the 'oral law'. Basically, G-d dictated to him. These laws still influence the lives and behaviour of all Jewish people in all aspects; hence the 'great Law-Giver'. The Ten Commandments are found in Exodus 20:1–17.

As his part of the Covenant, the Israelites promised to follow the Laws of G-d (the Ten Commandments and the 613 mitzvot), and in return the people would be the chosen people of G-d, receiving G-d's blessings. Moses also led the people to the Promised Land so completing the promise G-d made to Abraham in the earlier Covenant. Also it was with G-d's help that all this happened, as promised by G-d.

Obedience to the commandments – the 613 mitzvot including the Ten Commandments

The mitzvot (of which there are 613) are the rules of G-d. They are found in the Torah (the first part of the Tenakh). They govern many aspects of daily life for a Jewish person. They cover rituals to do with worship and ethical laws to do with morality. They were given to Moses who taught them to the Israelites in the desert. To keep these laws is to keep the Covenants; to disobey them is to break the Covenants. Some of the laws are judgements, and the reason for keeping them is obvious, for example, 'thou shalt not kill'. These are known as **mishpatim**. Others are statutes (known as 'hukim'), they are there as a test of faith because it could be argued that there is no real reason for them other than because G-d told them they had to be followed, for example, Jewish people must not wear a garment made of wool and linen fabrics together. Only G-d himself knows the reasons for these. The laws bind the Jewish nation to G-d and the well-being of the nation is dependent upon the keeping of these laws.

The Promised Land

This is the land promised to the descendants of Abraham by G-d. In the Tenakh (the Jewish scriptures) it is a theme throughout and the promise is made again to Isaac (Abraham's son) and Jacob (Abraham's grandson). These three are known as the Patriarchs of Judaism. The idea is that this promise is made to all Jewish people.

The Promised Land has had many names. In ancient times it was known as Canaan, later as Palestine and today Jewish people consider it is Israel. In fact, if the boundaries the Tenakh describe were mapped out, the Promised Land would include far greater territory than what Israel has today. It would include all of Israel, the West Bank and Gaza, Jordan, some of Egypt and Syria, Saudi Arabia and Iraq. Moses was shown the Promised Land by G-d from the top of Mount Nebo; he saw it with his own eyes. For Jewish people this land is the only place where it is possible to keep all of the mitzvot and where a third Jewish Temple could be built. Many Jewish people want a time in the future where all Jewish people return and the Temple will be rebuilt, which many Jewish people say will happen in the Messianic Age (see pages 172–174). Today Israel continues to encourage Jewish people to return 'home'.

The Basics

1 Find out why Moses only saw the Promised Land but G-d would not let him enter it.
2 How might Moses' story influence peoples thinking today about the Promised Land?
3 Do you think there a link between the Promised Land and heaven? Explain your answer.
4 **The Promised Land is just a dream.** Explore that statement, showing you have thought about more than one point of view.

The Ten Commandments (Decalogue)

Exodus 20:1–17

i	I am the Lord your G-d who has taken you out of the land of Egypt.
ii	You shall have no other gods but me.
iii	You shall not take the name of the Lord your G-d in vain.
iv	You shall remember the Sabbath and keep it Holy.
v	Honour your mother and father.
vi	You shall not murder.
vii	You shall not commit adultery.
viii	You shall not steal.
ix	You shall not bear false witness.
x	You shall not covet anything that belongs to your neighbour.

The Torah or the Five Books of Moses – Genesis (Bereshit in Hebrew), Exodus (Shemot), Leviticus (Vayikra), Numbers (Bamidbar) and Deuteronomy (Devarim) – are the direct words of G-d in Judaism. It is the first part of three which make up the Tenakh (Jewish scriptures). The Torah is often a term used for the whole of the Jewish scriptures and the oral law. Its importance is immense and it was Moses who brought it to G-d's chosen people.

Task

The ten rules stated in the Ten Commandments cover every aspect of life and there is therefore no need for other laws. What do you think? Analyse two sides of this statement being careful to refer to Jewish arguments in your answer.

The Ten Commandments (**Decalogue**) are found in the Torah. They have been called 'forever' commandments, that is, directed at every believer in every time. They are a condensed version of the 613 mitzvot, and are believed by Orthodox Jewish people to have been written on stone by G-d himself. The Decalogue is crucial to Jewish life today. The chosen people of G-d have the responsibility to serve G-d, and living according to His laws shows both respect and worship. Today, the Ten Commandments are often found over the Ark in synagogues in a form representing two tablets of stone. The Ark holds the Torah, and the Torah is the source of authority for Jewish life. The 613 mitzvot (which are the religious laws and which include the Ten Commandments), encompass all aspects of daily life, and, if followed, build a better person and a harmonious society. The command to keep the Sabbath Day holy is strictly carried out each week by many Jewish families. It is a day to focus on G-d and family, reminding them of their part in the Covenant.

The 613 mitzvot (the religious laws of Judaism)

The Talmud tells us that there are 613 mitzvot: 365 commands to 'not do' and 248 commands 'to do'. However, it does not list them. Maimonides was a great Jewish philosopher who lived in the twelfth century CE. He listed the 613 mitzvot in his Mishneh Torah, which is considered his greatest work, and one of, if not, the greatest Jewish legal text in history. Some laws require the Temple in Jerusalem, which was destroyed in 70CE, so it is not now possible to carry those laws out.

To learn the Torah and to teach it.

Not to wrong anyone in speech.

To love the stranger.

Not to curse your father or mother.

Not to break a vow.

Not to crave something that belongs to someone else.

Not for a man to wear women's clothing.

Not to tattoo the skin.

Not to punish anyone who has committed an offence under duress.

Those in war shall not fear their enemies.

Not to eat meat with milk in the same meal.

Not to lend with interest.

Tasks

1 Look at each of the laws above. The phrases around the edge of the page show the categories. Put each law into a category.
2 Write a brief explanation as to what you think the law is saying.
3 How relevant or meaningful do you think the mitzvot are for Jewish people in the world today?

God Torah Signs and symbols Prayers Love and brotherhood The poor Gentiles

Family Forbidden Sex Times Dietary Laws Business Practices Employees Vows Sabbatical Court Injuries

Wars Nazarites The King Leprosy RITUAL PURITY Sacrifices The Temple Tithes Priests The Firstborn

Property Criminal laws Punishments and Restitution PROPHECY Idolatry Agriculture Clothing

Mitzvot between humans and G-d

The idea of following the mitzvot is not simply a matter of obeying rules; it goes far deeper than that for Jewish people. It is seen as a way of communicating with G-d as they are His way of reaching out to His people. Keeping them is humankind's way of reaching out to G-d. However, some of the mitzvot are not entirely clear, for example, 'do not work on the Sabbath.' What counts as work? Orthodox Jewish people believe G-d not only gave Moses the mitzvot, but also the interpretation of these laws (the Halakah). This can be translated as 'the path that one walks'. If Jewish people follow the laws relating to G-d then they will walk in the way G-d wants them to. The Halakah continues to be added to by leading Orthodox rabbis and reinterpreted by Progressive rabbis so is applicable for Jewish life in an ever-changing world; like an ongoing process keeping Judaism up to date.

There are six constant mitzvot: to know there is a G-d, to not believe in other gods, that G-d is One, to love G-d, to fear G-d and to not be misled by your heart and eyes. Whatever Jewish people do should fulfil these mitzvot. Jewish people are encouraged to not just believe in G-d but to **know G-d**, by study (know in mind) and by love (know in heart). G-d is always with them, they can trust Him. He provides and leads humankind in the right way and, although that path might be tough, Jewish people have to keep on it. There are obviously mitzvot directly relating to G-d, such as for beliefs, prayer, rituals, worship and the Temple. However, if those related to one's actions towards a fellow human are done well then, as this is what G-d wants then they are related to G-d too. All mitzvot bring Jewish people 'closer' to G-d and that is what underpins the whole of Judaism.

Mitzvot between human and human

These mitzvot relate to Jewish people's actions towards their family and neighbours. If they were followed, then the world would be a far better place for humankind. They are ethics; a code of behaviour. The laws are not just laws, for example: from the laws on punishing a criminal Jewish people learn to act justly and seek the truth, from the laws on borrowing and lending money they learn to be compassionate, from the laws on agriculture and food they learn what is best for nature and health. Also, if Jewish people act in a responsible, caring way towards each other, then G-d is pleased, His goodness flows through people, G-d and humankind are closer to each other and so the central aim of the chosen people (to serve G-d) is fulfilled. Some observers might look at Judaism and say that it is too bound up by following rules. For a Jewish person, though, the rules have a far deeper and far more important meaning. Following the law is seen as walking in the path of G-d, fulfilling their part of the Covenant and bringing G-d's holiness into the world ready for the time when all humans will know G-d (Jeremiah 31:31–34).

The Basics

1 What are the mitzvot? Give some examples.
2 Why might it be difficult to follow the mitzvot as they are stated sometimes? Use examples to help demonstrate your points.
3 Explain the difference between mitzvot between humans and G-d and mitzvot between humans and humans. Use examples.
4 Explain why the mitzvot are important for a Jewish person in their daily life.

The relationship between free will and the 613 mitzvot

What is free will?

Free will is the ability to make decisions, to choose right from wrong. If humans do not have free will, then their actions have no moral or religious value. The Torah is clear that G-d has a role in determining what humans do. It is equally clear that, in most cases, human beings have free will and can choose what to do. Jewish tradition assumes that our actions *are* significant. According to the Jewish people, they were given the Torah and commanded to follow its Commandments – reward and punishment would follow their choices. In order for this to be true, then humans must have free will. G-d could not reward or punish people, if it were already decided what they would do. The 613 mitzvot tells Jewish people how to do good and avoid evil so humans have the power to do both. Jewish people believe they are urged to do good with G-d's help. Sometimes, though, there are exceptions to the Commandments. For example, if you are attacked and your life is in grave danger and you kill in self-defence, it is not considered to be breaking the Commandments. Sometimes humans do not control what is happening, but they can control their reaction to it. For example, a farmer chooses to plant a crop and to look after it, but whether it grows is out of his hands, that is the work of G-d. Hence human beings have free will but G-d can decide the outcomes.

How do Jewish people know humans have free will?

Genesis 3:22 says that humans know good from evil.

Deuteronomy 11:26–28 states, 'You can therefore see that I am placing before you both a blessing and a curse. The blessing is obeying the Commandments of your G-d, which I am prescribing to you today. The curse is if you do not obey the Commandments of your G-d, and you go astray from the path that I am prescribing for you today …'.

What do you think this means? How could it be interpreted in terms of following the rules and free will?

G-d said to Moses that in spite of clearly saying that those not following the Commandments would be cursed, G-d was aware that there was no guarantee that humankind would stick to them. *Why do you think that is true?*

Orthodox Jewish people believe they have to follow the mitzvot as written. As far as they are concerned, there is no room for exercising free will other than in using it to follow the mitzvot.

The Reform Jewish movement has a set of principles based in the mitzvot. They also believe that if Judaism is going to be progressive and inclusive, certain things need to be accepted/supported, such as the equality of women, the diversity in family structures today, mixed race families, same-sex couples and women rabbis, which are currently not in Orthodox Judaism. The mitzvot therefore are understood differently. There is an element of free will to make decisions about such things for the benefit of society. Laws always have to be interpreted and people will always have different opinions but the decisions should be made for the benefit of humankind.

Key moral principles – healing the world

Tikkun olam – where is this idea found in Jewish teaching?

Tikkun olam is the Hebrew word meaning to repair or heal the world. Humankind has a responsibility to heal or restore and change the world.

Keeping Shabbat – The idea of a day of rest has an effect on the other six days. The idea is that it is a day when Jewish people can renew their efforts to bring about a better world.

The Mishnah is the first rabbinic writing of the oral law: that is, laws which were passed orally before finally being written down by the rabbis. In it can be found the phrase 'tikkun olam,' which relates to the idea of doing something, not because holy texts say so, but because it helps create social harmony and a better community.

Ethical mitzvot directly provide 'healing of the world'. To be a Jewish person is to fully encourage people to work individually and as a collective towards a better world for everyone. Ethical mitzvot are about right thought and actions towards each other and if people can do this, then the world is healed.

Jewish people believe that the more people who practise tikkun olam, the more the world is repaired and they become nearer to what is known as the Messianic Age (a time in the future when there will be peace and togetherness on earth with no crime or poverty or war, see pages 172–174). In other words, the world will live in harmony and social justice.

The phrase is found within Jewish prayer. Joshua (the leader of the Israelites after Moses died) wrote the Aleinu prayer which Jewish people say three times a day. The prayer praises G-d for allowing them to serve G-d; they hope that the whole world will one day believe in the One G-d. Scholars debate the actual meaning with some saying it tells humans to heal the world, physically helping others and so the goodness of G-d can shine through. Others say it is to separate what is holy from the created world, so is a much more spiritual and contemplative act. The idea is also found in other prayers as well, even if not using the actual phrase 'tikkun olam'. For example, Jewish people pray for the harmony of nations, the uniting of people, where there is no hatred, where the sick are healed and the damage done by human to other humans ceases.

The Basics

1. What is tikkun olam?
2. Explain why Jewish people believe that healing the world is a key principle of the religion.
3. Give examples of the ways in which Jewish people might live by this principle.
4. **In the modern world, tikkun olam is the most important principle any Jewish person can follow.** Explore arguments for and against this statement. Try to use examples when you explain your arguments.

Jewish people believe they have a role/duty in creating a world of social harmony and peace. This will make life better for all and move forward towards a Messianic Age. Individually, Jewish people can set their lives up as an example and many believe they do this every day. For example, by following the mitzvot, giving personally to charity and working for good causes.

Isaiah 42:6 says that the Jewish people 'will be a light to the nations.' Many Jewish people believe that by carrying out the mitzvot their communities would be examples for others. Others would aspire to live in the same way. Orthodox Jewish people believe that following mitzvot can change the world so it is as G-d wants it, which heals it. So even though 'tikkun olam' is not a phrase used in the Torah, if a Jew adheres to the mitzvot then the world can still be healed. Progressive Jewish people believe practically healing the world is integral to being a Jew. Both believe that however the healing is achieved it is something that must be done.

The filmmaker Mimi Leder

Find out about this filmmaker. What motivates her films? How does she put the idea of healing the world in her films? Do you think doing this can spread the idea of tikkun olam to others?

Rabbi Lord Sacks received a knighthood from Queen Elizabeth II in 2005 for his work to bring together those of different faiths and his service to the community. He used his job to 'heal the world'.

Think about how they can heal the world.

Mitzvah Day (**www.mitzvahday.org.uk**) encourages Jewish people to volunteer their time for community projects; social action to bring about change at a community level. Look up (**www.tikkunolamisrael.org**) and see the social action programmes in which Arabs and Jewish people work for coexistence.

Make sure you have real-life examples of people/organisations that put 'healing the world' into action.

Tzedakah

This means 'doing righteous acts' and Jewish people are obliged to give as much as they can for the welfare of humanity. Many tithe their money (give 10 per cent of earnings), **tzedakah** boxes are found in synagogues and it is a Jewish custom to give something every day (except Shabbat).

Task

Look up the work of World Jewish Relief **www.worldjewishrelief.org**. *Write about this organisation, showing how its work contributes to the 'healing the world' principle.*

Key moral principles – justice and charity

Earlier we looked at the idea of G-d being the judge and as such G-d will judge people with justice and fairness

Religious quotes

'It has been told to you, O man, what is good and what the Lord requires of you; only to do justice and love kindness and walk humbly with your G-d.' *(Micah 6:8)*

'Turn from evil and do good; seek peace and pursue it.' *(Psalm 34:14)*

If your enemy is hungry, give him food to eat; if he is thirsty, give him water to drink.' *(Proverbs 25:21)*

What do you think these quotes are telling Jewish people?

Rabbi Sacks, the former Chief Rabbi of Orthodox Jewish people in the UK, explains tzedakah as both justice and charity. The word 'justice' in English refers to fairness and making things right. The Hebrew word tzedakah bonds together the ideas of charity and justice. Jewish people believe that G-d has gifted their wealth to them as a loan, and a responsibility of that loan is to use some of it to help those less fortunate or in need. This is an act of charity, which also brings justice. Rabbi Sacks said 'tzedakah is one word that has the power to change the world.'

Amos 5:24 says 'Let justice roll like water and righteousness as a permanent torrent.' The idea of working for a just world connects to the last topic on tikkun olam in that it contributes to repairing the world.

If we look at the world today, there are many areas where social justice is required. Civil rights for people of different races, sexualities and with disabilities, economic justice (for example, a living wage for all), religious freedoms, women's rights, the rights of people to live in a safe world, these are all areas that Jewish people can support. *Visit* **www.reformjudaism.org** *to see the kind of action for justice that can be taken.*

Tzedek is a Jewish charity whose vision is of the Jewish community involved in the reduction of abject poverty. It works to relieve poverty in developing countries, especially in Africa and India, supporting sustainable development, and also on educating the Jewish people about their responsibility to tackle such poverty. Tzedek tries to work with communities both in their homeland and on the move to resolve problems of poverty, sending volunteers to work to improve lives and create social justice.

Task

1 What is justice?
2 Explain, using examples, how the Jewish belief in justice leads Jewish people to work for social justice.
3 Explain how tzedekah leads to the righting of injustice.
4 **Resolving injustice would solve all the world's problems.** What is your opinion of this statement? Explain your reasoning.

Key moral principles – loving kindness

'The world is built on chesed' *(Psalms 89:3)*

Chesed is the Hebrew word for loving kindness. This Jewish virtue also contributes to tikkun olam. It is also central to the Commandments, which focus on people's relationships with each other. According to traditional Jewish belief, G-d's first act of creating the world was a clear act of chesed. G-d also sustains people through difficulties in their lives with His loving kindness. The word 'chesed' appears in the Torah over 245 times, two-thirds of these detailing G-d's loving kindness. When Jesus used the famous Christian teaching 'love your neighbour', he was simply quoting the Torah (Leviticus 19).

The Pirkei Avot (the ethics of the Jewish fathers) state that the world stands on three things: the Torah, the service of G-d and acts of loving kindness. There are always going to be problems in the world for which we may not have the solutions, however, acts of loving kindness can make many situations better. In the Tenakh, the prophet Micah actually says that it is not just the doing of loving acts that is important, but it is the loving of doing those acts which makes them chesed. It is also seen as even better than tzedekah because, according to the Talmud, it can be done for the rich **and** poor, the living **and** the dead and can be done with money **and** actions. The Laws of the Torah, healing the world and social justice and loving kindness are designed to create a society where no one takes from another or harms another or takes advantage of others' misfortune. At the same time, everyone gives to each other, helps one another and protects one another. So the focus is on personal service, personal attitudes and efforts from the heart. There are no restrictions to what can be done. This includes all aspects of life, Jewish person's relationships with each other, with the environment and with animals and with non-Jewish people as well.

Look at the following pictures – how do they show loving kindness?

Task

Research the work of one chesed organisation. There are many all over the world. Some are youth based groups whilst others are aimed at anyone wanting to be involved with chesed. Write a brief article about the organisation, what they do and explain how this work improves social justice and contributes to tikkun olam.

The Messiah

'He will be born of human parents, so definitely not G-d. He will be able to trace his family line back to King David (the second King of Israel, author of the Psalms) and he will restore the throne of David. The Hebrew term Moshiach (meaning anointed [one] Messiah) is used in the Torah, but to refer to kings or high priests rather than the Messiah himself. However, there are many references to the Messiah in the writings of the prophets ...'

'The scriptures tell of the prophet Elijah announcing the coming of the Messiah, who will ride into Jerusalem on a donkey; graves will open and the dead will rise. In Jewish history, as the kings failed to live up to creating a world of peace and following G-d, the hope grew that one day someone would usher in G-d's reign of peace. But the Jewish nation began to despair as they were exiled and Israel was occupied. This allowed the idea of a Messiah to become an even more prominent belief to cling to and to actively look for. Maimonides in the Mishneh Torah has the idea of Messiah as one of thirteen fundamental Jewish beliefs. The belief in the Messiah forms a part of the Amidah prayer said three times daily. This human figure would be sent by G-d to bring in a new era of peace – the Messianic Age. There have been many claims to be the Messiah – Christians (many of whom were former Jewish people) believe Jesus was the Messiah. Quite simply, though, the world and people are as cruel as ever, so … Jewish people still wait!'

Some Jewish scholars believe G-d has set aside a specific date, so it will happen when He decides.

Others say that it will not happen until the conduct of society needs it to happen. This could be when humanity deserves it the most because our behaviour is good and our beliefs are strong. Alternatively, it could happen when humans need it the most because it is at its most terrible!

Think about it

Think about how different the world will be when the Messiah arrives. Choose some examples from the image below and explain, by use of examples from the modern world, the differences that there will be.

He will be a great political leader descended from King David (Jeremiah 23:5). He will fully understand Jewish Law and observe its commandments (Isaiah 11:2–5). He will be a charismatic leader, inspire others to follow him. He will be a great military leader. He will be a great judge, making righteous decisions (Jeremiah 33:15). He is not G-d or semi-G-d or supernatural in any way. *Here are some of the statements about Him and the Messianic Age.*

1. Once he is King, leaders of other nations will look to him for guidance. (Isaiah 2:4)
2. The whole world will worship the One G-d of Israel. (Isaiah 2:11–17)
3. The spirit of the Lord will be upon him, and he will have a fear of G-d. (Isaiah 11:2)
4. Death will be swallowed up forever. (Isaiah 25:8)
5. There will be no more hunger or illness, and death will cease. (Isaiah 25:8)
6. All of the dead will rise again. (Isaiah 26:19)
7. The Jewish people will experience eternal joy and gladness. (Isaiah 51:11)
8. He will be a messenger of peace. (Isaiah 52:7)
9. Nations will recognise the wrongs they did to Israel. (Isaiah 52:13–53:5)
10. The peoples of the world will turn to the Jewish people for spiritual guidance. (Zechariah 8:23)
11. Weapons of war will be destroyed. (Ezekiel 39:9)
12. The people of Israel will have direct access to the Torah through their minds and Torah study will become the study of the wisdom of the heart. (Jeremiah 31:33)

The Basics

1. What is meant by the term 'Messiah'?
2. When will the Messiah come?
3. What will the Messiah be like?
4. Explain two Jewish teachings about the Messiah.
5. **The Messiah will be a humble man, nothing more.** Explore that idea by using the information on pages 172–174.

The role of the Messiah

So what will he do?

'Ezekiel tells us that before the time of the Messiah there will be war and suffering.'

1. He will bring political and spiritual peace in the land of Israel where Jerusalem will be restored.
2. He will establish a government in Israel that will be the centre of all government for both Jewish people and non-Jewish people.
3. He will rebuild the Temple and establish worship as it should be.
4. He will bring back the religious court system, so that Jewish Law will be the law of the land.

What will the Messianic Age be like?

'This is a bit like what people imagine the afterlife to be. People will live together peacefully, hatred and intolerance will stop. Animals will no longer prey on each other. Crops will be in abundance. All Jewish people will return home to Israel and the whole world will recognise the Jewish G-d as the true G-d. There will be no murder, robbery or any sin at all. Also, all people will have an understanding of religious truths, so religion will not divide us anymore.'

Compare this idea to other religious ideas of paradise and heaven. Do you notice any similarities?

As an Orthodox Jew I believe in a real-life Messiah. A real person who has the qualities described in my holy scriptures and promised by the prophets. I believe that every time we celebrate Shabbat we kind of get a glimpse of what life would be like – G-d's laws at the centre of what we do, time to worship G-d and where family and friends are central to life.

'As a Reform Jew I believe that the Messiah is a symbolic idea. Symbolic of a time when all people work together to bring the Messianic Age to earth. The world will be the place of social justice and kindness – a world repaired, if you like. I don't think we wait for it to happen. I think we have to make it happen.

The Basics

1. How might belief in a Messiah influence Reform Jewish people in their lives today?
2. Why is it important for Orthodox Jewish people to believe in a literal Messiah?
3. **Jewish people should fight for social justice to bring the Messianic Age more quickly.** Explore this idea, showing you have considered more than one point of view. Be sure to include Orthodox and Reform viewpoints.

The Jewish belief in life after death, judgement and resurrection

Judaism, compared to Christianity and Islam, does not place great emphasis on the idea of an afterlife. For Christians and Muslims, this life is short, a test for the eternal life to come where all human actions are seen as important to reach paradise and avoid hell and their holy books provide clear teachings about what the afterlife will be like. For Jewish people this is not the case, though most Jewish people do believe that death is not the end. Many Jewish people would say 'We know nothing about death and we cannot explain rationally what happens after death.' Varyingly, different Orthodox Jewish people might believe in righteous souls going to heaven, or resurrection at the coming of the Messiah, or some form of cleansing of the soul, or even reincarnation for souls that need to carry out unfinished business. At the same time, souls can be tormented or cleansed not by Satan, but by demons of their own creation. The world to come is also open to non-Jewish people who have observed the seven laws of Noah (see page 176).

It is difficult to pin down a single unifying belief about the afterlife in Judaism, so the course requires you to know about some specific aspects.

What do the Torah and Tenakh say about the afterlife?

The Torah itself says nothing about the afterlife or imagery to describe it. It concerns itself with the idea of rewards and punishments now from G-d. Look up Deuteronomy 11:13–15 to see an example. However, there are also passages which indicate that the righteous will be reunited with their loved ones after death and the not-so righteous will not. The Torah seems in favour of focusing more on life in the present, **olam ha-ze**. If Jewish people live properly now, what happens next will take care of itself. Now is the time for Jewish people to repair the world. However, later prophets like Daniel, sections of the Talmud and Maimonides do discuss the idea of an afterlife more. The physical man in G-d's creation came from 'dust', so the body is subject to decay and will return to dust. The soul comes from the essence of G-d and so lives on. Jewish people often call death the departure of the soul, Yetziat HaNeshama in Hebrew.

Resurrection

The resurrection of the dead is a key belief in traditional Judaism, though the Torah does not explicitly discuss it. Masorti Jewish people do believe in a bodily resurrection, but that our understanding is so limited as to stop us knowing what the afterlife will be like. Reform Jewish people also believe in an afterlife but that 'this life' is more important. What Jewish people do now, the efforts they put in to the repair the world, are far more important than gaining the perfection of an afterlife. Resurrection will happen in the Messianic Age. When the Messiah comes to bring peace the righteous dead will rise, the evil people will not be resurrected.

Reincarnation

Some Jewish people believe reincarnation is happening all the time, that souls are reborn to continue tikkun olam. This transmigration of souls (**gilgul** in Hebrew) is an example of divine compassion allowing a soul to fulfil the mitzvot. Hasidic Jewish people believe in reincarnation.

The world to come

Olam ha-ba means 'the world to come' and is mentioned in the Jewish scriptures and by the rabbis. It is like a perfect version of this world. It will physically exist at the end of days after the Messiah has come and G-d has judged the living and the dead. The righteous dead will rise to olam ha-ba, but a description of it is not given. However, it is also used to describe a spiritual realm where souls go at death. Olam ha-ba is said to be like the perfect Shabbat, but it must be prepared for by good deeds and knowing the Torah. However, the emphasis must be on the here and now; strive to live well and value our time here.

Generally olam ha-ba is seen in two ways:

1 It is not life after death but life after the Messiah, when the righteous dead will be resurrected for a second life. Therefore, there is the idea of who will be resurrected. Individuals and nations will stand to be judged.

2 It is the place where souls go either at death or in the future.

As well as olam ha-ba, there is reference to **Gan Eden** and **Gehinnom** which some describe like heaven and hell.

Gan Eden

There is no clear answer as to what Gan Eden is and how it fits in terms of the afterlife. Some say it is the place good people go after they die, but whether this is straightaway or in the future, or whether it is the souls that go there or the resurrected dead is unclear. According to Jewish tradition, the Messianic Age is a time when G-d will create peace and all nations will sit together and eat in Gan Eden. What it does not do is mention the dead! Some teachings in the Talmud describe Gan Eden as an earthly paradise based upon Genesis 2:10–14.

Only the really righteous go directly to Gan Eden.

Gehinnom

Those not going to Gan Eden go to Gehinnom, a place people associate with hell. This is not correct, though. Gehinnom is a place of cleansing for the soul, with the suggestion that no one is there beyond 12 months (at which point they move to olam ha-ba). It is not eternal torment in fires for most, rather a place where the soul sees the things they have done wrong, the harm they have caused and experiences remorse over these things. For the very wicked, some Jewish people believe that the soul ceases to exist after the twelve months, whilst others believe it continues in a state of remorse.

The term Gehinnom appears later in Jewish history. Some Jewish people claim it was created by G-d on the second day of creation. The rabbis believed anyone who did not live by the Torah would spend some time in Gehinnom. It was used to encourage people to do good, not to scare them. It is described in terms of fire, but not eternal fire.

Overall, the process of what Judaism believes about the afterlife is hard to describe. Even set ideas are difficult to explain. The afterlife is unknown and incomprehensible. This reinforces the idea that Jewish people need to concentrate on this life now, doing things out of a love for doing them, not for a good afterlife. The rest will take care of itself in the future ... whatever, wherever and whenever that happens.

The Basics

1 Write a short paragraph on each key term: olam ha-ze, olam ha-ba, Gan Eden, Gehinnom.
2 Explain why it is difficult to describe the afterlife for Jewish people.
3 How might a belief in the afterlife affect a Jewish person in their daily life?
4 **The afterlife is not as important as life now.** Do you agree? Give reasons for your answer.

The sanctity of human life

Life was created by G-d and humans were made in His own image.

Several of each species were created but humanity was created 'alone'.

As life comes from G-d it is a sacred/holy gift and should be preserved.

Each life has a purpose and is valuable.

G-d takes life just as He created it.

Think about the statements above.
What implications do they have for life today?

The sanctity of life is not an easy issue. The statements seem like common sense, but when you start to apply them to life issues today it may create some 'grey areas' and differences of opinion.

What do we know about the Jewish attitude?

From as early as the creation story in Genesis, it is clear that every part of creation was special. However, the Talmud suggests that as humanity was made 'alone' and in His image, G-d 'breathed' life into humanity, and gave him free will (unlike all other creations which are subject to nature, controlled by G-d and instinct). Humans do not own their bodies, they simply have them for use until G-d decides He wants to end that use. Humans were given a soul and were created to carry out tikkun olam and to seek out a close relationship with G-d. The former Chief Rabbi of Orthodox Jewish people in the UK, Rabbi Sacks stated that 'in whatever body or whatever disabled mind, there is a soul cast in the image of G-d.'

Life is sacred and must be preserved. Even Shabbat rules can be broken to save a life, for example, an ill person should be driven to hospital on Shabbat, even though driving is an activity not normally allowed on Shabbat.

Each Jewish person, it is believed, has a purpose. To live as G-d wants through the Torah and mitzvot. They are aiming to repair the world by their actions, changing the evil of this world to create peace and harmony and worship of G-d. Humans have a duty to make sure their lives are purposeful and that they make the most of the gift of life.

No human has the right to take a life, unless in self-defence, or as a punishment (capital punishment is still part of the law in many countries), or in the case of war. The 6th Commandment says 'Do not murder.' *This seems very clear, but when it comes to issues like abortion and euthanasia it can become more complicated. In these situations taking a life might prevent suffering. When there are rules, they might seem obvious, when they are thought about, they become more complex and less clear.*

Think about a special gift you have been given (and nothing can be as special as life), are you not expected to look after it at all costs as a sign of appreciation and also not to damage it deliberately?

Pikuach nefesh – the concept of 'saving a life'

It is Shabbat. Is what they are doing correct in Judaism?

Pikuach nefesh is the principle that the preservation of human life takes precedence over all else, because life is sacred.

> *Leviticus 18:5 says,* 'Keep my decrees and laws, for the man who obeys them will live by them. I am The Lord.'

The Talmud emphasises the word 'live' in this statement. The idea is that people will 'live by' the law – it will help them to survive and will protect their lives. The Talmud emphasises this, and making the point that they will not 'die' by the law. Hence the idea of saving a life is seen as more important than keeping the law.

Shabbat gives us a really good way to understand the principle of Pikuach Nefesh. The laws about Shabbat state that no work may be done. However, if a person's life is in danger, the laws of Shabbat should be broken in order to save that life. It actually becomes a requirement to break the law in cases where life is at risk. Life is the most important factor.

> 'I have set before you life and death, blessings and curses. Choose life so that you and your offspring shall live.' *(Deuteronomy 30:19)*

But what if it was not certain that life was at risk? The rabbis decided that in order to be safe, a person should act as if the life was indeed at risk. By acting this way, it saves the time which would be taken to think about the situation, and so makes the saving of life more likely, as well as reducing the chances of judging a situation wrongly, hence leading to someone's death.

> 'The Sabbath has been given to you, not you to the Sabbath.' *(Talmud)*

Pikuach nefesh is also extended beyond saving life to preventing life-shortening issues, so for example preventing the loss of a limb, or blindness. Pikuach nefesh demands a person do everything in their power to save the life of another, so includes organ donation. The Sephardic Chief Rabbi of Israel, Ovadya Yosef stated that this was the case, as long as donation does not put the life of the giver at risk, and the recipient is in a life-threatening situation. The example used most often is that of kidney transplant – a person can live with just one kidney, the success rate for transplantation is high, and even if it fails, the receiver can be supported by dialysis until a new kidney is sourced.

It has also been said that an autopsy can be a form of pikuach nefesh, if what is learnt from this action later helps to save the lives of others, so for example reveals new medical knowledge on an illness/condition. This attitude seems first to have been seen in the teachings of Rabbi Ezekiel Landau (1713–1793) who lived in Prague, and had been asked about it.

How is pikuach nefesh seen in action today?

There are many examples of this concept in the world today.

On certain festivals like Yom Kippur, Jewish people must fast. However, a sick person is obliged to break the fast. It is the right thing to do to observe fasting, but when fasting puts a person's life at risk then it is seen as sinful.

Hatzola (www.hatzola.org) provides a 24/7 emergency medical service, working closely with NHS services. Volunteers provide this service, which is based around being a first responder and ambulance provision. It also runs First Aid courses, gives First Aid advice and gives patient support. All their work is totally funded through donations.

In terms of **health issues**, for example, organ donation, Jewish law says that a body should be buried whole. However, if, when the person is dead, their organs can be used for a specific, named person (rather than organs being stored) to save their life then this should be done under the pikuach nefesh principle. Also, to give away a kidney for this use would also be acceptable from a living donor.

Health workers can work on Shabbat and use pagers and telephones to save lives. For many Jewish people, this means abortion is seen as acceptable if the life of the mother was in danger (even though to take a life is against the commandments). The mother's life is actual life, and so is more important than that of the foetus which is only the promise of or potential life. Pikuach nefesh again is the overriding idea here.

In terms of the environment, pikuach nefesh is the principle used to protect us. Go to www.greenfaith.org. One of the projects Green Faith has been involved in is an interfaith project to change chemical policy in the USA. It has been the case that too many chemicals are used on the land to fertilise crops which can get into and poison water supplies. Law change now means companies have to be more responsible, which helps protect the lives of all.

The Basics

1 Copy and complete this short paragraph:
Pikuach nefesh is the basic _______ of Judaism. It states that the _____________ of human _______ takes ____________ over all else, because life is ___________. ______ may be broken in order to save life. On ___________, it is a requirement to ________ the law if someone's life is at ______.

2 Explain why pikuach nefesh can be considered a basic principle of Judaism.

3 Give some examples of pikuach nefesh in action.

4 Keeping the idea of pikuach nefesh in mind, how might a Jewish person respond to the statement: **The mitzvot bring Jewish people closer to G-d, therefore they should be the ultimate guide for their actions.** Write a balanced answer using examples to explain your points.

Testing your knowledge

One-mark Questions

Multiple-choice question

For the one-mark multiple-choice question, you must choose the correct answer from the four you are offered.

Focusing on the first section of Judaism, on beliefs that you have now studied, try the following:

1 What is meant by Shechinah?

A a section of Judaism B Divine Presence
C G-d D Jewish Holy Day

2 What is the name of the Jewish homeland?

A Galilee B Israel
C Jerusalem D Jordan

3 Which of these is not one of the three key moral principles of Judaism?

A Dietary law B Healing the world
C Justice and charity D Loving kindness

4 What is the Jewish statement of belief called?

A Declaration of Faith B Shabbat
C Shema D Torah

5 What is meant by pikuach nefesh?

A a Jewish charity B coming of the Messiah
C justice D saving a life

Make up four answers to each of the following and test your partner. Do not forget: only ONE can be correct!

1 On which mountain did Moses receive the Ten Commandments?
2 Name the son of Abraham.
3 What is the word used for laws that are judgements?
4 How many mitzvot are there?
5 What is a Covenant?

Short response question

The one-mark short response question is asking you to write a brief response.

You will have to name or give an example of a belief, practice, key term or religious concept.

You may also be asked for a brief definition.

Do not waste time writing too much but make sure you write enough to fully answer the question. Don't leave the examiner guessing at what you mean, or how what you have written does answer the question. Don't be vague!

1 Give one Jewish belief about the Messiah.
2 Name one key moral principle of Judaism.
3 Give one reason why the Torah is important.
4 Name one of the Ten Commandments.
5 Give one way in which Jewish people can show tzedekah.

Make up three one-mark short response questions to test your partner.

Influence Questions

Four-mark questions

These questions are where you show your understanding of the religion you have studied, and how a person's beliefs have an influence on their lives. It is clear that when people believe things, their thoughts, words and actions become shaped by their beliefs – these questions want you to show that. They might look a bit scary at first, but if you get used to them, they become quite straightforward.

You will have to answer one of these questions in each of the beliefs sections of your chosen two religions. They are always worth four marks, and always ask you to explain two ways.

The wording will always begin: 'Explain two ways in which …'

Followed by one of these, or something similar:

- 'belief in/about …'
- 'learning about …'

Finishing off with: 'influences Jewish people today'.

Here are some examples for you to see how that works (and to try):

1 Explain two ways in which belief in pikuach nefesh influences Jewish people today.

2 Explain two ways in which beliefs about the mitzvot might influence Jewish people today.

3 Explain two ways in which believing in the sanctity of life influences Jewish people today.

Go back through your answers to these three questions and use AQA's mark scheme to see how you could improve them.

Look at the following answers. Which do you think is better, and why? Think about how clear the answer is, how detailed it is and whether you can clearly see the influence or effect on the believer.

Explain two ways in which believing in the sanctity of life influences Jewish people today.

Answer 1

One way that believing in the sanctity of life influences Jewish people today is that they think they should protect life when it is in danger. Another way is that they think they should cherish the life they were given by G-d, and enjoy it.

Answer 2

Jewish people believe in the sanctity of life – that life is sacred and special because G-d created it. For many Jewish people this means that abortion is always wrong, as it is the taking of life. The foetus is a potential life, which must be cherished and protected. Although, if it were to be the case that the mother's life was in danger, then an abortion would be allowed as her life is also sacred, and actually more important, as she is fully alive (the foetus isn't yet).

Answer 1: This gives two good ways, however, it doesn't explain either way. You could improve this for them by explaining their ideas.

Answer 2: This gives one way only, but does it in a lot of detail. You could improve this answer by adding a second way which you explain.

Explaining Beliefs and Teachings

Six-mark questions

These questions ask you to explain two beliefs and/or teachings from the religion.

The wording will always begin: 'Explain two Jewish teachings about ...'

Finishing off with: 'Refer to sacred writings or another source of Jewish belief and teaching in your answer.'

They will be marked against AQA's mark scheme which can be found on the AQA website.

From the question wording and the mark scheme you can work out how to answer the question effectively. Each question is different, but in this case you would:

- choose your two teachings and then explain each one
- develop your explanations fully
- use a relevant quotation/teaching, show how it links to the question and include its source of authority. This is where or who the quote/teaching comes from, for example a holy book (Torah), or religious leader.

Remember this is just one example to help you practice. In the exam, you will need to think carefully and respond to the actual question you are given.

What does 'fully develop' mean?

For these questions, you have to 'fully develop' your explanation, which means giving a lot more detail about each point you make. Below is an example. The explanation and further development are highlighted so that you can see them clearly.

Explain two Jewish teachings about the Messiah. Refer to sacred writings or another source of Jewish belief in your answer.

Sample answer

In the Tenakh, in Jeremiah[1], it says that the Messiah will be a great political leader descended from King David[2]. This means that the Messiah will be born a human, as he is a descendant[3]. King David was a great leader, so the Messiah will follow that trend, and be a great leader, which means he will be able to unite and lead the world into the time of the Kingdom of G-d[4].

Looking at the sample answer:

1 it opens by saying where the belief comes from, i.e. the source of authority, here the Tenakh;

2 this is what the Tenakh tells us about the Messiah – it is a general statement, not a direct quotation, but that is fine here;

3 this explains the teaching from the Tenakh by saying why the Messiah will be a human being;

4 this expands the point about the Messiah being a great leader.

Of course, the answer needs a second teaching about the Messiah, written in the same way.

Practise the following questions for yourself:

1 Explain two Jewish teachings about the creation. Refer to sacred writings or another source of Jewish belief in your answer.

2 Explain two Jewish teachings about G-d. Refer to sacred writings or another source of Jewish belief and teaching in your answer.

3 Explain two Jewish teachings about chesed (loving kindness). Refer to sacred writings or another source of Jewish belief in your answer.

Analyse and Evaluate

For GCSE RS you have to be able to show you can react to a given statement. This means that you consider what the statement says, present arguments to agree and disagree and come to a conclusion of what you yourself think of the statement. You have to also demonstrate what a Jewish person would say and what arguments they would use. In the religious section of the paper it will be impossible not to include religious ideas, so do not worry too much about this. This type of question takes the most thinking, so needs the most time. Together these questions will be worth 50 per cent of your exam, so it is essential to practise them.

It is a good idea to work to a formula when you answer this type of question. This structures your answer making it clear and ensuring you meet all the necessary criteria. Here is one formula you might consider using:

Reason to agree	Explanation of that reason	Further explanation	Example to demonstrate
Reason to disagree	Explanation of that reason	Further explanation	Example to demonstrate

Imagine you are building a wall of reasoning to answer the statement. In the formula above you can see that you have to develop your arguments from left to right: so you give a reason, and explain it. Your explanation is in depth and includes an example, so it is a strong argument in its own right. Follow this process two to three times in agreeing and two to three times in disagreeing.

After each argument, or at the end of your answer, you should make evaluative statements. This means explaining which side of the argument is stronger, and why that is so. It might include personal opinions as well.

1 **Sanctity of life is more important than keeping the law.**

Evaluate this statement. You should:
- refer to Jewish teaching
- give reasoned arguments to support this statement
- give reasoned arguments to support a different point of view
- reach a justified conclusion.

2 **It is easier to live as a Jewish person in a Jewish country.**

Evaluate this statement. You should:
- refer to Jewish teaching
- give reasoned arguments to support this statement
- give reasoned arguments to support a different point of view
- reach a justified conclusion.

3 **Every Jewish person should be a Reform Jew.**

Evaluate this statement. You should:
- refer to Jewish teaching
- give reasoned arguments to support this statement
- give reasoned arguments to support a different point of view
- reach a justified conclusion.

4 **If all Jewish people lived by tikkun olam there would be no need for such tight observance of Jewish law.**

Evaluate this statement. You should:
- refer to Jewish teaching
- give reasoned arguments to support this statement
- give reasoned arguments to support a different point of view
- reach a justified conclusion.

The more practice you get on this type of question, the better your technique. The point of these questions is to challenge your application of knowledge, and to make you show your skills in analysis and evaluation. In your conclusion, try not to repeat the same ideas you gave in your for and against sections, as you will have already been credited for these.

Want more practice? Go back through Topic 3.1 and pick out the evaluative statements. Have a go at answering them using the 'building bricks' formula or other formulae you know.

3.2 Practices

Judaism should not be seen as just a religion; it is a whole way of life. Over many centuries of persecution, Judaism has relied on family life for its continued existence and to flourish. Children learned through their families and the practices and traditions (**minhagim**) which were kept and, at times, this was the only way to follow the religion and keep it going. Much of this section is about how religion and family life intertwine.

The **halakah** is Jewish law. 'Halakah' is translated as 'the path one walks': in other words, halakah is the way that Jewish people should live their lives. It covers every aspect of life and it is quite comprehensive in giving guidance on behaviour. For example, it tells Jewish people about the food they can or cannot eat, the types of materials they may wear, the jobs they can do, how to keep themselves clean, how to worship, how to bring up a family, and much more. It is possible and correct to consult the halakah about everything in everyday life. Another way to look at it is to see halakah as giving a spiritual significance to everything done; everything becomes an act of worship, everything links back to faith, everything is a reminder of G-d and one's relationship with G-d. In this section, you will see mention of many traditions and rules, and although not specifically said, these mentions are all of halakah. Keep in mind the idea that Jewish people may be influenced in most, or even all, decisions by their religion.

Go back to pages 165–167 to reflect on the mitzvot, which show how all of life is governed by religious belief, or to pages 163–164 and the Ten Commandments to see how ethical decision-making is influenced. All of this lifestyle section gives you information about how life is influenced, and how the religion impacts on communities.

The way we behave, including towards others, indicates the values we hold. For example, if I believe we are all equal, I will not speak unkindly to someone (without provocation), I will not be greedy or selfish in my choices (so that someone else loses out). Often, if we go against our values, we actually feel bad or in the wrong, as if we have let ourselves down.

What are the guiding values which shape your actions? Can you give examples of where you have followed them? Do you operate consciously or unconsciously within these values?

The law in Judaism

You have read that Judaism governs nearly all aspects of life, that it is a comprehensive way of life. Here, we are going to look a little more closely at the law, namely the Tenakh, from whence most of the law comes, and the Talmud which is a comprehensive written interpretation of the law.

Refer back to the earlier pages on the Torah, and on the mitzvot. These all build into an idea of Jewish law and how it influences lifestyles.

The Tenakh

The Tenakh is the holy scriptures of Judaism as a whole. There are three parts: the Torah (the five books of Moses including the 613 laws), the Nevi'im (Prophets), and the Ketuvim (Writings). The word Tenakh comes from the first letter in Hebrew of each of the three sections. The most sacred part of the Tenakh is the Torah. It is this which is written onto scrolls for use in the synagogue and is read as a whole each year there. This part is considered by Orthodox Jewish people to be the word of G-d, written by Moses (and by Progressive Jewish people as inspired by G-d) and a crucial link between G-d and humanity. It is here we find the mitzvot, the rules which make up Jewish law.

The Torah

The contents make up the religious law of Judaism. Orthodox Jewish people believe that this was told to Moses on Mount Sinai by G-d, so it is of divine origin, hence being considered the word of G-d. Some Jewish people believe it existed before even the world existed, as part of G-d's divine law.

Torah means guidance or instruction. Following its rules means that the Jewish people stay close to G-d. These rules also separate Jewish people from other people in that they follow a specific path, which is true of any religion when followed fully. This is part of the 3rd Covenant, which G-d made with Moses (see page 157).

The Torah contains two types of law: mishpatim (judgements) – laws which are obvious to follow, such as 'Do not kill'; and chukim (statutes) – laws to be followed as a test of faith, such as the food laws.

According to Orthodox Judaism, the Torah is absolute, eternal and relevant everywhere, forever.

At synagogue on Monday, Thursday and Saturday a prescribed portion of the Torah is read. It is divided into 54 portions, and beginning on the festival of Simchat Torah, the final portion (from Deuteronomy) and the first portion (from Genesis) are read in the synagogue. Over the year, the whole of the Torah is read from start to finish in order.

Study of the Torah is crucial and many (particularly Orthodox) Jewish people devote their lives to this study. In Israel, many Haredi (strictly Orthodox) Jewish men are in full-time, state-financed study of the Torah instead of working.

The Nevi'im

These are the books of the prophets; their stories and their teachings. Prophets are people chosen by G-d to guide humanity, and make pronouncements for G-d; often warnings about behaviour.

They provide a historical narrative of early Judaism, as well as religious interpretations of those events and revelations from G-d. They also try to show the character of G-d through these events.

Some people see the prophets as 'G-d's spokesmen on earth'; a way to show that their main role was to obey G-d and deliver G-d's message. This was not always their preference though. The story of Jonah is an example of that, he tried to avoid doing what G-d wanted him to, got swallowed by a whale, and finally agreed to do as he was told.

The Ketuvim

This is a range of literature, from books of poetry (for example, Psalms), to books of historical stories (for example, Daniel), to books of philosophical debates (for example, Job). Ketuvim means 'writings', and they are a collection of unconnected books really. However, there is an underlying theme: every book demonstrates a commitment to G-d, which has been forged through difficulty and hard work.

Five books from the Ketuvim are also known as Megillot, and are used in specific festivals. These are Song of Songs (Pesach), Ruth (**Shavuot**), Lamentations (Tishah B'Av), Ecclesiastes (Sukkot), and Esther (Purim).

The Basics

1 What is the Tenakh? What are its parts?
2 Give two examples of books from each of the three parts of the Tenakh.
3 What is the purpose of each of the three parts of the Tenakh?
4 **The Torah is the only important part of the Tenakh.** Do you agree with this statement? Explain your opinion. Give an alternative view.
5 **Holy books are not relevant to life today.** Give reasons to agree and disagree with this statement. Refer to the Tenakh in your answer.

The Talmud

The Torah has laws for Jewish people to follow, but it was quickly realised that the laws did not give everyone an obvious answer to every question, and that life being as it is, it is difficult to apply the same law to every situation. Whilst the Torah is 'timeless', it still needs to be interpreted and applied if a person is to follow it correctly. The Talmud sets out to do this.

The Talmud is the entirety of Jewish civil and religious law, including commentaries on the Torah.

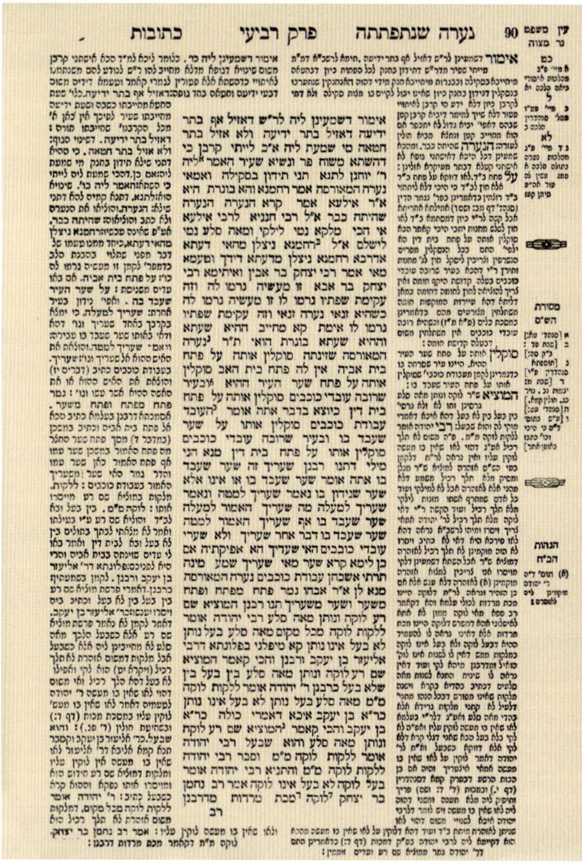
כתובות פרק רביעי נערה שנתפתתה 90

Take a look at the picture of the Mishnah – try to locate the following aspects.

1 The central and key aspects are the Mishnah (a study of Jewish law) and the Gemara (a commentary on the Mishnah). Immediately around it are the references to the Torah and Tenakh, so the reader can see where the origins of this Mishnah come from in their religion.

Rabbi Yehudah ha-Nasi (Rabbi Judah the Prince, who lived in the second century CE) was responsible for the most famous Mishnah, which splits the law into six categories and comments on each. These categories are: laws on agriculture and benedictions, festivals, women, civil law, sacred things, and cleanliness.

The Gemara (meaning 'completion') is the completed discussion of the law. It is written beside the part of the Mishnah it relates to, and its aim is to discuss, explain and simplify the Mishnah.

2 Around the central text, are two sections of commentaries. On its left, the Tosafot are commentaries which were written in the Middle Ages, and on its right is commentary by Rabbi Solomon ben Isaac (Rashi) from the eleventh century CE). The bottom left and bottom right sections are more commentaries: by medieval rabbis (on the left), and more recent ones (on the right).

3 In the outside left and right of the page, you can see references to Jewish law (left) and Talmud (right), so the reader is able to look up other laws which relate to the commentaries or are referenced in them. This helps their understanding.

4 The line of bits of text at the top is like a title line telling you the page number, what you are reading about, and so on.

Why is the Talmud important?

The Talmud is important because it helps a Jewish person to understand G-d's law and so live a correct life. The laws are there, but not absolutely clear. They might tell you that you have to do something, but not how to do it, for example: that meat has to be from a ritually slaughtered animal, but not what constitutes ritual slaughter.

The Torah is part of the Covenant with G-d made with Moses (see page 162), and is how Jewish people can understand how to fulfil the Covenant.

Time changes how people live and what people do, and even though the Torah is timeless, it does not mention many things, for example new technology. The commentaries apply today's problems to Torah law.

It has been said that the Talmud has moulded the Jewish people as a nation. Many aspects of Jewish culture are connected to, or based on, or inspired by the Talmud.

Talmud means 'study'. This is important because Jewish people don't just memorise the Talmud, they study it. Study brings greater understanding of the Torah, so helping Jewish people follow G-d's commands more effectively.

> 'The Talmud is really about the conversation, and the conversation never ends.' Rabbi Dov Linzer

> Albert Einstein was asked – shortly before his death – what he would do differently if he had his life again. 'I would study the Talmud' was his reply.

> 'If the Tenakh is the cornerstone of Judaism, then the Talmud is the central pillar, soaring up from the foundations and supporting the entire spiritual and intellectual edifice.' Rabbi Adin Even Israel Steinsaltz

The Midrash

Midrash is a kind of literature written by rabbis. It means 'story telling' and explores the ethics and values in texts from the Tenakh. There are two kinds – **Aggadah** (story) and halakah (interpretation of the law). It is used to interpret the texts or answer questions which arise from them, questions which are not clearly answered from the text itself.

> Studying the Talmud is like joining a conversation which spans centuries. You become part of that conversation and discussion with Jewish people great and otherwise which clarifies Jewish law.

The Basics

1 What is the Talmud?
2 Why is the Talmud important?
3 How does the Talmud influence the life of Jewish people today?
4 What is the Midrash?
5 Why is the Midrash important/helpful?
6 **Jewish people only need the Mishnah to understand how G-d wants them to live.** Do you agree with this statement? Explore and explain reasons for and against it.

Jewish dietary law

Kashrut is the word that covers things and persons which meet Jewish religious requirements. It is used mostly in describing the food laws and to indicate which foods are edible.

I keep kosher as fully as I can. My kitchen is adapted; I shop at kosher stores. It is part of what reminds me to be consciously Jewish, and consciously thankful to G-d for his love.

Philip

Where do these rules come from?

The key sections of the Torah are Leviticus 11 and Deuteronomy 14, which explain the animals that can be eaten, these are kosher, and the animals which cannot be eaten (**treyfah**).

Task

Read the text of Deuteronomy below (in the central column) and answer the questions (either side).

Looking at the list of animals a Jewish person may not eat, can you see any issues for Jewish people in the UK?	Do not eat any detestable thing. These are the animals you may eat: the ox, the lamb and kid, deer, gazelle, the antelope, ibex, chamois, bison and giraffe. And every animal that has a split hoof and has a hoof cloven into two sections, chews the cud among the animals that you may eat.	What does detestable mean?
	But you shall not eat of those that chew the cud, or of those that have the split hooves: the cloven one, camel, hyrax, and the hare, for they chew the cud, but do not have split hooves; they are unclean for you.	Looking at the list of animals a Jewish person might eat, can you see any issues for Jewish people in the UK?
	And the pig, because it has a split hoof, but does not chew the cud; it is unclean for you. You shall neither eat of their flesh, nor touch their carcass.	Why might it be said that the sanction against the pig is the strongest?
List fish that may be eaten, and those that may not.	These you may eat of all that are in the waters; all that have fins and scales, you may eat. But whatever does not have fins and scales, you shall not eat; it is unclean for you.	
	You may eat every clean bird. But these are those from which you shall not eat: the eagle, ossifrage, osprey; white vulture, black vulture, the kite after its species; and every raven; and the ostrich, owl, the gull and hawk; the falcon, ibis, and the bat; the pelican, magpie, cormorant; the stork, heron, the hoopoe and the atalef.	Use the list of what can't be eaten, and your knowledge of poultry to make a list of birds which can be eaten.
	And every flying insect is unclean for you; they may not be eaten. You may eat any clean fowl.	
A carcass is a dead body. This is a reference to an animal not ritually killed. Can you think of examples?	You shall not eat any carcass.	

You now have a list of clean animals which are kosher and fit to eat. However, if these animals are not ritually slaughtered their meat is 'neveilah', making it not kosher. Also, there are parts of kosher animals which are not to be eaten, for example, the internal fat of cattle, lamb and goat, called cheilev is considered in the same way that blood is (as the 'seat of life'), so is treyfah. This used to be burnt as sacrifice in the temple. The meat must be as clean of blood as possible. The sciatic sinew (which runs from the spine down the leg) must have been removed.

All fruit, vegetables and pulses can be eaten, and with either meat or milk because they are neutral food (**parev**). However, they should have been washed and checked for bugs and insects which are not kosher. They are neutral foods – **parev**.

Milk and milk products are fine to eat, but there are rules about combining these with meat, which we will look at on the next page.

Observing dietary law is very deep-rooted in Judaism. Many Jewish people keep dietary law very carefully, others loosely, and some do not keep it at all. However, all are at least aware of it. Considering that throughout their history, Jewish people have usually lived in non-Jewish countries, it has often been far from easy to follow dietary law. It should be respected therefore that it has been preserved by the community for centuries. Maimonides said that dietary laws train people to master their appetites, which is important when you think that food is a limited resource, especially meat.

I don't have two sets of everything, two sinks and so on – like you see in the books. I do check all that I buy to try to ensure it is kosher. Whilst I keep kosher, I think others are stricter in the way they do. This is about what works for me and my family, and as long as I am mindful of G-d, I think this is OK.

Anne

Eating kosher reminds us of our connectedness to G-d. We shouldn't eat just from hunger, we should always remember the Creator. So keeping kosher underlines that connection by making us think before we even eat.

Isaac

My family don't keep kosher very closely at all. To me it is important to live out principles which help others – chesed, tzedek, for example – than just think about what I eat. Of course, I don't just eat anything, but I also can't say I am very observant on this score.

Sue

With a partner, discuss which of these is kosher, and why. Which are not kosher, and why?

The Basics

1 What are kashrut, kosher and treyfah?
2 List four animals whose meat may be eaten by Jewish people if ritually slaughtered.
3 List four animals which are forbidden to eat.
4 What is parev?
5 Explain how the dietary laws have been important in Judaism.
6 **It is fine for Jewish people to eat non-kosher food if there is no kosher meat available.** Explore this statement, giving explained reasons to agree and disagree.

Ritual slaughter

For Jewish people who only eat kosher food, any meat cooked and consumed must have come from an animal which is, firstly, allowed by scripture, and, secondly, has been ritually slaughtered.

The animal has to have been slaughtered by a shochet (qualified kosher slaughterer), through a quick, deep stroke across the neck with a perfectly sharp blade. This leads to rapid blood loss and death. It is believed to be the most humane way to kill animals. A shochet is not only trained to be a butcher, he should be recognised as a good man, and should be well-trained in Jewish law.

Kosher butchers are regularly checked by the **Bet Din** (rabbinical court) to ensure they are observing kashrut at all times. They receive certification so that their customers can be sure of keeping the law.

Draining of blood

The blood is the life of an animal (Leviticus 17:11), and as such forbidden to Jewish people (Leviticus 7:26–27). So, the shochet will have removed most of the blood from meat by the way they slaughtered the animal. The remaining blood is removed by one of three processes: broiling, soaking or salting, each of which takes time. This has to be done within 72 hours of slaughter. It is most common to buy meat which has already gone through the process.

Research broiling, soaking and salting to find out what each involves.

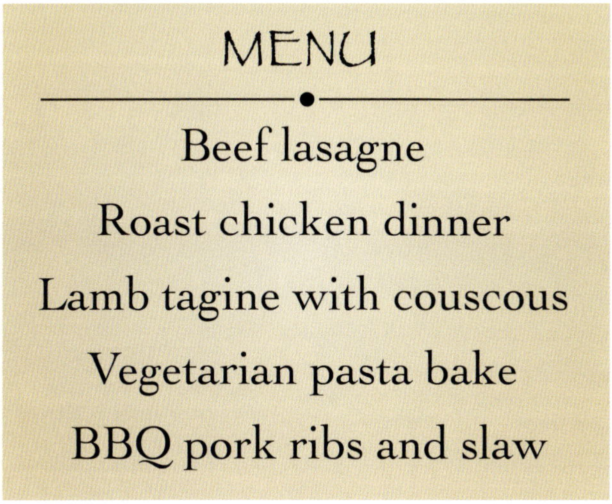

Meat and milk

In three places the Torah commands Jewish people 'You shall not boil a kid in its mother's milk', which is explained by the Talmud to mean: no eating, no cooking, no benefiting from a mixture of meat and milk. For some Jewish people this means not eating meat products and milk products in the same meal, for others not eating them within six hours of each other or three hours of each other, depending on custom. Historically, we know that the Canaanite people (enemies of the Israelites in the early period of the religion) ate meat and milk in one of their rituals, so this may be why Jewish people were not allowed to (distinguishing them clearly). In the first translation, there is a sense of compassion. To have mother seeing child or *vice versa* being killed/cooked would be cruel, this assigns a dignity and sanctity to the lives of both.

There are many non-milk replacement products now, which makes it easy to feed a mixed group of people the same meals. Many commercial businesses make good use of these products, for example soya or oat milk to use in coffee or to cook with.

Jewish cuisine

There are many traditional Jewish foods linked to Jewish festivals and the Sabbath. However, as Jewish people have lived in many areas around the world, everyday foods vary hugely. For example, Ashkenazi Jewish people may enjoy fried fish, cholent (stew) and bagels, Sephardic Jewish people may eat a more Mediterranean diet and Mizrachi Jewish people may eat more borekas (made of puff pastry), spicy foods and rice dishes.

Research these three types of Jewish cuisine.

The Basics

1. Explain what is meant by ritual slaughter.
2. Explain the rules about meat and milk.
3. Research a four-course meal which would be kosher for Jewish people.
4. Look at the menu board on the left. Explain which dishes a Jewish person could eat and which they could not.
5. **It is not difficult to keep a kosher diet in the UK today.** Explore this statement, thinking about such things as the ease of buying different foods, eating out, and so on. Explain arguments for and against the statement.

The synagogue – its importance and use

A little bit of history

The synagogue is the place of worship in Judaism. It is a special place to worship G-d. It is also a place to study Jewish texts, ideas and laws, hence it is also known by Ashkenazi Jewish people as 'shul' (school in Yiddish). It is also a community centre where celebrations and cultural events happen.

The idea of having a special place for worship goes back to the very beginnings of Judaism. Moses received the instructions to build a special sanctuary (Tabernacle) in which sacrifices were to be made, and which housed the Ark of the Covenant (Exodus 25–31), with the Ten Commandments. Until the Jewish people had their own homeland, this sanctuary was mobile.

In the tenth century BCE, King Solomon ruled a Jewish kingdom and the first permanent Temple was built in Jerusalem, within which was the 'Holy of Holies', housing the Ark. This Ark was lost in the sixth century BCE destruction of the Temple. A new Temple was built in the fourth/fifth century BCE, which was finally destroyed by the Romans in 70CE. If you go to Jerusalem today, you can see the remnants of the Temple, which include the Western (or Wailing) Wall, which is an external extension wall of the Temple complex. Today the Al-Aqsa mosque stands where the Holy of Holies in the Temple used to stand. Throughout the time of the Temples, animal sacrifices had been made there, with Jewish people being required to attend the Temple at three festivals during the year. When the second destruction occurred, animal sacrifice ended, and also the practice of having high priests. From this point, rabbis (teachers) slowly became community leaders in their local areas.

Where do synagogues fit into this history?

The first time synagogues are mentioned historically is in the sixth century BCE. The majority of the Jewish people were exiled in Babylon (modern-day Iraq), and they could not go to the Temple. 'Synagogue' comes from a Greek word which means 'a place of meeting/gathering', showing that Jewish people came together. The synagogue was a place for study and probably prayer. The first archaeological evidence for synagogues dates from the third century BCE, with actual synagogues still existing in Jerusalem from the first century CE.

Why is the synagogue important?

The synagogue emphasises the idea of community as it brings together the whole congregation to worship G-d, celebrate life events and festivals, learn and do cultural activities.

Also, it gave a space for the saying of specific prayers which require a **minyan** (ten members), for example, the **Kaddish** prayer which is both a prayer that praises G-d and expresses a yearning for the establishment of G-d's kingdom on earth. This prayer is said at every service and by mourners who have lost a family member recently.

Importantly, it is a house of worship or prayer, a Bet Tefilah.

Many Jewish people use the synagogue as a place of study (of scripture and law). Linked to that, it is a place of teaching, where Jewish adults and children can learn more about their religion and history.

Its role in the community means that many synagogues also provide space for meetings, events and celebrations such as weddings.

Joseph

I have grown up with the synagogue as part of my life. I attended shul to learn about my religion, I pray there, I was married there and my two boys had their Bar Mitzvah ceremonies there. Why is it important? Many personal reasons, but also it is a link – to my faith, my community and our history and traditions. Perhaps they are more important reasons than my personal ones.

The Basics

1. What is a synagogue?
2. How did the Temple and synagogue differ?
3. Why are synagogues important in Judaism?
4. **The most important role of the synagogue is as a place of worship.** What is your opinion on this statement? Explain several reasons for and against it.

Key features of a synagogue

From the outside, synagogues vary from being very plain to very ornate. They also vary in size and shape. The outside may have symbols such as a Star of David, menorah or Hebrew writing to mark it out as a synagogue. Some synagogues have stained-glass windows with Jewish symbols and images to make them beautiful. Synagogues are always built to face towards Jerusalem. *Find some images for your notes of synagogue exteriors. Label the recognisable Jewish features.*

There are a number of features which make a synagogue recognisable when you step inside. You would expect to see symbols such as the menorah, Star of David, Lions of Judah, and the Ten Commandments. Also specific furniture, such as a pulpit for sermons in certain synagogues, the rabbi's seat and a woman's gallery/section in Orthodox synagogues. You need to know about three specific elements of the synagogue, so we will look at them next.

Aron hakodesh

The holy ark is found at the front-centre of a synagogue and is the most important part of the building. It houses one or more Torah scrolls, which are used in services and which are the most sacred object in Judaism. In the UK, it will be on the Eastern wall, as when praying, Jewish people often face Jerusalem. It represents the Holy of Holies, which was the most sacred part of the Temple when it stood, and before it of the Tabernacle/Sanctuary. In today's synagogues this is like a cupboard in front of the wall, with a curtain (parokhet), doors or gates to safeguard and glorify the contents. Sometimes, the Lions of Judah holding the Ten Commandments are painted or sculpted above the ark, or on the curtain or door.

Ner tamid

In Exodus 27:20 and Leviticus 24:2, the people of Israel were commanded to keep a lamp burning in the Tabernacle all the time. Ner tamid means perpetual/eternal lamp. That it is kept alight always represents the idea of G-d being eternal and ever present. Traditionally, it was an oil lamp, though in modern synagogues it is usually electric, and it always hangs in front of the Aron hakodesh.

Bimah (or teba)

This is an elevated reading platform, from which the Sefer Torah is read during services. Traditionally, when the Sefer Torah was read, everyone would stand. Once the scrolls are in this holy place, in most synagogues, the congregation sit down (having been standing whilst it was brought from the ark). In Orthodox synagogues, the bimah is in the centre of the synagogue (facing towards the ark). This is, symbolic in a number of ways – when the Temple existed, an altar was in its centre, so the bimah reflects that; the Torah is read from the centre to show that its teachings should go out to the whole world; it also recalls that the Tabernacle was in the centre of the encampment when the Israelites were living in the desert before reaching the Promised Land. Practically, having the Torah in the centre of the synagogue means that it is equally audible to everyone at the service. In Progressive synagogues the reading platform is at the front of the synagogue, facing the congregation.

The Basics

1. For each of the three key elements of the synagogue, explain what it is and why it is important.
2. **Aron hakodesh is the most important part of a synagogue.** Explain reasons to agree and disagree with this statement.

Key differences between different synagogues

Orthodox Ashkenazi synagogue

Sephardi synagogue

Different synagogues

Reform synagogue

Hasidic synagogue

Progessive synagogue

Masorti synagogue

- In Orthodox synagogues, men and women sit in separate sections; in Progressive synagogues, men and women sit together.
- In Orthodox synagogues, the bimah is usually central to the room; in Progressive synagogues, it is a raised platform at the front where the aron hakodesh is, facing the congregation.
- Ashkenazi Jewish people are likely to call a synagogue a 'shul' and Sephardic or Mizrachi Jewish people are likely to refer to it as a 'Beit Knesset' (house of gathering/meeting).

If you went into 20 churches, you would not see two that looked exactly the same; you would expect them all to be at least a little different. This is true of mosques, of temples and of the religious buildings of any religious group, including synagogues. Local and national culture affect what they look like, but more importantly the strand of the religion that the building belongs to has an impact on what it will look like.

Look at the pictures on the previous page of the insides of some synagogues of different types of Jewish groups, and from different countries. Look at the list of key features of a synagogue on pages 193–194 and try to identify some of them in the photos.

Tasks

1. Look for the key features in each image – Aron hakodesh, ner tamid, bimah. How do they differ?
2. Can you spot other features such as the Ten Commandments, Lions of Judah, a pulpit, a menorah, Star of David?
3. Look at the decoration within the synagogues – how does it differ?
4. Look at the layout of furniture in the synagogues. How does it differ?
5. When you have compared the synagogues, and made notes about what you have spotted, answer the questions at the foot of this page.

The Basics

1. How can you tell that certain features of a synagogue are the key features? What are these features?
2. What differences did you find between the synagogues? Give examples to help make your points.
3. Can you explain why different synagogues look different? Explain your answer.
4. Do you think it matters that there are differences? Should synagogues all look the same? Explain your answers.
5. **A synagogue only needs a Sefer Torah.** Do you agree? Give reasons to agree and disagree with that statement, explaining them and including Jewish arguments in your answer.

Research Task

Find images of the interior of four synagogues. Explain the key features of each. Highlight the differences and similarities between these. Explain why they may differ.

Public and private worship

You have already read that Torah law covers many aspects of Jewish life. In the next few pages, you will be looking at practices which are about devotion to G-d, that is, acts of worship. Many acts of worship take place at the synagogue, but many also take place at home.

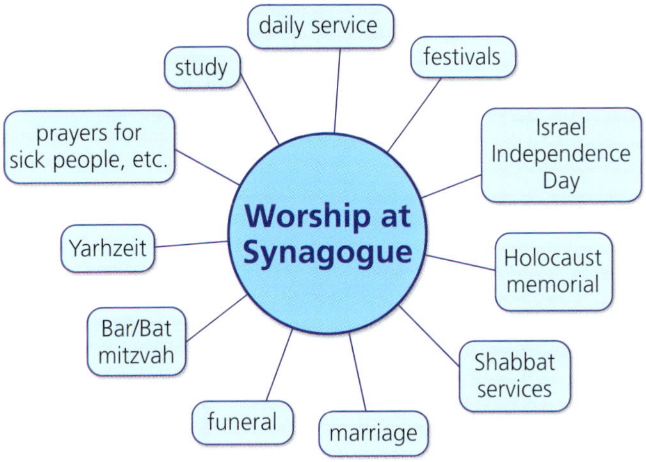

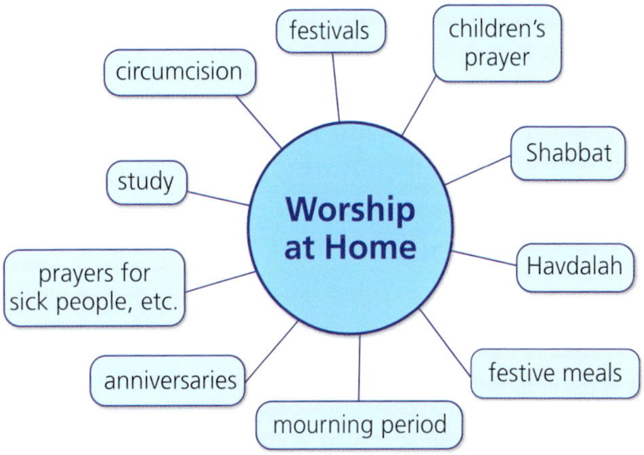

There are many areas of overlap which reinforces the idea that the home and family are key to the Jewish faith.

Note that Jewish people rarely use the term 'worship' themselves; you're more likely to hear them using terms like 'prayer' or 'practice'.

Why is it important to worship?

- It continues the Covenant with Abraham, so is a duty.
- It shows devotion.
- It encompasses the mitzvot: laws to keep.
- It keeps a person mindful of G-d's presence throughout the day.
- It is an act of praise to G-d.
- It brings a family or community together.

Jewish people can pray to G-d at anytime and anywhere. A simple prayer might be said. They might take part in a congregational prayer service. They might devote time to religious study. They might dedicate any actions to G-d as an act of worship.

The Basics

1. What is meant by worship?
2. Give some examples of worship in the synagogue and at home.
3. Explain why Jewish people believe it is important to worship.
4. Do you think it is more important to worship in the synagogue or at home? Explain your reasons.
5. **It is enough to remain mindful of G-d at all times, so there is no need for worship.** Do you agree? How might a Jewish person respond to this statement? Explain your ideas.

Talking about worship in the synagogue

Being dressed ready for prayer

You might have learned previously at school that Jewish people wear kippah, tallit and tefillin for prayer. In Orthodox Judaism, men will wear a head covering for prayer and some will wear a tallit for prayer and special occasions. Orthodox men will put on tefillin for morning prayers. In Progressive synagogues, most men and women will cover their head for prayer, usually with a kippah, and are able to wear tallit and tefillin if they wish. Generally people attending the synagogue dress well and do not wear scruffy clothes, as a mark of respect.

Key people

The rabbi is the spiritual leader of a Jewish community. They may lead prayers, though as they are scripted, others can also. This person (always male in Orthodox Judaism) must be of good character, and will have studied Jewish law and teachings to a very high level at a yeshivah (Torah school) and then rabbinical school. They are sometimes aided by a cantor, who sings at points throughout the service, leading the congregation through prayer, particularly at Shabbat and festival services. There has to be a group of ten adults for some specific prayers to be said. This is called a minyan.

The structure of worship

Worship is built around the reciting of different prayers. Two books are key: the **Siddur** or prayer book, which details the words and prayers which are said throughout a service, and the Chamash, which is the Torah in printed form. Depending on which prayertime in the day, the prayers said will vary. The key prayers are the Shema, the Amidah (18 blessings), the Kaddish, and **Aleinu** prayers. On Monday and Thursday, a portion of the Torah is read, whilst on Saturday, both the Torah and Haftorah (readings from the book of prophets) are read.

There are differences between the different groups within Judaism. For example, the number of prayers and readings, and the exact choice of them all vary. Not every synagogue has its own rabbi or cantor – anyone can lead the service (as long as they are of good character and knowledgeable about the faith). Minhag (tradition) has given differences as well as particular practices, for example, standing to certain prayers (other than the Amidah), which are specific to just one synagogue.

For each aspect, do some research to find out more detail, especially where there is diversity between the Jewish groups.

The Basics

1 What are the roles of the rabbi and cantor in a Jewish act of worship?
2 What is a minyan?
3 What might you observe about the appearance of those going to synagogue?
4 **Jewish acts of worship can be led by anyone.** Do you agree with this statement?

Prayer

The Hebrew word for prayer is tefillah and comes from a word which means to judge oneself. This shows that for Jewish people, prayer should be a time for reflection and thinking about how they are doing in their relationship with G-d, and in following their duties on Earth and not about begging G-d to change things. There are many prayers, blessings and benedictions used in Judaism. You are going to look at four which are used in the synagogue services. You will look at them in the order in which they happen in the service. They are all found in the Siddur (prayer book), so it is not necessary to know them by heart; however, many Jewish people do learn them. It is not just about the words, though. Judaism has many traditions (minhagim), and these along with the teaching of rabbis, have also shaped how the prayers are said and what is done whilst saying them.

The Shema

This is basically a declaration of faith. 'Shema' is the first word in Hebrew of this declaration, meaning hear or listen. It is traditionally recited three times daily in prayer. The Shema is taken directly from three paragraphs in the Torah, two from Deuteronomy (Devarim) and one from Numbers (Bamidbar). The way it is said varies: Orthodox Jewish people see it as study, so remain seated; some Reform Jewish people stand as a form of respect. The first line of the Shema is said aloud and clearly, because it is a declaration of the basic beliefs of the faith. It is common to see Jewish people close/cover their eyes to focus completely on the words in the first verse of the Shema. It is also common to see those wearing tallit holding the **tzitzit** (fringes) in their left hand whilst reciting the Shema. In its third paragraph, it mentions these three times, so it has become a custom to kiss the tzitzit as a sign of affection for the law at these three points.

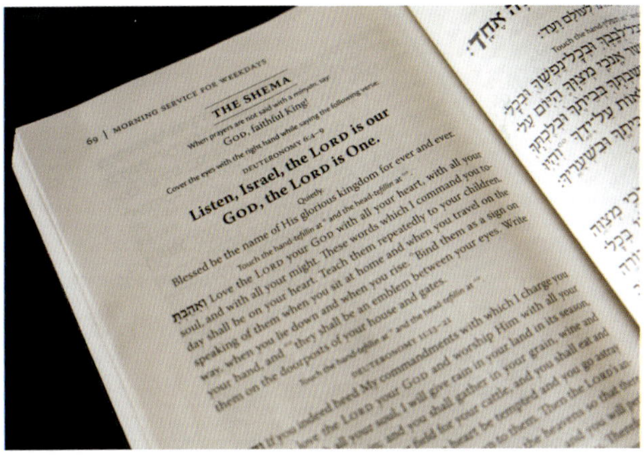

What does the Shema say?

It begins, 'Hear O Israel, the Lord is our G-d, the Lord is One G-d' which is the fundamental belief of Judaism, from which all other beliefs and the law flow. Then there is a sentence 'Blessed is the name of His Glorious Majesty forever and ever' which used to be said by the congregation in the Temple in Jerusalem after the priests had said the first sentence. It is not actually from the Torah, so is said more quietly. Then there are three paragraphs, all from the Torah. These are Deuteronomy 6:5–9, about G-d and religious duties to demonstrate love of G-d; Deuteronomy 11:13–21, about accepting and keeping the laws, and the consequences of doing this or not; and Numbers 15:37–41, which is about the mitzvah to wear tzitzit, and mentions the exodus from Egypt.

Look these up and make notes on their content.

We see some diversity here as Reform Jewish people in the USA do not include all of the second two of these passages, they have a different idea about G-d's retribution (what G-d will do if the mitzvot are not followed), and do not accept the mitzvot to wear tzitzit, so these parts are omitted from their Siddur. British Reform Jewish people, on the other hand, say them.

The Amidah

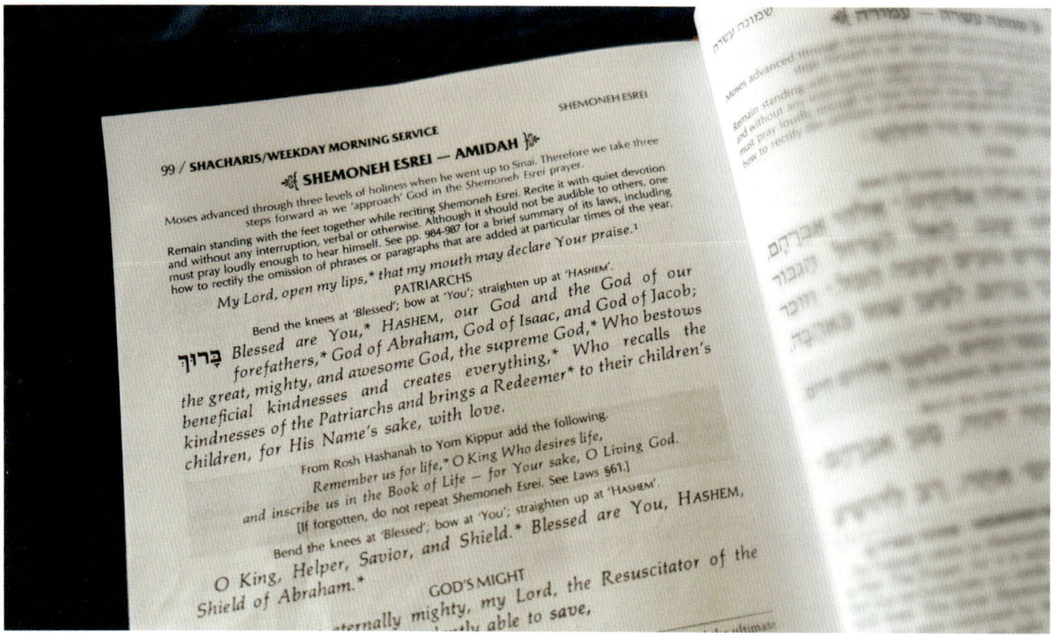

Another name for this prayer is the Shemonah Esreh or the 18 blessings. It is known as Amidah because it is said whilst standing, and Amidah means standing. There are actually 19 blessings now within the prayer. Tradition says that the blessings existed from the earliest times of Judaism, and as significant things happened, a new blessing was added, so that by the fifth century BCE, the 18 were in place. The nineteenth was added in the first century CE. The blessings take a specific and logical order, split into three groups: three blessings of praise, then 13 of requests, and finally, three of gratitude.

Find a copy of the Amidah in English, and make notes of the blessings within it. Which do you think are the most important, and why?

Most Jewish people follow the views of Maimonides (the man responsible for the Mishneh Torah) on how they say the Amidah (always standing, always facing Jerusalem). I Samuel 1:13 says that Hannah spoke to G-d merely by moving her lips – soundless – and so the Amidah is said in that way, as if the sound comes from the heart. During the prayer, rabbis have ruled that Jewish people must bend their knee at the word Barukh, then bow at Attah, standing up straight at Adonai. This happens twice. There are also two other bows where knees are not bent in the middle and end of the Shema. This is a sign of humility.

The Amidah is very sacred, as is the person's space when saying it, so it is traditional to take three steps forward and back before beginning. At the end of the prayer, a Jewish person once again takes three steps backward, and then bows to the left, right and forwards whilst saying a prayer asking for peace. Both actions represent approaching or leaving the presence of the King/Queen. They only return to their original place when the cantor begins his repetition of the Amidah. During this, the congregation will say Amen after each blessing.

The Amidah is modified for special occasions, for example, on Shabbat or on a festival celebration, but will always keep the first and last three blessings the same. It is said during each of the three daily prayers. Once begun, it must be completed.

The Kaddish

Kaddish means holy or sanctification. This is a prayer of praises to G-d, beginning, 'May His great name be exalted....'. It can only be said if there is a minyan (ten adults, and in the Orthodox tradition, males), as with the Amidah, so is recited at the synagogue at each prayer time each day. It is in the Siddur.

There are different Kaddishes, the most commonly known being the mourner's Kaddish. A Midrashic text explains its value to the deceased, but Jewish scholars have also shown it is of value to the living. Essentially, the congregation are praising G-d to remind themselves that death and loss are part of a greater plan, so words of the Kaddish in praising G-d help mourners restore their own faith and attachment to G-d.

It is recited aloud whilst standing. It is a *call and response* prayer, which means that one person says a phrase from the prayer, to which the congregation make a response.

Find the text of the Kaddish and make notes on the key elements, so that you can mention some if asked about the prayer.

The Aleinu

The Aleinu is the closing prayer of a synagogue service, and actually combines two prayers. It is a prayer to praise G-d and restate a Jew's dedication to G-d as one of the chosen people for whom there are many difficulties because of that choosing. It also reminds everyone that G-d's rule is without end, eternal.

On ending the service, each person is reminded of G-d, His power and splendour; that all hope is in G-d and the wish to see G-d. They are making a commitment to G-d, dedicating themselves again to Him. As a mark of that commitment, many Jewish people will bow towards the Aron hakodesh, as if they are bowing to G-d.

The Basics

1 Complete this chart which covers all four prayers. You will need more than one line per prayer, so complete the boxes for each prayer before writing the name of the next.

	Contents of prayer	**Conduct for prayer**
Shema		
Amidah		
Kaddish		
Aleinu		

2 How far do you agree with these statements? Give reasons to show you have thought about more than one point of view, including Jewish arguments.

a **The Shema is the most important prayer for Jewish people.**

b **For Jewish people, the words of a prayer are not the most important part of praying.**

Prayer at home

Judaism is also practised in the home. It is the case that not every Jewish person can get to the synagogue to pray for each of the three required prayertimes. It is also true that many Jewish people do not attend synagogue except for Shabbat. So it is the case that private prayer is common in Judaism.

Kavanah is the mindset for prayer. It is about having the right intention and focus. Just repeating the same prayers daily might lead a person to repeat them mindlessly and unthinkingly, so people need to have the right mindset.

Additionally, a person should be clean and tidy for their prayer, again as a sign of respect to G-d and for what they are about to do.

Kippah

Also called a yarmulke, this is a skull cap worn by Jewish men, though many women also cover their heads, including with a form of kippah in the different traditions of Judaism. Covering the head is one Jewish way of showing respect, and for some, to pray with the head uncovered would be breaking an important tradition of the faith.

Tallit and tzitzit

The tallit is a prayer shawl, often worn for prayers and special occasions. It is any garment with four corners and a hole in each corner. However, once the tzitzit (fringes) are attached, it becomes a sacred article and fit for prayer. It is traditional for there to be blue in a prayer shawl, though many Jewish people wear an all-white or multicoloured tallit depending on personal preference. Jewish people will wear the shawl across their shoulders, and some over their heads when praying. It has to cover the body, hence the practice of very large shawls being used. This represents that the person wants to wrap themselves in G-d's will. It is the custom of many denominations of Judaism that a tallit is worn regularly after marriage; however, Sephardic Jewish people and Ashkenazi Jewish people from Western Europe wear the tallit from their Bar/Bat Mitzvah or coming of age.

The tzitzit are the fringes which are affixed to each of the four corners of the tallit. They are twisted strands, tied and knotted in a very specific way, and hang loose. The number of strings and knots represents the 613 mitzvot, as well as the four corners of the earth; the idea is that the commandments are relevant everywhere. Specific prayers, for example, when reciting the Shema, require the holding of tzitzit (for those who are wearing them) in the left hand opposite the heart to show love for G-d and the commandments and as a physical reminder of the commandments.

Tefillin

These are two small boxes with straps which are worn on the forehead (tefillin shel rosh) and arm (tefillin shel yad), traditionally worn for morning prayers. Each contains parchment on which are written four passages from the Torah (Exodus 13:1–10, 13:11–16, Deuteronomy 6:4–9, 11:13–21). They are on one strip for the arm tefillin, and individual parchments for the head. These items are put on after the tallit. When being put on, the tefillin help the wearer to focus their mind on the act of praying. Prayers are said at each stage as the items are put on. The arm tefillin is put on first and has to be wrapped very specifically on the (non-writing, or weaker) arm and hand. The actual box points in to the body, toward the heart, as a reminder of G-d's love and of love for G-d and the commandments. The one on the head is to symbolise constantly being aware and thinking of G-d. A practice which ensures the commandments are followed and reward is gained, as only good is done.

The Talmud stresses the importance of wearing tefillin, saying many times that they must be worn. The tefillin help a Jewish person to focus on their past history, present duties to keep the mitzvot and their future destiny. Having said that, Shabbat does not require the wearing of tefillin because the day already symbolises the Covenant with G-d.

Siddur

This is the prayer book with all the prayers and words to be read at any prayer time. It is the guide for the period of prayer to be undertaken.

The Basics

1. Explain what each of these are: kippah, tallit, tefillin.
2. Describe how an Orthodox Jewish man might prepare for morning prayer, including the artefacts he will wear.
3. What is the difference between tallit and tzitzit?
4. **It isn't necessary to dress for prayer**. Explore this statement, giving reasons to agree and disagree with it, including what a Jew might say.
5. Do some research to find out more about the tefillin. How they are worn and the prayers said. Use this to show how important the actual process of getting ready for and carrying out prayer is for Jewish people.

When to pray

Some Jewish people pray three times daily. The first prayer is shacharit, in the morning. It recalls when sacrifices were made in the Temple, and was when Abraham chose to pray. He wanted to start his day with G-d, which then set him up to follow G-d's commands.

The afternoon prayer is minchah, to reflect when afternoon sacrifice took place in the Temple and follows Isaac's timing for prayer. To pray to G-d at this time is to interrupt the day and remind oneself of G-d's supreme importance.

The evening prayer is called maariv by Ashkenazi Jews and aravit by Sephardic and Mizrachi Jews. By praying in the evening Jewish people can ensure that G-d is the last thing on their minds before going to sleep.

On Shabbat, High Holy Days and the new Moon, an additional prayer, musaf, is added, traditionally combined with the shacharit prayer. This parallels the extra sacrifice that was brought in the Temple.

The importance of prayer

Read these comments to find reasons why Jewish people see prayer as important.

'It is a mitzvah, so of course we pray.'

'It shows my devotion to G-d, and my desire to be close to G-d so that I do what is right'

'It allows me to think forward and get in the right frame of mind for my day when I pray in the morning, and to reflect on my day when I pray at night. I sort of work things out in this time.'

'Jewish people have prayed since the start of the faith, and many of our prayers come from way back – they link us to our history, and we say them as a community. These are very important to me.'

'Prayer is a kind of cleansing act – it gives me a sense of well-being.'

'It is communication with G-d.'

Which is more important – praying at home or in the synagogue?

In Judaism, prayer is about communicating with G-d and introspection, but also about communal activity with other Jewish people. The rabbis said that congregational prayer was more important because the most important prayers (such as the Amidah and Kaddish) all demand a minyan for their recitation, so there have to be at least ten adults present. Maimonides said that G-d always answers the prayers of a community. Of course, it is also true that when people pray together in their place of worship, they can see the prayers being said and followed correctly, so they avoid mistakes, whereas when praying alone, they could teach themselves incorrectly, and so offend G-d. Additionally, the language of the prayers is to say 'us', rather than 'I' which shows that a group should be saying the prayer.

However, traditionally (and still in strictly Orthodox communities) women looked after the children and so could not easily attend synagogue as frequently as men. There are many reasons why Jewish people might prefer or need to pray mainly at home, and arguably as G-d sees everything it should be possible to pray anywhere at anytime. What matters is the sincerity of the prayers rather than where they are said.

The Basics

1 Explain the reason behind the several daily prayers.
2 Explain why prayer is important for many Jewish people.
3 Explain why congregational prayer is seen by most Jewish people as better than private prayer.
4 **All prayer should take place in the synagogue.** How far do you agree with this statement? Explain reasons for and against your view.

About Shabbat

'And the children of Israel shall keep the Sabbath to observe the Sabbath throughout the generations, for a perpetual covenant. It is a sign between Me and the Children of Israel forever, for six days the Lord made Heaven and Earth, and on the seventh day He ceased from work and rested.' *(Exodus 31:16–17)*

'Remember the Sabbath Day to keep it holy...for six days the Lord made Heaven and Earth, and rested on the seventh day.' *(Deuteronomy 20:8)*

'Six days you shall labour and do all your work; but on the seventh day, which is a Sabbath in honour of the Lord your G-d, you shall not do any work, neither you, nor your son, nor your daughter, nor your male or female servant, nor your cattle, nor the stranger who is within your gates.' *(Exodus 20:9–10)*

Shabbat is the Jewish day of rest, beginning at sundown on Friday and ending when the stars are out on Saturday evening. Jewish people keep Shabbat because it is a commandment, and a part of their Covenant with G-d. It reminds them that G-d created the world and they are copying G-d's example of resting from creative work. However, it can also be a day of family and friends, calmness, mindfulness and indulgence.

Not working

The Talmud forbids 39 areas of work on Shabbat. Many people think that 'work' can mean anything you do, but actually 'work' only covers *melachah* tasks (creative tasks, or ones which exercise control over one's environment). This word is only used in the Torah in terms of Shabbat, and building the Tabernacle, so the rabbis worked out the categories of forbidden work from what was needed to build the Tabernacle. However, the principle of pikauch nefesh (to save life) overrides Shabbat rules on work.

Find out some of the forbidden tasks. How might any of these make Shabbat more difficult to observe?

Getting ready for Shabbat

Why do you think Jewish people might want to be so prepared ahead of Shabbat?

Shabbat is a sacred time, so a person cannot just go straight from the hassle of work into the peace of Shabbat. Jewish people also have to prepare in advance for Shabbat so that they avoid breaking the rules around work during Shabbat. For example, any cooked food has to be already prepared.

Can you think of anything else which could be done in advance to avoid breaking the Shabbat?

Shabbat begins

Just before sunset, before the evening meal, traditionally the woman of the house lights two Shabbat candles, covers her eyes with her hands and recites a blessing to welcome in Shabbat. The two candles represent *zakhor* (remember Shabbat) and *shamor* (observe the Shabbat), which come from the two versions of the Ten Commandments in the Torah which describe the Shabbat. Whilst in Orthodox Jewish law this should happen at a set time (at least eighteen minutes) before Shabbat begins, in Progressive communities Shabbat does not have to start and end at exact times according to when it gets dark. In addition, in those communities living in a country where the stars are visible only very late, it might be done earlier. Candle lighting must happen before Shabbat begins, as it is traditionally forbidden to make fire on the Sabbath.

Many Jewish people attend the synagogue for the Friday evening service. Friday night prayers are in two parts, Kabbalat Shabbat (six chapters from Psalms) and then Maariv/Aravit prayers. During the second section, the Amidah is reduced to just seven blessings by omitting the middle twelve (the petitions) to reflect the belief that all is provided for on Shabbat. Instead, new paragraphs are inserted, reflecting the themes of Shabbat.

They return to enjoy a leisurely meal. Before the meal, many parents bless their children, and then recite Kiddush, a declaration that the day is holy and pray over wine to sanctify Shabbat. In Orthodox communities, Kiddush is said by the man of the house. If there are only women, it is said by a woman. In Progressive households it can be said by either a man or woman. This is traditionally followed by ritual washing of the hands and a blessing over two loaves of challah bread. During the meal, special songs are often sung that reflect the themes of Shabbat. After the meal, another long blessing is often said, called birkat ha-mazon. This can be said after any meal, but on Shabbat it is often sung by everyone together.

The rest of the evening is free for relaxing and spending quality time together.

Saturday

On Saturday at lunchtime, the rituals of Kiddush, hand washing and the two challah to start the meal are repeated. Whereas on Friday evening, Kiddush was to sanctify Shabbat, on Saturday morning it is just a mark of deference to Shabbat.

The Shabbat morning services at the synagogue can last for several hours. The service is similar to that described on page 198; however, the reading of the Torah is central to the Shabbat service. The Torah scrolls will be taken from the aron hakodesh, and processed around the synagogue before or after being taken to the bimah to be read. The Torah Scrolls are 'dressed' whilst not being read, so the coverings will be removed before the scrolls are opened and read. The congregation will all stand until the scrolls are on the reading lectern on the bimah, and as it is processed, some will kiss their tallit or hand and touch the casing to show respect. The same portion of the Torah is read in every synagogue all over the world, and its message will be the focus of a sermon which is delivered by the rabbi. The Siddur (prayer book) is used to structure the service, and ensure everyone says the right words. It is really important, as the service is long and difficult to follow from memory, especially when in Hebrew.

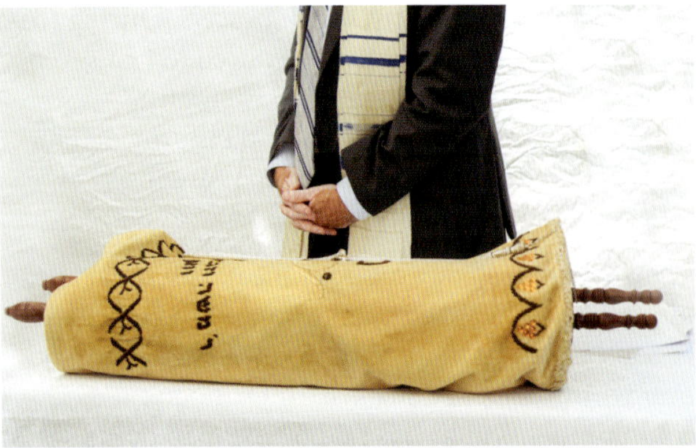

It is common for synagogue congregations to share Kiddush after the service; traditionally, wine and some cake. This is, after all, a time when the community comes together to reinforce their sense of community and friendship.

Whilst some Jewish people spend the afternoon in Torah study at the synagogue, for many it is an opportunity to spend quality time with family and friends. It is a day of rest, so time is given to study of Torah, Talmud and religion, but also to playing games or just resting/relaxing. Late afternoon is the time for a light meal – no one is allowed to work, so the meal has to be ready to just put on the table, prepared before Shabbat begins.

In Orthodox and Masorti communities, Shabbat ends at sundown, when three stars are visible. Traditionally a concluding ritual called **Havdalah** is performed. This recognises the difference between the sacred time of Shabbat and the rest of the week. Blessings are recited over wine, spices and candles. The candles are special, having multiple wicks. The spicebox is full of aromatic spices and everyone takes a breath of the smell. Shabbat is so special, the knowledge of it ending saddens people, so the scent of the spices is uplifting. Lighting candles is an act of work and it again indicates the end of Shabbat.

The Basics

1 Why do Jewish people observe Shabbat?
2 Explain the rules around work on Shabbat. Include examples of what counts as work and how Jewish people prepare ahead of Shabbat to eliminate the need for work.
3 Describe the Friday Shabbat rituals.
4 Describe the Saturday Shabbat rituals.
5 Shabbat is full of symbolism and tradition. Give three examples of this.
6 **Shabbat is the most important ritual in Judaism.** Explain different viewpoints on this statement.

Shabbat – importance, influence and diversity

Take a few minutes working with a partner to think about what you have learned about Shabbat. Can you think of reasons why it is important? Can you think of ways in which Shabbat might influence Jewish people in their daily lives? Can you recall any differences in the way that different groups of Jewish people might celebrate Shabbat?

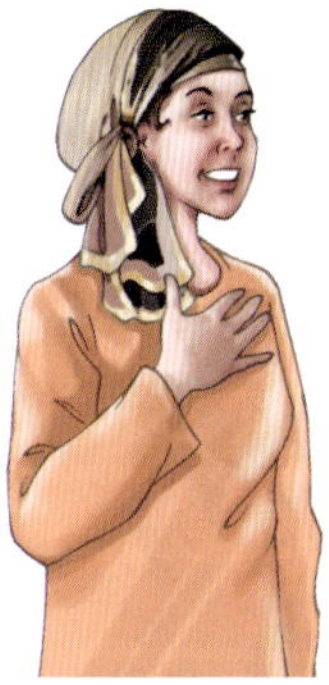

Rebekkah

My family are Orthodox Jewish people. On Saturday, I always follow the same routine. I get up early and have breakfast with my family. We live near enough to the synagogue to be able to walk – we couldn't drive as we don't drive on Shabbat. The whole family goes to the morning service, though my father and brother sit in different parts of the synagogue to myself, my mother and sister – we sit in the balcony. After the service, we go home to have a big meal, before my father and brother go back to shul. I will spend some time studying the Torah and Talmud. For me, this is really important to do when I have time; I get a chance to understand better how to fulfil the commandments. A final service at the synagogue takes place, and after that we have our final meal. We end Shabbat with the Havdalah ceremony where we are saying goodbye to Shabbat. This always makes me a little sad because I love the Shabbat atmosphere, and now I have to go back to the mundane ordinary life. You could say that Shabbat influences my whole life – I work toward it all week, and think about how I can be best prepared. That includes being right with G-d, fulfilling the commandments all week. Then Shabbat is a time for study and reflection for me and my family, a sacred, holy time.

My family are Masorti Jewish people. I think many Jewish people keep Shabbat for many different reasons really. It is a commandment but also a gift, given to us in Deuteronomy 20:8, and Exodus 20:9–10, 31:16–17. It is also a great tradition – throughout our history Jewish people have observed the Sabbath, and by continuing that, we honour them as well as the tradition. You know tradition (minhag) in Judaism is very important – it shapes the way we do many things. A well-known Midrash tells us that Shabbat is a sample of the Messianic Age, which shows how special and important it is – to then not observe it would be terrible. In my studies, I learned that G-d created the world in six days and rested on the seventh. I also know I am far below G-d, but I try to copy this day of rest to show respect to G-d, and also because G-d instructed us to do so in the Torah, for our own benefit. Wise rabbis of old tell us Shabbat is like a "queen", who is with us in our homes for the entirety of Shabbat. This makes the day more important, and means we try our best to be clean, tidy, and keep the commandment.

Binyamin

My family are Reform Jewish people. Whilst we observe the Sabbath, we do have differences in the way we observe it compared to Orthodox and Masorti Jewish people. For example, in my family we light Shabbat candles before our evening meal – whether it is sundown or not, because – in summer, for example, we would be eating too late if we waited for sundown, and in winter – too early. It also varies in my house as to who recites Kiddush – sometimes my mum does it, and I have done it myself. We drive to the synagogue and our family always sits together to pray, and we always go to share Kiddush after in the community hall. I love that time as I chat with my friends. On Saturday afternoon, my mum and dad always do stuff with us, quite often something to help others (tzedekah), for example, we have visited older relatives who are in care homes – taking Shabbos to them, you could say. We also made cards and cupcakes to take to them – some Jewish people would say this is work, but my family sees it as being together as a family, imbuing the things we make with our love, and then making someone's day a little brighter. My mum says this is part of the essence of Shabbat.

Carmel

My family are Reform Jewish people. In my lifetime observance of Shabbat has changed and evolved. I don't do with my family as was done when I was a child. My wife and I decided we needed to make attending the synagogue central to our family Shabbat. You'd be surprised how hard we work to make that possible – having a job, but getting everything ready to observe Shabbat as well, and managing young children. The key point is that the minute I get to the synagogue, I begin to relax, and I go into Shabbat mode. I am in a safe place, where I can pause and take time out from the hectic world and its many distractions. Shabbat gives a chance to be present in the moment, focusing on now, not what I need to do tomorrow. Shabbat isn't magic, but by making space for it, it feels magical.

David

Task

Read the information on Shabbat (pages 205–206). Answer these questions.

1. Explain why Shabbat is important to many Jewish people. Do you think it is more important to any particular type of Jewish person? Explain your answer.
2. Explain how Shabbat influences the lives of Jewish people. How important an influence do you think it is? Explain your answer.
3. How do different groups of Jewish people observe Shabbat? Why do you think this is the case? Explain your answer.
4. Do some research to find out differences in observance of Shabbat.
5. **Shabbat should be observed however much a person feels like it.** Analyse and evaluate this statement, showing you have thought about more than one point of view, and including Jewish arguments in your answer.

Jewish rites of passage – birth ceremonies

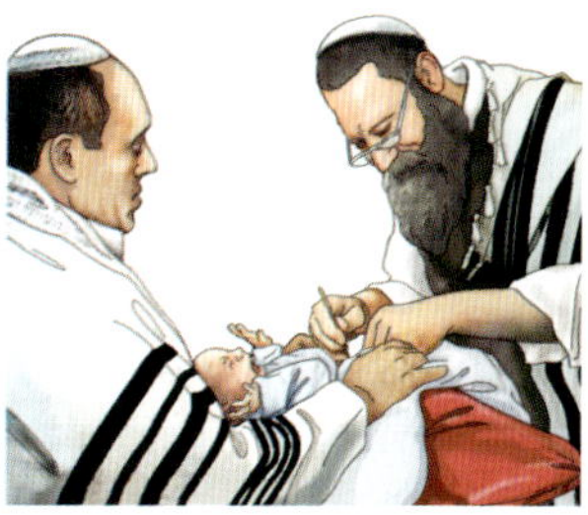

In Judaism the birth ceremony for boys is called the Brit Milah. In Sephardic and Mizrachi communities (where Jewish people are of Spanish, Middle Eastern, or North African heritage) and Italian communities, there is a tradition of welcoming girls with a celebration called Zeved Habat, meaning 'gift of the daughter'. It is now also common for Ashkenazi Jewish people to hold a celebration for baby girls, called a Simchat Bat ('celebration of the daughter') – or sometimes in Progressive communities Brit Habat ('covenant of the daughter'). This may include talking about the baby's chosen name, readings, prayers and blessings.

Brit Milah happens eight days after birth, unless there is ill health. The ceremony happens at home or in the synagogue, as early as possible after shacharit (morning) prayer, and a minyan should be present. A boy is circumcised as a mark of the covenant between Abraham and G-d. It is seen as a commandment. It is also the rite through which a newborn male becomes part of the Jewish people.

If the ceremony takes place in the home, a mohel (man trained to carry out circumcision) goes to the child. The kvaterim (godparents) take the child from the mother to give to the father. They wear a tallit and tefillin, as a reminder of the seriousness of this commandment they are following. They then give the boy to a special, male guest (sandek) who will hold the child whilst the circumcision is carried out.

Sometimes, candles are lit by those present. This is done for many different symbolic reasons.

Then the mohel will bless the child as he carries out the circumcision. The father reads a blessing from the Siddur Torah. Finally, after completing the circumcision, the boy's name is announced.

The baby is then given to its mother to be fed. It is traditional for there to be a celebratory meal.

For a girl, it is customary to name the newborn in the synagogue after the father (in Orthodox communities) or parents (in other communities) has been called up to the Torah. This happens on the first Shabbat after her birth. In some communities, this happens on the first day after birth at which there is a Torah reading. In the Sephardi tradition, the congregation will sing songs to welcome her. It has become tradition for the parents to treat the congregation to Kiddush in celebration after the service, or other food if the celebration is in the home.

Task

Find out about Shalom Zachar, which happens on the first Friday after a boy is born, and Wachnacht, on the evening before Brit Milah, and Pidyon Haben, which happens 30 days after the birth.

The Basics

1. Why are birth ceremonies important in religion?
2. Describe the Brit Milah ceremony.
3. Describe the ceremony for naming girls.
4. **Newborn children should always be welcomed into a religion.** Do you agree? Explain reasons for and against this statement, including Jewish arguments.

Coming of age – Bar Mitzvah and Bat Mitzvah

Bar Mitzvah can literally be translated as 'son of the commandments'. It is a recognition of the fact that a young man has reached the age by which he is personally responsible for his religious acts, and is marked by his first reading in the synagogue of the Torah. From this point on, he is regarded as an adult in all religious respects, for example, he should use tefillin in prayers and can count as one of the minyan. In fact, he remains Bar Mitzvah all his life, it is not just for one day, as it refers to the duty of keeping the mitzvot. Males lead the service in an Orthodox shul and so reading from the Torah is a way of showing the change in status from a child to an adult.

In Orthodox Judaism, girls have different roles within Jewish life and so they have different ceremonies.

Girls reach the age of maturity at twelve, and it is now common to recognise that through a Bat Mitzvah ceremony. There is no standard ceremony for this, and it is common for the girl to study a Jewish topic of interest to her or one linked to the Torah portion of the week, then present a speech to the community on it, as well as reading a prayer. Some Orthodox girls prefer to have a quieter celebration at home. Many girls also mark their Bat Mitzvah by doing a tzedakah (charity) project. In the Progressive (Reform and Liberal) traditions, in recognition of changing societal norms and a growing emphasis on equality, a girl celebrates at 13 years old and usually reads from the Torah in the synagogue, so the ceremony will be the same whichever gender.

Why are these important?

You have read that this is the day on which a child becomes responsible for their own religious duties. In other words, it is the day when – religiously – they enter adulthood. By going through the ceremony, a child consciously steps into the responsibility of living a Jewish life into adulthood, and they confirm their wish to keep the religion going.

Celebrations, festivals and rites of passage are central to Judaism. After all, these events reinforce one's faith and help young people to understand it more fully. For the community, the event promotes togetherness, as the event binds the young person to their community.

The Basics

1 What is the Bar/Bat Mitzvah?
2 Why are these ceremonies important in Judaism?
3 Describe the ceremony for Bar Mitzvah.
4 Describe the celebrations for Bat Mitzvah.
5 Explain how the two ceremonies might differ.
6 Apart from a synagogue ceremony, how do Jewish people celebrate the coming of age of their children?
7 Read these statements and write explained arguments to agree and disagree, including Jewish arguments:
   a **Coming of age ceremonies have no place in modern society.**
   b **Bar Mitzvah is more of a celebration than a serious religious event.**

Celebrating the occasion

Although the idea of Bar Mitzvah is in the Talmud, the custom of celebrating only began about six hundred years ago. It is common to give gifts to the young person and to have a family meal. Some families will pay for Kiddush at the synagogue for the congregation.

Some Jewish people believe that celebrations should be low-key, as there is no scriptural basis for over-the-top celebrations, like lavish parties. Some Jewish people now go abroad to celebrate, either to Israel (often to the Western Wall in Jerusalem) or to a place which is important to their family history.

Task

Research how Jewish communities are redefining the Bar and Bat Mitzvah ceremonies to find out about diversity within the religion, and also how things are changing in the modern world.

The ceremony

Anyone undergoing a ceremony has a lot to prepare, so there is a period of preparation during which a religious person will instruct the young person. For boys and girls in non-Orthodox communities, this will be in how to read and handle the Torah, as well as how to perform other religious obligations such as how to wear tefillin. It is quite common for young people to spend months studying the portion of the Torah they will read, and learning to wear the tefillin correctly. For Orthodox girls, the preparation may involve learning about mitzvot relating more to women, general Torah learning, and researching and writing a speech and certain prayers to read at their Bat Mitzvah ceremony.

For a boy, the ceremony usually takes place on the Shabbat after his 13th birthday as part of the usual service at the synagogue.

On the day of the Bar Mitzvah the Torah scroll is prepared on the bimah and then the rabbi calls the boy to read to the rest of the congregation. He goes up to the bimah and reads the passages in Hebrew for that Sabbath service. In many synagogues, his father (and mother in non-Orthodox communities) will then make a particular blessing: 'Blessed are You, LORD our G-d, King of the universe, for freeing me from being punished for this one's actions.' The Midrash states that a father is obligated to concern himself with bringing his child up well, and teaching him right from wrong and the correct way to behave before the age of 13, so when he becomes Bar Mitzvah, the father is no longer responsible for his child's negative choices and actions. In some communities, the boy will read all of the Torah portion, and will also lead the congregation in their prayers, which is a demonstration of them accepting him as an adult.

The rabbi then gives their sermon, part of this is for the boy to remind him of his duty to keep the Commandments throughout his life. Finally, he is blessed by the rabbi , starting with the words, 'May the Lord bless thee and keep thee.' Kiddush after the service allows the congregation to celebrate this event, and there is often a big family celebration.

For Reform, Liberal and many Masorti Jewish people, the girl's Bat Mitzvah would follow the same process in the synagogue. For Haredi (strictly Orthodox) Jewish people, the occasion is usually low-key, more of a private family affair, celebrated by a family meal, blessings and new clothes. However, in all Modern Orthodox communities, girls are allowed synagogue Bat Mitzvah, where they address the congregation with a reading about the Torah portion of the week or any other relevant Jewish topic, as well as reading prayers or psalms. In the Reform tradition, it is not unusual to see a young person design part of their own Bar/Bat Mitzvah ceremony, including them giving sermons after research and study.

Marriage in Judaism

This is the most elaborate ceremony in Judaism and is full of custom and tradition. Here we can only look at marriage generally, but you should do some research of your own to find out more about the differences between each Jewish tradition's way of doing this, and the origins of some of the customs.

Marriage is a fulfilment of the biblical verse 'It is not good for the man to be alone' (Genesis 2:18). Genesis 1:28 also commands: Be fruitful and multiply. In Orthodox Judaism, having children is only rightly done within marriage; hence marriage being necessary to fulfil one of the earliest commands given to humans. It is seen as the natural state of things to be married. From the time of Adam, Eve was created as a helper and companion for him, and so giving a template for living. Marriage is seen as a blessing, as it helps to overcome loneliness, both actual and spiritual. The idea is that the two partners complete each other, that marriage is a natural and ideal state and a blessing from G-d.

The ceremony

In Talmudic times (from 70BCE to c.500CE), there was a betrothal (kiddushin) ceremony and a separate marriage ceremony. These are now done either side of the reading of the Ketubah (marriage contract).

The betrothal ceremony begins with the signing of the Ketubah. It is signed by witnesses and in Progressive Judaism the bride and groom are also able to sign it. Traditionally, the Ketubah is a legal document protecting the bride's rights. In Progressive communities, many couples choose to have a Ketubah that is more egalitarian, expressing the bride and groom's commitment to care for one another.

The veiled bride then approaches and circles her husband to be a number of times. This is a custom which links to Jeremiah 31:21, where it says a woman encompasses and protects her husband, and also Hosea 2:21-22, where G-d speaks to his people saying 'I betroth you' three times.

The rabbi might make a speech about the responsibilities of marriage and about the couple. The man will then place the ring on his bride's index finger. The ring (or rings in Progressive Judaism) must be an undecorated, unbroken circle, showing the hope for a harmonious marriage. The husband will recite from the Talmud 'With this ring, you are wedded to me in accordance with the laws of Moses and Israel.' It is put onto the forefinger of the bride's right hand (she can move it to the ring finger of her left hand if she wants). This usually happens under the huppah (wedding canopy), which represents the home the couple will build together (and some say is a layer of G-d's protection over them).

Seven blessings (sheva berakhot) are then recited over wine; one specific blessing over wine, and six regarding the marriage and wishing the couple well. Finally, the groom crushes a glass under his foot to remember the destruction of the Temple in Jerusalem.

In most traditions, they go to a private room for about five minutes, this is called Yichud (privacy). This is because tradition dictates that the couple should not have sex before marriage and in Haredi (strictly Orthodox) communities, couples will not have any physical contact at all before marriage. This privacy therefore gives the couple an opportunity after the wedding ceremony for physical contact. It also gives them a moment's peace in an otherwise hectic day.

Some different traditions

As with all of Judaism, there are traditions which belong only to one or other of the strands within Judaism. Here are some:

Before the ceremony – some Jewish people fast on the day of the wedding until the ceremony, to show how seriously they are taking the commitment of marriage. Most Jewish communities do not allow the couple to see each other on the day of the ceremony. In the Orthodox tradition it is common for the couple not to see each other the whole week before.

Aufruf ('announcement') – on Shabbat morning before the wedding, it is traditional in Orthodox Judaism for the groom to attend synagogue, be called up to read the Torah and receive the congratulations of the congregation. In many communities, he will be showered with nuts, almonds and raisins, or more commonly today, sweets. Hebrew words have numerical values, and that for nut is the same as that for sin and good. So the point being made is that a marriage can be very good or very bad, depending on how married life is conducted. It is the duty of the couple to treat each other well to make the marriage work.

Veiling the bride – in the Ashkenazi tradition, the groom will go to the bride and put a veil over her face, which she wears until after they leave the huppah. It means he has seen who he is marrying, and is sure who is under the veil. This has Biblical origins as Rebecca covered her face before marrying Isaac, or alternately recalls that Jacob was tricked into marrying Leah when he should have been marrying Rachel, but her father had veiled her for the wedding and Jacob only saw her face once married. In some Progressive communities, the veiling of the bride is not done, or done in a modernised or different way, for example the bride reciprocates by putting a kippah on the groom's head, or cloaking him in a tallit.

Circling under the huppah – brides traditionally walk round the groom under the huppah either seven times, as seven is a number representing something being complete (like the seven days of creation), or sometimes just three times. In Progressive weddings, the couple usually both circle each other.

Kabbalat Panim ('welcome') – a chance for female guests to see the bride and male guests to see the groom before the ceremony. The groom greets his guests, who sing for him and toast his happiness and health. (This is sometimes accompanied by some Jewish learning or sharing wisdom, and called a 'tisch'.) The bride traditionally sits on a throne-like chair to greet her guests.

The Basics

1. Why is marriage important in Judaism?
2. Use these words to describe the marriage ceremony: kiddushin; ketubah; rings; huppah; sheva berakhot; wine; breaking the glass.
3. Explain how the marriage ceremony links to all Jewish people.
4. **Marriage ceremonies should be exactly as a couple want them, not dictated by tradition.** Explore this statement, giving reasons for and against it, including Jewish arguments.
5. **There is no need for a religious marriage ceremony nowadays.** Explore this statement, giving reasons for and against it, including Jewish arguments.

Death and the funeral

Rites of passage to do with death can often seem to be more about the family and friends rather than the dead. Whilst there is great respect shown to the dead, once buried attention turns to the bereaved and supporting them to get through a period of graduated mourning, which is designed to make them move on.

A person dies ...

The deceased is entitled to the same level of respect and dignity as a living person, so everything done to the body is done in that manner.

At death, the eyes and mouth of the deceased must be closed, if not already. Some believe a person cannot look on to this life and the life to come at the same time, so by closing the eyes, we close off this life and allow them to see the next. There is also scriptural authority to do this. The body will be covered and is sometimes put on the ground. Candles are lit and placed at the head, recognising Proverbs 6:23 '*For the commandment is a lamp and the law a light*', and 20:27 '*The soul of a man is the lamp of the Lord.*'

The corpse will be continually watched by someone (known as a 'shomer') until burial to show respect to the dead and ensure the proper treatment. They will recite psalms as this is thought to bring merit to the departed soul during its journey to the next world.

Each community has a Hevrah Kadishah (Holy Society) whose members are dedicated to preparing the body for and burying the dead. They work with the funeral parlour to wash the body, dress it in white linen shrouds (showing all are equal in death). Deceased males are wrapped in their tallit but with the tzitzit cut off so that it is not a holy article, and showing that they no longer have to fulfil the commandments.

The act of washing is done according to Jewish law and has both physical and spiritual elements. The work of Hevrah Kadishah can be said to represent the last link in a chain of care and concern for the deceased.

The Hevrah Kadishah keep the mitzvot of tahara. Tahara is purification, and is the term used to prepare the deceased for their final resting place.

Helen

Being part of the Hevrah Kadishah is all about teamwork. We are carrying out a sacred task. We act in the spirit of chesed (kindness). Our Hevrah has organised lectures from guest rabbis to help us do our work correctly.

Sarah

The work of the Hevrah Kadishah is so important, and such a kindness. After all, the dead cannot reward this kindness. I feel privileged to be able to be involved in this work.

Jack

The burial ...

Jewish people are traditionally buried not cremated, as '*man is formed from dust, and returns to it*' (Genesis 3:19). Burial should happen as soon after death as possible, preferably the same day. However, burials may not happen on Shabbat or on festival days. The casket must be of wood and completely biodegradable.

A eulogy is usually read about the deceased. A service is then held in a synagogue or prayer room at the cemetery, or at the graveside. But however they are carried out, they follow a similar process.

1. Keri'ah – the ritual of rending garments is observed, dating back to when Jacob tore his garments after he believed his son Joseph was dead (Genesis 37:34). Different communities do this at different stages. The Orthodox do it straight after death, others before the funeral procession or at or after the burial. Mourners' clothes are torn deliberately through the material (not along a seam) to represent emotional need and sadness. This copies scriptural practice. Many non-Orthodox Jewish people no longer tear clothes, but rather wear a strip of black ribbon on their outer garment, which, in the Reform tradition, is given to them at the funeral.
2. The casket is carried to the grave, and Psalm 91 is read. Seven stops are made along the way. This shows how difficult the task is and also that there is no desire to hurriedly complete it.
3. The casket is lowered into the grave, with the head facing east, as it is traditionally believed that the dead will be resurrected to rise facing east (to Jerusalem). Either during or just after this, prayers are recited.
4. El Malei Rachamim (prayer of mercy) is recited at the graveside, or sung by the cantor, followed by the mourners' Kaddish, by the family.
5. It is customary for those attending to help fill the grave. A shovel is used, which each person puts down onto the ground when they have used it, symbolising that they do not want to pass sorrow to the next person. Others throw soil onto the casket. This ritual shows service and love.
6. Those who are not mourners then make two lines between which the bereaved pass. The people then bless the bereaved, saying: *May G-d comfort you among the other mourners of Zion and Jerusalem.*
7. On returning from the funeral, the first meal, Se'udat Havra'ah, must be brought by neighbours or friends. It traditionally is a dairy-based meal (no meat), and it is customary for it to include eggs and bread. Often the bread will be round, to represent the cycle of life. Many of the meals consumed by the bereaved during the next seven days will be brought to them as gifts of comfort by members of the community which is part of the love and care given to mourners.

The Basics

1. Respect is given to the dead in all religions. Why do you think this is?
2. Explain the process of preparing a dead person for burial in Judaism.
3. Describe the funeral service, explaining symbolism within it.
4. **Funeral ceremonies should be the most important ritual in life.** Explore this statement, giving arguments for and against it, and including Jewish arguments.

Mourning

May G-d comfort you among the other mourners of Zion and Jerusalem. (Beracha for the bereaved)

Judaism structures the mourning period and shapes it so as to help the bereaved face the reality of having to move on. The rules of mourning are for when you have lost a parent, child or sibling. Traditionally there are four parts to the period of mourning.

1 *Aninut* – the period between death and the burial. During this period, the bereaved is excused from any and all commandments, even reciting the Shema. They may not wear tefillin, cannot eat/drink at a festive table, cut their hair, wash their clothes, bathe themselves, or have sexual relations.

Rules between death and burial

2 *Shiv'ah* – 'seven' – from the closing of the grave until seven days after. Only bereaved parents, siblings, children or spouses observe this period and the remaining two. It is often known as 'sitting Shiv'ah' because of the practice of sitting on a low stool and not working. The prohibitions of Aninut remain in place, plus they may not greet people, study the Torah (other than laws of mourning, or tracts about suffering, for example, the book of Job), cook for themselves or sit in normal chairs. All the mirrors in the house are covered, and a candle is lit which will last for seven days. People go to help comfort the bereaved; visitors often take food as mourners are not supposed to cook for themselves. Daily prayers will be held in the house of the deceased in many communities, with a minyan in attendance. The bereaved will go to Shabbat prayer, being greeted at the door by members of the congregation. It is customary for them to sit in a different place to their normal spot, which heightens their sense of loss and grief, as it is unfamiliar.

Seven days from closing of the grave

3 *Sheloshim* – '30 days', including the seven of Shiv'ah. Some of the restrictions are now lifted – they bathe (for cleanliness not pleasure), cook, use mirrors and go to work; many others are kept. This ends the official mourning period for those who have lost a sibling or child.

Some restrictions now lifted; lasts for thirty days

4 *Avelut* – For those who have lost a parent, mourning will continue for a full year. All the Sheloshim prohibitions are now lifted, though happy events, for example, weddings and going to shows or concerts, should be avoided. From the burial for eleven months, a bereaved son (in Orthodox Judaism) and daughter (in non-Orthodox communities) traditionally recites the mourners' Kaddish at synagogue. The belief is that this helps assist the transition of the soul into 'the world to come'. The Ashkenazi custom that the Kaddish is recited for eleven not twelve months, indicates there was good in the person, so they don't need a full year's 'help' to gain a place in the world to come.

Mourning for eleven months for those who have lost a parent

Remembering the dead – the gravestone (matsevah)

Gravestones are put up to ensure the dead are not forgotten and that the grave is clear for all to find, in order for friends and family to visit. They also make sure graves are marked so that Cohenim (Jewish people from the line of priests) do not come into close contact with dead bodies by mistake. In some communities, the erection of the gravestone happens at the end of Shiv'ah or Sheloshim and in some almost a year after the death. It is customary to have an unveiling ceremony for the stone. You might wonder why this does not happen earlier in these cases? For those waiting a year, they know that within that time, the person will not have been forgotten. For some who have been mourning for a year (and saying kaddish), it marks the end of that period.

Yahrzeit and Yizkor

Each anniversary of the death of a parent, child or sibling is recalled by Yahrzeit. A candle is lit which lasts 24 hours. Many Jewish people take time in the day to study the Torah, and it is customary for them to donate tzedekah on this day. Hasidic Jewish people have a celebration to recognise that their loved one is in the next life.

The Yizkor is a memorial prayer, which is recited by mourners in the synagogue on specific festival days: Yom Kippur, Sh'mini Atzeret, the last day of Pesach and Shavuot.

The Basics

1 How do practices in Judaism help and comfort mourners?
2 How does bereavement impact on a Jewish person's life?
3 Describe the four stages of mourning and explain the symbolism of any rituals.
4 How are the deceased remembered in Judaism?
5 **It is too difficult to complete Jewish mourning rituals in today's world.** Explore this statement, explaining reasons to agree and disagree, and including Jewish arguments.
6 **Jewish mourning rituals are designed to support the bereaved rather than remember the dead.** Explore this statement, explaining reasons to agree and disagree, and including Jewish arguments.

Rosh Hashanah and Yom Kippur

Rosh Hashanah

Rosh (meaning 'head of') Hashanah (meaning 'the year') is New Year. It is sometimes known as a High Holy Day, and happens on the first day of the month of Tishri (in September/October), and begins a ten-day period of reflection and repentance which ends with Yom Kippur. Its focus is the individual and their way of living on Earth, whether they are behaving appropriately and keeping the commandments so as to warrant more time on Earth. Jewish people traditionally observe this festival for two days, however Progressive Jewish people celebrate for only one day. There are ten days between Rosh Hashanah and Yom Kippur, so many Jewish people are mindful of this holy time throughout.

Rosh Hashanah represents the day G-d created the world, so you could see it as the world's birthday, which is actually emphasised in the Talmud. Therefore G-d is celebrated as creator on Rosh Hashanah. Given its focus around repentance, or being truly sorry for wrongs/sins done, it is referred to as Yamim Nora'im (Day of Awe) as many Jewish people believe that on this day all humankind stands before the throne of G-d to give a full account of all they have done in the past year, so that they can be judged. They hope to receive a promise of mercy from G-d, and the ten days are their chance to make sure of that. The Talmud says that there are three books of: the Wicked, the Righteous, and the in-between. The idea of the books is figurative, as G-d does not actually need to write down this information. In these books are recorded the deeds of every person and thus their destiny for the next year is fixed. The righteous gain another year of life, but everyone has the chance over Rosh Hashanah to make repentance for anything, and so secure another year and good things to come. The greeting 'May you be inscribed with a good year' is said often at this time and refers to these books. Even though there is a hugely solemn side to the festival, it is joyous and festive. The associated colour is white, representing purity and a 'clean slate', so white clothes are worn and Torah scrolls and some furniture in synagogues are often dressed in white covers.

Customs of Rosh Hashanah

The most obvious feature is the sounding of the shofar (horn), blown in different combinations of three notes as an announcement of the new year's arrival, a call to repentance, a warning and to make people think about how they can be better people. The horn is from any kosher animal, but not the cow or ox (as that links to the Golden Calf). Traditionally, a ram's horn is used, recalling the ram that was sacrificed in place of Isaac. Actually, this ritual starts in Elul, the month before Rosh Hashanah, giving advanced warning so that all Jewish people can prepare.

The custom of reciting Tashlich dates back to the fourteenth century. On the afternoon of Rosh Hashanah, processions take place to a riverbank or anywhere there is flowing water. Micah 7:18–20, and Psalms 33 and 130 are recited, and then all shake out their pockets to symbolically cast their sins into the water. Many Jewish people throw breadcrumbs into the water. The emptying out, and the breadcrumbs represent throwing sins away in the hope G-d will forgive.

Many Jewish people do not nap or sleep long hours on Rosh Hashanah, instead dedicating day and night to prayer, meditation and soul-searching. This means that the day has become maximised for personal, spiritual focus.

Attending synagogue on Rosh Hashanah is important for most Jewish people. Ashkenazi Jewish people usually have a special midnight service (Selichot) on the Saturday evening before Rosh Hashanah, when prayers saying sorry and seeking forgiveness are said. Many Sephardic and Mizrachi Jewish people say Selichot prayers in the month before Rosh Hashanah.

Any festival would not be complete without a mention of food. Round challah bread is eaten (instead of plaited) to symbolise both the world and the ongoing cycle of time/the seasons. Sweet food is favoured for Rosh Hashanah so sour or pickled food is banished. Ashkenazi Jewish people traditionally eat honey cake. It is also common to eat particular fruits: apples dipped in honey and pomegranates. It is the hope that a person will perform many good deeds in the year to come as there are many seeds bursting from a pomegranate. Sephardic and

Mizrachi Jewish people often eat many other symbolic foods in addition and even have a ceremony to eat them.

Family meals at home are also very traditional/ important. Many Sephardic and Mizrachi Jewish people eat or have on the table the head of a fish to represent the hope for Jewish people to be leaders, not followers. Fish is also symbolic of fertility and the Jewish people multiplying and becoming many.

Yom Kippur

This is the Day of Atonement. Over the period of Rosh Hashanah, Judaism asks people to think about what they have done in the past year, but also makes clear that everyone can find their way back to G-d if they show self-discipline – say sorry and change their behaviour for the better. It is a day of confession and prayer. Many Jewish people spend the whole day focused on this activity. It is believed that the day brings pardon for sin between humans and G-d; forgiveness between humans and other humans only comes if an attempt is made to repair any damage done.

Before Yom Kippur begins ...

Before sunset, a lavish meal is shared. This strengthens people ahead of the fast but more importantly is a celebratory meal in honour of Yom Kippur – the holiest day in the year. As Jewish people cannot eat on the day itself, the meal to honour the festival is eaten before it begins.

At the start of Yom Kippur is the Kol Nidre service in which the Kol Nidre prayer is chanted (sung in Ashkenazi synagogues) three times. This asks for release from all pledges made to G-d, recognising that at times people make rash promises that they simply cannot keep. Given how solemn the prayer is, it is appropriate for Yom Kippur. The prayer took on special significance for Spanish Jewish people during the persecution they faced in the Middle Ages. A person could not be seen to be Jewish, and had to pretend to be Catholic, so many Jewish people pretended to follow the Catholic faith (to save their lives) but each year went to a secret Kol Nidre service ahead of promises they would make in their 'Catholic faith'.

Yom Kippur is a day of fasting. Only children (pre Bar/ Bat Mitzvah), people who are ill and those who have recently given birth are excluded from the fasting. Taking prescribed medication is allowed. Numbers 29:7 says that they should 'afflict the soul', which is taken to mean fast. It is a tradition to wear white on Yom Kippur to represent purity and a clean slate. Although the day is difficult and serious, due to fasting and concentrating on prayers for many hours, this is the day the book of life closes, so Jewish people try to make the most of every hour. It is not a sad day as all sins can be released; rather it is about being thankful that G-d is loving and merciful.

The synagogue services at Yom Kippur all bear the theme of confession and repentance. The readings in the main service reflect the elements of the day, so for example, the book of Jonah features. Jonah's story shows that G-d is a G-d of all nations, but also that humans (Jonah) can abandon evil ways, accept responsibility for his actions and return to G-d. It will also include Yizkor (memorial) prayers. A shofar blast sounds the end of Yom Kippur and fasting.

The Basics

1. Rosh Hashanah and Yom Kippur are about repentance. What does that mean for Jewish people?
2. When do these festivals take place?
3. Describe the key motivation behind these two festivals.
4. For each festival, describe the key customs, and explain their significance.
5. Explain how observing these festivals can have an influence on the rest of a Jewish person's life over the next year.
6. **Yom Kippur is the most important day of the year for Jewish people.** Explore this statement, showing you have thought about more than one point of view, including that of Judaism.

Pesach

Pesach begins on the 14th Nissan. Pesach is a festival of joy due to the celebration of freedom from over 200 years of slavery, even though it recalls events of great sadness, such as the suffering of the enslaved Israelites and the effects of the ten plagues on the Egyptians. It is one of the three pilgrim festivals, where Jewish people historically attended the Temple to make a sacrifice. It is celebrated for seven days in Israel and in Progressive communities, with the first and last days being key, and a **seder** on the first night. Outside of Israel for Orthodox communities, it is an eight-day festival, with seders on the first two days. A seder is an evening involving songs, readings, questions, actions, prayers and a meal, generally attended by the extended family (multi-generational) to retell the story of the Exodus. The celebration is relatively similar whichever type of Jewish person is celebrating it; this was enshrined in tradition by rabbis historically. They realised the importance of the festival and of all doing the same. There are however slight variations in tunes, recipes and extra traditions of various groups for the seder and what foods are allowed to be eaten on Pesach.

Much of the festival is based around the home; certainly the key customs are, which many believe has enriched homelife, as well as reinforcing the religion and understanding of its history.

The origins of Pesach

Pesach commemorates the liberation of the Israelites from servitude in Egypt over 3000 years ago. It brings Jewish people into close contact with their history and the liberation, allowing them to celebrate their freedom and reminding them to continue to fight for freedom in every generation. It also emphasises that G-d will ultimately come to the aid of His people – so there is always hope. You can read the story for yourself in Exodus. This has an impact across the entire year, for example, when facing any difficulty, a Jewish person might think back to Pesach and know all will eventually work out; they might relish the freedoms they have in life which many believe were given by G-d. As well as this, there is the wish for 'Next Year in Jerusalem' which is the hope that Jerusalem (especially the Jewish Temple) can be rebuilt as the spiritual centre of the world, not just that a Jewish person might enjoy the festival there one day.

Try to think of some more freedoms which Jewish people believe were given by G-d.

Five key concepts of Pesach

1 Memory (remember…)

Only by becoming aware of the past can our lives become filled with purpose and meaning. The past give clues to the now and the future, and helps inform a better future.

2 Optimism (hope)

Without hope, the Israelites would not have survived. Jewish people are reminded to retain hope.

3 Faith (belief)

Jewish optimism comes from the firmly held belief that they are blessed with support from above by a caring God. This faith leads to faith in self, the future and an ability to help change the world.

4 Family (belonging)

In the home is sown the seeds of the future because the children are the future. They need to be educated and reminded about this festival and their history.

5 Responsibility to others

The experience of the Israelites shines a light on the need for people to care for others. This includes feeding those in poverty, fighting injustice and supporting the oppressed. Chesed and tzedakah are crucial principles.

Getting ready for Pesach

On the morning before Pesach begins, after shacharit prayer, it is traditional for first-born sons to attend synagogue for a study session on a portion of the Talmud led by the rabbi, called siyum bekhorin, as originally first-born males were required to fast on the day before Pesach (linked to the tenth plague – death of the Egyptian firstborns). Over time the tradition has changed to what is done now.

Many Jewish people give to charity, maot chittim (money for feeding people in poverty over the festival) directly before Pesach, due to the opening paragraph of the Seder: 'All who are hungry, let them come and eat.'

Traditionally, all chametz (leavened food) must be cleared from the house and a person's ownership by around 10 a.m. on the morning before Pesach begins. This is done formally, including renouncing any chametz which has not been found (just in case). The tradition of bedikat chametz (searching for chametz) sees the adults of the house with their children going to search for any remaining chametz around the house the evening before Pesach starts. It is traditional to use a candle for light, and collect breadcrumbs which have been left in each room on purpose, using a feather and a wooden spoon. Having collected the 'planted' pieces of bread, all is wrapped and left for the morning, when it is symbolically burnt.

My favourite festival? All of them, of course. Each festival is a celebration of our faith and community. It unites Jewish people everywhere in that celebration.

Avi

Most Jewish people have a special set of all kitchenware for use only at Pesach. All the things normally used are considered contaminated by leaven. New clothes might be bought. Special leaven-free and symbolic foods are prepared and eaten. This reinforces that this is a joyful festival.

The Basics

1. What is Pesach?
2. Explain why Pesach is an important festival for Jewish people.
3. What is chametz and why is it important at Pesach?
4. How do Jewish people prepare for Pesach?
5. Describe the seder meal.
6. Explain: Aggadah; seder plate; chametz; seder meal.
7. **Pesach has no influence on a Jew's life other than during the festival.** Explore this statement, giving explained reasons to agree and disagree with it, including Jewish arguments.

The Seder

> 'Anyone who has not said these three words on Pesach has not done his duty: Pesach, matzah, maror.' – *Rabbi Gamaliel II*

Seder is held on the first (and second for some) night of Pesach. There are 15 parts to the whole, which is rather like a service in some ways, and it follows a book of instruction called the Aggadah.

Sometimes, the leader of the seder wears a kittel (white, linen gown). Some say it represents the release from bondage of the Israelites and a fresh start after enslavement, as the kittel is simple like a burial shroud and therefore is a reminder that life is precious, and that Jewish people should be humble as they used to be enslaved. Some suggest that the kittel was worn when eating the Pesach offering in the Temple; Jewish people still treat their Pesach table as if they are eating sacrificial food.

The table will be set with three matzot, wine and the seder plate, as well as the usual dinner table items.

The recital of the Aggadah is the most essential part of the Seder. This book contains the story of the Israelites when they were enslaved in Egypt and how they were given freedom by G-d. It also explains the components of the seder plate, and why they are eaten: the Passover Lamb, the maror, bitter herbs and matzah. It also praises G-d.

There are three matzah, which replace the challah bread of a usual Shabbat meal. Of course, challah is forbidden because it is leavened. Chametz (leaven) can be made from five grains: wheat, barley, spelt, rye and oats. Matzah is made from wheat and water and baked within 18 minutes of the two being mixed. This is to ensure no fermentation, hence no chametz. Some Jewish people only eat hand-baked ('guarded') matzah, which are usually round. Some Jewish people eat shmurah ('guarded') matzah, which are specially made for Pesach and only at that time, and which have been made (from the grinding of the wheat to the actual baked product) under very close watch to strictly ensure no fermentation has taken place. This is especially common amongst strictly Orthodox Jewish people. The matzah reminds Jewish people of the eagerness of the Israelites when fleeing from enslavement in Egypt; they did not have time to make bread other than the unleavened type.

The seder plate is prominent when looking at the table. It has become customary for a special plate to be used, which has six sections to it, each containing a symbolic food. The maror (bitter herbs) represent the bitterness of the enslavement of the Israelites (horseradish is often used for maror). Karpas is a vegetable which is dipped into salt water before eating.

The vegetable (often celery or parsley) represents springtime (new growth), just like the Israelites had a new start and could start growing as a nation after leaving Egypt. The salt water (instead of salad dressing) represents the tears of the enslaved Israelites. The dipping of vegetables represents Joseph's coat being dipped into blood, which started the whole process of the Israelites ending up in Egypt. Some people choose to also have charazet, another vegetable which is bitter, as some say there need to be two bitter foods because the book of Numbers 9:11 speaks of eating bitter foods in the plural, that is, more than one kind. Charoset is made of fruit and nuts, chopped and turned into a paste with red wine. It represents the mortar made and used by the enslaved Israelites. Zeroa (shankbone) is symbolic of the 'mighty arm of G-d' and also the Paschal Lamb sacrifice. This can be a meat bone which has been baked, or the neck of a fowl. Baytza is a roasted hard-boiled egg symbolising the roast offerings from the Temple sacrifice and also the egg symbolises the continuing cycle of life.

The Aggadah leads the family through the seder service, giving readings from scripture, and giving children the four key questions which lead into the story of the original Pesach. The last section of the seder is made up of psalms of thanksgiving and joyful songs.

The number four is prominent: there are four questions, four sons/children, four cups of wine (reflecting the four references to redemption mentioned in Exodus). Wine is drunk at the meal, and it is traditional to spill ten drops, one for each of the plagues. This is a reminder to not rejoice too much at the misfortune of others (in this case the Egyptians). An extra cup is in place (Elijah's cup); this remains untouched. Elijah was a prophet and is a reminder of the Messianic Age, as some believe that he will re-appear to herald it in. The door to the house will be opened as part of the service, which is seen as a symbol of welcoming or wishing for Elijah and the Messianic Age.

Next year in Jerusalem

A wish stated out loud and often sung at the end of the seder. For some, this is wishing that all Jewish people will be reunited living in Israel in a time of world peace (Messianic Age), and for some this refers specifically to the wish that the Temple will be rebuilt in Jerusalem by next Pesach.

Testing your knowledge

One-mark Questions

Multiple-choice question

For the one-mark multiple-choice question, you must choose the correct answer from the four you are offered.

Focusing on the second section of Judaism, on practices that you have now studied, try the following:

1 What is the Talmud?

A Books of Moses
B five books of law
C Jewish civil and religious laws
D Jewish prayer shawl

2 What is the Halakah?

A Jewish law
B Jewish New Year festival
C Shabbat candle
D non-kosher food

3 Jewish dietary law forbids the eating of two foods together – which ones are they?

A fish and vegetables
B fruit and milk
C meat and milk
D pulses and chicken

4 Where is the Torah kept in the synagogue?

A in the Ark
B in the bimah
C in the gallery
D in the Ner Tamid

5 Which of the following Jewish festivals uses a seder plate?

A Passover
B Purim
C Rosh Hashanah
D Yom Kippur

Make up four answers to each of the following and test your partner. Do not forget: only ONE can be correct!

1 Which of these is the name for the birth ceremony for a Jewish boy?
2 Which of these is the name of the stand in the synagogue on which the Torah is unrolled and read?
3 Which of these is a place of pilgrimage for Jewish people?
4 What is meant by the term 'treyfah'?
5 What is the name for Jewish New Year?

Short response question

The one-mark short response question is asking you to write a brief response.

You will have to name or give an example of a belief, practice, key term or religious concept.

You may also be asked for a brief definition.

Do not waste time writing too much but make sure to write enough to answer the question fully. Don't leave the examiner guessing at what you mean, or how what you have written does answer the question. Don't be vague!

1 Give one religious reason why most Jewish people marry.
2 Name one key feature of a synagogue.
3 Give one religious reason why Jewish people celebrate Pesach.
4 Name one of the three parts of the Tenakh.
5 Give one of the rituals carried out during Shabbat.

Make up three one-mark short response questions to test your partner.

Differences Questions

Four-mark questions

These questions are where you show your understanding of the diversity within the religion you have studied – that there are different groups within Judaism, and they have different ways of practising their faith.

You will have to answer one of these in each of the practices sections of your chosen two religions. They are always worth four marks, and always ask you to contrast two practices.

The wording will always begin: 'Explain two different (Jewish) …'

Followed by one of these, or something similar:

- 'views on/about …'
- 'ways in which …'
- 'rituals associated with …'

Here are some examples for you to see how that works (and to try):

1. Explain two different Jewish views about the importance of the synagogue.
2. Explain two different Jewish rituals which are carried out during Pesach.
3. Explain two different ways in which Jewish people worship in Reform and Orthodox synagogues.

Go back through your answers to these three questions and use AQA's mark scheme to see how you could improve them.

Look at the following answers. Which do you think is better, and why?

Explain two different ways in which worship is carried out in the synagogue by reform and orthodox Jewish people.

Answer 1

In Reform Judaism, men and women sit together during services. Usually families sit together. In Orthodox Judaism, men and women sit separately, with only men involved in leading the prayers. Another way that they are different is that the service in an Orthodox synagogue is mostly done in Hebrew, whereas in the Reform synagogue it is mostly not in Hebrew.

Answer 2

In Orthodox Judaism, the service is in Hebrew, the language of the Torah – the word of G-d. Men and women sit separately in the synagogue, with men focused on and closer to the bimah and the Torah. Often women are seated in a gallery.

Answer 1: This gives two good ways but the explanation is simple, because it gives no detail. You could improve this for them by giving more detail to explain each way more fully.

Answer 2: This gives only one way, but in quite a lot of detail. You could improve this answer by adding a second way.

Explaining Practices

Six-mark questions

These questions ask you to explain two ways in which Jewish people put their beliefs into practice, or two ways in which Jewish people believe practices to be important.

The wording will always begin:

'Explain two ways in which …'

Finishing off with: 'Refer to sacred writings or another source of Jewish belief and teaching in your answer.'

They will be marked against AQA's mark scheme which can be found on the AQA website.

From the question wording and the mark scheme you can work out how to answer the question effectively. Each question is different, but in this case you would:

- choose your two ways and then explain each one
- develop your explanations fully
- use a relevant quotation/teaching, show how it links to the question and include its source of authority, for example a holy book (Torah) or religious leader.

Remember this is just one example to help you practice. In the exam, you will need to think carefully and respond to the actual question you are given.

What does 'way' mean?

The question wants you to explain the reasons why something is important. Don't get caught out in the pressure of an exam – practise a lot of questions beforehand.

Here is an example:

Explain two ways in which Jewish people celebrate Pesach. Refer to sacred writings or another source of Jewish belief and teaching in your answer.

Sample answer

One way Jewish people celebrate Pesach is by following the teaching of Rabbi Gamaliel II[1], who told the Jewish people that it was their duty to say three words – Pesach, maror and matzah.[2] This is saying Jewish people must remember the matzah, which the Israelites had to make in their flight from Egypt as they had no time to make bread properly. So it reminds them of their hardships[3]. It is also saying they have to remember the maror – bitter herbs – reminding us that the Israelites had bitter times and cried many tears in their enslavement[4].

Looking at the sample answer:

1 it opens by saying where the teaching comes from, i.e. the source of authority, here a respected 1st century Rabbi;

2 this is what Rabbi Gamaliel II said about Pesach;

3 this explains one part of what he said, making it clear how it relates to Jewish history;

4 this explains a second part of what he said, so further explaining the statement.

Of course, the answer needs a second teaching about how the Jewish people celebrate Pesach, written in the same way.

Practise the following questions for yourself:

1. Explain two ways in which Jewish people celebrate Rosh Hashanah. Refer to sacred writings or another source of Jewish belief and teaching in your answer.
2. Explain two reasons why pilgrimage to the Western Wall in Jerusalem is important to many Jewish people. Refer to sacred writings or another source of Jewish belief and teaching in your answer.
3. Explain two reasons in which Jewish people consider the Shabbat to be important. Refer to sacred writings or another source of Jewish belief and teaching in your answer.

Analyse and Evaluate

For GCSE RS you have to be able to show that you can react to a given statement. This means that you consider what the statement says, present arguments to agree and disagree and come to a conclusion of what you yourself think of the statement. You have to demonstrate what a Jewish person might say and what arguments they might use. This type of question takes the most thinking, so needs the most time.

It is always a good idea to work to a formula when you answer this type of question. This structures your answer, which makes it clear and also makes sure you meet all the necessary criteria to give a good answer. Here is one formula you might consider using:

SOCs

S = Some people might say …

O = Other people might say …

C = In Conclusion, I think the strongest answer is … because …

s = make sure you have several points in each of the above

Some other tips

- Focus on the statement itself, not the topic the statement sits within. For example, 'Birth ceremonies are the most important Jewish ceremony' isn't asking you to describe the birth ceremonies, but rather to compare their importance with the importance of other ceremonies.
- 'Some' and 'other' must be differing (opposing) views.
- Aim to give in-depth explanations of each argument.
- Examples are a good way to further develop your arguments and demonstrate good understanding.

Have a go at using the formula and tips to answer the following questions:

1 **The home is more important than the synagogue for the learning of the religion.**

Evaluate this statement. You should:
- refer to Jewish teaching
- give reasoned arguments to support this statement
- give reasoned arguments to support a different point of view
- reach a justified conclusion.

2 **Festivals just remember the past and are pointless in modern life.**

Evaluate this statement. You should:
- refer to Jewish teaching
- give reasoned arguments to support this statement
- give reasoned arguments to support a different point of view
- reach a justified conclusion.

3 **Prayer is more important than action in the world today.**

Evaluate this statement. You should:
- refer to Jewish teaching
- give reasoned arguments to support this statement
- give reasoned arguments to support a different point of view
- reach a justified conclusion.

4 **Jewish people should be able to live as they want not be dictated to by tradition.**

Evaluate this statement. You should:
- refer to Jewish teaching
- give reasoned arguments to support this statement
- give reasoned arguments to support a different point of view
- reach a justified conclusion.

The more practice you get at this type of question, the better. You could go back and use this formula to redo earlier evaluation questions.

Judaism Glossary

Aggadah the service text for the Passover seder

Aleinu closing prayer in synagogue

Amidah prayer in synagogue; standing; contains 19 blessings

Aron hakodesh the holy ark which houses the Sefer Torah scrolls

Bar Mitzvah the service for a Jewish boy to become a full member of the Jewish community

Bat Mitzvah the service for a Jewish girl to become a daughter of the commandment

Bet Din a Jewish religious court of law

Bimah Ashkenazi name for the reading platform in the centre of the synagogue

Brit Milah birth ceremony for boys in which he is circumcised

Cantor a singer, who leads prayer in the synagogue

Chesed Hebrew word meaning loving kindness

Covenant agreement made between humans and G-d

Creation the making of the world from nothing by G-d

Decalogue the Ten Commandments

Gan Eden the Garden of Eden, the place where Adam and Eve are supposed to have lived. Also the term sometimes used for 'heaven' in the world to come, where good people are thought to go when they die

Gehinnom a place of torment or suffering for those souls who do not deserve to go straight to heaven

Gemara found with the Mishnah, a large collection of texts of rabbis' discussions of the Jewish law

Gilgul the transmigration of the soul after death into another being

Halakah Jewish law made up of Talmud and Mishnah

Havdalah closing ceremony to end Shabbat

Jerusalem the capital city of Israel

Kaddish prayer in synagogue; often mourning prayers

Kashrut Jewish dietary system that covers what Jewish people can and cannot eat

Kosher proper or suitable for Jewish people

Maimonides the greatest philosopher and scholar of the Torah in the twelfth century

Messiah 'anointed one' who some Jewish people believe will come to make the world 'perfect'

Messianic Age the time that will see the arrival of the Messiah when the world will be improved

Midrash literature, including stories, written by the rabbis to help understanding of the Torah

Minhagim very established customs that are almost binding like laws

Minyan minimum number (ten) of adults necessary for some prayers

Mishnah Jewish oral law in a written format

Mishpatim laws that are judgements (contain logic)

Mitzvot (sing. mitztvah) 613 commandments in the Hebrew scriptures covering religious and moral conduct

Ner tamid perpetual light/lamp, found in synagogues and representing G-d

Olam ha-ba the world to come

Olam ha-ze the Jewish term for life here and now on earth

Oral laws the explanation of the Torah that is traditionally also believed to have been given verbally to Moses on Mount Sinai

Parev food with no meat/milk and so can be eaten with either

Pesach festival of the Passover celebrating the Israelites' escape from enslavement by the Egyptians

Pikuach nefesh the principle of saving a life which overrides nearly all other religious laws

Promised Land the land promised by G-d to the descendants of Abraham

Rabbi leader and teacher in a Jewish community

Resurrection the physical coming back of the body to life after death

Rosh Hashanah the Jewish New Year

Seder the service and meal shared by Jewish families at the start of Passover

Shabbat the Jewish holy day of rest

Shavuot also known as the Feast of Weeks celebrating the giving of the Torah

Shechinah the divine presence

Shema declaration of faith; prayer

Siddur a Jewish prayer book which contains the set order for daily prayers

Synagogue Jewish place of worship; means 'place of meeting' in Greek

Talmud commentary on the Jewish law

Tenakh the Jewish scriptures combining Torah, Nevi'im and Ketuvim

Ten Commandments the first ten laws/mitzvot believed by Orthodox Jewish people to have been given to Moses on Mount Sinai

Tikkun olam the principle of 'repairing/healing' the world

Torah first part of Jewish scripture, seen by Orthodox Jewish people as the word of G-d, and given orally to Moses on Mount Sinai

Treyfah food that it is not permitted for Jewish people to eat according to the Torah

Tzedakah this means charity and giving to those in need

Tzitzit the name for the knotted fringes attached to the four corners of the prayer shawl

Western Wall the only remaining wall of the Temple mount in Jerusalem built in 20BCE, which is the most holy of Jewish sites

Yom Kippur the Day of Atonement and the holiest day for Jewish people

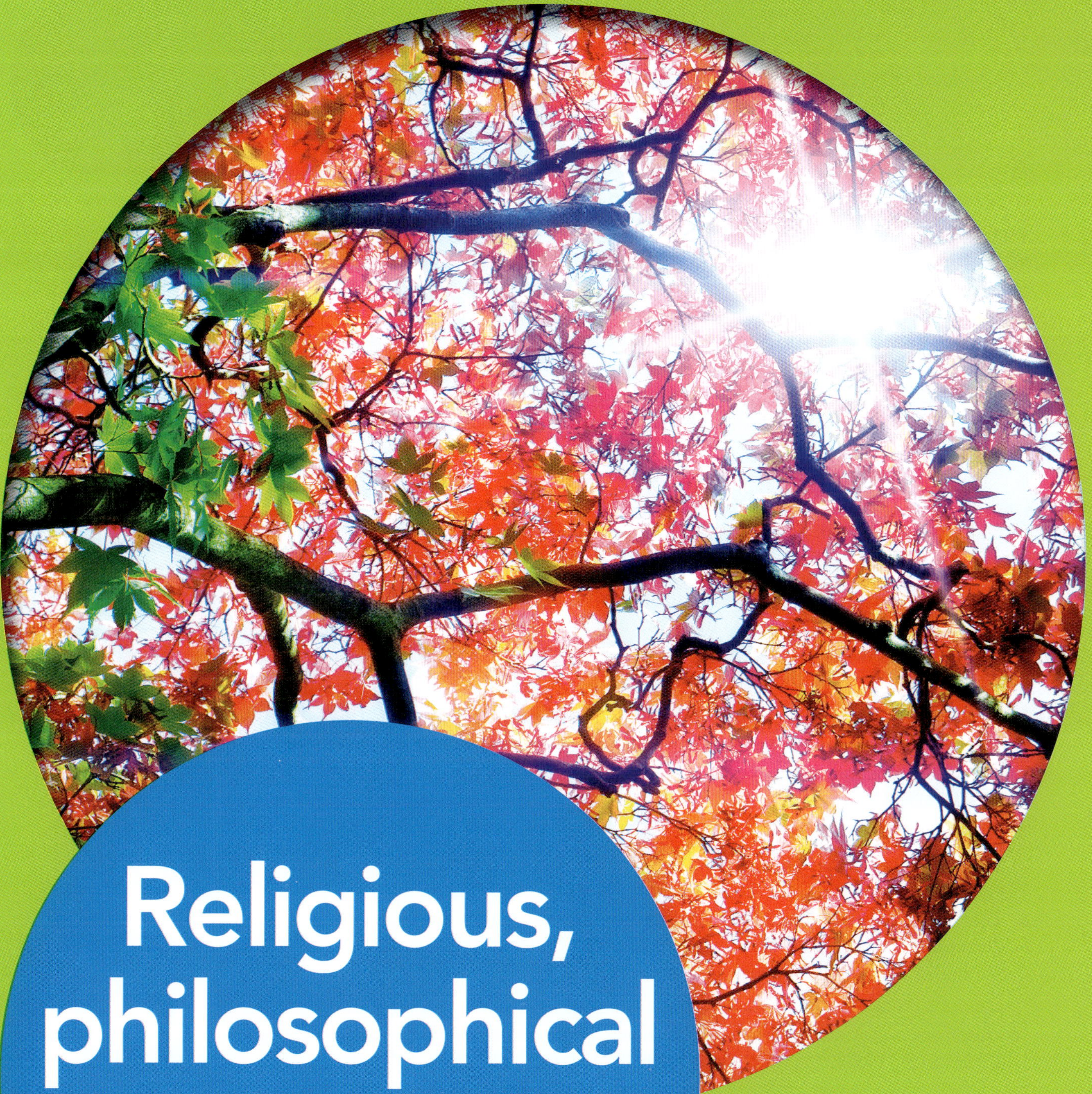

Religious, philosophical and ethical studies

What does the Specification say about the Themes?

Notes to Teachers and Students

In Themes A–F, you have to study the topics from two different religious perspectives or traditions. These can be consistently the same two throughout each of the themes or they can be different religions/traditions for different topics, therefore allowing you to refer to as many as you want. However, one of the areas of exam question focus is 'different views' and in these questions you must study two religious traditions. One of these must be the main religious tradition in Britain (Christianity). This means you **must** give a Christian perspective (generally or a specific denomination) as one of the two religious traditions you refer to in your answers. The other might be a different religion or a different Christian tradition.

In each theme three topics are specifically mentioned in the specification as requiring you to know different beliefs. The table at the foot of the page lists them for you and each of the different areas are addressed in this book at the end of each Theme.

In answering these 'differences' questions for each of the four Themes you have studied, you **must** present Christianity as one perspective. It is the main religious tradition of Great Britain.

You should know about different views. For example you might be asked:

- 'Explain two different beliefs in contemporary Britain about …'
- In your answer you should refer to the main religious tradition of Great Britain and one or more other religious traditions.

Marks will be awarded as shown in AQA's mark scheme. See the AQA website for details.

What are the traditions?

- They might be religions in their own right – Christianity, Buddhism, Hinduism, Islam, Judaism, and Sikhism.
- They might be denominations of Christianity – Roman Catholic, Orthodox, Protestant, such as Anglican (Church of England) or Methodist, or non-Conformist, such as Quakers or Salvation Army.

Note: If one of your chosen themes is Theme C, you must reference Christianity (or a tradition within it) and non-religious beliefs such as Atheism or Humanism.

Theme A	Theme B	Theme C	Theme D	Theme E	Theme F
Contraception	Abortion	Visions	Violence	Corporal punishment	Status of women in religion
Sex before marriage	Euthanasia	Miracles	Weapons of mass destruction	Death penalty	The use of wealth
Same-sex relationships	Animal experimentation	Nature as general revelation	Pacifism	Forgiveness	Freedom of religious expression

The religious bit …

Religion and religious people have opinions on all issues, just as you do. As this is an RS course, you are going to see the attitudes of the six major religions to the issues studied. Make sure you understand what those attitudes are and where they come from; in other words, the beliefs and teachings of the religions. In this book, you are given a small number of beliefs and teachings for each religion on each theme. Quite often, you can use these teachings in a few different themes. If a teaching will apply to more than one theme then you should use it, showing each time how it is relevant.

Below are some general teachings which you can apply to all the different themes. This cuts down the overall number of teachings you have to learn and ensures that those that you do use, you understand well. However, it is best to use beliefs and teachings which are specific to the themes, as well as the general ones. Do not forget to learn some of those when you meet them later. Copy them into the front of your notebook or file. Then use them as the basis for your work. When you study a theme, refer back to these to help you work out what the attitude of a believer will be to that theme.

Buddhism

1. Rebirth and karma – our words, thoughts and deeds create energies which shape our future rebirths. We need to make sure these are positive.
2. The Five Precepts (guidelines for living). These are: not harming others (ahimsa); using language kindly; not taking what is not freely given; not clouding our minds; no sexual misconduct.
3. Compassion (loving kindness).
4. The Noble Eightfold Path – the Buddha's system of self-discipline which gives an ethical basis to our actions, for example, Right Speech (using language kindly); Right Action (acting to help, not hurt, others).

Hinduism

Hindu holy books list many virtues. These include:

1. Ahimsa (non-violence)
2. Self-discipline
3. Tolerance
4. Service to others
5. Compassion
6. Providing shelter/support to others
7. Respect for all life
8. Wisdom
9. Honesty with others and oneself
10. Cleanliness

These virtues and many more are indicated throughout the Hindu scriptures as the basis of living a dharmic life.

Christianity

1. Jesus' two key teachings: love God; love your neighbour.
2. Equality of all, because in Genesis we are told that God made each person.
3. Justice (fairness): since everyone is equal, everyone deserves fairness.
4. Forgiveness and love are ideas taught by Jesus and shown in his actions.
5. Belief that God created the world, so it is special, as is all life in it. Hence stewardship is an important duty.

Islam

1. The ummah – brotherhood and collective unity of all Muslims. All Muslims are bound by mutual aid, brotherly solidarity and cooperation, which is treated as a religious obligation in Islam.
2. That everyone must follow duties set by Allah (God), for example, the Five Pillars (Sunni) or Ten Obligations (Shi'a).
3. Shari'ah Law, which is Muslim law stemming from the Qur'an and Hadith and how it is applied to modern life by Islamic scholars.
4. The afterlife – that Allah has created a paradise which people are rewarded with after death if they have been morally good.

Judaism

The Ten Commandments that are found in the Torah:

1 Love only G-d.
2 Make no idols of G-d.
3 Do not take G-d's name in vain.
4 Keep the Sabbath holy.
5 Respect your parents.
6 Do not kill.
7 Do not steal.
8 Do not commit adultery.
9 Do not tell lies.
10 Do not act on feelings of jealousy.

In addition, there are 613 mitzvot, or laws which are all found in the Torah (the holiest of Jewish scriptures, considered the word of G-d by Orthodox Jewish people). The mitzvot cover all aspects of life and religious practice.

Sikhism

1 Sikhism teaches that the divine spark is within all forms of life, so all life is sacred and should be protected.
2 God created everything, so all should be looked after.
3 The absolute equality of all – regardless of class, gender, religion – was taught by all the gurus.
4 The Khalsa vows – meditation and service to God; not to cut bodily hairs, use any intoxicants, or eat meat that has been ritually slaughtered; and to fight for justice.
5 Sewa (selfless service to others) is a religious duty.
6 Ethical virtues – sharing with others, including tithing (daswandh); dutifulness; prudence; justice; tolerance; temperance; chastity; patience; contentment; detachment; and humility.

Tasks

Check with your teacher which religious traditions you are studying. Create a cue card for your religious traditions with the teachings written on them from the boxes above.
Learn one a day so that you are familiar with each of them as you will need to use them in your answers to all types of questions. (Remember, if you use a teaching that does not directly apply to the topic in question (i.e. its relevance isn't obvious to the reader), you *must* explain how it applies. This will be true for these general teachings most of the time.)
Have them with you in lessons to refer to.
Carry them in your school bag or in your school planner, so you can access them easily.
Your teacher might give you specific teachings as you study each theme which you can add to the cards.
The greater diversity of teachings you can refer to, the better your answers will be.
If you learn them over the duration of the course it will make your final revision much easier as you lead up to your exams.

4 Theme A: Relationships and families

Key elements of this theme

This theme is about personal and sexual relationships, including **heterosexual** and same-sex relationships. Heterosexual relationships are between people who are attracted to the opposite sex. Same-sex or gay relationships are between people of the same sex. The term lesbian is often used to refer to women who are attracted to other women. The theme goes on to explore how people show their **commitment** through marriage and other forms of **cohabitation** and what the **family** in the twenty-first century looks like. Sometimes relationships end, so the theme also explores **divorce** as well as **remarriage**. Finally, it considers **gender equality**, particularly in the context of roles in the home, but also in society.

Let's talk sex!

Why do people have sex? Love, lust, fun, money, to make life. Can you think of any more reasons? Is it always all right to have sex? When do you think sex is not all right? Under what circumstances?

Think about the different types of relationships described on the next page. Which ones seem acceptable to you, and which ones do not? Explain why in each case.

It is true to say that society changes all the time in the UK. Fifty years ago, it was illegal to be gay and there was widespread persecution of gay and lesbian people; today it is much more accepted and most young people do not see sexuality as an issue (whether they themselves are gay or not). Fifty years ago, almost everyone got married and divorce was rare; now fewer than half of us marry and half of those couples get divorced. As society changes, our attitudes to sex change although religions tend to keep a more consistent attitude over time, because it is based on beliefs and teachings. For this course, you need to be aware of both secular (what society says/does) and religious attitudes.

Key concepts for this theme

These are the key ideas that come up throughout this theme. You should try to learn them so you can keep referring to them.

Commitment – this is an agreement with someone; a promise or pledge. In the case of relationships, it is usually based on being faithful and supportive.

Responsibility – with any commitment comes responsibilities. These are the things we have to do as part of the agreement we have made. For example, in marriage it might be that earning money to support the family is a responsibility.

Contract – these are binding agreements. Marriage vows and a marriage certificate are evidence of the contract made when two people marry.

Chastity – this is the idea of being sexually pure. In a relationship, it would be about being faithful to your partner. Outside a relationship, it would be about not behaving sexually. Most religious groups believe that sex is only appropriate within marriage, so to be chaste is important.

Sexuality

Sexuality

Age of consent

This is when you are old enough by law to choose to have sex. In the UK, the age of consent is 16 for everyone. Of course, you could have sex before then – but you aren't considered mature enough to be responsible enough and it is against the law.

Celibacy

I am celibate. I have no sexual partner. I have made a decision to wait until I marry to have sex. If I never marry, then I'll not have sex.

Adultery

Even though we are married, I had an affair. It lasted a few months. It has taken a long time to begin to make up for it. The marriage really took a battering, and is still fragile but we are working at it.

Heterosexuality

We met at school and just fell for each other. Broke up a few times and then drifted apart. But we got back together at a school reunion four years ago and knew we needed to make it work this time. Our relationship is really strong.

Sex before marriage

We all had sexual relationships before being married to anyone. Different circumstances and reasons – part of a relationship, lust – you know, one-night stands – in a relationship which led to marriage, everyone else was doing it.

Same-sex attraction

We met at university and have been together ever since. We are getting married this year. This is a strong, loving, sexual relationship and it works for us.

Task

Evaluative questions make up half the total marks. Work out as many reasons to agree and to disagree with each of these statements as you can:

1 **There should not be an age of consent for sex.**
2 **Only married couples should have sex.**

Take each of your reasons and explain them.

Contraception and family planning

If you have to learn about sexual relationships and having children you should really know something about **contraception**.

Read the statements and decide why these people use contraception.

Ben: *I'm not ready to be a dad, but I do have sex.*

Sarah: *I'm HIV+ and I don't want to pass that on to my partner. We still enjoy sex.*

Effie: *We have all the children we want to have, so need to use contraception.*

Shane: *Well, I like the feel and the fun of using contraceptives when I am having sex. It's all part of the enjoyment for me.*

The main reason for using contraception is **family planning**, that is, controlling the size of a family. Ben prevented his family from beginning, whilst Effie ensures it gets no bigger. They are both planning their families.

Task

You are the doctor. Recommend a form of contraception for each of the following:

- **a** Joshua has a family, but knows he could not care adequately for any more children. It is against his religion to have permanent methods of contraception, because that would be changing what God has made.
- **b** Jessica is married and wants no more children, who she sees as a gift from God. However, her religion does not agree with any artificial methods and she believes permanent methods are against God's wishes.
- **c** Xavier needs to protect his partner from an STI he carries. He needs to make sure there is no exchange of body fluids during sex.
- **d** Helena asked for a foolproof (100 per cent safe) form of contraception.

What kinds of contraception are there?

There are many kinds of contraception available and they work in different ways. That is why some people use one kind, but not another. Religious people in particular accept the use of some kinds, but not others.

- Artificial methods of contraception prevent sperm from fertilising the egg by means of a physical device or a barrier, such as a condom or the pill.
- Natural methods of contraception are aimed at limiting the chance of pregnancy such as the rhythm method, where a couple has sex only during the woman's least fertile part of her monthly cycle.
- Permanent methods of contraception are operations to prevent either the production of eggs or sperm permanently. These methods are the only ones guaranteed to prevent pregnancy.

Try to work out which type of contraception is being described in each of the following statements.

1. The withdrawal method (where a man withdraws from inside the woman before he ejaculates) is a commonly used, but very unsafe attempt to avoid pregnancy.
2. Barrier contraceptives make a barrier between the egg and sperm. If they do not meet, there is no pregnancy. Condoms and caps are two examples.
3. A man can have an operation, as can a woman, called sterilisation. This stops either eggs or sperm being released, so pregnancy cannot happen.
4. A woman's level of fertility varies during her monthly cycle. By working out these cycles of fertility and infertility, a couple can try to avoid pregnancy.
5. Using a coil (IUD) makes the woman menstruate, even if there is a fertilised egg in her womb. So the egg is lost with the blood.
6. Taking the pill affects a woman's hormones. She should not produce any eggs, so will not get pregnant.

Religious attitudes to sexual matters

Buddhism

- Buddhism, in all its forms, has a very strong **celibate** tradition, particularly within monastic communities. The energy which might have been put into sexual activity is channelled into spiritual activity to try to reach enlightenment. Having said that, there are many lay Buddhists who live as families. **Sex** is seen as natural, but most rewarding as part of a loving, caring relationship, so **chastity** is encouraged. Buddhists see using contraception to limit their family size, so practising family planning, as a skillful act. If a family cannot cope with or does not want a child, then family planning can prevent the suffering a new child might bring.
- The Four Noble Truths say that one must set aside desire and craving if one is to achieve enlightenment. Hence, Buddhist monks refrain from sexual relationships.
- Buddhism encourages people to follow the Precepts, such as the Precept to avoid sexual immorality, including **adultery**. Breaking that Precept generates bad karma, and will lead to suffering. Karma is what determines the quality of the next life.
- Buddhists do not condemn **sex before marriage** or **homosexuality**, as long as they are part of a loving, caring relationship. Where sex is just based on lust, such as one-night stands, then this is craving, which creates bad karma.

Task

Read pages 238–239. Write out the words in purple from the text from the religion/religions you have studied. Give each a definition and a brief idea of what their attitude is to each one.

Christianity

Many Christians believe that only married couples should have **sex**, and only with each other. **Chastity** is a virtue. Attitudes to the use of **contraception** also vary. There is a **celibate** tradition within Christianity (monastic life, and the priesthood).

Every sexual act must be within the framework of marriage. The Catholic Church teaches that only married couples should have sex, and the most important reason for sex is to have children. There should be a chance of pregnancy within every act of sex.

Any sex other than between husband and wife is wrong. **Sex before marriage** is called *fornication*, and is a sin. The same goes for masturbation, because it cannot lead to pregnancy. Using contraception is against Catholic teaching, because it cancels out the chance of pregnancy, though in Western countries this teaching is often ignored. Most Catholics follow natural methods of contraception.

Some Christians believe that gay or lesbian sex is unnatural and, as it cannot lead to pregnancy, is a sin. The Bible's stance on homosexuality is a complex issue with various interpretations. Some Christians interpret some biblical passages as condemning homosexual acts. Other Christians support committed same-sex relationships and same-sex couples can be married in some Protestant Churches, such as the Methodist Church.

Yet other Christians accept sex before marriage in a relationship which is leading to marriage, seeing it as an expression of love. They also stress the need for *responsible parenthood*; only having as many children as you can properly look after, so the use of contraception is encouraged. Many Christians disagree with sterilisation (unless for medical reasons) because that is damaging what God has created.

The Bible says 'Do not commit **adultery**'. Jesus says that even to look at someone lustfully is wrong, so affairs are also wrong and a sin. Having an affair means you break all the promises you made before God when marrying. Therefore, Christians do not agree with adultery.

ॐ Hinduism

For a Hindu man, life is split into four Ashramas or stages. Sexual relationships can only happen in the second stage, which is that of the married householder (grihastha). For the other three stages, the man should remain **celibate**. This means that women also have sexual relationships only within marriage. **Sex before marriage** and **same-sex attraction** are both unacceptable to some Hindus. **Sex** is seen as a gift from the Ultimate Reality (God), and must be treated with care and respect. It is for enjoyment and to have children.

Chastity is important in Hinduism and all are expected to be virgins before marriage, with their only sexual partner being the person to whom they are married. Two important Hindu virtues are self-discipline and respect, and **adultery** goes against both of these. Since adultery causes others to suffer, it brings bad karma to the adulterer, and negatively affects their rebirth.

Hindus do not object to using **contraception**; rather, they encourage it. *Family planning* is stressed, though. During the year, however, there are many days when couples should avoid sex, for example, festivals, full/new moon, holy days. There are up to 208 holy days in total, and this obviously acts as a form of birth control.

☪ Islam

Islam rejects celibacy, choosing never to marry and monastic lifestyles. It is a religious duty to marry and have children. Sex before marriage or outside marriage is prohibited.

The message is very clear in Islam; only married couples may have sex, and then only with each other. Prophet Muhammad ﷺ spoke of sex as being special within marriage. He said it was a source of pleasure and provided the blessing of children from God, if the couple so wished. This means that Muslims can and should use **contraception**. Muhammad ﷺ also said that couples should only have as many children as they could properly look after – *responsible parenthood*.

In several places, the Qur'an specifically mentions adultery, always saying it is wrong: 'Do not commit adultery. It is shameful and an evil way to act' (*Surah 17:32*). The Qur'an sets out a specific punishment, public flogging, for those who have **sex before marriage**, or who commit **adultery**, and some Hadiths prescribe the death penalty. The Qur'an also prohibits the sin of the people of Lot (*Surah 54:37*), generally understood to mean homosexual conduct, and some Hadiths specify the death penalty for it. In some Muslim countries, the punishment for adultery or same-sex relationships is severe, including the death penalty.

Task

Look at the couples mentioned in the image:

1. None of these couples are married. John and Sara only met last week, whereas Anand and Vijaya have been together for months, and Sameira and Mehmet for years. Explain what the attitude of each of the two religions you are studying would be towards each couple in relation to them having a sexual relationship.
2. What if John and Sara got married? What would be the attitude of each religion towards them having sex? What advice might be given by each religion about contraception?

Judaism

The family is very important in Judaism. Anything that goes against this ideal is wrong. Marriage is seen as the ideal, whereas a life of **celibacy** is not. The Torah states that woman was made from man to be his companion. This is interpreted to mean marriage.

A sex drive is healthy and **sex** within marriage is for pleasure and having children. The first command G-d gave was to *be fruitful and multiply*, which is understood to mean that couples should have children if they can. Different branches of Judaism have different attitudes to **contraception**. Orthodox Jewish people will accept it for medical/physical and mental health reasons. They often use the pill because it does not interfere in the actual act of sex, and does not directly cause the *wasting of seed* (forbidden in the Torah). Progressive Jewish people also accept contraception for social/economic reasons, so they use more forms. For those Jewish people who follow mitzvot, sex is forbidden at certain times within a woman's menstrual cycle.

The Torah lists punishments for **adultery**. Traditionally, Jewish people are expected to be virgins before marriage and observe **chastity** all their life. Committing adultery breaks one of the Ten Commandments.

Torah law forbids a man having sex with another man, therefore Orthodox Jewish people do not support or encourage gay relationships, though they believe that lesbian and gay people should be treated with respect, just as any other human should be. Progressive Jewish people generally accept same-sex relationships and marriage.

Sikhism

Sexuality is seen as a gift from God for continuation of human life on earth. However, Sikhs warn against being controlled by your sex drive and believe it should be controlled by marriage. So **sex before marriage** is wrong, and Sikhs try to protect even against the temptation of it, for example, discouraging dating before marriage. In the Adi Granth, Sikhs are warned to *avoid that which … produces evil thoughts in the mind.* Married life is seen as the norm and **celibacy** as a life choice is not encouraged. **Chastity**, though, is a virtue and highly valued before and within marriage as a form of self-control. Although most Sikhs see **same-sex attraction** as wrong as it does not follow the example of the gurus, some accept it as part of what God has created in a person.

In the wedding ceremony, Sikhs make promises including to be faithful. Those promises are made in front of God. The Rahit Maryada (see page 349) forbids **adultery**, saying *the touch of another man's wife is like a poisonous snake*, and adultery is one of the Four Abstinences of Sikhism.

When it comes to deciding on which **contraception** to use, Sikhs can choose for themselves. They are encouraged to follow *responsible parenthood* (only having as many children as one can properly look after). However, Sikhs do not use permanent forms of contraception except for medical reasons, since these change the body God has given you.

The Basics

Copy and complete this table for each of the two religions you are studying.
You will need to complete the entire row of information for each topic before moving on to the next, since you don't know how much writing you'll do so this way keeps it neat and easy to read later when you are revising.

Topic	Agree/disagree	Reasons why
a. Celibacy		
b. Chastity		
c. Sex before marriage		
d. Contraception		
e. Adultery		
f. Same-sex attraction		

Marriage and the family

Marriage is the joining of two people as a legal couple. When done religiously, it is done before God for God's blessing on the **covenant**.

Why do people marry?

You can answer this from your point of view and from what you have learned. People marry for many reasons. *Discuss them with a partner.*

love money family expectations
religious duty to legitimise a relationship
to legitimise a child for sex for companionship

It is likely that a couple who marry do so for many reasons, and their upbringing and culture have a big influence over their choice.

Who to marry?

Most people would say you marry who you want to. *Is it always that simple though?* Sometimes marrying who you want to has a cost; especially if your family do not approve of the person you want to marry. *Why might that make things difficult?*

Religious people are taught to honour their family and to honour their religion. You might then expect a religious person to marry someone who their family approved of, and someone who shared their religion.

So, should you get parents' approval of your choice, or should it be your acceptance of their choice? The latter is what we call an *arranged marriage*, which means that the parents have found a prospective spouse for their son or daughter. The two meet, whilst chaperoned, and then decide to go ahead or not with the marriage. Divorce is still less common in this kind of marriage than in 'marriages for love'. On the other hand, some religious people feel that getting their parents' approval of their own choice is the better way.

Why the same religion? Some religions discourage interfaith marriage due to possible conflicts in beliefs and practices, such as where to get married, or what religion will their future children follow. However, many couples today work through these differences through open communication, mutual respect and compromise.

Read these statements. Do you agree or disagree with each? Explain why.

1. The most important reason to marry is to have children.

2. A person should only marry someone their parents agree to.

3. People should always marry someone of the same religion as theirs.

4. There is no point getting married in our modern society.

Roles in marriage

During traditional marriage vows, couples express their commitment and love for one another. However, the roles and responsibilities in a marriage are also revealed during the vows.

Can you think of the traditional marriage vows or promises? If you cannot, think of how you would expect you and your spouse to behave when married. It is likely that you will come up with a similar set of commitments.

Married couples promise, either through vows/promises or through a contract, to be good to each other, to be faithful, to love and cherish each other, and to support each other through good and bad, until the marriage is ended by death. If you were setting up an agreement with someone about how you would live the rest of your life together as a couple, you would probably come up with the same or similar set of values.

Additionally, roles within a traditional marriage might include who keeps house (cooking, cleaning, etc.), who leads the upbringing of children, or their discipline, who earns money for the family. Traditionally, in a heterosexual marriage, the man went out to work and the woman stayed at home to look after the home and family. Today, however, it is more common for a married couple to share these tasks, and even for them to be reversed from what is seen as traditional.

The nature of families

Nuclear family – this refers to parents, traditionally mum and dad, plus the child(ren).

Single-parent family – this is a family of either a mum or a dad, plus child(ren). It is becoming more common to see this kind of family in the UK.

Extended family – this is the nuclear family plus other relatives, usually grandparents, living with the family, but can also include cousins, uncles and aunts and so on.

Polygamy – this is the practice of marrying multiple people, often having children with each. It is allowable under specific circumstances in the Islamic faith and some parts of the world, but illegal in the UK.

Blended family – this is a family where one or both parents have children from previous relationships. It is becoming more common to see this kind of family in the UK.

Marriage ceremonies

Buddhism

Buddhist wedding

Buddhism does not have a set ceremony for marriage, so the ceremonies are completely non-religious.

A couple will visit a monk to have their fortunes read and a lucky date is decided from that reading for their wedding.

Buddhists follow the local customs of their country for marriage, which may include registering their marriage officially.

Later, the couple might visit the monastery or temple to invite a monk to bless their marriage. He does this by reciting verses from Buddhist scriptures. He also gives them advice about being a married Buddhist.

The couple might then invite the monk to a feast, as a symbol of their thanks for his blessing.

Christianity

Christian wedding

Marriage is a sacrament in some Christian traditions; it brings a blessing from God. In the Roman Catholic ceremony marriage takes place as part of the Mass.

The couple will come to church to be united in marriage by the priest, who greets them before the whole congregation.

The priest then reads a *homily* (a moralising lecture) about marriage and what Christian marriage is.

The priest asks three set questions of the bride and groom to make sure they understand the responsibilities of marriage.

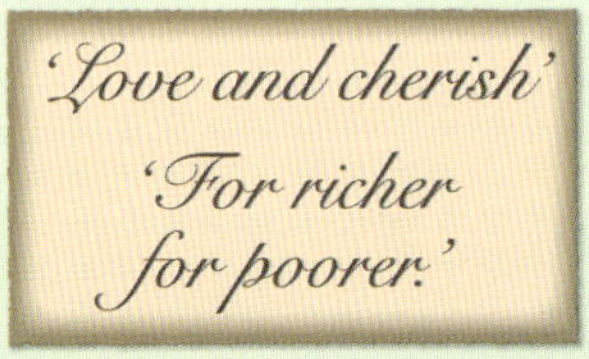

The couple make their vows to each other.

The priest declares they have agreed to marry before God and accepts their decision. It is at this point the priest says: 'What God has joined together, let no one put asunder.'

The rings are blessed and exchanged.

The priest blesses the marriage.

The couple sign the marriage register. This is the civil (legal) part of the ceremony.

🕉 Hinduism

Hindu wedding

The wedding ceremony is part of a whole set of ceremonies, which lead up to and form the actual ceremony. We will concentrate on the ceremony.

The groom, his family and friends arrive for the wedding to be received by the bride's family.

Under a specially built canopy, the priest begins the ceremony with a blessing on the couple. The bride and groom give each other garlands.

The father pours out sacred water to show he gives away his daughter, whilst the priest recites hymns from the Vedas. The groom also accepts his duties and responsibilities as a husband.

The bride and groom face each other. The end of her scarf is tied to his shirt to symbolise their eternal union. They exchange rings.

Holding hands, the couple offer *samagri* (a mix of sandalwood, herbs, sugar, rice and ghee) into the sacred fire to ask for the deities' blessing on their marriage.

The bride and groom walk four times round the fire, indicating the four goals of life, round the fire, reciting hymns and prayers.

At the end of each circuit of the fire, they both step onto a stone to pray that their marriage will be strong like the stone.

They then take seven steps round the fire, and with each one make a wedding promise.

The ceremony ends with a prayer that the marriage is a spiritual union and cannot be broken.

☪ Islam

Muslim wedding

Traditionally, Muslim weddings can last up to five days, depending on the cultural traditions of the Muslim country or region involved. We will concentrate on the actual wedding ceremony itself.

Some Muslims refer to the marriage ceremony as *nikah*. It is always a simple ceremony and is usually performed by an imam but it could be any respected Muslim male. Most nikah are performed at the home of the bride or groom, or at a banqueting location, and not the mosque.

The groom has to declare a *mahr* (a dowry), showing his respect for the bride. It can include anything she has asked for (for example, money, clothes, even a house). The groom can pay this over time, and is not allowed to take it back; it is hers.

The bride does not have to be there, she will normally have given her consent beforehand. The consent of the bride is asked for three times by the imam. He also asks the groom if he consents to the marriage. The imam announces their intention to marry and asks if anyone has any objections. He also recites some verses from the Qur'an, and the Nikah Khutba (wedding sermon), which explains the purpose of marriage to those present. After it is given, the marriage is complete.

Some couples sign marriage contracts beforehand about what they expect from the marriage and what the rights of each partner will be.

Judaism

Jewish wedding

Jewish weddings begin with the signing of the Ketubah (marriage contract) by witnesses. It details the legal terms of the marriage.

The ceremony begins at the huppah (wedding canopy), where traditionally the bride walks around the groom three or seven times. In Progressive communities, the couple may walk around each other three or seven times.

The rabbi often makes a speech about the responsibilities of marriage and about the couple. A ring is given to the bride or rings are exchanged. Rings must be an undecorated, unbroken circle, showing the hope for a harmonious marriage.

Seven blessings are said over wine, to represent the seven days of creation, and the start of the building of a marriage. Finally, the groom crushes a glass under his foot to remember the destruction of the Temple. With this act, the marriage ceremony is complete.

Sikhism

Sikh wedding

Visit **www.sikhs.org/wedding** for more details on and pictures of Sikh weddings.

Sikh marriage is called *anand karaj*. Only Sikhs can have this ceremony. Anyone who is a full Khalsa Sikh can lead the ceremony.

The groom listens to kirtan (call-and-response chants) in the gurdwara as he waits for his bride to arrive. When she arrives she sits on his left in front of the Guru Granth Sahib.

The Ardas prayer is said to begin the ceremony. This prayer begins and ends all Sikh ceremonies.

The end of the scarf is placed in the hands of the bride, whilst four lavan (verses of a hymn written by the fourth guru, Guru Ram Das) from the Sikh holy scripture, Guru Granth Sahib (the Sikh holy scripture) are read.

When the second lavan is reached, the couple stand and, groom first, walk slowly around the Guru Granth Sahib. They do this for each lavan.

The ragis (Sikh musicians who play the kirtan) read out the Anand Sahib, and a randomly chosen hymn from the Guru Granth Sahib is read out.

The ceremony ends with the Ardas prayer, and the distribution of karah parshad (blessed food) to all.

Task

Find more detail on each of the marriage ceremonies covered in this section. You could check out the GCSE RS section on the BBC Bitesize website, which has specific information on each religion. Try also to find pictures of aspects of each wedding ceremony to help your recall.

Cohabitation and same-sex marriage

Not everyone marries, but they may still have a relationship with someone. So how does that work?

Cohabitation is living together as if married. The only difference is the couple have no marriage licence and legally they do not have the same rights as a married couple (for example, to each other's pension). Not everyone feels the need to go through the marriage ceremony.

Civil marriage registration legally recognises a couple as being married, but there is no religious ceremony. It often takes place at a registry office, and may include promises. Same-sex marriage has been legal in England, Wales and Scotland since 2014, and in Northern Ireland since 2020, meaning same-sex couples have exactly the same rights as any other married couple.

Civil partnership is the legal registration of a same-sex couple. This means that in law they are treated as if married and they have many of the legal protections which a married couple are entitled to.

Attitudes to marriage and cohabitation

Dave: *My partner and I have lived together for 14 years. We have two kids. Marriage is just a piece of paper, and we do not need that.*

Jay: *We married but we are not religious, so we went to the registry office. It was a nice, quiet do – just right for our relationship. It gives us both protection if the relationship fails, but it also gives us financial benefits whilst in the relationship, like using the Marriage Allowance.*

Lucy: *We went through a civil partnership last year. As a gay couple, we were never going to be given the same rights as everyone else without this process. For example, now I am legally her next of kin. I couldn't even have visited her in hospital without her family's consent before the civil partnership.*

Sanjit: *My partner and I celebrated our gay marriage this year. We have been together 25 years and can finally, publicly show how we feel about each other.*

Musa: *I think if a couple love each other then marriage is the key. It is the only appropriate setting for sexual relationships and having children.*

Heather: *I live with my partner, and we might get married in the future. Right now, we are learning to live together, rather than getting married and then finding out we aren't compatible in that way.*

The Basics

1. What is the term for each relationship described below:
   - **a** Sally and Jane who legally registered as a same-sex couple.
   - **b** David and Emily who have lived together for four years.
   - **c** Callum and Aneela who had a registry office ceremony.
2. Use information from pages 238–240 for the religions you have studied. What might your chosen religions' attitude be to each of the three relationships in Question 1? Explain your answer.
3. Explain why some people choose not to get married in a religious building when they are in a relationship.
4. How do alternatives to religious marriage differ from religious marriages?
5. **In the modern world, there is no need for marriage.** What is your opinion on this statement? Include religious arguments in your answer.

Parenting – the purpose of families

We have seen that one of the main religious reasons for getting married is to have children. Think about these questions: *Why do people have children? Are there any specifically religious reasons for having children?*

Shows commitment – shows love – accident – fulfilment of relationship – duty – family tradition. You can probably come up with more reasons than these, but these are the most common.

What is the purpose of a family?

When two people marry or agree to set up home together, they make a commitment to each other. Very often that includes **procreation** (to have children) and this is just as true for same-sex couples as it is for heterosexual couples. When a relationship includes children, it acquires new purposes and responsibilities. They have a duty now to the children to work harder at issues in their relationship so that the children have *stability*. In other words, making sure there is a consistency of behaviour and life so the children know what they are coming home to every day, which is a safe and happy environment. Of course, the children have to be *protected* and cared for. They have to be given every chance to develop as confident and healthy young people, and kept safe from dangers. Part of caring for children includes making sure they have a good education, because that is part of protecting their futures. A good education is the best guarantee that they will be able to have successful, comfortable lives when they are adults. Many cultures and religions emphasise the idea that children have a duty to obey their parents, which is part of showing respect for them. In return, parents love and respect their children.

Educating children in a faith

Religious parents are like any other parent in wanting their children to have the best possible start in life. They want their children to be happy and ready to do well in their lives. They often would like their children to follow their faith, so they teach them its beliefs and practices, for example, how to behave by following its rules and how to worship. Many children are welcomed into the parents' faith and community early on. For example, most Christian parents arrange for their children to be baptised.

For people who are not religious, this might seem unfair and that the parents 'force' the religion on the child. However, they believe this faith is right, and that it is the key to happiness if not in this life, then definitely in the next. They want what is best for their child, and they believe this is it. For them, passing on a faith is an act of great love.

Many same-sex couples are also religious believers. If they have children (whether from previous relationships, through treatments such as IVF or by adoption), they will also want the best for their children, including that religious faith.

The Basics

1. Why do many people who marry choose to have children?
2. What are the purposes of families?
3. Explain the roles within marriage, including parenting.
4. **When a couple have children, those children should become their first priority.** Explain reasons to agree and disagree with this statement.

Divorce

Many marriages fail and are legally dissolved. This is what is meant by the term *divorce*. In the UK, more than one in three first marriages ends in divorce.

Why do marriages fail?

Any difficulties in a marriage can put strain on it, for example, money, arguments, different attitudes or beliefs, affairs, illness, job issues, abuse. When those difficulties become too great for one or both to cope with, they might turn to divorce as a solution.

Should it be easy to get a divorce?

Many religious people think divorce is always wrong. Many of them do see a need for divorce, but feel that it should not be an easy option, which might encourage people to not even try at their marriage. In 1969, the Church of England was key in getting the divorce laws relaxed. The situation at the time meant people were living in loveless marriages, or separating and being unable to move on. Jesus taught compassion, forgiveness and second chances – allowing divorce is compatible with that. Religions argue that people made a very serious commitment, so should work hard at their marriage, and work even harder when it is in difficulty. Divorce should only be the last option.

Support for marriages in difficulty

Since divorce is not a welcome option, many religions try to support couples in these times. Obviously, families will support them, for example, look after the children, listen and help them problem solve, and so on. Religious people will also do those things, but they might also encourage them through their religion, such as through prayer, reading their holy books, and so on.

Some couples turn to marriage counselling, which allow couples to try to talk through problems or to come to amicable agreements ahead of divorce. This is important because many people feel anger and many negative emotions when their relationship ends, which they need help to get through. Look at **www.relate.org.uk** which is a charity which focuses on relationships (of all kinds).

Religious attitudes to divorce

Buddhism

Any vows made are serious and should not be broken easily. Buddhists see marriage as important for a stable society, and divorce is discouraged, although not forbidden.

Buddhism teaches:

- Keep the Five Precepts.
- Be compassionate.
- Thoughts, deeds and actions should always be positive, because they have a karmic value which shapes our next lifetime(s).

Divorce has to be seen as the right option. If two people are causing themselves and others great suffering by staying together, this breaks Precepts, creates bad karma and goes against Buddhist principles of compassion and ahimsa.

Christianity

The Roman Catholic Church does not recognise divorce. Marriage is a sacrament, which cannot be broken. Promises are made to God and each other to stay together 'until death do us part', and these promises are binding. It is possible to have an **annulment**, which is where the marriage is set aside, as if it never was real.

For most other Christian traditions, divorce is discouraged but accepted as a last resort. It is sometimes the *lesser of two evils*, and also a *necessary evil*, so divorcees should not be made to be villains.

Christianity teaches:

- God hates divorce. (Old Testament)
- Whoever divorces … then marries another; it is as if he committed adultery. – Jesus
- We should forgive those who wrong us, and show love to all. – Jesus

ॐ Hinduism

Hindu law forbids divorce according to ancient scriptures, however, it does happen throughout Hindu society, though is considered undesirable.

Hinduism teaches:

- 'I promise never to abandon her, whatever happens.' – wedding vow
- Marriage is one of the spiritual stages in life.
- Divorce is granted for specific reasons. – Hindu Marriage Act (1955) and Manusmriti scriptures

The Manusmriti scriptures said that a man could replace any wife who was quarrelsome or difficult; the law allows for divorce in the case of cruelty, non-production of children and other reasons. Divorce is available within the religious teachings for specific reasons. However, it is not common as it carries social stigma especially for women. Couples tend to stay together because of some of these pressures but also because they believe married life is positive.

Judaism

Marriage is a sacred commitment and union. Although divorce is allowed, it should be a last resort.

Judaism teaches:

- God hates the fact that divorce has to happen. (Malachi 3, Nevi'im)
- When a man puts aside the wife of his youth, even the very altar weeps. (Talmud)
- A court can grant a woman divorce, if she can show that she can no longer live with him. – Maimonides

Technically, it is easy to get a divorce in Judaism. However, it is not desirable, and every effort will be made to help the marriage stay together. A period of time has to pass which allows attempts at reconciliation. If these fail, the husband will serve the bill of divorce (*get*); as he put forward the original contract with its promises, he is the one who cancels it. The get must be written by a trained scribe with black ink on parchment – it is an official document, and is served before the Bet Din (Jewish Court of Law). Then the marriage is ended.

Islam

Both men and women can divorce. It is seen as the absolute last resort. Islam teaches:

- Marry and do not divorce. (Hadith)
- If you fear a breach between a man and his wife, appoint two arbiters. (Surah 4:35)

A Muslim couple and their families must work hard to fix any problems and seek to avoid divorce. There has to be mediation between them, and time given for reflection and solving problems. If divorce is the only solution, the husband will state 'I divorce you' before witnesses. After the first pronouncement, the wife enters a waiting period that lasts three menstrual cycles or three months (if she is not menstruating). The waiting period serves to confirm whether the wife is pregnant and allows for the possibility of reconciliation.

At the end of the waiting period, the divorce becomes final. At this point, the husband must pay any outstanding part of the dowry. Importantly, the husband may pronounce divorce up to three times in separate instances, and after the third pronouncement the divorce becomes irrevocable.

Sikhism

Divorce is not the Sikh way, but is accepted by the faith.

Sikhism teaches:

- Marriage is a sacrament.
- Marriage is the union of two souls and a lifelong commitment.
- If the husband and wife dispute, their concern for their children should reunite them. (Adi Granth)

If a marriage is in difficulty, both families will try to help solve the problems – after all, given that many Sikh marriages are arranged, its collapse reflects badly on the families as well as the couple. Divorce used to carry a stigma but this is changing, however, it is still avoided if possible. It is a matter for a person's individual conscience.

The Basics

1 Explain what is meant by divorce.
2 Explain the attitude of religious believers to problems in marriage and divorce.

Remarriage

This can be a person marrying a new partner after a divorce, making this their second (or more) marriage. It is also sometimes the case that people who divorced later remarry again. Some people talk about marriage after the death of a partner as being remarriage, others call this a second marriage.

Most people who get divorced believe they will have other, positive relationships, and often find themselves wanting to marry again to show their commitment to a new partner. Marriage is the ultimate commitment and the failure of one marriage does not mean that every relationship will fail. It is to be expected that people will look for and try to find happiness again.

What do you think about remarriage? Do you agree with any of the statements on the right?

I have to have sons to carry on my faith and so I will remarry. My first marriage was not blessed with children, and that led to our divorce.

Bilal

Love and marriage go together. I think if the love is strong enough, then a marriage will survive. But just because one marriage ends, doesn't mean never again.

Jesse

Sounds silly really, but my wife and I divorced. Then years later we met again and it was love. I think we were too young the first time, but now we are remarrying and it will last this time.

Karl

I have been married four times. Each marriage broke up for different reasons. I am due to marry again in two months.

Nia

After my husband died, I never thought I would find another love. I am so lucky to have met Ben and I think we can be happily married.

Denny

Religious attitudes to remarriage

For most religious believers, getting married again after the death of a first partner is not an issue. Of course, they believe the person deserves to be happy and this will help them to be happy. Some cultures disagree with a woman remarrying after her husband has died; they believe she is eternally married to that one man.

If it is marriage after divorce, whether a religion agrees or not depends very much on their attitude to divorce. For those religions which disagree with divorce, of course, remarriage would be wrong. As far as they are concerned, the original marriage still exists. Roman Catholic teaching says that divorce is not recognised by God, so remarriage is not allowed. Other religious believers might allow remarriage, but not allow a religious ceremony. Some Anglican vicars will not perform a marriage ceremony for divorced persons. They recognise that people might have found new happiness, and do believe that marriage forms the basis of a strong, good society. However, they also see the original ceremony as having a sanctity and vows made before God cannot just be laid aside to remake with someone else.

In the Roman Catholic tradition, it is possible to get an annulment of the marriage. This means that the marriage was never valid, usually because it was not consummated (no sexual relationship), or because one or both did not properly understand the responsibilities of marriage (for example, when a Catholic marries a non-Catholic and the religion becomes an issue between them). Technically, any marriage after an annulment is not remarriage (there was no first marriage).

The Basics

1 What is meant by remarriage?
2 Use information from pages 248–249 for the religion(s) you have studied to explain what their attitude to divorce and remarriage might be.
3 **There is nothing wrong with divorce for religious believers.** Do you agree? Give reasons to agree and disagree, including religious arguments.

Gender equality – gender prejudice

This is prejudice against someone because of their gender. Reread page 242 to remind yourself about religious attitudes to the various roles within marriage.

Can you state reasons why some people might consider the roles in some marriages to be unequal?

Why are some people prejudiced?

Prejudice is the pre-judgement of others based on a characteristic they have, rather than what they are like as a person. People are often prejudiced because of the way they were brought up; they were taught this kind of attitude and behaviour. There is often an element of tradition. In some societies, women don't hold positions of power and so they are seen as less important. Or perhaps their attitude to women was shaped by personal experience, or situations they were in which made them think women should be treated in a certain way. Attitudes are changing but in some cultures that change is very slow.

What is the effect of gender prejudice against women?

It can lead to different treatment (discrimination), so that women are given fewer opportunities, for example, by not getting the same chances or promotions at work. It may be that the culture within which they live sets stricter rules for women than for men, for example, where women are not allowed to leave the house, or can only leave when chaperoned, or where girls are not allowed education beyond a certain age; they seem not to have the same rights as men. It may be that women are not allowed to contribute to decision-making or leadership roles, so a female perspective is never considered. Prejudice and discrimination within power structures can mean that when women are treated negatively, there is no consequence for the perpetrator, and this further encourages that negative behaviour. If you read the newspapers, or watch TV shows, you get the impression that women are the usual victims of violent crime. When no punishments are given to men who commit these crimes, the message seems to be that violence against women is not so bad, which encourages more of it. **Gender discrimination** spans from misogynistic comments to murder; it definitely has an impact.

Ultimately **gender prejudice** (when applied to women through discrimination) keeps women less powerful, and makes society work for men rather than for the balance of society. It is true that in the UK, laws exist to prevent gender discrimination, and that employment law is being changed to equalise pay and conditions, but there is still a long way to go.

65% OF SECONDARY HEADS ARE MALE

Businesses still mostly run by men

Women outnumber men going to university in the UK

Fewer than 35% of UK MPs are female

Only 30% of girls are educated beyond the age of 12 in the world today

What impression do you get from these headlines?

The Basics

1 What is gender prejudice?
2 Why are some people gender prejudiced?
3 How does gender prejudice affect women?
4 Look back at page 242 to read about roles within marriage. Do you think these encourage gender prejudice? Explain your answer.
5 **Gender prejudice cannot be ended.** How far do you agree with this statement? Give reasons to support and argue against it, and include religious arguments in your answer.

Religious teachings about gender equality

Buddhism

- If a man denies the possibility of enlightenment of women, then his own enlightenment is impossible. (Lotus Sutra)
- There is no legal basis in Vinaya (monastic) law to deny a woman the right to full ordination.
- The practice of Buddhism in some traditions (such as Mahayana and Vajrayana Buddhism) is the same for men and women, showing no inequality of demands on either.

Christianity

- Some of the earliest converts, and leaders of churches were women, for example Priscilla at Ephesus.
- There is neither Jew nor Gentile, neither slave nor free, nor is there male and female, for you are all one in Christ Jesus. (Galatians 3:28)
- So God created humankind in His own image, in the image of God He created them; male and female he created them. (Genesis 1:27)

Hinduism

- Good treatment of women is seen as a blessing. (Laws of Manu)
- Where women are honoured, there the gods are pleased. (Manusmriti)
- There are no differences between men and women on a spiritual level as the true essence of each (the atman) is the same – differences only exist at a physical level that can be seen outwardly. (Sruti)

Islam

- Men and women have the same spiritual nature, according to the Qur'an.
- Prophet Muhammad ﷺ said, 'I command you to be kind to women.'
- I shall not lose sight of the labour of any of you who labours in My way, be it man or woman; each of you is equal to the other. (Qur'an 3:195)

Judaism

- In Progressive Judaism, women can be rabbis.
- The equality of men and women begins at the highest possible level, as God has no gender. Both men and women were created in God's image. (Genesis)
- Men and women were created equally; in Orthodox Judaism, their methods of connecting to God through the mitzvot are different but of equal value.

Sikhism

- While either a man or woman may read the Guru Granth Sahib at services, it is unusual to see women fulfilling this role.
- Man is born from a woman … woman is born from woman; without woman, there would be no one at all. – Guru Granth Sahib
- Waheguru (God) is neither male or female. – Guru Granth Sahib

Task

Using the teachings of the religion(s) you have studied, and the information from pages 388–390 (about prejudice generally), explain what might be their attitude to gender equality.

Attitudes to the role of men and women

Traditionally men have held positions of authority in most religions. They usually are the decision-makers, the leaders in the home, community and religion and generally have more power. This is true in patriarchal societies in general. Look at the headlines on page 251 and think about what this means for both men and women. For example, it is clear that patriarchal societies often restrict leadership roles for women, in religion and other areas of society.

Within religion there is a debate about the role of women. They are treated differently to men and there is often the accusation that women are being discriminated against despite the fact that all religions condemn any kind of discrimination. Here are some examples:

- In Christianity women cannot be priests in the Roman Catholic Church and the first female bishops in the Anglican Church were appointed in 2015.
- In Islam religious leaders are generally men, and women do not pray at the front of the mosque.
- In Orthodox Judaism women sit separately to men, often upstairs, and do not lead prayers in a mixed gathering.
- Hindu scriptures do not stop women becoming priests and there have been many female Hindu priests in Indian history. There are more male priests today as there are in all world cultures. However there are also increasing numbers of women priests and there are institutions in India which offer courses for women who are interested in becoming priests.
- In some branches of Buddhism, women pray that their rebirth will be as a man.
- In Sikhism, whilst either gender may read the Guru Granth Sahib at services, it is unusual to see women fulfilling this role.

If women are denied access to certain roles then this could be said to be discriminatory. However, many religious traditions say that roles are different but equal. If women are happy in their roles and what the religion permits to do and not to do then to them discrimination is not an issue. The issue arises when women want to do something as part of their religion but are not allowed because rules or traditions say they cannot.

As time moves on, changes around gender discrimination are occurring, but women have to fight hard for those changes. They would argue that if we are all creations of God, then if, for example, a woman wants to devote herself to the service of God and serve the community of believers, would God not want her to simply because she is a woman? Perhaps a woman could deal with community issues and help people in a different way to a man?

Some religious people view gender discrimination as hurtful and wrong in any form.

The Basics

1 What is meant by the term 'gender prejudice'?
2 Explain religious teaching about gender prejudice. Look at the teachings about prejudice on pages 388–392 to be able to comment on how these might affect attitudes towards gender prejudice.
3 Give some examples of sexist behaviour.
4 **Should women be allowed to be leaders in religion?** Explain two reasons to agree and two to disagree.

Different beliefs

Contraception

Roman Catholicism

The Roman Catholic Church's teaching on contraception is that **all sexual acts must be open to procreation – this is natural law**. Anything done to prevent natural law is wrong. In Humanae Vitae, the Pope declared that '**any act which deliberately prevents procreation is an intrinsic evil**'. Use of artificial contraception is a deliberate act, and that is a sin. So Catholics should not use contraception.

Anglicanism

The Church of England does not regard contraception as a sin or against God's teaching. The Lambeth Conference in 1968 stated that **sexual love is good in itself** and that there can be **good reasons for limiting or delaying parenthood**.

Judaism

In Judaism, Orthodoxy accepts the use of contraception for **medical/health reasons**. The 'wasting of seed' is forbidden in the Torah, so it is considered acceptable for women to use the pill.

Islam

Prophet Muhammad ﷺ indicated that Muslims should practise **responsible parenthood**. They should only have the children they can care properly for.

Question

Explain two different beliefs in contemporary British society about contraception.

In your answer you should refer to the main religious tradition of Great Britain and one or more other religious traditions. *(4 marks)*

Sex before marriage

Christianity

Christian teaching generally states that sex should only be experienced within marriage, so sex before marriage is wrong. Sex is a gift from God, for the **purpose of procreation**, but also a sign of a couple's loving bond. However, this is a **gift to a married couple**. Sex before marriage is seen by many Christians as **fornication**, which is a sin. St Paul said: 'Now to the unmarried and the widows I say: It is good for them to stay unmarried, as I am. **But if they cannot control themselves, they should marry, for it is better to marry than to burn with passion.'** (I Corinthians 7:9).

Buddhism

Marriage is not a rite of passage in Buddhism – marriages are culturally based events. So sex before marriage – as long as it is within the context of a **loving relationship** – is acceptable.

Anglicanism

The General Synod of the Church of England recognises the variety of family forms today. It stresses that whilst marriage is the ideal context, sexual relationships must be **within permanent, loving relationships** (which allows sex before marriage).

Quakerism

The Quaker Society sees marriage as the ideal context, but accepts changing society norms. It accepts that a couple can be **faithful to each other in a loving, non-exploitative relationship outside marriage**.

Question

Explain two different beliefs in contemporary British society about sex before marriage.

In your answer you should refer to the main religious tradition of Great Britain and one or more other religious traditions. *(4 marks)*

Same-sex relationships

Quakerism

Quakers in the UK fully accept lesbian and gay people into their community and do not condemn those who have same-sex relationships. 'Quakers were one of the first churches to talk openly about sexuality. We feel that the **quality and depth of feeling between two people is the most important part of a loving relationship, not their gender or sexual orientation**.' The true consideration should be whether there is **genuine (selfless) love** between the couple. They point out that Genesis says that **all people are created in the image of God** – which must include lesbian and gay people.

Roman Catholicism

The Roman Catholic Church does not accept same-sex relationships. Church teaching classes same-sex attraction as an 'objective disorder' (only leaning toward sin), **same-sex relationships are a 'moral disorder'** (committing a sin).

Islam

The overwhelming majority of Muslims see same-sex attraction as a **crime against Allah**, punishable under Shari'ah Law. Prophet Muhammad ﷺ said 'If you find anyone doing as Lot's people did, kill the one who does it, and the one to whom it is done.'

Buddhism

Buddhism does not condemn same-sex relationships between gay people where they are long-term and committed. However, short relationships **based on lust is seen as 'craving' – one of the Three Poisons**. This is unskilful living.

Question

Explain two different beliefs from contemporary British society about same-sex relationships.

In your answer you should refer to the main religious tradition of Great Britain and one or more other religious traditions. *(4 marks)*

Getting prepared

The importance of key words

The key technical words of a Theme are the start point of your journey to getting to grips with the content. You need to look at them on three levels. If you do not know the key words, you cannot answer any questions which might include them.

Key word definitions

Each Theme requires you to answer a simple one-mark question first, and this might be a definition question. You must choose the right definition for a key word from four choices.

Here are some examples:

1 Which of the following means to live together as if married?

A civil marriage B civil partnership C cohabitation D polygamy

2 What is meant by the term 'divorce'?

A ending a relationship B legal ending of a marriage C living together D separation

In larger tariff questions, you need to explain yourself, so need to understand fuller definitions of the words.

Have a go at these:

1 Can you explain what is meant by marriage vows?

2 Can you explain what religious believers mean when they say that marriage is a contract?

3 Can you explain what is meant by the term 'commitment'?

You can find all the key words for each Theme in a glossary at the end of each chapter – you can find the glossary for this Theme on page 258, for example. Why not make your own glossary book, and include **any** word you meet which is new or important. You could do this for any of your subjects as the need to know key words is true for all of them.

The next level

Key words can also form the basis of questions worth more than 1 mark.
If you do not know the word then you cannot answer the higher value questions.
So, the message remains – learn the key words!

You could be asked for the religious attitude to, or view on, something, or to describe the key features of ceremonies. Here are some examples:

1 Explain two different beliefs in contemporary British society to sex before marriage. In your answer you should refer to the main religious tradition of Great Britain and one or more other religious traditions. (4 marks)

2 Explain two different beliefs in contemporary British society about contraception. In your answer you should refer to the main religious tradition of Great Britain and one or more other religious traditions. (4 marks)

3 Explain two different beliefs in contemporary British society to remarriage. In your answer you should refer to the main religious tradition of Great Britain and one or more other religious traditions. (4 marks)

A little tougher is to be asked how religious beliefs relate to an aspect of the topic. So for these questions, you will also need to know the key word to be able to give an answer. Some examples might be:

1 Explain two religious beliefs about gender equality. Refer to sacred writings or another source of religious belief and teaching in your answer. (6 marks)

2 Explain two religious beliefs about the role of parents in a religious relationship. Refer to sacred writings or another source of religious belief and teaching in your answer. (6 marks)

3 Explain two religious beliefs about adultery. Refer to sacred writings or another source of religious belief and teaching in your answer. (6 marks)

And another level …

Half of the marks are for questions which require analysis and evaluation. Remember, analysis is the exploration of a reason to agree or disagree; evaluation is weighing up how weak or strong the analysed reasons (arguments) are. These questions start with a statement, followed by the instruction to argue about it (worth 12 marks). If there is a key word/phrase in the statement you have to analyse/evaluate, and you do not know it, then you might have trouble answering. Again, you must learn the key words!

1 'Religious believers should never be sexist.'

2 'Ceremonies for remarriage should not be allowed in places of worship.'

3 'Marriage ceremonies are out of date nowadays.'

So, overall, hopefully you see the need to learn the key words – start learning!

Relationships and families glossary

Adultery having an affair, a sexual relationship with someone you are not married to

Age of consent the age at which a person is considered old enough to be able to decide to have sex, according to the law

Annulment a legal procedure that declares a marriage void from the beginning, as if it never legally existed

Civil marriage non-religious marriage ceremony

Civil partnership the legal union of two people of the same gender

Celibacy not having sexual relations; to be celibate

Chastity keeping oneself sexually pure, for example, waiting until marriage before having sex

Cohabitation living together as a couple

Commitment the act of making a promise or pledge

Contraception precautions taken to prevent pregnancy, and to protect against sexually transmitted infections

Contract a binding agreement between two sides

Covenant an agreement based on promises between two sides; often linked to religion, so includes an agreement before and with God

Divorce legal dissolution (ending) of a marriage

Extended family the nuclear family plus other relatives, usually grandparents, living with the family, but can also include cousins, uncles and aunts

Family parents and their children as a group

Family planning the planning of when to have a family using birth control/contraceptives, or natural methods

Gender discrimination acting on prejudices against someone because of their gender

Gender equality the idea that men and women are of equal worth

Gender prejudice the idea that men and women are not equal

Heterosexual someone physically attracted to the opposite sex

Nuclear family traditionally, a family unit consisting of a mum and dad, plus the child(ren)

Polygamy the practice of having more than one husband or wife at the same time

Procreation the production of offspring; reproduction

Remarriage a second or subsequent marriage

Responsibility a duty; something we have to do, like looking after a younger brother or sister

Sex before marriage sexual relations prior to being married

Single parent family a family of either a mum or a dad, plus child(ren)

Vows promises that a couple exchanges with one another in a wedding ceremony

5 Theme B: Religion and life

Key elements of this theme

In this Theme, you will firstly be thinking about **science** and religion; how they compare and how they clash, especially on ideas about the origins of the universe and life. This leads logically to the other parts of the Theme as, secondly, you think about the value of the world, including environmental issues and **animal rights**. Then finally, you consider the value of human life, including the issues of **euthanasia** and **abortion**. The key concepts for this theme are split across each part.

Scientific truth *versus* religious truth

Scientific truth

Scientific truth comes from *making a* **hypothesis**, then *testing* it to see if it is true. Seeing something happen again and again is important; this is called *repeated observation*. Think about how you do experiments in science. You write what you are trying to do and what you think will happen. Then you do a lot of testing to check. So your tests confirm or disprove your idea.

Science includes things like $E = mc^2$, or that the Earth is in orbit around the sun, or that the Northern Lights are a reflection of space dust hitting the atmosphere. In other words, scientific truth is describing our world and how it works.

Science answers the *what* and *how* questions; function and process.

Scientific truth is always open to being developed and added to, as we find out more information, or find out new circumstances. It can be challenged and tested by other theories, so is not absolute. It is always *conditional*, that is, true when based on the conditions in which the testing/observation took place.

Religious truth

Religious truth comes from religions and holy books. We read it, or we get taught it, or some people think they were told it by God. Many religions, or versions of a religion, are based on a person's experience of God.

Religion tries to explain things like why we are here, who God is, how we should behave, and what will happen after we die. In other words, it gives us answers to ultimate questions; the questions no one else has an answer for, and which are really important to humans.

Religion answers the *why* questions; purpose and meaning.

Religion, and holy books, can be open to interpretation, but their words do not change. The truth of religion is considered to be *absolute*, that is, unchanging and relevant for all times.

The Basics

1. What do we mean by *scientific truth*? How is it found?
2. What do we mean by *religious truth*? How is it found?
3. What similarities are there between scientific and religious truth?
4. What differences are there between scientific and religious truth?
5. Which kind of truth is more important? Explain why.
6. **Religion is about ideas not truths.** Explain reasons to agree and disagree with this statement.

The origins of the universe and life

How the universe began is one of the areas in which it seems that science and religion disagree. You need to know what each side says, and also whether they can agree or not; are they *compatible* or *conflicting* kinds of truth?

The Big Bang theory

The **Big Bang theory** is a description of how scientists believe the universe began. Scientists say the universe began about 13.7 billion years ago. All the matter in the universe was concentrated at one point and began to expand very rapidly with a big explosion, eventually creating the universe as we know it today. The earliest signs of life appeared millions of years ago, before the land and sea settled. The Earth was very hot, and covered in a *primordial soup* (a mix of liquids, chemicals, minerals, proteins and amino acids). These fused to give the first life forms, which were simple single-cellular beings. From these, all other life developed, including humans.

What is the evidence behind this scientific theory? What makes people believe it as a truth?

Scientists know that the universe is still expanding and that the movement can all be tracked back to a single point. This supports the Big Bang theory.

Another bit of evidence is what we call *background microwave radiation*. Explosions cause radiation and this can still be detected in space.

This was not the first theory of how the universe came to be. As scientists find new evidence, they reshape their ideas. In the case of the Big Bang, it replaced the Steady State theory as the accepted view of the origins of the universe. There might be another theory waiting in the wings for that extra bit of persuasive evidence – like the Pulsation Hypothesis theory. That is one of the 'problems' of scientific theory and truth – it is open to change, development and revision. We could say that science is an evolving, changing description of the world and its workings. It is the truth for the time we are in with the knowledge we have.

Task

Find out more about the Big Bang theory: who proposed it, what all the evidence was, and whether it is still considered the best explanation of how the universe began.

Charles Darwin and evolution

Charles Darwin (right) was a natural scientist. He wrote a book called *On the Origin of Species*, published in 1859. This was the culmination of years of research including travels on the scientific exploration ship, HMS *Beagle*. In this book, Darwin suggested that the world is a place of change, and that the huge variety of creatures and species is the result of thousands of years of change and adaptation (**evolution**). He said that there is a struggle for survival between species because of competing demands and limits of resources like food, space, etc. Where species failed to adapt, they became extinct, so that only the fittest (best-suited) could survive. He called this **natural selection**. Darwin also realised that different places caused different varieties of the same creature to develop, because the places made different demands on the creatures. For example, finches (a kind of bird) had different-shaped beaks depending on whether they lived in an area where berries were abundant, or in an area where shellfish were the main food (see image below). The great variety of species we see in the world is a result of million of years of evolution.

We can use an analogy to make the concept easier to grasp.

Look around you at the world and everything in it. *Do things change? Do people change? Is there anything that does not change?*

When you started secondary school, it was probably a big change from life at primary school. If you have moved from one school to another, that is a big change too. *How did you cope with the difference? Do different people cope in different ways?*

If you went to live from a hot to a very cold country, things would be very different for you. You would have to make changes to your life. *What would happen if you did not?*

These are the main elements of evolutionary theory. When we look at the world around us, we can see many, many different varieties of animals, birds, fish and insects.

Among the scenes which are deeply impressed upon my mind, none exceed in sublimity the primeval (tropical) forests … temples filled with the varied products of the God of Nature. No one can stand in these solitudes unmoved, and not feel that there is more in man than the mere breath of his body. (Charles Darwin, 1879)

I see no good reason why the views given in this volume should shock the religious feelings of anyone. (Charles Darwin, On the Origin of Species*)*

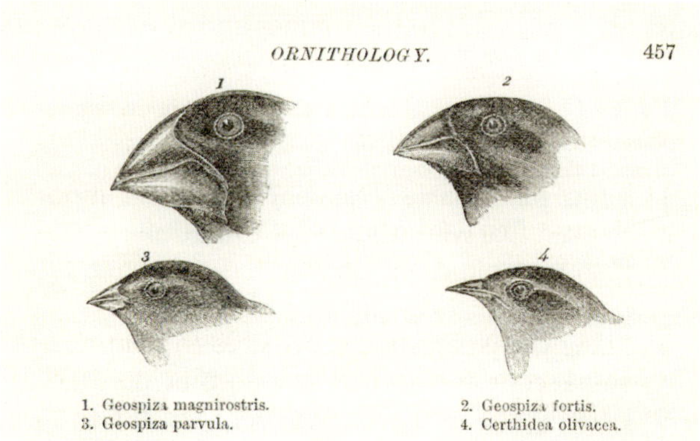

If we look at the **environment** in which these species live, we can see there are great differences. For example, some places are much hotter than others.

We can also see that the creatures in an area are suited to living in that particular environment. For example, a polar bear has special fur, which makes it possible for it to live in cold temperatures.

Environments are always changing, for example, volcanoes may erupt covering the surrounding area with ash, altering the shape of the landscape. Many scientists believe that the world has always been changing. Creatures have had to get used to the change and adapt to it, or they have died. Where a whole species could not adapt, it has become extinct. Where a species did adapt, its biology has changed so that the species survived.

This theory suggests that nothing was designed to look like it does today, or to work in the way it does today. Things have changed so that they could survive, which means it is wrong to believe some power designed things as they are, or to believe the world has always been the same. Many religious people believe that God created the world, so they are at odds with accepted scientific theory.

No God?

You would think that Darwin's theory completely discarded God. No longer could people claim the world was the same perfect **creation** of God. The idea of the seven-day creation was also challenged, as evolution suggested that the world developed over many millions of years. So was it time to forget about God? Was science finally getting rid of God?

However, Darwin still claimed God was involved in all this. In the final chapter of *On the Origin of Species*, he asks where all the intelligence within nature, and the complexity and interdependence came from. He finds it difficult to believe that without some sort of guidance, there is not just total chaos. He puts it down to God. God created the original lifeforms with the ability to adapt and change. It is not design down to the fine detail, it is design via intelligence and adaptability.

Now, God is even greater than was first thought; his creations adapt and change. Many Christians find this something they can agree with – after all, it just adds to the wonder and awe felt towards God.

The Basics

1 Who was Charles Darwin? Why is he important?
2 Explain Darwin's theory of evolution.
3 Many people claim Darwin has explained God away, so God is not needed. Why do they say that?
4 Many Christians find it possible to continue to believe in God and accept evolution. How do they do that?
5 Look at the three quotes on pages 261 and 262. What do you think they are trying to say?

The existence of science is 'not a mere happy accident, but it is a sign that the mind of the Creator lies behind the wonderful order that scientists are privileged to explore'. (John Polkinghorne, Physicist and Theologian)

The Genesis creation story

A *creation story* is a story telling us how God created the world and universe.

The Christian creation story is written in the Bible. The first book of the Bible is called Genesis, which means *beginning*, and it begins with God's creation of the world. This version is known as the *Genesis creation story*, or the *Christian creation story*, or the *seven days of creation story*. It is also believed by Jewish and Muslim people. You may have already learned a little about it.

In Genesis, it says that at the beginning there was nothing. God decided to create the world. On each day of this creation, He made a new thing.

On the first day, God created light. God separated light from dark, so that there was day and night.

On the second day, God created the heavens.

On the third day, God collected the water together to give land and sea. God also made plants of every kind grow on the land.

On the fourth day, God created the sun, moon and stars, so that there were lights for the day and the night, and to mark the seasons.

On the fifth day, God created the fish and birds.

On the sixth day, God created animals, and then humans – in His image.

Finally, on the seventh day, God rested. Each day, God had looked back at the creation and said that it was *good*. God had created a good world.

That creation story is understood in different ways. However it is interpreted or understood, it is what we call a *religious truth*. Religious truth does not change, it is a truth for all time. Religious people believe this is so because it is a truth which came from God. God is eternal, and without fault, so it must be true.

For some, the creation story as told in Genesis is literally (word for word) true. They believe in an all-powerful, all-loving, all-knowing God – so it is easy to believe that God really could do this in the way described. This is a fundamentalist view of the Bible, and hence of creation.

The order of the creation makes sense: the planet, then vegetation, then fish and birds, then animals, finally humanity. Genesis perhaps seems a little quick in comparison to what science says, but it was a story first told thousands of years ago. It is told in the only way it could be told, using the language and knowledge of the time, so many believe that the order of the story is correct but the seven 'days' of creation represent much longer periods of time.

There are some key messages in the story. It is telling us that humans have a purpose; they were deliberately made by the Creator. This was a designed and considered creation – not just an accidental, chaotic happening.

Science … or religion … or both?

Can you believe both science and religion on the matter of the origins of life? Read each of these people's understanding of Genesis. Which of them could believe in both Genesis and the Big Bang?

Jasprit believes the Bible is the word of God. Everything written in it is absolutely true. God told people exactly what to write. This includes Genesis. So Josh believes that every word of Genesis is true. He believes that the Genesis story is exactly how the world began. It is word for word true. The world was created in seven days by God.

Jasprit says God can do anything and God is really clever. This means God could create the world. He says we will never understand how, because we are humans not gods, so we should just believe it.

Ronnie believes the Bible is true, but not word for word. He believes God told people things, but they made some mistakes when they wrote them down. So the story in Genesis is right, but not exactly. For example, the story you have read uses the word 'days', but the original language uses a word which means 'periods of time'. Maybe the story was really saying that over a long time, God made the world change and develop. Ronnie believes that. Ronnie believes Genesis is more or less what happened.

Lucy believes the Bible is people's ideas about things that happened. She thinks people thought about events and believed that God had been involved. This means that someone was saying how they believed the world began because of God. This means Genesis is not word for word true. Lucy still believes God created the world. Scientists did not exist when the story was first told. People had to tell the story in the way that made sense. Genesis makes sense, and it matches the way that scientists say the universe was formed and life developed.

Whether someone could believe both depends on how strictly they follow their religious story. The Big Bang theory and the religious creation story obviously say different things, so a literal understanding of Genesis would make believing both a problem. However, the less literally we take Genesis, the easier it is to see it as a non-scientific way of understanding the world around us. If we think of Genesis as having a message, then it is not even answering the same question as science. Science is telling us *how*, whilst religion is telling us *why*.

It is the same with science though; the more completely you believe that theory, the less room there is to believe anything else.

And anyway, who did make the Big Bang go bang?!

Comparing these truths

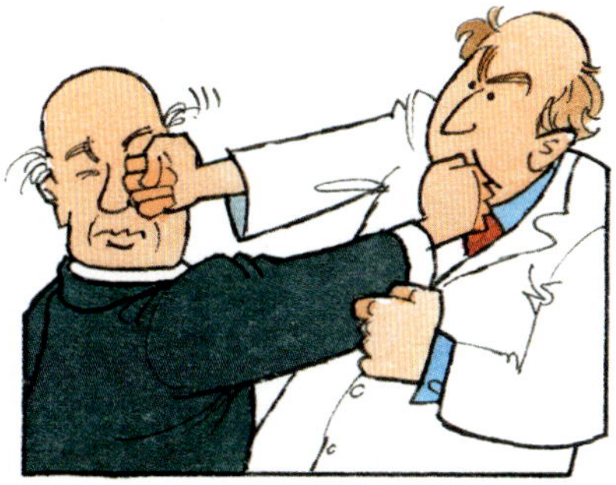

Which is more important, science or religion? If you look at the number of faith schools compared to the number of science schools, you might think religion was more important. If you compare how much time science takes up on your timetable with how much RS does, you might get a different answer. How many science programmes are on TV, compared to religious programmes? What about in the news? Is there more science or more religion? Does either dominate news as a whole or does it all depend on what is happening in the world at the time?

Science, as you have learned, is about hypotheses and testing. It describes observed regularities in the world around us; it helps us make sense of how the world works. Religion is about giving a sense of purpose and meaning to our lives; it can act as a control on behaviour, because of its rules and the promise of an **afterlife**; it gives people a sense of well-being and comfort. *Are those things the same?*

Science and religion are different kinds of truth, telling us different things. So maybe they do not even contradict each other. Many people dismiss religion because it tells us things without scientific proof. However, science works on theories, like the Big Bang – there is evidence for the theory, but not absolute proof. Is there a difference?

With a partner, try to work out why society seems to favour science over religion?

You might say because science has proved lots of religious ideas wrong. Or because we live in a modern world. Or because religion is not relevant today. Or that science has greater logic – so is more attractive.

Why does religion still prove strong in the world?

You might have said because it answers questions nothing else can. Or it makes us feel special. Or it is a tradition. Or simply that it is right.

In our society, science holds a high place. It is very important to society's development and improvement right now, and it seems to have overtaken religion for many people. Science does challenge religious beliefs, and this course wants you to explore two of the biggest challenges science made.

The Basics

1. Explain what we mean by *science* and *religion*.
2. Which is more important science or religion – and why? Use the reasoning you have just read in your answer.
3. **Both science and religion are valuable in our world today.** What do you think? Give three arguments to agree and three in disagreement. Remember to explain each.

The value of the world

You have already learned that most religious believers think God created the world. This part of the Theme looks at key environmental issues, and how religious believers might think about these issues, or might try to be part of the solution to them.

Key concepts

All religious believers believe that *life is sacred*, or special. This must extend to all life and so the world becomes sacred as it is the home to all. It should be treated with respect.

The idea that God created the world, means it has to be looked after. In fact, religious people believe they were given a responsibility or duty by God to look after the world (**stewardship**).

As humans are the prime species, religious believers think that God gave us the right to decide what happens to the world and all the species in it. This is called **dominion**. Humans have power over nature by permission of God.

When people look at the beautiful things in nature, they can be struck by a sense of wonderment. They are amazed and 'wowed' by beautiful sunsets, landscapes, waterfalls and the power of nature. This is called **awe**. For religious people, that sense of awe makes them praise God even more because they believe God created the world. He is responsible for the things that make them feel this way. They want to worship Him more as a result.

Is the world important?

Of course it is! We live on it. Our children will live on it after we have passed away. We need to look after it, if only because it is in our own personal interests.

For religious people, they also have the duty of stewardship, and the hope that they will be rewarded in heaven, or the next rebirth, for their positive work for the environment.

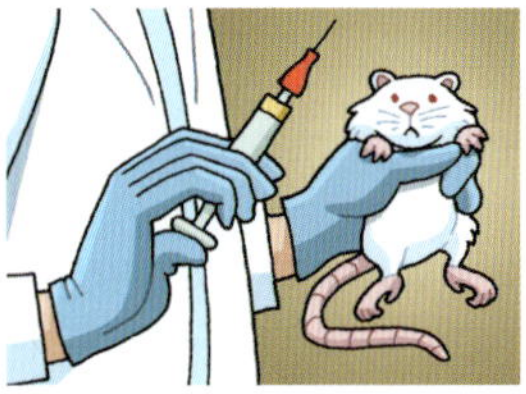

Abuse of the environment

Buddhism

Buddhist attitude to the environment

Buddhists believe that all life, in whatever form, should be respected. So, Buddhists respect the natural world. Since everyone must live many, many lifetimes, it is important to protect the world for our own future, as well as our children's. Two key values for Buddhists are therefore *respect* and *compassion*.

The Dalai Lama has said:

- Destruction of nature and **natural resources** results from ignorance, greed and lack of respect for the Earth's living things ... This lack of respect extends to future generations who will inherit a vastly degraded planet.
- The Earth is not only the common heritage of all humankind but also the ultimate source of life.
- **Conservation** is not merely a question of morality, but a question of our own survival.

Buddhism also teaches:

- Support the life of all sentient beings. (First Precept)
- Compassion for all life.
- There are karmic consequences to all of our actions.

Looking after the environment is about the people of the future, it is about the other forms of life now and in the future. Ignorance and greed are two of the three poisons which keep people from enlightenment, and much environmental damage is because of people and business wanting more for themselves – money, space, anything.

Pollution

Pollution basically means there is too much of something which is toxic and causes damage to the environment. It can affect air, water or land. We now even talk about light and noise pollution. Usually, it is a result of human actions.

Busy roads and factories cause air pollution. That affects our health and drives some wildlife away. It also produces *acid rain*, where chemicals dissolve in water droplets in the atmosphere so that when rain falls it poisons the land and water, and damages buildings and structures.

Factories can cause water pollution by emptying waste into rivers poisoning them. Fertiliser running off farmers' fields can kill off all the fish, as it makes the algae grow too fast, taking the oxygen from the water. This is just one form of *toxic chemical*. Too much **pesticide** does more damage to the ecosystem than intended and can change its whole balance.

You have probably added to land pollution because of dropping litter. This does not just look bad; it also kills lots of wild animals who eat it or get trapped in it.

In towns and cities, you see fewer stars than when you are in the countryside. The lights at ground level block out the stars causing light pollution.

People living near airports, for example, suffer from noise pollution because of the sound of planes taking off and landing. Even if it does not affect their hearing, it makes life unpleasant, and affects the value of their homes.

Pollution is a big part of the reason for global warming and climate change. Our waste produces greenhouse gases which heat the Earth.

The Basics

1 Explain what we mean by *pollution*.
2 **Pollution is a fact of life; it cannot be stopped.** Choose three reasons to agree with this statement and three to disagree and explain each.

Global warming and climate change

Climate change is the idea that the Earth's temperature is increasing and therefore causing more extreme weather, such as flooding and more storms. This will lead to temperatures everywhere getting higher and this is what is meant by *global warming*. The questions are: why that is happening; what the consequences will be; and, how we can try to stop it, because it is a problem.

Why is it happening?

The Earth's cycle is to get hotter and cooler over time. You have heard of the ice ages, when the Earth froze over; global warming is the opposite. So climate change and global warming is all part and parcel of the Earth's life. However, scientists know that the activities of humans over the last 250 years, and especially the last 100, have speeded up temperature change. They estimate that the surface temperature of the earth will increase between 1.4 and 5.8°C before 2100. This is mainly because of greenhouse gases, particularly CO_2 released by burning **fossil fuels** for energy, transport and industry. Following the *precautionary principle*, scientists are telling us we need to act now.

What are the consequences?

Imagine British summers so hot you do not need to go to Greece for a sunshine holiday! It sounds good, so what is the problem?

Hotter usually means dryer and so plants and animals have to adapt or die. Hotter everywhere means some places become just too hot to exist in. The ice caps melt, so the seas rise and lands flood (and Britain is surrounded by the sea). If it gets too hot, the diseases found in hot countries come too, for example, malaria, dengue fever, and so on. Everyone will need air-conditioning which will cost money and resources.

With a partner, work out what it would be like in school all year if climate change caused the place where you live to become too hot. What problems would there be? What solutions can you see?

Solutions?

Scientists say the key solution is to change our energy use. We need to find alternatives to fossil fuels (coal, gas and oil) so that the fuels we use do not add to the problem. This is called **sustainable energy** – in other words, we can keep using it without doing more harm. It is energy which meets the needs of the present without compromising the ability of future generations to meet their own needs.

With a partner, list as many forms of renewable energy as you can. You have probably covered this in Science – so use that knowledge here as well.

The Basics

1 What is meant by climate change and global warming?
2 Why do scientists think the Earth is getting hotter?
3 What is the main change we can make to try to slow this effect?
4 **Religious believers should work harder to fight climate change.** Choose three reasons to disagree with this statement and explain each. If you have time, choose three reasons to agree, and explain them.
5 **Global warming is the biggest problem facing humans today.** Explain reasons to agree and disagree with this statement. Include religious arguments in your answer.

Christianity

Christian attitude to the environment

Christians believe God created the world, and gave humankind stewardship – the responsibility to look after the world. Christians, in modern times especially, have seen the need to work to *heal the world* and look after the environment.

The Bible teaches:

- God made the world and gave the duty of stewardship to humans. (Genesis 1:28)
- The Earth is the Lord's, and everything in it. (Psalms 23:1)
- Respect for life extends to the rest of creation. – Pope John Paul II
- More than ever – individually and collectively – people are responsible for the future of the planet. – Pope John Paul II
- I want to awake in you a deep admiration for creation, until anywhere thinking of plants and flowers, are overcome by thoughts of the Creator. – St Basil

Christians also believe that humans have dominion over the earth – God put humans in charge. But this does not mean we can just do what we want with the earth. Christians believe we need to be responsible in our dominionship, otherwise there will be negative consequences both on earth and in the afterlife. Clearly, humans have a special role on Earth, which is to look after the Earth and animals. Since humans must face God on the Day of Judgement, all must carry out their given duties. If humans did not look after the world, or did nothing to stop its destruction, they should expect to be punished by God. Many Christians are motivated to do environmental work because of this belief.

My house was flooded three times in two years. Torrential rain has made the river break its banks. I'm not the only one to suffer, but it has been devastating. We will have to move – but I have lived here all my life.

David

Destruction of natural habitats (deforestation)

Land is cleared in Borneo for palm oil plantations. Orang-utans lose their habitat, and are now an endangered species.

You just read about pollution. Pollution is one reason why natural habitats are being destroyed. For example, if a tanker spills oil into the sea it can wipe out life in that area, and degrades the land for many years. Research the *Torrey Canyon* spill to get a better idea of this.

Another reason is deforestation, where huge areas of forest are cut down, for example, to create grazing land for cattle, or areas for building, mining and roads. Trees, of course, are habitat for many species and so these species are affected, with some even dying out. Also, trees take in carbon dioxide and release oxygen that we breathe, so they help the fight against global warming; but cutting them down, the climate crisis worsens.

The rainforests also contain many plants that can be used as medicines, which are lost with deforestation. There are thought to be many species of animals and plants which we have not yet even recorded in the rainforests; they could become extinct before we have studied them. Even without knowingly causing extinction, natural habitats are destroyed and species endangered.

How could we make up for destroying these habitats?

ॐ Hinduism

Hindu attitude to the environment

Traditionally, Hindu life was very simple, and relied on nature. This was linked with beliefs about the **sanctity of life** and non-violence to form the religion, which is peaceful towards the environment. Brahman (the Ultimate Reality) is in all life.

Hinduism teaches:

- There should be respect for all life, including the created world.
- There should be ahimsa (non-violence).
- You should focus on environmental values. (the hymn, Artharva Veda)
- Trees have five sorts of kindness which are their daily sacrifice: to families they give fuel; to passers-by they give shade and a resting place; to birds they give shelter; with their leaves, roots and bark they give medicines (Varaha Purana)
- Everything rests on me as pearls are strung on a thread. I am the original fragrance of the earth ... the taste in water ... the heat in fire and the sound in space ... the light of the sun and moon and the life of all that lives. (Bhagavad Gita)

All life is seen as interdependent, and that includes animal and plant life. All life depends on the environment, so everyone has a vested interest in protecting and looking after it. Additionally, Hindus believe our souls will all be reborn into more lifetimes on Earth, so we have to look after it for our own future sakes. God is seen as part of nature, so protection and worship are important as the Artharva Veda states.

The Basics

1 What is *destruction of natural habitat*? What does this lead to?
2 Give some reasons why this happens.
3 How could we avoid this destruction?
4 **When God gave humans dominion over the world, it meant we could do what we like.** Explain reasons to agree and disagree with this statement.

Use and abuse of natural resources

Islam

Muslim attitude to the environment

Islam sees the creation in its entirety as the work of Allah. Humans are *khalifa* (stewards) of the world. Looking after the world shows respect to Allah.

Islam teaches:

- The world is green and beautiful, and Allah has appointed you His stewards over it. (Qur'an)
- 'The heavens and the earth declare God's glory.' (Surah 17:44)
- When Doomsday comes, if someone has a palm shoot in his hand, he should still plant it. (Hadith)
- The earth has been created for me as a mosque and a means of purification. (Hadith)
- Prophet Muhammad ﷺ gave the example of not wasting. He only ever washed in water from a container, not the river or other running water.

Humans are the trustees of Allah's creation. Trustees look after things, rather than destroy them.

The whole creation reflects Allah, and Allah knows everything that happens in it. Allah knows who damages and who looks after His creation. So it is a good idea to look after the world, because those who do not follow their duty will be punished on Judgement Day by Allah.

The Muslim community is one *ummah*, a brotherhood, including those in the past and future. Everyone has a duty to their family and fellow humans to make sure they pass on to them a world fit to live in, not one damaged beyond repair because humans were so selfish as to think they could do what they wanted with it.

Natural resources include vegetation, minerals and fossil fuels. Humans are using these in greater quantities and at a faster rate now than at any other time in our history. This is because of how technologically advanced we are. We can take materials out of the ground faster and in greater quantities than ever before. Modern technology, for example, cars and all forms of transport, often needs more resources to run. More people use more technology more often.

Some fossil fuels, for example, coal, are already running out. These fuels are limited in quantity, and take millions of years to be formed. We have to find a different source of energy, which is renewable. If we do not stop using fossil fuels, they will run out, and we will have to find a new source anyway.

Can you think of all the fuel sources we use? What new ones could we try? What will be the problems caused if, for example, oil runs out?

It is not just that these fuels are limited. They give off lots of greenhouse gases and pollution. The more we use, the more the problems stack up. So finding an alternative helps us with those problems too; it is not something we can hide from.

The Basics

1. What do we mean by use and abuse of natural resources?
2. List the ways we use, overuse and abuse material resources.
3. Why do we need to find new ways to get energy?
4. What new energy forms could there be?
5. **We must ban the use of fossil fuels now.** Explain reasons to agree and disagree with this statement.

Caring for the world

Sustainable development

This is the idea that new technological developments should all be infinite, or very long-lasting, as well as within the reach of all nations. Developments should support, not damage the environment. It would be no use swapping coal as a fuel for something else which will quickly run out. Similarly, it would be no good finding a new technology which was simply too expensive for anyone to use.

Conservation

Conservation means when we try to protect an area or species. Sometimes it involves repairing damage that has already been done, for example, to maintain the environment for an endangered species. It might include planting trees to protect an area from landslides. It might be declaring an area a nature reserve in order to protect wildlife and the environment there. This has happened in Borneo to help protect orang-utans.

It is becoming more common for people to take holidays which are based around conservation, either of animals, like working on a lion reserve for a few weeks in Kenya, or environmental, like rebuilding dry stone walls in Scotland to protect vegetation in fields beyond the pathways.

Find out about a conservation project which is going on near to you.

Judaism

Jewish attitude to the environment

Jewish sacred writings begin with G-d's creation of the world, and go on to state that G-d gave humans the duty of stewardship. There are many mitzvot (rules) about looking after the environment.

Judaism teaches:

- Genesis creation story. All is made by G-d and is good. Humans are given stewardship over the creation.
- The *bal tashchit* (do not waste) precept can be interpreted as an instruction to conserve resources. (Torah)
- The earth and everything that is in it is the Lord's. (Ketuvim)
- All that I created for you ... do not corrupt or desolate my world ... there will be no one to repair it after you. (Midrash Ecclesiastes Rabbah 7:13)
- Love your neighbour as yourself. (Leviticus)

So, clearly Jewish people have a duty to look after the world and should do this by treating it with respect. For example, land is to be left fallow on a regular cycle. Increasingly, Jewish people are becoming more active in environmental work and are linking existing Jewish values to the issue. For example, tikkun olam (healing the world) could be interpreted as tackling environmental problems; tzedek (justice) is being extended to mean justice for all of creation, including animals and the world itself. It is not possible to 'love your neighbour' if you are damaging the environment they live in.

I was brought up to believe in tikkun olam, healing the world. I joined a local volunteer group, and have made lots of friends whilst helping with the cleaning of the local area. For example, we helped to get rubbish out of the local pond, and it is now attracting more birds. It feels good to be doing something good.

What can individuals do?

Religious believers are like every other person on the planet and so can do what any other person can do. They can start from their own personal practice, for example, recycling, reusing, not wasting. They can join in local efforts, for example, clean-ups, not buying goods that are harmful to the environment, buying local produce. They can join in with campaigns, and donate to charities that try to resolve environmental problems. They might also work within their local religious community, encouraging others to also help or focusing worship on this issue.

The difference is their motivation to help, as you have already read. They have a *religious motivation* to look after the environment.

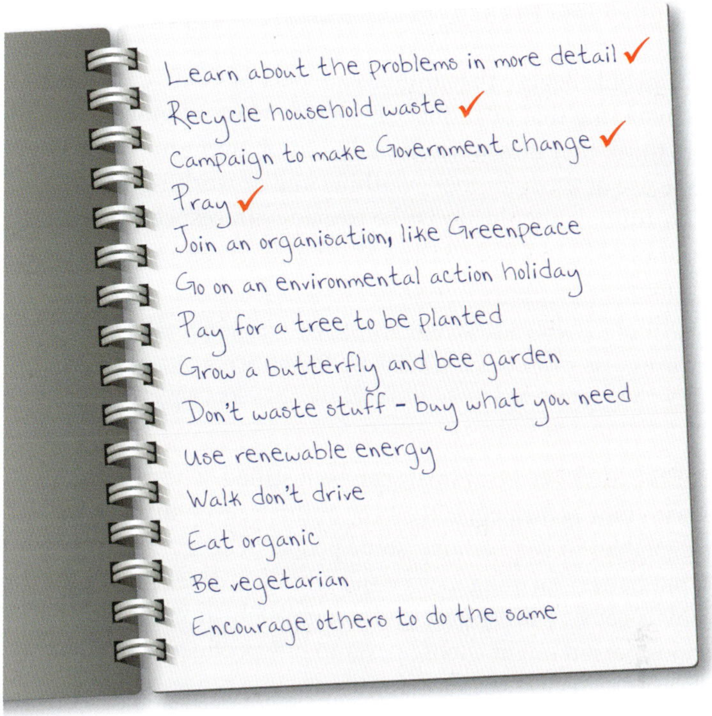

The Basics

1. What is meant by sustainable development?
2. What is meant by conservation?
3. Explain why religious believers think they should look after the environment.
4. Explain how religious believers can help to solve environmental problems.
5. **The environment should be everyone's first priority.** Do you agree? Explain your reasons, showing you have thought about more than one point of view.

I am a Sikh, and I have a job in scientific research. The projects I am working on are all about sustainable forms of energy. We need to stop using up the earth's resources, and begin to show respect to our planet. God created this world, and it is sacred.

Japnoor

I am part of the local ecology group. As I am the best with technology, I am the one who keeps the website up-to-date and running. I also keep environmental issues at the front of people's minds by putting up reports, displays and posters in church regularly. Everyone needs to help – it is their duty of stewardship.

Casey

I know that when I go to be judged before Allah, I will be asked what I did for His creation. I work in the local nature reserve one Sunday a month, helping to manage the plants and trees in there. Quite apart from being a good deed, it is really healthy, and I have learned loads.

Mo

Animals and animal rights

Religious people believe that animals are part of God's creation. All life, including that of animals, is sacred. Most religious believers think that they were given dominion over animals, so can make use of them for food, clothing and as working animals. However, animals should always be treated with respect, fairness and kindness.

Think about all the ways humans use animals. Make a list of the ones which are fine – in your opinion – and those which are not. Now compare your list with a partner, and try to challenge the answers they give.

Many of the ways we use animals can be justified. The problem comes with how some people treat the animals, even in a use we find acceptable. So, for example, some people believe that farming is fine, but battery farming may be thought of as cruel, given that the animals get very little space and a completely unnatural life. A religious person might choose never to buy produce which has come from a battery farm, choosing always free range.

There are two specific issues you have to know for the course. They are animal experimentation and the use of animals for food.

Sikhism

Sikhs believe the natural environment is a gift from God and that we have to take care of it. It only exists because God wants it to, so God could make it just stop existing.

Sikhism teaches:

- The universe comes into being by God's will. – Guru Nanak
- In nature we see God, and in nature, we hear God speak. – Adi Granth
- There should be respect for all life.
- God created everything. – Guru Nanak
- The Sikh ideal is a simple life free from conspicuous waste.

So, Sikhs should look after the environment out of respect for life, and as worship to God. Sikhs believe they must perform *sewa* (service) for others, and this can be understood to include the natural world. Of course, looking after the world means that it is safeguarded for future generations, so Sikhs are doing sewa for people in the future. They believe that it is not possible to care for the environment without thinking about society's needs too, because often environmental damage is a result of poverty.

The gurdwaras in India have signed up to a plan to replace fuel with solar power to use in langars (communal meals) which feed hundreds of thousands every day.

Sikh gurus have said that God is within everything, so in some ways damaging the world is like damaging God.

Animal experimentation

When you mention animal experiments, many people often instantly think they are very cruel. It is experiments on live animals which usually have this impact. The animals (mainly guinea pigs, mice, rats, rabbits, dogs and monkeys) are specially bred in farms.

However, animal experiments have resulted in enormous benefits for both humans and animals, which is why many people, including religious believers, support them. Animal experiments further our medical knowledge so that surgical procedures are improved. They are used to test new drugs for effectiveness and so that they do not cause harm. They are also used to test some new products, although animal testing for cosmetics is banned. Medical science has always used animals. Many surgical procedures, such as transplantation surgery, were perfected on animals. While some experiments may cause injury or death, many just mean a change in diet. At the end of the experimentation any remaining live animals left are humanely destroyed. Since 1986, in the UK, there have been specific laws to regulate animal experimentation.

What are some of the issues?

1 It is cruel. Even scientists accept the animals can suffer, though they believe it is for the greater good.

2 Modern science has now developed some other alternatives, like using human tissue cultures to test for toxicity.

3 Animal genetics and human genetics are different, and often reactions are not the same. So some animal experimentation is pointless as it tells us nothing helpful.

I work in a science research lab. We test new drugs on animals, before they go for human testing. These tests help us to develop drugs which can save lives. Although the animals must be tested on and must die at the end of the experiment, we have to use them. We couldn't just test on people without knowing anything about the effects of a drug.

Adil

The Basics

1 Explain why scientists do experiments on animals.
2 Explain why some religious believers disagree with animal experimentation.
3 **Humans are misusing their power over animals.** Do you agree? Explain your reasons, showing you have thought about more than one point of view.

As a Buddhist, I revere all life. However, I know that we need to protect life, and I think human life needs the greatest protection of all. I work in a research laboratory where we use human skin and tissue cultures to test products. This means that no animal is ever harmed, and that our products should be safer as all their testing has been done on human materials. Animals and humans don't always react the same way to the same things. It means I do not disrespect animal life in my work, rather I protect it.

Rita

Whilst I know that all animals are part of the greatness of creation, I also know that humans are the highest form of it. God has given us the capacity to use animals for our own good. We can perfect surgical procedures on animals. Trainee doctors can learn how to be better surgeons – cutting, stitching, transplanting – all on animals, before they have to operate on people.

Danial

Use of animals for food

Why be vegetarian?

There are many reasons why people are vegetarian. They are usually to do with health, upbringing, religion and concerns about farming methods. Some people eat no meat or dairy products at all (vegans); some choose to eat no meat or meat products (vegetarian).

The Christian, Muslim and Jewish faiths all allow meat in their diets. Some Christians fast at certain times of year, for example, not eating certain foods during Lent. Many Christians do not eat red meat on Fridays out of respect for Jesus' sacrifice on Good Friday. Muslims and Jewish people may not eat certain meats, for example, the meat of a pig, of shellfish, and of birds of prey. They may only eat ritually slaughtered meat (halal for Muslims, kosher for Jewish people). This reflects the idea that God/Allah/G-d gave humans dominion over animals, and so they could be used by humans, including as food. Hindus on the whole are vegetarian, reflecting two important beliefs: ahimsa (non-violence) and respect for all life. Hindus are usually vegetarian and all food cooked or offered in Hindu temples to distribute to those in need is strictly vegetarian. For Buddhists, it very much depends on the culture in the country and on available diet. For example, in Tibet a healthy diet is only possible if it includes meat. Many Sikhs are vegetarian to show respect for God's creation and the Sikh langar is always a vegetarian meal.

The Basics

1. Check pages 267–274 to find the religions you have studied. For each write any teachings which link with animals. Add any other ideas you have come across in your studies (for example, that God created all life).
2. Use what you have written to write a paragraph on the attitude of each of your two religions to animals.
3. Re-use those teachings to explain the attitude of each to eating meat.
4. Why do some people choose to be vegetarian?
5. **Eating meat is disrespectful to God's creation.** Do you agree? Give reasons and explain your answer, showing you have thought about more than one point of view.

Task

Find out about the dietary requirements of followers of the religion(s) you have studied.

The value of human life

There is no doubt that religions say human life is the most important and special of all kinds of life. There are two key concepts: sanctity of life and **quality of life**.

Sanctity of life

This is the idea that all life is special. Many religions believe life is sacred because God created it (Christianity, Hinduism, Islam, Judaism and Sikhism). Some religions believe human life is special because it is the way we can achieve enlightenment (Buddhism and Hinduism). No one in the world believes that life is worth nothing. Generally, legal systems consider murder to be the worst crime you could commit, and it carries the toughest punishments. All religions believe that life is special and deserves to be protected and cherished. Religions extend this belief to plant and animal life. Be sure to use this concept when talking about animals and the environment as well.

The status of human life

Religious believers think that humans are the highest form of creation, or that they are within the highest levels of spiritual development. This means that the value of human life is beyond measure, and as such it should be protected and cared for. Most religious believers are '**pro-life**' in many questions of life or death. For this part of the Theme, you need to consider the issues of abortion and euthanasia.

Quality of life

This is a description of how good someone's life is. It includes how comfortable they feel, how easy it is for them to live through each day, perhaps how much they have in terms of money and possessions. For this Theme, it concerns whether or not life is worth living because of the medical situation a person finds themselves in. Giving someone a good quality of life is part of the most basic teaching of all religions; we should treat others as we wish to be treated.

Task

Look at the scenarios listed below. In each case, decide if the key consideration is sanctity or quality of life, or both. Explain your decision each time.

- Sarah is pregnant, but has cancer and needs treatment. Treatment will lead to the termination of the foetus.
- John kills people who are dying of terminal illnesses.
- Gillian visits her mother regularly to make sure she has everything she needs and is comfortable.
- David does not agree with abortion because he says it is a life God created.
- Kulpna is a doctor in the Intensive Care Unit. She makes decisions about life support.
- Jacob is very ill with cancer and is in a lot of pain. He is in a hospice.

The Basics

1. Explain what is meant by sanctity of life.
2. Explain what is meant by quality of life.
3. Explain why a religious believer might say that sanctity of life is more important than quality of life.
4. How might belief in sanctity of life affect the way religious believers behave?
5. **Religious believers should always fight for life to be preserved.** Explain reasons to agree and disagree with this statement.

Abortion

When does life begin?

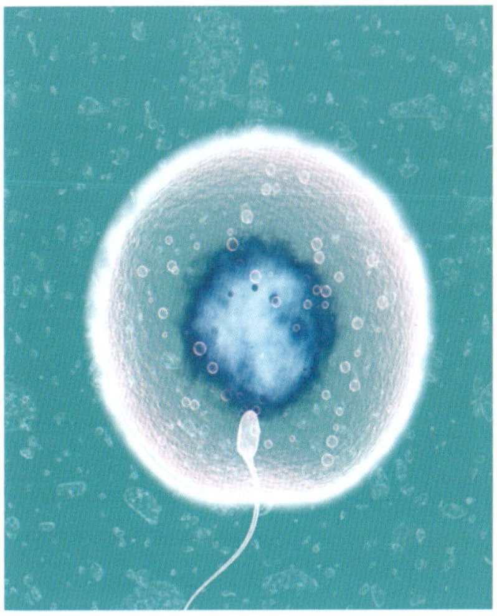

Is it at **conception**?

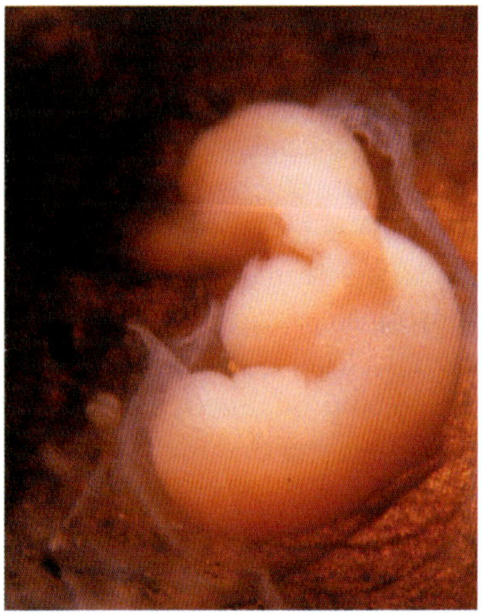

Is it when the foetus has a heart of its own, which beats?

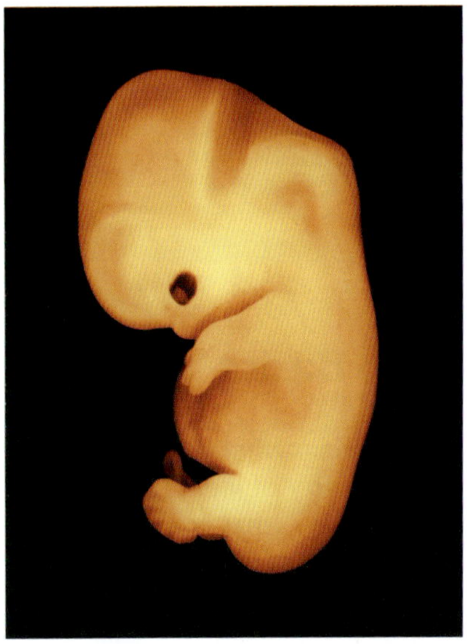

Is it when there is a backbone?

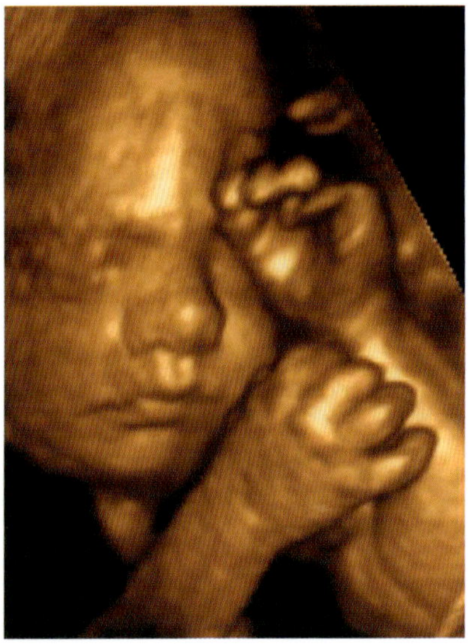

Is it when the foetus would likely survive if born prematurely (viability)?

Is it when the baby has been born?

The question of when life begins is key because many people see abortion as murder or killing and there has to be a life before there can be a murder. So, it affects whether or not we see abortion as wrong.

In UK law, life begins when the baby is born, but given that the Abortion Act (as amended in 1990) does not allow abortions beyond 24 weeks; is that when life begins? Some people think that when the foetus looks like a baby, it should be treated as such, whether it is fully formed or not.

What we *can* say is that at every stage the foetus is a potential life.

The law on abortion in the UK

UK law defines abortion as: 'The deliberate expulsion of a foetus from the womb, with the intention of destroying it.' It is different from a miscarriage, which has the same result (that the pregnancy ends without a baby living), because miscarriage is accidental, a turn of nature.

The law in the UK (excluding Northern Ireland) begins by stating that abortion is illegal. It then goes on to say that there are some exceptions.

Abortion can only be carried out if two registered doctors agree that at least one of the following is true:

- There is a danger to the woman's mental and/or physical health.
- The foetus will be born with physical and/or mental disabilities.
- The mental and/or physical health of existing children will be put at risk.

The abortion has to be carried out at a registered place, by a registered doctor before the 24th week of pregnancy.

A registered doctor is a doctor who has passed medical exams and is recognised by the Medical Council. So a doctor who has been struck off the official list can neither give advice, nor carry out an abortion. A registered place is a hospital or clinic that is registered with the government, and can perform such medical procedures as abortion because of that registration. Any other place is not legal.

Breaking the law carries great penalties for all those involved.

The Basics

1. Explain what the UK law says about abortion.
2. Explain three situations in which a woman might seek an abortion. For each, say whether a religious believer might agree with it.
3. Thinking about the belief in sanctity of life, how would you expect a religious believer to view abortion.

Some scenarios – what do you think?

Before you look through these scenarios, there are some rules. You cannot just agree or disagree with any case, you have to explain why you agree or disagree. Also, you have to say what the consequences of each woman not having an abortion are because they are all asking for the abortion, even if they do not feel good about having to do that. Finally, you have to say whether you think they had another reasonable option and why.

I carry a genetic disease; doctors have tested my baby and it has the disease. If I allow it to be born, my baby will suffer greatly.

I am only 14 – too young to have this baby.

I was raped, which left me pregnant.

I am 46, and pregnant. My baby has Down's Syndrome.

I have cancer, and the doctors have advised me to have treatment (which will also end my pregnancy) for my best chance of recovery.

I am single and have no wish to have children – ever. I am pregnant because the contraception I used failed. I neither want nor planned this pregnancy.

Reasons for and against abortion

Pro-life

Pro-life is the term we use for those arguments against abortion, usually in any circumstances. Pro-life pressure groups include PROLIFE and SPUC. Since they support the foetus' right to life, their arguments are all in favour of protecting the foetus to ensure it is born.

Read these comments and pick out the pro-life arguments in each one.

I believe that all life is sacred, and must be protected. So, abortion is completely wrong.

God has created life, and as stewards of this world, humans have to protect life.

Abortion is the murder of another human being. Murder is wrong.

The foetus cannot defend itself – so someone else has to.

When a foetus will be born with disabilities, we cannot say what the quality of its life would be, so should not decide to forbid it that life.

The foetus has a right to life and not to be discarded as if it is just waste.

Pro-choice

Pro-choice is usually associated with supporting the use of abortion, but it actually means the arguments which defend a woman's right to choose what happens to her body. Since they support the woman's right to choose, the arguments are about the woman, rather than the foetus.

Read these comments and pick out the pro-choice arguments in each one.

A woman should have the right to decide what happens to her body.

Where a woman is pregnant as a result of rape or incest, it would be wrong to not allow her an abortion.

Some foetuses are so damaged that it would be cruel to allow them to be born.

If having a child is going to put a woman's life at risk, or is going to make her postpone medical treatment which she needs, then she should have the right to an abortion.

Up to a certain point, the foetus cannot survive outside the womb, so should not be thought of as a life in its own right.

If we banned abortions, women would still have them – but not in a safe way. We need to protect women.

Task

Find out about the work of a pro-life (against abortion) and a pro-choice (for a woman's right to choose) group. In a presentation, explain what they do and how they campaign.

Thinking about the lives involved

When we consider abortion, we are immediately thinking about the foetus involved. However, the law considers the women first not the foetus. Her life and well-being take precedence in law. *So, how might her life become a greater consideration? Have a look at these examples:*

Jess has been told she has cancer of the womb. The only option is to remove her womb, which of course means removal of the foetus and the ending of the pregnancy. Without following this option, the cancer will be terminal.

Saira has a heart defect, which means that any strain could be lethal. Obviously, pregnancy is difficult even for healthy women, especially in the last few months. The actual birth will also require a lot of work on her part. Whilst she could have a caesarean section, the doctors are not sure her heart is strong enough to cope with that operation.

Demi has a form of cancer which requires chemotherapy. The chemotherapy needed will affect the foetus, either by affecting its formation or causing miscarriage. If she does not have the treatment, the prognosis for her is very poor.

How would religions view the argument that a woman's life is at risk unless she has the abortion?

All religions believe in the sanctity of life and that life should be preserved/protected. Without the woman's life, the foetus has no chance of life.

Buddhists believe the key intention must be compassion, so helping save a woman's life is compassionate.

In Judaism and Islam, the life of the mother takes precedence – she is a fully developed human with responsibilities, whereas the foetus is not even born and will need everything doing for it.

The Roman Catholic Church sees abortion as wrong, but where it is the 'side effect' of a procedure to save a woman's life, it can be accepted.

The Church of England has said that abortion is a great moral evil, but that where the continuance of a pregnancy threatens a woman's life, then it is justifiable.

In Hinduism, abortion is condemned as the taking of life, unless it is absolutely necessary to prevent the mother from dying or experiencing severe mental health issues. There may be exceptions such as abortion on compassionate grounds if it is known that the foetus will be born with a painful terminal illness.

It seems clear, then, that religions believe the woman has the right to an abortion, albeit still considered a moral evil, if her life is at risk.

The Basics

1. Refer to page 279 to explain what the law in the UK says about a woman's right to an abortion. On what grounds does it support her rights?
2. Explain why religious believers believe a woman's life is more important than that of the foetus.
3. **The only acceptable reason to have an abortion is when the woman's life is at risk.** Argue for and against this statement and use religious arguments in your answer.

Other questions about abortion

When students discuss this topic, they often get into debates in two areas not covered so far: whose right is it to decide that an abortion is the appropriate action, and what else could a woman choose to do to avoid abortion?

In the image above, you can see there are a number of people who contribute to the decision. The woman is probably the first – after all it is her body. You would expect her to discuss it with her partner – he is the father. She might also discuss with her own parents or siblings – we often talk to them about issues. She will have to talk to a doctor – and under UK law, doctors are the ones who sanction and carry out abortions (without their say-so, she cannot have an abortion legally). The question is who gets the biggest say and the final decision?

What do you think? What rights do you think each person in the image has to support or block abortion?

What other options are available?

If the woman has a medical condition, she may have no choice but to have the abortion or she forfeits her own life. That seems quite straightforward, but it is still difficult because it involves taking potential life.

A woman could decide against abortion, complete the pregnancy and have the baby fostered or adopted. At some point, by law, that child would be able to find out about their birth circumstances and might come back to the mother to ask questions.

Or, she could decide against abortion and continue the pregnancy. She would be choosing to work through or in spite of the problems that made her consider abortion. If there had been a risk to her mental or physical health, this is even more difficult.

Can you think of the pros and cons of each of these alternatives to abortion?

Practising debate

Write arguments for and against each of these statements, giving at least three reasons which are explained on each side.

1 Only the pregnant woman should have any say in deciding to have an abortion.
2 Women in the UK should not be allowed to have abortions.
3 There is no need to have an abortion in the UK as there are better alternatives available.

Care for the dying – the hospice movement

Hospices are the preferred Christian response to the issue of euthanasia. A hospice is a home for those who are terminally ill (dying). They are for both children and adults of all ages, for example, those with cancer. People may go there until they die or to give their families respite from looking after them for a while. On average people stay there for two weeks.

Originally, hospices were places for travellers, the sick and the needy to stay. They were set up by Christians. Over time, some of them began to specialise in looking after those who were dying.

When someone is dying, they cannot be cured – only cared for. Hospices try to provide care for all aspects of a person's illness and suffering. Many religious people believe that if the care is good enough, then euthanasia would not even be considered.

The aims of hospices:

1 To relieve the physical symptoms of illness. In other words, to get rid of as much pain as is possible. This includes whatever it takes, for example, massage, meditation and relaxation. Often, medical treatment for the dying is very specialised. It is called palliative care.

2 To care for the emotional and spiritual well-being of the patient. Many dying people have unfinished business, which is a worry to them. The hospices help them to sort things out. Many patients are angry, for example, asking questions such as 'why me?', and hospices help them to come to terms with dying. Many patients need to be listened to and often relatives cannot cope with this, but the hospices do.

3 To support the families of patients who also suffer. Hospices provide many support networks and services for family members, even after the death of the patient.

4 To educate others caring for the dying, and to work out new, better ways to care for the dying which will be invaluable in the future. The experience built up in hospices can be used in other places.

Religious groups see hospices as the way forward for terminally ill people. They believe that God wants us to care for these people, to look after them, to express God's love for them, not to kill them.

St Ann's Hospice (www.sah.org.uk)

This hospice was opened in 1971 and serves the Greater Manchester community. Its aim is to improve the quality of life of people with life-threatening illnesses. It aims to do this while supporting families and carers.

In a year, the hospice treats over 5500 patients, of whom about 5000 are outpatients. In 2018, it cost over £12 million to run St Ann's, meaning that the hospice has to raise £20,000 a day. The NHS provides only 37 per cent of funds, so most of the money comes from voluntary donations.

95 per cent of patients are suffering from a cancer-related illness. Each patient is given a personal care plan, which is tailored to meet their individual needs. This is what makes the support so unique and effective.

Task

Find out about a hospice local to your school. Learn something of the work it does, the numbers of people it helps each year, and whether it specialises in certain illnesses or age groups. Produce a report on that hospice for others in your class.

www.hospiceuk.org.uk is the national charity for hospices. You can learn much about the hospice movement from their website.

Religious attitudes to life

Buddhism

Buddhism teaches that:

- Life is special and must be protected.
- The First Precept is to not take life.
- A primary guiding principle of Buddhism is to reduce suffering.
- The Dalai Lama has said: 'Where a person is definitely going to die, and keeping them alive leads to more suffering, then termination of life is permitted under Mahayana Buddhism.'
- Buddhists must show compassion (loving kindness) and practise ahimsa (non-violence).

The first and most important precept is not to take life; abortion and euthanasia both do this. So, your initial reaction might be that neither would be supported by Buddhism. However, the key element is the *intention* behind any action, and this may lead to the conclusion that either abortion or euthanasia is more of a right action than a wrong one. Every situation has to be judged separately.

Many Buddhists would point to the belief that suffering has come as a karmic consequence and so a person suffering may need to work through that so as not to face the same in a future life. It is important to make death as comfortable as possible, as our state of mind when we die is the key to shaping our next life. If we face death with anxiety, anger and upset, our next rebirth is negatively set. Facing death with acceptance is better. Hence, Buddhism supports hospices which help people to face their death calmly.

Christianity

Christianity teaches that:

- God created life in His own image. (Genesis)
- Do not murder. (Ten Commandments)
- I, your God, give life, and I take it away. (Old Testament)
- The Catholic Church teaches that life must be respected from conception until natural death.
- Doctors do not have an overriding obligation to prolong life by all means possible. (Church of England)

It is clear that on most occasions, Christians do not agree with either abortion or euthanasia. All life is believed to be sacred as it was created, and belongs to, God. Whilst death might mean going to heaven to be with God, it should not be hastened. Life should always be protected. For most Christians, abortion is always morally wrong. Some accept it rarely as a *necessary evil*.

In the case of abortion where the mother's life is at risk, this makes it difficult because her life is also sacred. Most Christians would accept procedures that save her life, even if they lead to the ending of the pregnancy. Many would also point to the fact that in many cases there are options other than abortion, for example, adoption.

In the case of euthanasia, few Christians support active euthanasia, regardless of what a person might themselves wish for. They see it as killing, so it is wrong. Christianity teaches care for the most vulnerable in society and some Christians fear that very vulnerable people could be pressured to agree to euthanasia against their will. However, in countries where euthanasia is legal, there are Christian groups who also agree with it, for example, the Dutch Protestant Church in the Netherlands, which sees it as an act of love and compassion and a good use of the medical knowledge God has granted humans.

Hinduism

Hinduism teaches that:

- Those who carry out abortions are among the worst of sinners. (Arthava Veda)
- Compassion, ahimsa and respect for life are key. (Hindu virtues)
- The result of a virtuous action is pure joy; actions done from emotion bring pain and suffering. (Bhagavad Gita)
- The one who tries to escape from the trials of this life by taking their own life will suffer even more in the next life. (Yajur Veda)

Life is very special and sacred, and must be protected. Hindu teachings are strongly against abortion. In each lifetime, a soul creates new karma for the next and 'pays off' the consequence of bad karma. By terminating a pregnancy, we deny the soul that chance to create/repay karmic consequences in a lifetime. So we block the soul's progress towards union with the Ultimate Reality. Some scriptures say that those who have abortions will themselves suffer that fate many times. Where a woman's life is at risk, abortion is acceptable as her life takes priority.

Many older Hindus see it as acceptable to refuse food and treatment so that they will die, rather than be a burden on their families. So, in this sense, passive euthanasia is acceptable. It is also expected that families will care for their older relatives as a mark of respect, which suggests euthanasia should not be necessary. However, active euthanasia is considered murder and wrong. Hindu principles support care for the dying, not the ending of their life.

Islam

Islam teaches that:

- Neither kill nor destroy yourself. (Surah 4:29)
- No one can die except by Allah's leave, that is a decree with a fixed term. (Surah 3:145)
- Each person is created individually by Allah from a single clinging form (sometimes translated as clot of blood). (Surah 96:2)
- Do not take life – which Allah has made sacred – except for a just cause. (Surah 17:33)
- Euthanasia is zulm – wrongdoing against Allah. (Shari'ah Law)

Allah creates every life and Allah has a plan for each one; both abortion and euthanasia go against Allah's plans. Hence, for most Muslims, abortion is always wrong, as is any form of self-harm or self-killing.

Prophet Muhammad ﷺ told the story of a man who helped a friend die because he was in so much pain. The man and his friend were both denied paradise as a result. No one knows the plans of Allah; this is called al-Qadr or Allah's perfect foreknowledge. In other words, Allah has planned for this experience, so it must have some value. Life will end when Allah wills it, so euthanasia is not acceptable. This prohibits assisted suicide, but does not prohibit withdrawal of medical treatment where there is no hope of recovery.

Muslims disagree about when ensoulment (when the soul becomes part of the growing foetus) takes place. It is varyingly said to be at conception, at 40 days or at 120 days. Before that time, technically an abortion is acceptable because no life is being taken. Where a mother's life is at risk, most Muslims would prioritise the woman's right to life.

Task

With a partner, discuss whether the religion(s) you have studied would agree with abortion in these scenarios:

- a woman who is suffering from an ectopic pregnancy
- a woman whose pregnancy came about through rape
- a woman who feels unready to have a child.

Judaism

Judaism teaches that:

- Do not kill. (Ten Commandments)
- G-d gives life and G-d takes away life. (Psalms)
- The foetus has the spiritual status of 'mere water' until the fortieth day of pregnancy. (Talmud)
- If there is anything which causes a hindrance to the departure of the soul then it is permissible to remove it. – Rabbi Moses Isserles
- The emphasis in Judaism is on life and new life, not the destruction of life.

In Judaism, life is sacred. Foetal life is not a life in its own right (it is regarded as a part of the mother's body and not a separate being) and there are no rights until a baby is born. Hence, there are many situations in which abortion would be allowed in Judaism, for example, if the woman's life is in danger, and for medical reasons (therapeutic abortion). Some rabbis have extended this idea of endangerment to include a woman's mental health, for example, after rape. Across the spectrum of Judaism, there are many different attitudes to what counts as therapeutic abortion.

Judaism believes death should be a calm experience, and attitudes to euthanasia vary greatly. The central question is whether euthanasia shortens life or shortens the act of dying. Shortening the act of dying, that is, not doing things which extend and prolong the pain, allows a person a 'good death', and so is acceptable. It is important to protect life and to care for the dying. Active euthanasia is considered to be wrong because it actually causes death. Euthanasia can be seen as throwing life away, which is absolutely and always wrong.

Sikhism

Sikhism teaches that:

- God sends us and we take birth, God calls us back and we die. – Guru Granth Sahib
- Life begins at conception.
- God fills us with light so we can be born. – Guru Granth Sahib
- All life is sacred and should be respected. – Guru Granth Sahib

According to Sikhism, all life is sacred and every soul is on a journey through many lifetimes to achieve liberation. That life begins at conception means abortion is generally considered to be morally wrong, as it is a form of murder. Abortion is also the destruction of God's creation and the opposite of Sikh ideals for life. This does not mean that a Sikh will never contemplate abortion – seeing it on certain occasions as a *necessary evil*.

In Sikhism, there is no place for euthanasia. The Sikh gurus set up hospitals and many Sikhs work in the caring services because of the duty of sewa (service to others). This means looking after and healing, not harming or ending life. Active euthanasia is wrong, it is killing. Any suffering may be seen as working through the negative karma of previous lifetime(s), so must be lived through, not avoided. A Sikh's duty when someone is dying is to care for them until God decides they die, not to hasten their death.

Task

1 With a partner, discuss whether the religion(s) you have studied would agree with euthanasia in these situations:
   - a man on life support in a persistent vegetative state
   - a man suffering horrendous terminal cancer pain
   - a woman with end-stage motor-neurone disease.
2 Read the information about the religion(s) you are studying. Explain what their attitude might be to: euthanasia, abortion, life support. Use religious teachings to support your explanation.

Religious beliefs about death and an afterlife

Death is when our brain and body stop functioning permanently. Religious people believe that at death the soul/spirit/self leaves the physical body. Beliefs about what happens to it vary from one religion to another, but all believe there is a continuation and some other kind of life.

Buddhism

Buddhists believe in rebirth. There is no permanent soul, rather a mix of ever-changing skandhas: emotions, feelings, intelligence and so on. After the death of the body, this mix fuses with an egg and sperm at conception. The thoughts, actions and intentions of each life shape the quality of the next. The goal is to achieve enlightenment and stop being reborn.

Hinduism

Hindus believe in reincarnation. Their atman (soul) lives through many lifetimes, each one shaped by the thoughts, words and actions of their past lifetime(s). The actions of each life result in consequences that can be experienced in the same life or future lives. Living a dharmic life does not generate new karma and builds good karma that eventually leads to liberation from the cycle of birth and death. Its goal is to achieve enlightenment and become one with the Ultimate Reality, so stopping being reincarnated.

Judaism

Judaism focuses on this life rather than the next. Some teachings mention a heavenly place. Jewish people talk of the 'world to come', which can refer to two things – firstly, the place souls go to after death and secondly, a Messianic Age when the world will be at peace. That is a form of life after death because there is an idea that the righteous dead will be 'woken' to live through that time.

Christianity

Christians believe in the physical resurrection of the body. At death, the body waits until Judgement Day. Catholics call this Purgatory. At judgement, each person faces God and Jesus to evaluate their deeds. If they were good in life, they go to heaven, which is paradise and wonderful forever. If they were bad, they go to hell for eternal punishment.

Islam

Muslims believe in resurrection. After death, the body waits in the grave (barzakh) and sees the events of its life. This can be quick or very slow and painful. On Judgement Day, people are sorted according to their beliefs and actions. The wicked are cast into hell; the truly good go to paradise across the As-Sirat bridge. A Hadith says that some will be transported across almost instantly, others will cross with some scratches, while some will fall into hell due to their evil deeds.

Sikhism

Sikhs believe in reincarnation. The soul is born into many lifetimes, whose quality is decided by the words, thoughts and deeds of the previous lifetime(s). The point of each life is to serve and worship God, so that eventually the soul can be reunited with God (waheguru) and stop being reincarnated.

Think about this statement: If I believe any of these to be true, how might that belief affect my behaviour now in this life?

Different beliefs

Abortion

Roman Catholicism

Roman Catholics believe that abortion is always wrong. They say **life is sacred** because it was created by God. They also believe that **life begins at conception**. This means life must be protected from conception, so any abortion is wrong. The Didache states **'Do not kill your children by abortion.'** Vatican II says **'Life must be protected with the utmost care from the moment of conception.'**

Anglicanism

Many Anglicans accept abortion as a necessary evil. For example, the mother's life may be at risk (e.g. ectopic pregnancy) – her life is also sacred.

Judaism

In Judaism, the life of the mother takes priority as hers is an actual life, whilst that of the foetus is only a potential life. Should there be any risk to her life, the principle of **pikuach nefesh** comes into play – an abortion should be carried out.

Islam

In Islam, abortion is frowned upon. Opinions vary on whether **ensoulment** (when the foetus acquires a soul) takes place at conception, at 40 days, or at 120 days. Before ensoulment, an abortion may be permitted.

Question

Explain two different beliefs from contemporary British society about abortion.

In your answer you should refer to the main religious tradition of Great Britain and one or more other religious traditions. *(4 marks)*

Euthanasia

Roman Catholicism

Roman Catholics believe that euthanasia, especially active euthanasia (where action is taken to end life directly), is always wrong. They say **life is sacred** because it was created by God. The Old Testament says **'I, your God, give life, and I take it away'**, which shows that no one else has the right to end life – so euthanasia must be wrong. Also the Ten Commandments clearly state **'Do not murder'**, and euthanasia would break this rule.

Dutch Protestant Church

The Dutch Protestant Church believes that all life is sacred. However, for those with terminal illness their life can become very undignified. In these cases, they believe **God wants Christians to help the person** from their suffering.

Christianity

Christians generally accept passive euthanasia (letting nature take its course), for example, switching off life support. This fits with the Old Testament teaching that **'There is a season for everything – a time to live and a time to die.'**

Judaism

In Judaism, euthanasia might be acceptable where it shortens the act of dying. So switching off life support would be acceptable in some cases. **'Anything that causes a hindrance to the departure of the soul is permissible to remove.'** (Rabbi Moses Isserles).

Question

Explain two different beliefs from contemporary British society about euthanasia.

In your answer you should refer to the main religious tradition of Great Britain and one or more other religious traditions. *(4 marks)*

Animal experimentation

Christianity

Some Christians think experiments on animals are wrong because God gave us **stewardship** over animals – the duty to look after them. Experimenting on them and causing them to suffer is not stewardship. Pope John Paul II declared **'We must abandon laboratories and factories of death'**, showing that laboratories for experimentation are simply places of death. Many Christians believe that testing such as for **cosmetics is cruel and unnecessary**, bringing suffering to God's wonderful creation, and going against St Francis of Assisi's teaching that **as part of the creation, animals deserve respect and protection**.

Roman Catholicism

The Roman Catholic Church accepts experiments on animals **'within reasonable limits'** and only if it is **'caring for or saving human lives'**. (Catechism of the Catholic Church).

Judaism

Judaism recognises the duty to **improve the welfare and well-being of humanity**. This includes improving medical science. Where experiments are for this purpose, and there is no other option, they would be acceptable as **human life has more value**.

Sikhism

Sikhism accepts experimentation which leads to improving human life. **Life is sacred**, and Sikhs have a **duty of service** (sewa) to others, so where **experiments advance medicine**, they are tolerated. Where experiments are repeating research already done, they are not acceptable.

Question

Explain two different beliefs from contemporary British society about animal experimentation.

In your answer you should refer to the main religious tradition of Great Britain and one or more other religious traditions. *(4 marks)*

Getting prepared

Four-mark AO1 Influence Questions

In your studies, it is not enough to only know and understand what religious people believe; you have to be able to write about how those religious beliefs and teachings affect the way believers act in our society today. The most obvious questions seeking this skill are 'influence' questions, and they are worth 4 marks each. You will have to answer one in each topic on the exam paper.

The crucial aspect of showing your understanding well is that you can explain beliefs and teachings in terms of the topic you are being asked about. So, for example, writing about abortion, you might use the teaching of 'Do not murder'. You could then go on to explain how that applies to the issue of abortion, and from there how that affects a person's decision about abortion. Where possible try to show how one teaching can be interpreted differently, depending on the circumstances; 'Do not murder' might seem to suggest abortion is always wrong, but what if the woman's life is at risk?

To answer these questions well you could use some key building blocks:

1 Know the key term and what it means.

2 Know the relevant beliefs and teachings which might be applied to this.

3 Know a general religious attitude to the term/issue.

Make sure you show how the beliefs and teachings actually influence the decisions made by the religious believer. That is the key element of the question. You could also combine the building blocks to show their influence.

The question might give you a belief/teaching to focus on in your answer. If it does this you must focus on that, or you will waste time. For example:

Explain two different beliefs in contemporary British society about abortion. In your answer you should refer to the main religious tradition of Great Britain and one or more other religious traditions.

If all you do is list some teachings (like compassion, and 'Do not murder'), you will limit your answer – so you have to make them relevant to abortion (showing how abortion could be seen as being compassionate).

You also have to present **different beliefs**, that is, show that the attitudes of religions vary to any one ethical issue. The specification names three specific topics for each Theme to be contrasted. Make sure you know different views to each of those.

For each question complete the chart provided opposite before writing a comprehensive answer.

Definition of term	Potential beliefs and teachings relevant to this	General attitude
Abortion is….	In ______, it says……	This means that Christians agree/disagree with _______ because…….

1 Explain two different beliefs in contemporary British society about abortion. *In your answer you should refer to the main religious tradition of Great Britain and one or more other religious traditions.*

2 Explain two different beliefs in contemporary British society about euthanasia. *In your answer you should refer to the main religious tradition of Great Britain and one or more other religious traditions.*

3 Explain two different beliefs in contemporary British society about animal experimentation. *In your answer you should refer to the main religious tradition of Great Britain and one or more other religious traditions.*

For Theme C, the 'In your answer…' part changes. It says '*In your answer you should refer to the main religious tradition of Great Britain and non-religious beliefs*.' You are expected to show a secular attitude – what a humanist or atheist might say as your different belief.

So what are the different/contrasting topics in each Theme?

Theme A	Theme B	Theme C	Theme D	Theme E	Theme F
Contraception	Abortion	Visions	Violence	Corporal punishment	Women
Sex before marriage	Euthanasia	Miracles	Weapons of Mass Destruction (WMD)	Death penalty	Wealth
Same-sex relationships	Animal experimentation	Nature as General revelation	Pacifism	Forgiveness	Freedom of religious expression

As you study these topics, pay particular attention, and make sure that you learn different/contrasting views on each – that will mean you can cope well in the exam whatever topic is chosen.

Religion and life glossary

Abortion deliberate expulsion of foetus from womb with the intention to destroy it

Afterlife beliefs about what happens after we die to our self/soul

Animal rights the idea that animals should have rights because of respect for life

Awe an overwhelming feeling often of reverence with a link to God

Big Bang theory the scientific view of the beginning of the universe

Charles Darwin the man who put forward the theory of evolution in the nineteenth century

Conception when the male sperm fertilises the female egg so allowing pregnancy

Conservation the practice of protecting, preserving, managing or restoring natural environments and the plants and animals that inhabit them

Creation idea that God created the world/universe from nothing

Dominion idea that humans have the right to control all of creation

Environment the world around us

Euthanasia mercy killing; ending life for someone who is terminally ill or has degenerative disease can be voluntary (a person deciding for themselves) or involuntary (being decided by others as the individual is incapable)

Evolution change in inherited traits in a species

Fossil fuels the earth's natural resources – coal, oil and gas

Hospice a place that cares for people who are dying usually from an incurable disease

Hypothesis a proposed explanation of something

Natural resources the resources the earth provides without the aid of humankind

Natural selection one of the basic mechanisms of evolution

Pesticide chemicals used to kills pests especially on crops

Pro-choice advocating for a woman's right to choose whether or not to have an abortion

Pro-life opposing abortion and euthanasia

Quality of life how good/comfortable life is

Right to die the belief that a human being should be able to control their own death

Sanctity of life the idea that life is special; life is created by God

Science knowledge coming from observed regularity in nature and experimentation

Stewardship duty to look after the world, and life

Sustainable energy resources that are renewable, for example, solar, wind and nuclear power

6 Theme C: The existence of God and revelation

Key elements of this theme

This theme is about God and experiencing God. It lets you consider some of the arguments for God's existence and whether they are effective arguments or not. It introduces you to how God is described (the nature of the divine), including some of the key terms used to describe aspects of God. It also takes a look at the concept of **revelation**, that is, how we might claim to see God directly and within the world, including whether what we think we have seen/experienced can be trusted. It is from this that we gain our ideas of the nature of God/the divine.

What is God like? What is your idea?

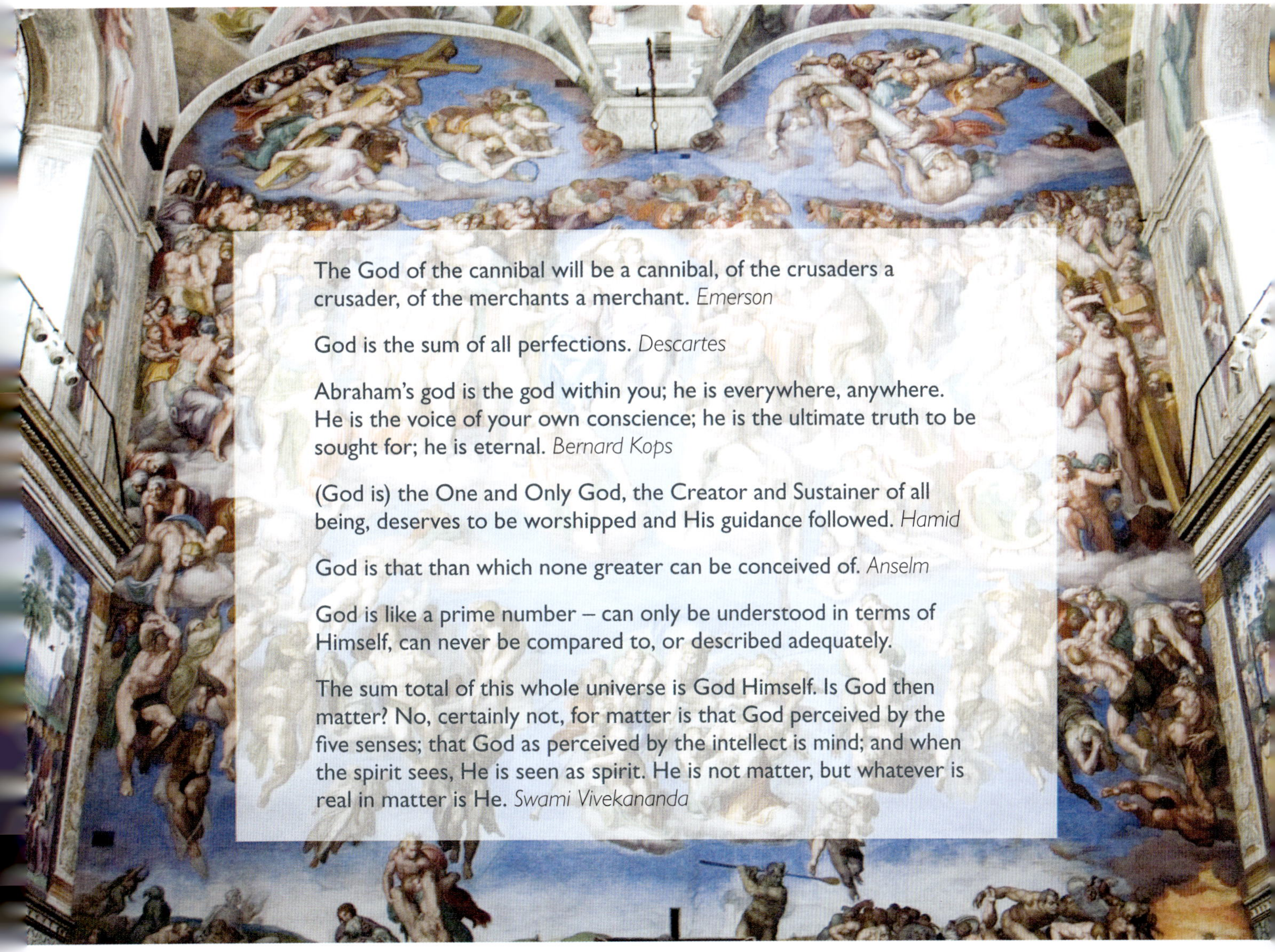

The God of the cannibal will be a cannibal, of the crusaders a crusader, of the merchants a merchant. *Emerson*

God is the sum of all perfections. *Descartes*

Abraham's god is the god within you; he is everywhere, anywhere. He is the voice of your own conscience; he is the ultimate truth to be sought for; he is eternal. *Bernard Kops*

(God is) the One and Only God, the Creator and Sustainer of all being, deserves to be worshipped and His guidance followed. *Hamid*

God is that than which none greater can be conceived of. *Anselm*

God is like a prime number – can only be understood in terms of Himself, can never be compared to, or described adequately.

The sum total of this whole universe is God Himself. Is God then matter? No, certainly not, for matter is that God perceived by the five senses; that God as perceived by the intellect is mind; and when the spirit sees, He is seen as spirit. He is not matter, but whatever is real in matter is He. *Swami Vivekananda*

Religious traditions of God

Religions have their own ideas about God and this is the key difference from which flow many other differences. On these pages we are looking at the idea of God as expressed differently in three religions.

Christianity

What do Christians believe about God?

The main belief of Christianity is that God expresses Himself in the form of the Trinity. This is One God, but three forms or persons. Forms or aspects are not individual gods. For Christians, God is One.

In the Apostles' Creed, we see an explanation of Christian belief. It includes descriptions of the three aspects of God: the Father, the Son and the Holy Spirit.

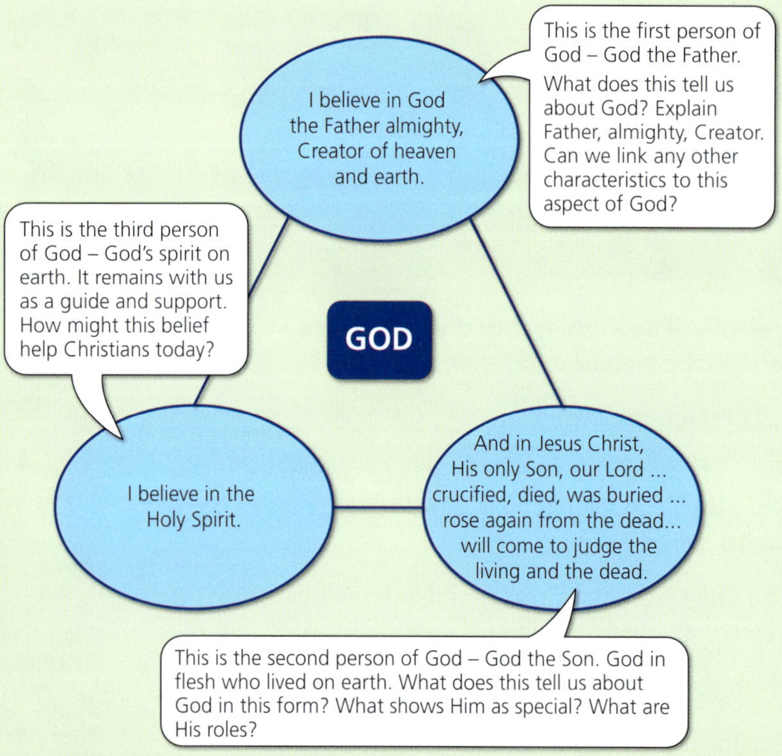

God is all three of these; they are all aspects of God. They each have different roles, but are still the same God. Think about yourself for a moment. Are you exactly the same when in school as you are when at home? What about when with friends? What about at a club you belong to? We have different personas for the different situations we are in. We can use this analogy to help us to understand the aspects of God. God expresses Himself in many ways but it is always the same God.

Islam

What do Muslims believe about God?

> 'Say He is Allah the One. Allah is eternal and absolute. None is born of Him, nor is He born. And there is none like Him.'
> *(Surah 112)*

One of the basic beliefs of Islam is **Tawhid**, that is, the Oneness of God. Allah is the name of God in Arabic and appears in Arabic language translations of the Bible. Muslims worship the same God that Abraham, Moses and Jesus worshipped. Allah cannot be split up in any way. Islam follows strict monotheism.

There are many names for Allah. The Qur'an lists 99 names, such as the merciful, the compassionate, the preserver. There is a story that there are 100 names, but only the camel knows the hundredth. It is just to show that we can never completely know Allah.

Allah is the Creator of the universe, and is all-powerful and all-knowing. Allah is eternal, He was never born and will never die. Allah does not change, because Allah is perfect. Allah guides us through the Qur'an and the prophets.

ॐ Hinduism

What do Hindus believe about God?

Hindus believe in the **Ultimate Reality**, which they call Brahman. Brahman is transcendental, eternal and unchanging. We cannot know Brahman, we can only know and understand ideas of Brahman.

Brahman manifests in three forms (the Trimurti). This lets us try to understand three of the major roles of God/Brahman. These are Brahma (Creator), Vishnu (Sustainer) and Shiva (Destroyer).

Brahma

Vishnu

Shiva

Hindus believe that the universe is in a continuous cycle of creation and destruction, then creation again. When it is time for the creation, Brahma has most influence and power, then Vishnu sustains the creation before Shiva is instrumental in the destruction. We can see this sharing of power on a lower level around us, for example, seeds grow into plants (creating), which live and flower/fruit (sustaining), and finally die (destruction), before rebirth after winter or through their seeds.

Hindus usually devote most of their worship to one of these three.

You may have seen statues or pictures of other gods. Ganesha, Lakshmi, Parvati, Durga are all children or consorts (partners) of the Trimurti. They are ways of relating and understanding the transcendental Brahman, through their manifestations in creation.

Try to imagine something that is beyond your senses and mind, for example electricity. You cannot *directly* see electricity, but you can see the *effects* of electricity through the name and form of the appliances, like the fridge which cools and the cooker which heats. Hindus have representations of the divine that express the Ultimate Brahman that is not available to us directly.

The Basics

1. Explain the idea of God in any religion.
2. Explain what it means to believe God has many forms, and why some believers find this helpful.
3. Explain why some religions say it is wrong to think of God in many forms.
4. **Humans could never understand God.** Explain reasons to agree and disagree with this statement.

One God – many gods – no God – aspects of God

If I believe in one God, I am a **theist**.

If I believe in many gods, I am a **polytheist**.

If I do not believe in God or gods, I am an **atheist**.

If I do not think it is possible to prove or disprove the existence of God, so am unsure, I am an **agnostic**.

Do not forget that some religions believe that one God can be split into different forms or aspects, for example, Hinduism and Christianity. Others, like Islam, believe there is only one God who cannot be broken into elements.

Read the following statements. Which definition word from the left is an appropriate label for each?

I believe there is a god for each one of us.

I do not know whether there is a God or not. Sometimes I think there is, other times I am sure there is not.

God is all around us, in everything.

You cannot prove God, so as far as I'm concerned there is not one.

When someone proves God exists, then I will believe.

A god of the moon, a god of the sun, a god of the trees – all forms of God.

God is a crutch for the weak to lean on.

God is here now.

God is nowhere.

There are different gods for every element of life.

So, I am an atheist – what does that mean?

To start with it means 'I believe there is no God'. It is a more definite attitude than 'I do not believe in God', because we can say we do not believe in something yet it may exist. An atheist will base their attitudes and actions on things other than God and an afterlife in which we can be rewarded/punished.

But isn't that a humanist?

Well, humanists also do not believe in a God. They see the universe and all of nature as totally without design or creator. Humanists trust **science** and can see how it is used to help our development. They believe in the fundamental value of each human and that we should make the most of the one life we have. We have the opportunity and responsibility to be decent human beings based on our ability to reason and empathise with others. Humans are the key, and what we can do to and for each other. There is no reliance on a divine being to get us out of trouble etc. So, you could say that being an atheist is actually a strand of being a humanist, but actually **humanism** is much more than just an idea about 'no God'.

Religious people follow rules set by God, because of what they believe will happen when they die. What motivation might humanists have for behaving in a positive way in life?

Is the motivation for humanists more effective than that for religious people in your opinion?

What explanation might humanists give for the stories of people meeting God, or seeing God through nature and the work of other people?

Interesting point to bear in mind …

Humanist opinion is a useful way to look at statements that you are asked to evaluate and argue. Do not forget to try to bring in the 'non-religious, but morally good' thinking of humanists.

Immanent or transcendent … or both!

Immanent

When talking about God, this means God is involved in His Creation, He is active in the world (**immanent**). This is possible because of God's almighty power. It is a sign of His love for us.

Why is God's immanence a sign of His love?

Jesus was an example of God's immanence. Jesus was God on earth, trying to show people the way to live and so to attain heaven. Jesus' ability to perform **miracles** was due to his divine status. This was God active in the world.

Find out about one of Jesus' miracles.

Many people believe that God makes things happen, which are naturally impossible, for the purpose of good. For example, a person is diagnosed with a brain tumour, which should kill them, yet it suddenly begins to shrink. When questioned, doctors can only say what it is doing (disappearing), not why. The person involved may see this as God's intervention.

Do you know of any stories of modern-day miracles?

Examples of people meeting God or having religious experiences are also examples of God's immanence. God has to be involved in the world to be able to let people experience Him.

Transcendent

When we talk about God as **transcendent**, we mean God is beyond this world and its limits. That does not mean God is far away, not in distance terms anyway. It means that God is distinct from the world. God is not controlled by time, so is eternal, never born and never to die. Nor is God limited by space, so He has no physical qualities.

What does this mean for any efforts to prove God exists by scientific means?

God does not need the world or rely on it, though the world needs and relies on God. This means that if God did not exist, then neither would we.

It also means that we cannot ever hope to understand God because God is beyond our limited intelligence, which is exactly what you would expect of the being that created the world. This is why some people claim that we should not try to understand why God allows evil and suffering – we simply cannot.

The Basics

1 What do immanent and transcendent mean?
2 Make a list of reasons why people might prefer God to be (a) immanent and (b) transcendent. What problems might each cause for religious believers? (Think of how people might feel, to help you answer these.)
3 Can God be both immanent and transcendent? Explain your answer.
4 Can a human have a meaningful relationship with either? Explain your answer.

Personal or impersonal

Personal

If you have a **personal** relationship with someone, what does that mean?

It is about being close, about knowing someone, being able to speak frankly with them and to confide in them. It is about knowing they are concerned for you and will listen to you.

When we say God is personal, we mean all those things about God. We can have a one-to-one relationship with God, and can experience God in our lives. We can each relate to God as a friend. God can have such a relationship with everybody at the same time because He is **omnipotent**.

In practical terms, what would this mean in the life of the believer?

It also means we can describe God in human terms, even though God is clearly beyond human comprehension. This is how we can call God Father, or speak of Him with human qualities (loving, forgiving and so on).

Do you know of any other such expressions for God?

Impersonal

When we use this term to describe God, we are saying that we cannot relate personally to God, because God is God. We can worship God, though, as a sign of our acceptance of God's superiority. We cannot describe God because our terms are inadequate for the vastness that is God. God is beyond our understanding.

Why might religious believers think this of God?

Impersonal also means that God is distant from us, because God is not like us in any way.

God's influence is on the world as a whole, not on our individual lives.

Does this explain why evil and suffering exist?

Task

1 You must learn these four words: transcendent, immanent, personal, impersonal. Can you spot which statement relates to each?
   a Mr Smith says God is beyond our understanding, because we are human.
   b This book says God is pre-existent – never born, never to die.
   c The vicar says God came to earth as Jesus to die for us.
   d She believes God is with her all the time, listening and concerned for her happiness.
2 Try to make up more sentences which demonstrate each of the four words.

The Basics

1 Explain the terms personal and impersonal.
2 Make a list of reasons why people might prefer God to be (a) personal and (b) impersonal. What problems might each cause for religious believers? (Think of how people might feel to help you answer these.)
3 Can a human have a meaningful relationship with a God described as either of these? Explain your answer.

Why the different ideas about God?

How people learn about God

If you belong to one religion and your friend belongs to another, it is likely you will have different ideas of what God is like. Look back to the page about ideas of God in three faiths (pages 296–297) to see. How do they differ?

What a person is taught in their places of worship, through holy books or teaching from religious leaders, will differ. For example, in the Qur'an, we see that Allah is totally beyond man's reach (transcendent). In the Christian faith, however, God is very much accessible (an immanent God).

You might also meet others who claim to have met God. They might show you a different idea of God to which you have no access through your own faith.

Probably your first impression of God comes from your parents. Upbringing is our number one influence.

How people experience God

People claim to have met God in various ways and at various times. This will affect their understanding of God.

If someone meets God when they are very unhappy (because of a tragic event, for example), they might feel that God is helping them through it. They might see God as a caring, loving figure, who is very much active in the world. That idea would help them through the difficult time, and encourage them to pray more often. On the other hand, if they have done something wrong, and they meet with difficulties in their life, they might see these as punishment from God. In this case, they might feel that God is like a judge, and to be feared, so they worship Him more strictly.

Can you think of any more examples?

Personal preferences

Maybe a person just prefers one idea about God to another.

They look around the world and see much suffering and evil. How do they reconcile this with the existence of the God they worship? They could say God is transcendent, because that helps with their dilemma. It makes the whole problem easier.

Alternatively, they might want to follow a God who is active in the world, so they do not feel alone. Even in the blackest hour, there is hope, because God is by their side.

Can you think of any more examples?

The Basics

1. In what ways do people find out about God? List them, and give examples to show your understanding.
2. Why might different people have different ideas of God?
3. **It does not matter if people have different ideas about God.** What is your opinion on this statement? Explain some reasons to agree and disagree with it.

Can we prove God exists?

When you have heard people say they 'believe in God', what do they mean? Is it that they believe God exists? Or that God will do something for them, or that God starts some religions, or is it something else? To 'believe in' God doing anything, means you believe God exists in the first place, so what they are saying is they *believe God exists*. Not everyone believes God exists, so what is it that has proved God's existence to some people and not to everyone? Any ideas?

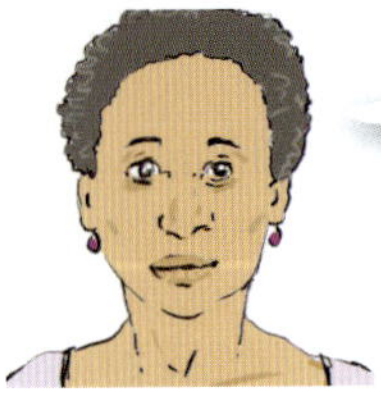

These five statements represent some reasons why people believe in God. Of course, people also believe because their parents, or some other significant person, told them God exists, or they believed what it said in a holy book. However, those reasons are not really useful to us as proofs. This course wants to know the 'proofs' of God's existence and whether they really are proofs or not.

The 'proofs' you are going to look at are summed up in the above statements. Can you can spot which is which?

- **Design argument** (**teleological argument**)
- **First Cause** argument
- argument from miracles

You are going to find out a bit more about each in this topic. You might be asked what the argument says, whose argument it is (because that helps you understand the way they thought), what is good about the argument (its strengths), and what is bad about it (its weaknesses).

Apart from saying what is wrong with the arguments, you also need to look at why people *do not* believe God exists. And lastly, the arguments you will meet are not the only arguments for God's existence, they are just the ones covered by this course.

The Basics

1. Can you think of some reasons why people believe God exists?
2. Can you think of some reasons why people believe God does not exist?
3. What are the three types of arguments for God's existence that the course covers?
4. Write a simple explanation of each type. You could use the statements to help you.

The Design argument (teleological argument)

1

This is **William Paley**. He said that the world itself was enough evidence of God's existence. It is too amazing to have just happened by chance.

Can you think of something amazing about the world? Why is that amazing?

2

Paley used the example of a watch. He said that if you found one, you would know it was human-made, even if you did not know what it was. Unlike the stone, it would be obvious that the watch did not get there by chance as it shows such evident signs of design.

Look at this object. What is it? Has it got a purpose that you can recognise? Is it human-made or natural? How can you tell?

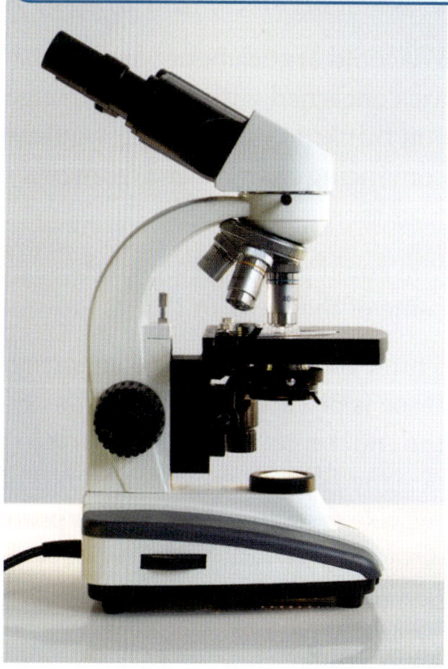

You probably said that that object was not natural. Even if you do not know what it is, it is human-made. We can tell that things were deliberately made because they obviously have some sort of use and purpose.

3

Paley said that the world is like that watch, or the object you just looked at. There is a difference though: he said the world is even more obviously designed.

4

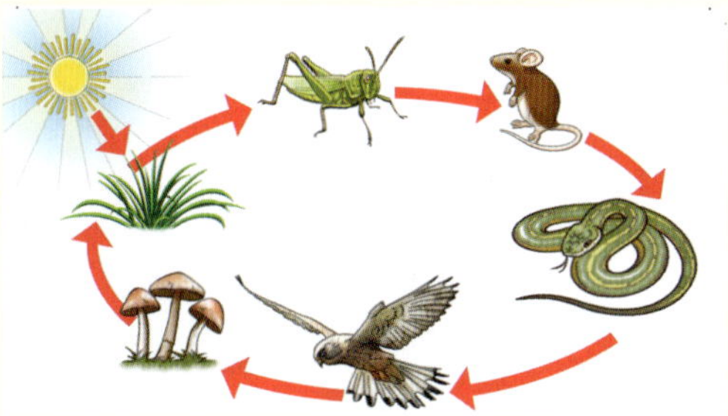

There are many patterns in nature, for example, food chains, the seasons.

5 There are so many unique things, for example, each one of us, our iris pattern, our fingerprints, our DNA.

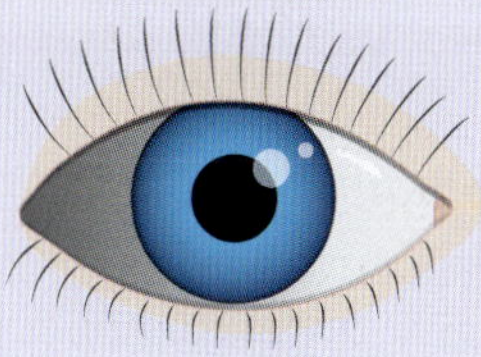

6

So many things seem perfectly suited to their environment, like polar bears, which have special fur and an extra layer of fat to keep them warm.

7 Paley said that all these things are too amazing to have come about by chance. Something or someone must have thought about it all, and deliberately made it all. That someone must have been God.

Doubts about the Design argument

Answer these questions before you read on:

1 *Outline Paley's Design argument for the existence of God.*

2 *Is that argument convincing to you? Explain your answer.*

We could argue about whether the world does look designed. Here we are concerned with what is wrong with the argument itself. What do you think? Is this a strong argument? Does it convince you? Is it more convincing than other arguments such as First Cause when you read them?

You could get asked any of those questions, so you need to find out some of the flaws in Paley's argument to support your answer to them.

Think about what he is comparing at first: a stone and a watch. The stone is discarded because it has no design, but the watch has. Then at the end, he compares the watch to the world by saying the watch is designed, but the world is even more obviously designed. That's great, it makes sense, but could it be a proof? Small question – is the stone (not designed) part of the world (very designed)? So, should it not also show design? It sounds like he changed the rules in the middle of his argument.

Something else – just because something looks designed, does that guarantee that it really was designed? Penicillin, which is brilliant as a medicine, was discovered by accident. The person who made Post-its© was trying to invent a glue which bonded two sides forever and never came unstuck! So, things that look designed might not have been intentionally designed.

Further consideration might lead to these ideas. Perhaps God just designed the world, meaning He may no longer exist. Also our world could just have been one of many different designs. Looking at the world, there are many reasons to suggest that God's design of this world wasn't as perfect as Paley claimed.

Person profile

The most famous person to use the argument of design to prove God's existence was William Paley. He was an eighteenth-century archdeacon in Carlisle. He wrote many books, including *Natural Theology*, which contains his 'proof'. His argument followed the process described on these pages. It is basically saying the world looks designed, so it must have been and that God was the designer.

The Basics

1 Explain some of the problems with Paley's argument.
2 Do you think the problems make his argument weaker? Is it still as convincing as it was to you before you explored its problems? Explain your answer.

Tasks

1 Find out about other Design arguments, for example, Newton talked about the design of the thumb being proof enough for him.
2 Find out what 'teleological' means.

The First Cause argument

Person profile

St **Thomas Aquinas** was a Christian monk, who lived from 1225 to 1274CE. He wrote several books, including *Summa Theologica*, which gave his proofs of God's existence. He spoke of five different proofs. The second is about God being the Uncaused Cause, the First Cause of everything else. So, according to Aquinas (using the steps of the argument on this page) God was the cause of the universe. However, Aquinas, being a monk, could be accused of bias; of course his solution to any question about the cause of the universe would be God – it is his job to say that.

Aquinas' argument

Step 1 – We can use the idea of a row of dominoes. Why do they fall? If nothing pushes them or acts on them to make them fall, will they ever fall? Now, think about the world around you and all the things in it. What causes each thing? Can you think of anything which is not caused by something else? Anything that is totally independent, not relying on something else for its existence?

Step 2 – Bet you could not think of anything. It seems that everything relies on something else so that it can exist, or be. For example, that row of dominoes does not just fall over; something has to make the first domino move, so that the whole chain of dominoes falls in a sequence. Usually someone pushed it.

Step 3 – So, we have to accept everything is caused by something else. But, how did the universe start? It had a beginning, it did not cause itself, so what caused it?

Step 4 – So if there was a beginning to the universe, we have to have something to start it all off. That something had to be Uncaused – had to just exist. At some point in the history of the universe there had to be something which is not caused by anything else – an Uncaused Cause, Aquinas called it. Can you guess?

Step 5 – Some people say it was God. Thomas Aquinas said *everyone* did (but then he was a monk, so we should expect that).

Some might say: 'Of course, it is the Big Bang! The Big Bang is the First Cause.' But, then the question is 'what caused the Big Bang?' Do you think it might have been God?

Task

Research Aquinas, and try to find out the other 'ways' he used to prove God exists.

The Basics

1. In your own words, explain the idea of God as First Cause. You could use the domino idea to help you explain.
2. Do you think Aquinas is right to say 'everyone believes the Uncaused Cause to be God'? Explain your answer.
3. Can you think of anything else that might be the First Cause other than God?
4. How convincing an argument for God's existence is this for you? Explain your answer.

The trouble with Thomas Aquinas

You need to consider some of the weaknesses in the arguments for the existence of God.

Can you see any flaws in it? Remember Thomas Aquinas was writing hundreds of years before the internet and modern science. Also remember he was a monk, so more inclined to believe in what the Bible said and see God as the explanation for the universe.

Use these clues to work out some of the bigger problems with his argument:

a Who does he say believes the Uncaused Cause to be God? Is that realistic?

b How does he know *everything* is caused by something else? What would be his evidence?

c What is his God like? What does the God in this argument do and does that sound like the Christian God?

There are other problems, such as whether Thomas Aquinas was biased and so assumed certain things because of that.

Referring to clue a, do you really think Aquinas could have asked everybody if they agreed with him? Hundreds of years ago there were no phones or internet. Even if he asked something totally obvious like *do you think water is wet?*, he cannot really say everyone says *yes*, because he cannot ask everyone. He is making a claim, which he cannot prove.

There is a similar problem in clue b. Can anyone – in their entire life, doing nothing but study – be sure they have seen everything in existence? If he hasn't seen everything, how can he claim everything has been caused by something else? It is another claim he cannot prove.

What about clue c? His God causes the world – that is it. He could have just caused the universe and then ceased to exist. He might have caused an imperfect universe and not have been able to fix it. Or He could have deliberately caused evil. This God only has one role to cause everything, which is a problem, because it leaves too many unanswered questions.

A word about *problems* in philosophy

You are going to see the word *problem* lots of times in this course. You just need to be sure you understand what it means in 'philosophy-speak'. It is not like a health problem, or a problem between people or a maths problem. It is one of those times where you say 'Yes, but …' and pose a difficult question for the person who is trying to explain something to you. You will have done it with your parents, or with your teachers. And when they cannot answer, we usually feel quite proud of ourselves! In this course, the *problems* are usually questions which challenge an argument or challenge belief. You must be able to talk about the problems (the flaws) in all the philosophy we cover, because that is part of the course.

The Basics

1. What do we mean by *problems* in philosophy?
2. What problems are there with Aquinas' First Cause argument?
3. Do you think the problems make his argument weaker? Is it still as convincing as it was to you? Explain your answer.

Miracles

Many people believe that God reveals Himself through miracles. They say God makes miracles happen, and the miracle is the proof God exists. The miracle is an example of God reaching into our world to help us. Religions are full of stories of miracles. Miracles can confirm what someone already believes, like a proof for their faith. They can also make someone believe in God; the trigger for belief. Without God there are no miracles.

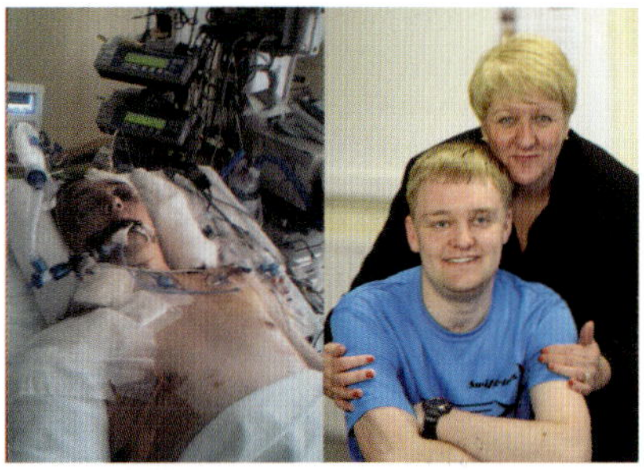

Brought back from death

The name of God in Arabic was spelled out in seeds inside an aubergine

Every single person survived

On 21 September 1995, hundreds of *murtis* (statues) of Lord Ganesh were reported to be drinking unlimited quantities of milk. Individual *murtis* case-tested by leading journalists from around the world were found to be drinking milk

These events have all been called miracles. What is a miracle? From the images above, how can you explain the idea of a miracle?

Choose the appropriate word from each pair below:

- expected/unexpected
- possible/impossible
- bad/good
- disaster/saving
- people/God

(You probably picked the second word of each pair – most people would. Can you explain why you picked each one?)

An 'act of God' means God did it. Many religious people believe God is immanent and that He interferes in our world through events like miracles. So, the family whose house is destroyed by a tornado whilst they sleep on is protected by an act of God.

When we say miracles go against what we understand of nature, we mean they seem impossible, like they should not have happened. If the doctors say someone is dying, with no cure, but they live, that is against nature.

Miracles are always good. God uses His power (omnipotence) to help because of His love for us (benevolence). You would not call a plane crash in which everyone dies 'a miracle'. But you would if anyone survived, and you might even say God helped them.

Miracles are often very personal. People see the miracle as God showing Himself to them by acting in their life for their good. For example, if I believe I have been blessed with amazing luck, I might believe that luck came from God for me personally. This miracle has proved to me God exists and it does not matter what anyone else says, I believe in God.

The Basics

1 Explain what a miracle is.
2 Give three different examples of a 'miracle'.
3 How does a miracle prove God exists?
4 If you recovered from a serious illness that should have killed you, would you think it was a miracle? Explain your answer.

Evil and suffering as an argument against God's existence

If we read the news, we might see a number of terrible events. Some are clearly caused by humans; others are definitely part of nature.

Take a look at these headlines – which ones are the fault of humans, and which ones of nature?

ANOTHER COLLEGE SHOOTING LEAVES THIRTY-FOUR DEAD

Man jailed for torture and murder of his own baby

Religious extremists bomb tourist paradise

Hurricane Joe devastates Haiti – thousands missing

Tsunami death toll hits 9,000

Crop failure due to drought – a country starves

It is a fact of our lives that every day we are confronted with new stories of suffering where people have to endure mental, emotional or physical pain because of something that has happened. We also experience suffering personally. Suffering is a very real part of our world, which we cannot deny and which makes our lives more difficult on a number of levels.

Religious believers believe God has the following qualities:

- God is **omniscient** – He knows all there is to know, and all that can be known.
- God is all-loving – He loves each and every human as an individual and without reserve. Christians believe He even came to earth as a human and died in order to make it possible for humans to enter heaven.
- God is omnipotent – He is all-powerful and can do anything. This is how it was possible for God to create the world and all in it.

Does the amount of evil and suffering prove there is no God? For many people it is obvious they know there is suffering as they see examples all the time. However, God is part of a *belief system*, and beliefs are not proven, so God may not be real. Many Christians struggle to explain why God seems to allow evil and suffering to exist, and this is a problem for their faith.

I see evil and suffering in the news all the time. Sorry to those that believe, but for me it proves there is no such thing as God. A loving, powerful God just wouldn't let so much of it happen.

If God really loved us, God would use His power to make our world kinder and safer. After all, God must know about everything that is happening, and must know how to fix it. That God doesn't fix the mess, to me, proves God is either not loving or powerful, or simply doesn't exist.

I lost all belief in God when my mum died. She had given her life to her religion, brought her kids up in it, done loads of charity work – a genuinely good person. She died horribly in extreme pain, ravaged by cancer. What kind of a God does that to His own?

Task

Look back to pages 7–8 of Christianity where you can read how Christians try to resolve this problem.

The Basics

1. What is meant by evil and suffering? Give examples.
2. Explain why the existence of evil and suffering makes some people not believe in God.
3. **God must not exist because of the suffering in the world.** Do you agree with this statement? Explain your ideas.

Science as proof that God does not exist

Many people believe in science, and that science answers all the questions we have. Or that if it does not right now, it will at some point in the future. There is no need to believe in God.

Hundreds of years ago people didn't have the scientific knowledge we have now. I'm not surprised they believed in religion – it gave them answers to questions they puzzled over. But nowadays, we do not need to rely on a mystery being – we know how things work because science tells us.

I know religious people believe God made the world, but to me I look at scientific answers. The Big Bang theory may only be a theory, but there is a lot of evidence. It makes more sense to me than some ultimate being. Science has evidence – I can relate to and rely on that; religion doesn't.

Some people say God must exist because if he didn't neither would we. They say the Big Bang was caused and controlled by God, that the conditions which made it happen, and the conditions caused by it (temperature of blast, distance from sun, and so on) are so precise, they had to be deliberately created. I just think we are here and asking questions because we are here – one big, lucky fluke, not God. So be a nice person and get on with it!

When I prayed, nothing happened – I didn't get better. When I went to the doctor and got checked out, he gave me medicine – I got better. Science works, religion doesn't. Science is real, religion not.

It is clear that for these people, science is more important and more realistic to them than religion.

Many religious people also believe very strongly in science; there are many religious scientists. For these people, science is how God works in the world, or is a description of God's natural law (which we are still learning about). To them, scientific advances just add to the glory of God.

The Basics

1 Explain why some people believe science disproves God's existence.
2 **It is impossible to believe in both science and religion.** Refer to pages 259 and 265 in Theme B to help you argue for and against this statement. Explain your points.

Buddhism

Buddhism aligns with science in teaching that something can be said to be 'true' when it has been proven through rational thinking, reasoning and experience. From this, Buddhists believe that no creator God has been proven to exist, having not been experienced through meditation. There are references to deities in Buddhist teaching and stories, but these are not the idea of God met in the Western faiths.

General and special revelation

Many people say they will only believe in God when they meet God. Maybe you are one of them. Think about this though: if you met God, could you prove it?

Could you prove it to yourself or anyone else? Would you later dismiss it as an **illusion** or something other than God?

Revelation is when God reveals Himself, so that humans can know something about God. There are two kinds:

Special revelation

Direct revelation, God communicating directly with you (as an individual or a group). For example, talking to you in a dream, hearing His voice whilst you are praying.

General revelation

Indirect revelation, God revealing something of Himself through other things, for example, nature, people, events. You interpret what you see as being linked with God, and this leads you to say you have experienced God. Your interpretation is based on a feeling.

Learn these terms. You may be asked to explain them.

Try to guess some of the questions we can ask about revelation. Then as we look at some examples of different types of revelation, we can keep those questions in mind. Philosophy is about those questions and our efforts to find solutions.

Sort these questions into the ones which apply to **special revelation**, and those which apply to **general revelation**. Some might apply to both.

- Where is the concrete proof that this really happened?
- Can you believe someone who already believes in God?
- Are our feelings and interpretations always right?
- Is there any other explanation?
- Does a particular place or context make us see things in a certain way?

Try to answer some of the questions.

Special revelation

Special revelation is a direct revelation. God comes directly to the person involved and makes Himself known. It is not that we guessed God did something, like cure someone because we prayed for it. It is that God spoke directly to a person. The event can have a massive impact on the life of that person. Unfortunately, there is no scientific evidence of this experience being true that we can show to someone else, or even to ourselves. We cannot prove it was real by using science or forensics. How can we show it was real?

If we cannot prove God by scientific means, we will not be able to prove that someone did meet God. All we can do is listen to their account of what happened and judge the impact it had on them. Then we have to decide if we believe that they met God or not, and from that, whether or not we can say God exists.

Let's look at the example of St Paul from Christianity:

1 Saul was a Jewish man, who rounded up Christians to be executed as blasphemers against the Jewish faith.

2 On his way to Damascus, he was blinded by a light which only he could see, and from which came Jesus' voice 'Saul, why do you persecute me?'

3 For three days he was blind, then a Christian came to cure him, saying 'God has sent me to give you back your sight.'

4 He immediately became a Christian, changing his name to Paul. He travelled around the Mediterranean spreading the message of Christianity: 'I speak to you of Jesus Chris, Son of God.' His teachings form the basis of much of the Christian faith.

We can say that Saul became enlightened through this experience; he learned religious truths through it, which then changed his life. He was also the beneficiary of a miracle: his blindness was cured. To be enlightened is to have a new understanding or insight. In religions, we are always talking about religious understanding. For some religions, for example, Buddhism, Hinduism and Sikhism, the aim of religious study is enlightenment; to truly understand the nature of things. Achieving enlightenment in Hinduism and Sikhism means to be reunited with God; it brings revelation and knowledge.

You may need to be able to describe special revelations from each of two religious traditions. There is another example on the next page. When you read such examples, think about the impact they had on the person involved. What difference did it make to their lives?

More about special revelation

1 Muhammad ﷺ was a business man. He would go to a cave in the hills to pray and to think about life.

2 On one of these visits, he was met by a huge man who ordered him to read.

3 Muhammad ﷺ could not read, but the man grabbed him and squeezed him tightly, and again ordered him to read.

4 This happened three times. At the last, Muhammad ﷺ read – as if the words were burnt onto his heart, and he knew them already.

5 The man was Archangel Gabriel (Jibril in Arabic), and he told Muhammad ﷺ that Allah (God) had chosen him as a prophet (the final prophet) of Islam.

If you had been either St Paul or Muhammad ﷺ, what would you have believed had happened? Explain why.

Do you think that this type of direct experience is the best evidence for God's existence? Explain your view.

When someone has a direct special revelation, they feel they have met God in some direct, clear way. Maybe they have spoken to God, maybe they have heard God, or felt God's presence. Whatever happened, they are convinced this was God, and they know God through this meeting. These experiences can be life-changing. In the two cases you have just read, the lives of both men completely changed, and they put their own lives at risk many times because of their new beliefs.

Can we prove what happened though? To ourselves? To anyone else? That is a problem. But, why would anyone lie about these experiences? Would you tell anyone if you had such an experience? If not, why not? It is a big deal to describe these experiences to anyone because of how sceptical we all are.

But then again, fame, popularity, money: all of these are enough to encourage some people to lie, or see things that happen to them in a certain way. So maybe some of these experiences are 'invented'.

Also, can we trust people who believe in God already? Do they expect it to be God, so are biased and unconsciously invent these experiences? There is always the fact that our senses can be deceived by many things, for example, drink and drugs, tiredness, illness.

Tasks

1. Research one or both of the examples of direct revelation discussed here. Think about how it was not easy for either man to make or stick to these changes to their lives.
2. Find out some other examples of people who have claimed to have met God.

The Basics

1. Define revelation.
2. What is the difference between general revelation and special revelation?
3. Write accounts of two direct revelations of God and state which religious tradition each comes from.
4. What problems can you find with the idea of direct revelation?
5. **We should always believe it when someone says God spoke to them.** Do you agree? Explain the reasons for your answer.

Enlightenment as a source of knowledge about the divine

Enlightenment means *awakened*. It is a term used to describe a person who has come to understand religious truths. The course wants you to know how enlightenment helps believers know, and perhaps understand, the nature of God or the divine. It is a term used mainly in eastern religions, such as Buddhism and Hinduism, although the religious study by Orthodox Jews is also designed to gain a similar insight.

Buddhism began through the enlightenment of the Buddha, so enlightenment is crucial to the religion, and is an aim of all Buddhists. The Buddha's was a complete enlightenment, so that he understood the true nature of everything. These are the key points of his enlightenment:

1 The Buddha sat beneath a Bodhi tree and made a commitment to meditate until enlightened.

2 He was visited, tempted and threatened by the demon Mara along with Mara's daughters and armies, to stop him from meditating.

3 The Buddha called to the earth as a witness that he was ready for enlightenment and was able to see all his past lives (as human and animal) in evidence that he was fit for this step forward in his spiritual nature.

4 He finally understood the true nature of all things and of suffering, and how suffering could be ended. This meant he was fully enlightened.

Believers are realistic enough to realise that it takes much to achieve full enlightenment (for the Buddha, thousands of lifetimes). Most of them aim to achieve lesser levels of enlightenment. Imagine standing behind a wall. A small hole gives a glimpse of what is behind: this is like a partial enlightenment. Destroying the whole wall to get the full view and so properly understand, would be like full enlightenment.

Religious believers can study and learn about God, and the insight they gain from their study, meditation and worship may give them an insight (a partial enlightenment, or an insight into a religious truth). From this they understand more about God and the nature of the divine. All Hindus believe that the real purpose of life is to gain liberation from the cycles of birth and death. The way in which this is to be attained is to follow the path of dharma in each stage of one's life, doing one's duty according to the roles one has. Then through deep devotion and meditation, one realises the true nature of the divine and hence attains enlightenment. There are clear instructions in the scriptures about the attainment of enlightenment. Some Hindus devote their whole lives to the study of the divine through their holy books, and enlightenment is seen as the main aim of life. Hinduism splits life into four Ashramas (age-based life stages) – the first is that of student, where the beginnings of studying sacred texts happens, whilst the last two are focused entirely on religious study and the pursuit of enlightenment. In Hinduism, enlightenment leads to moksha which is a complete release from reincarnation and reunion with the divine.

The Basics

1 What is meant by the term 'enlightenment'?
2 What do religious believers hope to gain from enlightenment?
3 **Religious believers should make it a priority to gain enlightenment.** Do you agree with this statement? Explain your arguments.

General revelation – knowing God ... through nature

Nature is beautiful.

Nature is complicated.

Nature is clever.

It seems that there is design and purpose in nature.

These ideas provoke a sense of awe and wonder in many people.

Make a list of examples of how nature is each of these things.

Many people would say that the sense of awe and wonder they feel when experiencing nature is a sense of the divine on earth. It could be seen as evidence that God is immanent, because God is visible through His creation, or in the workings of His creation. This idea can be difficult to understand. Let's explain it in a different way. If you like art or music or film or books, you may like a particular person's work. There is something about their style that draws you to them. Even when you have not heard or seen or read their latest work, you might buy it. You can also recognise their work, because of the style. When you get used to their style, you may feel it tells you something about them as a person; their thoughts or feelings. *Can you think of any examples of this?*

This is very much how some people see the world. It is God's creation, and so is full of hints about God. Generally speaking, the world and nature are good, so God is good. The elements of the world, although we try to use the ideas and imitate them, are vastly greater than those we could devise. We could, therefore, say that God is much wiser, cleverer and more powerful than we are.

Can I prove that whatever I feel is the correct interpretation of what I see? Can I use it to prove God's existence to anyone else? In other words, is it real or illusion?

The Basics

1 How can we know God through nature? Give examples to support the points you make.
2 How strong a proof is nature for God's existence? Explain your answer.
3 How strong a proof is this for God? Could we ever prove it was real (or illusion)?

General revelation … through holy books, scripture and religious writings

The Basics

1 What are holy books and religious teachings? Give examples of each.
2 What can we learn of God from these? Give examples.
3 How useful is either in helping us to know about God? How well can we know God through these?

Holy books (scripture)

What do we learn about God from holy books?

The Qur'an gives 99 names for Allah. The Bible describes God in many ways.

The Torah gives 613 mitzvot (laws). Qur'anic law forms the basis of Shari'ah (Islamic law).

The Old and New Testaments mention God in historical events.

The holy books are all about God, but these three elements stand out: what God is like, how God has acted in the history of the world to influence it, and how God wants us to live our lives.

We can look at holy books in many different ways. Indeed, their believers make different claims for them. The way we view a holy book will decide how closely we follow it, how we treat it, and how we understand what it tells us about God. If I take a book literally, for example, I believe every word to be accurate, so my God will be exactly as described.

Religious writings

How are these different from holy books?

They are the writings of religious people to explain what is written in the holy books, or their own experiences of God, or the teachings of their religious tradition.

Do we really need people to do this for us?

Perhaps the most famous religious leader in the world is the Pope. As head of the Catholic Church, every Pope has written papers about Church teaching. They are also said to be speaking the infallible word of God when speaking '*ex cathedra*'. Roman Catholics look to the teachings of the Pope for guidance in their religious lives.

The Dalai Lama, leader of the Tibetan Buddhist faith, is respected worldwide. He has written and published many books which try to put ancient Buddhist teachings into modern language, to make them accessible and readable for the West. One of his books, *Ancient Wisdom, Modern World* was top of the bestseller list for many weeks.

The value of revelation

Special revelation, general revelation – what is the value of either?

Read the following statements and make a list of all the ideas they give you about why revelation is important and valuable.

Shaun

I had a religious experience – I saw God in a ***vision****. I now have absolute proof that God exists and that I am right to live my life by following a religious code. It has given me the strength to keep living that way, even when I meet difficulties – as if that experience is my protection and security.*

Narindar

I am aware of God often every day. God's presence is in everything all the time. I try to link everything to God – my thoughts are on God, and my actions devoted to God. Through this I feel comforted and protected.

Jacob

Through the scriptures, I learn about G-d. They give me insight into G-d's nature and what G-d wants from me. The rabbis of old explained the scriptures, and these religious writings, like the Talmud, help me to understand more clearly and deeply. By understanding these, I can live more closely following my faith – I get it right and that is important.

Helen

The beauty of nature reassures me that God is immanent, and that the world is a wonderful creation. This has encouraged me to be more aware and active in environmental work.

Djimi

Prophet Muhammad ﷺ received the Qur'an through revelations. That has given us our religion. Without the revelations, we would not know about Allah or how we have to act in Allah's world – they were crucial to starting our religion, and are crucial in knowing how to secure a place in paradise in the afterlife.

Megan

I am studying for a PhD which focuses on some religious writers of the Middle Ages. These people claimed to have had revelations, and the truths they learnt through those revelations are given in their work. The revelations are important because they educate other people through them.

There are many reasons why revelations are important. Perhaps the single most important is that most religions are based on one or more revelations; they are central to a religion. For an individual, perhaps the most important factor is that they confirm their faith and they provide personal proof of what they believe in, often against a context of many reasons not to believe.

The Basics

1. Explain why revelation is valuable.
2. Do you think special revelation is more important than general revelation? Explain your reasons.

The problem of revelation

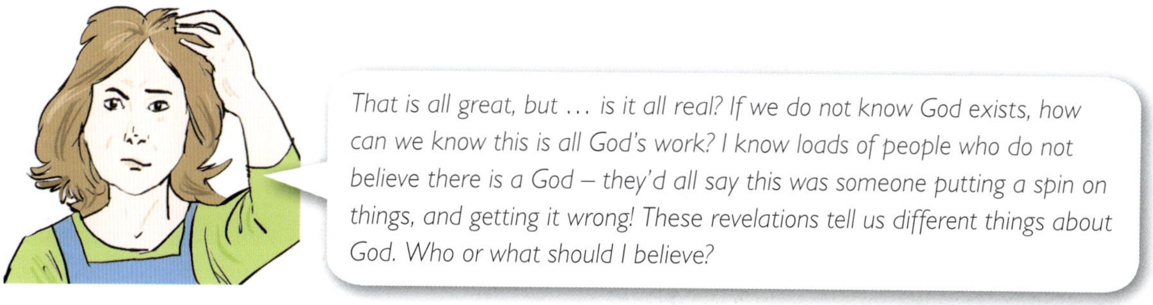

That is a valid point. Is it all **real** or just an **illusion**?

The big question is whether people have really met God, or have just imagined it. **Reality** is what has really happened, you existing is a reality. Illusion is a false or misleading perception, you think you saw a leprechaun in your garden, for example.

Some people say religious experiences are real. Some people say religious experiences are illusions. Some say they can be either and it all depends on the person and the circumstances.

If someone does not believe in God, they will think all religious experiences are illusion. You cannot meet something that does not exist. These people say there is no proof of God. They also say there is no proof of the experience, it is just what someone says. That person could be mistaken or ill, or deliberately lying. They could make themselves believe something that was not real, because they are so desperate to see God. They might interpret something as God that was not, like if someone was very ill but got better. They would see that as God, but the atheist would not. There is no proof of either, in spite of how strongly convinced they each may be. That is the big problem with religious experiences: they cannot be proved, they can only be persuasive.

Can you work out why each of the characters in the image might be disbelieved if they said God revealed Himself to them? Whilst most people claiming to have met God are not these characters, the reasons you gave for not believing the characters on this page are routinely used against perfectly ordinary people who make the same claims.

What about general revelation? There is even less evidence of that; everything is an interpretation. I might be convinced that God exists because I read a holy book, but was I really reading God's words (so having a revelation)?

For the individual, a special revelation is strong evidence, and general revelation may be less so, although many millions follow religions based on revelations, so maybe we can say this is strong enough evidence.

The person who has the experience might be convinced that it was God, even if they cannot prove it. We trust our own instincts and feelings. We cannot prove them to anyone else. We might be able to persuade someone else that we met God because of what we say. To the person meeting God, their experience is real; others might see it as an illusion.

Thinking about revelation

You have seen a range of examples of special and general revelation. These all tell us some things about God and that we can know God.

Are we really seeing God or are we deluding ourselves? Can we explain religious experiences in any way other than God? If God is transcendent, can we expect to meet Him? If we can meet God does that mean He cannot be impersonal?

This page is designed to get you thinking about these questions. Look upon it as a sort of brain aerobics session!

I had been reading all about Saul, and later God came to me.

Choose the simplest answer and that's usually true.

I only trust my gut instincts.

I'd believe anything she told me.

Do you know anyone? Really know them? How can you justify that answer?

Do you think you could 'really know' God? Explain yourself.

How well can you know God? What makes it difficult?

Are revelations real or illusion? Which types of revelation are more likely to be real? Why?

If I cannot prove a revelation happened, did it happen at all?

If I am religious, can you trust what I claim to have seen?

Why do different people have different ideas about God?

Does accepting that revelations are real lead to any problems for believers?

Why do believers have different ideas about God?

There's got to be another answer.

When I meet God, I'll believe in God.

If God's not physical, can we prove God?

How well do you know yourself? Do you really know how you'd respond in every situation?

If a tree falls in a forest, and no one hears it fall, and no recording is made, does it still make a sound?

She's my best friend. We went to primary school together.

The Basics

1. Explain what we mean by 'real' and 'illusion'.
2. What other explanations could someone give for a 'religious experience' other than God?
3. **God is an illusion.** Do you agree? Explain reasons to agree and disagree with this statement.
4. **'As revelation is based on belief, it will always be subject to doubt.'** Do you agree with that statement?

Different beliefs

Visions

Christianity

Visions are a **form of revelation** from God, allowing humans to **better understand God and have a relationship with God**. Many Christians have written about their revelation, and gave insight because of it, for example, St Teresa of Avila (sixteenth-century nun), Bernadette Soubirous (twentieth century), and Fred Ferrari (twenty-first century). Christians believe **God speaks to humans directly** through these revelations, telling them religious truths, and helping them understand His wishes. The vision often has a **profound impact on their lives, causing great change**, so for example Fred Ferrari became an evangelical Christian, having been a dangerous criminal.

Atheism

Atheists might see these experiences as **hallucinatory**. They believe there is **no God, and so there can be no source for the revelation** other than our own brain.

Humanism

Humanism takes a non-theistic stance, and does not look for supernatural explanations for events. A vision may be caused by hallucination, illness, drugs, or many other reasons – but not a divine being.

Islam

In Islam, **Allah does not reveal Himself directly to humans**. It would be impossible for humans to be able to look upon Allah. Any message has been sent through the medium of an angel.

Question

Explain two different beliefs from contemporary British society about visions.

In your answer you should refer to the main religious tradition of Great Britain and one or more other religious traditions. *(4 marks)*

Miracles

Christianity

Christianity has recorded many miracles, **where God has intervened in His creation to make something good happen, often healing** the incurable. Mother Teresa was a Christian nun who devoted her life to helping the needy in Calcutta. On the **first anniversary of Mother Teresa's death**, a non-Christian Indian woman was **cured of a huge abdominal tumour** – it simply disappeared over night as she slept. Members of the Missionaries of Charity had **prayed to Mother Teresa** for this cure. The belief is that the prayers showed the necessary faith to allow Mother Teresa's soul to bring God's power to this problem. Doctors have been unable to find any other explanation.

Atheism

An atheist would **dispute that God performs miracles**, as (to them) **God does not exist**. They might see this event as **something which can occur naturally (spontaneous regression**) though is not yet understood by medical science.

Humanism

A humanist would look to a **non-supernatural answer** for this event. They can show that events previously classed as miracles are now **explainable through medical science**, and that those calling them miracles already had a **religious bias** to affect them.

Question

Explain two different beliefs from contemporary British society about miracles.

In your answer you should refer to the main religious tradition of Great Britain and one or more other religious traditions. *(4 marks)*

Buddhism

In Buddhism, the approach is to resolve issues from one's own resources and strengths. The **Buddha told his followers not to look to some supernatural being for help or answers**. It is believed miracles are possible for any person who has mastered higher forms of meditation.

Nature as general revelation

Christianity

Revelation is when God reveals Himself. Nature is seen as a source of revelation by Christians because it is **God's creation**. Just as an artist leaves clues of themselves in their work, so God had left **clues in His creation**. For example in the beauty of nature, the fact that it seems to have been designed, the patterns found in nature (the seasons, life cycles etc.). **William Paley** tried to prove God exists by using the world and nature as His evidence. Many Christians believe that **in a beautiful sunset, they see God at work, in new life they see God at work** – this is nature revealing God.

Humanism

A humanist would say that as there is **no such thing as God**, a non-existent being cannot be revealed in any way – nature or otherwise – as there is **nothing to be revealed**. We should **just appreciate** the beauty and the patterns.

Further, a humanist might say that seeing God in nature is **simply a person's interpretation of things, and not the reality**. There are many reasons why they might **interpret something as God**, but no proof it ever was. Hence their interpretation is wrong.

Atheism

An atheist would say that as much as nature might reveal to a believer that there is a God, **it reveals nothing to others especially those who believe there is no God or divine being**.

Question

Explain two different beliefs from contemporary British society about nature as general revelation.

In your answer you should refer to the main religious tradition of Great Britain and one or more other religious traditions. *(4 marks)*

Getting prepared

Command words

Command words tell you how to answer a question in the exam. Understanding what they mean helps you to know what the question requires. Don't confuse them with the key words, which are key terms that form the basis of your answer (for example, 'special revelation); rather, the command words *instruct you how* to answer (for example, 'Explain').

Explain – when you make a point, expand upon it

Give – same as 'write down' or 'list'

How – same as 'in what ways', for example, 'How do religious people work for animal rights?' is asking 'in what ways' do religious people help animals – practical answers are required

Name – is asking you for the actual technical word or actual name of something

Refer to ... – same as include in your answer, for example, you may be asked to refer to religious beliefs and teachings (scripture and sacred writings) or to examples, so you must include some to meet the requirement of the question. Scripture and sacred writings just means the holy texts of a religion, for example the Bible, or another text that a religion gives special respect to, such as the Talmud for Jewish people.

What is meant by ... – say what something means – a definition usually

Why – give reasons for something, for example, why people choose to fight in a war

Different beliefs – the two beliefs cannot be the same. You are being asked about different attitudes to an ethical issue, and the diverse ways in which religious people approach it

Influences – this is how something influences something else, for example, how a belief affects the way a person behaves

Importance – significance; why something is important either in itself or to/for something else.

In your answer you should refer to the main religious tradition of Great Britain and one or more other religious traditions – this is telling you to give an answer from Christianity, as that is the main religious tradition of Great Britain. You could choose another attitude from within Christianity, or from another religion to give a different view (which the earlier part of the question has asked for).

Evaluate this statement – this is only found in the 12-mark questions. However, the bullet points below will help you develop the skills needed to tackle these questions:

- give reasoned arguments to support this statement – reminding you that you must give a number of reasons, and must explain them for one side of the argument; using the word 'developed' suggests you have to give more than just a simple explanation, you really have to apply the points you make.
- give reasoned arguments to support a different point of view – reminding you to give a second side, again with well-explained arguments for that view.
- should refer to religious arguments – you must discuss many arguments for and against various religious viewpoints. It will not be enough to give one simple religious point.
- may refer to non-religious arguments – there are probably good arguments you can use from non-religious traditions, for example, what atheists and humanists might say, or what any ordinary person on the street might say
- to reach a justified conclusion – finally, you must draw a conclusion – which side is strongest from the arguments you have put forward, when considering the statement?

Make sure you learn those words and phrases so that you do what the question asks of you. This will guarantee your answer is stronger. It is no use knowing lots of information if you do not know what the question wants you to do with it!

The existence of God and revelation glossary

Agnostic a person who believes there is not enough evidence to say whether a God exists or not

Atheist a person who believes there is no God

Design argument the idea that the world is designed so God exists as the designer, also known as the teleological argument

First Cause the idea that the world was the result of something causing it

General revelation indirect revelation, for example, seeing God through nature

Humanism a belief system that does not include God, but sees as central the morally good behaviour of humans

Illusion that something is not real, but a trick of the mind

Immanent that God is at work in the world, for example, performing miracles

Impersonal that God is beyond human capacity to understand; distant (in intellectual and emotional terms)

Miracles good events that are considered impossible, so should not have been able to happen, and are inexplicable by science

Omnipotent all-powerful

Omniscient all-knowing

Personal relatable; humans can meet and connect with God

Polytheist person who believes in more than one God

Reality what is real or actual

Revelation God revealing Himself

Science the collection of knowledge from observation and testing

Special revelation direct revelation, for example, seeing God in a vision

Teleological argument the idea for the existence of God through the design of the world

Theist a person who believes in One God

Thomas Aquinas an Italian philosopher and Catholic priest in the thirteenth century, who wrote five arguments (Five Ways) for the existence of God, including the Argument from Cause

Transcendent that God is beyond space and time, controlled by neither

Ultimate Reality the idea of One God which is absolute

Vision an image said to be seen as part of a religious or supernatural experience

William Paley an English clergyman who in the eighteenth century put forward the Design argument for the beginning of the world

7 Theme D: Religion, peace and conflict

Key elements of this Theme

The first part of this Theme considers the religious concepts relating to violence, **terrorism** and **war**. You need to know the key concepts of **peace**, **justice**, **forgiveness** and **reconciliation**, and the religious beliefs and teachings about these. You also have to explore religious beliefs and teachings about violence and terrorism, both of which some religious people are involved in. We need to look at beliefs and teachings about war itself and attitudes to fighting war, including when religious believers will go to war. We will also look at how religion causes **conflict**, and religious attitudes to **nuclear war**. We also need to understand religious attitudes to peace, including how individuals have fought for peace and how religions support victims of war.

Key concepts

Justice – this means fairness; making right and fair a situation which has been unjust. Religion is meant to bring justice to the world, and to fight injustice where it is seen. Many wars are about, or include the abuse of, justice, so many religious people feel duty-bound to fight against that. For example, Sikhs vow to fight injustice.

Peace – this has to be the aim and goal of all people, as it means to live in harmony and without fear. Many religions talk about a time to come where there is peace. It may be the Kingdom of Heaven, paradise, or enlightenment, but it is a goal for all to reach and work towards. Having peace on earth (no wars) is a step towards that.

Reconciliation – most religious people will be involved in reconciliation after war. The Quakers are pacifists who try to bring sides together and help them resolve issues so they can live peaceably. If we do not bring the opposing sides together and resolve their issues, how can we expect any peace to last?

Forgiveness – this is the belief that we should be able to move a relationship forward with someone who has done wrong to us, by accepting their apology and putting the wrongdoing behind us. It is a central teaching of Christianity and important in all religions.

Conflict – before the actual fighting starts, there is conflict. Conflict is disagreement; armed conflict is the actual fighting. Religious people might have been involved in trying to resolve the original disagreements, but might also then get involved in the armed conflicts as often they feel they have no other option. For example, Dietrich Bonhoeffer, a German pastor, was involved in a plot to kill Hitler. Many religious people have died in battle.

The Basics

1. Give a definition for each of the following words: justice, reconciliation, peace, conflict.
2. For each definition, give an example to demonstrate its meaning.
3. Do you think war is the biggest problem in the world today? Explain your reasons.
4. **The most difficult thing to do is reconcile after conflict.** How far do you agree with this statement? Explore arguments for and against it, explaining the arguments you give.

Religious beliefs, teachings and attitudes about the meaning and significance of justice

In terms of justice there are two elements of justice:

- to put right injustice; making right a situation which has been unjust
- to carry out this fight in a just way.

Justice

Buddhism

The idea of justice does not apply easily to Buddhism because Buddhism teaches that there is no God upholding universal laws of morality. There is no absolute good and evil in the world, and no divine reward and punishment. Buddhists try to act appropriately, avoiding harm, which includes avoiding violence, conflict and abuse. Out of compassion and using right speech and right action one can peacefully challenge laws and policies that go against these principles. Buddhists will favour negotiation and arbitration to resolve difficulties.

Christianity

Christians will fight for justice under the conditions of the **Just War** theory, which is that war should be fought with justice too; the cause, weapons used, treatment of captured soldiers, should all be just. While God desires peace, He also desires that humans should live in justice and freedom. However, some Christians believe that the conditions gained from war are never better than the injustice that started it. War does go against Jesus' teachings, but is sometimes necessary for the greater good.

Hinduism

Hinduism teaches that war should be avoided unless absolutely necessary. Being forceful is against Hinduism, and the most desirable method of settling differences is through dialogue and compromise.

The Bhagavad Gita teaches that there are different levels of settling differences between individuals and nations, in which the most peaceful method is held in highest regard, and war must be the very last resort once all other options have failed.

Hindus will only take up arms in self-defence.

Islam

Muslims believe in jihad, 'striving for justice', which means both the inner religious struggle to be a better person and the collective armed struggle to protect the common good. Shari'ah Law has strict rules about who can declare jihad. War has to be carried out in the right way and has set rules. The killing of innocents is prohibited, and no individual Muslim can decide for themselves to wage jihad.

Judaism

Justice is a key issue in Judaism, for example, tzedekah is all about justice, even though people often think about it as charity. War in self-defence is justifiable where the Jewish nation is under attack, as this is about bringing justice. However, it must be carried out in a just way throughout.

Sikhism

Sikhs will fight for justice. Dharam yudh (a righteous war) is the idea that minimum force should be used; only enough to achieve an objective. Nuclear war and terrorism are never right as they indiscriminately take life, which is the highest expression of the Supreme Self, God.

How do religious believers view justice in regards to war?

Religious beliefs, teachings and attitudes about the meaning and significance of forgiveness and reconciliation

Forgiveness and reconciliation are two of the most difficult challenges we have, both as individuals and nations, especially after a war or period of conflict. We hear much about the horrors of war, but what happens after it very rarely gets reported or seen. Nations very rarely apologise for their actions (as this would seem to say they were wrong to act in the first place), or forgive opposing nations, but reconciliation sometimes appears to happen over time despite this.

However, on an individual basis there have been many stories of people coming to terms with war, their actions and the actions of others by both seeking forgiveness and indeed giving it. This has then led to a kind of reconciliation. As a religious person of whatever faith, it is looked at as the right thing to do … to forgive.

Look at these two examples of people who have forgiven others for their actions in war.

Corrie Ten Boom was a Dutch girl who helped save Jewish lives in the Netherlands in the Second World War. She was caught with her father and sister, both of whom were killed by the Nazis. She was for some reason released – an act of God, she claimed.

Later, when giving talks about her experiences in the Holocaust, she met the SS man at a church in Munich who had guarded them in Ravensbrook concentration camp. As he held out his hand to shake hers, all her memories flooded back. She kept her hand by her side, even though she had preached many times that we should forgive those who hurt us. She recalled the treatment in the camps, her anger growing alongside a desire for revenge. Then she felt that her emotional state was a sin, and began to tell herself off because she believed Jesus had died for all, including this man. So she prayed for God to help her forgive him. She tried to smile and to raise her hand to shake his. However, she still could not engage with this man, so she prayed again for the help from Jesus. This time, she said, when their hands touched, it was as if a current was flowing from her to him and she felt love (agape) for this man who had formerly been her cruel guard. Corrie interpreted this to mean that the rifts in the world are healed by God's love. She believed that through Jesus' command to his followers to love their enemies, the ability to love enemies also comes from Jesus.

Eric Lomax was a British soldier who was tortured by the Japanese while being held as a prisoner during the Second World War, but who was able to forgive one of his tormentors. He was one of thousands of British soldiers who surrendered to the Japanese in Singapore in 1942. Many were relocated to Thailand and forced to build the Burma Railway, also known as the Death Railway. After his captors found a radio receiver he had made he was repeatedly tortured; his captors broke multiple bones and poured water into his nose and mouth. One of his constant torturers stood out: Nagase Takashi, an interpreter. 'At the end of the war, I would have been happy to murder him,' Eric told *The New York Times* in 1995. Eric had actually searched for the man, and his wife wrote a letter to arrange a meeting between the two in Thailand. He learned that after the war Nagase had become an interpreter for the Allies and helped locate thousands of graves and mass burial sites along the Burma Railway. 'When we met, Nagase greeted me with a formal bow,' Eric said on the website of the Forgiveness Project (a British charity that seeks to bring together victims and perpetrators of crimes). 'I took his hand and said in Japanese, "Good morning, Mr Nagase, how are you?" He was trembling and crying, and he said over and over again: "I am so sorry, so very sorry."

Eric had gone to the meeting with absolutely no sympathy for his former torturer, but was turned around by the complete humility Nagase showed. In the following days they spent a lot of time together, talking and laughing, and became good friends. That friendship remained until their deaths.

'I haven't forgiven Japan as a nation,' Eric told *The Times*, 'but I've forgiven one man, because he's experienced such great personal regret.'

When people forgive, they can start to heal and move on from their wartime suffering. All religions would commend these two individuals for what they were able to do. Whether it is inspired by religion or simply human action, Corrie Ten Boom and Eric Lomax set an example for others. Neither found it easy, but both had the strength to do it.

You can read Corrie Ten Boom's story in *The Hiding Place*, and Eric Lomax's in *The Railway Man*.

Religious ideas about forgiveness

All religions teach that their God is one who will forgive. God forgives everyone, as long as they are truly sorry. God's nature is to be loving and just, hence God forgives. Religious believers think they should try to show forgiveness as God does – it is a virtue.

Forgiving someone does not mean that they shouldn't face justice, but that they should be treated fairly and with compassion.

'Holding on to anger is like grasping a hot coal with the intent of throwing it at someone else – you are the one who gets burned.' Buddha

'To be a Christian means to forgive the inexcusable, because God has forgiven the inexcusable in you.' C.S. Lewis

'One should forgive, under any injury. It has been said that the continuation of the human species is due to human forgiveness' Mahabharata

'Dispelled is anger as forgiveness is grasped.' Guru Amar Das

'We achieve inner health only through forgiveness – the forgiveness not only of others but also of ourselves.' Joshua Loth Liebman (American rabbi)

'Although the just penalty for an injustice is an equivalent retribution, those who pardon and maintain righteousness are rewarded by God. He does not love the unjust.' (Qur'an 42:40)

The Basics

1 What is meant by forgiveness?
2 How does the story of either Corrie Ten Boom or Eric Lomax show forgiveness?
3 **Religious people should always forgive those who do wrong to them.** Explain arguments for and against this statement.

Religious beliefs, teachings and attitudes about violence including violent protest

Buddhism

Buddhists do not believe in violence, and **protests** should be non-violent. Protests have taken place and speaking out about injustice can be seen as right speech and right action. Trying to change injustice is a compassionate act. The Dalai Lama has said that peace can only happen with mutual respect. However, there have been occasions where Buddhists have taken protest to an extreme, for example, the very famous incident of Thich Quang Duc, a Buddhist monk who set fire to himself to protest the persecution of Buddhists during the Vietnam War.

Christianity

Christianity teaches non-violence, as Jesus said 'Blessed are the peacemakers' and told his followers to turn the other cheek in the face of violence. Christians are told to love their enemies and love each other. However, sometimes non-violent protest may be used to demonstrate against unjust laws. Some Christians accept that force may be necessary to oppose injustice.

Hinduism

Hinduism teaches that violence should not be used for its own sake or as a means of intimidation. The Bhagavad Gita talks about how disagreements and war-like situations should be dealt with. It teaches that there are different ways of settling differences between individuals and nations, following principles that uphold dharma, which is the sanctity of life and civilised society.

The most peaceful method, settling differences through dialogue, is held in highest regard. Violence must be the last resort.

Islam

Islam means peace and Muslims should be peaceful, but violence may be used in self-defence. Muslims have a duty to protest about anything unfair, and in the UK there have been many peaceful protests over wars and issues in the Middle East, Islamophobia and racism.

Judaism

Judaism encourages protest against injustice for many reasons. Having been the subject of persecution over thousands of years, many Jewish people want to help others in the same situation. The books of the Nevi'im contain stories of the prophets protesting. Jewish people have protested about anti-Semitism and issues in Israel. Sometimes civil disobedience (active refusal to obey certain laws) is used, but violence should not be.

Sikhism

Sikhism teaches that we should not harm others, but should also be prepared to use force to resist injustice. The primary symbol of Sikhism, the Khanda, features crossed swords. Sikhs believe in sewa (service) and as such they will defend the persecuted.

The Basics

1. What is meant by violent protest?
2. Why might religious people feel the need to protest?
3. **It is always wrong for religious believers to protest violently.** Do you agree with this statement? Explain reasons, giving examples to illustrate your arguments.

Religious teachings, beliefs and attitudes about terrorism

Terrorism is an act of violence that is intended to create fear. A terrorist is anyone who plans or carries out such an act. Terrorist acts are often directed at civilians and because of this, many consider them to be unlawful acts of war and violence. The United Nations Security Council regards terrorist attacks as criminal: *Acts intended to cause death or serious bodily harm to civilians or non-combatants with the purpose of intimidating a population or compelling a government or an international organization to do or abstain from doing any act.*

TERRORIST THREAT BRINGS FEAR TO OLYMPICS

Suicide bomber kills 20 children in school

Terrorists use hospital as base to launch bombs

White supremacist kills 51 worshippers in mosque shooting spree

Museums of ancient history destroyed by terrorists

In the modern world there have been many recorded acts of terrorism. These have taken countless numbers of lives, such as the shootings by white supremacist Brenton Tarrant at two New Zealand mosques, which took the lives of 50 people in 2019. In some attacks, the terrorists take their own lives as well as those of others, such as in suicide bombings, as happened in the London Underground bombing (7 July 2005). There have been other kinds of attacks, for example, cyber terrorism has targeted hospitals and national security systems. Terrorism aims to disrupt and frighten, for example, between the 1970s and 1990s the Irish Republican Army bombed British government and economic targets in England and Northern Ireland as part of their campaign to end British rule in Northern Ireland. In Syria, ISIS/ISIL destroyed the ancient historic site of Palmyra in an act of terrorism in 2015.

Why do terrorists carry out attacks? They claim that:

- they are fighting against social and political injustice, where a group of people are being denied their human rights
- they are fighting to assert their religious beliefs, especially where they feel these are denied to them.

When people are fighting for a cause they believe in, some are prepared to go to any lengths to have their voice heard. It has been said that, 'One man's terrorist is another man's freedom fighter.' There are many examples where a person was labelled as a terrorist, but later seen as a legitimate leader, for example, Martin McGuiness in Northern Ireland and Nelson Mandela in South Africa.

The Basics

1 What is meant by the term 'terrorism'?
2 Give two reasons why many religious people would consider terrorist acts wrong. Explain your reasons.
3 Use the images and headlines on this page to describe the effects of terrorism.
4 Why do some people feel they have to carry out terrorist acts?
5 Explain religious beliefs or teachings which show that all acts of terrorism are wrong.

Religious teachings, beliefs and attitudes about reasons for war

At any point in time there is always a war happening somewhere in the world. We have fought wars throughout history and there is little sign of them stopping. Wars between nations, **civil wars**, and threats of futuristic wars including nuclear and cyber wars all threaten our existence on a daily basis. We have reached a point where weapons exist that could destroy us all.

All religions promote peace, and the majority of the global population would claim to have a religious belief … so why do we continue to have conflicts?

We can look to history for some of the reasons.

Name as many wars/conflicts as you can in the last 100 years.

Have you written a long list? It is probably true to say you know something about each of them, but do you know the reason why they started? Many reasons have been used to justify wars, but whether they are valid is debatable. This could depend on the side you support, previous events in history, where the war is happening and, of course, whether you find yourself in the middle of a war zone.

Can you think of any reasons why wars begin?

Your list might include: disputes over land, in self-defence, to get power, to re-establish human rights, for resources, to keep an agreement (treaty) with other countries. There are many more reasons. However, which reasons are valid, and which are just about greed? It all depends on your viewpoint.

For the purpose of this theme you need to focus on three reasons in particular: greed, self-defence and retaliation.

Greed

This can explain a war to gain, for example, more land, more power or more resources. Most religious teaching would not support this as a reason for war. Greed comes from selfishness, which all religions do not approve. Considering the numbers of soldiers and casualties in war, greed could never be seen as a justifiable reason for it.

Self-defence

Religious holy books and texts describe many wars. The Hebrew Bible, the Qur'an, the Bhagavad Gita, the Guru Granth Sahib all suggest that war may be necessary in self-defence. If a country or religion is under attack, then conflicts can happen. It would therefore be seen as entirely right and proper to defend your own country against attack. The problem comes when the response is disproportionately large, and self-defence turns into aggression for its own gain.

Retaliation

At times, a country will be attacked in a way which provokes retaliation. For example, one of the triggers for the First World War was retaliation against a political assassination. The problem with retaliation is that it is often a spontaneous reaction which leads to the escalation of a situation, and hence war. All religions would say that it is preferable to resolve issues of conflict through peaceful negotiation and discussions rather than simple retaliation because this can help to defuse rather than exacerbate the situation.

The Basics

1 Use religious teachings from pages 324 and 331–333 to explain whether war can ever be justified.
2 **For religious people, greed is never a good reason for war.** What do you think?
3 Explain religious views about fighting in self-defence.

Religion and belief as a cause of war and violence

When asked the question about the causes of war, religion is always an answer. Is this true or not though?

Religion/religious teachings themselves do not cause violence or war. How they are put into practice or how they are interpreted is the problem. Religious teachings are all about peace and understanding, but sometimes teachings can be ambiguous or difficult to understand, which may cause problems. The Bible says 'Do not murder' but also 'an eye for an eye'; the Qur'an allows Muslims to fight for the name of Allah, yet 'the greatest sin is to take another man's life'. This means that for some people there is room for violence/war in the name of religion, and as long as people believe that, then innocent people will die in war and great mistrust will continue to grow between people of different cultures. Some may think they are fighting for their religion, but for the people at the top organising the fight/war, perhaps their own power is the most important.

Task

Find out about the work of an organisation which tries to work for peace, for example, Médicins san Frontiéres, Pax Christi, Buddhist Peace Fellowship.

1 It is definitely true that **religion** is *involved* in war, for example, the Israel-Gaza conflict or the Syrian civil war, both of which have complex religious, ethnic and political dimensions.. However, both these conflicts are more about politics than about religion. The War on Terror has been seen as a conflict between Islamic extremists and other religions in the West, yet Western leaders would define it as a war on terrorist organisations. So, religion is **not** the *actual cause.*

2 Throughout history, **religious beliefs** have divided people. Where splits have occurred *violence* has erupted. For example, after the death of Muhammad ﷺ there was a terrible violent struggle for power resulting in the split between Sunnis and Shi'as; the Bosnian War (1992–95) saw bitter fighting between different ethnic groups, and Christian ethnic cleansing of Muslims. Therefore, we can say religious beliefs sometimes **do** cause violence.

3 People are quick to discuss the differences between different religions, yet if we look more closely, the similarities between religions and what they want for the communities are far greater. This is what we need to hold on to bring people together in faith and understanding. Many people are doing exactly that. For example, many groups work across religious divides to help others, save lives, solve conflicts and bring peace, and these people are far greater in number than those causing the conflicts. True religious beliefs do not cause war, and these people are a testimony to that.

Is it right to say that religion causes war? Explain your ideas.

Religious attitudes to war and peace

Buddhism

Buddhism, war and peace

Buddhism is a religion of peace. Although Buddhist countries have armies, they usually exist for defence purposes and as a secondary police force.

Buddhism teaches:

- The First Precept – to refrain from harming others; this is ahimsa and is a core principle of Buddhism.
- The Noble Eightfold Path – for example, Right Action and Right Awareness.
- Hatred does not cease by hatred, hatred ceases by love. (Dhammapada)
- He should not kill a living being, nor cause it to be killed, nor should he incite another to kill. (Dhammapada)
- Peace can exist if everyone respects all others. – Dalai Lama

The message of Buddhism is one of peace, not war. Buddhists believe their actions have consequences for their future rebirths. It is wrong to harm others, yet soldiers must kill. Buddhists believe all peaceful means must be tried, because war can lead to greater problems than it solves. War is often the result of the Three Poisons (greed, hatred, ignorance), and war also encourages them, whereas Buddhism seeks to get rid of them. In 1950, China invaded and annexed Tibet. While China claims it was a 'peaceful liberation', Tibetans and many international observers say the invasion ended Tibetan independence. However, the Dalai Lama still believes the only resolution can be a peaceful one. He won the Nobel Peace Prize in 1992.

Task

Hold a class discussion about this statement:
Peace is an impossible dream.
Take a vote at the end of the debate.
Which side won? What arguments were the most persuasive?

Christianity

Christianity, war and peace

The teachings of Christianity are peaceful. Jesus taught a message of love and Christianity that has a strong pacifist tradition. However, many Christians accept that there are circumstances when it is necessary to use armed conflict and they will fight in a Just War. However, no Christian denomination would support the use of nuclear weapons.

Christianity teaches:

- Put away your sword. Those who live by the sword die by the sword. – Jesus (Matthew 26:52)
- Blessed are the peacemakers. – Jesus (Sermon on the Mount)
- Love your enemies, and pray for them. – Jesus (Sermon on the Mount)
- Peace I leave with you, my peace I give to you. – Jesus (John 14:27)
- Everyone must commit themselves to peace. – Pope John Paul II.

Christianity is a peaceful religion if we look at the teachings of both Jesus and St Paul. The Kingdom of Heaven is a place of peace and love, not violence and fighting. All the earliest Christians were pacifists and most Christians today are pacifists. The Quaker Movement is a good example of this attitude.

Many Christians only agree with war in certain circumstances, for example, to defend against an invading force. Many Christians disagreed with the War on Iraq (2003–2011) because they felt the reasons for it were wrong, and that it led to thousands of innocent people being killed. Where Christians do accept war, it has to be the last resort after all peaceful efforts have failed.

ॐ Hinduism

Hinduism, war and peace

Hinduism follows a system of *varna* (social division) which traditionally categorises society on the basis of profession. One of the four main *varna* is *kshatriya* which means 'to protect from harm'. They are warriors. Hindus believe in following dharma (duty), so for kshatriyas fighting is acceptable in just wars. However, Hinduism promotes ahimsa (non-violence) and tolerance as key virtues, both of which are against fighting.

Hinduism teaches:

- Kshatriyas (warriors) are expected to be the first to battle, and the bravest in battle; their main duty is to defend and protect others.
- Even an enemy must be offered appropriate hospitality if he comes to your home. (Mahabharata)
- Key Hindu virtues include ahimsa (non-violence), tolerance, compassion and respect, as well as protection of others.
- The pursuit of truth does not permit violence being inflicted on one's opponent. – Mahatma Gandhi
- If you do not fight in this just war, you will neglect your duty, harm your reputation and commit the sin of omission. (In Bhagavad Gita, Lord Krishna says this to the warrior Arjuna.)

So, where a war is seen as just, for example, in defence against an invading nation, kshatriyas must follow their duty and fight. Not doing so would gain bad karma, and negatively affects future rebirths. Where it is necessary to protect others, fighting may be the only way, and so is acceptable.

However, Mahatma Gandhi stressed that justice can be achieved through non-violence. Since all life is sacred because Brahman is within all (in the atman, or soul), war destroys this ideal.

☪ Islam

Islam, war and peace

One meaning of the word Islam is *peace*. Allah has 99 names known to Muslims. One of them is *As-salaam*, which means 'the source of peace'. It is said that if all people followed the Muslim way of life, there should only be peace. Muslims should work to keep the peace; war should only occur when all peaceful means have been exhausted. Only then do Muslims have a duty to fight to defend the weak and oppressed.

Islam teaches:

- Greet others *salaam alaikum*, which means 'peace be upon you'.
- Greater jihad is every Muslim's personal struggle to follow Allah. Lesser jihad refers to the shared struggle to uphold justice and protect the faith, which in certain situations may include armed defence.
- To those against whom war is made, permission is given to fight. (Surah 22:39)
- Those who die in Allah's cause will be rewarded with paradise. (Surah 3:16)
- Hate your enemy mildly; for he may become your friend one day. (Hadith)

When Muhammad ﷺ was alive, the Muslim community had to defend themselves by fighting and Allah gave them permission to do this. If they had not, they would all have been killed. Islam does not teach pacifism.

Task

Working with a partner: write a discussion between two believers, one who would fight in a war and one who says it is wrong to fight. Remember they could both believe in the the same or different religions.

Judaism

Judaism, war and peace

Judaism does not question the right to defend a just cause by war. The Talmud says that whoever sheds the blood of humanity, by humanity shall that person's blood be shed. However, in fact there are rules which exist for fighting war only as a last resort. It is forbidden to take delight in the war or its victory, and those Jewish people who believe that a Messiah will come, believe that all weapons will be destroyed and turned into peaceful tools. Peace remains the ideal.

Judaism teaches:

- The Jewish greeting is *shalom* – peace.
- Get ready for war. Call out your best warriors. Let your fighting men advance for the attack. (Joel, Nevi'im)
- The sword comes to the world because of the delay of justice and through injustice. (Ethics of the Fathers, Talmud)
- It shall come to pass ... nation shall not lift up sword against nation, neither shall they learn war any more (Isaiah, Nevi'im) (about the future Messianic Age).
- When siege is laid to a city, surround only three sides to give an opportunity for escape to those who would flee to save their lives. (Maimonides Code)

In early Judaism, war was a religious duty. There are many descriptions of wars fought in the Bible, where G-d is on the side of the righteous Israelite army, and they win. The Ark of the Covenant was taken into battle with them as a talisman. Today, war is still acceptable, but as a last resort, and only for just reasons, for example, self-defence, or when the Jewish people or Israel are threatened.

There are rules about fighting wars, including that chances for escape and surrender must be given, that there is no scorched earth policy, and that civilians and prisoners are treated with dignity.

The ideal is peace, and justice is vital for peace.

Task

Use the information provided to create a booklet that explains the religious teachings about war and peace for the religions that you are studying.

Sikhism

Sikhism, war and peace

Sikhs have duties to fight for justice and to protect minorities. War should be a last resort and should be fought in a just manner.

Sikhism teaches:

- The Sikh Khanda is made up of two swords, 'Miri' and 'Piri'. Khalsa Sikhs wear the swords to show willingness to defend their faith when necessary.
- When all other methods have failed it is permissible to draw the sword. – Guru Gobind Singh
- A true warrior is one who fights for the downtrodden, the weak, and the meek. –Guru Granth Sahib
- The Lord is the haven of peace. (Adi Granth)
- Peace is believed to come from God.

Whilst Sikhism aims for peace, it also allows fighting, particularly in self-defence and for justice. Early Sikhism saw many threats from other communities, including the rulers of the land in which they lived. Being able to fight was the only way Sikhism could have survived. Several of the Sikh gurus instructed Sikhs to do physical and military training. Guru Hargobind Singh swapped prayer beads for two swords, showing a stance against oppression and injustice. Guru Tegh Bahadur led the Sikhs into battle for the right to religious freedom. Guru Gobind Singh organised the Sikhs into an effective army after setting up the Khalsa, whose members were prepared to give up their lives for their religion. Even in the modern world, many Sikh men are soldiers and very highly regarded for their skill and effort, fighting for the country in which they live. For example, many Sikhs fought in the British Army during the First and Second World Wars.

This does not mean that Sikhism looks for wars to fight. Peace through justice is the ideal. However, there is an obligation to fight to get justice, where necessary.

Some Sikhs are pacifist out of respect for the sanctity of life and the belief that God created all life, meaning it deserves both respect and protection.

Religions allowing war – holy war and just war

We have seen that all religious traditions believe in peace not war. However, most also accept that there are times when it is necessary to go to war to avoid a greater evil. Within religious teachings there are different views on war and so religious believers must use their **conscience** in deciding if they believe a war is morally justified.

There are three possible stances a religious believer may take:

- **pacifist** – believing all war and killing is wrong
- **holy war** – believing it is right to fight a war in the name of God
- **just war** – believing it is right to fight a war in the interests of self-defence, justice and the greater good.

Within some religious traditions there is clear guidance on the rules and legitimacy of wars.

✝ Christianity

Declare a Holy War, call the troops to arms. *Old Testament*

Holy war

Within Christian history there was once a strong concept of holy war. In the Old Testament there are many examples of wars fought in the name of God. The soldiers believed God was on their side and indeed had influence over the outcomes of battles. For example, Joshua's army followed God's commands to blow trumpets and bring down the walls of Jericho. The Crusades (1095–1291) were fought to capture control of the Holy Land. The Christian soldiers believed they were fighting for a sacred and noble cause. They believed God was with them and the Muslim Turks they were fighting against were the pagan enemies of God.

Just war

It is impossible to conceive of a just war in a nuclear age. *Pope John XXIII*

St Paul said Christians should obey their rulers, who had been given power by God. When those rulers demanded Christians be soldiers, a compromise had to be found. St Augustine was the first to try to write a set of rules regarding this, and eventually the just war rules were written in detail by St Thomas Aquinas. The message is clear: sometimes if you do not fight, you allow a greater evil to happen than a war would have caused, so you have to fight.

Christian Just War Rules

- War must be started and controlled by a legitimate political authority such as a government.
- There must be a just cause for the war; it must not be based just on aggression towards an enemy.
- The war must have a clear aim to promote good and overcome evil.
- War must be a last resort; every effort must have been made to resolve conflict peacefully.
- There must be a reasonable chance of success, as it would be wrong to risk lives with no chance of success.
- The war must be conducted fairly. Only reasonable force should be used and the risk to civilians minimised.
- There must be a good outcome and peace restored.

Islam

'Fight in the cause of Allah those who fight you, but do not transgress limits ... if they cease let there be no hostility.'
Surah 2:190-192

Lesser jihad refers to armed struggle under specific conditions. If Muslims are attacked, self-defence may become a religious duty. Since that is sanctioned by the Qur'an, it is sometimes called 'holy war', and follows clear ethical guidelines.

Holy war

For Muslims a holy war is a just war. There are rules for how Muslims should fight a war. These are based on the Qur'an, and were set out in more detail by the first Caliph (successor or ruler). A jihad may only be fought as a last resort and must never be against another Muslim nation.

1 Who fights?
- Muslims have a duty to join the army and fight, if a just leader begins a war.
- Not all Muslims have to fight. Muhammad ﷺ said one man from each two should fight, so that there are still men to defend and look after the towns and villages.
- Sane Muslim men, not boys, whose families will cope without them fight.
- Soldiers on the battlefield must fight; running away is wrong, because that makes it more difficult for other soldiers.
- If a town is attacked, everyone (men, women and children) has to fight back.

2 How is the war fought?
- It may only begin when the enemy attacks and it ends when the enemy shows they want peace.
- Civilians must not be harmed, attacked or mistreated.
- Crops should be left alone. Holy buildings especially should not be damaged.
- Prisoners of war should be treated well. Money collected for zakat can be used to pay for food for them.

3 How does the war end?
- When people regain their rights.
- When the enemy calls for peace.

Sikhism

Just war

When Guru Gobind Singh formed the Khalsa it was his intention to create an army of warrior saints committed to the cause of justice. Accepting the need for Sikhs to be prepared to fight, he outlined the teachings of a just war. In Sikhism this is called **dharam yudh**, which means in defence of justice.

The soldiers were to be **sant sipahi** (saint soldiers). As well as their training, they had an obligation to do **nam simran** and meditate daily. In other words, they had to practise their religion devotedly, as well as do their military training and preparations. Guru Gobind Singh once said: *Without power, righteousness does not flourish, without dharma everything is crushed and ruined.*

The Basics

1 What does the term holy war mean?
2 Why do you think some religious believers would fight in a holy war?
3 Choose either Christianity, Islam or Sikhism. Write a detailed explanation of their teachings about a just war.
4 **There can be no such thing as a just war, because the innocent always suffer.** Do you agree? Give reasons to argue more than one point of view, including religious arguments in your answer.

Victims of war

War has obvious consequences – soldiers die, civilians die.

Think about the reports you have seen on TV, online and in the papers. What other consequences of war are there? Think about all the things on this page.

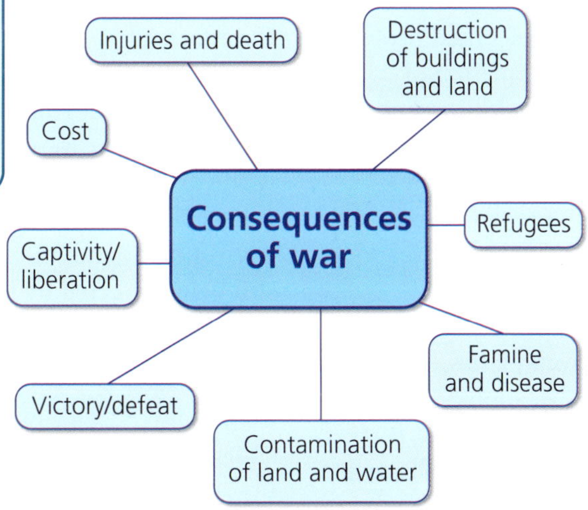

Which of these consequences is worse? Are the victors of war likely to suffer the same as the losers?

Helping the victims of war

There are many organisations which try to help the victims of war, both when war is happening and after it. Part of their mission is to try to bring about peace. It is part of all religions to help those in trouble and defend those who cannot defend themselves, so it is natural that religious organisations also help the victims of war. To do so fits with the basic teaching of the Golden Rule 'Treat others as you would be done by' which every religion follows.

Here are some examples of relgiious organisations that provide assistance to the victims of war:

Christian Peacemaker Teams (**www.cpt.org**) – was founded in 1984 by three historic pacifistic Churches, Mennonite, Church of the Brethren and Quaker, though now has support and membership from a wider range of Christian denominations. It sends small teams to work on peace-making in conflict zones (third-party non-violent intervention) trying to end conflict between sides by peaceful means, and brings aid and support to the victims of war.

The Buddhist Peace Fellowship (**www.buddhistpeacefellowship.org**) – was founded in 1978, and works by applying Buddhist principles to issues in the world, and Buddhist teachings to resolve them. It speaks publicly to raise awareness of issues, tries to strengthen leadership in the areas where there are issues, and acts with other groups to make change happen. This supports victims of war, by helping to return peace to an area. It also undertakes relief work for victims of war.

Khalsa Aid (**www.khalsaaid.org**) – was set up in 1999 as an international organisation. Its work is based on the Sikh principles of selfless service (sewa) and universal love. It has provided relief assistance to victims of war, funded through donations from Sikhs all over the world, as well as other disaster and relief work. Many Hindu voluntary organisations help war victims.

Task

There is a civil war in a country, and aid is urgently needed for refugees and civilian victims of the fighting. Imagine you have been asked to raise funds for a Humanitarian Aid Agency. Design a full-page newspaper advert appealing for funds. Remember you will need to tell people about why the funds are needed and what you will do with the donations.

Religious attitudes to weapons of mass destruction and nuclear weapons

Most religious people disagree with **weapons of mass destruction** (WMD), and many have joined protests against their use. WMD are a phenomenon of modern warfare. They are capable of killing and maiming large numbers of people. They can also cause massive levels of destruction to both the natural landscape and human-made structures, such as cities. It is almost impossible to use such weapons solely to target military operations. They are controlled from far away, and are either in the form of missiles or bombs dropped from planes. This means that whoever releases the weapon does not experience or see the weapon's effect directly. It is very different to soldiers on the battlefield. There are several types of these weapons:

1 Nuclear weapons – also known as atomic bombs; they cause widespread destruction of life and structures within their range. The radioactive 'fallout' has long-term effects.

2 Biological warfare – also known as germ warfare; involves using living disease-causing bacteria or viruses such as anthrax, to bring about death or serious illness.

3 Chemical warfare – involves using non-living toxins such as nerve agents and mustard gas, to cause death, incapacity or illness.

4 Radiological weapons – also known as 'dirty bombs'; weapons that disperse readioactive material, often through **conventional** explosives. As well as killing people, they make the impact area useless because of contamination.

Religious attitudes

No religion agrees with the use of nuclear weapons and all other weapons of mass destruction are unacceptable. They are seen as too extreme, and uncontrollable. They do not fit with any just or holy war theories, or with ideas of moral behaviour in war.

Religious people believe in the sanctity of life and so the effects of WMD go completely against this belief. When the US military a chemical weapon called Agent Orange during the Vietnam War, thousands of civilians died or were left permanently disfigured or with various long-term health problems, such as cancer. The toxic chemical also contaminated the environment and, more than 50 years on, people are still being affected by birth deformities, cancers, and other conditions.

Religious people also believe that wars should be fought only to gain justice for the people. WMD are considered unjust because they arbitrarily kill and maim civilians. During Saddam Hussain's reign in Iraq, his government ordered the use of nerve gas on Kurdish people and Shi'a Muslims in Karbala. The weapons were being used as a tool of oppression to bring terror upon the people who opposed his rule.

Nuclear deterrence

Some religious believers accept the existence of nuclear weapons as a deterrent. They stop others attacking a country, but there is no intention to use them. In other words, they help to keep the peace. Many religious believers, however, think nuclear weapons are completely unacceptable. Even when not used, they cost huge sums of money, which could be better spent. Also, if the technology gets into the wrong hands, there is no guarantee they will not be used. The fact that they exist means they could be used, which is immoral.

Roman Catholic Church

Though the monstrous power of modern weapons acts as a deterrent, it is feared that the mere continuance of nuclear tests, undertaken with war in mind, will have fatal consequences for life on earth ... nuclear weapons should be banned.
– *Second Vatican Council*

'Nuclear deterrence' is a phrase used to show that nuclear weapons can deter others from attack. A country that has nuclear weapons 'feels' safe because of those weapons.

The role of religion and beliefs in war and peacekeeping in twenty-first century conflicts

Do you agree with John? Does religion start wars? Is religion the defining factor of each side? Does religion play a part in ending war or keeping the peace? Let's consider evidence for each of those.

Does religion cause wars?

Yes ...

... on occasions people have claimed that religion is the cause of a war by claiming that their religion is under attack. Some Muslims have claimed that the Gulf Wars and the Israel-Gaza Conflict are because the West were, or still are, making a direct attack on Islam. Some fundamentalist groups like ISIS/ISIL believe that an Islamic state needs to be created. (However, many Muslims would say that what ISIS/ISIL is trying to create is not an Islamic state and that its methods are not Islamic either.)

Ah but ...

... if it was the religion under attack in these cases wouldn't someone just bomb their holy city, and hit the religion directly?

No ...

... power, land and self-defence are the real causes of war – war creates tensions and that is when religious divisions may surface. Also, some people claim religion as the cause to get support (money/people/weapons) from people of the same religion around the world.

Mmm however ...

... perhaps it is religion that causes wars, but countries do not want to admit it.

Is religion the defining factor between sides in a war?

Yes ...

... religion may not be a cause directly, but often religion becomes a key issue as communities are divided. The Israel-Gaza Conflict is an issue over land and living conditions yet it is often seen as a conflict between Jewish and Muslim people. In other parts of the Middle East, civil war has led to conflict between Sunni and Shi'a Muslims.

Ah well ...

... it is just easier to see who is fighting who by separating on religious grounds, isn't it?

No ...

... although many claim it is. Historical divisions often rise to the surface even between members of the same religion, but this is secondary to the root cause(s). Tensions bring out the worst in people and religion often gets caught in the middle. All religions speak of peace not war, especially with people or nations of the same religion.

Mmm true ...

... but if religious tensions rise to the surface so easily does this not say that religion could be the root cause?

Does religion play a part in ending war?

Some people would say yes ...

... as religious leaders often call for the end of conflict. For example, the Pope has called for the end of conflict in Syria and in Northern Africa where militant groups like Al-Shabab and Boko Haram wage war against Christians and indeed other Muslims. Also, he has called for peace in Russia and Ukraine. Many religious leaders and groups are involved in working towards peace or speaking out against violent actions.

Mmm ...

... but the Pope calling for the end of a war does not actually end it, does it?

Some people would say no ...

... as, where religious extremism is concerned, some groups often want to perpetuate war and they only want to see an end if everyone conforms to their demands. Even then they will find another excuse to continue the violence because of their need for power.

Ah ...

... but extremists are only a small part of a religion ... the majority in the religion do want to see the war end.

Does religion keep the peace?

Some people would say yes ...

... as Christianity and Judaism teach to 'Love your neighbour'; Islam means 'Peace'; Buddhism has the idea of non-harm in its precepts; Hinduism has the concept of 'Ahimsa'; Judaism and Christianity say 'Do not kill' in the Ten Commandments; Sikhism in the words of Guru Nanak says 'No one is my enemy'. If all these were adhered to, then there would be peace. Religious groups are regularly involved in peacekeeping in war-torn areas and in negotiations to prevent wars happening.

Mmm ...

... it may be true to say teachings want peace, but many believers ignore these teachings and start wars!

Some people would say no ...

... as, sometimes even with all the best efforts, religion cannot keep the peace because there are greater overriding factors, such as the craving for power, the need to react to attack or to join allies to help protect them.

True ...

... but without the efforts of religions there would be more wars, so is it win some, lose some?

Task

Answer the following evaluation questions. Explain reasons to agree and disagree with each statement.

1. **Religion does not cause war.** What do you think?
2. **Religion does not keep the peace.** What do you think?
3. **Religion cannot end war.** What do you think?

OK, maybe it isn't quite as simple as I thought it was. You have given me lots to think about. Maybe religion doesn't start all wars, and maybe it does help solve some of them, but then maybe I was right in the first place. I will have to think more about this.

Religious attitudes to peace and pacifism

Peace is not just the absence of war, but a state of harmony, where justice exists for all and freedoms are respected. All religions teach the importance of peace on earth and encourage their followers to live peacefully. Throughout history there have always been people prepared to refuse to use violence or fight in wars, even if it meant they faced imprisonment for their beliefs.

Pacifists believe that all violence is morally wrong. They will not participate in any war, regardless of the reasons for that war. *Conscientious objectors* are people who refuse to participate directly in fighting wars on the grounds of conscience. However, they will assist in non-military ways such as medics, relief work and mediators. Many believe they have a peace-making role.

Revisit pages 330–332 and re[illegible] your chosen religion(s) attitude(s) to peace[illegible]

Working for peace

Quakers

This is a pacifist group within Christianity. As a Church they believe they are following the true teaching of Jesus by maintaining a completely pacifist stance. Their Peace Testimony makes clear that they will not use violence under any circumstances. It says that they denounce all violence, whatever its form. They totally oppose all outward wars and strife, and fighting with outward weapons, for any end, or for any reason. They believe that all relationships should be loving ones, including those between countries. During wars they will take on peace-making roles, for example, mediating for peace between warring nations. They also undertake non-combat work such as training, acting as medics for any side, and providing support to refugees and victims of war.

Swami Vivekananda

Swami Vivekananda (1863–1902) was a Hindu yogi. He preached and practised peace and harmony, and his teachings included the following:

'I and the whole universe are one and you will find this conclusion has not only been reached through knowledge and philosophy, but also through the power of love. There are therefore many stages in the development of the human spirit and there is no need for quarrels. Manifest the divinity within you, and everything will be harmoniously arranged around it.'

Dietrich Bonhoeffer

Dietrich Bonhoeffer was a Christian living in Germany during the rise of the Nazi party. He believed in pacifism and helped found the Confessing Church which spoke out against the human rights abuses of the ruling Nazis. Once war broke out, he believed even more strongly that helping the oppressed was a test of faith. He defied Nazi rule by helping Jewish people escape the death camps and also worked to overthrow the Nazi party. Eventually, even though he opposed all killing, he felt that he had to be prepared to sacrifice his principles and even his life, so he joined a group that was planning to assassinate Hitler because he believed it was necessary for the greater good. He was eventually arrested by the Gestapo and executed for treason.

Dalai Lama

The Dalai Lama is the spiritual leader of Tibetan Buddhists. He is recognised around the world as a symbol of peace. When the Chinese invaded his country, Tibet, he was forced into exile. However, despite this injustice he refuses to condone physical fighting against the Chinese. He says that hatred and violence will lead to more hatred and violence. He believes peace will only exist when everyone respects each other. He received the Nobel Peace Prize in 1992. Buddhist monks in Tibet have maintained peaceful protests against Chinese rule despite being subjected to threats and violence.

The Golden Rule

Buddhism

'I will act towards others exactly as I would act towards myself.' *Udana-varqa*

Christianity

'Treat others as you would like them to treat you.' *Jesus*

Hinduism

'This is the sum of duty: do nothing to others which if done to you could cause the pain.' *Mahabharata*

Islam

'None of you truly believe until he wishes for his brothers what he wishes for himself.' *Prophet Muhammad* ﷺ

Judaism

'What is harmful to yourself do not do to your fellow man.' *Rabbi Hillel*

Sikhism

'As you value yourself, so value others – cause suffering to no one.' *Guru Granth Sahib*

Think about these statements. How do they fit with the idea of going to war? Or, being a pacifist?

Task

Make a PowerPoint presentation on the theme of peace. You should include what peace means: religious teachings, beliefs and attitudes to peace; and the work of at least one person or group that works for peace. You could also select a suitable song to go with your presentation. Show your work to the rest of your class.

Different beliefs

Violence

Christianity

Whilst Christianity follows Jesus' teachings of peace, there are Christians who see violence as **acceptable in given situations**. Catholic, Orthodox and Anglican denominations accept the Just War theory, which provides **conditions within which war may be fought**. Certain groups believe it is acceptable to chastise children physically (**'Whoever spares the rod hates their children, but the one who loves their children is careful to discipline them.'** Proverbs 13:24). Many Christians accept the **use of violence in self-defence**. Some agree with the **use of the death penalty** out of a sense of abhorrence for certain criminal acts.

The Quaker Society

The Quaker Society is **non-violent**. Believers **refuse to participate** even as soldiers in times of war. They will carry 'no outward weapon'. They claim the '**Spirit of Christ will never move us to fight**.' There is **something of God in every person**, and appealing to that **resolves issues better than violence** can.

Roman Catholicism

The Roman Catholic Church's stance on violence is that there is dignity to being human. Inflicting violence, or receiving it is a denial of that dignity. Pope Francis spoke out against the death penalty.

Buddhism

The Buddha gave the Five Precepts, including to **not harm other sentient beings**. The skilful way to keep this is to help others – not to hurt them. **Violence breaks several of the Precepts** (sexual immorality, being untruthful, stealing being forms of violence), and is **against much of the Noble Eightfold Path** (e.g. Right Action).

Question

Explain two different beliefs from contemporary British society about violence.

In your answer you should refer to the main religious tradition of Great Britain and one or more other religious traditions. *(4 marks)*

Weapons of mass destruction (WMD)

Roman Catholicism

The Roman Catholic Church does not agree with the use of WMD but thinks they are acceptable as a deterrent.

The Quaker Society

The Quaker Society **utterly condemns WMD**. Believers are pacifists, and no outward weapons are acceptable. WMD are **indiscriminate and beyond control**.

Buddhism

Buddhism would argue that **WMD bring death and suffering on a massive scale**, so their use **can never be justified** under the **Precept of not hurting other sentient beings**. Not only do these weapons impact now, they **impact negatively on many generations in the future**.

Question

Explain two different beliefs from contemporary British society about weapons of mass destruction.

In your answer you should refer to the main religious tradition of Great Britain and one or more other religious traditions. *(4 marks)*

Hinduism

Hinduism would argue that use of WMD goes against the teaching of **ahimsa** and dharma (righteous action) based in the principle that creation is divine. It **is not possible to restrict the impact** of WMD, and they affect humans, animals and nature alike for very long periods of time. There is no justifiable reason for this destruction and the suffering caused.

Pacifism

Anglicanism

The Church of England is **not a consistently pacifist** church. Go into any cathedral and it is clear that **soldiers have been supported and are honoured**. The Church accepts the **Just War theory**, and **sees war as necessary** in certain conditions, **especially in situations where war is waged to fight injustice**. It is seen that pacifism is the ideal to which we should strive, but given that others exploit and abuse, and **pacifist methods seem not to have made a difference, then war may be sanctioned**, for example against Nazi Germany in the Second World War during which **Anglican chaplains served in all the armed forces units**.

Buddhism

Buddhism is a pacifistic religion. The **Five Precepts** demand a pacifistic approach to life. The **Noble Eightfold Path** seeks positive (hence peaceful) ways to live. The Dalai Lama said that **'Peace can exist if everyone respects all others.'**

The Quaker Society

The Quaker Society is pacifist. They **do not join armies, and refuse to participate in any violence**. They are **committed to peace making**. As Jesus said '**Blessed are the peacemakers, for they will be called the children of God**.'

Hinduism

Hinduism is a peaceful religion. It is based on the principle of the Supreme Truth as this Creation, and therefore the virtue of **ahimsa** (**non-violence**). Key virtues include **tolerance**, **compassion**, and **respect for all life** – all qualities leading to pacifism.

Question

Explain two different beliefs from contemporary British society about pacifism.

In your answer you should refer to the main religious tradition of Great Britain and one or more other religious traditions. *(4 marks)*

Getting prepared

Attitudes

For the six-mark question you will be asked to explain two beliefs or teachings about one of the ethical issues discussed in the theme.

Here are some examples from each of the six themes:

Theme A: Explain two religious beliefs about the use of contraception. Refer to sacred writings or another source of religious belief and teaching in your answer.

Theme B: Explain two religious beliefs about euthanasia. Refer to sacred writings or another source of religious belief and teaching in your answer.

Theme C: Explain two religious beliefs about revelation. Refer to sacred writings or another source of religious belief and teaching in your answer.

Theme D: Explain two religious beliefs about holy war. Refer to sacred writings or another source of religious belief and teaching in your answer.

Theme E: Explain two religious beliefs about the aims of punishment. Refer to sacred writings or another source of religious belief and teaching in your answer.

Theme F: Explain two religious beliefs about racial prejudice. Refer to sacred writings or another source of religious belief and teaching in your answer.

Sacred writings could include holy books like the Qur'an, Bible or Tenakh, or other respected religious texts, like Vatican II for Catholics. However, often holy books don't have specific teachings about these ethical issues, especially if they are issues arising from advances in medicine or science. This means that religious believers need to take the teachings of their holy books and other sources of authority and apply them to the issue. This is what shapes their attitudes.

What might be a good strategy for answering this type of question?

So, for example, let's take that question about the aims of punishment from above.

Holy books tend not to have direct teachings about the aims of punishment, rather they talk about whether and how we should punish, and the religion has a set of virtues its believers aspire to.

- You could start by giving a relevant teaching, including saying where it is from – 'Christians believe ...'. We might use:

'Christians believe there is something of God in everyone, because it says in the Bible that humans were made in the image of God.'

- Then you could show how that belief shapes attitudes to the topic, so for example, so we have to apply that teaching. In this question then:

'If this is the case, then punishment should aim to reform the person, as they are redeemable because they are a child of God.'

- You could then develop your point further, clearly linking it back to the question, for example:

'This means that punishments which help the convicted person to improve their behaviour and become a good member of society are favoured by Christians.'

Here are some examples of questions for you to practise from this Theme:

1 Explain two religious beliefs about helping victims of war. Refer to sacred writings or another source of religious belief and teaching in your answer.

2 Explain two religious beliefs about war. Refer to sacred writings or another source of religious belief and teaching in your answer.

3 Explain two religious beliefs about peace. Refer to sacred writings or another source of religious belief and teaching in your answer.

They can be marked against AQA's mark scheme which can be found on the AQA website.

From the question wording and the mark scheme you can work out how to answer the question effectively. Each question is different, but in the case of the above questions you would:

- choose your two beliefs and then explain each one
- develop your explanations fully
- use a relevant quotation or refer to a relevant teaching and include its source of authority, for example a holy book or religious leader. It is fine to use a more 'general' teaching or quotation in your answer but you *must* show how it is relevant. For example, if you use the teaching 'Love your neighbour' for a question about peace, but don't explain how it is relevant to peace, then you can't get the marks for the teaching and source (2 marks altogether).

Religion, peace and conflict glossary

Civil war armed conflict between factions within the same country

Conflict disagreement which escalates

Conscientious objector a person who is opposed to bearing arms or fighting in war due to moral or religious reasons (their conscience)

Conventional (warfare) war using conventional weapons – weapons acceptable under Geneva Conventions

Forgiveness willingness to not blame a person any more for the wrongs they have done

Holy war rules around fighting a war acceptable to Islam

Justice making things fair again

Just war rules around fighting a war acceptable to Christianity and Sikhism

Nuclear weapons/war a weapon/war of mass destruction

Pacifism belief that all violence is wrong

Peace the opposite of war; harmony

Protest voicing disagreement with something

Reconciliation restoring friendly relations after a disagreement

Retaliation hurting someone in response to an actual or perceived harm, especially to get revenge

Terrorism the unlawful use of violence/threats to harm or intimidate civilians, especially for political or ideological reasons

Violence causing harm to someone

War armed conflict between two or more sides

Weapons of mass destruction weapons that cause uncontrollable and untold damage, for example, nuclear weapons

8 Theme E: Religion, crime and punishment

Key elements of this theme

This Theme is about **law** and **order**. It is about what we mean by **crime**, why people commit crimes, including the idea of **evil** people and actions, and the way society deals with offenders. It looks at the impact of crimes, the suffering they cause, and how we should help **victims** of crime. It is also about why we punish offenders and the debate about the death penalty. Key to the Theme are religious teachings and beliefs about human nature, repentance and **forgiveness**. You must be able to show your understanding of religious attitudes to crime and punishment.

Key concepts

There are several concepts which underpin this topic and you need to learn them.

Law and order – the rules of our society and how they are enforced. These rules exist to maintain a calm and peaceful society. They are based on ideas of *right and wrong*. Most of the rules are common sense, and we usually agree with them most of the time.

Evil – an act that is very wicked or immoral. Many people associate these kind of acts with an evil being. They are not understandable to ordinary people, going beyond what most see as simply wrong or bad, and even sickening people.

Forgiveness – a process that a victim goes through to change their feelings of resentment, hate or vengefulness towards an offender in order to move on. It is a central attitude in all religions.

Justice – a belief in what is right and fair. It is also the main aim of any criminal system, that is to judge, punish the guilty and bring justice to the victims.

Suffering – a feeling of pain, harm, distress or hardship caused by the actions of others when they commit crime.

Morality – a person's or a religion's beliefs of what is right and wrong in terms of behaviour and actions. Most religious people have had their sense of morality shaped by their religion.

Conscience – the voice in our head that tells us right from wrong. It is also seen as the sense of feeling guilty when you have done something wrong. Many religious people believe it is God's guidance.

Sin – an act that goes against God's will; a religious offence. Many laws are there to enforce against sins, for example, taking life and stealing. For religious people, committing sin is a great wrong and can be punished by God in the afterlife.

The Basics

1 How might someone's conscience prevent them from committing a crime?
2 Why might it be difficult for someone to forgive a criminal?
3 How might criminal acts lead to suffering? Use examples in your answer.
4 Do you think that getting justice makes it easier to forgive someone? Explain your ideas.

Religion and rules

All religions have their own rules and laws that believers are told to follow. These rules give people a framework and guidance to help them live their lives in a way that will help them achieve their spiritual aims. For example, the Ten Commandments apply to Jewish people and Christians, and Sikhs follow a code of conduct called the Rahit Maryada. When a believer does something that breaks one of their religious laws they commit a religious offence (sometimes called a sin). Just as in society when someone breaks a law they are punished, there is also the belief in religious traditions that believers who sin will be punished in some way. Ultimately their afterlife could be affected, for example, they could go to hell or be reborn in a lower life form.

Deciding what is right and wrong can be a tricky business. Religious people have several sources of authority to guide them. However, they should always be guided by their *conscience*. This is sometimes described as the voice of God inside your head telling you what is right or wrong. Have you ever felt guilty, ashamed or disgusted with yourself because of a wrong action? Your conscience is what causes these feelings.

Religious traditions accept that everyone makes mistakes, but they also teach the ideas of *punishment for the wrongdoing*, *repentance* by the individual and compassion from the victim which then allows them to *forgive*. To repent is to recognise that we have done something wrong and to be truly sorry. It involves learning from the mistake and doing our best not to repeat it. Forgiveness is accepting that a person is sorry for what they have done wrong and allowing them a second chance. Forgiveness can be given by a victim even if the criminal shows no remorse and therefore must continue with the punishment. Some people believe that forgiveness is the best way for both criminal and victim to rebuild their lives. Punishment, though, is a clear part of the process. Jesus discusses forgiveness on many occasions but that does not mean to the exclusion of punishment. When Jesus was on the cross his comments about the two criminals being crucified with him can be interpreted as forgiveness. However, there was no reference to their punishment being stopped or cancelled.

Most religions also instruct their followers to keep the laws of the country in which they live. They should only break a law in certain circumstances, such as to protect life, for example, or if they are being challenged to break a key principle of their own religion. Religions recognise that laws are for our own and society's good and safety and so must be right. Most laws are not unlike religious ones anyway. Some examples are shown in the box to the right – *would you agree with them?*

Do not hurt others.

Do not steal from others.

Do not damage other people's things.

Do not tell lies about other people.

The Basics

1. What is meant by right and wrong, religious offence, sin, conscience, repentance, forgiveness?
2. Explain how the behaviour of religious people is guided by their faith.
3. **Religious people should always forgive those who do wrong.** What do you think? Explain reasons to agree and disagree with this statement.

Different types of crimes

All societies have laws to protect individuals, protect property and make society a safe place for everyone. When someone breaks the law they commit a crime. In the UK, millions of crimes are committed each year. Many are not reported or followed up because they are considered trivial or the victim is too embarrassed or scared to say anything. At some point in our lives most of us will experience the effects of crime.

There are two kinds of laws in the UK.

Bye-laws – made by elected councillors and apply to a local area. They cover things like parking restrictions, alcohol-free zones and environmental concerns such as dropping litter and dog fouling. Breaking a bye-law can result in a fine, but you do not get a criminal record. Some laws are centuries old, and appear out of date, but as they have not been repealed, they are still laws.

Parliamentary laws – made by the government and apply to everyone in the country. These laws also put crimes into two categories. *Non-indictable offences* include minor crimes and driving offences. These are usually dealt with in a Magistrates' Court. *Indictable offences* are much more serious crimes. These are dealt with in Crown Courts with a judge and jury, and usually carry much harsher potential penalties.

MAN DIES IN SUSPECTED HIT AND RUN

MUM KILLS AND BURIES HER OWN CHILD

THREE ARRESTED IN COUNTER TERRORISM STING

MAN JAILED AFTER SETTING UP CANNABIS FARM

BOY OF 16 PUNCHES MAN TO DEATH

CAR THIEVES TO DO COMMUNITY SERVICE

WOMAN CHARGED WITH FRAUD AFTER STEALING MONEY FROM HOSPITAL

Why do you think there are local and national laws and not just one set for everywhere?

There are three key types of crimes:

- *Crimes against the person* – offences causing direct harm to a person, for example, murder, rape, GBH and **hate crimes**.
- *Crimes against property* – offences that damage or deprive people of their property, for example, arson, burglary, trespassing.
- *Crimes against the state* – offences that potentially endanger everyone or affect the smooth running of society, for example, terrorism, selling state secrets, perjury.

It is very difficult to say which of these is the worst. The victim of an assault may say that crimes against the person are the worst as they have personal experience of them. Where a country is put at risk by someone's actions, millions can be affected, so maybe crimes against the state are the worst. Crimes against property, such as burglary have long-term negative impacts on the victims, and often these take longest to get over.

With a partner, try to come up with reasons why each type of crime is the worst and also least bad. Thinking of examples often helps make those points.

The Basics

1. Write definitions for all of the italic key words on this page.
2. Using examples, explain the three types of crime.
3. Religion should dictate the law. What do you think? Explain your opinion.
4. **Crimes against the state are the worst kind of crime.** Do you agree? Explain your reasons showing you have thought about more than one point of view.

Causes of crime

You have just looked at the types of crime that are prevalent in society today. More importantly, though, the question we should all be asking is why are they happening? If answers can be found, then society can try to prevent them in the first place.

In pairs make a list of the reasons people might have for committing crimes. Next, look at the diagram below. Can you place the reasons in your list under the appropriate headings?

Complete the task in the box to the right. Were there any debates about where to place the reasons? There probably were, as these are not always separate reasons. For example, an addiction can be classed as a mental health problem, a person's upbringing might lead to addiction. It is important to see these links.

Reasons for crime

Upbringing – This might include the environment a person is brought up in, such as experiencing an unstable family life, neglect, physical or emotional abuse, or being surrounded by crimes/criminal activity.

Mental health problems – The state of mind of a person may lead them into crime. They might have serious psychological issues with no understanding of right or wrong; might feel no guilt or compassion for others; might enjoy hurting others; might have educational learning issues and be easily led into crime; or are themselves victims of some event which has disturbed their minds, for example, depression or an abusive upbringing.

Opposition to existing laws – Some crimes are committed in protest about laws that exist that are considered either unfair or for the benefit of a select few in society. Sometimes laws have to be broken to get laws to be changed.

Poverty – A person might commit a crime because they see no other alternative way to survive. They may have no money, no job or cannot provide for themselves or their children.

Greed/hate – Emotions can be responsible for crime. Greed can drive crime focused on wanting more, while hate can drive acts of violence, revenge or discrimination.

Addiction – A person may have an addiction, for example, to alcohol, drugs, sex or money, which may lead them to commit a crime to feed their habit or their cravings. They may even be addicted to crime itself, for example, stealing.

What would religion say about this?

All religions would say that the law should be followed. St Paul tells Christians to 'obey the laws of the land'. In all religions, a law is a law and if you break that law, then punishment shall follow. However, although crime is never right, sometimes there are understandable reasons why it does happen. If all people lived by the principles of 'love your neighbour' or 'treat others as we wish to be treated' or the Buddhist Noble Eightfold Path or the Hindu idea of 'ahimsa' and righteous action (dharma) then many causes of crime might disappear. The phrase to 'hate the sin not the sinner' can be used here. Criminals often need our help rather than our judgement. However, punishments have to be given or society would be chaotic but at the same time the causes of crime have to be removed.

The Basics

1. Explain briefly two of the reasons for crime.
2. Explain religious attitudes to those who break the law.
3. What might a religious person mean by 'hate the sin not the sinner'?

Good and evil

There are those who suggest that people who commit the worst crimes are evil. But what exactly is 'evil' and where does it come from? Similarly what is meant by 'good' and where does that come from?

Definitions:

- Evil is something that is profoundly immoral and wicked and is usually seen as depraved and malicious.
- Good is defined as morally excellent, virtuous, righteous and pious.

Where does evil come from?

Buddhism

Buddhism teaches that all unenlightened beings are capable of both good ('skilful') and evil ('unskilful') acts. Evil acts are those strongly motivated by the Three Poisons – greed, hatred and delusion. Such acts are considered harmful because they cause suffering both to the person acting and probably to other people as well. We are each responsible for our actions and the consequences of our actions. How we manage our intentions, thoughts, words and deeds impacts other people for good or ill.

Christianity

Evil is seen as the abuse of the free will God gave to humans that allowed them to choose right from wrong. Many Christians believe in a figure called the Devil or Satan, who is an evil power, though ultimately less powerful than God. The Devil continually tries to tempt people and encourage them to behave badly. So, evil is a combination of internal and external factors.

Hinduism

According to Hinduism, there is a constant struggle in the universe, the world, and our individual selves between light and dark, good and evil. Good and evil can exist in creation. Certainly, a human's free will allows them to do evil, and, as people are ignorant of the divine reality of the world, their dharma selfishness can encourage them in the wrong direction. In Hinduism the concept of right and wrong action is related to dharma or righteousness, where living according to dharma is good.

Islam

The Qur'an says that Iblis is a devil who was previously an angel. When Allah ordered the angels to bow to Adam, Iblis refused and was expelled from paradise, but was later able to cause Adam and Eve's expulsion from Eden. Iblis continually tempts humans to be wicked. Humans fail to show self-discipline, and give in to Iblis' temptations. Evil is a mix of temptation by Iblis and human weakness.

Judaism

In Genesis, we read the story of how Adam and Eve were tempted by the serpent to disobey G-d, resulting in their expulsion from Eden. The serpent represents an evil malevolent force, which continues to tempt humans into bad deeds. However, we have free will, so there has to be evil – this allows us to exercise our free will for good or bad. By being obedient to the mitzvot (laws), a Jewish person avoids evil.

Sikhism

Sikhism puts selfishness at the heart of evil. The concept of selfishness (haumai) is what prevents people from following their religion, and encourages them to break rules and hurt others. The more selfish a person, the more evil they are capable of. So, for Sikhs, evil lies within the consciousness of any person, and the level of selfishness we have makes it more or less controlling of our actions.

What about other ideas?

If you do not believe in a devil or the Fall (the story of Adam and Eve), or any other religious beliefs, you could still believe evil exists. With a partner, can you think of any examples you would class as evil that you have heard of – what were they, and why do you label them as such?

Some people believe that all people have the capacity to do evil, that it is part of a human's make-up. But we do not all show evil, and those who do, do it to different degrees. You might say that someone who kills their child is evil, but are they the same level of evil as someone who goes out hunting people only to torture and eventually murder them? So why isn't everyone evil? The argument goes that it depends on our upbringing, the influences in our lives (and when those influences occur), and experiences we have. Any of these can trigger or sow the seeds for evil to manifest in us, but evil is not a force within us, rather a psychological phenomena. In all these, we are saying that it is the person themselves who is evil.

Evil person or evil action?

It is common to hear the phrase 'hate the sin, not the sinner'. This is making the point that it is actions which are wrong, not the person themselves. However, the fact remains that we cannot punish the action or sin, we have to punish a person *for committing the sin or carrying out the wrong/evil deed*. So, when we see something as evil, regardless of how we think that evil originated, we have to punish the perpetrator. Most religious people believe that people who do wrong are still redeemable, that they are not themselves evil, and can be brought back to good ways. Religions believe in evil actions rather than evil people.

How do we deal with evil?

Through a country's justice system, a person will be punished when found guilty of a crime. We will look at punishment later in the topic, but punishment in the UK takes a range of forms, from **imprisonment** through to fines and exclusions. In other countries, punishment can be harsher, through **corporal** and **capital punishment**. However, crimes affect people beyond the actual event; they have an emotional impact, which can be very long-lasting. Evil events disturb people's sense of well-being and safety, so have an even greater impact. The victims have to be helped, and everyone else reassured.

Is it ever right to cause suffering?

If I had to make someone suffer to protect myself or my family, I would. But that is 'necessary', not 'good'.

Ian

I think it is wrong to cause anyone to suffer – indeed it is evil to do so, and we should avoid it.

Jamal

The question is 'would it bring about a greater good?' That is the only time making someone suffer might be justified.

Tovi

The Basics

1. Define 'good' and 'evil'.
2. For your chosen religion(s), explain how evil originates, and the relationship between good and evil.
3. Explain why some crimes are considered 'evil'. Use examples to help your explanation.
4. **Following a religion prevents evil from happening.** Do you think this is true? Explain your answer, trying to show more than one point of view.
5. **People are not evil, some just do evil things.** Do you think this is true? Explain your answer, trying to show more than one point of view.

What is the worst crime to commit?

For the course, you have to think about murder, theft and hate crimes. But, are you clear on what these are? Murder is the deliberate killing of someone; theft is to permanently deprive someone of something they own; hate crimes are any crimes motivated by **prejudice** in the negative sense. Religions are very clear about murder and theft, but hate crimes are not mentioned in any scriptures and are relatively new to the British legal system.

So which is worst?

Use these teachings plus information from page 352 and page 363 to work out what the religion(s) you have studied might say about each of the crimes.

All religions believe life is sacred, that it should be protected and cherished. So, any murder must be wrong by definition, as it is the opposite of that. They all include severe punishments for murder in their laws. There is no way to repair the damage; you cannot bring someone back to life, and their families suffer the loss for the rest of theirs. It is the biggest insult to God because it is deliberately destroying God's creation. Both Islam and Judaism describe the taking of a life as akin to the annihilation of a whole world.

Theft is also against the laws of religions, but punishments are less harsh than for murder. Depending on what is taken, theft might have a bigger or lesser impact on someone's life. For example, to steal an older person's savings leaves them with only their pension to live on, whereas to steal a person's car might only be an inconvenience until their insurance replaces it. Theft shows disrespect to someone, and all religions preach **equality** and respect, therefore theft goes against fundamental ways of behaviour.

'Hate crime' really refers to the reason why the crime is committed, not the type of crime itself. You could say that because any type of crime could be a hate crime and be motivated by prejudice, then these are the worst type of crime. These examples are considered hate crimes: the murder of Antony Walker in 2005, just because he was black and the desecration of Jewish cemeteries because of anti-Semitism. It is also true that hate crimes go against fundamental religious teachings of equality and love, community and brotherhood.

Look at these examples. What is each an example of? Which do you see as worse, and why?

David murdered John after he had an affair with David's wife.

Siobhan stole £50,000 from her job in a hospital to pay for medical treatment for her son who is sick.

Jayden poured petrol through a letterbox, and set fire to it. The family inside died. He did it because of the colour of their skin.

Felix cheated an older couple out of their savings by telling them their money was going into Christian investments in developing countries, but he was really spending it on himself.

The Basics

1 Define murder, theft and hate crime.
2 Explain why religious believers would disagree with each of murder, theft and hate crime.
3 **Hate crimes are the worst type of crime.** Do you agree with this? Explain more than one point of view and include religious arguments in your answer.

Is crime linked to evil?

When you read stories in the newspaper or see some of the real-life programmes about the crimes some people have committed, you can be really shocked. Sometimes crimes are labelled as evil actions, their perpetrators as evil people. So, why do we use the word 'evil'? Usually it is because we are sickened by what we know has happened and we cannot imagine doing it so feel there must be something wrong with the perpetrator. Often their offences harm children or vulnerable people (or animals). Fred West, John Venables and Robert Thompson, Ian Brady and Myra Hindley are all people who committed crimes of this type that might make us say they are evil.

So, why might some people be evil or behave in this way? Look back to the previous pages for the reasons behind crime. Many religious people also believe the Devil is at work in the minds of these people, making them do terrible things and that this is where evil comes from.

Crime and punishment exercise

Look at the list of crimes in the pink box. Identify the type of crime being committed in each case. Is it against a person, property or state? Now look at the list of punishments available under the English law (the green box). Which is the most suitable punishment in each case? For each one, what do you think the punishment will achieve? Do you think any of the perpetrators should have a different punishment? Explain why. Would you class any crimes as 'evil'? Explain why?

1 a young woman who killed her husband after years of domestic abuse by him
2 a woman who neglected, tortured and eventually beat her own child to death
3 a schoolgirl who stole items worth £85 from a department store
4 four football fans who kicked a rival fan to death after a match
5 a schoolboy who covered a railway bridge with racist graffiti
6 a woman who defrauded a charity of £50,000
7 a young man who sold drugs in a school playground
8 a man who sexually abused a number of children
9 a gang of men who held up a train at gunpoint, stealing millions in bank notes being taken for destruction
10 a drunk driver who hit a pedestrian, leaving them with a disability
11 a young man who raped a woman he had been dancing with all night at a club and had walked home
12 a couple who downloaded terrorist materials from the web.

Life imprisonment — Fixed term imprisonment
Suspended prison sentence (only enforced if they reoffend) — **Community service order**
Curfew order — Fine — Disqualification (e.g. from driving) — Electronic tagging
Probation order (required to meet probation officer weekly) — Restraining order
Exclusion order — Compensation order — Police caution

The aims of punishment

On the previous page, it was important for you to justify the decisions you made regarding the choice of punishments. Society sets up rules and we have to obey them or face the consequences. However, what one person thinks is very wrong, another person might consider less so. That is why we have a judicial system that sets tariffs for punishments to guide judges in the sentences they hand down.

A judge also knows other information before they give a sentence. For example, if the person has offended before, information from psychologists and perhaps about their home background.

There are six main aims of punishment and you probably came up with all of them in the punishment exercise. For the course, you need to know more about three of these.

Would some of your decisions in the previous task have been different if you knew more about the person? Did you think about the reasons why you were punishing someone? How might this have influenced the decisions you made?

Deterrence

A punishment is meant to be unpleasant and a **deterrence**, so that the offender (and wider society) is put off committing crimes in the future. A burglar who gets sent to prison for five years will hopefully not want to experience that again and will find some other legal means to obtain money and possessions. Also, we learn very quickly that when we do wrong we may be punished, so if they know what the punishment is going to be, many people would be put off committing the crime in the first place. For example, the penalty for drink driving in the UK is a minimum 12-month driving ban, a fine and potentially a prison sentence which deters most people from drink driving.

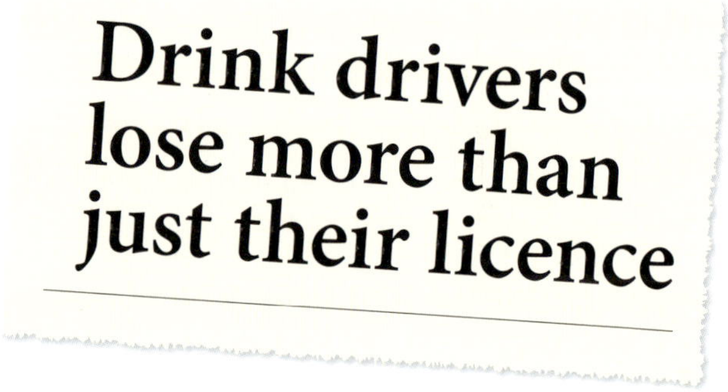
Drink drivers lose more than just their licence

Task

Read these statements. How does each one demonstrate deterrence?

a Bilal – I lost my driving licence because of drink driving. No one got hurt, but I still got punished. That cost me my job as well, as I was a driver. I have really learned my lesson – so I won't drink and drive.

b Chris – I was sent to prison for 12 months. I never want to go back inside, so am working with my parole officer to make sure.

c Jane – Even though I really needed cash, I didn't steal it when I had a chance, because of the consequences of getting caught.

BRING BACK HANGING FOR MURDERERS

Government to set up new prisons which aim to reform not just punish

Retribution

This is taking revenge on the offender; simply put it means 'getting your own back'. When people break the law someone somewhere is almost always hurt, even if it means they are just upset or angry. Most people follow the law so it is not fair that a few people want to just ignore the rules and do as they please. Society uses punishment to make the offender pay for what they have done and show support for the victim. They do this by demonstrating that the criminal has not got away with hurting them. In some cases **retribution** can be very severe. In the UK, criminals can receive lengthy prison sentences; other countries use capital or corporal punishment.

Reformation

Obviously society cannot simply lock up everyone who breaks the law and throw away the key. Many punishments are given to try to change the nature of the person who has offended. This is because most people who break the law will continue to be part of society. It is important to try to get these people to realise the effects their action(s) had on others and then hopefully they will not do it again. For example, a graffiti artist might be sentenced to work in the council parks and gardens department. In prisons there are usually education and work programmes to support offenders in their rehabilitation; this helps prepare them to rejoin society as a constructive member. Religious groups feel this is an important aim of punishment.

Task

Look at this list of punishments. Which ones suit each of the three aims of punishment? Explain why:

- Prison
- Large fine
- Corporal punishment
- Drink-drive rehabilitation course.

Task

How might a punishment system based on each of:

a deterrence
b retribution
c reformation

influence criminals and society?

Thinking questions

1 **The only good aim of punishment is deterrence.**
2 **Religious people should ensure all punishment reforms criminals.**

Explore these statements, analysing arguments to agree and disagree, and include religious arguments.

Aims of punishment continued …

Although you will not need to know these in detail, there are three other key aims of punishment to be aware of. **Protection** – the whole point of having a legal system is to protect society. Some criminals are dangerous, and society must be protected from them. The criminal must also be protected from society. When a person shows no remorse for what they have done and continues to be a threat, most people agree that they should be locked up. **Vindication** – the courts must impose proper punishments for crimes committed, so that laws are respected. Without penalties, some people would ignore the law. Rules are rules and have to be justly applied to the crime done. **Reparation** gives offenders the chance to make up for damage they have caused to the victim and/or society, for example, through community service..

Religious attitudes to the aims

Deterrence

This is key for all religions, because if it works there is no need for any other aims as there would be no crime. Islamic law has tough consequences for the criminal in the hope that this will deter criminals. Christianity agrees with deterrence but not through such harsh punishment. For example, many Christians are against the death penalty. Breaking the law does not fit with Buddhist principles either, but Buddhism does not agree with harsh punishments that could harm the criminal. They would encourage positive punishments, such as community service, or education programmes to deter future crimes.

Retribution

Religions share similar views on retribution as they do to deterrence. The punishment should fit the crime even to the point where it can be seen as revenge. In some religions it is taught that retribution is an appropriate punishment which God allows. For example, the teaching 'an eye for an eye' is often used to justify retribution. Many Christians believe that a criminal should serve their time, but that the death penalty makes the law as bad as the criminal. Revenge is not an appropriate reason for punishment.

Reformation

All religions agree with this but in different ways. The basic idea of reformation is that helping people to change is best for them and for society, as then they would not reoffend. Many religions believe that people can be reformed through counselling, education programmes, and so on. Reformation as an aim has been central to all prison reform in Britain since the early nineteenth century. Quaker Christian Elizabeth Fry was a major force in prison reform at the time.

The Basics

1. Explain why some people commit crimes.
2. Explain each of the three aims of punishment – deterrence, retribution and reformation.
3. Look back at the punishment exercise. Which aim of punishment was most important in each case? Why?
4. **Protecting people from criminals is the most important aim of punishment.** Do you agree? Give reasons for your answer showing that you have thought about more than one point of view and include religious arguments in your reasoning.

Suffering and religious attitudes to it

Suffering happens when people cause pain, hardship or distress to themselves or others. It can be physical or emotional. Crime may directly cause suffering because it is done to you directly (for example, assault) or indirectly (for example, property or possessions being stolen or damaged). In some cases a country can suffer (the crime is against the state), or an entire religion. Rarely is it the case that only one person suffers because often their families and friends do too.

Who suffers?

1. a bomb blast in a major city
2. an older person having their purse stolen
3. a young child being abducted
4. a house being broken into
5. a woman who is raped

Think about …

1. Does the number of victims make the suffering worse?
2. Is physical suffering worse than mental suffering?
3. Should a criminal who makes many people suffer be dealt with more harshly than one whose crime involves only one person?

Religious teachings for you to think about …

Religions condemn suffering caused by human action towards others. Our wrong actions and decisions are unacceptable as they hurt other people. Religious teachings tell us it is wrong to cause suffering. There is also a responsibility to deal with people who cause this suffering. Buddhism stresses that suffering is everywhere and we all have to look within ourselves to stop this suffering, whilst other religions look to a god to help them overcome suffering or be forgiven for the suffering they have caused. Religious teachings give humans the path to righteous actions, but human nature (emotions, reactions and needs) make it virtually impossible to choose the right actions all the time, so we cause suffering.

1. All religions have rules that are there to try to prevent suffering.
2. All religions have a 'love your neighbour' concept to prevent suffering.
3. All religions stress how our emotions (for example, love, hate, greed and desires) easily lead to suffering and so they give us teachings to keep these in check.

Religions support the law to prevent suffering. However, they believe law-breakers should be punished fairly and with justice, and that victims must be helped. Religious people should care for all people, good and bad, even those who cause the greatest amount of suffering. The law must provide this help, whilst religions try to provide wrong-doers with the means to right their wrongs, and heal suffering on both sides.

The Basics

1. What is meant by suffering?
2. How can religion help prevent suffering?
3. Explain religions' attitudes to suffering.
4. **Those who cause suffering should not be helped.** What do you think?
5. **Suffering will never stop.** Refer to religious ideas and different viewpoints in your answer.

Helping those who are suffering because of crime

Sometimes we get preoccupied with what should happen to the criminal and justice being done. However, there is the other side to crime … the victim. What happens to them? Is there support out there or are they just left to get on with it and move on?

If you are a victim of a reported crime, then the police will send you the contact details for a charity called Victim Support (**www.victimsupport.org.uk**). Many victims of minor crime do not need this service but it is offered because we can never know how an individual may react to such crimes. You can turn to Victim Support yourself to overcome the effects of the crime. Witnesses can also receive support, as the process of giving evidence can be traumatic, especially in the case of serious crime.

Victim Support

Victim Support offers six key areas of support:

- Emotional and practical support
- Practical tips to keep safe
- Specific support in certain areas, for example, abuse or rape
- The **rights** of a victim
- Help for young victims
- Help for foreign language speakers

'As a victim I didn't know where to turn … my house was broken into and I was a wreck, nervous and couldn't concentrate at all … Simply to talk to someone helped and getting advice about the criminal justice system gave me a way forward.'

'As a victim of serious assault I could not come to terms with the crime. I didn't even know how to report the crime, how to write a personal statement to show how the crime had affected me, what would happen in court and what was meant by restorative justice. Victim Support helped me.'

'The support I got was tailored to my needs … see I was abused as a child and only now can I talk about it. I needed someone specific to help me. Victim Support has given me that.'

'As an advisor for Victim Support I am often contacted by victims who cannot speak English well enough to get the help they need. We can find interpreters in over twenty languages. They are victims just like anyone and I help them get the help they need.'

'I suffered abuse on social media and no one understood how it made me feel … Victim Support did! Young people can react totally differently than an adult and so we need different support. The bullying made me feel helpless but now I get help.'

'I didn't know I had rights! I do now though! There is a code for victims about how I should be helped and kept informed of my case which means I feel more secure and protected.'

Task

Read the six cases above and use that information to explain why the work of Victim Support is important.

Forgiveness as an attitude to criminals

Forgiveness is a process that victims go through where they let go of the offence and the negative ideas of revenge, to move on and allow the criminal to move on too. It does not mean the victim condones, accepts, excuses or forgets the crime. Whereas society deals with criminals through punishment, victims can deal with it through forgiveness. To forgive is very hard to do and some never can, whereas others find it within themselves to do so. Some people show forgiveness through words, others through actions.

Forgiveness is very important in Christianity, with Jesus saying we should forgive 'not seven times but seventy times seven'. Islam states 'whosoever forgives and makes amends, his reward is upon Allah' (Surah 42:40). In Judaism, the Torah explicitly forbids Jewish people to take revenge or to bear grudges (Leviticus 19:18). In Buddhism, forgiving practises two essential virtues: compassion and understanding. Without it the world remains vengeful and troubled. Sikhism states that 'forgiveness is as necessary to life as the food we eat and the air we breathe' (Guru Granth Sahib). In Hinduism, forgiveness is one of six cardinal virtues in the Rig Veda.

Although religions clearly teach forgiveness as a very important quality, they also teach justice when the law is broken. So for them, the law deals with the criminal as it has to. It can be described as a process: crime' committed → criminal caught and punished → time served → repentance shown (maybe) → new start. The crime is not forgotten, but the criminal has the opportunity to move on from that mistake. Some criminals, through their repentance, earn forgiveness as the victim can see that the criminal regrets what they have done and the forgiveness allows both parties to move on. However, a victim's forgiveness is not dependent upon the criminal's repentance. A victim can forgive even though the criminal does not repent and this allows them, as the victim, to move on. Christians often turn to prayer to help them forgive; they do so with the help of God. Most religions state that forgiveness is a quality of God, to be copied by the believer. However, it is not an easy virtue to put into action as many people have suffered terrible crimes and will never be able to forgive, but at the same time the hatred can ruin their lives. Others have shown forgiveness and many positive things have come from it. Religion would always urge people to forgive, but never demand it as it is a personal decision. Those who are able to forgive need to be commended and those who cannot forgive need to be helped.

Religions *do not* teach 'forgive, forget, don't punish'. All religions teach that those who commit crime **should receive a punishment** for their crime. Forgiveness is separate – a personal matter for the victim.

The Basics

1 What does forgiveness mean?
2 How does forgiveness allow victims to move on?
3 Explain religious attitudes to the forgiveness of criminals.
4 **It is the religious duty of all victims to forgive.** Give arguments to support and arguments to disagree with this view. Explain your own views.

The treatment of criminals

Punishments in the UK

Custodial sentences	Locking the offender up
Prisons (adult)	The UK has different types of prisons. High security are category A and B and house the most dangerous offenders. Category C is for those serving shorter sentences and category D are open prisons for first-time offenders and those due to be released.
High security mental health institutions	House offenders with serious psychological disorders, who threaten the safety of others and themselves, for example, psychopaths, sociopaths, schizophrenics.
Young Offender Institutions	House offenders classed as children (under 18 years of age). Routines are specifically targeted at children's needs.
Non-custodial sentences	**Alternatives to prison**
ASBOs	Anti Social Behaviour Orders set restrictions that the offender must stick to, for example, curfew, barred from going to certain places.
Community Service	Unpaid work in the community, for up to 300 hours. Offenders do not have a choice in what they do although their offence and experiences may influence magistrates.
Curfew	Must return home by a set hour, often used with tagging.
Electronic Tagging	An electronic surveillance device attached to the offender's leg.
Fines	A set amount of money must be paid for committing the offence.
Probation	Offenders must meet regularly with a probation officer who monitors behaviour.
Restorative Justice	Young offenders attend sessions to discuss their crime, why it was wrong and its effect on the victim; often includes meeting and talking with their victims.

Look at pages 356–358 on the aims of punishments. What aims of punishment are met by each of the punishments described in the above table?

Attitudes of religions to offenders

For a religion to assess its attitude to offenders, various issues have to be looked at:

- the type of crime committed – lesser or serious
- the violence used and the suffering of the victim
- the reasons that caused the criminal to commit the crime
- who has committed the crime and their circumstances
- is the criminal old enough to be responsible for their actions?
- the best punishment considered to serve the aims desired.

Each religion has general attitudes to punishments, but also has the belief that each case has to be assessed individually on its own merits. No crime is exactly the same as another and for that reason punishments can be different.

Task

Look at each of the issues in the bullet list above. Give reasons why you think each one could make a difference to the type of punishment that is given.

Task

Criminals must always get what they deserve.
Do you agree? Explain reasons to agree and disagree.

Buddhism

Buddhists believe that if people don't commit crime because they are afraid of the punishment (it has acted as a deterrent) this is the wrong motive; instead, people should avoid criminality by thinking and acting in the right way. Buddhism would teach criminals the law of karma like it teaches everyone else. Understanding karma means taking responsibility for your actions. Buddhists would generally recognise the need for punishment and prisons as part of the justice system and to keep others safe. Cruel punishments and the death penalty would not be encouraged by Buddhists.

Hinduism

To punish is seen by smriti texts as a ruler's right and through fearing the threat of punishment all beings should follow their dharma. Punishment maintains social order. In the past, punishments allowed for compensation rather than for retribution. This allows for society and criminals to be reconciled and **social justice** to be restored. In modern UK law not only are punishments given by the state, but the victims need to be compensated too for loss or injury.

Judaism

There is a strong belief in repentance and whilst a person can repent to G-d, this is pointless if they try to avoid the punishments from society. One of the seven laws of Noah states that there is a need for a proper legal system to establish a moral society. With this in mind, treatment of offenders must be just and fair with a focus on reform. Revenge as in retribution, according to the Talmud, is not a Jewish principle.

Christianity

Christians believe the law has a responsibility to punish and care for the criminal whilst trying to reform them. Whilst prison removes freedoms, separates prisoners from families and removes their rights, it also has concern for their reform to be released back into society. Therefore, there can be conflict between severe punishments and the Christian belief in help, love and reform. Some Christians want more of an emphasis on 'justice' based on the 'an eye for an eye' teaching from the Bible. However, most Christians do believe in treating offenders humanely and fairly, giving them a chance to face up to their crime, having them serve a fair punishment and giving them a second chance to turn their lives around.

Islam

The Qur'an emphasises the justice of Allah and the idea of accountability for one's actions. Also, it teaches mercy and forgiveness. Shari'ah Law prescribes punishments for crimes such as murder, rape and theft. Justice must be done and the victims should be compensated equitably. Hence, under Shari'ah Law victims can accept compensation from the criminal who then is given a lesser sentence, and Allah looks favourably on that. Most Muslim countries have modern prisons and principles of fair treatment of criminals; some still use Shari'ah Law for crimes.

Sikhism

For Sikhs there are religious laws and criminal laws. For the former, community service in the gurdwara is used, with an emphasis on penance, humility and renewal of vows broken. Sikhs do not hold power in any state country and so do not determine punishments. Some agree with capital punishment to keep society safe, but many believe it is against the nature of God as He decides life and death. Punishments should be just and allowing for reform and forgiveness is consistent with trying to be like God.

Focus on prisons

Prison is used as a punishment all over the world. There are many types of prison in the UK, from high-security to open prisons, and there are many crimes which result in people being given a prison sentence. There is great debate about the following:

- which criminals should be sent to prison
- the conditions that prisoners are kept in
- the work that is done with the prisoners to reform them
- whether prison actually achieves its aims, especially in light of the high cost.

Christianity in Britain has played a big role in the prison debate. Whilst Christians support their use, they are concerned about the way they are run and levels of reoffending. Many prisons contain individuals who need social and/or medical help, education work and life skills and as Christians there is a **duty** of care and help which is based in religious teachings. Even though they have committed a crime, criminals deserve fair and humane treatment and are more likely to respond positively to them than harsh punishments. Other Christians have different views and believe that life in prison should be tough to act as a deterrent. If prison life was tough enough, then prisoners would not want to reoffend. The Jewish charity Jewish Prisoner Services International (JPSI) works to bring loving kindness to prisoners, by addressing the needs of Jewish prisoners and their families through chaplaincy, advocacy and social services, because to treat anyone with mercy and humbleness is all part of being Jewish.

Organisation profile

The Prison Reform Trust was founded in 1981. It works to create a more humane and effective penal system. It provides advice, information, educational work, research and campaigning. Its work has been very effective in achieving change in prisons, as well as in the policies and practices of the penal system. Find out about this charity through its website. **www.prisonreformtrust.org.uk**

Fact! 57 per cent of prisoners in the UK have a reading age of below 11 (2021)

I work for the Prison Reform Trust and have direct experience of how damaging locking people up can be. It's easy to say that prison life is easy when you have never been inside one. The reality is very different. Conditions in some prisons are very poor, inmates can be locked in their cells for 23 hours a day. Problems such as over-crowding, lack of exercise, poor diet, boredom, violence and drug abuse are a daily experience. I think it is really important that prisoners have the opportunity to reform and the hope of reward for good behaviour.

I was imprisoned 20 years ago for armed robbery. It wasn't my first offence, I had done prison time before. I thought it was important to be hard and to stand up for myself. I got into a disagreement with a prison warden and ended up with another sentence for GBH. I should have been paroled by now, if it wasn't for that. Somehow it just doesn't seem important anymore. My wife divorced me by mail a few years back. Joey and Tina were just toddlers when I was sent down, I didn't see them grow up. I sometimes wonder what they are like now. Simple things like having a beer in the pub, driving a car, cuddling on the sofa are just distant memories. I'm used to life in prison, the routines, not having to make decisions and I've learned to just do as I'm told!

Fact! In April 2025, 383 under-18s were being held in prisons in England and Wales

I'm doing two months in prison because I allowed my teenage daughter to stay off school. I didn't think it would come to this. I was so frightened when they brought me here and embarrassed by the admittance procedures. I cried constantly for the first three days. It is hard to adjust to having your life run by someone else. I can't stop worrying about the kids. My mum isn't well so they have had to go into foster care. I know I'm going to lose my job too, because they don't know I'm in here, unless they have read the local papers. Going home will be really bad; everyone will know and they probably think I'm an awful mother.

Parole means that a person can be released early having served some of their sentence. When on parole they must live within the law and are supported by a parole officer, who will help them to reintegrate into society. The parole order may require them to have treatment, for example, for drug abuse. The aim is to help them avoid re-offending and become active and purposeful members of society.

Fact! Prisons spend on average just £2.70 on each inmate's food daily (2023)

Fact! 31 per cent of women prisoners have children under 16 at home (2018)

I'm in this young offender's institute because they want to change me – reform, they call it. I have to go to sessions and talk about the stuff I've done and how it affects others. I've done loads of stuff. I've had warnings, three ASBOs, paid fines and done community service a couple of times too. I didn't do the last one though because it was boring. I'd have gone if it was working on cars or something like that. Me and the gang like hanging out in the street. I'm only in here because a copper saw me with a knife. I miss home and my mates and I'm fed up with all the rules.

Fact! There were 399 deaths in prisons in England and Wales between March 2024 and March 2025.

The Basics

1 Describe the long-term and short-term effects of prison sentences on the offender.
2 Make a list of advantages and disadvantages of non-custodial sentences.
3 Explain three reasons why young offenders are dealt with differently to adults.
4 **A life sentence should mean life in prison.** Do you agree? Give reasons for your answer, showing you have thought about more than one point of view.

Community service as punishment

Community service is often called 'community payback' when referring to it as a punishment. Community sentences can be given if the criminal is convicted of a crime but is not sent to prison. The punishments involve doing unpaid work in the local community, like cleaning up a park.

Community sentences can be given for less serious crimes such as damaging property or drink driving. It is seen as more positive than prison and the judge might think that it could have a better effect on the offender than sending them to prison. Also, it allows offenders to carry on working and do the payback in the evenings. This enables them to keep their job.

Payback is working in a local area and managed by a community payback supervisor. Offenders must wear high-visibility clothes. Punishment time is between 40 and 300 hours dependent upon the crime and if the person is unemployed, they may be required to work up to 3–4 days a week.

Community payback is intended to help offenders address the behaviour that caused them to commit a crime, and encourage them to not do it again. Individuals can receive help for addictions and mental health issues, and learn new skills. Payback programmes can include: counselling sessions, drug tests, anger management and mental health help, literacy skills and help with job applications. Many people see community payback as a positive punishment, as opposed to locking someone up in prison. Dangerous criminals are not considered for the programme; it is lesser punishment for lesser crimes.

Religious attitudes to community service (payback)

If you look at the aims of payback, religions would support its use. Organised properly, it is suitable for the type of criminal it is designed to reform. Also, communities can benefit, with damage repaired or expertise shared. Prison can mean people mixing with individuals far worse than them and therefore it can have a negative influence. Also, separation from families and loss of jobs can lead to long-term problems, whereas community service does not have this impact. However, this punishment does not work for some people, and they get involved in further crime. Also, on some occasions the type of service or payback has not been suitable or indeed run very well. Some religious people might believe it is too soft a punishment and does not bring the reform necessary or create the deterrent it needs to. If the punishment had been tougher, then perhaps further crime could have been prevented.

The Basics

1. Describe how community service works.
2. Why do religions support community service/payback?
3. Explain why some religious people believe community service might not be a suitable punishment.

Corporal punishment

What is corporal punishment?

Corporal punishment is to use physical pain as a punishment for a criminal act. It deliberately inflicts pain through whipping, branding or amputation (removal of a body part).

This type of punishment only remains in parts of Africa, the Middle East, Asia and South America.

Religious attitudes to corporal punishment

Most religious people today disagree with the use of corporal punishment, although many holy books allow it.

☸ Buddhism

In Buddhism 'An action, even if it brings benefit to oneself, cannot be considered if it causes physical and mental pain to another being' (Buddha). Corporal punishment causes that pain, so should be considered to be against Buddhist principles. Buddhism states that cruel treatment of an offender does not make right what they did, and does not improve them. The Dalai Lama said that hatred is not ended by hatred, rather by love – meaning that corporal punishment is wrong. It also harms the person giving the punishment as they are intentionally hurting another – so breaking a Moral Precept.

✝ Christianity

Most Christians do not agree with it, believing it does not help reform criminals, as it is more about retribution and taking revenge. Jesus himself was flogged before he was hung on the cross. The quotations 'and a rod for a fool's back' (Proverbs 26:3) and Psalm 89 'I will punish transgressions with the rod' allow some Christians to justify physical punishment of children as chastisement. No Christian country in the developed world uses corporal punishment in its justice system.

ॐ Hinduism

With Hinduism, corporal punishment has been used historically in cases where reform has not worked. If a person says they are not guilty of the crime then a trial should be held. The evidence should be followed and appropriate punishment given.

Islam

Shari'ah Law allows corporal punishment, 'A thief male and female cut off the hand of both' (Surah 5:38), and 'If a woman or man is guilty of adultery, flog each of them 100 stripes' (Surah 24:2). In many Muslim countries, the Law of Compensation can be used which swaps corporal punishment for paying compensation. However, many Muslims today don't agree with corporal punishment and believe that Allah is merciful and forgiving.

Judaism

Jewish text does state punishments for breaking certain laws, which include using physical and capital punishments for certain things. However, these were used extremely rarely in exceptional circumstances by Jewish courts. The Mishnah states that a religious court that executed someone once in 70 years was considered excessive. It is widely accepted that these punishments are laid out as a deterrent.

Sikhism

Sikhism does not agree with inflicting pain as a way of punishment, rather it encourages reformation and rehabilitation within society. Within India, Sikhs follow Indian law. 'Show kindness and mercy to all life, and realise the Lord is pervading everywhere' (Guru Granth Sahib) – this suggests that corporal punishment would be wrong.

Reasons for the use of corporal punishment

1 Some see it as a deterrent.
2 It can fulfil the aim of retribution and quick reformation.
3 Physical pain is a harsher punishment for more serious crime.
4 It is more effective than prison as people fear pain.

Reasons for not using it

1 It is barbaric and inhumane.
2 It makes criminals more hardened and does not reform.
3 Revenge is wrong.
4 To purposely inflict pain is unacceptable.

Sanctity of life in relation to corporal and capital punishment

Even the lives of criminals are sacred. Most religious believers agree there is an aspect of God to each individual. So, as corporal and capital punishment damage/end life, they are both incompatible with this idea. However the offences committed have already disregarded 'sanctity of life', so do the offenders deserve that same consideration?

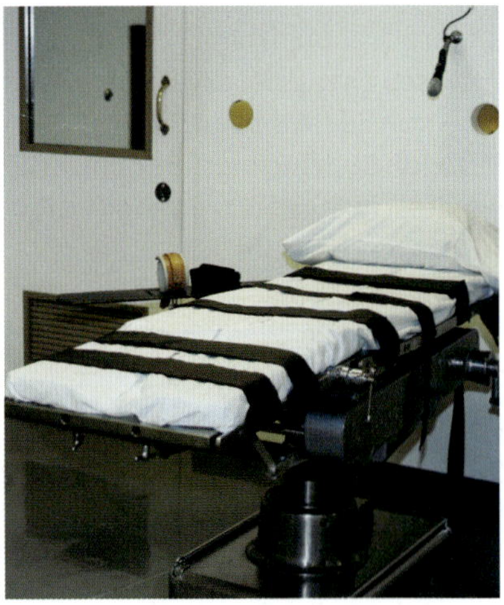

Lethal injection is a form of capital punishment

The Basics

1 What is meant by corporal punishment?
2 Explain why some religious believers agree with corporal punishment.
3 **Religious believers should never agree with corporal punishment.** Give reasons to agree and disagree with this statement, and explain them.

The death penalty – capital punishment

The death penalty is *capital punishment*. Where it is used, it is usually reserved for the most extreme offences, for example murder. Worldwide, other crimes such as blasphemy, adultery, drug offences, corruption, fraud, smuggling, treason, hijacking and war crimes are capital offences.

Are any crimes so bad they merit the death penalty? What do you think?

Why use such an extreme punishment?

The crimes are seen as so bad that no other punishment would be suitable. People who commit such horrific acts must face the most severe punishment, so that justice is seen to be done and others are deterred from committing these crimes. It is the principle of 'an eye for an eye' and is seen as the law of equality of retribution in Islam. A murderer shows no respect for human life, so the state shows no respect for the murderer's life. Many holy books name certain offences as being punishable by death.

USA executions (1976–2018)

Lethal injections	1318
Electrocution	160
Lethal gas	11
Hanging	3
Firing squad	3

In 1977, the USA allowed individual states to choose whether they wished to use capital punishment. Currently, 27 states have the death penalty. Texas is responsible for over one-third of all executions that take place. Between 1977 and June 2025 there were 1,630 executions in the USA. As of 1 January 2025, there were around 2,100 prisoners in the USA awaiting execution on death row. Amnesty International has said that the USA is savage, barbaric, cruel, prejudiced and uncivilised. This is because the USA has executed: people who offended as a child; people who have mental health problems; black people sentenced by all-white juries and many other seemingly unfair cases. If this is what can be said about what is considered to be the most democratic country in the world, what might be the situation in other countries?

See page 370 for more information on the work Amnesty International undertakes.

Facts and figures

- 144 countries have abolished the death penalty in law or practice.
- 58 countries retain and use the death penalty.
- This century 88 per cent of all known executions have taken place in China, Iran, Iraq, Saudi Arabia and the USA.
- Between 1976 and 2003 the USA executed 22 people (all of them men) who were under the age of 18 at the time the crime was committed – more than half of those executed worldwide.
- In March 2005, the USA abolished child executions, affecting over 70 juvenile offenders on death row in 12 states.
- In the USA, since 1973, over 150 prisoners on death row have been released after their convictions were overturned.
- Methods of execution worldwide include: firing squad, hanging, lethal injection, stoning, beheading, gas chamber, electric chair, crucifixion (Sudan).

Discuss the information above. What issues does it raise about the death penalty?

Did you know? Over 1,400 people have been killed by lethal injection in the USA, some of them dying in excruciating pain. Victims have been seen gasping for air, convulsing and grimacing in agony, and some have received chemical burns 30 cm long. Some executions have lasted as long as an hour.

Did you know? In California in 2008, the legal system cost $137 million per year to run. Without the death penalty it would have cost just $11.5 million.

Should the UK reintroduce the death penalty? Discuss.

Task

Find out more about the work of Sister Helen Prejean and the move to abolish capital punishment in the USA. Watch the film *Dead Man Walking*.

Some arguments for capital punishment

- An 'eye for an eye, life for a life' means that murderers should pay with their life.
- It is a deterrent, therefore it puts people off committing horrendous crimes.
- It brings justice for the victims and their families.
- Life sentences do not mean life; murderers walk free on average after 16 years.
- It is a waste of resources housing criminals for their entire life.
- This is the only way to totally protect society from the worst murderer. Many people believe these individuals cannot be reformed.
- The Principle of Utility states that an action is right if it brings happiness to the greatest number of people. Capital punishment protects society at large and brings satisfaction to victims' families, so could be argued to be right under this principle.

Some arguments against capital punishment

- Retribution is uncivilised; two wrongs do not make a right. It is a contradiction to condemn murder and then execute (kill) a murderer.
- Most murders are done on the spur of the moment, so capital punishment would not deter this crime.
- Victims' families still grieve; killing the murderer does not end the pain of loss.
- Legal systems can fail and innocent people can be executed.
- All life is sacred and murderers should be given the chance to reform.
- It is inhumane and degrading to put anyone through the mental torture of death row.

Amnesty International was founded in 1961 by Peter Benenson, a British lawyer. Today it is the world's biggest **human rights** organisation, informing the world about human rights abuses and campaigning for individuals and political change. Amnesty disagrees completely with execution, seeing it as cruel, inhumane and degrading. In its reports about the death penalty in the USA, it has highlighted the degrading nature of the system, giving examples of prisoners being taken from intensive care to be executed, wiring up prisoners who were still awaiting last-minute appeals, executing people who were clearly mentally ill, and a person who is paraplegic being dragged to the electric chair. Campaigning against and monitoring the use of the death penalty worldwide is just one part of Amnesty's work. The organisation campaigns to end all human rights abuses and recognises the inherent value of all human life. Find out more about Amnesty International by visiting their website at **www.amnesty.org.uk**

AMNESTY INTERNATIONAL

The Basics

1. What is capital punishment?
2. Explain three reasons why the death penalty is used.
3. Use the information from pages 371–373 to explain religious attitudes to the death penalty.
4. **It is never right to execute a murderer.** Analyse and evaluate this statement. Explain reasons to agree and disagree, so that you show you have thought about more than one point of view. Include religious arguments in your answer.

Buddhism

Buddhism teaches that people should follow the laws of the country in which they live. The Noble Eightfold Path relates to living life correctly. Each of the steps in the path starts with the word 'right' and they emphasise the importance of correct action. A life of crime would not be Right Livelihood and criminal activity would certainly be against the First Precept because it causes harm to other people. Furthermore, the motivation behind crime is often linked to selfish human traits and desires. Breaking the law would lead to bad karma and this would affect future rebirths, preventing a person from achieving enlightenment.

Buddhism teaches:

- Suffering is caused by attachment to the material world.
- The Three Poisons (greed, hatred, ignorance) are the cause of evil actions.
- The law of karma – the sum total of good and bad actions.
- Buddhists should practise Metta (loving kindness) and Karuna (compassion).
- The story of Milarepa illustrates that all people are capable of change.

Although Buddhists teach that all people can change and bad actions will have karmic consequences, they recognise the need to punish criminals. Buddhists would agree that the public needs to be protected from dangerous criminals. However, imprisonment should not prevent someone from changing and should provide opportunities for the offender to reform and be helped. Meditation has been successfully introduced in prisons in Asia and the West for this purpose and has reduced reoffending. The principles of non-harming, loving kindness and compassion mean Buddhists would not agree with punishments that were unduly severe or would cause direct harm to the offender. The Angulimala society provides support for prisoners.

Look up the stories of Angulimala and Geshe Ben. What do they teach about Buddhist attitudes to crime and punishment?
https://angulimala.org.uk

Christianity

Christianity teaches that the laws of a country should be followed unless they are unjust. The Ten Commandments concern both religious and moral practice. Many of them are reflected in the laws of the UK. St Paul taught that the state should be obeyed because it only has authority because God has given permission for it to exist. For Christians, law breaking would therefore mean they were committing sins as well as crimes. This could affect them in the afterlife because they believe they will be judged by God who will decide if they are fit to enter heaven.

Christianity teaches:

- Love your neighbour (Jesus – Mark 12:30–31) – Christian love (agape) should be shown to all people.
- Pray for those who persecute you. (Jesus – Sermon on the Mount)
- The Ten Commandments – a law code that guides behaviour.
- Forgive your brother 70 × 7 times (Jesus – Matthew 18:22) – meaning that a Christian should always be prepared to forgive those who wrong them.
- The Lord's Prayer – recognises that everyone sins and needs forgiveness.

Christians accept that offenders must be punished to protect people from crime and deter others from offending. Punishments should be fair and just, offenders should be treated humanely. The Quaker Elizabeth Fry devoted her life to prison reform. Amnesty International which was founded on Christian principles works worldwide to campaign for the protection of prisoners' human rights. The story of Adam and Eve (The Fall) shows that human nature is such that everyone sins. Christians believe that people should have the opportunity to repent for their wrongdoing and make amends. They also emphasise that it is important to follow the example of Jesus and be prepared to forgive others. This is why most Christians do not agree with the death penalty. Some, however, follow the Old Testament teaching of an eye for an eye, a life for a life.

Look up the Parable of the Lost Son (Luke 15:11–32) and the story of the woman caught in adultery (John 8:1–11). What do they teach Christians about repentance and forgiveness?

ॐ Hinduism

Hindus believe all people should follow the law and rulers have a responsibility to ensure that justice is carried out and people are protected from offenders. In the Hindu scriptures dharma (duty), varna (social division) and the belief in karma are important influences on attitudes to crime and punishment. Criminal activities bring bad karma and would cause a person to be reborn into a lesser life form. The principle of ahimsa (non-violence) would also be broken, since crime causes harm to others physically and/or emotionally.

Hindu teachings:

- Karma – all evil actions result in bad karma that influences rebirth.
- Reincarnation and Moksha – the cycle of rebirth (samsara) depends on karma. Moksha can only be achieved through good actions.
- An eye for an eye and the whole world would be blind. – Mahatma Gandhi
- When a person claims to be non-violent … he will put up with all the injury given to him by a wrongdoer. – Mahatma Gandhi

Hindu teachings make clear that just punishments should appropriately provide retribution, deterrence and reformation. In the past the severity of punishment was greater the lower the caste (hereditary classes in Hindu society) of the offender. In modern times many Hindus follow the example of Gandhi and would expect offenders to be treated humanely and that punishment should make provision for the offender to learn from their mistake and reform. The Laws of Manu make clear that the death penalty is acceptable for crimes such as murder, theft and adultery, but in India today only murder and treason are capital offences.

Find out how Mahatma Gandhi led a campaign of peaceful civil disobedience against British rule in India. Write a report on your findings.

☪ Islam

Some Muslim-majority countries have purely secular criminal law, others have only Shari'ah criminal law, while many have a mixture. Under Shari'ah Law, an offender breaks Allah's laws. There is no reason to steal because *zakat* is provided for those in poverty, so criminal activity is an offence against Allah and will be punished on earth and in the afterlife. Some of the earthly Shari'ah Law penalties are set out on page 368.

- The penalty for murder is death. (Surah 5:45)
- The afterlife penalty arises on the Day of Judgement – when Allah will decide who goes to paradise or hell

Crime in Islam can be divided into four groups: *Hudud* – the seven worst crimes: murder, blasphemy, theft, adultery, false accusation, treason, highway robbery and drinking alcohol. There are capital and corporal punishments for these offences. *Jinayat* – involves killing or wounding and the victims have the right to claim compensation. Offenders can pay *diya* (blood money) as part reparation for their crime. *Ta'azir* – lesser crimes and punishments are decided by a judge who will consider social pressures and change. *Mukhalafat* – covers laws related to the smooth running of the state such as driving offences; a judge decides the punishments. Punishments should ensure justice is served and Islam accepts there may be mitigating circumstances to be considered and allows for the forgiveness of offenders.

Find out more about the use of capital and corporal punishment in Muslim-majority countries. Write a report on your findings.

Judaism

The Torah includes 613 mitzvot (rules). These outline the conduct expected of all followers. There is also guidance on repentance for wrongdoing. Jewish people believe that G-d will forgive and be merciful if a wrongdoer makes *atonement* – repents their sins and makes amends. They can do this through prayer, fasting and charitable giving. The *Bet Din* (Jewish court) makes decisions about religious matters. Apologising to another person is also needed in cases where the wrongdoing is against another person.

Jewish teaching:

- The Ten Commandments.
- G-d created the world with justice and mercy so that it would last. (Midrash)
- The Lord does not enjoy seeing sinners die, He would rather they stop sinning and live. (Nevi'im)
- If anyone takes the life of a human being on purpose (not by accident or due to self-defence) they could potentially be put to death. (Torah)
- Yom Kippur – the Day of Atonement when Jewish people make confession and atonement for sins.

Judaism teaches that society should be protected and that people should be deterred from committing crimes. Punishment should be just and rehabilitate the offender. The Torah does allow execution for some crimes. Judaism considers it important for offenders to have the opportunity to atone for their crimes.

Look up the Ten Commandments (Exodus 20:1–17). Explain how they guide religious and secular behaviour.

Task

For the religions you are studying, use the information you have learned in this topic to explain believers' attitudes to:

1. the law
2. punishment of offenders
3. capital punishment.

Sikhism

Sikhs regard the law as important for ensuring justice and the protection of weaker members of society. All people need God's guidance to avoid the evils of anger, greed, lust, pride and attachment to worldly possessions. Human nature means that sometimes people fall into sin, but they should have the opportunity to repent and make up for their mistakes. Khalsa Sikhs follow a strict code of discipline (Rahit Maryada) when they commit to the community. If a Sikh were to break this code they would have to make reparation before the rest of the community. In society, Sikhism teaches its followers to be law-abiding, but to be prepared to fight against injustice and oppression.

Sikhism teaches:

- Law of karma – evil actions result in bad karma and lower rebirth.
- Kurahits – religious vows guiding personal conduct.
- Kirpan – a symbol of the fight for justice and truth.
- If someone hits you, do not hit him back, go home after kissing his feet. – Guru Granth Sahib
- He who associates with evildoers is destroyed. – Guru Granth Sahib

Sikhs believe in *nirvair* – trying to be without hatred. They accept that it is important to punish criminals in order to protect society and reform the offender. They do not accept physical or mental torture, as they respect the dignity of all human life and the essence of God within all. Many Sikhs support human rights organisations like Amnesty International and would offer support and counselling to convicts. Sikhs are told to follow their conscience and many would not support the death penalty because of the belief in the sanctity of life. However, some may regard it is a useful deterrent and just punishment for some crimes.

Look up the Sikh kurahits. Write a report on how they would influence a Sikh's life.

Different beliefs

Corporal punishment

Christianity

Christianity as a rule **does not support the use of corporal punishment**. Many point to the idea of **human dignity** and that this kind of punishment breaches that. As a form of violence many Christians see it as wrong, and as vengeful rather than merciful. The belief that **violence begets violence** means that criminals dealt with in this way will not be reformed. Christian groups such as the Quakers worked to reform this kind of punishment in UK law, to the end that it is now illegal in the UK.

Some Christian groups allow parents to physically chastise their children for misbehaviour. This follows the teaching in Proverbs 'Whoever spares the rod hates their children, but the one who loves their children is careful to discipline them.' (13:24)

Hinduism

Hinduism has **historically allowed corporal punishment** where other means of punishment have not worked. Hinduism says that physical punishment should be avoided as far as possible.

Islam

Shari'ah Law includes corporal punishment, for example 100 lashes for adultery (Surah 24:2) and amputation for theft (Surah 5:38). Muslim-majority countries applying Shari'ah Law for crimes use these punishments.

Question

Explain two different beliefs from contemporary British society about corporal punishment.

In your answer you should refer to the main religious tradition of Great Britain and one or more other religious traditions. *(4 marks)*

Death penalty

Christianity

Christianity generally does not support capital punishment. The Church of England was at the forefront of the move to end its use in the UK. It is seen as a breach of the commandment **'Do not murder'**, because a life is being deliberately ended. It also **denies the sanctity of life** for the offender, and is against their **human dignity**. There is no chance of reform of this person as death is too final.

Islam

Shari'ah Law includes the use of capital punishment. The Qur'an, states certain **crimes are punishable by death** (Surah 5:32). Surah 6:151 insists **'Take not life except by way of justice and law',** so the crime must merit the death penalty.

Christianity

Some Christians believe it is right to use the death penalty for those criminals who have committed the **worst crimes**, such as murder. Since they have taken life, for example, they forfeit their own – **'An eye for an eye'** (Exodus 21:24).

Question

Explain two different beliefs from contemporary British society about the death penalty.

In your answer you should refer to the main religious tradition in Great Britain and one or more other religious traditions. *(4 marks)*

Judaism

Judaism prescribes the **death penalty for murder** in extreme cases with very specific circumstances. This is seen as a huge deterrent, but also **justice** and essential to the **preservation of the community**. However, Israel has only executed two criminals in its history, one being the Nazi Adolf Eichmann, preferring instead to **commute death sentences**.

Forgiveness

Christianity

Forgiveness is a central teaching of Jesus. When asked how often a person should forgive, in Matthew 18:22, he said **'seventy times seven'** – in other words, innumerably. The Lord's Prayer includes the injunction to **'Forgive us our trespasses as we forgive those who trespass against us'**. Jesus' **crucifixion was necessary so that humans could be forgiven their sins and so enter heaven for eternity with God**. Humans must try to follow Jesus' example, so should be forgiving.

Some Christians, who have been victims of very serious crime – for example having a family member murdered – **do not see a way to forgive**. They seek **justice rather than forgiveness** for these serious crimes.

Islam

In Islam, whilst **forgiveness is a quality of Allah**, it is conditional. A human must be sorry, recognise the wrong, commit to not repeat it, and seek forgiveness. **Without these conditions, forgiveness cannot be given**.

Buddhism

Buddhism recognises that whilst forgiveness is the ideal, it can be very difficult to grant. Where a person has suffered greatly, the negative emotions they hold because of that suffering can prevent them from forgiving. That is why **meditation practices are taught specifically to cultivate forgiveness.**

Question

Explain two different beliefs from contemporary British society about forgiveness.

In your answer you should refer to the main religious tradition of Great Britain and one or more other religious traditions. *(4 marks)*

Getting prepared

Using quotations for maximum effect

Every year, candidates do not make the best use of the quotes in their answers, leading to less effective responses. It is an important skill to learn and practise as it will improve your writing. Look at the following examples:

Explain two religious beliefs about the treatment of offenders. Refer to sacred writings or another source of religious belief and teaching in your answer. (6 marks)

Christians say love your neighbour. They think everyone should be punished. So they think you have to punish them but fairly.

This candidate has mentioned one teaching and has indicated a value (fairness). Look at the next version. How do you think this compares?

In the Bible it says love your neighbour, so while Christians think everyone should be punished, so they think you have to punish them fairly. They believe in justice which makes it important that treatment is fair and not cruel.

Explain two different beliefs in contemporary British society about using the death penalty as a punishment. In your answer, you should refer to the main religious tradition of Great Britain and one or more other religious traditions. (4 marks)

In the Bible it says 'do not murder'. It also says that life is sacred. You should love your neighbour, not hurt them.

This gives us three valid ideas, but does not answer the question. Rather the reader has to work out the relevance of each point. Sometimes, it is not obvious enough. Make sure that you apply the quotes you use to the actual question.

In the Bible it says 'do not murder'. Sometimes, a criminal has murdered someone, and they have broken this teaching so gone against a fundamental rule of Christianity. It also says that life is sacred. So we should always condemn and punish harshly when someone commits a crime against the person (which is always doing damage to someone). You should love your neighbour, not hurt them, so religious believers would say this kind of crime goes against this teaching by Jesus. All of these teachings show that when a person commits a very serious crime like murder, then the death penalty would be an appropriate punishment.

Do you think this second version is a better answer than the first one? If you do, what makes it better?

Religion, crime and punishment glossary

Capital punishment also known as the death penalty; the legally authorised killing of someone as punishment for a crime

Community service order type of punishment; the offender must undertake a set number of hours' work in the community as their punishment

Conscience sense of right and wrong; usually the guilty voice in our head

Corporal punishment physical punishment, such as caning or flogging

Crime breaking the law; can be against a person (e.g. assault), against property (e.g. arson), or the state (e.g. terrorism)

Deterrence aim of punishment; where the punishment puts someone off committing the crime

Duty something we are bound to do

Evil something (or someone) considered morally wrong; wicked; often linked to the idea of a malevolent force, e.g. the Devil.

Forgiveness letting go of anger towards someone for a wrong they have done us

Hate crime a crime committed because of prejudice, e.g. beating someone up because you think they are gay; in UK law, it can mean the doubling of a sentence if found guilty

Imprisonment locking someone up as a punishment

Justice making things fair again

Law the rules which govern a country to keep us safe

Order the enforcement of rules, e.g. by a police force

Parole release of a criminal from prison, but continuing to monitor their behaviour

Probation order punishment; monitoring of behaviour with the threat of greater punishment for offending again

Protection aim of punishment; to keep people safe

Reformation aim of punishment; helping the person see how and why they should behave better

Reparation aim of punishment; making up for, compensating

Retribution aim of punishment; getting back at the person for what they have done

Victim the one against whom a crime is committed, can also include friends and family of the victim, and the wider community

Vindication aim of punishment; the punishment exists because the law does

Young offenders persons under 18 who commit crime

9 Theme F: Religion, human rights and social justice

Key elements of this Theme

This Theme is broken into two parts.

Firstly, **human rights** – what they are, why we should have them and how religious people may view them. From this comes the issue of **prejudice** – what it is and why it may happen; religious attitudes to prejudice and **discrimination**, both generally and in specific situations. Secondly, **poverty** – both in the UK and across the world; why there is poverty; exploitation of those in poverty; religious attitudes to poverty and to helping those in poverty.

These topics can all be viewed through the idea of human rights and **social justice** – that society should be a fair place, and those who are victims must be helped and protected.

Key concepts

There are concepts which apply to all three aspects of this Theme. First is the idea of *rights and responsibilities*. Many people argue they have a right to something, often without thinking of other people's rights. For you to have a right to something, for example, freedom of speech, you have to have the **responsibility** to speak appropriately, that is, not hurting others by telling lies about them. Where prejudice and poverty exist, it is often the case that someone somewhere is not meeting their responsibilities.

Given that people are individual and different, it is important to be *tolerant* of people's differences. This means accepting differences, and not making a big deal of it, especially not targeting people because of them. You can see that if we are tolerant, there is no place for prejudice. You can also see that where people are tolerant of each other, they can live in **harmony**.

All religious believers agree that life is special and sacred. Many believe we were all created equally by God. This means we have equal worth and value, and should enjoy equal rights (**equality**). Anything to deny these rights would be wrong.

Lots of people are disadvantaged in life for many reasons. Religious believers would see a need for systems to bring social justice to those people, as they believe that things have to be made fair. They also call for all people to show **compassion** (loving kindness) to all others. This means giving help where it is needed, simply because it is needed.

Overall, religious people believe they have the duty of **stewardship** (a responsibility to look after the world and the people in it). If we are serious about this responsibility, we will try to defend the rights of all to live in harmony and in a just world.

The Basics

1. Write definitions for the following words – **tolerance**; **rights**; responsibilities; **justice**; compassion; stewardship.
2. Explain how a religious believer who believes in tolerance, equality, justice, rights and responsibilities might view the following:
   - prejudice
   - poverty.
3. Explain how belief in compassion and stewardship might affect how a religious person lives their life in regard to others.
4. **Rights are more important than responsibilities.** Do you agree? Explain your reasons, showing you have thought about more than one point of view.

Social justice

This means justice in terms of **wealth** distribution, the law, equal rights and opportunities for all people. For social justice to exist, society must be fair to all regardless of race, age, **gender**, **sexuality** and disability. It also means that society has to be organised so that it is open to all in terms of education, healthcare, housing and social welfare. The United Nations' 2006 document *Social Justice in an Open World* states 'Social justice may be broadly understood as the fair and compassionate distribution of the fruits of economic growth'. Social justice is a reason why religions fight for human rights and against prejudice and exploitation of all people including people in poverty.

Social justice in the modern world is difficult to achieve. Different political methods have been tried, but there are always those who feel things are not fair. Different political parties manage a country's economy in different ways, and promote social justice differently. It is probably true to say that there are people in society who can look after themselves despite political systems, but there are always those who cannot. Some will argue that those in poverty need preferential treatment and a society is judged on how it treats its most vulnerable. Others believe too much help can make people reliant on that help so they do little to help themselves.

All religions have teachings on social justice.

Buddhism

In Buddhism, along with the idea of selflessness, Buddhists believe that right action, livelihood, speech, effort and intention should, if carried out properly, lead to social justice.

Hinduism

In Hinduism, there is a conscious move away from caturvarnya (the caste system) which has separated people and has created social issues through misunderstanding and misrepresentation. Hinduism teaches that each person is an undivided part of a whole world community.

Judaism

In *To Heal a Fractured World: The Ethics of Responsibility*, Rabbi Lord Jonathan Sacks states that social justice is central to Judaism. He explains that the concepts of simcha (gladness), tzedakah (the religious obligation to perform charity), chesed (deeds of kindness), and tikkun olam (healing the world) all allow for social justice.

Christianity

In the UK, Christians have fought for prison reform since the eighteenth century, organisations like Christian Aid work in inner cities, and the House of Lords includes clergy who discuss the law – all examples of involvement in social justice.

Islam

The Qur'an contains references to social justice. One of Islam's Five Pillars is zakat, or alms-giving. Charity and assistance to those in poverty (concepts central to social justice) have historically been important parts of the Islamic faith.

Sikhism

Sikh scriptures promote the message of equality of all beings and reveal that Sikh believers should deal with all humankind with the spirit of universal brotherhood and equality.

The Basics

1 What is meant by social justice?
2 Why is it correct to say that religions believe social justice to be important?

What do we mean by human rights?

There are many descriptions and declarations of human, but essentially they are what humans should be able to expect as a minimum because they are human. They include basic rights and freedoms: the right to life, to not be persecuted by others, to have a fair trial, to free speech, and also the right to have food, shelter, education, healthcare and work.

The **Universal Declaration of Human Rights** starts with the fundamental statement that: *All humans are born free and equal in dignity and rights. They are endowed with reason and conscience and should act towards one another in a spirit of brotherhood.* Everything else comes from that. Laws are built on this, and our behaviour towards and with others should be governed by it.

Task

Imagine you and 99 others have been stranded on a bio-sphere on Mars. There is no hope for anyone else from earth to get to you for many years. The bio-sphere allows for the production of food and recycling of all waste. It will sustain you all for as many years as you manage it properly (do not overuse resources, and maintain systems so that they do not break down). You all realise very early on that a set of rules needs to be drawn up which everyone will live within. You are a mix of cultures and nationalities, with different expertise and experience. Your rules will only work if they are designed to protect a set of human rights. Your task is to decide what the rights of humans on Mars should be.

Rights issues

Read these statements. In each case, do you think there is a human right being denied or broken? Which right(s)?

Luke was beaten up because he kept making extremely racist comments.

Chris was told by the council they could not house him after his parents had thrown him out at the age of 19.

Sash did not get into the school her parents chose because it was full – so they did not send her to another school.

Wayne was found guilty of murder and sentenced to death.

Rights … and responsibilities

People have the right to voice their opinion. But that right brings a responsibility to also listen to the opinions of others, as they also have a right to their opinion. It also brings the responsibility of speaking in a responsible and respectful way, and of taking the consequences of exercising our right. It is the same for any human right, for example, if I have a right to education, then so do you; if I have a right to good healthcare, then so do you. We cannot say only we have rights, and we cannot say that we do not need to take responsibility for exercising those rights. Sometimes our rights affect others in a negative way, and we have to be mindful of that.

If I am to have my human rights, then I have to be prepared to respect and protect the human rights of others. If I am blessed with wealth, I should use my money responsibly – I have a right to my money as I earned it, but also a responsibility to help those in poverty. I have a right to live free from prejudice, but a responsibility to not behave in a prejudicial way as well as to actively try to fight prejudice and support victims.

The Universal Declaration of Human Rights

Statements of rights have been written all through history. We can trace British human rights back to Magna Carta (1215CE), which stated the ruler's commitment to his people. Setting out a code of rights is perhaps the first step in building law and legal systems.

The Universal Declaration of Human Rights was written and then adopted by many nations in 1948, coming about partly because of the atrocities that nations fighting the Second World War had carried out. Although many nations today adopt the Declaration, there is no binding requirement for them to keep it. The rights are in two distinct groups: civil and political rights, and economic, social and cultural rights. The UN claims that these are part of the way to build freedom, peace and justice in the world.

Here are some examples of human rights:

Everyone:
- is equal
- is born free
- should be treated in the same way
- is innocent until proven guilty.

Everyone should respect everyone else.

Everyone has the right to:
- legal protection
- a public trial
- asylum
- belong to a country
- marry
- own things and keep them
- free speech
- meet peacefully with others
- vote
- work
- rest
- an education
- basic rights – water, food, shelter, healthcare
- artistic freedom and enjoying the arts.

No one should be:
- tortured
- unfairly imprisoned.

No one may destroy the rights of others.

There must be laws to protect these rights.

Visit **www.un.org.uk** to find out more information about the Universal Declaration of Human Rights.

Do you think there are any rights missing from the list? Or any that are wrong? Which do you think is the most important? Why? Do you think that everyone should always have rights? Is there ever a time when someone's rights should be reduced, or taken away?

Tasks

1 Reread the four human rights cases on the previous page. Using the list of human rights opposite, try to work out what, if any, rights are being broken in those cases, and who by.
2 Read the newspaper headlines below. Discuss how the events in each headline are a human rights issue.

MAN CLAIMING ASYLUM TURNED AWAY AT AIRPORT

Tsunami victims denied help by their own government

More than one million children under 14 forced into prostitution each year

125 million children aged 5–14 work full-time to support their families

New laws rushed in to stop protestors

Racist fights for absolute freedom of speech for himself

The Basics

1 What do we mean by 'human rights'?
2 Explain how the Universal Declaration of Human Rights came to be written.
3 List four human rights.
4 **The most important human right is for everyone to be free.** Do you agree? Explain both sides of the argument.

The Human Rights Act (1998)

The **Human Rights Act** (HRA) gave a legal standing in the UK to the fundamental rights and freedoms contained in the European Convention on Human Rights (ECHR). These are based on the Universal Declaration of Human Rights (UNDR). The HRA is supposed to ensure that people's human rights are protected and respected by public authorities. It makes it illegal for public authorities to act against a person's human rights. Everyone in the UK is protected by these rights.

However, the rights are not absolute. The government has the power to limit or control people's rights under certain conditions, such as in wartime. They also rely on people respecting each other, and not behaving in a way which would go against other people's rights. *Respect* is the key to everything, because respect for others leads to all those rights.

Respecting human rights as a religious citizen

A *citizen* is someone who is a member of a country or nation. You are probably a British citizen; you might have citizenship of another country, because some people have dual citizenship (usually because of having parents from different countries, or by living in another country for a number of years). Being a citizen brings rights within that country, but also responsibilities to respect and follow the rules of that country.

A *religious citizen* is simply someone who is a citizen, but has religious beliefs. Those beliefs should mean they respect the law of the country in which they live or have citizenship. Generally speaking, British law has as its basis the Ten Commandments. Both are based on *respect* – that word keeps coming up, doesn't it? So religions would all agree with laws based on respect.

Sometimes religious laws and secular laws do not match up. What happens then? Read these stories, and try to work out what the people did in the end. The answers are at the foot of the page for you to check.

David

My grandfather died suddenly. The doctors want to do a post-mortem. In my religion, we should not desecrate a body, and should bury it whole. The post-mortem goes against both of those beliefs. Should we agree to the post-mortem, or fight it?

I belong to the Quaker faith. My grandfather was a Quaker, and when the Second World War started, he was called up to fight. Quakers are pacifists – they do not believe in violence. The draft papers said he had to join the army – in wartime, of course a soldier has to fight. What do you think he did?

Sarah

I am a Christian. My teacher won't let me wear my silver ring which represents my vow to stay celibate until marriage – it breaks school uniform rules. I have not been to school whilst banned from wearing it in school. I use the internet and books to help me study for my GCSEs. What should I do?

Lucy

David's family did not give permission, but the law can take that right away. His grandfather's body was subject to post-mortem exam before being released to the family for burial.

Sarah's grandfather claimed his right to be a conscientious objector. He was given a job in the UK for the war effort, but was subject to much persecution and abuse, being called 'unpatriotic' and a 'traitor'.

Lucy's case went to court, and the House of Lords. It was ruled that wearing a ring is not a religious duty, so the school need not respect that claimed religious right.

Freedom of religion and belief including freedom of religious expression

In the UK today, the right to religious freedom is protected, and freedom from persecution because of religion is also possible because of discrimination laws.

Freedom of religious expression – this is the right of any person to follow the religion of their choice and to be open about what they believe. In the UK, you cannot be told (legally) that you are not allowed to follow a particular religion and none are banned. Nor can you be ordered by law to follow a particular group's interpretation of that religion, so you could not be told that the only legal denomination of Christianity is the Church of England. This was not always the case. For example, in the sixteenth century, first the Protestants under Queen Mary and then the Catholics under Queen Elizabeth I were executed for their beliefs.

Freedom from persecution because of religion – this is the right to be legally protected if someone targets you because of the religion you follow. They would have committed a hate crime, which is a criminal offence. So, for example, if a person attacked another person in the street, simply because they thought they were Muslim, then that would be a hate crime. That does not mean that a person who is refused the right to wear a religious symbol whilst at work is a victim of religious discrimination, unless the symbol was compulsory to their religion (like a Sikh's turban).

All religions will argue for their right to both of these freedoms. But do they also seek to protect the rights of others to their (different) religion?

Buddhism

Buddhism teaches that, if properly understood, religion is a way or means to realise the truth, and that there are many ways to the same religious truths. When asked about his religion, the Dalai Lama once said 'My religion is kindness.' The Buddha himself, after enlightenment, did not try to convert anyone; he explained and discussed what he had learned, allowing people to decide for themselves. Scriptures give many examples of where a non-Buddhist listened to the Buddha, and converted. Additionally, the Buddha did send followers out to spread his teachings.

Christianity

Some Christians believe that the only way to salvation (earning a place in heaven) is through belief in Jesus. This excludes all other religions, and is the main reason why Christianity has always been a missionary religion that tries to convert others. Some believe that as long as a person leads a morally good life, then they too can earn salvation, which opens the door to accept all other faiths, given their key principles fit with Christianity's. Whatever the belief about who can and cannot go to heaven, it is important to treat everyone with equanimity and kindness, so Christians should not be involved in any form of religious discrimination.

Hinduism

Hinduism is a wide-ranging religion and is open to all other faiths. It does not agree with trying to convert others as it is a way of life and not a prescriptive religion. In the modern context, Hinduism continues its tolerance for other viewpoints.

Judaism

In traditional Jewish thinking, other religions could be seen as either G-d-fearing or those who seek to deny or demote G-d. The latter will always be wrong. Jewish people are clear that Judaism is the best way to live, but they do not say others should not live how they choose to. To be a Jewish person is usually by birth (unless someone is a convert to Judaism). Regarding people who are not Jewish, the deciding factor is how they live their lives, not who they choose to worship, so there should be no intolerance or religious discrimination shown.

Task

All religions accept each other.
Research your religion(s) of study to explore how true this statement is.

Islam

Islam sees Jewish people and Christians as 'People of the Book'; they have received revelations from Allah, although have allowed them to be corrupted. In essence, there is still a form of the right religion to their beliefs. Prophet Muhammad ﷺ had to build relationships with people of each of these faiths, and a lot of his teachings show the principles of tolerance and peaceful coexistence, as well as inclusiveness and mutual acceptance. In particular, they were allowed to practise their own faiths in their own way. There is also a sense that those who are morally good will also be rewarded in the afterlife, so should be respected now.

Sikhism

The Rahit Maryada states that 'Sikhs must in no way give offence to other faiths.' Guru Nanak said 'There is no Hindu, no Muslim ... I shall follow God's path.' Guru Gobind Singh said that different clothes and cultures did not stop all being the same flesh and blood creations of God. There are many examples from the life of Guru Nanak where he shows there should be no boundaries and no discrimination because of religion – often rejecting the exclusiveness which others claimed for their own religion.

Should religious people openly express their beliefs?

A public display of a person's beliefs can be as simple as how they live their life. You might not even notice they are religious, just that they are generally a good person (since all religions promote morally good behaviour). It might be something obvious – like wearing or having a particular symbol of the faith, perhaps a Jewish person wearing a kippah (skull cap), a Sikh wearing a turban, a Muslim carrying tasbi (prayer beads). It might be really overt, for example, someone talking to you about their religion and why you should convert.

Is there any problem with being open about what you believe in?

In the West, fewer people follow religions, and it seems acceptable to make fun of religious believers and their beliefs. Society is not guided by religion any more, so religion has less authority.

Read these real situations. What is your opinion on each? Do these show we live in a society tolerant of religion?

- An incident took place where a check-in desk worker at an airport was banned from wearing a cross and chain because it might offend passengers who were not Christian.
- A discussion took place as to whether shops should display Christmas cards in their windows because it might cause offence to people who are not Christian.
- A nurse was suspended because, as a Christian, she offered to pray for a patient who was in the hospital she worked at.
- A Muslim woman employed as a teacher was asked to remove her full face veil because it was deemed not appropriate when teaching young children.
- Some people made insulting remarks about the appearance and behaviour of Hindus who were on their way to celebrate a festival at their temple. As a result, the Hindus stopped wearing their traditional clothes for the festival.
- A head teacher lost her job because she decided that all assemblies should be given to all students, and not split for particular religious or non-religious groups.

Is it easy to follow a religion in the modern world?

More and more countries are becoming more 'religion-rich', as immigration brings new faiths in, and new places of worship are built. The internet means anyone can access any religion, or group within it, for information or worship from their own home, without having to be part of a physical **community**. As a society, it could be said we know more about other faiths, so are more tolerant. Laws protect religious freedoms. All this makes it easier than ever to follow a religion.

The Basics

1. What is meant by the terms 'religious freedom' and 'freedom of religious expression'?
2. Explain religious attitudes to other religions and people of other religions from the religion(s) you have studied.
3. What can make it difficult to openly express religion in our society? Use examples in your answer.
4. **Freedom of religion and religious expression is not possible in the modern world.** Do you agree with this statement? Explain your arguments.

Prejudice

The two key words for this part of the Theme are *prejudice* and *discrimination*. If you can learn what they mean it will help with this whole Theme. The two words are linked, but their meaning is slightly different.

Prejudice means to pre-judge something or someone usually without any real evidence to base that judgement on. In most cases it is negative. We use the word to describe a person's dislike of certain other people, when they have no good reason. We talk about prejudice against race, religion, age (**ageism**), nationality, sexuality or appearance. Prejudice is about what we *think* – it is about the ideas in our head.

Discrimination is when we put these prejudiced ideas into action. We treat people differently or say things because they are not the same as ourselves or what we know. We make known to them our dislike and therefore it can have a great effect on a person's life. In Britain it is against the law to discriminate against a person with certain protected characteristics in certain situations.

Prejudice and discrimination break people's human rights, because they stop them having the same chances as others and they lead to harm.

What kinds of prejudice can you see illustrated here?

What might the attitude of religious believers be to each of these, based on their beliefs in equality, justice and tolerance?

Positive discrimination

Discrimination can be positive as well as negative. Positive discrimination is used to promote opportunities for minority groups in society, especially so that those groups are better represented in public services. For example, the police service may advertise specifically for black, Asian or gay officers – members of all these groups have an understanding of minority issues. The aim is to create a police force which better reflects and so can better serve our society, both locally and nationally.

Can you see any examples of positive discrimination in the images on this page?

Can you think of any examples of positive discrimination?

What makes someone prejudiced and want to discriminate against others?

Everyone can be prejudiced at times, even by accident. However, not everyone will discriminate against others because of their prejudice. Which is the more serious – the thought or the action?

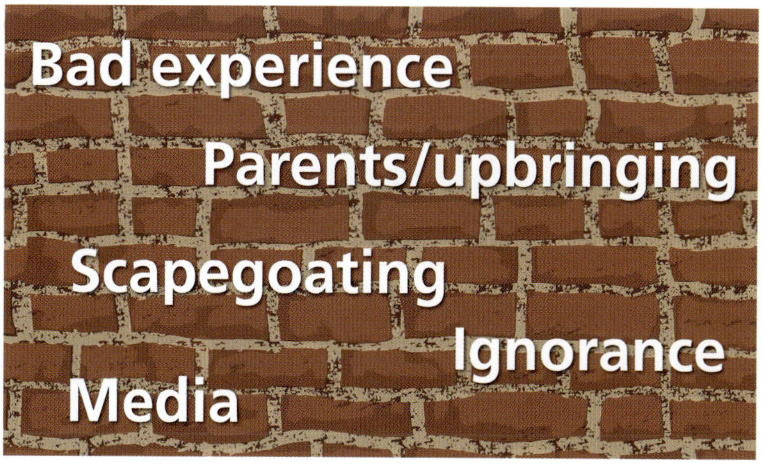

Prejudice can be a barrier which stops people living, working and learning together as a community. It is very unfair and it only takes someone to be seen as 'different' by someone else to be singled out for discrimination. The victims are almost always in the minority and find it very hard to deal with or to fight against or get justice after the fact.

There are five main reasons that lead to prejudice.

1 Having a *bad experience* with someone might make you think anybody else like them is like that. For example, maybe when you were young you were frightened by a grumpy old man and now you think all old men are grumpy.

2 Having been told bad things about a certain group of people by your *parents/carers* you might be prejudiced without even getting a chance to know any differently. Their words and attitudes often shape our own, so we copy and repeat them. Our upbringing has a big influence on us, and our parents' or carers' words have a huge effect.

3 Having seen something on television or read something in a newspaper (or other forms of *media*) that was very biased (it focused on only one fact or idea, taking it out of context), you might have believed it and so now are prejudiced.

4 When you do not have enough detail about something to base an opinion on, yet you think that you are able to judge someone. This is called *ignorance*. For example, having a negative opinion about a group of people, who you have never met or actually learned anything about – you do not know them, but you insult them anyway.

5 *Scapegoating* is when you use others to blame or as an excuse for a problem. For example, Hitler blamed Jewish people for the economic problems in Germany, which led to the devastating events of the Holocaust. In actual fact the Jewish people in Germany had done nothing wrong.

The Basics

1 What is meant by the terms 'prejudice' and 'discrimination'?
2 Explain how the pictures on page 386 are examples of discrimination.
3 Give some other examples of discrimination.
4 Why is *tolerance* important in helping prevent prejudice?
5 Explain some reasons why some people might be prejudiced.
6 Choose three of the reasons you gave in your answer to Question 5 and give an example to demonstrate each one, which is different from the examples here.
7 **You need to change the way people think to prevent discrimination.** What do you think? Explain reasons to agree and disagree with this statement.

Types of prejudice ... religious teachings

The following pages show a type of prejudice with examples. The religious teachings provided here are general teachings that can be applied to all forms of prejudice. *You only need to focus on the religion(s) that you are studying.* Think about how each teaching/religious idea can be applied to each of the forms of prejudice. Remember that *tolerance, justice, community* and *harmony* are key religious ideas too.

Sexuality

Some people face prejudice because of who they are attracted to. In the past, it was illegal to be gay in Britain. Even today, many gay and lesbian people still suffer homophobia because some people do not agree with their relationships. It is often difficult for gay people to come out to their families (who may themselves be unsupportive, or even homophobic) and as a result members of the LGBTQ+ community can feel alone. For religious people who are gay, there are also fears of how their community might respond, and it may be the case that their religion forbids same-sex attraction. Also, many religions *do not agree* with these relationships, although they *do agree* that people *should not* be discriminated against. For religion, a key role of sex is to accept God's blessing of children – same-sex couples cannot do this naturally and in holy books there are teachings against same-sex attraction. In the UK, same-sex marriage is now legal, and with the help of science, having children outside heteronormative relationships is also possible, so things are changing. Some religions do now accept that some people are attracted to the same sex, but still disagree with them having sexual relationships.

Thinking question

As a young person, you may have experienced prejudice/discrimination. What happened? How did it feel? Has it had a continuing impact on you?

☸ Buddhism

Buddhism states that as discrimination leads to suffering, it must be wrong and should be avoided.

- The Five Precepts ask Buddhists not to harm others or use harmful language.
- Everyone should try to develop metta (loving kindness).
- We are all unique as individuals, but we share the fact of suffering and the capacity for awareness and compassion. We are equal in our potential for enlightenment.
- Prejudice creates bad karma and has a negative effect on rebirth.
- The Dalai Lama stated that the best way to live life was to 'Always think compassion'.

✝ Christianity

Christianity states that all forms of discrimination are wrong.

- God created everyone equally. (Old Testament)
- There is neither Jew nor Gentile, slave or free, male or female. We are all equal in Christ. (Galatians)
- So in everything, do unto others what you would have done to you. (Matthew 7:12)
- Jesus told us to love our neighbour. (Sermon on the Mount)
- In the Good Samaritan story, the man is helped because of his need, not because of who he was or was not (in fact, the victim and helper were from enemy nations). (Luke 10:25–37)

Disability

Sometimes people who have a disability are discriminated against. Remember, a disability encompasses a wide variety of conditions, categorised into two types: physical, for example, being blind, being in a wheelchair, not having a limb; mental, for example, having a learning problem or a mental illness. By law a disability is a long-term issue that has a significant impact on the day-to-day life of the person with the disability, so that they cannot do (some) things as normal.

People with a disability often face barriers of access to certain places; for example, could a person in a wheelchair access your school? Have you ever witnessed someone call another person names who is hearing or sight impaired? Discrimination may affect people with disabilities in all sorts of ways. However, religions state that all people are equal and God creates people in many different ways. We are all valued despite our differences. Ellie Simmonds (see photo above) is a multiple Paralympic swimming champion. Her achievements show that people with disabilities can overcome the biggest challenges and achieve great success, and this should be an inspiration to all of us.

Discrimination is totally wrong where disability is concerned. *Research the Disability Discrimination Act for more information.*

ॐ Hinduism

Hindu dharma states that the divine is found in everything, so therefore any prejudicial thoughts or discriminative actions would be viewed as wrong.

- Hindus believe in non-violence (ahimsa) love and respect for all things.
- Compassion is a key belief with the desire to improve things for others, not persecute them.
- Hurting others can lead to bad karma which affects future reincarnations.
- Hindus believe that the true self is the atman and as everyone has one this must mean everyone is equal.
- The Bhagavad Gita suggests that to reach liberation, one should work for the welfare of all fellow human beings.

☪ Islam

Islam teaches that Allah created everyone and made them into nations and tribes, equal but different, so discrimination is unjustified. (Surah 49:13)

- Allah loves the fair-minded.
- The Five Pillars (beliefs and actions) apply to all – equally.
- Muhammad ﷺ chose a black former enslaved person to call prayers in Madinah. He welcomed everyone regardless of wealth, status or creed.
- The Muslim Declaration of Human Rights states that everyone is equal.
- On hajj everyone, no matter their status dresses in the same white sheets, equal before Allah.

The Basics

1 How might people discriminate with regards to disability?
2 What is the religious attitude to any form of discrimination?
3 **Discrimination is the worst thing a person can suffer.** What do you think of this statement? Explain your own opinion, then argue the opposite view.
4 **Being discriminated against because of a disability is worse than sexism.** Explore reasons to agree and disagree with this statement, including religious arguments on both sides.

Gender prejudice

People can often be discriminated against because of their gender. This is called sexism. Traditionally there were roles for men and roles for women in society and within religion. However, these have not been equal roles with equal opportunity. Religions would argue that the roles are equal but different. In society in the last 100 years the role of women has changed. There are now far more women in top jobs, in male-dominated sports, in politics and in the armed forces. However, in terms of leadership in religion, most religious traditions are still male-dominated.

March 2015 marked the start of the ministry of the first female Anglican Bishop. Libby Lane, who had been consecrated Bishop at York Cathedral in January 2015, began her work as Bishop of Stockport. This had been a long journey through a time of change for the Church of England. Before 1994, there had been no female vicars in the Church of England, and it took 20 years for one to become a Bishop. During that time, some Anglicans left the church in disagreement. Archbishop John Sentamu – at her consecration – said 'In a few years' time, when more and more women will be Bishops, I predict we shall be wondering how we ever managed without them.' She said 'The Church has moved so quickly into a new normal where the appointment of women Bishops is as expected as the appointment of men.'

Refer to pages 251–253 for more detail on gender prejudice and gender in religion.

Judaism

Judaism teaches that prejudice and discrimination are incompatible with Jewish law. Over centuries, Jewish people have faced persecution and discrimination, and they therefore have strong opinions on the issue.

- G-d created everyone equal. So prejudice is seen as an insult to G-d.
- The Torah tells Jewish people to welcome and not persecute strangers.
- Treat others as you wish to be treated. (Torah)

Sikhism

Sikhism believes in the principle of justice and to fight for justice where it does not exist. Equality and sewa (service to others) would clearly indicate that discrimination is wrong.

- Using the same mud, the Creator has created many shapes in many ways – Guru Gobind Singh
- Those who love God love everyone.
- God created everyone so all are equal so deserve the same treatment and respect.
- Everyone is welcome to take part in communal meals (langar) at Sikh gurdwaras across the world, regardless of their gender, ethnicity or religion.
- God is without caste – Guru Gobind Singh.

Racism

Racism is the belief that the colour of a person's skin, or their race, makes a person less valuable than others, so that they can be treated unfairly. We use the word 'racist' to describe someone who discriminates against people of other races in a negative way. Hate and discrimination against some groups of people have specific names, for example anti-Semitism is the name for hatred of Jewish people and Islamophobia the name for hatred of Muslim people.

The trade in enslaved people in the seventeenth and eighteenth centuries was based on the belief that people of colour were somehow of less value than other people, and so could be bought and sold, and treated in any way, with no rights at all. It cost the lives of tens of thousands and destroyed many communities. This attitude of superiority still exists in the world today. The statistics in the UK show that if you are black, you are more likely to get excluded from school, to achieve less highly than others, to get stopped by the police more often, to get sent to prison, to be murdered – it goes on.

The police keep records of race-related crimes, which show that those of Asian heritage suffer most hate crimes, often because they are thought to be Muslim. This is in direct relation to society's perception of the nature of Muslims as portrayed by groups such as the Taliban, Al Qaeda and ISIS/ISIL.

> 'All human beings are born free and equal … should act in a spirit of brotherhood … everyone is entitled to all the rights and freedom.' *Universal Declaration of Human Rights*

Equality and justice

Religions believe in equality (that we all have the same intrinsic value, and are special beings) and in justice (that things must be made fair, and wrongs made right). So it seems impossible that religious believers could support prejudice of any kind. Prejudice clearly suggests a sense of superiority (not equality) and leads to injustice (not justice).

However, positive discrimination (see page 386) can help to bring about both as it tries to raise up the life and well-being, as well as the profile and status of minority groups.

The Basics

1. List the types of prejudice covered by the course, and explain what each one is.
2. Use the teachings from pages 388 and 390 to explain what the attitude of the religion(s) you have studied might be to racism.
3. **Religious believers should fight racism more than other forms of prejudice.** What do you think? Explain your opinion.

What does the law say in the UK?

There are laws in the UK to deal with discrimination. As prejudice is about the way people think, the law cannot do anything about this, but when that prejudice turns into discriminative actions then the law can act. However, discrimination is not always easy to prove.

The 1976 Race Relations Act (RRA) made it illegal to discriminate against anyone because of race, nationality, ethical or national background in four main areas: jobs, education, housing and the provision of services, and to use threatening or abusive language in regard to race. It also made it illegal to publish anything to stir up racial hatred.

The Fawcett Society: **www.fawcettsociety.org.uk**

The Commission for Racial Equality was set up to deal with cases of discrimination and to act as a watchdog against racism. In 2000, The Race Relations Amendment (RRA) Act was introduced as a way of strengthening the 1976 Act. It stressed the need to promote harmony and tolerance among all people.

There have also been laws passed about Equal Pay (1975), Sex Discrimination (1975), Disability Discrimination (1995) and Sexual Orientation Regulation (2007). All these Acts have been superseded by the Equality Act (2010).

As well as the law there are organisations that support victims and try to improve awareness of the discrimination certain groups face.

There are also many other organisations that fight prejudice and support victims. Here are just some examples:

JCORE is the Jewish Council for Racial Equality. It believes that concern for social justice should be an important part of Jewish identity, and that Jewish people have a duty to both work with and for others in the struggle against discrimination. It does a lot of work to educate Jewish children about this duty and to support asylum seekers in the UK.

FAIR (**www.fairuk.org**) is the Forum Against Islamophobia and Racism. This organisation is all about making the UK less Islamophobic, less anti-Semitic and less racist. It sees no place for attacks on Muslims and Jewish people in a civilised society, and rejects the extreme actions of some Muslims as being against Islam. Part of its work is to encourage and facilitate discussion between Jewish people and Muslims, rather than fuelling hatred between the two or against them.

The Hindu Forum of Great Britain (**www.hfb.org.uk**) undertakes activities to build community cohesion and encourage religious understanding. It fights against racism and advocates for equal opportunities.

The Basics

1. Explain how discrimination affects its victims.
2. How does the law in the UK try to fight prejudice? Refer to UK laws in your answer.
3. **Not enough religious people stand up to fight prejudice.** Clearly explain arguments both for and against this statement, including religious arguments.

Religious attitudes to wealth

What – to you – counts as being wealthy?

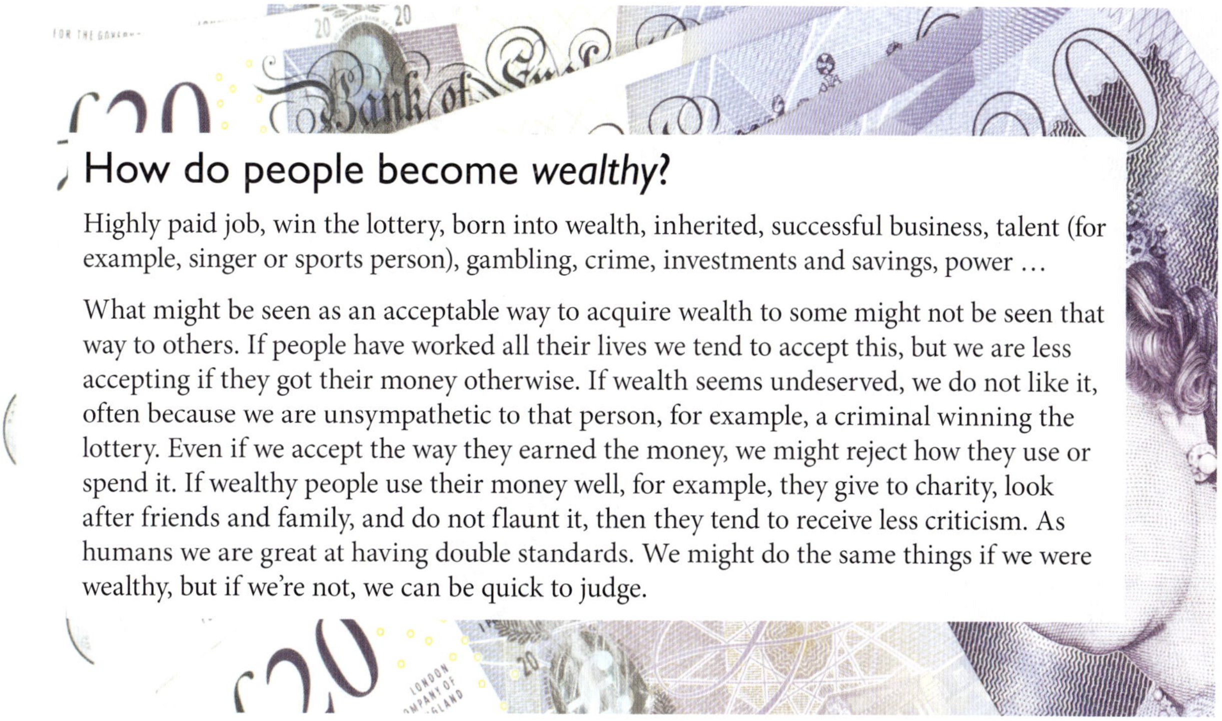

How do people become *wealthy*?

Highly paid job, win the lottery, born into wealth, inherited, successful business, talent (for example, singer or sports person), gambling, crime, investments and savings, power …

What might be seen as an acceptable way to acquire wealth to some might not be seen that way to others. If people have worked all their lives we tend to accept this, but we are less accepting if they got their money otherwise. If wealth seems undeserved, we do not like it, often because we are unsympathetic to that person, for example, a criminal winning the lottery. Even if we accept the way they earned the money, we might reject how they use or spend it. If wealthy people use their money well, for example, they give to charity, look after friends and family, and do not flaunt it, then they tend to receive less criticism. As humans we are great at having double standards. We might do the same things if we were wealthy, but if we're not, we can be quick to judge.

Think about how people become wealthy. What do you see as the wrong ways to acquire wealth, and why?

Buddhism

Buddhism states that there is essentially nothing wrong with having wealth; what is important is how it is used.

- Riches ruin the foolish ... through craving for riches, the foolish one ruins himself. (Dhammapada)
- Acquiring wealth is acceptable if, at the same time, it promotes the well-being of the community or society. – Phra Rajavaramuni
- Unskillful thoughts founded in greed keep people circling in samsara, in an endless round of repetitive, habitual attachment. – Kulananda, member of The Triratna Buddhist Order

Buddhism encourages right action, right thought, right intention and livelihood. For the wealthy to see poverty and ignore it would be wrong.

Christianity

Christians believe that there is nothing wrong with wealth in itself; it is how we use it that matters, as it can be used for good or bad. Wealth is seen as a gift from God. Our money should come from lawful means. The Bible warns that having the wrong attitude to money could lead people away from God.

- For the love of money is a root of all kinds of evil. Some people, eager for money, have wandered from the faith and pierced themselves with many griefs. (1 Timothy 6:10)
- No one can serve two masters … You cannot serve both God and money. (Matthew 6:24)
- Be on your guard against all kinds of greed: a man's life does not consist in the abundance of his possessions. (Luke 12:15)

Hinduism

For Hindus, it is important to create wealth (artha) to provide for their family **and** maintain society. Rich devotees should not hoard wealth, but use it in a stewardship role. Excess wealth can bring problems as it can lead to overindulgence and materialistic rather than spiritual living.

- Hindus believe that all wealth is a gift from Goddess Lakshmi and must be earned righteously.
- Happiness arises from contentment, uncontrolled pursuit of wealth will result in unhappiness. (Manu)
- Act in the world as a servant, look after everyone and act as if everything belongs to you, but know in your heart that nothing is yours – you are the guardian, the servant of God. – Sri Ramakrishna

Hindus believe that life is all about good deeds here and now. This not only helps the receiver but it helps the giver's own rebirth.

Judaism

Judaism states that wealth is a gift from G-d and can be used for the self and others. The Tenakh clearly states that money should only be earned in the correct way. Materialism can lead to people sinning – if your heart is filled with the desire for money then there is no room for G-d. The Talmud does see that a decent standard of living is needed for the well-being of the individual.

- Do not weary yourself trying to become rich. (Proverbs)
- He who loves silver cannot be satisfied with silver. (Ecclesiastes)
- He who has a hundred, craves for two hundred. (Midrash)

Money should not be desired but it is necessary.

Islam

In Islam, all wealth is a gift from Allah; humans are caretakers of Allah's wealth, and will be judged by their use of it to benefit humanity.

- Wealth is sweet for him who earns it lawfully and spends it rightfully. He who obtains wealth wrongfully is like one who eats but is never satisfied. (Hadith)
- Nobody has ever eaten a better meal than that which one has earned by working with one's own hands. (Hadith)
- It is not poverty which I fear for you, but that you might begin to desire the world as others before you desired it, and it might destroy you as it destroyed them. (Hadith)

Sikhism

Sikhs believe that anyone possessing riches has been blessed by God as they are able to help those in poverty. Livelihoods should be made by honest means. Anything that is earned dishonestly is seen as the 'blood of the poor'.

- One who lives by earning through hard work, Then gives some of it away to charity, Knows the way to God. – Guru Granth Sahib
- Be grateful to God for whose bounties you enjoy. – Guru Nanak
- Those who are too greedy for money have anxiety. – Guru Granth Sahib

Task

The more important question is where the money comes from, not what a person chooses to do with it. What do you think of this statement?

Causes of poverty

Disease/disability · Bad investments · Climate/natural disaster · Idleness/lack of effort · High-interest loan · People trafficking · War/corrupt governments · Addiction · Family and upbringing · Lack of education/employment · High taxes · Austerity measures · Debt · Immigration · Unfair trade/poor wages

Task

Which causes from those mentioned above apply more in the UK? Explain why for each of your choices. We seem to believe the wealthy have a responsibility to help those in poverty. We are looking here at two areas: 'giving money' to help those in these situations, and preventing the underlying causes where we can. It is the creation of social justice we referred to earlier. Look again at the examples above – people often experience poverty due to one or more of these. Can you connect some of them? Solving one issue may not lift a person out of poverty. Poverty is very complex.

Religious teachings that tell us we have a duty to tackle poverty

Buddhism

- Karuna (compassion) wishing others freedom from suffering.
- 'Today everyone is looking for personal happiness. So, I always say, if you wish to be happy and aim for self-interest, then care for others. This brings lasting happiness.' Dalai Lama

Christianity

- If anyone has material possessions and sees his brother or sister in need how can the love of God be in him? (I John 3:17)
- If a brother or sister has no clothes or food what good is it to wish him well without caring for his physical needs? (James 2:15)

Hinduism

- Some Hindus believe that by helping those in poverty, they can improve their own karma and rebirth.
- It is taught 'it is the same God shining out through so many different eyes. So helping others is no different than helping ourselves.'
- In Hinduism, the Vedas and the Mahabharata refer to *dana* (to give) as one of the most powerful characteristics within the self that can quickly lead one towards the realisation of the *atman*.

Islam

- He who eats and drinks whilst his brother goes hungry is not one of us. (Hadith)
- For a debtor, give him time to pay – but if you let it go out of charity this is the best thing to do. (Qur'an)

Judaism

- You shall not burden your heart or shut your hand against your poor brother. (Torah)
- The Torah forbids charging a fellow Jewish person **interest** on loans.

Sikhism

- A good person always seeks the welfare of others. – Bhai Gurdas
- A place in God's court can only be attained if we do service to others in the world. Guru Granth Sahib

The Basics

1. **If you have wealth you have a responsibility to tackle the causes of poverty.** Why might people agree and disagree with this?
2. Explain why religious people should be helping to tackle the causes of poverty.

How those in poverty are exploited

Fair pay

This means being paid at a rate that is appropriate for the work done. Also, that there is equal pay between men and women for the same job. It is a difficult issue because what is appropriate pay? Pay can be based on hours worked, qualifications needed, the necessity of the job and the type of job. A person might work a lot of hours but be low paid whereas another might work fewer hours at a highly qualified job and get paid more. There are some who are paid very high wages, like the heads of big companies, whereas an NHS nurse is paid much less. The minimum wage in the UK protects the very low paid. As of April 2019, the mandatory Living Wage was equalised with the minimum wage for those aged 25 and over. Low-paid workers often do jobs of great necessity for our everyday living, yet the wages they are paid don't reflect this. Remember *fair* does not mean *equal* as this would be impossible to achieve.

In the UK, religions have played a big part in campaigning for an increase in the minimum wage and working for the interests of people who are low paid. Regular statements are made, particularly by Church bishops to highlight this issue for those in poverty. There is a balance to be found as paying higher wages might mean fewer jobs are available, but even so there are many people who are working really hard for long hours of work but little money.

UK minimum wage (April 2025)

21 and over £12.21

18–20 £10.00

Under 18 £7.55

Apprentice £7.55

UK National Living Wage (April 2020)

21 and over £12.21

Excessive interest on loans

Some people experiencing poverty may feel forced to take loans to pay for things that more wealthy people take for granted. It might be to pay for Christmas as their wages are not enough, or an unforeseen expense, like replacing a broken fridge. Loan companies exploit these needs by offering same-day release of money, but the rate to pay it back can be huge – even thousands of per cent more in interest. People paying weekly only at the minimum rate will see that what they owe actually increases over time, rather than reduces. Each payment only pays off some of the interest on the loan which gets bigger the longer it takes to pay the loan back. It is all too easy to fall behind on payments and some people must take out additional loans to pay off the first loan. This is a vicious circle of increasing debt. Loan companies make a lot of money this way. In 2015, the UK government implemented restrictions on interest rates on loans, but it was nowhere near enough to solve the issue.

I needed cash quickly. The wages had gone and I had bills, so I took out a payday loan. I didn't read the small print carefully. I have already paid back ten times what I borrowed, and I still owe them money.

All religions disagree with excessive interest on loans. In fact, Islam does not allow interest for fellow Muslims, and Judaism for fellow Jewish people. Religions accept that companies have to make profits, but disagree with the extent that loans can exploit people. They exploit their need, their inability to pay and their lack of understanding as to how the system works. The loans do not help; rather they make situations worse.

Human trafficking

Human trafficking is the modern-day trade in enslaved people. It can take place both domestically (within a country) and internationally (across borders). Trafficking gangs exploit vulnerable people by taking large amounts of money from them in exchange for the promise of a better life, but often the victims find themselves in terrible situations that they cannot escape.

Victims can be men, women and children. They tend to be from war-torn countries, or regions with little opportunity. Traffickers charge high fees to move them – often thousands of pounds, and families work hard to save up to give their family member a better chance. But often victims find themselves in a situation where they are forced into sexual exploitation or enslavement/forced labour, and they are forced to work in degrading conditions to obtain their freedom. Many are victims of violence and intimidation. Some never regain their freedom.

In recent years there has been an increase in people being trafficked across Europe. They are migrant workers who cannot get into the UK legally, so gangs offer to smuggle them in for a high price. Some pay it and get here, whilst some are caught and often deported back to their country of origin. Some are successfully smuggled only to find themselves at the mercy of the gangs who demand more money, which they have to work, often in dire, usually illegal conditions, to get.

From 2015, there was an increase in people trafficking of those trying to escape war-torn countries, including Afghanistan, Iraq, Syria and Somalia. Desperate people pay large sums of money to illegal smugglers with the intention of travelling to safety, usually in Western Europe. People are moved in the back of lorries and on small boats, and often placed in grave danger on the journey. Boats are often inadequate and many have sunk, killing large numbers of migrants. For those who make it across borders, they have no right to claim status in the new country. Millions have been left displaced in this way.

Religions see people trafficking not only as illegal, but also as inhumane and totally unacceptable in a modern world. It goes against every kind of moral principle and religious teaching about our treatment of each other.

Think about the religious teachings you know already – which ones would tell us trafficking is wrong?

The Basics

1. Why is fair pay an important practice?
2. Explain what 'excessive interest loans' are and why many religious people disagree with them.
3. Explain why religions see people trafficking as wrong.
4. **People in poverty will always be victims.** Do you agree with this statement? Explain arguments on both sides, including religious arguments.

Responsibility for those living in poverty

This section looks at who should help people living in poverty.

The government

We elect a government to look after the best interests of society and this includes people living in poverty. MPs provide for the needs of the country as a whole and for individuals.

MPs should help because they have the means to help: they collect the taxes to finance the running of public services. People will not vote them into power if they do not help.

The government has the health services, educational services, welfare services, links to business and the means to bring all these together to help people living in poverty. It has the money, expertise and the access to co-ordinate helping these people. Also, MPs policy decisions on saving and spending directly affect the wealth of individuals – for example, cutting benefits or spending more on alleviating homelessness.

Charities

A charity by its very nature is set up to help someone or something. It collects money to help its cause and therefore has the means to help.

They should help because that is the reason they exist. They are set up on religious or humanitarian principles, that is, compassion and wanting to reduce suffering. People who belong to these charities perhaps just want to 'give something back' to society, to help those who have not had the same opportunities they had.

They fund-raise through organised events, national charity shops, donation collection and so on. They then decide through experience how to best spend the money raised.

Who should help people living in poverty?
Why should they help?
How should they help?

Religions

At their core, religions are about communities and helping each other. The worship of God has to be seen in action as well as in words.

Religious believers should help as the teachings of holy books tell them it is their duty, and throughout history, helping people living in poverty has been at the heart of their work. Also, helping these people is seen as doing God's work, or showing loving kindness or bringing social justice to the world. God rewards such actions.

Religions organise community events, donate to religious charities, work with vulnerable people here and abroad, pray for them and are simply there for people in times of need.

Those living in poverty

Most people living in poverty want to improve their financial situation:

- They might do training or work towards qualifications that will help them secure better-paid employment.
- If they suffer from physical or mental health conditions that stop them being able to work they might seek help for these.
- They might seek out organisations that are designed to help those living in poverty.

However, it is up to society to provide the support to those living in poverty who want to improve their financial situation.

Task

In pairs, research one of these four groups. Make a case to present to the class that it is your chosen group's responsibility to help people living in poverty.

Charity

Buddhism

International Buddhist Relief Organisation

History – The aim is to give practical and direct help to all living beings anywhere in the world. It sees itself as having a duty, especially to the most vulnerable, particularly children to whom the future belongs. It sets up sponsorship for many children in many countries.

Recent project – In Malawi, IBRO has financed the digging and building of wells so that villages have access to clean water. Communities have been able to redirect time previously spent fetching water into projects such as growing more food. This is helping to lift them out of poverty.

www.ibro.org.uk

Christianity

CAFOD

History – CAFOD was set up in 1962. Historically, Catholic churches generated charity funds on one specific day of each year. They themselves decided what to do with this money. CAFOD was the organisation set up to centralise this fund-raising, and be more effective and wide-ranging with it. Work which began as disaster relief and aid work now includes campaigning for a fairer world, and a vast array of educational work, including a schools magazine, as well as church magazines.

Recent project – Nicaragua is the second-poorest country in the Americas. CAFOD is contributing to a range of revival and urban projects to transform people's lives, for example, projects to give emotional and educational support for women and girls so that they do not get forced into sexual exploitation.

www.cafod.org.uk

Hinduism

Sewa International

History – This is a UK charity, entirely run by dedicated volunteers from all sections of the community, working towards serving humanity. It funds long-term projects for economic development. It tries to combine modern and indigenous techniques to improve living conditions in affected disaster areas of India. It focuses on education, orphanages, village amenities and employment.

Recent project – The Women's Empowerment Project runs in Odisha, India. Its major focus is to form village women's committees. This tries to give women a greater say in the decisions made in their village. It also educates women, because it is proven that for every year of education a woman has, the better her children's lives will be and the better their life chances in the future. Her education encourages theirs, empowering families and communities to see more pathways to change.

www.sewauk.org

Tasks

1. Read about the six projects on this page and the next. In each case, how important do you think the work has been? Explain your ideas.
2. Do you think that any of the projects are more important than the others? Explain your ideas.
3. If these charities were all UK-based, do you think they should focus on UK-based projects? Explain why.

Islam

Muslim Aid

History – Founded in 1985, this UK charity works in over 70 countries across Africa, Asia and Europe. It responds to emergencies but at the same time sets up strategic programmes to eliminate poverty, focusing on education and skills, provision of clean water, healthcare and ways to generate income. Muslim Aid also runs a qurbani programme whereby Muslims from all over the UK donate during Ramadan. This allows poor communities all over the Muslim world to receive food packages.

Recent projects – Beity Syrian Orphanage Appeal was set up in Turkey to provide care and support to children orphaned by the Syrian crisis. Muslim Aid provides food, medicines and accommodation at the orphanage, as well as counsellors for orphaned children, who are often traumatised by their experiences. This gives them a chance to rebuild their lives.

www.muslimaid.org

Judaism

World Jewish Relief

History – The charity was founded in 1933 to rescue Jewish people from the horrors taking place in Nazi Germany and brought 70,000 Jewish people to safety before the start of the Second World War. After the war, work began to respond to the needs of Jewish refugees and communities all over the world, with the aim of supporting Jewish people in distress. Its work involves empowering local communities by teaching them to be self-sufficient. Today WJR stands as the leading UK international agency responding to the needs of Jewish communities at risk or in crisis, outside the UK and Israel. At times of major international disaster, it leads the UK Jewish community's response to others in need all over the world.

Recent project – WJR funds three centres that support over 100 former children living on the streets to give them a chance of escaping poverty. It provides food and shelter, and access to medical and social workers as well as trauma counsellors. It ensures these children have an education and vocational training.

www.worldjewishrelief.org

Sikhism

Khalsa Aid

History – Based in Slough, UK, this is a humanitarian organisation run on Sikh principles, especially sewa (service to humanity). It runs entirely from donations and volunteers even pay their own expenses. One of its aims is to strive to assist in any possible way to combat poverty wherever there is a need. Following the central Sikh belief in equality, Khalsa Aid works with any group anywhere in the world, regardless of gender, age, religion or any other barrier. Khalsa Aid was one of the first agencies to help victims of the Grenfell Tower disaster in 2017.

Recent project – The Punjab region regularly experiences catastrophic flooding. Many villages are destroyed and crops devastated. Khalsa Aid responds by supplying food rations, blankets and clothes to affected people. They also send equipment to help ensure clean water is available. Khalsa Aid works with communities to help them rebuild, and to get them through to the time when their new crops can be harvested.

www.khalsaaid.org

The Basics

1 Give two reasons why the work of charities is important.
2 Why do religious people want to work for and give to charity?
3 **The work of charities is the solution to poverty.** What is your opinion?
4 Research the work of a charity which helps internationally, and one which focuses its work in the UK.

Poverty in the UK

There are some charities that focus on key areas of poverty in the UK. Sometimes when we see poverty in other parts of the world, we forget that actually there are many people living in poverty in the UK too.

Shelter

Shelter is the UK's leading housing and homelessness charity.

Shelter helps millions of people every year struggling with bad housing or homelessness through their advice, support and legal services.

And they campaign so that, one day, no one will have to turn to them for help.

They are here so no one has to fight bad housing or homelessness on their own.

The charity was formed in 1966 by Bruce Kenrick (founder chairman) and Des Wilson (founder-director), in response to the country's massive housing crisis. Their vision – along with co-founders Edwin Barker, David Reid, Rev. Eammon Casey and Lewis Waddilove – was to establish one organisation to speak for the millions of 'hidden homeless' living in overcrowded slums.

In 2019, a spokesperson from Shelter said that we are now again facing a national emergency that is the housing crisis, with 6 million households across England and Scotland denied the right to a safe home, or threatened with losing it.

The Salvation Army

You might have seen members of the Salvation Army at Christmas time, in shopping centres playing music and with collecting tins. But, they actually work all year round on:

- rebuilding lives – offering a hand-up to homeless people, a family tracing service, drug and alcohol rehabilitation, anti-human-trafficking services
- offering – food parcels, lunch clubs for older people, supporting the emergency services during major fires and incidents, visiting prisoners
- giving people the chance to belong – organising and providing youth clubs and music groups, for example.

As a Christian Church and registered charity, The Salvation Army also runs a Christmas Present Appeal each year for children, homeless people and older people who have little or nothing at Christmas time. It runs homeless resettlement centres, care homes for older people, employment services for long-term unemployed people, support services for the armed forces and home-visiting services in local communities. All this is done through volunteers and ministers who believe in putting their Christian beliefs into action and following Jesus' example to help (not judge) anyone who is in need.

Issues with giving to charity – interesting dilemmas

- Do we give to charity or directly to the individual?
- Do we give money, for example, to a person begging or buy them food?
- How do we know the money we give actually helps the people who need it?
- How much of every £1 we give to charity is actually spent on helping people living in poverty?
- How much does it cost to fund the charity work?
- Which charities do we choose to give to when so many are so deserving?

Discuss the bullet-point questions in pairs and share your answers as a class.

The Basics

1. Explain the work of one charity that focuses on helping people living in poverty in the UK.
2. **People living in poverty in the UK are just as deserving as those living abroad.** How far do you agree or disagree?

Different beliefs

Status of women in religion

Christianity

Women have status in Christianity. Christians believe that **God made all people free and equal – in the image of God** (Genesis 1:27). St Paul said **'There is neither Jew nor Greek, male nor female, for you are all one in Christ Jesus'** (Galatians 3:28) – demonstrating equality. The first people to see Jesus after his resurrection were female, and **early church leaders included women.**

Roman Catholicism

In the Roman Catholic Church, women **may not hold positions of authority**. While women could publicly pray and prophesy in church (1 Cor. 11:1–16), they **could not teach or have authority over a man** (1 Tim. 2:11–14). These are **two essential functions** of the clergy, so women are **scripturally excluded** from these roles.

Islam

Women can be Islamic scholars and jurists and can lead other women in prayer. Most Muslims consider that women may not lead prayers of both men and women. Two female commercial contract witnesses are equivalent to one male witness (Surah 2:282).

Christianity

In the Orthodox Church, women may not have leadership roles. Women have a **God-given role and task as a mother**; nothing is more important than this and nothing should detract from it.

Question

Explain two different beliefs from contemporary British society about the status of women in religion.

In your answer you should refer to the main religious tradition of Great Britain and one or more other religious traditions. *(4 marks)*

Use of wealth

Christianity

Many Christians believe in **tithing** – the giving of charity up to a tenth of a person's income. Jesus taught the early community to give – **Go sell everything you have and give it to the poor and you will have treasure in heaven** (Mark 10:21). In Luke 12:15, Jesus cautioned people **against greed, saying that life does not consist of having many possessions**. Wealth should be used to **benefit others, not just for selfish reasons**. There is **no fixed rate** of giving though.

Islam

Muslims give zakah (2.5%) of their wealth (minus a lower limit) each year. **They see it as a duty, not charity, as not giving will be problematic in the afterlife.** Shi'a Muslims also give khums, which is 20% of their income from specified sources, on top of zakah.

Sikhism

Sikhs should give 10% of their wealth to charity (daswandh), with the expectation that they will give more where they can. **It is more than a personal choice whether to give.** 'One who lives by earning through hard work, then gives some of it away to charity, knows the way to God'. Guru Granth Sahib

Question

Explain two different beliefs in contemporary British society about the use of wealth.

In your answer you should refer to the main religious tradition in Great Britain and one or more other religious traditions. *(4 marks)*

Hinduism

In Hinduism, **wealth is seen as the consequence of previous rebirths**. Hence, a person's lack of it is also a consequence, and a few might believe poor people **should not be helped, as they have bad karma to work through**. However, **giving still brings good karma to the giver, and helps those in need, so is encouraged and practised**.

Freedom of religious expression

Christianity

Christians believe that **God made all people free and equal**. All were made in **the image of God** (Genesis 1:27). This entitles all to rights including that of freedom of religious expression. **Dignitas Personae states that the 'human person has a right to religious freedom'.** They point to the fact that Jesus invited people to follow him, and did not force them – allowing them to choose their religious path.

Islam

Muslims **accept Christians and Jewish people as believers in God** – both are 'people of the book' although Muslims consider Islam preferable to either religion. Some Muslims consider converting from Islam to any other religion to be punishable by death; others consider that there is no earthly penalty, only one in the afterlife. Other religions beyond Islam, Christianity and Judaism are considered invalid and often idolatrous.

Most religious people would say that freedom of **religious expression is a vital element of society**. However, many would say that religious expression needs to be within reason – **not disrespecting or offending other religions, and not forcing one's own religious rules onto others**, for example.

Question

Explain two different beliefs from contemporary British society about freedom of religious expression.

In your answer you should refer to the main religious tradition of Great Britain and one or more other religious traditions. *(4 marks)*

Getting prepared

Points of attack

A total of 50 per cent of the marks are allocated to analysis and evaluation; that is, challenging or supporting statements. It is essential you answer using proper technique. For each topic, you must answer a 12-mark evaluation question.

When faced with a statement, it is often the case that we can only think of one way to argue – either for or against – so our answer becomes either one-sided or very limited on a second side. But there are phrases you can use to give yourself a better chance, for example:

Best Most Everyone/All Always Must

When we are faced with a statement that we feel very strongly about, we can find it really difficult to think in a different way or be open-minded. But each of these words gives you an opening – a way to challenge the statement. Take a look at these examples:

All *religious believers should help people living in poverty.* Should they really? What if people living in poverty are poor because of activities like gambling (which is against most religions)? What if the religious believer is themselves experiencing poverty (so they have nothing to give)?

Religious people should always *fight for human rights.* Should they really? Always? Are there any people who have forfeited some of their rights, for example, a murderer who loses their right to freedom? What if those rights lead to the persecution of others, or diminish another individual or group's rights, for example, allowing freedom of speech to the extent of religious hatred?

Discrimination is the worst *thing a person can suffer.* Is it really? What if the discrimination is very limited? Might there be other things more dreadful, like being wrongfully accused or convicted of a serious crime? Thinking about the potential repercussions gives you a huge scope for your answers.

Brainwork

Our brains are actually quite lazy, preferring not to have to think – which is actually quite hard. We know that our brains prefer to just go back to what they already know and have already experienced, rather than work things out anew. So a great phrase to help our brains open up to more options can come in the answer – 'it depends'. Take a look at this:

A special tax is the best way to solve poverty. Well it depends – if the tax is an affordable one, then yes. However, if the tax is a flat rate, so everyone pays the same – well that is not fair, and means even those in poverty have to pay (which is pointless!).

Planning an attack on an evaluative question

When faced with an evaluative question:

- Make sure that you are writing about the statement and not just giving religious attitudes to the topic – there is no point writing what Christians and Muslims think about prejudice generally, if the statement says 'Prejudice is the biggest issue for the world today.'
- You must give arguments to agree and disagree – giving a one-sided answer will limit your answer.
- You must have strong religious content – not just one religious argument or point.
- You must use religious teachings to prove those religious arguments.
- You must explain your arguments – just listing reasons to agree or disagree is not going to get you far enough. Each time you give a reason, explain it by extending the point – try to give examples to illustrate what you mean.
- You must use examples to help support your reasons – they are very effective for showing the point clearly.

A useful checklist for writing higher-mark answers

- Did you agree with the statement? What are your reasons?
- Did you explain all of those reasons?
- Did you include at least one religious argument which was explained in those reasons?
- Did you disagree with the statement? What are your reasons?
- Did you explain all of those reasons?
- Did you include at least one religious argument which was explained in those reasons?
- Is your opinion different? If so, add it.

Let us practise ...

Use the knowledge you have gained from this page and your notes to write detailed answers to the following statements:

There is no point fighting for human rights.

Prejudice can never be ended.

Religious believers should make the ending of poverty their top priority.

Religion, human rights and social justice glossary

Ageism discrimination on the grounds of a person's age

Community a group of people who belong together because of a shared characteristic

Compassion loving kindness; helping because help is needed

Discrimination actions based on prejudice, often negative

Equality the idea that everyone is equal, of equal value and worth

Fair pay equal payment for equal work

Gender the characteristics of being male or female that are socially constructed

Harmony living together without argument and conflict

Homophobia prejudice against someone on the grounds of their (perceived) sexuality

Human rights the rights a person is entitled to simply because they are human

Human Rights Act a law which protects the rights of all human beings and allows us to challenge when these are violated

Interest the money paid to a lender from a borrower on top of the initial sum borrowed

Justice fairness, moral rightness

Loan borrowed money which has to be paid back, usually with interest; excessive loans are where the rate of interest is very high

Minimum wage the legal minimum a person can be paid per hour in a job in the UK

People trafficking the illegal trade of humans to exploit them through sexual exploitation and/or forced labour

Positive discrimination discriminating in favour of a person with a protected characteristic

Poverty having less than the basic needs of life, so that life is a struggle

Prejudice pre-judging someone based on a characteristic they have, for example, their race, religion, sexual orientation or gender

Racism prejudice based on a person's racial/ethnic origins

Responsibility duty, for example, the responsibility to work to earn money

Rights entitlements, for example, the right to education

Sexuality a person's sexual orientation, for example, straight, gay or bisexual

Social justice justice in terms of wealth and opportunities in a society

Stewardship duty to look after, in this case, other people and those less fortunate

Tolerance acceptance of difference

UN Declaration of Human Rights a statement adopted by the United Nations organisation to protect all human beings

Wealth the total value of assets (money, possessions) owned by an individual, group, company or country

Index

It is a disturbing privilege to be at the epicentre of any kind of disaster. We now know what it is like to live in the wreckage. We nurse ourselves along, trying to deal with a range of issues – from huge personal loss to property loss to wear and tear on the nerves. We cannot be foolishly brave and risk families and ourselves for the sake of 'sticking with it'.

Lyttelton's location has a charm that other towns, villages around the world, can only dream of. The advantage we have is our tight-knit community. Notice has already been served that the people will have what they want in the re-build. Thus, we will have a new Lyttelton and a London St (among others) which will be both charming and successful.

To slightly adapt a poem I wrote 30 years ago:

Still waters, Lyttelton.
I come to you for shelter.
Lover and harbour,
you are.

Gary McCormick

THANK YOU *to the many contributors who have made this Earthquake Edition of "Harbour Kitchens" possible. The many local amateur photo-journalists alongside local photographers – Frank Visser, Mick Stephenson, Nick Groves, Stacy Paton and Louis Russell. Thank you to local writers Ben Brown, Bruce Russell, Roy Montgomery, John Sellwood, Gary McCormick and the talented children of Lyttelton West and Lyttelton Main Schools. We also acknowledge the generous support from Project Lyttelton Earthquake Fund.*

Lastly, we would like to pay tribute to the tireless and heroic efforts of the Lyttelton Volunteer Fire Brigade and Lyttelton Civil Defence.

Published by the Combined Lyttelton Schools' Charitable Trust
c/- Lyttelton West School, 41 Voelas Road , Lyttelton, Christchurch, 8082, NZ

This edition published December 2011.
First published October 2009.

ISBN 978-0-473-15695-4

Printed by Maxim Print
Graphic design by TimeZoneOne
www.timezoneone.com
Cover photograph by Dean MacKenzie

HARBOUR KITCHENS

CELEBRATING LYTTELTON, ITS FOOD AND PEOPLE

Room 3 mural, Lyttelton Main School

CONTENTS

This book is dedicated to the people of Lyttelton:
to those who have built this community, to those who are carrying it forward now,
and to our children who represent its future.

"When a earthquake happens and you are in class go under your desk like this."

Rhiannon, age 8

12.51pm, 22 February, 2011

"I dived for a desk under a rain of dictionaries and maths books as the ground twisted and turned like a tumble dryer and then, as quickly as it started, it ended. The only sounds were the cries of the children and the creaky groan of the Lyttelton houses."

Hektor, age 12

"We buddy up with little kids and took them to the Rec Centre to wait for our mums and dads. Everyone had something to eat. Two brave men went into the supermarket and grabbed lots of food for us."

William, age 8

"In the earthquake mum and dad were very proud of me. I did what I was supposed to do."

Elaina, age 6

"BOOM another one struck, mother nature must be having a tantrum."

James, age 10

CANTERBURY ST
THE
VOLCANO
LAVA
BAR
FIRE
RESCUE

NO EXIT
Port of Lyttelton
NO PUBLIC ACCESS
Sumner
Lyttelton
Town Centre

"This is a picture of when I went in the car into town after the earthquake. When I looked out the window this is what I saw (sort of)."

Joshua, age 9

"My dad is the Chief Fireman and he was very busy after the earthquake. We didn't see him much. I was proud of him."

Connor, age 8

THANK U

AUCKLAND
AIRPORT
FIRE
RESCUE
FIRE
RESCUE

JUST ADD PORK

Two days after the February quake we were going up Canterbury Street to check out the naval field kitchen behind the Rec Centre. It was late afternoon, and we'd heard that the navy was putting on a spread, which seemed a good way to catch up with the neighbours, and see what was what round town. One of the good things about a disaster is that there's plenty of time to enquire after people, and see if they need anything - such as chimney pulling down, some hydrated lime for the long-drop, or a go under our solar shower.

Everybody seemed to be at the field kitchen, and the soup was excellent. Even though we weren't short of food, having a chance to get fed without all the hassle that ensues in a quake-ravaged home seemed like a nice idea. So there was a lot of chat, which was very therapeutic – nothing like a shared episode of utter terror to stimulate the need to engage with your friends, it turns out. Eventually we were heading off in a homeward direction when suddenly my daughter appeared with an enormous pork roast in her arms.

'Where'd you get that?' I asked, understandably curious, due to a lifelong enthusiasm for pork roasts of any size. 'They're clearing out the chillers at Ground' was her matter of fact answer. The delicatessen had suffered a considerable degree of damage, there was no power on, and obviously a salvage operation was in progress. Walking down the hill, my curiosity piqued by the enormous free slab of meat, I encountered a similarly-sized slab coming towards me under the arm of a neighbour. 'Good score', I commented. 'Yes, but what are we going to do with it all?' was the reply. It didn't take long to decide that roasting them would be the best way to handle such an embarrassment of porcine riches. 'Put the word about – we'll have 'em tomorrow.'

Our generously-proportioned oven was amazingly undamaged by its unexpected flight across the kitchen: an unforeseen argument in favour of long gas connection pipes. There was still a bit of tidying to be done, but the next evening saw a considerable throng gathered to see off the meat. The rule was: bring your own water, and anything you could muster for the table, as well as anything handy in the liquor department. Everyone was pretty lively. Hell, we actually were alive! The cooking took a while, which allowed for several toasts to Ground Culinary Centre, and a hearty guffaw greeted the neighbour who asked the question of the hour: 'Can I just go to the toilet anywhere in the garden, or do you have a special spot?'

And that's how we got through it, people pooled their resources, shared what they had, and looked out for their neighbours. I think as people we're the better for it, despite what we've lost. Having 25 friends over for dinner three days after a natural disaster is the only way to respond. Life must be affirmed, and it turns out that food and drink are the best way to do it.

Bruce Russell

"Then I helped my dad fit some piping to the drain that gets spring water and started to fill buckets of water to boil so we can have a cup of hot milo. We were lucky because we had a gas stove with lots of gas."

William, age 8

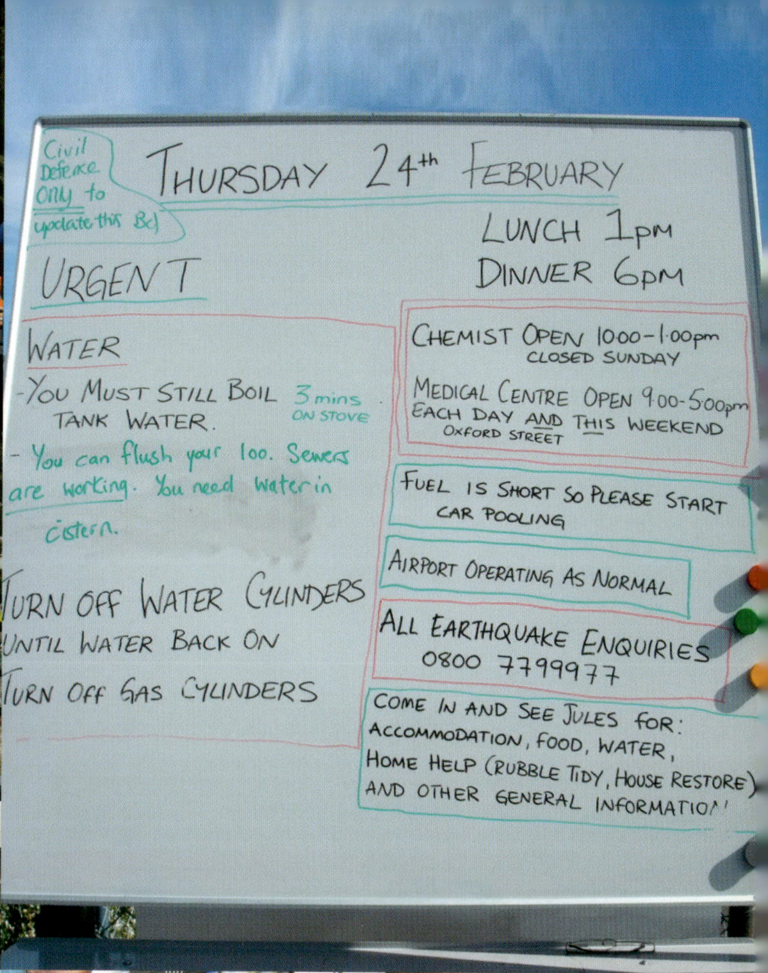

"The following days were boring and depressing, but still people cheered each other up. People who didn't know each other were asking if they were okay and others were doing nice things for the community. Yet, you still couldn't call it a holiday."

Tom, age 12

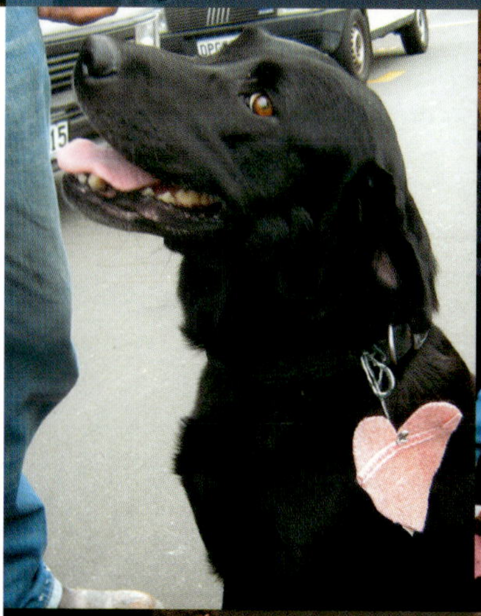

"And as we sat stitching amongst the rubble of our beloved buildings, we discovered a small way to grieve a little for what we had lost. This is no small thing."

Jacinda

We take them for granted

We pass them by and don't
give them another glance

We barely remember what
they look like

We think,
"I'll walk by it tomorrow"

But then once they are gone

We just look at them

Covered in rubble.

Alex, age 12

"The Harbourlight
has criss-cross cracks"

Finn, age 8

"One day I woke up and looked up the hill and the Timeball was not there!"

Sonny, age 6

NZ TRANSPORT AGENCY
WAKA KOTAHI

TRANSFIELD
SERVICES

APPROVED TUNNEL

TRAVEL PERMIT

COMMANDING OFFICER
26 FEB 2011
HMNZS CANTERBURY

SIGNED

STAMP

RED STICKER BLUES

The cat has been away for a day or two, which is so unlike
the sanctimonious sod, predisposed as he is to enjoying all the
luxuries of life from the comfiest chair in the house.

The Empire has fallen.

The grand old pub is dead and buried, red sticker for an epitaph.

I wonder; did I pay my tab?

My children now understand the Richter scale, and the difference
between incremental and exponential, and the fundamental
nature of tectonics, and the latent potential of stress as two
heads butt against each other for sixteen thousand years. My
children understand that mum and dad do that sometimes, but it
usually goes away in the end.

A house I used to live in swayed but did not fall. I'm glad.
I love that old house, something to do with the jam of its doors
and the suicidal creak of the stairs.

If you think about it, the hills above this town should not have
houses on them, angry hills do not like houses on their faces,
which is precisely why the ancestors built them here in the first
place, something to do with defiance.

If you tell me I cannot live here, then I will.

Ben Brown 2011

These days our skyline is very different, so much is gone but we're still here. We have a café in a garage, a bakery in a porta-cabin and the bookshop is in a back-room office behind the medical centre. During the winter The Loons' performed Macbeth outdoors in a demolition site where once the Volcano stood. And without a local supermarket, volunteer cooks feed the elderly from a meeting-room kitchen.

We are all in a place of transition, the narrative of our lives has changed suddenly and dramatically, the future we each dreamed of will now be something different. But we're all in this together, we share a common experience and that's where our strength lies. It's okay to be fragile, to be unsure – letting go is hard, but with it comes renewed hope, opportunity, a new narrative by which to live.

John Sellwood

AFTERSHOCKWORD 2011...

In the text below, written in 2009, there are a number of lies laced with what at the time was more or less true. Lyttelton was indeed hip and it still had a handful of old hotel buildings and it was charmingly gritty. Two years later it looks like it could do with a hip operation, the pubs are gone and there is more grit in the air, thanks to the dust from the demolition of most of the central business district, than any of the locals could ever have desired.

But for the loss of two of its inhabitants on February 22, 2011 I might have quipped that such adversity would merely be grist to the mill for the true Lytteltonian. After all, the CBD had been destroyed once before in a fire on October 24, 1870. Now is not the time for glibness or the type of rhetoric about rapid reconstruction of which many have tired as they sit in their unchimneyed homes and stare out at a largely downed downtown. Now is the time for the food that fuels the thought and the action that builds and rebuilds communities like Lyttelton.

This book is for the hard yards and kinder years to come. Oh, and Marmaduke Lyttelton III? It turns out that, thanks to some recently discovered papers, he did not perish on the shores of Whakaraupo but instead made it all the way to Lanzarote in the Canary Islands in 1728 only to fall, a few years later, into one of the 32 new volcanoes that appeared on the island in the swarm of eruptions that occurred between 1730 and 1736.

LYTTELTON
An informal introduction

A very unreliable legend has it that Lyttelton was originally and accidentally founded by Marmaduke Lyttelton III – in 1727. This heir to an extinct branch of the Lyttelton dynasty attempted to establish, with the as-yet-undiscovered Terra Australis, a trade in cotton, saffron and, most enterprisingly, opium. Unfortunately the young man was no entrepreneur, a poor sailor, and not particularly likable. By the time he reached the distant harbour of Whakaraupo his circumstances were dramatically reduced. Jettisoned by common-sense mutineers into a leaking longboat with only his diary and some strips of dessicated albatross, he expired on the beach along which the town later grew, scattering the pages of his diary to the wind. It was fragments from these pages, found by later explorers, that gave substance to this melancholy legend, and a name to the town they established.

Canterbury people usually have even vaguer ideas than this about the age, name, and original function of Lyttelton. The town remains a working port for shipping of various types. The steep walls of the extinct volcano in which it sits has limited the degree to which the place can grow. The flatlanders also tend to think the place is cold because it faces south - and that it is a long way from civilisation (as they term Christchurch). The locals, of course, know better.

What is less well-known is the fact that in the early months of 1849, when the initial surveys were being carried out, the first choice site for Lyttelton was a few bays west at Rapaki, while Christchurch was pencilled in for the head of the harbour at what is now known as Teddington. The resident Ngāi Tahu at Rapaki had other ideas – so Lyttelton moved east to a seasonal site of Maori occupation called Ohinehou. We know the exact, if unofficial, date for the founding of Lyttelton because Charles Torlesse noted in his journal that on 3 July 1849 the survey team 'moved tents to Cavendish Bay'. The town was surveyed from 23-28 July and fully laid out by August, a month before a notional town of similar size was laid out at Sumner, and several months before Christchurch was laid out in the following year.

Since then Lyttelton's star has waxed and waned a number of times. It was regarded as prime commercial real estate in the 1850s and a real rival to Christchurch in terms of which would prevail as the capital. However, as industry on the waterfront developed over the following century, it came to be seen as a less desirable place to live. The town's reputation, from an outsiders' perspective, could perhaps best be described as sooty, shady, salty and, well - slutty - if one was to put it alliteratively. However, throughout its history it has been steadfastly defended by the majority of its residents, most of whom were either imprisoned in the jail, or had some connection to the operation of the port. The unofficial town motto remains – 'love it or leave it'. In the 1970s a new wave of colonisation began: including solo mums looking for affordable housing, 'media types' looking for something different, refugees from Europe fleeing the threat of nuclear winter, and people who liked old houses and who knew that even if it took twenty years to 'do up' the place, the neighbours would understand.

Right now, Lyttelton is hip. While Christchurch has sprawled and sprawled Lyttelton has stayed more or less within the boundaries set in the first decades of settlement. Ironically, this enforced village scale is part of what now makes Lyttelton so 'cool'. The grid pattern of the streets and houses means that the town serves people on foot best, not cars. Once the calf muscles thicken up it is eminently walkable. Although once the 'last port of call' for homebuyers, it is now thought to be as desirable as the hill suburbs through the tunnel.

A new Lyttelton parochialism has emerged in the twenty-first century. The old pubs are still there, even if they are no longer the dens of iniquity they once were. Cafes and festivals abound. Babies, toddlers and 'new invader' parents clutter the main street, and mingle with the genuine old guard, and the late twentieth century arrivistes – who like to think they have done enough time to almost qualify as locals. They all unite in their consternation at the weekends when the town hordes pour through the tunnel and overrun the village. New forms of resistance are emerging. Once upon a time locals pleaded for street upgrades to make it more like other towns and cities. Now they campaign against 'improvements' that might compromise the gritty ambience of the place. Once upon a time there were church groups for the 'ladies' and clubs for the 'working men'. Now there are community gardens, radio stations, book groups and school fundraisers...

Roy Montgomery

Spring

As the days grow longer and warmer the first blossom appears, and the hills turn green with new growth. While unwelcome, the yellow flowering broom and gorse remain timely reminders of the changing season. Vegetable plots are dug over and summer crops planted.

The cruise ships return and Antarctic-bound boats pull in to restock for their journeys south.

The weather can be volatile, with unseasonal winds taking their toll on local moorings. This makes for trying times for those tending blooms for the Lyttelton Rose Show.

/FOT
8
6
4
2
13M
8
6
4
2
12M
8
6
4
2

spring food

Ricotta hotcakes

Kate McRae
serves 4-6

When we started No 6 cafe this was one of the most popular dishes on the breakfast menu. The addition of ricotta makes them lighter and gives them an interesting texture.

4 eggs, separated

1¼ cups self-raising flour

½ cup sugar

pinch salt

1 cup ricotta

¾ cup milk

butter for frying

Beat the egg whites until stiff and set aside. Sift the flour, sugar and salt into a large bowl. In a separate bowl mix the ricotta with a metal spoon to make it smooth. Add the yolks and the milk and mix until just combined. Add the ricotta mixture to the flour and mix lightly. Add the whites and mix until just combined. Melt the butter and cook in batches in a non-stick frying pan. Two tablespoons of batter makes a good sized hotcake.

Serve with seasonal fruit, crispy bacon if you want, and plenty of maple syrup.

"I like baking pancakes with my mum and all my friends like Bethny and Lili and Samantha and Jaspah and Ngaio." Grace, age 6

Yoghurt bread

Michael Herman
makes 1 large loaf

When I was child in Cape Town my mother Chia made this bread every day for my school lunches – a perfect sandwich with lettuce, cheese and tomato.

4 cups whole grain flour (a premixed variety is fine)

2 tsp salt

1 tsp baking soda

2 tbsp honey

500ml plain non-Greek style yoghurt, unsweetened

Preheat oven to 180°C.

Mix all the ingredients together and bake in a greased loaf tin for approx 1 hour. If it is still not quite cooked then turn the oven off and leave for another 10mins.

Enjoy!

Thai fish cakes

Clare O'Regan
serve 4-6

500g fish, gurnard or terakihi is best

3 spring onions, finely sliced

2 tbsp fresh coriander, chopped

1-2 tbsp Thai red curry paste, depending on degree of hotness required

1 tbsp lime juice (lemon will do)

a little salt

Place all the ingredients in a food processor and blend until you have a reasonably finely minced texture. Form into small balls about golf ball size and flatten. This can be done up to several hours before required and stored in the fridge.

To cook, sauté in very hot oil – only a few minutes required for each side.

Serve with rice and Thai chilli sauce, or with sticky rice.

Maki-sushi (rolled sushi)

Jeremy and Keiko Orczy
makes 6 rolls

4 cups short grain rice

4 cups water

7 tbsp rice wine vinegar

6 tbsp sugar

1 tbsp salt

Wash rice and drain in a sieve. Let it stand for 30 mins to 1 hour in water so rice can absorb water. Transfer the rice to rice cooker and cook.

To make vinegar dressing: Mix together vinegar, sugar and salt in a small saucepan and heat but don't boil. Let the cooked rice stand for 10 mins.

Transfer the cooked rice to a large bowl. Sprinkle the vinegar dressing over the hot rice. Mix quickly in bowl with a chopping motion. Then let it cool.

To roll sushi: Place a sheet of seaweed on a bamboo rolling mat. Spread rice thinly over seaweed, leaving 2.5 – 3cm space on the edge away from you. Lay out each ingredient in a line along the centre of the seaweed then roll the rolling mat tightly to form a sushi roll. Gently but firmly press the rolling mat around the roll to shape it. Cut into 8 pieces.

Suitable Sushi fillings: cooked chicken, tuna, avocado, peppers, omelette, cucumber, spring onion, chives.

sticky rice with scallions

Shelley McCabe
serves 6

1½ cups sticky rice soaked for at least 1 hour or preferably overnight - use a glutinous rice available from Asian supermarkets

2 tbsp peanut oil

2 tbsp soya sauce

½ cup scallions, chopped

juice of 1 lime, or to taste

¼ cup coriander, minced

salt & pepper

2 tsp sesame oil

Steam rice for about 8 mins until tender. While rice is hot toss with peanut oil, soy sauce and scallions. Stir in lime juice and ½ of the coriander. Just before serving, add remaining coriander, sesame oil and more lime juice, salt & pepper.

Serve at room temperature.

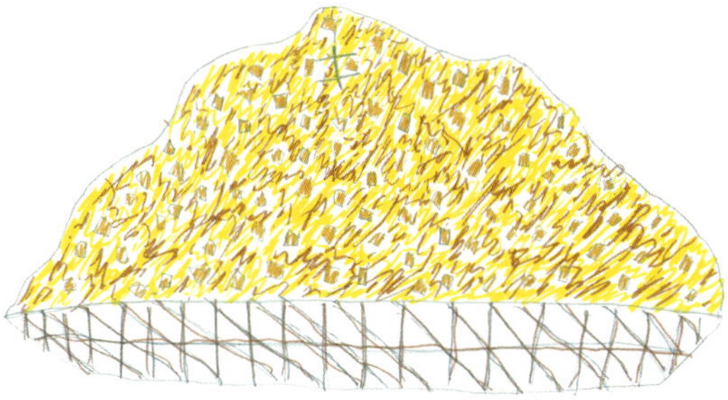

"Never eat food cold" Isla, age 8

MSA 100072
lpc
PILOT

Helen's mussel morsels

Helen Hobson, Harbour Light, Lyttelton
serves 6

10 gourmet Nadine potatoes

2kg fresh live mussels (approx. 40 mussels)

1 cup white wine

4 cloves garlic, finely chopped

3 dried chillies, finely chopped (don't discard the seeds)

rock salt & black pepper

good dollop butter

To serve:

1 loaf of Turkish bread

1 bunch Italian parsley, coarsely chopped

Steam potatoes until just cooked through, and set aside to cool. Prepare a large pot for cooking the mussels in with the wine, three-quarters of the garlic, the chillies and salt & pepper. Dice potatoes and brown in a frying pan with a good dollop of butter and remainder of the chopped garlic. Add mussels to the prepared pot and cook until they just open. Remove mussels from heat as soon as possible after opening and plate up. Scatter potatoes, then parsley over the mussels and serve with Turkish bread.

Enjoy with a slightly sweet but spicy bottle or two of Gewürztraminer and some good company.

Tomato & fresh herb mussel soup

Gael Abraham
serves 6

The beauty of this soup is that any fresh herbs will work – try coriander, Italian parsley, watercress or even sorrel.

2 doz fresh mussels

1 cup white wine

2 tbsp olive oil

1 large onion

5 cloves garlic, finely sliced

2 tsp ginger, finely sliced

2 red chillies, finely chopped (or sweet chilli sauce)

2 limes, zested & juiced

500mls tomato juice

1 tbsp Worcestershire sauce

1 tbsp mirin (sweetened rice wine)

1 bunch fresh herbs

Clean the mussels discarding the broken or open ones. Cover the bottom of a pan with about 1cm of water and a dash of white wine. Steam the mussels until they open, discard any that haven't opened. Remove from the shell but retain the cooking liquid. In a large saucepan sauté onion, garlic, ginger and chilli in olive oil until onions are translucent. Add zest plus remainder of the liquids, including the stock from the mussels. Finally, when ready to serve, chop mussels into bite-sized bits and add back into the pan with the chopped fresh herbs. Warm and serve.

Tuna surprise

John Sellwood
serves 4

The surprise part of this recipe is that if a ham-fisted numb-nut like myself can actually cook something worth eating - and this is worth eating - then anyone can! Even better, this recipe doesn't actually involve cooking, well not real cooking, not like you see Richard Till doing on the tele. I may have low standards and an unsophisticated palate but I reckon this is a winner, particularly for those awkward unexpected, 'oh-do-stay-for-tea moments,' when the cupboard is all but bare.

And you only need to be able to boil water, open a tin and slice bits and bobs. Skill level 0.5.

½ pkt macaroni or similar pasta

2 eggs

3 stalks of celery

½ red pepper

2 small tins tuna (lemon pepper flavoured)

1 lemon

1 tsp butter

mayonnaise (optional)

salt & pepper to taste

Boil pasta and eggs (no, not together, it will all end in tears and I won't be held responsible. Use two pots for goodness sake). Cut celery and red pepper. Mix with cooked pasta, slice in boiled eggs and add tuna from tin. Mix it all together, add a squeeze of lemon juice, a bit of butter and salt & pepper to taste. If you're a real fancy pants, or perhaps a trying to impress the "Mrs", you might want to add mayonnaise.

All this can be achieved whilst taking a shower and clipping your nails – I know.

"The surprise part of this recipe is that if a ham-fisted numb-nut like myself can actually cook something worth eating - and this is worth eating - then anyone can!"

Prawn curry

Captain John Cleaver
serves 2

When I was based in Bombay (Mumbai) working passenger ships running to and from East and South African ports, we carried about 150 saloon passengers and about 1000 deck passengers. We had Hindu sailors on deck, Muslims in the engine room and Goanese (Christian) stewards. This required three galleys and store rooms for the three religions! In addition, the deck passengers travelled 'without food' and prepared their own (two more galleys). They could also purchase their meals from contractors travelling in the ship (more galleys). The smell of curry cooking was all pervasive! In order to check on the standard of food supplied by the contractors, we used to send down for lunch every so often - curry - it was delicious, prepared with spices from scratch (no curry powder) and gave me a lasting taste for curry dishes.

For the curry sauce:

1-2 tbsp oil

1 onion, chopped

1 small apple, peeled & chopped

2 tsp curry powder

2 tbsp flour

1 cup stock or water

1 tomato, peeled & quartered

½ tsp of sugar

handful sultanas

2 tsp chutney, or gooseberry or plum jam

2 tsp lemon juice

salt

To serve:

200-300g cooked prawns

rice or mashed potatoes

lemon slices

Sauté the onion in the oil and then add the apple. Sprinkle in the curry powder and flour cook thoroughly. Gradually add the stock, tomato, sugar, sultanas and chutney. Bring to the boil and simmer for a few minutes. Transfer to a covered casserole dish, season with salt and lemon juice and cook over low heat for approx an hour.

To serve: Add 200-300g cooked prawns to the curry sauce. Reheat in the oven at 175°C for 25 mins. Serve with boiled rice or mashed potatoes. Decorate with lemon slices.

Diced, lightly-cooked chicken may be used instead of prawns.

"In order to check on the standard of food supplied by the contractors, we used to send down for lunch every so often - curry - it was delicious, prepared with spices from scratch" Captain Cleaver

John, Judi & Andrew's salmon

John Thawley, principal, Lyttelton Main School

An incredible meal prepared by our son. Judi and I have adopted it. We eat it once a week! In April 2008, Judi and I visited Andrew in London. We hadn't experienced the pleasure of his culinary talents for some time, so when he suggested that he cook a meal we were delighted, but also slightly apprehensive. The meal turned out to be the best salmon dish we had ever tasted.

Per serve:

approx 200g salmon fillet (one large fillet can be cut into 3 or 4 pieces)

1 tsp of lime juice

1 tsp of brown sugar

pinch of salt

Preheat the oven to 180°C.

Remove all bones from the salmon (I use tweezers). Make a pocket out of tin-foil and place the salmon fillet skin side down in it. Add lime juice and sprinkle over brown sugar and salt. Seal the pocket. Place in a baking dish and bake for 20 mins.

Serve with a salad or on creamed potatoes with poached asparagus.

Aunty Anne's fish dish

Diana Saxton
serves 4

Super easy, super quick, super tasty!

1 cup cream

500g red cod

1 tbsp capers

½ cup grated Gruyere cheese

salt & pepper

Preheat oven to 190°C.

Whip cream and spread over fish. Sprinkle on rest of ingredients. Bake uncovered for 20 mins.

Serve with asparagus, salad and French bread.

Finn, age 6

Captain Joanne Laing, Port Mistress with LPC, arranged port access for Jason Larraman and Yosay Briels for a behind the scenes look inside the working port of Lyttelton. On the Altair 2, a fishing boat taking NZ quota for Independent Fisheries, the Polish crew work six months on, and six months off. Our guide Konrad, the second mate, considers himself a very lucky man. He has just arrived from Poland for the November to May stint. His job allows him to experience summer all year round. To top it all he will be back just in time for the birth of his second child in July.

The smell of baking reached us long before we reached the kitchen. Janek is the cook and baker. He works all day and night catering for the needs of the eighteen crew. Apparently he does not sleep! Fourteen shiny loaves, fresh from the oven and clad in poppy seeds, would last the crew about five days. It tasted great, chewy and almost sweet. Beef borscht was simmering away on the central stove.

A clever smoking contraption on deck provided the crew with some delicately smoked monkfish. The Manuka chips were from The Warehouse, naturally. When they go out to sea the crew swells to around 50, which is hardly surprising when you see the onboard fish processing factory - able to process 75,000 tonnes of fish at full capacity.

Risotto primavera

Jonny Schwass
serves 2

Simple things always sound better in a foreign language and this dish of 'Spring Rice' is no exception. Feel free to substitute any of the bounty from your spring garden to replace or in addition to the ones below.

600ml chicken stock

4 tbsp olive oil

2-3 knobs of butter

1 garlic clove, finely chopped

½ onion, finely chopped

200g Arborio rice

small glass of white wine

3-4 asparagus spears

3-4 stringless beans

1 courgette, diced

30g freshly grated parmesan cheese, plus extra to serve

salt & black pepper

Heat the chicken stock in a pan to a very gentle simmer. Heat 2 tbsp of the olive oil in a large pan with a knob of butter. Gently fry the garlic and onion over a medium heat, until the onion is softened and translucent. Add the rice and coat with the olive oil, garlic and onion mix. Cook for a minute or so. Pour in the white wine and cook until the liquid is absorbed. Once absorbed, add a ladle of the simmering stock and cook until absorbed. Continue until all of the stock is absorbed and the rice is al dente. Meanwhile, cut the asparagus, stringless beans and courgette into bite size pieces. Heat the remaining 2 tbsp of olive oil in a frying pan and then add the vegetables and cook for a 3-4 mins. Season with salt & pepper. Stir the remaining knobs of butter, 30g of parmesan cheese and the cooked vegetables into the risotto.

Season to taste and serve with an extra grating of parmesan.

Rice pilaf

Bob Parker
serves 2

The recipe was handed down to Bob from his Mum. He and Audrey love it because of its simplicity and fresh taste. He uses it often when wanting something quick and tasty.

1 onion, chopped

1 tbsp butter

1 cup basmati rice

1½ cups chicken stock

4 cardamom pods

¼ cup toasted cashews (optional)

Cook the onion in the butter in a medium saucepan until tender. Stir in the rice and cook until the grains turn from opaque to white. Add the stock and cardamom pods and bring to the boil. Reduce the heat and cover. Simmer gently for 12 mins. Remove from the heat and discard the cardamom pods. Add the cashews and serve.

Lemon & ginger chicken stir-fry

Emma Champers
serves 4

1 tbsp oil

2 cloves garlic, thinly sliced

4cm piece ginger, peeled & sliced

2 chicken breasts, trimmed & sliced

1 lemon, sliced

¼ cup oyster sauce

¼ cup chicken stock

½ cup fresh basil leaves

Heat a wok with the oil until hot. Add the garlic and ginger. Cook for 30 seconds stirring all the time. Add the chicken and lemon slices. Cook for several minutes, until the chicken is cooked through. Add the oyster sauce and stock. Cook for a further 2 mins until the sauce has thickened. Remove from the heat and add the basil leaves.

Serve with rice.

Gingered rice & asparagus salad

Jo Hay
serves 6

1 cup cooked brown rice

2 cups roasted pumpkin

1 bunch blanched asparagus

1 cup cooked corn kernels

½ cup crystallised ginger, chopped

1 cup tinned chickpeas, rinsed

½ cup coriander, chopped

2 tbsp roasted pumpkin seeds

Dressing:

2 tbsp soy sauce

2 tbsp olive oil

2 splashes sesame oil

1 tbsp salt

1 tbsp lemon juice

1 tbsp balsamic vinegar

black pepper & honey to taste

Gently toss all salad ingredients together in large bowl. Drizzle over dressing.

Asparagus & ricotta ravioli with herbed butter

Nick Freeman, Freemans Restaurant, Lyttelton
40 pieces of ravioli
serves 4

At Freemans fresh pasta is part of our story in Lyttelton and my story as a chef and restaurateur. Our ravioli is a beautiful dish to be enjoyed with family or friends in the warm sunshine, with perhaps a nice glass of pinot grigio. This delicious ravioli dish is best served with more grated Parmesan and a good glug of quality olive oil.

Filling:

24 asparagus spears

150g good ricotta

50g mascarpone

150g Parmesan cheese, grated

1 tbsp herbs, freshly chopped (chervil, chives, parsley)

grated zest of 1 lemon

sea salt & freshly ground pepper

200ml vegetable stock

24 basil leaves

50g unsalted butter, in pieces

A glug of olive oil, to finish

Ravioli dough:

400g flour

4 eggs

1 egg yolk beaten with 1 tsp water (egg wash)

Peel and trim asparagus if necessary, then blanch and refresh. Finely chop stalks (reserve spears for garnish). Mix chopped asparagus with the ricotta, mascarpone, 100g of the Parmesan, half of the mixed chopped herbs, lemon zest and salt & pepper to taste. Combine well and put aside.

To make the ravioli dough, put the flour into a food processer and whizz. Then with the motor running add the 4 eggs, one a time, until the mixture comes together to form breadcrumbs. Empty the mixture onto a lightly floured bench top and knead well until dough is smooth and soft. Wrap in plastic food wrap and let stand for 20 mins.

Divide the dough into 4 equal pieces. Shape each piece into a neat square and roll in a pasta machine starting at grade 10 and working down to grade 1 until you end up with a sheet of pasta about 60-70cm long. Cover with a clean tea towel (to stop it drying) and repeat with rest of dough.

Working with one sheet at a time, place about 10 teaspoon-sized pieces of the asparagus mixture down one half of the sheet. Brush around the filling with the egg wash and then carefully fold the sheet in half to enclose the fillings. Press firmly but gently around each mound to seal then use a fluted pasta cutter or sharp knife and cut between the portions. Repeat with rest of the sheets. You should end up with 40 pieces of ravioli.

To serve: Bring a large saucepan of salted water to boil, add the ravioli all at once and cook for 4 mins. Drain. Add stock to the pan, add the drained ravioli, and bring back to the boil. Add remaining chopped herbs followed by the diced butter, while continuously tossing the ravioli. The butter and stock will emulsify with the starch of the ravioli pasta to create a lovely shiny sauce.

Garnish with basil and warmed asparagus spears.

"I like those long green things with spears that you dip in butter" James, age 5

Deck
Freeman
ningToward
47

POLICE STATION
POLICE
1880

Bruce's meatloaf

Rebecca Rennie
serves 6

Whenever I see these types of recipes I shudder and think of meat sweating in a tin meant for banana loaves. But in this case my dad makes a great meaty yet dry loaf which is totally child friendly. You can flash this recipe up by dividing the meat mixture into individual-size loaves and draping with streaky bacon.

500g sausage meat

500-800g mince

1 large red onion, finely chopped

½ tsp salt

½ tsp mixed herbs

4-6 slices bread, crumbed (use blender or grater)

1 egg

4-6 weetbix, crushed onto a large flat dish

Preheat oven to 150°C.

Mix sausage meat, mince, onion, salt, herbs and bread together. Add egg and combine well. Roll the mixture in the weetbix. Bake uncovered in a roasting dish for 1¼ hours. Turn over half-way through cooking. Allow to stand for 10 mins and then slice and serve.

For individual loaves omit weetbix and criss-cross loaves with streaky bacon and reduce cooking time to 30-40 mins.

Perfect served with smash hot potatoes.

smash hot potatoes

Rebecca Rennie
serves 6

16 small round potatoes eg. Desiree

1 tbsp extra virgin olive oil

1 tsp sea salt

1 tbsp fennel, cumin or caraway seeds

1 tbsp fresh thyme or rosemary

pepper

Preheat oven to 250°C.

Clean but don't peel potatoes. Boil whole in salted water for 15 mins. Test with a skewer until just cooked but not soft. Transfer to a greased baking tray. Use a potato masher to squash each potato flat. Brush top with oil and scatter sea salt, pepper, herbs and spices on top. Bake on top shelf of oven for 20-25 mins until crisp and golden.

Stack a couple on top of each other and serve.

Tagine of chicken with lemon & olives

Janet Foley
serves 6

We love this recipe. It's very green due to the amount of parsley and coriander. It's a fabulous combination of flavours and easy to prepare. The recipe comes from a Mediterranean cookery course I did once.

2 onions

2 tbsp oil, rice bran is good

4 cloves garlic

1 tsp cinnamon

2 tsp cumin

1 tsp ground ginger

2 tsp ground coriander

2 tsp ground black pepper

6 threads of saffron

12 chicken drumsticks (2 per person)

2 cups vegetable stock

1 cup white wine

½ cup water

½ cup stuffed green olives, or more to taste

1 preserved lemon, or zest of 2 fresh lemons

salt to taste

generous bunch of coriander and parsley, chopped

Chop onion finely and sauté in oil in a pan. If you don't have a ceramic tagine any heavy wide pan with a lid will do. Add garlic, then spices. Add chicken and turn to colour. Make sure you have sufficient oil so spices don't dry out. Add stock, wine and water. Simmer with lid until cooked, around 30 mins. Add olives and lemon to warm. Season to taste. Just before serving add parsley and coriander.

We like it with couscous, chopped and toasted almonds, soaked currants and seasonal steamed vegetables.

Rat & Roach mustard honey dressing

1 tbsp whole grain mustard

1 tbsp honey

250ml white vinegar

500ml oil

Put the whole-grain mustard and honey into a blender. Add white vinegar. Turn on the blender and slowly add the oil until the dressing becomes thick and creamy. Using a blender rather than a processor helps the dressings to emulsify much better.

Beziers pies

Lisa West
makes approx 12 small pies

I have seen recipes for these pies which use a sprinkling of brown sugar when sautéing the lamb, zest and currants. I usually omit the sugar as there is often enough sweetness in the currants, but a hint of brown sugar does work well, just not too much. The pies are intended to be slightly sweet and are a picnic favourite.

1pkt flakey pastry

500g lamb, suitable for dicing (I usually buy a good cut so that it is reliably tender)

butter for sautéing

currants, a handful to taste

lemon zest, to taste

salt & pepper

Preheat oven to 190°C.

Cut the pastry to fit your small pie dish. I usually use a muffin tray to make small picnic-sized pies. Grease the dishes and position the pastry.

Dice the lamb and gently brown in a frying pan. Add the currants and zest. Season to taste. Spoon the mixture into the pastry and cover with pastry tops. Do use tops as the meat filling will dry out if the pie is not covered. Cook in a very hot oven just long enough to cook and brown the pastry. 10-15 mins.

"Babies, toddlers and 'new invader' parents clutter the main street, and mingle with the genuine old guard"

KoL
LYTTELTON LOCAL LADS

BACKROOM

the Loons
www.theloons.co.nz
THE LOONS

Mobil
DUAL
PORT NZ
DESIGNER
CLOTHING

Lyttelton Rose Show

The biennial Lyttelton Rose Show is a local institution that has been held for the last 100 years. Contestants vie with each other for an array of cups and trophies. There are over forty categories, including sections for roses, cookery, cut flowers, vegetables, preserves, photography and home industry. The Norton Cup is the most prestigious and is awarded for the premier bloom of the show.

School children make fruit or vegetable creations, and pre-school entrants create colourful sand saucers. There is always a fiercely contested interschool competition, and the great chocolate cake challenge and auction is a highlight.

The organising committee hopes that with the recent increase in popularity of home baking, preserving and the growing of fruits and vegetables, the Lyttelton Rose Show's future is assured.

SECTION A
ROSES

The following recipes all in some way have an historic association with Lyttelton. Some come from local institutions such as the Rose Show, and some have been given to us by older women, or their families.

Bran muffins

The Coffee House, Lyttelton coffee shop and ice-cream parlour, 1977-1980
Pauline Goodfellow

"14 cents each and 15 cents buttered"

The Coffee House became a communal meeting place and was the focus of many local projects. The delightful brickwork paving in the ice-cream parlour by Zoe's dad, the wooden gate with tongue and cone by Jess and Joe's dad, the posties Jim and Dave's interior design flair, Muncher's 3rd storey, Keith's photos on the walls, Rex's pottery exhibits, Richard's organic herbs and veges delivered by bike, Ann's exclusive baking – who can forget the flaming Baked Alaska on late night Thursday, Wendy's fresh horseradish sauce, Joe Fitz's Devonshire teas on Sunday and her slices.

Tobin summed up the homemade signature of the Coffee House by naming Pauline as "Mrs Muffin".
Ingredients prepared the night before to allow more time during the busy period before opening.

½ cup dried fruit

1 cup milk

1 cup flour

1 tsp baking powder

½ tsp salt

1½ cups bran

1 tbsp butter

1 tbsp golden syrup

1 tbsp molasses

1 tsp baking soda

1 beaten egg

Soak dried fruit (sultanas, raisins or currants) in 1 cup of milk – cover and leave overnight.

Sift flour with baking powder and salt. Add the bran and cover.
In a saucepan put butter, golden syrup, and molasses.

In the morning put saucepan on gentle heat and stir until boiling. Mix baking soda in a little milk and add to soaked fruit, stir in the egg and mix. Add to dry mixture. Pour in ingredients from saucepan and combine all.

Preheat oven to 220°C.

Quickly put into greased muffin pans. Bake for 15 mins.

Await the rush.

Hilary Downer's famous pavlova

"The fabulous Sunday pavlova". Hilary would always offer to "bring the pav" and it would always be a great success
– Judith M Priddy

5 egg whites

1½ cup castor sugar

1 tsp vinegar

1 tsp cornflour

1 tsp vanilla essence

Preheat oven to 100°C

Beat egg whites till smooth & shiny. Add ½ of the sugar, beat on high for 1 minute. Fold in rest of sugar, vinegar, cornflour, vanilla essence with metal spoon.

Put in oven for 1 hour then turn off oven & leave for ½ an hour.

Rose show toffee apples

This recipe has been made for over 80 years and came to me from Mrs Stevenson of 'Stevenson's Steep'. She made the toffee in kerosene tins on top of her coal range and could turn out dozens of apples at a time. Her house (and her 12 or so children) is still standing. It is unbelievable that they could fit into such a small space. Now that I run the Lyttelton Rose Show with Chris Parrett we continue the tradition of the toffee apple stall. – *Ann Stanaway*

8 cups sugar

8 cups water

2 tbsp malt vinegar

2 tbsp butter

1 tbsp cream of tartar

food colouring

apples

icecream sticks

Boil all ingredients to the hard crack stage (150°C). Keep in a tall pot to make the dipping easier. Use clean and dry apples only. Insert an ice-cream stick into each apple then dip the apple into the toffee mixture and coat well. Place apples on squares of baking paper to harden.

Hint: to check for the hard crack stage put a few drops of the toffee into very cold water. It will separate into brittle threads when hard crack has been reached.

"Mrs Stevenson turned out dozens of toffee apples from the top of her coal range every year for the Rose Show"

Nana Mahar's raisin drops

125g butter

75g sugar

1 tbsp golden syrup

1 tsp vanilla essence

½ cup sultanas

225g flour

3 tbsp milk

½ tsp baking soda

Preheat oven to 180°C.

Cream butter and sugar, add golden syrup and vanilla, then the dry ingredients. Lastly add baking soda dissolved in milk. Bake for 15 mins.

Queen cakes

Moira Fitzgerald

Queen cakes were Moira's specialty and a favourite in the Fitzgerald household. Grandchildren still returned to Moira's home to bake Queen cakes with her in her 90th year.

125g butter

125g sugar

2 eggs

175g flour

1 tsp baking powder

50g sultanas

Preheat the oven to 200°C.

Cream the butter and sugar well. Beat the eggs until thick. Sift the flour and baking powder. Add alternately the egg and the flour to the creamed butter and sugar. Add the sultanas with the last of the flour

Put mixture into greased patty tins. Bake for 10 -12 mins.

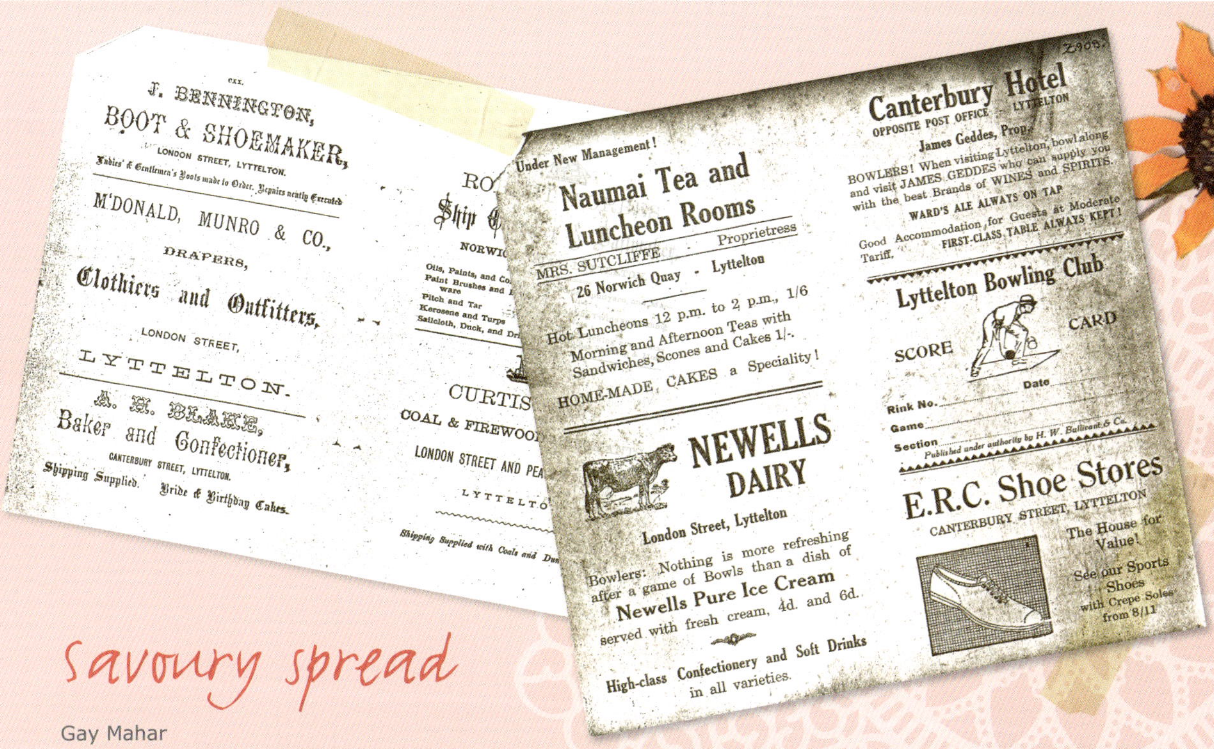

Savoury spread

Gay Mahar

125g butter

2 tbsp grated cheese

pinch of salt

1 egg, beaten

1 tbsp butter

2 small onions, finely chopped

pinch of cayenne pepper

Mix all the ingredients together with the beaten egg. Cook for 2 mins on a slow heat until the vegetables are soft.

Serve as a spread on crackers or bread.

Cornish pasties

Alice Tyro

short pastry

225g lean minced beef

1 small onion, finely chopped

1 small potato, finely diced

1 small carrot, diced

1 tsp flour

small amount water to moisten

salt & pepper to taste

a few drops Worcestershire sauce

Preheat over to 200°C.

Brown the mince and vegetables in saucepan. Add flour and cook over low heat for 1 min. Add small amount of water, salt, pepper and Worcestershire sauce. Cook until the vegetables are just soft. Remove from heat and allow to cool.

To assemble: Roll out pastry thinly and cut out rounds. Divide the filling between the rounds. Wet the edges of the pastry – join the edges at the top. Seal well shaping with finger and thumb. Prick either side with fork.

Bake for 20 - 25 mins.

STEVENSONS STEEP

Clafoutis (baked cherry custard)

Ilda Inglis
Serves 6

The origin of the clafoutis is not known, but both Limousin and Auvergne - where they make the similar millard, claim it as their own. This is my favourite dessert and kids love it too! The cake batter is based on a pancake recipe. It is very versatile and the fruits can be changed according to what is available in the cupboard. I have used fresh or tinned peaches, cherries and plums.

750g ripe black cherries (or equivalent)

2 eggs

1 egg yolk

½ cup sugar

5 tbsp butter, melted

½ cup all purpose plain flour

1 cup milk

vanilla sugar or icing sugar, for dusting

Preheat an oven to 200°C.

Wash, dry and stem the cherries. Butter ovenproof china or glazed earthenware dish which is large enough to hold the cherries in a single layer. Place the cherries in dish. Combine the eggs and yolk in a bowl, add the sugar and whisk until the mixture is pale in colour. Whisk in the butter. Sift in the flour and mix well, then add the milk. Beat until batter is smooth and then pour over the cherries. Bake until lightly golden on top. Remove the clafoutis from the oven and sprinkle with vanilla sugar.

Serve lukewarm, from the baking dish. Voila!

Boysenberry dessert

Ann Jolliffe
serves 4-6

This is a great favourite with friends. I'm always being asked for the recipe.

1pkt raspberry jelly crystals

300ml whipped cream

1pkt Krispie biscuits, crushed

½ pkt frozen boysenberries (or 2x tinned boysenberries)

Mix the jelly crystals with 1 cup of hot water and leave for 10 mins, stirring occasionally. Mix the boysenberries with the jelly and fold in the whipped cream. Place a layer of crushed Krispie biscuits in a bowl, pour over some of the boysenberry mixture and then repeat in layers. Top with crushed biscuits. Leave for at least an hour in the fridge before serving.

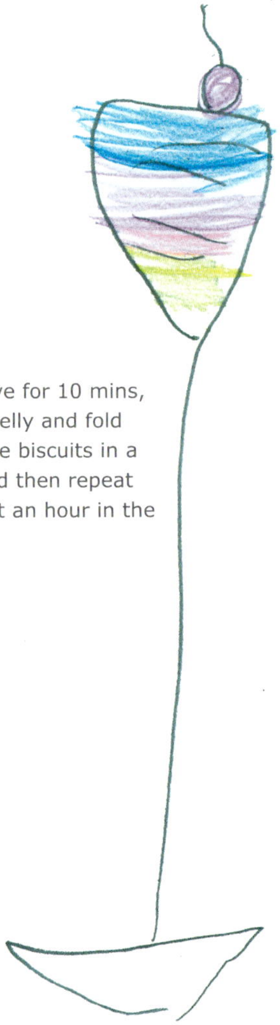

Mae, age 5

Lemon dee-liter

Pam Jacomb

Base:

1 cup butter

½ cup sugar

2 cups flour

Topping:

3 eggs

pinch salt

2 cups sugar

juice of 2 lemons

grated zest of 1 lemon

4 tbsp flour

1 tsp baking powder

Preheat oven to 180°C.

Cream butter and sugar, add the flour and spread into 30cm greased tin. Bake for 20-30 mins until lightly golden.

Beat the eggs then add the rest of the ingredients. Mix well and spread over the baked layer. Bake for a further 25-30 mins. Cool, cut into squares and sprinkle with icing sugar.

Lemon yoghurt cake

Jane Simmonds

zest & juice of 2 lemons

1¾ cups sugar

2 eggs

1 cup yoghurt

¾ cup oil – use a mild flavoured oil such as canola or rice bran

2 cups self-raising flour

Preheat oven to 180°C.

Beat together the lemon zest and the sugar. The sugar will absorb the oils from the lemon which gives a great flavour to the cake. Add the eggs and beat well. Then add 2 teaspoons of lemon juice, the yoghurt and the oil. Beat well. Finally add the flour and mix together. Bake for 30-40 mins in 20cm greased tin. This cake works particularly well in a ring tin.

Yummy with cream or yoghurt or both.

"Don't let your eyes get bigger than your plate"

Camille, age 9

Vegan chocolate crazy cake

Meg Devane

1½ cups flour

4 tbsp cocoa

1 tsp cinnamon

1 tsp ginger

1 tsp baking soda

1 tsp salt

1 cup sugar

½ cup oil

2 tbsp vinegar

1 tsp vanilla

¾ cup water

Preheat oven to 190°C.

Measure out the first six ingredients and sift them all into a large bowl. Add sugar and stir well with a fork. Add the oil to the dry ingredients, without stirring. Then add the vinegar, vanilla and the water, and stir well with the fork until smooth.

Pour mix into prepared 20cm round or square tin and bake 30-40 mins. Great with chocolate sauce and raspberries as a dessert. For kids I generally leave out the ginger. But adults like the unusual spicy flavour of the cinnamon and ginger combo.

Eccles cakes

Megan Collings

Fruit filling:

1 tsp nutmeg

1 tsp cinnamon

2 cups sultanas or currants

2 tbsp brown sugar

1 lemon, zested and juiced

grated apple (optional)

Flakey pastry:

225g flour

¼ tsp salt

175g butter

cold water

Glaze:

egg yolk

milk

Preheat oven to 180°C.

Mix fruit filling ingredients together and microwave for a minute to soften the fruit.

Flakey pastry: Put the flour and salt in a large bowl. Chop in the butter with a knife and add enough cold water to make a stiff dough. Roll out 5mm thick, fold several times to the centre and roll out again. Stand for at least an hour in a cool place. Then roll out again and cut out cup size circles.

Put a spoonful of fruit in the centre of each dough circle and fold inward pinching to hold the pastry together. Turn out on trays with pinched side facing down on the tray. Put two small knife cuts in the top and brush with egg yolk and milk. Sprinkle castor sugar over the top.

Bake for about 20 mins until golden top and bottom.

Ishbel, age 9

SEAS MARINER
NASSAU
50
SCHOOL
ZONE
ENDS

Summer

Summer in Lyttelton is a time to relax. Nor'west winds turn the hills brown and the sea aquamarine. Swimmers head to Corsair Bay or the Norman Kirk pool in Oxford St. Boats take to the harbour and Wednesday evening yacht racing becomes a fixture. Locals, hill-walkers, and tourists fill London St enjoying ice-cream and fish and chips. Seagulls fight noisily for their share.

In February people pack Lyttelton for the Summer Street Party where revellers enjoy food and music into the night.

EXIT
STACE
WORLD
Cerebos
TABLE SALT

summer food

Muesli

Rebecca Rennie
makes 1 large jar

This recipe came from my brother.

3 cups rolled oats

2 tbsp vegetable oil

80g raw almonds

1 cup sunflower seeds

¼ cup pumpkin seeds

¼ cup sesame seeds

½ cup flaked coconut

1 cup dried cranberries, raisins or other dried fruits

1-2 tbsp honey

Preheat oven to 160°C.

Place all ingredients, except for fruit and honey, in a large baking dish and stir. Place in oven for 30 mins stirring occasionally. Remove from oven, add dried fruit and honey, stir well, allow to cool. Store in an airtight container.

▼ "The dock has been used as a swimming pool on many occasions. Here, Christ's College students take part in their annual swimming races in 1889. Before concerns about health, safety and security changed the dock's operating rules, local schools used the dry dock for their swimming races. The dock remained in use as a swimming pool until the mid 1950s." LPC Dry Dock 125th Anniversary, 2008

Image courtesy of Lyttelton Port of Christchurch

Holiday bread

Phoebe Clay
Note: takes 1 day to prepare

This recipe originally came from Brigid Chunn on a holiday at Bethels beach, but the recipe she gave me has changed and evolved over many batches of bread. I always cook this recipe as flat bread, but depending on the size of the tin it will vary in size. It is great for cooking on holiday because, although it takes all day to make, it actually requires little effort. The yeasty smell as it cooks is lovely and the bread is different every time. It has been crunchy, super fluffy, even overcooked, but it is always devoured within minutes.

water

1 tsp yeast granules

1 tsp sugar

4 cups plain white flour

1 tbsp salt (approx)

1 tbsp olive oil

olive oil, sea salt & herbs to dress

Preheat the oven to 200°C.

In a bowl put ¼ cup warm water. Add the yeast and sugar. Leave so that the yeast starts to activate and froths up. Put the flour and salt in a separate bowl. Once the yeast is ready add it and the oil to the flour mix. Form into a dough with 1-2 cups water - start with 1 cup and add more bit by bit. Cover the bowl with a tea towel and leave in a warm place to rise to almost double its size. When it has finished the first rise, knead the dough. Cover the tin/tray you are using with olive oil, put the dough in, and leave to rise again. The second rise can be as long or short as you like. I have even skipped it and it made the bread crusty rather than fluffy - but it still tasted delicious. Cover the dough in heaps of olive oil, sea salt and herbs - I always use rosemary. Bake the bread for around 20 mins. I have cooked this in many temperamental ovens, including a traditional wood oven and a barbeque and the cooking time has changed accordingly. The bread is ready when it turns gold on top.

The long-awaited hummus recipe

Helen Taylor
makes a good sized bowl

Yummy as a dip or as a spread. Wheat, soy and additive free unlike the pre-made 'off the shelf' rubbish! Adapted from the 'Morrison St Café' recipe my sister gave me and a friend gave her!

2 x 390g tins of chickpeas, drained

2 cloves garlic

1 tbsp ground cumin

2 tbsp sweet chilli sauce

2 tbsp lemon juice

¼ tsp each salt and pepper

1 tbsp honey

1 tbsp tahini

handful of very fresh coriander chopped (optional)

¼ cup olive oil

Blend everything together except the oil until smooth. Slowly pour in the oil. Check the seasoning. You may prefer more spice if you like it hot!

"I like white bread sandwiches but mum always gives me brown."

Josh, age 7

Gran's bacon & egg pie

serves 6

2 sheets flaky ready-rolled pastry

6 eggs

1 onion, finely chopped

2-3 rashers of bacon, diced

1 tomato, diced

3 cooked potatoes, diced

ground black pepper

Preheat oven to 180°C.

Line a pie dish (approx. 30 x 20cm) with the pastry. Break eggs into the pie case and lightly whisk with a fork. Add the onion, bacon, tomato and potato. Season with pepper. Fit the remaining sheet of pastry over the pie to make a lid, being careful to press the edges to form a good seal.

Cut small slits in the pastry lid. Cook for 30-35 mins or until golden.

Courgette slice

Bev Wood
serves 4-6

375g grated courgette

½ cup cooking oil

3 lean rashers of bacon

1 cup self-raising flour

1 large onion, finely chopped

3-5 eggs beaten

1 cup grated cheese

Preheat oven to 180°C.

Combine all ingredients together thoroughly. Pour into oven-proof dish (approx. 30 x 20cm) and bake for 30-40 mins.

"When I was in the house
I could smell pie" Mae, age 5

Pesto pasta salad

Rei Couch
serves 4-6

1 pkt pasta spirals

250g pesto & cashew nut dip

2 tbsp olive oil

1 tbsp sweet chilli sauce

1 tsp crushed garlic

unsalted peanuts and raisins to serve

Cook pasta, strain and cool. Mix all other ingredients in a small bowl and combine with the pasta. Top with peanuts and raisins to serve.

Couscous salad

Jane Simmonds
serves 2-4

1 cup couscous

handful fresh basil

6-8 sundried tomatoes, chopped

1 red onion, finely chopped

125g feta cheese, crumbled

handful olives (red or green)

plenty of lemon juice

salt & pepper

handful of pinenuts

Cook the couscous. Add all other ingredients and mix.

Green bean salad with red onions & fresh pomegranate

Kate McRae
serves 4-6

We are lucky here in the southern hemisphere because we get to enjoy pomegranates (even though they are imported) in the summer, which means we can use them for all sorts of great summer salads. If you haven't used pomegranates before it's the seeds that you are after, but be warned they are messy to deal with and it can be tricky to prize them out of their little beds - but it's worth it! This recipe is so simple, and it looks and tastes spectacular. I also love pomegranates mixed with sliced fresh strawberries for a super quick summer fruit salad. Apparently they are very good for the prostate.

500g fresh green beans

1 medium red onion

1 pomegranate

juice of 1 lemon

1 tbsp olive oil

salt & pepper to taste

Trim the beans but leave them whole. Steam quickly for a few minutes - you want them tender but still with some bite. Refresh under cold water and then set aside in a bowl. Cut the red onion into thin slices and add to the beans. Halve the pomegranate and scoop out the fleshy seeds from both halves, trying to save as much of the juice as you can. Add to the beans and just before serving add the lemon juice, olive oil, salt & pepper to taste. Perfect summer barbecue food!

Moroccan tomato & preserved lemon salad

Ground Culinary Centre, Lyttelton
serves 2

This fresh salad is best if you use vine ripened tomatoes. Any variety of summer tomato will do, but a mix of several varieties looks good. Never keep your tomatoes in the fridge as they lose their flavour.

½ red onion

1 clove garlic, sliced

4 tbsp extra virgin olive oil

handful cherry tomatoes

4 plum tomatoes

slivered rind of 1 Moroccan preserved lemon

¼ tsp sweet smoked paprika

juice of 2 lemons

2 tbsp flat-leafed parsley, torn

3 tbsp mint, chopped

sea salt

Gently cook the onion and garlic in the oil over a low heat, stirring occasionally until the onion is just beginning to soften. Transfer to a wide mixing bowl using a spatula to get all of the oil as well. Cool for 5 mins then add tomatoes, preserved lemon, paprika and lemon juice. Stir once to combine. Just before serving add the herbs and the salt.

► "As a prelude to the British Commonwealth Games, an Auckland - Lyttelton Yacht Race took place on 12 January 1974. Yachts were moored in the marina, as well as the dry dock. The HMS Britannia, which brought the Queen, Duke of Edinburgh, Prince of Wales and Princess Anne to New Zealand, is shown on Wharf 4. Accompanying it are several military vessels from New Zealand and Australia."
LPC Dry Dock 125th Anniversary, 2008

Aioli

Richard Till

This is garlic mayonnaise. It's become a very widely used item for lots of New Zealanders who a few years ago would never have heard of it. It's almost become the Highlander mayonnaise of the 21st century. Try adding a little sweet chilli sauce to part of a batch to make a sensationally good dip for chips, squid rings or any other fried food item that takes your fancy. Add finely chopped gherkin, capers and spring onion and you've got a good tartare sauce. But all that aside, if you've ever bought aioli and liked that you'll love this homemade version even more.

I've made aioli for years and even to this day every so often it'll 'split' when I'm making it. When this happens the aioli doesn't thicken. It remains runny and it looks like the word split suggests. Should this happen to you, you've probably added the oil too quickly and if it happens get a clean bowl, another egg yolk, add a little bit of salt and a tiny drip of lemon and then add to the split aioli instead of the oil. When this is used up go back to using the oil. I fear I'm making it sound harder than it is - you'll get the feel for it and it's well worth the effort!

2 cloves garlic

½ tsp salt

200-300ml light oil

2 eggs yolks

juice of ½ a lemon

2 tbsp cider vinegar

pepper

Very finely chop the garlic. Once you have chopped it finely, chop it more. Tip the salt on top of the garlic and crush the salt and garlic together with the back of the knife's blade. Throw the egg yolks, crushed garlic and lemon juice into a bowl. Begin whisking the mixture. As you beat, slowly–ever so slowly–pour in the oil in a fine stream. As the mixture begins to thicken and lighten, start pouring the oil a little faster. Once the aioli has reached about half a cup in volume, stop pouring in the oil, and add a tablespoon of cider vinegar. Continue beating in more oil until the mixture is a pale yellow hue and the volume is to your liking. Stir in a little cracked pepper.

Image courtesy of Lyttelton Port of Christchurch

Two Mexican salsas

Gabriela Gerstein Vazquez

Mexican guacamole

makes about 2 cups

This is a traditional guacamole recipe. We use it as a dip and also eat it with fish and steak...very versatile!

4 ripe avocados

juice 1 lemon

1 small onion

1 small tomato

1 fresh chilli

1 clove garlic

handful fresh coriander

salt & pepper

Peel the avocados and cut into pieces, dousing well in lemon juice. Chop the onion, tomato, chilli, garlic and coriander. Mix into the avocados. Season with salt & pepper to taste.

Picode gallo salsa

makes about 2 cups

This salsa is fresh and chunky and good served with grilled chicken or fish along with burritos, tacos, or other Mexican style meals.

4 plum tomatoes, seeded & chopped

½ cup onion, finely chopped

2 fresh chillies, seeded & finely chopped

2 tbsp red or yellow peppers, chopped

1½ tsp coriander, chopped fresh

1 tsp lime juice

salt & pepper

Mix everything together in a glass or other non-reactive bowl and refrigerate for at least 20 mins before serving. Season with salt & pepper to taste.

Ceviche Acapulco

Gabriela Gerstein Vazquez
serves 4-6

This is a very traditional seafood cocktail suitable for summer barbeques.

500g fish fillets

8 lemons

1 small onion

2 tbsp olive oil

½ cup green olives, chopped

10 capers

pinch oregano

salt to taste

5 tomatoes

¼ cup coriander, chopped

Cut the fish fillets into pieces and put into a glass or other non-reactive bowl, add the juice of 6 lemons. Cover and refrigerate for at least 6 hours to 'cook' the fish in the lemon juice. After marinating, remove the fish and wring excess moisture out of the fish. Chop the onion and add the juice from the remaining 2 lemons, along with the olive oil, chopped olives, capers, oregano and salt. Cut the tomatoes in half, remove the seeds, and then cut into small pieces. Mix together all the ingredients and add the coriander. Serve in cups or dishes along with fresh avocados.

LIFE BUOY

Volcano fish

Lois Ogilvie, Volcano Café, Lyttelton
serves 4

This is a favourite recipe at the Volcano. The fish is locally caught and fresh; the lime and banana give the dish a tropical flavour and tang. The pickle we use is called Fadel's Hot Lime Pickle, it's made by Frances and Paul de Latour from locally grown limes in Lavericks Bay on Banks Peninsula.

4 serves firm white fish fillets, such as gurnard or monkfish

½ cup seasoned flour

2 tbsp olive oil

1 tbsp butter

2 bananas, sliced lengthwise

¼ cup white wine (optional)

1-2 tsp hot lime pickle, according to how hot you like it

250ml coconut cream

salt & pepper

Dust the fish fillets lightly in seasoned flour. Heat the olive oil and butter in a good sized frying pan at a medium heat. Place the fish fillets and banana in the pan and fry on one side for a couple of minutes, then turn both and add the white wine, lime pickle and coconut cream, in that order. Pan fry for about 2 mins until the fish is cooked. Test with a fork or skewer, which should insert easily into the flesh. Remove fish and banana from the pan, then stir the sauce and reduce it for another minute to the desired consistency. Season with salt & pepper to taste.

Serve fish, banana and sauce with steamed jasmine rice and either steamed spinach, or a fresh green salad.

Cured salmon

Wendy Everingham
serves 8
Note: takes 48 hours to prepare and if using raw salmon, it must be frozen first to kill any bacteria

I love food and food preparation. This is one of my favourite recipes, given to me by a special friend and a reminder of my time living in Stockholm. A great 'special-occasion' recipe, that tastes delicious and is easy to prepare. This recipe can also be easily halved.

2kg raw salmon, either a whole fish or large fillets

150g cooking salt

100g sugar

2 tbsp coarsely ground black or white peppercorns

2 sprigs dill, finely chopped

Mustard sauce:

2 tsp sugar

2 pinches salt

2 pinches finely ground pepper

4 tbsp American mustard

2 tbsp Dijon mustard

2 tbsp vinegar

200ml oil

1 cup dill, chopped

Defrost fish. If using a whole fish, remove the head, tail and fins. Slit along the backbone and carefully lift out the bone, making sure not to damage the fish. Mix the sugar and salt. Cut the fish or fillets in half and create two fish 'sandwiches'. Open the fish sandwich and coat the fleshy sides with salt, sugar, pepper and dill. Close sandwich. Place each fish sandwich into a clean plastic bag, skin side out. Pat the remaining sugar and salt mixture onto the skin sides of the fish. Place the two plastic bags of fish into a shallow dish and weight down the salmon. Leave in the fridge for 24 hours. Turn the fish over and leave, weighted down, for another 24 hours. The fish is now ready for serving. Cut into very thin slices and serve with a mustard sauce (see below).

For the mustard sauce: Mix all the dry ingredients with the mustards and vinegar. Gradually add the oil a little at a time, beating hard. Finally, fold in chopped dill.

"If you don't eat food you could die. My favourite food for sometimes is fish and chips"

Bella, age 7

Fossie's tomato sauce

John & Sue Fitzgerald

Lyttelton is a treasure that only the people who live here can know. We have lived in Lyttelton all our lives and follow a long heritage of family. We are Ships Provedores, which means we supply anything a ship may need, from a pound of butter to a new anchor. This has lead to a varied and cosmopolitan life for both John and I and our family. Our three children have visited Antarctica, working on research vessels. Many funny stories have evolved from these times, such as, when our daughters were running the Deluxe Café, John sneaked in and put on the specials board "Pan Fried Hector Dolphin Steaks", which did not sit well with some customers, or telling visitors on the Port Open Day that the research ice-breaker we were servicing was a nuclear powered whaling vessel.

Much of our time in Lyttelton has been spent working in the hospitality industry, from helping family run the Empire and the Canterbury Hotels in the 1960s and 1970s, to the Deluxe Café (1980s- 2006) where many local young people learned how to wash dishes and make coffees, to our business J.Voyce & Co (1970). So, in that vein, we have chosen a recipe which reflects our family's history. This is my father's tomato sauce recipe which has been served in our varied establishments since the 1960's and was a 'secret recipe', well sought after by customers at the Deluxe Cafe. It's very old so still in pounds...

12 lbs ripe tomatoes

3 lbs sugar

1 ½ pints vinegar

3 oz whole allspice

3 oz salt

Chop tomatoes and all ingredients and boil for about three hours or until a nice sauce consistency

You can cheat and use chopped tinned tomatoes.

Rice volcano

Carmel Courtney, Volcano Radio
serves 4

Volcano Radio hit the airwaves on February 25th 2008 with 35 volunteer DJs. From the first broadcast a simple ethos has prevailed; to produce community radio that presents a diverse and personal cultural collage of music, people and place. This approach has seen the original crew swell to nearer 100 Djs, techies, sound engineers, and hosts.

2 cups raw brown rice

3 cups water

1 tbsp butter

1 cup chopped onion

1 large clove garlic, crushed

½ tsp dill

¼ tsp dried mint

salt & pepper

cayenne pepper

3 large eggs

¼ cup parsley

2 cups grated Cheddar

Pre-heat oven to 190°C.

To make rice volcano: Combine the brown rice and water, bring to the boil, lower heat and cover. Cook until just done. Set aside. Combine butter, onion, garlic, dill, mint, salt & pepper in a saucepan on medium heat and sauté until the onion is translucent. Add this to the rice. Stir the eggs, parsley and cheese together and then beat into the rice mixture.

To shape the rice volcano place a cylindrical oven-proof vessel (eg. a skinny coffee cup) in the centre of a buttered oven proof dish. This is to create a hole to pour the Lahar Dip into. Pour the rice mixture into the dish and around the vessel creating a volcano shape. Cover with tin foil and bake for 30 mins. When the Volcano is baked remove tin foil and grill the Volcano for a few minutes. Remove from oven and take the cylindrical vessel out from the middle.

To serve, pour the Lahar Tofu Dip into the middle of Volcano. Then pour the Lava Tomato Sauce from the top to the bottom of the Volcano.

Serve with a platter of steamed and raw veges for dipping. Decorate with brussel sprout boulders, broccoli bushes and carrot trees.

Lahar tofu dip

makes about 2 cups

1 block soft tofu

2 tbsp sesame oil

2 tbsp tamari sauce

2 tbsp fresh lemon juice

2 tbsp cider vinegar

¼ cup water

1 clove garlic, crushed

½ cup tahini

1 spring onion, finely chopped

½ cup parsley, finely chopped

salt, black pepper, cayenne to taste

Combine the first seven ingredients in a blender and puree until smooth Then beat tahini into the puree and stir in remaining ingredients.

Lava tomato sauce

children friendly or lava hot

1 can tomatoes

1 red bell pepper, chopped

1 onion, diced

1 large clove garlic, chopped

salt, black pepper & chillies to taste

Combine in a saucepan and cook on medium heat until your taste buds say Yes!

5658
Wildwood

seared lamb fillets with Zydeco sauce

Sue Curtin
serves 4

I work as a chef at the Volcano Cafe and also have a stall at the Farmers' Market selling marinated olives and other goodies. In 1992 I opened a little cafe in Manchester St with my good friend Jo Chiverton, called the Zydeco Cafe. We served very tasty Cajun food. We sold the Cafe when darling Phoebe came along. We had fantastic times there and ate some great food. This recipe was something we just couldn't take off the menu - people kept asking for it.

1kg lamb fillets – marinate in garlic, rosemary and olive oil

Zydeco sauce:

2 cups pumpkin seeds

1 cup shelled pistachios

1 cup cashew nuts

3 red peppers, roasted & peeled

1 red chilli

2 tsp cumin powder

1 tsp salt

1 tbsp white vinegar

2 tbsp corn syrup (you can use golden syrup if you don't have corn)

1 cup olive oil

Zydeco sauce: Roast seeds and nuts in oven. Put all other ingredients, excluding the lamb, in the food processor with the roasted nuts and seeds and whizz. The sauce will have the consistency of a thick pesto.

Sear lamb fillets on a hot skillet until medium rare. Serve on top of Zydeco sauce. Eat and enjoy, delicious!

"I love going to my Nana and Grandad's and having roast lamb" William, age 7

Warm venison & blue cheese salad

Linda Baker
serves 2

500g Denver leg of venison

fresh salad leaf mix

2 ripe pears

blue cheese - amount to suit personal preference

handful of cherry tomatoes

ranch or similar creamy dressing

Pan fry venison on medium heat for 10-15 mins each side - the middle should remain tender to touch. Rest for 10 mins. Arrange salad leaves with pear slices, crumbled blue cheese and tomatoes on individual plates. Slice venison into diagonal strips and arrange on salad. Drizzle with dressing and serve.

Vege burgers (dairy free)

Liza Rossie
serves 4

425g tin red kidney beans

½ onion, chopped

1 clove garlic, crushed

½ cup fresh breadcrumbs

½ cup rolled oats

1 tsp chilli sauce

1 tbsp sweet fruit chutney

1 tbsp pesto (optional)

breadcrumbs for coating

Drain the beans. Put all ingredients in a food processor and chop on pulse to combine. Make sure you don't puree the mixture, it should be firm enough to mix into 4-6 balls. Flatten each ball and coat in breadcrumbs. Cook in a little oil on both sides until lightly browned.

Serve in a bun with salad and sauce or chutney. For a wheat-free option simply stack with salad greens.

Roasted nectarine chutney

Kate McRae
makes 2-3 large jars

In our garden we have an ancient nectarine tree. Some years it's laden with fruit and on other years it has hardly any. It's always a race to get the fruit before the ants do but I hate to waste any. This chutney recipe is great for using up fruit that is less than perfect. You can use a combination of stone fruit if you don't have enough nectarines - over the years I've added peaches, apricots and even the odd apple. Roasting really brings out the flavour of the fruit.

3kg nectarines (or combination of stone fruit) stoned & quartered

2 cloves garlic, chopped

2 onions (I use combination of red and white)

1 large lemon, chopped (pips removed)

small handful fresh rosemary, chopped

2-3 bay leaves

1 tbsp cumin seeds

1 tbsp fennel seeds

4-5 small bird eye dried chillies

750g brown sugar

approx 500ml white vinegar

2 tbsp salt

Preheat the oven to 150°C.

Put the first nine ingredients into a large roasting dish. Add the sugar and mix together gently making sure the fruit is well coated. Add the vinegar – you may need to adjust the amount of vinegar as you want enough liquid so that it comes approx half way up the sides of the roasting dish. Add salt. Cover the dish with tinfoil and bake for about an hour. Remove the foil and continue to cook until the mixture is soft and has darkened. It will almost begin to look a little caramelised. You can use a potato masher to break up the fruit if you want to or else leave it chunky. Bottle in sterilized jars, and if you can, leave it for a week or two before using.

"Resolve dog-staring problem by tipping remaining food onto separate plate and giving to dog."

Dinner for two adults for one night, or one adult for two nights, or, realistically, for one adult & one dog

Joe Bennett

$22

1 telephone (mobile or fixed line)

1 car

Pick up phone in hand of choice. Dial 3288819.

Say 'Good evening. This is (insert name here). I'd like to order number two and number eleven please. I'll pick them up at (insert time here. Do not insert 8.15pm because you'll have to wait in line behind me). See you then. Thank you. Bye.'

Drive dog to hills for hunger-whetting possum hunt.

On way home from possum hunt double-park outside Lyttelton Chinese Takeaway on north side of London Street near BNZ.

Crack joke with proprietor.

Hand over $22.

Collect food.

Drive home swiftly, not because the food cools rapidly but because you are salivating. Keep dog away from food by regular swerving.

Tip half of number 11 (combination fried noodles) onto plate.

Tip half of number 2 (lemon fried chicken) over number 11.

Push remaining food to back of bench to avoid dog-theft.

Open beer.

Carry plate and beer to lounge.

Tell dog to stop staring.

Wedge book open under rim of plate on lap.

Eat.

Tell dog to stop staring.

Resolve dog-staring problem by tipping remaining food onto separate plate and giving to dog.

Eat.

Relax.

Your day is done.

There is only drinking to go.

Then bed.

Jenny's gooseberry shortcake

Geoff Knight (recipe from his mum)
makes approx 10 slices

Perched on top of an old corrugated iron fence at the bottom of our section (Ripon Street) to get at our gooseberries. Baking hot sun, surrounded by the 1980's. If you can sneak some into the fridge and eat it the next day, well, you've won.

100g butter

½ cup sugar

1 egg

1½ cups plain flour

1 tsp baking powder

500g green gooseberries

Preheat oven to 180°C.

Cream butter and sugar, beat in egg. Sift dry ingredients then mix thoroughly into creamed mixture. Press half of the mixture into a 20cm cake tin. Cover with gooseberries. Sprinkle with sugar, cover with remaining mixture. Bake for 40 mins. Serve with cream.

Raspberry & peach cheesecake tart

Jillian Frater
serves 6-8

This pudding is quick, simple and no fuss and it's easy to get the ingredients together. Simon Holst adapted it from a dessert he remembered fondly from his childhood.

Base:

1½ cups flour

100g cold butter

¼ cup sugar

Topping:

125g sour cream

125g cream cheese

½ cup sugar

2 large eggs

½ tsp vanilla

825g can sliced peaches, drained

½ cup raspberries , fresh or thawed frozen

Preheat oven to 180°C.

Place the flour, butter and sugar in a food processor and blend until the butter is evenly mixed (the mixture should resemble breadcrumbs). Line a swiss roll tin (18 x 28cm, or similar) with a Teflon liner or baking paper, then tip in the flour mixture. Firmly press the mixture evenly into the pan and cook for 10 mins.

While the base cooks, tip the first 5 topping ingredients into the (unwashed) food processor and whiz until smooth. Arrange the sliced peaches in rows over the hot base, then sprinkle with the raspberries. You can also use other fruits such as apricots and strawberries. Pour the custard mixture over the fruit. Bake for 20-25 mins until the topping is beginning to brown around the edges and has set in the middle.

Leave to stand for 15-20 mins before lifting carefully from the tin and cutting into serving-sized pieces.

Raspberry & cream cheese soufflé

Jason Dell
serves 2-4

This recipe brings back memories of my Nana Rakena and her wonderful raspberry jam steamed pudding, which featured religiously on the dining table at Christmas time and for special Sunday lunches. As kids, we used to often gather wild raspberries from the nearby bushes just up the hill behind Nana's house in Rapaki. Nana Rakena was a fantastic preserver of fruits (often used in the terrific trifle she also used to make) and there was always plenty of homemade jams and poached fruits in her pantry.

180g cream cheese

70g icing sugar

20g cornflour

2 eggs, separated

2 tsp raspberry jam

10 fresh raspberries

salt

Preheat oven to 160°C.

Line your soufflé ramekin moulds evenly with softened butter, using either a pastry brush or a small piece of baking paper scrunched up. Dust the ramekins with castor sugar, tipping out any excess.

Using a wooden spoon, cream the cream cheese with half (35g) of the icing sugar, the cornflour and the 2 egg yolks. Beat until smooth. Stir through the raspberry jam. In a separate stainless steel bowl, whisk the egg whites with a pinch of salt until stiff and firm. Add the remaining icing sugar and beat again until glossy. Gently fold the meringue into the soft cream cheese mixture. Do this in 2 stages, so as to allow the mixture to amalgamate and be sure not to knock all the air out of the meringue. Carefully fold through the fresh raspberries.

Spoon the mixture into your prepared ramekins to ¾ full. Wipe all the edges clean, so that as the soufflé rises it does not stick to the ramekins. Place into the middle shelf of oven and cook for 20 mins. Carefully remove from oven, dust with icing sugar and place on plate, then serve. Accompany with warm raspberry sauce and your favourite ice-cream.

"Fruit is healthy for you and veges are healthy too but my favourite is... raspberries and strawberries." Meg, age 7

Raspberry and almond cake (gluten free)

Gill Hay
serves 10-12

Gill Hay started *The Preservatory* in Fendalton, which she ran for 10 years. This successful business was one of the first deli/cafes in Christchurch at the time. Gill is a well-known New Zealand artist, and still does some catering.

3 cups icing sugar

1 cup rice flour

2 cups ground almonds

350g melted butter

2 tbsp vanilla

12 egg whites

1½ cups raspberries

50g slivered almonds

Preheat oven to 180°C.

Sift icing sugar and flour together with ground almonds. Melt butter and add vanilla. Beat egg whites until stiff. Fold dry ingredients into egg whites then gently fold in butter and vanilla. Place in lined round cake tin (approx 26 cm) and sprinkle top with raspberries and slithered almonds. Bake for approx ¾-1 hour.

"I love taking Hester, my dog, to Corsair Bay. She goes crazy."

Tommy, age 4

French caramel flan

Sally Green
serves 8-10

This is a recipe that I was taught to make by an Egyptian chef in a restaurant in Marseille.

250g sugar

7 eggs

1 litre milk

1 tsp vanilla

Preheat oven to 170°C.

Put 100g sugar in a pot with a little water and bring to the boil to make a caramel sauce. Gently move the pot from side to side until the caramel is a brown colour and pour into a high-sided glass dish or loaf tin (approx 21 x 15cm). Beat 5 eggs and 2 egg yolks along with a splash of milk. Bring the remaining milk, sugar and vanilla to the boil. When the milk starts to bubble remove it from heat, beat in egg mixture, and pour over hardened caramel. Place loaf tin into a high-sided oven dish half-filled with boiling water. The water level should reach at least half-way up the sides of the loaf tin. Cook for an hour or so (the flan should never boil or bubble in the oven). Test with a knife to ensure that the mixture has set. Cool and when ready to eat flip it on to a long dish so that the caramel sauce runs down the sides. Bon appétit!

Italian ricotta cake

Kate McRae
serves 10-12
Note: best made the day before

I ate something like this years ago in a café but could never work out how to make it. Then much to my delight I found a very similar recipe in a magazine and have made my version of it ever since. It's all made in the food processor so minimal cleaning up! Keep refrigerated until needed.

Crust:

3¼ cups flour

3 tsp baking powder

¾ cup loosely packed brown sugar

1 cup ground almonds

1 egg beaten

1 tsp vanilla

250g very cold butter

Filling:

400g ricotta

400g cream cheese

2 tbsp dark rum

½ cup slivered almonds, toasted

100g dark chocolate

1 cup castor sugar

Preheat oven to 180°C.

Crust: Line a 23cm spring-form tin with tin foil. Put all the crust ingredients, except the butter, in a food processor and pulse to combine. Add the butter in small chunks and process till the mixture resembles breadcrumbs. Set aside approx ¼ of the crumb mixture for the topping. Press the remaining crust into the lined tin making sure it's evenly distributed and it comes up the sides of the tin. It doesn't need to be too thick (1½ cm is good) as it does rise. Refrigerate while you make the filling.

Filling: Combine ricotta, cream cheese, and rum in the processor. Then add the remaining ingredients and pulse very gently. You don't want to over-process the chocolate and the almonds as you want some decent sized chunks in the finished cake. Fill the chilled crust with the ricotta filling and then crumble the remaining crust over the top. Bake until the crust is lightly golden (approx 1 hour). Refrigerate in its tin until required. To serve, remove from the tin. The cake should lift out easily – then simply peel away the foil and place on a serving plate.

Serve at room temperature with whipped cream. Fresh berries or a berry coulis are also good with this.

Easy chocolate cake

Janice Moore
Note: recipe can easily be doubled

Perfect for a crowd of hungry children.

3 eggs

2 tbsp milk

125g flour

90g butter, melted

1 tbsp cocoa

185g sugar

2 tsp baking powder

Preheat oven to 180°C.

Put all ingredients into the bowl and beat for 5 mins with an electric beater. Bake 15 -20 mins in a greased sponge roll tin (approx 30 x 22cm). When cool, cut in half and fill with cream (or leave whole). Ice or sprinkle top with icing sugar.

"I know that vegetables are good for you. Eat veges everyday. I love brownies."

Jade, age 7

Nimbupani (traditional indian lemonade)

Michael Herman
makes 1 large jug

2 litres water

250ml freshly squeezed lemon juice

¼ tsp rose essence

1 handful fresh mint, chopped

1 cup sugar

Combine ingredients and refrigerate. Add two trays of ice to serve.

Antipodean eggnog

Whaea Gillian
makes 4 litres

This recipe came from the Supervalue checkout in New Brighton at Christmas time about 30 years ago. Once tasted, it has been requested by relatives from all over the world ever since.

2 litres vanilla ice-cream (low-fat if you feel guilty)

12 eggs

1 bottle rum, brandy, whisky or sherry (we prefer brandy)

Soften the ice-cream and mix in a food processor. Add the eggs and continue to mix. Pour in the alcohol gradually with the processor going. Serve in glasses with a little grated nutmeg on top. Can be kept in the fridge for up to 2 days - but it never lasts that long.

Christmas fruit mince filo cigars

Anne Carne
serves 12

A low fat Christmas treat - very easy too. These look really cool and you don't have to make the pastry.

4 tbsp butter or margarine

12 sheets filo pastry

1 cup Christmas fruit mince

Preheat the oven to 190°C.

Line an oven tray with baking paper. Melt the butter. Using one sheet of filo at a time, fold both of the edges on the long sides into the middle and lightly brush with the butter. Place 4 tsps of fruit mince in a 1cm roll along the short edge of the pastry, leaving a 1cm gap at each end. Roll up and place on the tray. Brush with butter. Repeat the process. Bake for 15 mins, or until browned. Cool and store in an airtight tin in a cool place.

Serve reheated for 5 mins in a hot oven and lightly dusted with icing sugar.

Panforte margherita

Carolyn Bruce
makes one 20cm cake

A traditional Italian cake served at Christmas time.

1 cup whole hazelnuts, lightly toasted

1 cup blanched almonds, lightly toasted

1 cup candied peel

1 cup dried apricots, chopped

1 tsp lemon zest

½ cup flour

1 tsp cinnamon

¼ tsp coriander

¼ tsp cloves

¼ tsp nutmeg

¾ cup sugar

¾ cup honey

2 tbsp butter

Preheat oven to 160°C.

Chop the nuts coarsely and put into a large bowl, add the fruit, flour and spices. In a saucepan, heat sugar, honey and butter. Stir until dissolved and cook until the mixture reaches soft ball stage. Add to nuts and blend well. As it cools it will become hard to mix so work quickly. Press into a well buttered 20cm round tin. Cook for 30-40 mins. When the mixture just begins to bubble at the edges it will be cooked. Cool before removing from the tin. It should be much firmer than a normal Christmas cake. Dust liberally with icing sugar. If wrapped well, it will keep for weeks.

To serve cut into paper-thin wedges.

Hint: To test for soft ball stage either use a jam thermometer – it should read 114°C – or drop a small amount of the hot mixture into very cold water. It will form a soft ball in the water when squeezed but this will flatten when removed from the water.

"Food is fuel" Benjamin, age 9

shortbread

Shirley & Richard McGuigan
makes approx 30 pieces

This recipe was given to me by my mother many years ago.

225g butter

¼ cup sugar

¾ cup icing sugar

1 cup cornflour

1½ cups flour

Preheat oven to 150°C.

Cream the butter, sugar and icing sugar. Add the sifted flours. Combine well. Roll into a log shape and cut into slices. Bake for about 30 mins.

Christmas chocolate fruit cake

Andrew Barker, principal, Lyttelton West School
serves 10-12

This recipe comes from my mother. It is of unknown origin but was discovered on a hand-written piece of paper between the pages of an old fundraising cookbook!

2 tbsp golden syrup

1x 400g tin condensed milk (not lite)

125g butter

4 eggs

1 tsp pure vanilla extract (with seeds if possible)

1 tsp pure lemon essence

1 tsp almond essence

1.2kg dried fruit

1 pkt chocolate bits (don't use chips or buttons)

¼ cup rum, brandy or port (optional) + 2 tbsp for soaking the cooked cake at the end

½ tsp baking soda

¼ cup milk (not trim)

350g white flour

Preheat the oven to 130°C.

Line a 20cm square tin with baking paper. Melt the golden syrup, condensed milk, and butter together in a large saucepan over a gentle heat, stirring constantly. Beat the eggs with the essences until pale and thick. Place the dried fruit and chocolate in a bowl and add the first measure of alcohol, stir. Dissolve the baking soda in the milk. Sift the flour. Fold the egg mixture into the butter and condensed milk mixture. Add half the fruit mix and half the flour mix to the saucepan as well. Add the remaining flour and fruit. Add the milk and soda and stir gently till combined. Bake for approx 3½ hours or until a skewer comes out clean. After cooking sprinkle the top with the second measure of alcohol. Cover with a cloth and leave to cool before turning out of the tin.

"I like to cook with my Mum and make Christmas cake" Francesca, age 5

autumn

Autumn lingers here with misty mornings and mellow afternoons, but as the days shorten thoughts turn to winter. Crops are harvested. Firewood deliveries block footpaths as home-owners face the arduous task of negotiating a score or more of steep steps. The plane trees on Winchester Street lose their leaves. Eventually gutters clog as rainwater streams down the roads. The shadows at the Farmers Market lengthen and the stall-holders don their hats, gloves and cheerful smiles.

ERING
PHONE
328 8105

autumn food

Yoghurt with fresh fruit, nuts & honey

Kate McRae

This makes a great breakfast at any time of the year - just vary the fruit you use. It's especially nice when you don't feel like anything too heavy, although it is surprisingly filling.

per serve:

150ml Greek style yoghurt

a handful of selected nuts

2 tsp manuka honey

a selection of fruit to serve

Into the bottom of each individual glass put a small teaspoon of manuka honey then fill each glass with a good quality plain yoghurt, leaving some room at the top of each glass.

Sprinkle over nuts of your choice - I like almonds and pistachios. Then drizzle over another teaspoon of honey and let it run through the yogurt slowly, you don't need to mix it through.

Arrange each glass on a large plate with some assorted fruit cut into pieces big enough to dip into the yoghurt.

Hint: a couple of drops of rosewater mixed into the yogurt at the start gives a wonderful additional flavour but be careful not to use too much.

slow baked tomatoes

Kim Hickford

Fantastic as a brunch or lunch dish - melt in your mouth!

5 tbsp peanut oil

8 medium tomatoes

2 tsp sugar

½ tsp salt

½ tsp freshly ground black pepper

3 medium cloves garlic, minced

1 tbsp olive oil

½ cup parsley, minced

Preheat oven to 150°C.

Spread the oil in a lamington tin. Cut off the stem end of the tomatoes, place tomatoes cut side down in pan and bake for ½ hour. Turn and bake for another ½ hour, basting with pan juices occasionally. Sprinkle with the sugar, salt & pepper. Cook for another 1½ hours until tomatoes are flattened.

Sauté the garlic in the olive oil until soft, do not brown. Stir in parsley and sprinkle over cooked tomatoes.

Silverbeet, bacon & chickpea soup

Jillian Frater
serves 4-6

This soup is yummy and is chunky enough for a light dinner. I like it because silverbeet is one of the few vegetables that will grow in my garden and I often have canned chickpeas, tomatoes and bacon in the house.

8 silverbeet leaves

3 tbsp olive oil

1 onion, finely chopped

1 stick celery, thinly sliced

1 carrot, finely diced

3 cloves garlic, finely chopped

½ cup rindless bacon, finely diced

1 tbsp rosemary, very finely chopped

2 x 300g cans chickpeas, rinsed & well drained

400g can Italian tomatoes, mashed

500ml chicken stock

salt & freshly ground pepper to taste

extra-virgin olive oil for drizzling

Coarsely chop the silverbeet leaves and drop them into a saucepan of boiling water. Boil about 5 mins until tender. Remove from heat, drain, cool under cold running water, drain again, squeeze dry and chop again finely. Put aside. Heat the olive oil in a saucepan and add the onion, celery, carrot, garlic, bacon and rosemary. Fry gently, without browning, for about 10 mins or until the onion is soft. Add the chickpeas, tomatoes and stock and bring to the boil. Add the cooked silverbeet, bring back to the boil and simmer 10 mins. Taste, and season with salt & pepper.

Serve drizzled with extra-virgin olive oil.

Bianca, age 8

Minestrone soup

Deb Wood
serves 4-6

2 onions

5 cloves garlic

olive oil

1 carrot

½ aubergine

2 tsp of any Italian-style herbs

1 courgette

1 red pepper

1½ cans tomato puree

1 can cannelloni beans

1 cup pasta

salt & pepper

Using a food processor, blend onion and garlic together, then sauté in olive oil for a few minutes. Next, blend together the carrot and the aubergine, add to the onion and sauté for another few minutes. Add the herbs, and then blend together the courgette and the pepper and add to the mix. Once the vegetables are soft, pour in the tomato puree and an equal amount of water. Once boiling, add drained beans and the pasta. Simmer until pasta is cooked. Season with salt & pepper.

Connor & Sophie's favourite pumpkin soup

Helen Taylor
serves 4

1 onion

2 garlic cloves

½ a decent sized pumpkin

1 kumara

a sprinkle of curry powder

a dash of sugar

salt & pepper

splash of orange juice

½ cup tomato puree

In a heavy pan add enough butter to fry onions, garlic, pumpkin and kumara, with a good sprinkling of curry powder and a dash of sugar and salt & pepper. Once all are caramelised and spicy add a splash of orange juice to deglaze the pan. Stir in ½ cup tomato puree.

Add enough water to cover the veges - simmer till well cooked. Puree completely so that no veges can be identified by a fussy child! Add more seasoning if you like. Dish up with a dollop of sour cream and serve with fresh bread.

Spicy pumpkin tortilla baskets

Anne Carne
serves 6

Tortillas and salsa are available from most supermarkets. Recipe best made close to serving.

50g butter, melted

3 x 25cm flour tortillas, quartered

Filling:

300g pumpkin, peeled & chopped

2 tbsp olive oil

1 medium onion, sliced

1 clove garlic, crushed

1 tbsp ground cumin

310g can red kidney beans, rinsed, drained, mashed

1 tbsp mild sweet chilli sauce

¼ cup sundried tomatoes, drained & chopped

310g can corn kernels, drained

¼ cup water

¼ cup sour cream

¼ cup tomato salsa

Preheat oven to 180°C.

Grease 6-hole Texas muffin pan (¾ cup capacity). Brush 2 tortilla quarters with a little butter, press quarters into a muffin hole with points overlapping. Repeat with remaining tortillas and butter.

Filling: Cook pumpkin until just tender, then drain. Heat oil in pan, add onion, garlic and cumin. Cook, stirring until onion is soft. Add pumpkin to pan with remaining ingredients, stir until hot.

Divide filling between tortilla baskets. Bake about 20 mins or until tortilla baskets are crisp. Serve topped with sour cream and coriander, if desired.

Barbecued aubergine, tomato & mozzarella pie

Yosay Briels

Quite a rich number! Great with barbecued meats or fish and green salad or for lunch served as a main course with a side salad. You can even make it the day before and gently reheat it in a warm oven for about 30 minutes.

4 aubergines

500g mozzarella cheese, grated

100g cheddar cheese, grated

For the sauce:

2 tbsp olive oil

2 onions

1 clove garlic

500g fresh tomatoes, skinned and finely chopped

1 tbsp tomato paste

1 tsp thyme leaves

1 tbsp fresh oregano

2 bay leaves

salt & pepper

1 tsp sugar

Preheat oven 180°C.

Slice the aubergine, grill it on the barbecue until nicely softened. Set aside to cool.

To make the sauce sauté the onion in the lightly warmed oil until very soft and golden. This will take about 15 mins. Add the garlic and cook for a further 2 mins. Add the tomatoes, paste, herbs and sugar. Cook uncovered on a low heat for about 30 mins. Season with salt & pepper. Cool. Remove bay leaves.

Line a 23 cm spring-form tin with baking paper. Cover the bottom with the aubergine slices, top with a good ladle of tomato sauce, a handful of grated mozzarella and repeat until all ingredients are used up. Top with the grated cheddar.

Bake for 30 mins. Then grill the top until it is nicely browned. Cool slightly before cutting into wedges.

Harvest salad of roasted beets, pears & walnuts

Kim Hickford
serves 4 as a main course or 6 as a starter

I love this salad of roasted vegetables, especially in the autumn and winter. It's a meal-in-one.

4 large beetroot

3 large red onions

3 large pears

¼ cup olive oil

2 tbsp balsamic vinegar

2 tbsp brown sugar

1 cup walnut halves

1 tbsp pesto

2 tbsp lemon juice

3 tbsp olive oil

salt & ground black pepper

French bread, 10-12 slices

150g goats' cheese

5 handfuls mixed salad greens

Preheat oven to 220°C.

Peel and chop the beetroot into batons. Peel and slice red onions. Core and cut the pears into eight wedges. Place the vegetables in separate roasting dishes. Divide the oil, vinegar and sugar evenly between the dishes and toss through. Roast for 40-50 mins, stirring a couple of times until the liquid has evaporated and the veges are tender. Bake walnuts for 12-15 mins. Allow all to cool separately.

Pesto dressing: Combine pesto, lemon juice and olive oil. Season with salt & pepper.

Goats' cheese croutons: Spread slices of French bread with goats' cheese.

To assemble: Toss pesto dressing through salad greens. Add beets, onions, pears and walnuts. Garnish with goats' cheese croutons.
Serve at once.

Stuffed autumn vine leaves with feta & thyme

Yosay Briels
makes approx 36

60ml olive oil

2 small onions, chopped finely

1 cup short-grain rice

1½ cups water

2 tbsp thyme, finely chopped (lemon thyme is best)

100g feta cheese

600g vine leaves, fresh off the vine

2 tbsp lemon juice

300ml water

2 tbsp olive oil

Heat the oil in a heavy based pan and cook onions until soft and golden. Add the rice, water, and thyme and bring to the boil. Give one stir with a fork, cover, turn down the heat and cook for 18 mins. Turn off the heat and leave the rice to sit until cooled. Mix in the feta once cooled.

Blanch the vine leaves in boiling water. Rinse under cold water. Place vine leaves with vein side up and put about 2 tsp of filling in each one. Fold in the sides and roll up into a parcel. Put parcels in a single layer in a heavy-based pan. Pour over the lemon juice, water and oil. Place a plate on top of the parcels to stop them from moving around. Simmer for one hour. Cool in the pan and serve with pre-dinner drinks.

Herbed polenta & fresh tomato sauce

Lyttel Piko, Lyttelton

4 cups water or vegetable stock

1 tsp sea salt

200g polenta

black pepper to taste

freshly grated nutmeg

Sauce:
2 tbsp olive oil

1 onion, chopped finely

1 garlic clove, minced

1 tbsp fresh rosemary or 1 tsp dried

1 tbsp fresh thyme or 1 tsp dried

1 tbsp fresh marjoram or 1 tsp dried

2 bay leaves

pinch chilli powder

200g chopped tomatoes

½ cup tomato puree

salt & pepper to taste

Place water and salt into a large saucepan, bring to the boil. Gradually pour polenta into the boiling water, stirring continuously. Reduce heat and simmer uncovered for about 30 mins or until the water is absorbed. Stir frequently until the polenta is thick. When it pulls away from the sides of the pan easily, remove from the heat, season with pepper and nutmeg, and then spoon into a tin. Set this aside to cool. In a saucepan sauté the onion, garlic and herbs in the olive oil. Add tomatoes, tomato puree and bring to the boil. Simmer for 10 mins or until slightly thickened. Season with salt & pepper and serve.

William, age 7

WEATHER STONE
CONDITION OF STONE FORECAST
STONE IS WET: RAINING
STONE IS DRY: NOT RAINING
STONE CASTS SHADOW: SUNNY
WHITE ON TOP: FROSTY
CAN'T SEE STONE: FOGGY
SWING STONE: VERY WINDY
BOTTOM OF STONE WET: VERY HIG TIDE
STONE SWING OR GONE: TORNADO
STONE BOUNCING UP AND DOWN:
EARTHQUAKE

Pears in tarragon cream

Ann Stanaway
serves 4

I inherited my 'cooking' genes from my mother, and in turn have seen them appear in my three sons, who share my love of eating first, and cooking second. This recipe is a classic favourite that my mother and I were taught at a Cordon Bleu class we attended in 1970. It later became a staple dish on the menu at the many weddings I catered for with my friend, Christine Sandford, in a business we called Stanford Cuisine. We ran this for 20 years, taking our new babies with us and stashing their bassinettes under the bench, next to the coleslaw. Our husbands worked as lawyers by day, and carved hams at our buffets by night. We burned a lot of "midnight oil" and gathered a lot of great stories.

My first home was a small, 100-year old worker's cottage in Lyttelton. Here the food for a 100 guests was prepared on a scrubbed pine bench and transported by a yellow volkswagon down the steep incline to its destination - the "Old Stone House" in Cashmere. At this time we were one of the only companies doing food that was really different and this recipe stretched the boundaries between what was sweet and what was savoury. As an entree or a salad you can't go past this flavour combination. It is easy to prepare and still a contemporary taste that will challenge your guests to identify its components. I hope you like it as much as we do.

3 or 4 pears
(I think tinned are best)

lettuce leaves to serve

toasted walnuts, chopped

For the tarragon cream dressing:

1 egg

2 tbsp castor sugar

3 tbsp tarragon vinegar (essential)

250ml cream

Tarragon vinegar:

2 cups fresh tarragon leaves

4 cups white vinegar

Break egg into a bowl and beat with a whisk. Add sugar. Gradually beat in vinegar. Over a pan of hot water, whisk until thick - or this can be done in the microwave on 4. Chill. Partially whip cream and fold it into dressing. Place half a pear on a lettuce leaf. Spoon over dressing. Sprinkle walnuts on top. The custard can be made up and stored in the fridge for at least a week.

For the vinegar: Bruise tarragon leaves and put in a screw-top jar. Cover with the vinegar and steep 6 weeks. Strain and put in decorative bottles with a fresh sprig of tarragon and seal.

"It helps you stay alive. It gives you energy and there is healthy food and unhealthy food and my favourite is icecream." Brydee, age 7

"Our husbands worked as lawyers by day, and carved hams at our buffets by night. We burned a lot of "midnight oil" and gathered a lot of great stories."

Mussel patties

Alan Goodmanson
serves 4 as a starter

I have gathered shellfish for years at Port Levy. I prefer wild mussels from the ocean rather than the commercial ones. These mussels seem to taste better and are larger than the cultivated species. The premium mussel is the green lip variety.

6-8 clean mussels

Batter:

4 tbsp self-raising flour

salt & pepper

**¼ cup beer
(I prefer CD, our beer)**

oil for frying

lemon wedges to serve

Place 6 to 8 mussels into a bowl and put in microwave for 4-6 mins on high, depending on the size. Repeat the process if required. The purpose of this is to open the mussel and partially cook the meat.

Discard mussels that have not opened. Open shell and remove beard. I prefer to also remove the lip around the mussel. Cut the mussel into small pieces about 25mm square. Place in bowl and prepare the batter.

Batter: Place self-raising flour into a bowl. Add salt & pepper, slowly pour in beer while stirring, add extra flour and beer until you have sufficient to cover your mussels. Leave to sit at room temperature for 10 mins. The texture needs to be smooth and runny, continue stirring until lumps disperse. Place mussels into the batter mix.

Cooking: Preheat oil in a frying pan. Spoon in mussel mixture and cook until golden brown. Serve on a platter. Squeeze lemon juice to suit.

Fish in tempura batter

Karen & Chris McMullon
Known as 'posh fish fingers' in our house!

One of the things I love about living in Lyttelton is that you can buy fresh fish from the guy at the harbour on a Saturday morning. Unfortunately he won't fillet it for you so you have to attempt that yourself (Rick Steins Seafood Cookbook is brilliant at teaching you how). I'm lucky that although Chris is an accountant he has hidden talents on the cooking side and he is quite adept at it! Despite him loving to serve up beautifully presented fine French cuisine (he has even appeared on a BBC cooking programme with the famous French chef Raymond Blanc ...embarrass him and ask him about it), the following simple recipe is my favourite way that he cooks fresh fish.

fish eg: sole, flounder, brill - filleted (most fishmongers will do this for you)

150g plain flour

100g corn flour

5g baking powder

handful of ice

soda water

oil

Preheat deep fat fryer to 180°C.

Cut the fish fillets into strips and set aside.

Put the plain flour, corn flour, baking powder and some ice in a bowl. Mix in enough soda water, using a fork, until the mixture becomes the consistency of thick cream. Don't worry about the lumps.

Dip the fish into the batter and place into the deep fat fryer for about 2 mins until crisp and golden. Take out and drain on kitchen towel. Don't try to cook too many at the same time - they will keep hot for a while.

Serve with a wasabi mayonnaise (just mix some wasabi paste with mayonnaise) ...or tomato ketchup for the kids!

Chicken & bacon pasta

Diana Hardy
serves 4

I came upon this recipe during a holiday in Brittany in 2002. We stayed in converted stone farm buildings and our neighbours were a group of French businessmen from Nantes who had come away for a week of fishing. During the week they caught one fish between the six of them and one managed to break his leg! Stories of quite how it happened varied depending on the amount of Pastis consumed at the time.

1 tbsp olive oil

6 rashers streaky bacon, cut into small pieces

1 large onion, chopped

2 fat cloves of garlic, peeled and crushed

400g dried pasta spirals or penne

2 skinless chicken breasts, chopped into bit sized pieces

1 tsp herb de Provence or sage

1 x 250g crème fraiche

salt & pepper to taste

1 cup frozen peas (optional)

fresh parsley, chopped

Heat the oil in a pan over a medium heat. Add the bacon and cook for a couple of minutes until starting to colour. Add the onion and garlic and cook, stirring occasionally, until the onions are softened and the bacon is cooked. Put pasta on to cook in a large pot of salted water.

Add the chicken and herbs to the bacon mixture. Stir well. Put a lid on to the pan and leave to cook for about 5 mins. When time is up, give it a good stir and scrape any sticky bits from the bottom of the pan. Add the crème fraiche and stir well to coat everything. Adjust seasoning and let it simmer on a gentle heat for a few moments.

Add the peas to the pasta pot a few minutes before the end of cooking time and cook for a couple of minutes. Drain and pour over the chicken mixture. Stir well to combine. Divide into bowls and serve with parsley.

"Carrots are my favourite food because they are good for you. My other favourite food is cake." Eva, age 7

Cassoulet

Jo Hay
serves 10-12

A trusty favourite that always tastes good. Freezes well. Makes two medium sized casseroles, or one very large!

2 onions

garlic cloves

4 chorizo sausages, chopped

4 rashers of bacon, chopped

2-3 chicken breasts, chopped

2 tins cannelloni beans, drained

2 tins tomatoes, diced

4 carrots, grated or equivalent of red peppers, chopped

2 tsp chicken stock powder

thyme & bay leaves

Preheat oven 150°C.

Sauté the onion and garlic. In batches, brown the sausage, bacon and chicken. Divide these sautéed ingredients into two casserole dishes, and add the vegetables, chicken stock and herbs. Add ½-1 cup of water as required, this depends on tomato juice, etc - best to add minimum at the beginning and add more if necessary.

Cover with a lid and cook for 2½ hours. Stir occasionally. Serve with bread or brown rice, salad etc.

steak casserole parcels

Megan Jamieson

Tasty, yummy and easy. A beautifully colourful way to stretch steak. Great for families as you take advantage of cheaper cuts of meat and individualize the casseroles according to taste.

blade or chuck steak (fat removed)

seasoned flour

onions

mushrooms

capsicum

tomatoes

chutney

salt & pepper

Preheat oven 150–180°C.

Cut meat into chunks and roll in seasoned flour.

Place the steak on a piece of foil. Layer your choices of vegetables over the meat in a pile up, with the chutney in a big dollop on the top and season generously. Fold the foil over to make a parcel. Bake for at least 40 mins to an hour depending on size of meat.

Serve with baked potatoes and vegetables or crisp salad. Put the foil parcel onto the plates, as when you open them the meat has its own delicious gravy/sauce.

Charlie's ratatouille fillet

Cassandra Davis

No idea who Charlie is but...

2kg whole scotch fillet (I use a 2.3kg rump roast)

2 onions peeled

1 red pepper

1 green pepper

2 courgettes

2 cloves garlic

¼ cup parsley

90g butter

½ tsp dried basil

salt & pepper to taste

Preheat oven to 170°C.

Slice meat at 3cm intervals being careful not to slice the meat all the way through.

Slice the onions, peppers, and courgettes. Chop the garlic and parsley finely.

Melt butter in a pan, add prepared vegetables and herbs, cook gently for 3 mins. Season with salt & pepper. Fill the meat cavities with the vegetable mixture. Put meat into a large ovenproof dish. Pour over the remaining butter from the pan and bake.

1¼ hrs for rare

1½ hrs for medium

1¾ hrs for well done

Serve beef in thick slices, allowing each portion a serve of the vegetables.

Risotto with leeks, beetroot & goats' cheese

Kate McRae
serves 4-6

3 medium beetroot, scrubbed

100g butter

2 tsp olive oil

1 large onion, chopped

3 cloves garlic

2 medium leeks, washed trimmed & chopped

1 stalk of celery, chopped

3 cups Carnaroli or Arborio rice

1½ litres warmed vegetable stock, & the reserved liquid from cooking the beetroot

1 cup dry white wine

½ cup Parmesan cheese

juice 2 lemons

salt & pepper to taste

150g goats' cheese

Italian parsley

Begin by cooking the beetroot (scrubbed not peeled) in a pot of water until tender. This could take up to 45 mins depending on the size of the beetroot. Don't let them boil dry as you need some of the cooking liquid.

Sauté the onions in the butter and olive oil in a large heavy-bottomed pan until tender. Add the garlic, leeks, and celery and cook until the leeks are soft. Add the rice and stir until the grains of rice look semi-transparent in colour. Turn pan down to a medium simmer. Begin adding the stock, one ladle at a time, stirring continuously with a wooden spoon until the liquid has been absorbed. Continue doing this until you have used all the stock, then add 2 ladles of beetroot juice and the cup of white wine.

Once you have added all the liquid the rice should be al dente, and wet looking. If it still feels very hard then continue adding a little more liquid. Cover and leave to stand for a couple of minutes. Add the Parmesan, lemon juice and salt & pepper to taste. Peel the beetroot, the skins should slip off easily, and chop into small pieces.

To serve, put the beetroot in a pile on the top of the rice, then sprinkle over the goats' cheese, parsley, extra salt & pepper, and lemon juice if it needs it. You can also serve extra Parmesan at the table as well.

Hint: The secret of a good risotto is to use the best rice you can, Carnaroli will give a creamer result than Arborio. Also the more the risotto is stirred the creamier it will be.

Braised shanks of lamb with parsnip puree

Rosalind Dixon
serves 4

This is a great recipe for cold dark winter nights for the family or a few friends, as you can do a lot of the hard work early and finish it up an hour or less before serving. It is an impressive looking dish and with the right cooking the shanks come out beautifully. The slower and longer the cooking, the better the results.

4 lamb shanks

olive oil

sea salt & ground pepper

1 carrot, roughly chopped

1 onion, roughly chopped

1 leek, roughly chopped

1 celery stick, roughly chopped

½ a head of garlic

a sprig of fresh thyme

1 bay leaf

sprig of fresh rosemary

2 star anise

300ml dry white wine, or whatever you have available

1 litre of dark chicken stock (preferably a brown chicken stock, but you can make do with the standard packet liquid stuff, just strengthen it a bit with some stock powder)

Parsnip Puree:

100g butter

4 large parsnips, peeled & chopped

100ml double cream

sea salt & ground pepper

Heat a little olive oil in a large pan or pot. Season the lamb shanks and brown them all over in the oil, then remove from pan and set aside. Add a little more oil to the pan, add the chopped vegetable, garlic, herbs and anise, and cook gently until browned. Pour in the wine and continue cooking until it has reduced down to a syrup. Put the shanks back into the pan and pour on the stock. Season to taste.

Cover the pan and cook gently for 2½ - 3 hours or until the meat falls off the bone and is very tender. If you are finding it hard to keep them covered in the stock you will have to keep turning them so they stay moist.

About 30 mins before the end of cooking time make the parsnip puree.

Parsnip puree: Melt the butter in a frying pan over a low heat and cook parsnips until completely soft and falling apart (about 25 mins). Add the cream and bring to the boil. Season, then blend or liquidise it to a smooth puree. Keep warm.

Remove the lamb shanks from their liquid and keep warm. Strain the stock, pour it back into the pan and cook over a high heat until it forms a sauce consistency (don't be tempted to thicken with flour, as it will reduce).

Place each shank on top of a good spoonful of the parsnip puree then pour the sauce over the top.

Mutton bird

Mark Whyte

Take a mutton bird out of the brine and bung it in a pot of cold water.

Bring it to the boil (preferably outside) and boil for an hour. Drain.

Refill with cold water and bring to the boil for a further hour. Drain.

Grill for 5 mins on each side

Gob using your fingers, either hot or cold, by itself or on white bread, in company or as selfishly as you like. Bones must be picked clean.

Suggested beverage: any single malt from the lowland or on hot days anything fizzy, brown and beginning with b.

▼ The inner harbour 1923. "In dry dock is the original Wahine, which had only arrived at 9:30am with passengers and mail. Within 13 hours she was painted with water-cured paint, and sailing back to Wellington. Vessels at the time were cleaned by school children in small punts. Water in the dock would be let out a few feet at a time so that cleaning could move progressively downwards." LPC Dry Dock 125th Anniversary, 2008.

Image courtesy of Lyttelton Port of Christchurch

Project Lyttelton

Project Lyttelton is a grassroots, non-profit community organisation working to make Lyttelton a better place to live. Projects include the Summer Street Party and Winter Festival of Lights, the Timebank, community education and welcome bags for new residents. One of the greatest successes of Project Lyttelton is the weekly Farmers' Market, attracting 35 regular stalls and hundreds of people each week to the town.

Project Lyttelton has a vision of food gardens all around Lyttelton. They would love Lyttelton to be self-sufficient for all its food needs. To this end, organic vegetables are grown in Opawa for the Lyttelton community, and volunteers communally grow food at the Community Garden in Oxford Street, finishing their weekly sessions with a shared lunch.

"One of the greatest successes of Project Lyttelton is the weekly Farmers' Market, attracting 35 regular stalls and hundreds of people each week to the town."

Caramelised fresh figs

Yosay Briels
serves 6

There are quite a few fig trees growing in Lyttelton. Figs are wonderful eaten raw, skin and all, just plucked from a tree. This recipe makes a perfect autumn dessert, served with a good dollop of cream, beaten quite stiff, with a little vanilla sugar. Alternatively serve with a good vanilla ice-cream. We like the sauce so much that we often make double...it all seems to get eaten.

9 fresh figs

90g unsalted butter

¾ cup soft brown sugar

cream or ice-cream (or both)

Preheat the grill to 200°C

Melt the butter and sugar together in a heavy-based saucepan, stirring continuously until the sugar has dissolved into the butter. Cut the figs in half with a very sharp knife. Brush a small amount of the sauce onto the figs and grill for about 3 mins until the tops of the figs are nicely caramelised.

Serve 3 halves per person on individual plates, with the rest of the sauce poured around the figs and a dollop of cream or ice-cream.

Tarte Tatin

Jean-Pierre & Megan Ribotton

Tradition says that the Tarte Tatin was first created by accident at the Hotel Tatin in Lamotte-Beuvron, France in 1898. The hotel was run by two sisters, Stéphanie and Caroline Tatin. Stéphanie, who did most of the cooking, was overworked one day. She started to make a traditional apple pie but left the apples cooking in butter and sugar for too long. Smelling the burning, she tried to rescue the dish by putting the pastry base on top of the pan of apples, quickly finishing the cooking by putting the whole pan in the oven. After turning out the upside down tart, she was surprised to find how much the hotel guests appreciated the dessert.

This is a recipe that Jean Pierre and I use a lot over winter when apples are plentiful and comfort food is necessary. I recommend making your own pastry which in this case is quick and easy if you have a food processor. This pastry can also be used for egg and bacon pies, pasties, quiches and fruit tarts.

Pastry:

200g plain flour

salt

100g butter

1egg

2 tbsp cold water

Filling:

1kg golden delicious apples, peeled

15g butter

175g sugar

¾ cup water

Preheat oven 200°C.

Pastry: Make the pastry by placing flour, salt and butter into the food processor and whizzing until the texture of bread crumbs. Add the egg and water and pulse until mixed. Turn out onto a lightly floured bench and lightly knead. Refrigerate while making the filling.

Filling: Cut the butter into small pieces and dot over a 28cm round shallow flan dish. Chop the apples into quarters and arrange in the flan dish.

Place the sugar and water in a saucepan and bring to the boil (once boiling do not stir). Just before the syrup turns to toffee take it off the heat and pour over the apples (prepare the apples while the sugar syrup is reducing). Once the apples are covered with the syrup (toffee) cover them with the rolled pastry, tucking it down the sides of the dish and prick the top.

Bake in the bottom of moderately hot oven for 30 mins. When cooked turn out onto a large plate so the fruit is on the surface. Serve warm.

Easy fresh fruit cake

Caro Davidson

A friend was giving cooking lessons at her home in the port. She gave us this simple and delicious cake recipe – that is good for using up any old stone fruit. It can be made in a roasting dish, or 2 x 20cm cake tins. No weighing required...

6-8 plums or other stone fruit (or canned fruit)

3 tsp sugar

300g butter

1½ cups sugar

3 eggs

lemon zest

1 tsp vanilla

1 cup milk

3½ cups of white flour

1 tsp cinnamon

2 tsp baking powder, heaped

Preheat oven 180°C.

Slice or halve the fruit and sprinkle with the sugar (or use drained tinned fruit). Cream butter and sugar together and add eggs, lemon & vanilla. Beat well then add milk, flour, cinnamon and baking powder. Put into desired tin or tins and arrange the fruit over the top. Bake for approximately 1 hour. The fruit will sink while cooking. Freeze if not using immediately.

"I love fruit and my favourite fruit is apples"

Taine, age 10

LONDON STREET

Bank of New Zealand

Crème brulee

Chef Adrian Lowrey
London St Restaurant, Lyttelton
enough for 6 small ramekins

This classic French dessert was always on the London Street Restaurant menu. It represented the restaurant's food philosophy, 'simple flavours done well using the best ingredients'. The free range egg yolks give this dish a richness on the palate while the shallow brulee moulds allow a caramel to crème ratio that has to be eaten to be believed. Enjoy!

1 vanilla pod

500ml cream

7 free-range egg yolks

80g castor sugar

Preheat oven 110°C.

Slice the vanilla pod in half length-wise. Scrape the vanilla seeds into the cream. Bring the cream and vanilla pod to the simmer. Whisk the yolks and sugar till pale and creamy. Pour the hot cream onto the yolk and sugar mixture, stir, then put aside to rest. Pour this mix through a sieve then into your brulee moulds. Place these moulds into a shallow tray and fill that tray with water 1cm up sides of moulds. Bake in the oven for approx 15-20 mins. When ready the brulee should have a slight wobble. Remove from oven and allow to cool.

Sprinkle a light layer of castor sugar over the top of each crème brulee and using a gas blow torch, caramelise the sugar.

Cape brandy tart

Clare O'Regan

This sweet and delicious pudding is the South African version of sticky toffee pudding. Makes one very big pudding, best served in small slices.

Syrup:

1½ cups sugar

¾ cup water

1 tsp vanilla

¼ cup brandy

Cake:

250g dates, chopped

1 tsp baking soda

1 cup boiling water

125g butter

1 cup sugar

2 large eggs, beaten

2 cups white flour

1 tsp baking powder

pinch salt

¼-½ cup nuts, chopped (walnuts or macadamias are best)

Preheat oven 180°C.

Boil the first 3 syrup ingredients for 5 mins (add the brandy at the end, or it will all evaporate). Mix dates, baking soda and water and allow to stand. In a separate bowl, cream butter and sugar, then add eggs slowly. Add to this mixture the sifted flour, baking powder and salt. Add date mixture and nuts. Mix together. Bake in large pie dish for 45-60 mins. Allow to cool slightly. Pour over the syrup.

Serve warm or at room temperature with vanilla icecream or lashings of whipped cream.

"Cooking is about making a basic masterpiece" Alexandra, age 10

Banana fritters

Arthur Collins
serves 4

I cannot claim culinary expertise, but this passes the "yum" test from sons Josh and Tom.

3 bananas (riper the better, black is fine but yellow works too)

5 tbsp plain flour (self-raising is fine, omit the baking powder)

1 egg

2 tsp baking powder

3 tbsp oil

Mash the ingredients with a fork in a medium sized bowl until gooey. Place a dollop into a frying pan with 3 tablespoons of hot oil (rice bran oil best). Flip once. Serve with maple syrup, ice cream and lemon juice.

Enjoy the compliments from wife and kids. Retire to the sofa with a glass of wine!

Tarta de Santiago

Ground Culinary Centre, Lyttelton

This tart is originally from Galicia where it is traditionally eaten on St James Day.

1 x sweet pastry sheet for the tart shell

Filling:

130g Membrillo (quince paste)

1 tbsp water

1 tbsp lemon juice

230g blanched almonds, ¼ processed till chunky and the rest medium

grated zest of ¾ orange & ¾ lemon

1¼ cinnamon sticks, roasted and finely ground (old coffee grinder is excellent for this)

40ml sherry (Spanish is best)

115g unsalted butter

75g castor sugar

2 large eggs

Preheat the oven to 180°C.

Bake the pastry shell blind then cool. In a saucepan melt the Membrillo with the water and the lemon juice over low heat so it doesn't stick. Spread this evenly over the cooked pastry shell. Set aside.

Mix the almonds, zests, cinnamon and sherry and leave for 5 mins for flavours to infuse. Beat the butter and sugar until pale, soft and fluffy. Add the eggs one by one. The mixture will look lumpy. Now fold the almond mixture into the egg mixture and ease it into the pastry shell spreading it roughly.

Bake in the middle shelf for about 30–40 mins until a golden brown crust has formed.

.espresso

Coffee fudge slice

Gill Rowe
makes 30 squares

250g butter

2 x tins of condensed milk

2 tbsp golden syrup

About 2½ packets wine biscuits, crushed

200g walnuts, chopped (and some extra chopped walnuts for the top)

Preheat oven 170°C.

Melt the butter, remove from the heat and beat in the condensed milk and golden syrup. Add wine biscuits and the walnuts. Put into a sandwich tray 28x32cm lined with baking paper. Bake for 20 mins until lightly golden. Once cold, ice with coffee-flavoured icing and cut into small squares.

Almond biscotti

Sonja Kingsbury

A 'tried and true' from my good friend Chrissie, a part Italian Aussie. It is a 'leave overnight' recipe.

4 egg whites

⅔ cup castor sugar

1 cup flour

1 cup whole almonds with skins on

vanilla

Preheat oven 180°C.

Beat egg whites stiffly, gradually add sugar and continue beating until glossy. Fold in flour, almonds and vanilla. Place in a greased and floured loaf tin. Bake in a moderate oven for 60 mins. Leave to cool. Wrap in foil. Refrigerate overnight. Slice loaf finely, place onto a baking tray and bake in a cool oven at 110°C for 30mins to dry out. Store in an airtight container.

Dutch apple cake

Yosay Briels

3 cooking apples, cored

lemon juice

185g butter

185g castor sugar

3 eggs

1 tsp vanilla

250g self-raising flour

150ml milk

icing sugar for serving

Preheat the oven to 180°C.

Core and cut the apples into slices and brush with lemon juice to avoid them going brown. Grease and line a 20cm spring-form with baking paper. Beat the butter and the sugar until almost white and light and creamy. Add the vanilla and eggs one at a time and beat well. Fold in the flour with a large slotted spoon until combined. Mix in the milk after warming it slightly on the stove or in the microwave. Spoon the mixture into the tin, press in the apple slices and bake for 1 hour or until cooked. Leave tin inside oven with the door open for about 10 mins and then turn it out onto a rack to cool completely. Top with sifted icing sugar.

Date nut slice

Gail Davey

125g butter

1¼ cups flour

1 tsp baking powder

1 cup sugar

1 cup coconut

1 cup dates, chopped

½ cup walnuts, chopped

1 egg

Preheat oven to 180°C.

Melt the butter and put aside. In a bowl mix the dry ingredients, then add the dates and nuts and the egg. Finally add the butter. Cook for approx 20 mins. When cool ice with chocolate icing.

Courgette bread

Richard McGuigan
makes 2 loaves

2 cups grated courgette

3 eggs

2 cups sugar

1 cup vegetable oil

3 cups flour

1 tsp baking soda

2 tsp cinnamon

1 tsp salt

¼ tsp baking powder

2 tsp vanilla (optional)

½ cup walnuts (optional)

Preheat oven 180°C.

Grate the courgette and drain off the excess liquid. Beat the eggs lightly. Add the sugar, oil and courgette. Combine all the dry ingredients and add to the egg mixture, beating until smooth. If desired add vanilla and nuts. Pour batter into 2 greased loaf pans. Bake for about an hour.

Felix, age 9

Lemonade scones

Dawn Kottier

1 cup cream

1 cup lemonade

4 cups self-raising flour

2 tsp baking powder

pinch of salt

Preheat oven 200°C.

Stir cream and lemonade together. Gradually add dry ingredients to the wet mixture.

Roll out on board and cut into six pieces. Bake for 11-14 mins on a floured tray.

Using quinces

Glyn Abbott

The quince is a favourite fruit of mine. Not only is it beautiful to behold and wonderfully fragrant, but it is also delicious and versatile and surprisingly easy to use.

Any Aunt Daisy book or the Edmonds Cookbook will tell you how to make quince jelly. Put one or two perfect quinces into your linen cupboard to perfume your sheets and pillow cases.

Baked quinces

Preheat oven 180°C.

Simply wipe quince clean and remove the soft down that appears on a ripe quince. Put, as is, into oven and bake until soft (40 mins–1 hour).

To serve, drizzle with honey and a good spoon of plain yoghurt, or a simple caramel sauce is great (½ cup cream, 2 tbsp brown sugar, 25g butter – simmer together until thick).

Oven roast quinces

Syrup:

220g sugar

2 cups water.

Peel, core and quarter quinces and put them into a baking dish. Bring sugar and water to boil, pour over the quinces, cover with tinfoil and bake in a moderate oven for 2 hours. The cooked quinces will have transformed to a wonderful mahogany colour. Allow them to cool in the syrup.

Cooked like this, quinces can be used in a number of ways. They are delicious served cold with plain yoghurt or ice cream, sprinkled with toasted pistachio nuts. They can be drained and chopped to use as the fruit portion of your favourite muffin recipe.

Simple & quick quince paste

Kate McRae

1kg quinces

750g sugar (approx)

Peel and core the quinces and cut them into medium sized chunks. Put them into a saucepan with just enough water to cover them, and bring to the boil. Simmer until the quinces are soft and most of the water has evaporated. Put them into a food processor and process to a pulp. Measure the pulp cup by cup and return to clean saucepan. For every cup of pulp add 1 cup of sugar. Bring to the boil, stirring the mixture to prevent it sticking. Continue to boil until the mixture is thick and has darkened in colour. Quickly pour into a shallow, very lightly greased rectangular dish. Put this into a very low oven – 120°C for about half an hour to allow the paste to dry out. When cool cut into squares and wrap each square in waxed paper. Store in the fridge. The paste will keep for months.

Serving suggestions:
Great with cheeses, or as a way to add flavour to sauces, gravies and casseroles. Or use in desserts such as the Tarta de Santiago.

winter

Snow paints a wintry stripe across Mt Herbert. Wood and coal smoke fills the air but disperses quickly in the sea breezes. Grit trucks fight the frosts, garlic is planted and roses pruned. Hardy walkers still tramp the muddy hill tracks.

The Festival of Lights brings crowds to brave the cold and enjoy mulled wine and lamb shanks on the illuminated streets.

Families head for the ski slopes, and the football fields. Blackboards advertise soup and locals fill the cafes and bars seeking warmth and company. Impatient dogs shiver on the pavements.

BELLS PHARMAC
nt Bell
macist
DOGS PROHIBITED IN THIS SHOPPING AREA UNLESS ON LEASH
LONDON ST
LONDON

winter food

Mary's kidneys and bacon

Barbara and William Lee
serves 4

The non-cook's successful brunch used only when William goes on strike. Many years ago my very Irish mother-in-law prepared this dish for brunch I said, "There is absolutely no way I am eating kidneys ...they are too disgusting". They were delicious and I've been cooking them ever since. If like me, kidneys have always repulsed you, I suggest you try these. They are fabulous, incredibly easy – and guests think I'm so clever.

knob of butter

6 lamb kidneys, skinned with the fatty bits trimmed off & chopped into small pieces

6 bacon slices, chopped up small

chopped tomatoes, drained if tinned

mushrooms (optional)

Worcestershire sauce

ground black pepper

cornflour

water

toast

Place the following in a small saucepan with a lid and layer in this order: butter, lamb kidneys, bacon, tomatoes and/or mushrooms. Top with a very, very generous shake of Worcestershire sauce. Add freshly ground black pepper (doesn't need salt). Do not disturb the layers. Put on saucepan lid and bring to boil then simmer for 20 mins. Thicken by stirring in a little cornflour and water. Serve on thick-toasted Vogels, or whatever. This can be doubled or more, if larger quantity required.

Oatmeal pancakes

Baden Norris

During a recent voyage to the Antarctic, a German lady and I formed the lecturing staff. On this voyage we encountered very bad weather, making the work of the ship's cooks very trying. To relieve the pressure on them, the ship's staff decided to cook a breakfast for the passengers and give the cooks a break. To this end, each staff member chose to prepare his or her favourite recipe. I chose scrambled eggs, others put their hand to sausages, porridge, some less adventurous chose toast. The German lady produced oatmeal pancakes. They proved the most popular with the passengers; simple to prepare, tasty and very filling.

Per person you will need:

½ cup rolled oats

½ cup white flour

½ tsp baking powder

1 egg

½ cup milk

Mix all ingredients to a paste and pour into a preheated frying pan, not too hot and previously greased with butter. Cook over a low heat but keep checking to prevent sticking, and turn over when brown. Serve with maple syrup, fruit (tinned plums are great) and whipped cream. Enjoy!

Lyttelton Coffee

LESLIE'S BOOKSHOP
Agency
CHRISTCHURCH PRESS CO LTD
CLASSIFIED ADVERTISING
Prepaid Cards
London
Paris
Back o'
Bourke
THE PRESS
ON
SALE
HERE

Mulligatawny soup

Lyttelton Coffee Co, Lyttelton
serves 6-8

Stock:

2 chicken legs

3 carrots

2 onions

3 stalks celery

3 cloves garlic

1 tsp oregano

2 bay leaves

Soup:

2 onions, chopped

3 cloves garlic

3cm ginger, grated

4 tsp curry powder

1 cup rice

oil or butter

salt & pepper

sweet chilli for seasoning

½ can coconut cream

fresh coriander, chopped

For the stock: Chop vegetables into 5cm chunks and cover with water. Boil with the chicken for 1 hour 20 mins. Strain, shred chicken and set aside. Remove bay leaves and process vegetables and set it all aside.

To finish the soup: In a large pot, sauté first five soup ingredients in oil or butter, add stock and simmer to cook rice. Add everything else.

"Don't play with your food" Tanchoz, age 8

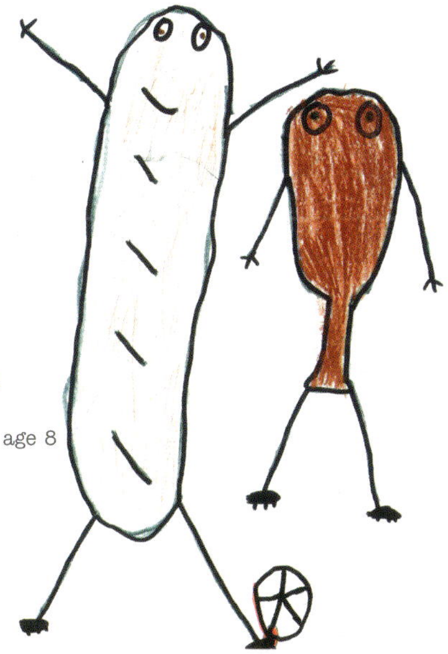

Sweet potato & corn soup

Rob and Lisa Swann
serves 4

1 onion

2 stalks celery

2 carrots

½ leek

oil/butter

1 tsp Chinese five spice

2 small kumara, cubed

1x400g tin coconut milk

1-2 cups of vegetable stock

1x400g tin sweetcorn kernels

Roughly chop onion, celery, carrots and leek, sauté in oil or butter until soft and golden. Add five spice, kumara pieces and liquids. Bring to the boil and simmer until kumara is soft. Puree or liquidise, season with salt & pepper to taste. Add corn kernels. Warm through and serve with crusty bread.

Bacon & lentil soup

Frances Berkhout
serves 6-8

This is one of my favourites, with the lentils and paprika bought from Piko Wholefoods, and a rummage through the bargain bin at Verkerk's for the bacon scraps and sausage.

2 tbsp olive oil

1 large onion, finely chopped

1 carrot, peeled & finely chopped

4 strips smoked streaky bacon

3 tbsp tomato paste

2 cloves garlic, crushed

2 tsp smoked paprika

1 bacon bone (or bacon scraps)

120g smoked kransky, chorizo or salami

2½ litres chicken stock (good quality/homemade)

2 x 400g cans tomatoes (crushed or roughly chopped)

2 cups brown lentils, washed

1 bay leaf

salt & pepper

Heat oil and sauté onion, carrot and streaky bacon. Add tomato paste, garlic, paprika, bacon bones or scraps and diced sausage. Stir over heat for another minute. Add chicken stock, tomatoes, lentils and bay leaf and simmer for 1-1½ hours. Season with salt & pepper to taste. Can be made in a slow cooker, after the sautéing stage. Perfect for a winter's night and it freezes well.

"I love going to the market on Saturday mornings with my mum and eating bacon butties!" Hamish, age 9

Borscht

Kate McRae
serves 4

This is a simple and quick version and would make a great lunch dish.

1 tbsp olive oil

100g bacon or pancetta

1 onion, finely chopped

3 large beetroot, peeled & grated

3 carrots, grated

3 sticks celery, cut into matchsticks

1 litre beef stock

1-2 cups water

1 tbsp wine vinegar

salt & pepper

1x400g tin chopped tomatoes

sour cream or yoghurt

chopped gherkins & parsley

In large pan heat the oil and gently cook the finely chopped bacon, then add the onion and cook until soft. Add the beetroot, carrot and celery and cook for about 5 mins or until the vegetables begin to soften. Add the stock, water, vinegar and seasoning. Cover and simmer for about 30 mins. Add the tomatoes and cook for a further 10 mins. Serve with sour cream or yoghurt, chopped gherkins and parsley.

Cheesy crumpets

Sarah Wild
serves 4

This is an old family recipe that my father used to make sometimes on Sunday evenings. As children, our family would have a cooked Sunday lunch at about 1pm. So in the evening we used to have easy snack-style food for dinner. Cheesy crumpets always remind me of my father. These probably sound strange but they are really tasty and delicious.

1 cup cheese, grated

1–2 tbsp milk

wholegrain mustard

crumpets

Put cheese, milk (start with smaller amount and add more if needed) and mustard into a bowl and mash/mix together with a fork. This will form a stiff paste-like mixture.

Toast the crumpets on the bottom side only. Spread cheese mixture on the top of the crumpets and grill until melted (not too close to the grill) – they will be golden brown.

Sweet onion tart

Sarah Wild
makes 1 x 25cm tart

I have been using this for years – a favourite of my son, Sebastian. I add more eggs and cream depending on how big I want the tart to be.

Ready-bought flaky or savoury short-crust pastry enough to line a 25cm flan dish (you can make your own of course)

2–3 tbsp olive oil

600g onions, peeled and finely sliced

3 eggs

150ml cream

¼ tsp salt

black pepper to taste

nutmeg, a good grating (optional)

Preheat oven to 180°C.

Line a 25cm flan dish with pastry and put into fridge until needed. Put the oil into a large saucepan or cast-iron frying pan and add onions. Cook over low-medium heat, uncovered, stirring from time to time, until onions are pale and golden. This will take about 20-25 mins and should not be hurried as sautéing develops the onions' sweet flavour. Take care not to let the onions catch and burn towards end of cooking. Set aside to cool.

In large mixing bowl, add the eggs, cream and seasonings and mix. Add the cooled onions and combine. Pour mixture into the pastry case and bake in oven for approx 45 mins – or until pastry is golden-brown and custard is set. Leave for 15 mins to settle before slicing.

"I love food. Yum. I love it so much." Sophie, age 8

Adie's mum's sausage rolls

Adie Guest
makes 8 medium sized rolls

2 slices bread, crumbed

1 onion, chopped

2-3 cloves garlic

450g sausage meat

Worcestershire & tomato sauce

1 carrot, grated

1 potato, grated

2 pastry sheets

1 egg

Preheat oven to 200°C.

Mix bread, onion and garlic together and set aside. In a separate bowl put sausage meat, Worcestershire sauce, tomato sauce, carrot and potato. Add the crumbed mixture to the sausage mixture and mix well together. Place mixture onto pastry sheets and roll up to form a sausage-shape, seal with an egg wash, then brush top with the remaining wash. Bake for approx 20 mins.

Ivy's parsnips

Rebecca Rennie
serves 4-6

My mum was an amazing cook, not only did we have great dinners but we biked home for wonderful cooked lunches. Friends used to say you only ever saw Ivy at the kitchen bench or ironing and I suspect either of these places were where she was the happiest.

1kg parsnips

¼ cup oil

3 tbsp butter

1 tomato, sliced

5 tsp brown sugar

¼ tsp salt & pepper

grated cheese

¼ cup cream

fresh breadcrumbs

Preheat oven to 180°C.

Core parsnips by slicing vertically and using a small knife to cut down either side of the woody core to remove it. Sauté parsnips in oil and butter and drain. Layer parsnips in an ovenproof dish with tomato, brown sugar, salt & pepper. Sprinkle over cheese. Pour cream over top. Sprinkle breadcrumbs on top and cook for 20-30 mins.

Roasted cauliflower with cumin & sesame

Shelley McCabe
serves 4-6

1 medium cauliflower

2 tbsp tomato puree or paste

3 tbsp olive oil

2 tsp cumin seed

2 tbsp sesame seed

fresh dill/coriander

sea salt & ground pepper

Preheat oven to 230°C.

Separate cauliflower into similar-sized florets. In a bowl put tomato puree, oil and seeds, and stir thoroughly. Smear over the cauliflower and lay in a baking tray. Roast towards the top of the oven for 15-25 mins until black in patches or soft enough to insert a knife through. Sprinkle with coriander and/or dill and serve. Season with salt & pepper.

Fish fillet pie

Caro Davidson
serves 4-6

A friend made this dish for us after the delivery of our first baby. A fabulous meal-in-one and a great source of Omega 3, which birth and lactation deplete from new mothers. Lyttelton has a fresh fish delivery to our doors every Thursday. Mediterranean-inspired and a fish dish the children will actually eat...

fresh fish fillets (terakihi or gurnard)

dried tarragon

frozen baby whole beans

potato, sliced thinly

olive oil

paprika

Preheat oven to 180°C.

Grease ovenproof dish with olive oil and line the bottom of the dish with fish fillets. Sprinkle tarragon over the fillets. Layer beans on top of fish. Pour over more olive oil. Layer potato on top of beans, overlapping. Add more olive oil. Sprinkle with paprika. Place in oven until the potato layer is golden and cooked (don't over-cook, or fillets dry out). Cooking time about 20 mins.

Creamy pasta with smoked salmon & spinach

Ange & Graeme Bachop
serves 4

Graeme likes this recipe because he is a seafood lover. It is quick to prepare and doesn't require any complicated ingredients. It's his favourite pasta dish and is one of Donna Hay's recipes, with a bit of a twist.

400g fettuccine or spaghetti noodles

1 cup cream

2 tsp lemon zest, finely grated

2 tbsp lemon juice

½ cup Parmesan cheese, grated

½ cup basil leaves, chopped

black pepper

2 large handfuls baby spinach leaves

100g cold-smoked salmon, chopped

Parmesan cheese to serve

Boil pasta in plenty of salted water and cook until al dente. Drain and return to the pan. Add the cream, lemon zest, lemon juice, Parmesan, basil, black pepper, spinach and salmon. Stir through pasta (the heat of the pasta wilts the spinach and cooks the salmon). Place on plates and top with grated Parmesan. Really easy and very tasty.

SMITH

Samsun

Cecily's old food pie

This is a bit of a favourite with flatmates of my past. Actually I'm not sure if that's true, but I'm often reminded of my having inflicted it upon them. It's difficult to list the ingredients, as they tend to be whatever's in the fridge on a Sunday evening. I don't necessarily choose to make it but have the decision thrust upon me by the mountain of leftovers and threatening-to-go-off vegetables pushing my frugal button. Bon appetit!

vegetables: e.g. potatoes, pumpkin, carrots and parsnips, remove any rotten bits and cut into chunks

1 onion, chopped

2 cloves garlic, chopped

olive oil

broccoli, cauliflower, tomatoes, chopped

4 eggs

salt & pepper

cheese – with mould cut off, grated

Preheat oven to 200°C.

Cook (microwave) the vegetables until cooked. Sauté onion and garlic in olive oil. Add broccoli, cauliflower and tomatoes. Sauté for a further 5 mins then place everything in a casserole dish. Beat eggs, add seasoning and pour over the vegetables. Sprinkle cheese on top. Bake for 30 – 40 mins. Can be complemented with any dessert that hasn't been lurking in the fridge for more than a week.

Cecily found living alone a constant battle with old food.

sausage & lentil casserole

Clare O'Regan
serves 6 hungry appetites

800g good pork sausages

2 tbsp olive oil

2 onions, cut lengthwise into slices

4 cloves garlic, thinly sliced

4 slices streaky bacon, chopped

2 carrots, finely chopped

2 celery sticks, thinly sliced

2x400g cans tomatoes, chopped

250g brown or puy lentils

750ml water

2 bay leaves

salt & pepper

parsley

First brown the sausages in the olive oil in a casserole pot. Put on a plate and set aside. In the same pot, cook the onions, over a medium heat. When soft, add the garlic and the bacon. Add a little more oil if required. Cook for a few minutes and then add the carrots and celery. Cook until softened. Add the tomatoes, lentils and water. Bring gently to the boil. Add the sausages and the bay leaves. Cover with a lid and simmer gently for 45-60 mins or until the lentils are soft. If there is too much liquid, remove lid halfway through. Add salt & pepper to taste. Garnish with parsley. Serve with crusty bread or mashed potatoes, with a green salad on the side.

steak on the barbecue, winter recipe.

Gary McCormick

The important thing to remember about cooking is that it's not terribly important. Chefs call me from all around the world for this recipe. I am rude to them and then hang up. We chefs all do that kind of thing. It makes us feel important and we have done a jolly good job of elevating cookery to a religion and have made ourselves the high priests and priestesses. Well done us!

steak, good quality second-grade

onions

potatoes

Colman's Hot English mustard

Fire up the barbie (not the doll, the metal thing in the back yard. You'll need it to melt the snow). Pour yourself a drink - gin at this stage. Stare at flames of barbie until you start seeing faces. Change to beer. When hot plate evaporates spit, hurl good quality steak onto it. One of the key ingredients in cooking is/are the ingredients. No good trying to cook an old boiler, and in this country, cooking your mother-in-law is illegal. So buy good quality second-grade meat - the best gets exported of course.

Meantime, boil potatoes. Fry onions on barbecue - this is a good opportunity to move on to a Sav Blanc. Flip steak over. Slightly mash potatoes and add to onions on hot plate. Go inside and forget what you went in for. Return to barbecue. Go inside again and put frozen peas in boiling water. Dash outside for second Savvy so wife won't notice. At about this time, you will be overcome by a torrent of fantastic ideas for solving social and political problems. Regale wife with them - she may feign indifference -Winston Churchill had the same problem. Collect mound of potatoes and onions in one bowl and steak on plate. Stir up enormous quantity of Colman's Hot English mustard. Serve. Pour glass of red. If guests turn up, grab plateful and hide in garage.

Steak au poivre (pepper steak)

Ilda Inglis
serves 2

Invented around 1920 in the kitchen of the Trianon Palace at Versailles, steak au poivre has become one of the classic dishes of French cuisine. In order to give a lift to some very tender but rather tasteless beef from Argentina, the chef, Emile Lerch had the idea of covering it with crushed peppercorns before cooking it. Today, mignonnette or coarse ground pepper is also referred to as poivre à steak. This is a fantastic dish accompanied by homemade potato chips (thin cut) and a good Merlot or Cab Sav.

1 porterhouse or rump steak, about 400g and 3cm thick, trimmed and cut into two steaks of equal size.

salt

1 tbsp cracked peppercorns

60g butter

2 tbsp cognac

3 tbsp double cream or crème fraîche

Pat steak dry and season with salt. Spread the peppercorns on a plate and roll the steaks over them to coat each side lightly. Melt half the butter in a 26cm skillet. Cook the steak over high heat for 2-3 mins on each side, according to taste. Pour the cognac over and ignite. When the flames subside, remove the steaks from the pan and keep warm on a plate. Discard the butter from the pan and add the cream. Boil for one min over high heat, them whisk in the remaining butter. Pour this sauce over the steaks and serve immediately.

italian braised lamb

Gill Rowe

serves 2

Note: start the day before.

We like to cook this in winter as it smells great when it's cooking. We serve it with creamy mashed potatoes and/or hunks of bread. It's adapted (only slightly) from a Nigel Slater recipe.

4 lamb neck chops, 6-7 cm thick

2 bay leaves

a few sprigs thyme

2 stalks of celery

2 carrots, peeled & sliced

1 medium onion, diced

3 cloves garlic, squashed

1 large dried red chilli, chopped

black peppercorns

1 orange

1 bottle red wine

olive oil

1 tbsp balsamic vinegar

2 flat brown mushrooms (opt)

Put lamb, bay leaves, thyme, celery, carrot, onion, garlic and chilli and a few peppercorns in a bowl. Peel the orange and add the skin and the sliced flesh of the orange to the bowl. Pour over sufficient red wine to cover the meat and set aside overnight.

You will need a heavy-based casserole with a lid. Allow as much of the liquid from the chops to run off (this will ensure both sides of the meat brown nicely). Add a good splash of olive oil to the pan and brown the marinated chops. Lift these out of the pan and set aside. Now add the remaining vegetables and herbs from the marinade and the mushrooms (if required). Cook for a good 10 mins until the vegetables have softened. Pour in the wine from the marinade and the rest of the bottle. Bring to the boil over a medium heat, turning the heat down so that it simmers. Add the balsamic vinegar and the lamb. Cover the casserole with greaseproof paper (helps prevent evaporation) and then the lid. At this stage you can leave the casserole on a gentle simmer on the stovetop for about 1½ hrs. Check the meat for tenderness. It should fall off the bone.

Remove the lamb, and turn up the heat and cook uncovered until the liquid has thickened slightly. Put the lamb back in, warm through and serve.

Marsala chicken fillets with caramelised onions

Yosay Briels
serves 2

This recipe can be doubled or tripled when feeding a crowd. The most important part is the caramelising of the onions until they're really soft, as that gives a beautiful texture to the sauce. Serve with mash and greens, or a green salad with lemony dressing.

2 tbsp butter

1 tbsp good olive oil

2 red onions, sliced thinly

2 large or 4 small chicken fillets

3 tsp cornflour

1 cup homemade chicken stock or the pantry variety

1 cup Marsala (dark sweet fortified wine)

Heat butter and olive oil in a heavy-based pan and add the onions. Cook on a low flame until golden and very soft, but not brown. Set aside. Cut the chicken fillets in half if large or leave whole if small. Cook the fillets for about 4 mins on each side or until done. Mix the cornflour with a little of the stock, add the rest of the stock and the Marsala. Bring to the boil and turn down to a simmer for about 5 mins until nicely thickened.

Venison medallions with Guinness glaze & horseradish mashed potatoes

Linda Baker
serves 4

After many years of living under the shadows of the wild and rugged Ruahine and Tararua ranges, venison became a regular staple of our family diet as there were so many wild deer in the hills. Pot luck teas always included a venison dish of some sort. If you don't like too gamey a taste, then farmed venison has a mild flavour and is easy to source every Saturday at the Lyttelton Farmers' market. Twelve medallions of venison, about 60g each (3 per person), or a boneless Denver leg (800g or so). The Denver leg will need longer cooking, as it's a thicker cut of meat.

potatoes to serve 4

1 large red or brown onion

1 tbsp butter

2-3 cloves garlic, crushed

1 tsp malt or balsamic vinegar

1 can of Guinness

1 tsp English mustard

1 tbsp soft brown sugar

100ml or so of meat stock

1 tbsp horseradish sauce

pinch nutmeg

salt & pepper to season

Get potatoes on to cook. Sauté onion and garlic in butter until golden. Deglaze pan with the vinegar and Guinness then reduce. Add mustard, sugar and stock to sauce. Reduce heat to just keep warm whilst preparing meat and potatoes.

Mash potatoes with horseradish, nutmeg and seasoning. (I also add milk and butter for super creamy mash). Keep warm till meat is cooked. Get the pan hot and sauté medallions in hot oil for about 2 mins each side. They should remain tender to touch in the centre. Rest the meat for at least another 2-4 mins. Slice venison sideways into smaller pieces and serve on the bed of mash. Drizzle with the Guinness glaze and enjoy with freshly steamed seasonal veges.

Note: with the Denver leg, you will be sautéing for up to 15 mins each side depending on the central thickness and then resting for at least 10 mins.

MUSEUM

HOW MY DAY STARTED
WOOF!
WOOF!
WOOF!

Baingan bhartha

Guy Stanaway

makes 1 bowl

India is a place of colour, smells, amazing people and a country I have always wanted to travel to. When the opportunity arose to go to Rajasthan to run a kitchen for the Aman hotel group, I couldn't pass up the opportunity. I have always wanted to learn more about spices and their uses both for cooking and medicinal purposes. I love the deep history behind such amazing cuisines. Those recipes that have been in families for generations. Here is a really simple dish that is great with bread or crackers. This is a favourite of mine, a simple quick vegetarian dish that is great hot or cold. I would eat this with fresh Indian breads or a nice baguette. The garam masala recipe is also a must for every pantry. Enjoy ...

500g aubergine

100ml oil

2g cumin seeds

20g garlic, chopped

10g ginger, grated

200g red onion, chopped

200g tomato, chopped

salt

5g turmeric powder

2g red chilli powder

10g green chilli, chopped

10g coriander, chopped

Grill the aubergine on the chargrill (or tandoor) in their skins until cooked. Once cooked scoop out the flesh and finely chop. In a heavy-based saucepan, heat the oil and roast the cumin seeds until you hear them pop. Add the chopped garlic, ginger and sauté for thirty seconds. Add the onion and caramelise slowly. Add the tomato, salt, turmeric, and chilli. Sauté for 3 mins. Add the aubergine and cook until the liquid has evaporated. Season to taste and garnish with chopped coriander.

Garam masala

Guy Stanaway

This is a common spice-mix used in almost all Indian dishes. It's usually a family recipe that has been passed down from generation to generation. This is the one we used in the hotel.

6 tbsp coriander seeds

4 tbsp cumin seeds

2 tbsp green cardamom pods

1 tbsp cinnamon stick, lightly crushed (about 3 sticks)

1 tbsp cloves

½ tbsp black peppercorns

½ a nutmeg, grated

Preheat oven to 150°C.

Roast together all spices (except the nutmeg) in a dry roasting pan in the oven or in a dry frying pan on top of the stove. Roast until aromatic, stirring occasionally. Grind all spices together until smooth in a coffee grinder or similar. Add the nutmeg. Store in a glass jar out of strong sunlight and away from direct heat. Use within 1-2 months for maximum flavour.

Anari gosht lamb curry with pomegranate

Indian Harbour, Lyttelton
serves 6

¼ cup cashew nuts, chopped & soaked in ½ cup water for a few hours, then processed to a smooth paste

2 tbsp canola oil

1 large onion, chopped

3 cloves garlic, coarsely chopped

large knob fresh ginger, peeled and coarsely chopped

700g well-trimmed lamb shoulder, diced 2cm

2 tbsp garam masala

2 tsp ground pomegranate seeds *(sold as anardana powder at Indian grocery stores)*

4 tbsp tomato paste

1 tsp sugar

1 tsp salt

coriander to garnish

Puree onion, garlic and ginger in a food processor until smooth. Heat the oil in a frying pan and stir-fry the onion paste for 2 mins. Add the meat and cook gently until just tender, about 40 mins. Make sure the mixture does not brown. Add the spices and cook for a further 2 mins. Add the rest of the ingredients and cook for another 2 mins, adding a little water if necessary to achieve a consistency similar to that of butter chicken. Serve with basmati rice and naan bread and garnish with fresh coriander.

Premdeep's dish

Crile Doscher
serves 2-4

This is a yummy Sikh bean dish. We often make it the night before we want to eat it as the flavours really come out that way. Premdeep was an Indian Sikh I met at university. He was very tall, with a large moustache and beard, and more often than not, a brightly coloured pagri (or turban), usually a shade of magenta. I had invited him over to teach me how to make this particular dish and asked what spices or ingredients I should have on hand. He was quite insistent that he brought all his own spices and all his own ingredients. While he was quite adamant that we not double the recipe, we've done so many times with no problem...please don't tell Premdeep.

oil for sautéing

1 onion, diced

garlic to taste, diced

1 tsp chilli powder

1 tsp garam masala

1 tsp turmeric

2 tomatoes, roughly diced

1 can kidney beans*

1 can black beans*

1 tbsp tomato paste

dash of salt

Sauté the onions and garlic until soft and then add the spices, sautéing for a minute or so more. Next add the tomatoes and sauté until soft. Finally, add the beans, black bean liquid, tomato paste and salt, turning the heat down to a simmer to cook it down a bit. Serve over rice with garlic naan and a bit of mango chutney. Yum.

**kidney beans drained and rinsed, black beans drained but retain about half the liquid.*

Kuchamber

John McCallum
serves 4-6

It's a hearty Indian-style relish. Tailor it or tone it down with whatever else you have at hand. The raw onion is very, very good for the blood. The best onions will often be found early in the season or at farmers' markets. They will feel softer, be larger, thin-skinned, have thick (7mm plus) rings and are often flatter than the hot, hard, thin-ringed storage onions (i.e. export rejects) that are often sold here. This is a nice side dish with curries, rice and so on but would be okay with Mexican dishes too.

1 onion, finely diced

lemon juice

½ tsp red wine vinegar

pinch salt

3 tomatoes, chopped

½ cup (or less) coriander and/or parsley, chopped

½ cucumber, peeled & diced

Combine all the ingredients and serve.

Lentil & spinach dahl

John McCallum
serves 4-6

This is a recipe from Alec, who is a keen nine-year-old cook. Alec loves vegetarian food, especially curry. This dahl is a favourite because "it tastes nice, and has a nice texture," with the three different beans. He cooked it at the Canaan Downs music festival at New Year. "It was raining when we cooked, but not when we served." It went down well with the vegans, as well as the wet revellers. The recipe is from 'Easy Indian' by Das Streedharan, given by Alec's mother to his father, because John loves cooking (and Anna loves him cooking too).

100g split red lentils

50g mung beans

50g chana dahl or yellow split peas

1 potato, peeled & chopped

3 onions, peeled & diced

3 green chillies, finely diced

3 tomatoes, chopped

1 tsp ground turmeric

1 tsp chilli powder

650ml water

100g spinach leaves, stalks removed

4 tbsp vegetable oil

¼ tsp cumin seeds

3 cloves garlic, crushed

Put the split red lentils, mung beans and chana dahl or yellow split peas in a saucepan. Add the potato, onions, chillies, tomatoes and ground spices and stir well. Pour water and bring to the boil. Lower the heat, cover and simmer for 15 mins or until the lentils are tender. Add the spinach leaves and cook for 5 mins. Heat the oil in a frying pan, add the cumin seeds and chopped garlic and sauté briefly. Pour this mixture over the dahl to serve.

"My favourite food is chicken curry because the sauce is melty in my mouth" Lili, age 5

CHRISTCHURCH
WILDLIFE CRUISES
MUSEUM

Lemon snow

Clare O'Regan
serves 4

My mother's baked lemon pudding.

½ cup white flour

1 cup sugar

grated lemon zest

¼ cup cold water

1½ cups milk

3 eggs, separated

1 tbsp butter, melted

juice 2 lemons

Preheat oven to 180°C.

Mix flour, sugar, lemon zest, water and milk. Beat the yolks until thick and add to mixture. Add melted butter and lemon juice and lastly stiffly beaten egg whites. Put into buttered soufflé dish and stand in bain-marie (dish of hot water). Bake for 45-60 mins.

Kentish well pudding

Ann Jolliffe

serves 8

This is a traditional farmhouse pudding recipe that has pleased hungry men and delighted children since the 17th century and probably earlier, almost never made now, which is a pity. It is possibly too heavy for the sedentary and urban lives we all lead today, but splendid for a cold day in winter.

½kg self-raising flour

180g shredded suet (Shreddo)

water

180g currants

240g unsalted butter, in one piece

120g soft brown sugar

Mix the flour, suet and currants with water to form soft dough. Roll out 4cm thick. Grease a large stainless steel, china or heatproof bowl. Press dough into the bowl, reserving a quarter of the crust for the top. Put the butter in one piece in the centre and the sugar around the butter to fill up the well. Cover with the remaining crust, pinching the edges firmly together. Cover closely with foil. Place the pudding bowl in a saucepan of simmering water so that the water reaches ¾ of the way up the outside of the bowl. Steam for 2 hours at a constant simmer until a skewer inserted into the middle comes out clean. Turn out carefully. When cut, the melted butter and sugar should run out, though some will be absorbed, making a rich and delicious centre. You could also serve extra caramel sauce or custard (children love it) with this if you wish.

Finn. age 6

One minute chocolate sauce

Margaret Dann, new entrants teacher at Lyttelton Main School

This is a rich, smooth, grown-up chocolate sauce that you can make while someone clears the table from the main course.

1 tbsp butter

1 tbsp cocoa

½ cup boiling water

1 cup sugar

2 tbsp golden syrup

Bring butter, cocoa and water to the boil. Add sugar and golden syrup. Mix and bring back to the boil. Boil for 1 min. This sauce can be used straight away but it thickens on cooling.

Nana's no-fail sticky date pudding

Marie Henry
serves 6

1½ cups dates, chopped

1 tsp baking soda

1½ cup boiling water

75g butter

1 cup brown sugar

1 tsp vanilla

1 lemon, zested

2 eggs

½ cup orange juice

juice of one lemon

1 cup flour

1¼ tsp baking powder

Caramel sauce:

1 cup brown sugar

1 cup cream

50g butter

1 tsp vanilla

Preheat oven to 175°C.

Place dates and baking soda in a bowl and pour over water. Leave for 15 mins. Cream the butter and sugar, add vanilla, lemon zest and eggs beating well. Add the orange and lemon juice to the date mixture. Mix the flour and baking powder together then add to creamed mixture, alternating with the dates. It will be very sloppy. Bake for 40-45 min. Stand for 10 mins before serving with the caramel sauce.

Caramel sauce: Combine all ingredients. Bring to the boil and simmer for 5 mins.

Francesca, age 5

Granny apple pie

Sarah Wild

makes 1 x 25cm pie

I am not an apple pie fan but this recipe is actually really delicious. The pastry cannot be replaced with store-bought as it would not be the same pie. It is great on a cold winter evening with cream, mascarpone cheese or vanilla ice-cream.

Pastry:

150g butter

150g castor sugar

1 egg

250g flour

1 tsp baking powder

Filling:

50g butter

1.2kg granny smith apples, peeled, cored and thickly sliced

milk, for glaze

50g butter

1 heaped tbsp castor sugar

Preheat oven to 180°C.

Pastry: Cream butter and sugar in a food mixer until light and fluffy. Add the egg and combine. Gently add the flour and baking powder. Remove and roll into a ball. Knead to combine for about 30 seconds. Cover with plastic wrap and chill for 30 mins.

Lightly butter (I use an oil spray) a 25cm flan dish. Cut pastry in half and use one half to line dish. Re-wrap other half and put dish and pastry into fridge.

Filling: Melt butter in a non-stick frying pan and when it sizzles add the apples. You want them to colour here and there and soften but not break up. Sprinkle sugar over and continue to cook until they are very lightly caramelised. Remove from heat and pour off any liquid that has been formed. Set aside to cool a bit.

Roll out the other half of the pastry. Put apples into chilled pastry case and carefully lay the pastry on top. Seal edges with the juice from the apples. This pastry is very soft so patch where necessary. Carefully brush the pastry crust with milk and sprinkle with extra castor sugar. Bake on lower shelf of oven for 40-45 mins. Check after 20 mins and if brown put a sheet of aluminium foil over pie to stop further browning. Cool briefly and sprinkle with more castor sugar before serving.

Telephone pudding

Chia Herman

serves 4-6

1 egg

½ cup milk

1½ cup flour

1 cup brown sugar

2 tbsp butter or margarine

1 tsp ground ginger

1 tsp bicarbonate of soda

2 tbsp fine apricot jam

3 cups boiling water

1½ cups sugar

Preheat oven to 180°C.

Mix egg with milk. Add next 6 ingredients and set aside. In a separate dish (in which the pudding is to be baked) place boiling water, add sugar. Stir until sugar dissolves. Pour first mixture into sugar mixture, but do not stir. Bake for 1 hour. Serve with custard.

"The mandarin is the yummiest. The apple is the second yummiest." Connor, age 6

another
SELF OPENING GATE
BUMP AT 3 M.P.H.
DON'T STOP
FENCE & GATE COMPANY LTD.

Banana loaf

Gail Davey
Note: It is recommended to wait a day before turning the loaf out.

80g butter

1 cup sugar

1 egg

2 bananas, mashed

1½ cups flour

½ tsp baking powder

1 tsp baking soda

4 tbsp milk

Preheat oven to 180°C.

Cream butter and sugar, add the egg, banana, flour and baking powder. Dissolve the baking soda in milk then add to the mixture. Cook for approx 1 hour. Turn out the next day. This keeps well.

Chocolate cake with vodka infused cranberries

Clare O'Regan

250g butter

1½ cups espresso coffee (or strongly made instant using 1 tbsp instant coffee and 1½ cups boiling water)

200g dark chocolate (70%)

2 cups castor sugar

1½ cups self-raising flour

¼ cup cocoa, preferably Valrhona

2 eggs

2 tsp vanilla

½ cup dried cranberries

100ml vodka

Icing:

125g dark chocolate (70%)

½ cup cream

Preheat oven to 170°C.

Soak the dried cranberries in vodka either overnight, or put in microwave for 20 seconds and leave for 20 mins. Melt butter in pan, add coffee, chocolate and sugar and stir till smooth. Add dry ingredients and beat with electric beater until smooth. Add eggs and vanilla and beat for about 2 mins (this will be very runny). Drain cranberries and add to pan. Pour into greased and lined cake tin and bake for 1¼–1½ hrs. Allow to cool before icing.

Icing: Melt together and smother cake.

Eva, age 7

Chocolate fudge square

makes approx 20 pieces

250g pkt malt, wine or digestive biscuits

½ cup brown sugar

¼ cup cocoa

3 tbsp milk

1 tsp vanilla

75g butter

1 cup sultanas (optional)

Chocolate icing

1 tbsp cocoa

2 tbsp boiling water

1 tbsp butter

½ tsp vanilla

1 cup icing sugar, sifted

Crush biscuits evenly. Mix the sugar and cocoa in a medium-sized pot, then stir in the milk, vanilla and butter. Bring to the boil, stirring all the time. Remove from heat. Add the crushed biscuits and sultanas (if using) and stir together. Press mixture into sponge-roll tin, and flatten surface until fairly smooth. Cover with chocolate icing.

Chocolate icing: Measure cocoa into a small bowl, add the boiling water and mix to a paste. Add the butter, vanilla and icing sugar. Beat until smooth. You may need to add a little more icing sugar if mixture is too thin.

Cut into squares when set. Store in the fridge during hot weather.

sultana malt biscuits

Jo Hay

makes approx 30 biscuits

This recipe originally came from my grandmother and was one my mum always baked at home. I often cook these biscuits as the recipe is quick and easy, makes heaps and kids love them!

125g butter

2 tsp golden syrup

½ cup sugar

1 tbsp milk

1 tsp vanilla

1 cup sultanas

½ tsp baking soda

1 cup flour

Preheat oven to 180°C.

Melt butter, golden syrup, sugar, milk and vanilla in a saucepan. Remove from heat and add sultanas and baking soda. Let the mixture cool a little and then add flour. Roll spoonfuls of mixture into small balls, place onto a greased oven tray, and flatten with a floured fork. Bake 10-15 mins.

"The best way to eat cookies is to make crumbs" Reha, age 11

Thermette

Lyttelton West's rosemary & riesling mulled wine

A favourite at the Lyttelton Festival of Lights winter street party.

½ cup water

½ cup white sugar

¼ cup honey

2 sprigs fresh rosemary

4 lemons

2 bottles Riesling

In a large pot put the water, sugar, honey and rosemary. Simmer but do not boil for about 10 mins, until the mixture becomes slightly thick and syrupy. Remove from the heat. Using a potato peeler, peel 2 lemons and add the peel to the pot, along with lemon juice. Then add the wine and let the mixture sit for at least an hour for the flavours to develop.

To serve, strain the mixture to remove the rosemary and the peel. Add 2 more sliced whole lemons and gently reheat, being careful not to let the mixture boil.

LAW
ROAD CLOSED

NINETEEN

kids

"I love Lyttelton because it has a great community and interesting history. I like looking at the scenery and the boats and the hills. My school is cool."

Hamish Laing (9), Lyttelton Main School

"We love living in Lyttelton because... I've got all my friends just around the corner. The ice-creams at the Empire Dairy are the biggest and the best. There are lots of activities to do in Lyttelton like sailing, soccer, the Loons, swimming, mountain-biking and art."

Jack (10) and Jemma (11) Ballard, Lyttelton West School

Madi's meatballs

Madisyn Tucker, age 5¼

Great for kids to help with, their little hands are a perfect size for forming the balls! You can alter the spice flavourings to suit other tastes.

250g minced beef

½ carrot, grated

1 stalk celery, finely chopped

½ courgette, grated

½ onion, finely chopped

1 egg

bread crumbs, alter the quantity to suit desired consistency

dash Worcestershire sauce

celery salt

paprika

moroccan spices

cumin

1 tsp garlic, crushed

Preheat oven to 180°C.

Mix all ingredients together and form into small balls with hands. Bake in oven in a dish for about 30 mins. Enjoy hot or cold. Because they cook in their own fat, you don't need to grease the baking dish.

This recipe can also be made with pasta sauce poured over the meatballs before baking but they may need a little longer to firm up.

"Fruit is healthy for you, like an apple and an orange. My favourite food is spaghetti bolognaise" Eli, age 7

sweet potato chips

Karen McMullon

2 tbsp orange juice

1 tsp onion powder

salt & pepper

2 sweet potatoes (cut into chunky fry-shaped sticks)

Preheat oven to 180°C.

Combine orange juice, onion powder and salt & pepper in a bowl. Add the sweet potato and coat well. Layer sticks on a greased oven tray. Bake in oven for about 10 mins or until cooked.

Serve with light sour cream.

Hannah, age 7

Becky's homemade spaghetti

Becky McMullon, age 5 (Mum helped me write this!)

Becky has enjoyed making this with her Dad since she was about two-years-old. It's easy, fun to make, healthy... and tastes delicious! All the ingredients, as well as the pasta machine can be bought in Lyttelton!

250g 00 pasta flour

4 free range egg yolks

pinch of saffron, dissolved in 1 tbsp hot water (optional but does make the pasta a brighter colour)

1 tbsp olive oil

1-2 tbsp water

Put the ingredients in the given order into a food processor and mix for 30-45 seconds until just blended. Knead the dough on a very lightly-floured board/work surface until perfectly smooth. You may need to add a little extra water while doing this. Wrap the dough tightly in cling film and put in the fridge to rest for 1-2 hours.

Set up the pasta machine and cut the dough into four pieces. Flatten each piece and roll out on the work surface. Put the dough through the pasta machine – it is important to keep folding the pasta and turning it, before changing the setting on the pasta machine as per the instructions. Practice makes perfect!

You can cook the pasta straight away, but it tends not to stick together so much if you dry it out for a while - just hang it over anything convenient; the back of our wooden chairs is the favourite place in our house.

Tip from Becky: if you have a cat make sure it is out of the way. Becky's cat Poppy loves to play with the hanging spaghetti if she gets a chance!

Cook the spaghetti in a large pan of boiling water for about 2-3 mins and serve with favourite sauce.

Although you could make a sauce to go with it, this pasta is quite rich and tasty just on its own...or even better with a little Parmesan cheese on top.

Sweet & sour pork

Hineata McGregor

900g pork pieces

1 tbsp cooking oil

2 tbsp cornflour

milk

1 small can pineapple pieces

¼ cup brown sugar

½ cup vinegar

1 tbsp soy sauce

½ tsp salt

½ cup water

½ cup onion, thinly sliced

2 green peppers, sliced

Brown pork slowly in oil. Add water, cover and simmer till tender (about 1 hour). Drain pineapple, reserving syrup. Mix cornflour with a small amount of milk to the consistency of thin cream. Add this to the pineapple syrup along with the sugar, vinegar, soy sauce, salt and water.

Cook this mixture over low heat till thick, stirring constantly. Pour over hot cooked pork. Let stand for 10mins or longer. Add pineapple, green peppers and onion. Cook about 10mins longer and serve over noodles or rice.

"I like pizza and pies and rainbow drinks and carrots. I like peas too. I like icecream and cookies too and I like soup and fudge brownies"

Zachery, age 7

Patrick's favourite quick pasta, with tomato & chorizo

Patrick O'Regan

Easy enough for a 12-year-old boy to make

2 tbsp olive oil

2 onions, finely chopped

2 cloves garlic, crushed

5 chorizo sausages, sliced diagonally

2 x 400g cans crushed tomatoes

1 tsp sugar

salt & pepper to taste

torn basil leaves

500g spaghetti or penne

Saute the onion and garlic in olive oil until soft but not brown. Add the diagonally sliced chorizo and cook for a few minutes more. Add the tomatoes, sugar and salt & pepper. Simmer gently for 20-30 mins. While the dish is simmering, cook spaghetti or penne in the usual way. Just before serving add the torn basil leaves.

Serve with a green leafy salad with mustard vinaigrette, and maybe some crusty bread to mop up juices.

"I like looking out the window and seeing the harbour"

Thomas, age 9

“I love cooking but I hate it when Mum takes over”

Olive, age 11

Best-ever cupcake recipe

Olive Russell, age 11
makes approx 30 small cupcakes or 12-15 medium cakes

This recipe is so easy - everything just gets mixed in one bowl. You can vary the flavours as you wish. For example, try lemon, orange & poppy seed, vanilla or chocolate (add a splash more milk to compensate for the cocoa). Ice with traditional butter icing or try our special cupcake icing.

2 cups self-raising flour

¾ cup sugar

125g butter, melted

3 eggs

½ cup milk

½ tsp vanilla

Preheat oven to 180°C.

Sift the flour and sugar into a mixing bowl. Add the butter, vanilla then the eggs one at a time and lastly the milk. Beat well to a smooth batter.
¾ fill greased muffin tins or patty cases with the batter. Bake for 10-15 mins or until golden.

Ice and decorate when cool. These cupcakes will keep well for several days.

Special cupcake icing

This icing is like old-fashioned animal biscuit icing. It will set hard and is great for decorating the tops of cupcakes with different colours. A simple way to do this is to divide the basic icing mixture into different bowls and colour each one individually. By cutting a tiny corner in a small snaplock bag and filling it with the coloured icing, you can make a simple piping bag. Just seal what you don't use in the snaplock bag and it will keep for next time.

2½ cups icing sugar

3 tbsp orange juice

Beat together the icing sugar and the orange juice until smooth. Add more icing sugar if mixture is too runny. Colour as desired and store in the fridge until required.

Connor & Logan's best banana chocolate chip muffins

Belinda Buckley
makes 12

2 cups self-raising flour

½ cup sugar

½ cup chocolate chips

¼ tsp salt

100g butter

1 cup milk

1 egg

1 tsp vanilla

1 cup mashed banana

Preheat oven to 220°C.

Stir together the flour, sugar, chocolate chips and salt with a fork, in a large bowl. Melt the butter, add the milk, egg and vanilla essence and beat well. Stir the mashed banana into the butter mixture. Tip the liquid mixture into the dry ingredients. Fold everything together carefully until all the flour is mixed in but the mixture is not smooth.

Grease muffin pan. Three-quarters fill each cup with the mixture. Bake for 12-15 mins or until they spring back after being gently pressed in the centre.

Chocolate brownie

Alex Simmonds, age 10

100g butter, melted

1 cup sugar

2 eggs

1 tsp vanilla essence

¾ cup self raising flour

¼ cup cocoa

You can also add a handful of chocolate chips to make it richer if desired

Mix together all the ingredients in a large bowl. Put in a greased microwave dish and cook on high for 6 mins. Sprinkle with icing sugar

Yummy hot or cold.

"I like making cookies and I love when I come home after school and my mum is making cookies. My favourite food is chocolate and I like chocolate icecream"

Ngaio, age 6

Nicki's fudge deluxe

George family

125g butter

½ cup sugar

3 tbsp cocoa

¼ cup condensed milk

1 egg

1 tsp vanilla

1 pkt wine biscuits

¼ cup coconut

100g marshmallows

½ cup mini M&M's

Lightly grease 20cm square dish. Melt together butter, sugar, cocoa, and condensed milk until the butter is melted and the sugar dissolved. Cool. Quickly mix in the egg and vanilla. Crush the biscuits, add the coconut, marshmallows and M&M's. Pour the cocoa and butter mixture over the biscuit mix and mix thoroughly. Press into the dish and chill until set. Ice with chocolate icing and cut into squares.

"The only way to cook is to make a mess"

Ruby, age 11

Octopus biscuits

Rebecca Rennie

These are James and Megs' favourite biscuits. Makes approximately 10 octopuses.

125g butter

125g sugar

175g flour

3 tbsp cocoa

1 egg

Sweets (pebbles) for eyes

Icing:

25g butter

50g icing sugar

1 tbsp lemon juice

Preheat oven to 160°C.

Cream the butter until fluffy and white. Add sugar and beat well. Sift in flour and cocoa. Add the egg and mix well. Make into a large log shape. Wrap in plastic wrap and chill for 30 mins.

Slice log into 10 pieces. Gently flatten each round and make four cuts to make legs approximately two-thirds of the way up the shape. The uncut area is the octopus face or body. Lift octopuses onto a tray and bake 10-12 mins. Cool on an oven rack. Using icing, stick the pebbles onto the body to make the eyes.

"Food is fuel" James, age 9

White hot chocolate

Jim Visser
serves 4

This recipe can be halved or quartered depending on how many people you're making this for. I wound up using a quarter of the ingredients as I just made one cup. Make sure to use the same amount of vanilla extract though for any version of the recipe. Top with nutmeg or cocoa powder for decoration.

4½ cups milk

½ tsp pure vanilla extract

½ cup best-quality white chocolate, finely chopped

In a medium saucepan, heat milk and vanilla over medium heat just until milk begins to steam 5-6 mins. Add white chocolate, and whisk until completely melted and combined. Divide among four mugs.

Serve immediately. Enjoy!

Fruit smoothies

1 banana

1 can pineapple

1 cup strawberries

1 cup strawberry yoghurt

Drain the pineapple. Blend all ingredients together until smooth.

Fruit tingle mocktails

orange juice

raspberry cordial

lime cordial

lemonade

Place a scoop of crushed ice into each glass.

Pour in the different ingredients over a spoon to keep the layers separate. Decorate the glass with fruit such as pineapple or orange.

Watermelon ice blocks

Sonja Kingsbury

Cool summer idea.

watermelon

Cut watermelon into small wedges. Place wedges in an air-tight container and freeze for 6 hours. A great after-school treat on a hot day. Use within three weeks.

"Healthy food is good. And so is fruit. But I like icecream and chocolate" Palace. age 8

adidas
ALL BLA

Acknowledgements

The pupils, whanau, and staff of Lyttelton West and Lyttelton Main Schools.

PHOTOGRAPHY
Maree Henry
Jason Larraman
Dean MacKenzie
Frank Visser

CREATIVE DIRECTOR
Kate McRae

GRAPHIC DESIGN
Kim Hickford, Timezoneone
Rose Wells, Liz Bissland, Henriette Nass

WEB DESIGN
Wired Internet Group
Bruce Russell

FUNDRAISING
Thea Mickell Consulting

MARKETING ADVISOR
Jan van der Heyden

PORT LIAISON
Captain Joanne Laing
Doug Cockerell
Hal Upton
Jocelyn Patel

CONTRIBUTORS
Richard Till
Nick Freeman
Gary McCormick
Jason Dell
Joe Bennett
Ann Stanaway
John Sellwood
Roy Montgomery
Guy Stanaway
Jonny Schwass
Glyn Abbott

SPONSORS

Premier
Stark Bros Ltd
Bells Pharmacy Lyttelton Ltd
Solid Energy New Zealand Ltd
Lyttelton Engineering Ltd

Gold
Pub Charity
Air Rescue Services Ltd
Lyttelton Port of Christchurch
Veveritz Properties Ltd
Gordons Quality Produce
Project Lyttelton

Silver
DUAL Design Ltd
Harbour Light Entertainment & Function Venue
Lyttelton Coffee Company
Ingrid Geldof Design
Portico
Bookkeeping & Beyond
Ann Stanaway
Lyttelton Video Ezy

Bronze
Elaine Ferguson, Harcourts Harbourside
Leslie's Book Shop
Min Sarginson Real Estate Ltd
Vic's Bakehouse
SBA Small Business Accounting (Lyttelton)
Wear on Earth
Ground Culinary Centre
Heather Chick, Harcourts Phoenix Estate Group Ltd
Kingswood Skis
Home Fresh Deliveries
Monster Bar

WE WOULD ALSO LIKE TO THANK THE FOLLOWING:
Anne & Graeme Bachop, Captain John Cleaver, Alan Goodmanson, Barbara & William Lee, Betty Purdue, Bill Hammond, Sarah Freeman (Freemans Restaurant), Jenny Garing (Ground Culinary Centre), Gill Hay, Carmel Courtney, Bob Parker, Vanta Kaur & Dilip Singh (Indian Harbour), Jane Purdue & Mark Whyte, Lyttelton Coffee Company, Lisa West (Haunt), Baden Norris, Brian Rick (Lyttel Piko), Megan & Jean Pierre Ribotton, Shelley McCabe, Carol Anderson (No. 6 Café), Lois Ogilvie & Peter Evans (Volcano Café), Sally Green, Gay Mahar, Alice Tyro, Rei Couch, Hilary Downer, Jo Fitzgerald, Helen Hobson, Wendy Everingham, Carolyn Bruce, Pauline Goodfellow, Megan Collings, Adie Guest, Anne Joliffe, Rachel Barker, Dawn Kottier, Celia Allison, Adrian Lowry.

Index